ISBN 978-1-332-75426-7
PIBN 10051490

For support please visit www.forgottenbooks.com

1 MONTH OF
FREE
READING

at

www.ForgottenBooks.com

By purchasing this book you are eligible for one month membership to ForgottenBooks.com, giving you unlimited access to our entire collection of over 1,000,000 titles via our web site and mobile apps.

To claim your free month visit:

www.forgottenbooks.com/free51490

English
Français
Deutsche
Italiano
Español
Português

www.forgottenbooks.com

Mythology Photography **Fiction**
Fishing Christianity **Art** Cooking
Essays Buddhism Freemasonry
Medicine **Biology** Music **Ancient**
Egypt Evolution Carpentry Physics
Dance Geology **Mathematics** Fitness
Shakespeare **Folklore** Yoga Marketing
Confidence Immortality Biographies
Poetry **Psychology** Witchcraft
Electronics Chemistry History **Law**
Accounting **Philosophy** Anthropology
Alchemy Drama Quantum Mechanics
Atheism Sexual Health **Ancient History**
Entrepreneurship Languages Sport
Paleontology Needlework Islam
Metaphysics Investment Archaeology
Parenting Statistics Criminology
Motivational

THE LIFE

OF

SAMUEL F. B. MORSE, LL. D.,

INVENTOR OF THE

ELECTRO-MAGNETIC RECORDING TELEGRAPH.

BY

SAMUEL IRENÆUS PRIME,

PRESIDENT OF THE NEW YORK ASSOCIATION FOR THE ADVANCEMENT OF SCIENCE AND ART;
CORRESPONDING MEMBER OF THE NEW YORK HISTORICAL SOCIETY;
AUTHOR OF "TRAVELS IN EUROPE AND THE EAST,"
"THE ALHAMBRA AND THE KREMLIN," ETC.

NEW YORK:
D. APPLETON AND COMPANY,
549 AND 551 BROADWAY.
1875.

PREFACE.

In his last will and testament Professor MORSE gave to his executors authority "to place his manuscripts in the hands of some suitable person for the purpose of examining and using the same in preparing a biographical or historical note," relating to himself. The family of the great inventor and the executors of his estate united in an urgent request that the author of this volume would take charge of the papers and "prepare and present to the public a biography of Professor Morse in such a style that it would be generally read."

With great reluctance, and after repeated solicitations, I consented to attempt the service. My studies and pursuits had not qualified me for the task, and it would have been far more in harmony with my wishes and judgment, had the work been confided to other hands. But, having been associated with the brothers of the Professor more than thirty years, and during that time on terms of friendly and pleasing intercourse with him, having heard from his own lips again and again the story of his struggles and triumphs, I had some peculiar facilities to understand and interpret the man. But I would have decisively declined the honorable service assigned me, had I anticipated the difficulties and labors it involved. During his lifetime Professor Morse was often applied to for materials out of which his biography might be prepared. To one of the applications he replied by letter, " My time is so much absorbed in making my life, I have none to spare for writing it." And so literally true is this remark, that, in the huge mass of manuscripts left by him, there is not a page that appears to have been written with the expectation that it would be employed in his biography.

If it were possible to compensate my lack of preparation, it · would be supplied by the remarkable ability, extent, and value of the assistance which has been generously, and I may add nobly, rendered by others. Professor E. N. Horsford, at my request, cheerfully prepared the admirably lucid and condensed history of "Electro-Magnetic Science," and the measure of Morse's indebtedness to his predecessors. The Hon. F. O. J. Smith furnished the most important letters and memoranda of the early years of the Telegraph. Colonel T. P. Shaffner put at my service his vast telegraphic collections and illustrations. Hon. Ezra Cornell, with his own hand, wrote for me his recollections of the construction of the experimental line from Washington to Baltimore. To the Hon. William Orton and to George B. Prescott, Esq., I am indebted for those important facts which bring the history of telegraphy down to the present time. Robert G. Rankin, Esq., Benson J. Lossing, Esq., General T. S. Cummings, Daniel Huntington, Esq., General James Grant Wilson, Rev. Dr. Wheeler, and others, have contributed sketches with incidents and observations that enliven and enrich the volume.

The life of Professor Morse is very naturally divided into three parts, to each of which has been assigned about one-third of the volume. The first includes his career as an artist, which was precisely one-half of his life. The second was employed in the construction and establishment of the Telegraph, a period of twelve years. The third and last presents the rewards that he received, and the benefits he conferred upon mankind. These portions of time have distinctive values and interest; combined, they form an epoch in the history of the human race. Freely and thoroughly as the history of Morse and his work has been sifted and searched by critics and courts, by friends and foes, it was left for his biographer to discover and present facts which explain with simplicity and ease the phenomenon that an artist suddenly grasped the profoundest secrets of science, and welded them into an invention to revolutionize the intercourse of the civilized world. We have learned that Samuel F. B. Morse was a born inventor, with a genius for mechanism; that he invented machinery and secured patents long before he made the Telegraph; that his education and habits of thought, his antecedents and associations, fitted him for the task; and, when the hour arrived, the instrument was ready and the work was done! This was at least the third of his mechanical and scientific contributions. Electrical science was his favorite study in college and afterward; evidence of this is here given unknown to himself as in existence. He propounded the idea of the Electric Telegraph to familiar friends before he seriously undertook to make it practical. He wrought out his invention and made it a mechanical, working instrument, doing all that it now does, before any man, scientist or artisan, gave him a particle of assistance. As the recording Telegraph is the sublimest of all human agencies, so the conception and construction of the instrument by a solitary, unaided man, mark it as one of the most extraordinary facts in human progress.

Embarrassed by the wealth of material that would easily have filled many volumes as large as this, and being compelled by want of space to suppress hundreds of letters and documents that would honor the memory of Professor Morse, I have conscientiously executed a trust most reluctantly accepted. With all its imperfections, with which no one can be made better acquainted than the author is already, the volume, with unfeigned diffidence, but with confidence in its justice and truth, is committed to the public.

S. I. P.

NEW YORK, *July* 8, 1874.

CONTENTS.

CHAPTER I.

MORSE.

Genealogy—Characteristics of Ancestors—His Grandfather Rev. Dr. Samuel Finley—His Father Rev. Dr. Jedediah Morse—His Brothers Sidney Edwards and Richard Cary Morse—Birth of Samuel F. B. Morse—Predictions . . . . Pp. 1–12

CHAPTER II.

1791–1811.

Early Education—His School-mistress—Drawing with a Pin—At Grammar-school—Yale College—President Dwight—Professors Day and Silliman—Studies in Electricity—Germs of the Telegraph—Portrait-painting—Recollections by Fellow-students 13–27

CHAPTER III.

1811–1815.

Washington Allston—Morse goes to London under his Tuition—The Voyage—Longings for a Telegraph—Benjamin West—Morse's Letters to his Parents—To a Friend at Home—Impressions of West—Leslie the Painter—He and Morse become Room-mates—Samuel Taylor Coleridge—Triumphs of the Young Artist—Meets with William Wilberforce, Henry Thornton, Zachary Macaulay, Lord Glenelg, and Others—Visit at Mr. Thornton's—Intercourse with Coleridge—Travels to Oxford, and Incidents—First Portrait abroad—Leslie and Morse—Letters to his Parents—Zerah Colburn—Dartmoor Prisoners—Attempts to serve them—Dunlap's Account of Morse—Dying Hercules—Judgment of Jupiter—Gold Medal—Mrs. Allston's Death—Scene at Mr. Wilberforce's—Return Home 28–88

CHAPTER IV.

1815–1823.

Return to America—Opens a Studio in Boston—No Success—Invents Improvement in Pump—Travels in Vermont and New Hampshire as Portrait-painter—Meets his Future Bride—Pursues his Invention—Goes to Charleston, South Carolina—Dr. Finley—Success—Allston's Encouragement—Returns North—Marriage—

Charleston again—The Pump—W. Allston—Morse paints the Portrait of President Monroe—Third Winter in Charleston—New Haven—Painting "House of Representatives"—History of the Picture . . . . . Pp. 89–126

CHAPTER V.

1823–1828.

Invents a Machine for cutting Marble—Goes to Albany—Little Success—Returns to New York—Portrait of Chancellor Kent—Ichabod Crane—Arrangements to go to Mexico as Attaché to the Legation—Letter from Hon. Robert Y. Hayne—The Scheme abandoned—In New Haven—Travels in New England—Settles in New York—Commissioned to paint Portrait of General Lafayette—Goes to Washington—Sudden Death of his Wife—Death of his Father—Founds the National Academy of Design—Sketch-Club—Letter from General T. S. Cummings—Lord Lyndhurst's Letter—Studies in Electro-magnetism—Professor Dana's Lectures—His Own Lectures—Escape from Death . . 127–171

CHAPTER VI.

1829–1832.

Commissions to paint in Italy—Journey to Rome—Letter to his Cousin—England—Paris—Avignon—Marseilles—Nice—The Cornice Road—Geneva—Pisa—Rome—The Vatican—Galleries of Art—Notes—Thorwaldsen—Portrait—James Fenimore Cooper—H. Greenough—Letters—Return to Paris—Friendship with Lafayette—Sympathy with Poland—Imprisonment of Dr. Howe—Fall of Warsaw—Letters to his Brother—Suggests Lightning-Telegraph—Humboldt—Presides at Fourth-of-July Dinner—Letters of Lafayette—Interior of the Louvre—Humboldt and Morse—Dunlap's Notices of Morse in Paris and London . 172–250

CHAPTER VII.

1832.

Packet-ship Sully—Electro-magnetism—Dinner-table Conversation—Idea of the Telegraph—First Marks made—The Invention announced to Passengers—Drawings exhibited—Prediction to Captain Pell—Prof. E. N. Horsford's History of the Science—Stephen Grey—Leyden Jar—Franklin's Experiments—Charles Marshall—Le Sage—Lomond—Reusser—Cavallo—Wedgewood—Ronalds—Dyar—Galvanism, or Voltaism—Volta—Schweigger — Coxe — Magnetism — Electromagnetism—Ampère — Schilling — Cooke and Wheatstone—Oersted — Spiral Coil, 1821—Arago—Sturgeon—James Freeman Dana—Joseph Henry—Fechiner—Ohm's Law—Steinheil — Daniel—Soemmering—Samuel Finley Breese Morse—Invention and Discovery—Claims of Discoverers and Inventors—Successive Steps in Telegraphic Invention 251–284

CHAPTER VIII.

1832–1838.

Arrival in New York—The Brothers' Testimony—Mould and Type the First Things made for the Telegraph—Castings preserved—Struggles of the Inventor—Poverty and Distress—His Brothers' Sympathy and Aid—Making the Telegraphic

Instrument—At the Lathe—Faith in God and Himself—Rejected as One of the Painters of a Picture for the Capitol—Artists' Sympathy—Elected Professor in University of New York—Rooms in Building—Apparatus—Cooks his Own Food in his Room—Announcement of his Invention—French Idea of Telegraph—Professor Gale's Statement—Daniel Huntington—Hamilton Fish—Rev. Mr. Seelye—Commodore Starbuck—Robert G. Rankin—Rev. Dr. H. B. Tappan—Alfred Vail becomes a Partner—Letter to Secretary of Treasury—Secretary's Report to Congress—Professor Gale a Partner—The Instrument at Speedwell—Three Miles of Wire—Experiments—Exhibition in New York—Ten Miles of Wire—First Dispatch preserved—Exhibited to the Franklin Institute—Report—The Instrument in Washington—Exhibited to the President and Cabinet—Hon. F. O. J. Smith—Professor Morse's Letters to Mr. Smith—Report of Committee of Commerce—Partnership with Mr. Smith—Letters to Vail—Preparations for a Journey to Europe . . . . Pp. 285–346

CHAPTER IX.

1838–1839.

Professor Morse goes to England—Application for Patent—Refusal—Reasons—False Statement of an Official—Goes to Paris—Letters to his Daughter—Dr. Kirk's Recollections—Arago—His Great Kindness—Exhibition before Academy of Sciences—Baron Humboldt's Congratulations—Report upon it—Letters to Friends—Hon. H. L. Ellsworth's Letters—Patent in France—Count Montalivet —Professor Morse's Letters to Mr. Smith—Lord Lincoln's and Lord Elgin's Interest in the Telegraph—Professor Morse goes to London—Exhibits the Telegraph at the House of Lord Lincoln 347–393

CHAPTER X.

1839–1843.

Return to New York—Russian Contract—Disappointment at Inaction of Congress—Mr. Smith's Views of the State of Things—The Daguerreotype introduced—Experiments—Success—Teaches Others—Sully and Allston—Russia fails—Deep Depression—Letter to his Partners Mr. A. Vail and Hon. F. O. J. Smith—Consultation with Professor Henry—Letters of Professor Henry—Struggles of Morse under Poverty—Letters to Mr. Vail—An Agent employed at Washington—Failure—An Old Sorrow—Hon. W. W. Boardman, M. C.—Letter to Hon. F. O. J. Smith on Professor Henry's Encouragement—First Submarine Cable laid by Professor Morse—Report of American Institute—Hon. C. G. Ferris—Letter to him—Professor Morse in Washington—Favorable Report in Congress—Debate—Passage of Bill in the House and the Senate appropriating Thirty Thousand Dollars for an Experimental Line of Telegraph—Death of Allston 394–472

CHAPTER XI.

1843–1844.

Preparations to lay the First Line—Use of Tubes underground—Ezra Cornell—Tubes abandoned—Wires put upon Poles—Experiments with 160 Miles of Wire—Professor Henry's Letter—Progress of the Work—National Whig Con-

vention—Nomination of Henry Clay announced at Washington by Telegraph—
The Line complete—The First Message—Triumph of the Inventor—His Letter
to Bishop Stevens—National Democratic Convention—James K. Polk nominated — Conference with Silas Wright — Working of the Telegraph — Professor Morse's Report of the Completion of the Line — Enthusiasm of the
Press and the Public—Telegraph offered to the Government—Determining the
Longitude . . . . Pp. 473–509

CHAPTER XII.

1845.

Congress refuses Further Appropriations—Letter of Professor Morse to his Daughter
—Hon. Amos Kendall engaged as Agent—Formation of the Magnetic Telegraph
Company—Letters to Mr. Vail—Mr. Vail's Replies—Professor Morse goes
abroad—In London—General Commercial Telegraph Company—Hon. Louis
McLane—Professor Morse in Hamburg—Returns to London—Exhibitions of
the Telegraph in Hamburg, St. Petersburg, Berlin, and Vienna—Mr. Fleischmann's Account of its Reception—Professor Morse in Paris—Arago—Exhibition
before Chamber of Deputies—Return to America 510–538

CHAPTER XIII.

1846–1847.

Extension of Patent—The Inventor's Claim—New Lines established—Sidney E.
Morse's Predictions—Report to the Postmaster-General—Artists' Petition—
Line between Baltimore, Philadelphia, and New York — French Chambers
Debate—Letter to Arago—First Fruits—Smithsonian Institution—Professor
Henry appointed Secretary—Printing-Telegraph—Letter to Daniel Lord—Pi-
ratical Invasions—Ocean-Telegraph 539–556

CHAPTER XIV.

RIVAL CLAIMS AND LAWSUITS.

Invasion of Patent-right—O'Rielly Contract—Injunction—Lawsuit in District Court
of Kentucky—Decision—Morse Patent sustained—Incidents of the Trial—Distinguished Men engaged—Judge Pirtle's Epigram—The Case appealed—Supreme Court of the United States sustains the Morse Patent—Opinion—French
and Rogers Case—Judge Kane's Opinion—Sustains Morse's Patent—House's
and Bain's Instruments—Dr. Jackson's Pretensions—Improvements in the Telegraphic Instrument—Extent and Value of the Telegraph Business—Morse
Instruments compared with Others—Western Union Telegraph Company—
William Orton—George B. Prescott—The World's Verdict—Only One System,
that of Morse 557–588

CHAPTER XV.

1847–1854.—REST AND REWARDS.

A Home at last—Purchase of a Country-seat and Farm at Poughkeepsie—Marriage—Social and Domestic Life—Love of Nature—Birds—His Neighbors' Esteem—Letter to his Daughter—Rembrandt Peale visits Morse—Letter of Benson

J. Lossing—House in the City of New York—Letter to Arago—Adoption of the Morse System by the German Convention—Extension into Denmark, Sweden, Russia, and Australia—Honorary Distinctions and Testimonials—Scientific Bodies—Yale College—Foreign Governments . . . Pp. 589-613

CHAPTER XVI.

1854-1855.

Submarine Telegraph—The First Experiment—Newfoundland Electric Telegraph— Cyrus W. Field—Lieutenant Maury's Opinion—Formation of a New Company —Morse to Faraday—Extension of Patent—Letters to Mr. Field and Mr. White —Dr. Steinheil's Letter—Hon. D. D. Barnard—Professor Morse's Predictions— Expedition to Newfoundland—Attempt to lay the Cable—Failure—Renewed Attempt, and Success . . . . · 614-625

CHAPTER XVII.

1856.

Professor Morse visits his Native Place—Goes to Europe—Consultations in London on the Atlantic Telegraph—Mr. Peabody's Dinner—Landseer and Leslie— Whitebait Dinner—Letter to the Children—Goes to Paris and Hamburg—Attentions shown to him there—Copenhagen—Visit to the King of Denmark— Goes to Russia—Reception—Presentation to the Emperor—Visit to Berlin— Reception by Humboldt—Return to London—Scientific Experiments—Letters to Mr. Field—Banquet to Morse—Legion of Honor—Tupper's Sonnet—London *Times*—Robert Owen 626-648

CHAPTER XVIII.

1857.

Submarine Cables—Early Attempts—Construction of the Cables—Congressional Action—Professor Morse, the Electrician—Embarks on the Niagara—Letters to Mrs. Morse—Experiments with Dr. Whitehouse in London—Lord Mayor's Banquet—In Paris—Mr. Mason—Professor Morse's Claim—Return to London —Embarking—Narrow Escapes—Cable Festival—Cove of Cork—An Accident —Valentia—Sailing of the Expedition—Parting of the Cable—Attempt abandoned for the Season—Return to New York—Mr. Field's Efforts—The Second Expedition—Failure—Third Expedition—The Cable laid—The Continents connected—First Message—Great Rejoicing—Celebration—The Cable silent Eight Years—Fourth Expedition—Great Eastern—Failure—Return—Fifth Expedition—Success at last 649-666

CHAPTER XIX.

1858-1859.

Return to America—Winter in New York—Bridal Party and Festivities—Invited to Paris—Preparations for the Journey—Instruction to Farmer and Coachman— Voyage—Remarkable Prediction and Fulfillment—Paris—Banquet—Memorial to Foreign Powers—Hon. Lewis Cass—Hon. John Y. Mason—The French Government—Convention called—Governments represented—Count Walewski's

Letter to Professor Morse—Proceedings of the Convention—Amount of Award —Proportion of the Several Governments—Summary of Foreign Distinctions— Visit to the West Indies—Erection of a Telegraph—Southern Atlantic Telegraph—Correspondence—Letter from Professor Steinheil—Morse's Reply—Proposal to raise a Testimonial to Steinheil—Professor Morse's Return—Reception at Poughkeepsie . . . . Pp. 667–694

CHAPTER XX.

1860–1870.

At Home—Views on Secession and the War—Education of his Children—Letters to them—Applications for Aid—Last Visit to Europe—Düsseldorf and Artists— Paris—Attentions paid him—Reception at Court—The Great Exhibition—Habit of Life in Paris—Labors in the Committee on Telegraphs—Isle of Wight— Dresden—Presentation at Court—Berlin and the Telegraph Corps—Return to America—Purchase of Allston's "Jeremiah" and Present to Yale College— Allston's Portrait by Leslie he presents to Academy of Design—Donation to Theological Department of Yale College — To New York Union Theological Seminary—Banquet in New York—Chief-Justice Chase's Remarks—Professor Morse's—Mr. Huntington's—Summer at Poughkeepsie—His Leg is broken— Prostrate for Three Months—Statue of Humboldt—Statue of Morse—Erected by Telegraph-operators—Ceremonies in the Central Park—Academy of Music— Address by Professor Morse 695–724

CHAPTER XXI.

LITERARY AND RELIGIOUS LIFE.

A Ready Writer—Studies in his Department—Authorship—Lucretia Maria Davidson—The Serenade—Roman Catholic Controversy—Foreign Conspiracy—Confessions of a Priest—General Lafayette's Remark—Our Liberties defended— Imminent Dangers—Defense of his Invention—Religious Life—Analysis of his Christian Character—Sketch by Rev. Dr. Wheeler—Anticipations of Death— Death of his Brother Richard—The Three Brothers—The Tortoise and Hare— In his Library—Asiatic Society—Evangelical Alliance—Literary and Benevolent Labors—Domestic Peace—The Evening of Life 725–737

CHAPTER XXII.

1870–1872.

An Old Painting—Letter to the Convention in Rome—Death of Sidney E. Morse— Last Public Service—Unveiling the Statue of Franklin—Sickness—Death— Funeral—Memorial Services in Washington—Boston—Action of Congress— Legislature of Massachusetts—Telegraphic Sympathy—Tributes of Respect— Sketch of Character 738–753

APPENDIX 754–776

ILLUSTRATIONS.

MORSE, ÆT. 75.................................. *Frontispiece*

REV. DR. MORSE AND FAMILY.................. *To face page* 26

THORWALDSEN................................. " 205

MORSE, ÆT. 45............................... 251

MORSE'S WORKSHOP........................... 289

ARAGO, HUMBOLDT, AND MORSE............... 365

MORSE, PEALE, AND LOSSING................. 596

TURKISH DIPLOMA... 608

HUMBOLDT................................... 641

MORSE IN HIS STUDY......................... 726

Drawings illustrative of the invention will be found in their appropriate places in the text and the appendix.

LIFE OF SAMUEL F. B. MORSE.

CHAPTER I.

MORSE.

GENEALOGY—CHARACTERISTICS OF ANCESTORS—HIS GRANDFATHER REV. DR. SAMUEL FINLEY—HIS FATHER REV. DR. JEDEDIAH MORSE—HIS BROTHERS SIDNEY EDWARDS AND RICHARD CARY MORSE—BIRTH OF SAMUEL F. B. MORSE—PREDICTIONS.

THE name of Morse is readily traced to the time of Edward III. of England. It is variously written Mors, Moss, Morss, and Morse. During the last five hundred years the family coat-of-arms has borne the motto, "In Deo, non armis, fido:" IN GOD, NOT ARMS, I TRUST.

Anthony Morse, who was born at Marlborough, in Wiltshire, England, May 9, 1606, came to New England in 1635.

He settled in Newbury, Massachusetts, about half a mile south of the most ancient cemetery in the old town. The house in which he dwelt was on a slight eminence in a field that is known as the Morse field to this day. He was a man of courage, energy, enterprise, and great integrity of character, traits which have been transmitted through the successive generations of his family. His son Anthony succeeded to the paternal acres, lived upon them, and died February 25, 1677–'78.

Peter Morse, grandson of the first Anthony, and son of the second, removed about the year 1698 to New Roxbury, Massachusetts, and died there November 2, 1721.

John, the oldest son of Peter, resided in the same place, and was married to Sarah Peak, who lived within a month of a hundred years. She died March 15, 1801, having had ten children, seventy-two grandchildren, two hundred and nineteen great-grandchildren, and fourteen great-great-grandchildren. Their tenth and last child was Jonathan, who (it is not strange to say) died at the age of three years and four months, having read the Bible through twice, committed many passages to memory, and conducted family worship, for which he must have been emiuently qualified!

Dolly Morse died in West Woodstock, Connecticut, on the 29th of November, 1870, in the eighty-seventh year of her age, leaving one sister, in her eighty-fifth, and two brothers, one in his eighty-first and the other in his ninetieth year—all cousins of Professor Morse. The grandfather of these seven cousins died in the ninety-fourth, their grandfather's brother in the ninety-third, one of his sisters in the eighty-eighth, another in her seventy-eighth, his oldest son in the eighty-fifth, and his mother in the ninety-ninth year of their respective ages. The descendants of the great-grandmother, at the time of her death, numbered three hundred and nineteen, of whom thirty-one were of the fifth generation; and one or more of each of the last four generations resided under the same roof with the old lady when she died. If the great-grandmother, who was born in 1701, had at the time of her birth any living ancestor over eighty-one years old, three lives, viz., the lives of this ancestor, of the great-grandmother, and one of her surviving great-grandchildren, would cover the whole period of American history from the landing on Plymouth Rock to the death of Professor Morse in 1872. Professor Morse compiled a table of longevity in his family, leaving a blank in it for his own age at the time of his death, which was eighty-one. In this table he records the age of his great-great-grandmother seventy-nine, great-great-grandfather eighty-one, great-great-grandmother ninety, great-grandmother ninety-nine years and eleven months, grandfather ninety-four, grandmother eighty-one, great uncle ninety-three, great aunt eighty-eight, cousins ninety-one, eighty-seven, eighty-seven, eighty-two.

Jedediah was the oldest son of John and Sarah Morse. He was born July 8, 1726, in New Roxbury. In the year 1749 the town passed from the jurisdiction of Massachusetts to that of Connecticut, and was called Woodstock. Here Jedediah Morse, with seventy-three others, took the oath of allegiance to Connecticut at the first freemen's meeting. He was a strong man, in body and mind, an upright and able magistrate, for eighteen years one of the selectmen of the town, twenty-seven years town clerk and treasurer, fifteen years a member of the Colonial and State Legislature, and a prominent, honored, and useful member and officer of the Church. He died December 29, 1819, at the age of ninety-four.

Jedediah Morse, D. D., father of SAMUEL FINLEY BREESE MORSE, was the eighth child of Jedediah Morse, and was born in Woodstock, August 23, 1761. Dr. John Todd said of him, " Dr. Morse lived before his time, and was in advance of his generation." He was a projector, author, founder, inventor. His works were in the line of intellectual and moral progress, but to him the world owes large and lasting gratitude, as well as to his illustrious son. In early years he exhibited a fondness for books; and a delicacy of constitution unfitting him for the severe labors of the farm, his ardent desire for education was gratified by his judicious and intelligent father. In the spring of 1779, in the midst of the War of American Independence, he was admitted into Yale College. Before the term began he was drafted as a soldier in the Connecticut Line of the army. His health was so frail, there was no probability of his being able to endure the hardships of the camp and field, and at the request of his father, the Governor of the State, Jonathan Trumbull, issued an order, as captain-general, to Colonel Samuel McClellan (grandfather of Major-General George B. McClellan), directing his discharge, if in the judgment of the colonel it was proper. He was accordingly excused from the service, prosecuted his studies, and graduated in the class of 1783. He studied theology under Rev. Dr. Jonathan Edwards, son of President Edwards, and Professor Samuel Wales. Before he was licensed to preach, and while teaching school in New Haven, he projected and began his " American Geography," which afterward was inseparably identified with his name. He was licensed to preach and began his ministry at Norwich, whence he was called back to be tutor in Yale. His health was inadequate to the work, and he went to

Georgia, and spent the winter preaching at Medway. On his journey he became acquainted with Benjamin Franklin in Philadelphia, George Washington at Mount Vernon, and Dr. Ramsay, the historian, in Charleston, South Carolina, all of whom, and many others, including Drs. Rodgers, Green, Witherspoon, and Keith, made valuable contributions to the material with which he enriched his geography, and afterward his " Gazetteer of the United States."

After returning from the South with improved health he spent a few months in the city of New York, and then was settled as pastor of the First Congregational Church in Charlestown, Massachusetts, April 30, 1789, the same day and hour when Washington was inaugurated, in New York, President of the United States. Here he became the champion of that system of religious doctrine which he professed, preaching with boldness and power, publishing pamphlets and essays, establishing a religious magazine, the *Panoplist*, and subsequently a religious newspaper, the *Boston Recorder;* with others laying the foundations of the Theological Seminary at Andover, the American Board of Foreign Missions, the American Bible Society, the American Tract Society, and other benevolent institutions which have marked the first half of the nineteenth century with moral grandeur unequaled since the morning of the Christian era. Dr. Eliot, speaking of Dr. Morse, said, " What an astonishing IMPETUS that man has ! " Judge Jonas Platt pronounced him " one of the most industrious men our country has produced." President Dwight said, " He is as full of resources as an egg is of meat." Daniel Webster spoke of him as " always thinking, always writing, always talking, always acting.''

Having preached a sermon in 1799 on the " Duties of Citizens," he sent a copy of it when published to General Washington, which was acknowledged in the following letter, the original of which is preserved.

" MOUNT VERNON, *May* 26, 1799.

" REV. SIR : I thank you for your sermon ' exhibiting the present dangers and consequent duties of the citizens of the United States of America,' which came to hand by the last post, and which I am persuaded I shall read with approbating pleasure, as

soon as some matters in which I am engaged at present, are dispatched.

"With esteem and regard,

"I am, Rev. sir,

"Your obedient and obliged

"Humble servant,

"The Rev. Mr. MORSE.   G. WASHINGTON."

He was a man of genius: not content with what had been
and was; but originating, and with vast executive ability combining, the elements to produce great results. To him more
than to any other one man may be attributed the impulses given
in his day to religion and learning in the United States. A polished gentleman in his manners; the companion, correspondent,
and friend of the most eminent men in Church and State; honored at the early age of thirty-four with the degree of Doctor
of Divinity by the University of Edinburgh, Scotland; sought
by scholars and statesmen from abroad as one of the foremost
men of his country and time, such a man was the father of the
inventor of the Telegraph.

On the 10th of May, 1821, in the City Hotel of New York,
at the anniversary of the American Bible Society, Dr. Morse
delivered an address, in which he said, in substance:

"This is one of the signs of the times; one of the grand
prodigies of external Providence. But all we now see is less the
end than the beginning. It will be prodigy on prodigy, wonder
following wonder, greater as they go, till wonders become the
order of the day; wonders on wonders, the steady and established method of Providence. Besides, they will anticipate us,
not we them. New resources will be opened. New truth will
be learned—new only to us, though old itself as its Eternal Author! For God is our 'king of old, working salvation in the
midst of the earth.' Like himself always, ever original, as well
as supreme, He will do his own pleasure, and illustrate his own
word, as equally 'wonderful in counsel, and excellent in working.'"

Such were the visions of future progress before the mind of
Dr. Morse, and which he was wont to impress upon the minds
of his children.

The mothers of great men are deservedly held in honor.

On the corner of Wall and Hanover Streets, in the city of New York, where is now standing the banking-house of Brown, Brothers & Co., the mother of Morse was born, September 29, 1766. Elizabeth Ann Breese was her maiden name. She was the daughter of Samuel Breese, Esq., of Shrewsbury, New Jersey, and his wife Rebecca, daughter of Samuel Finley, D. D., President of Princeton College. Dr. Finley was of Scotch parentage. He was born in Ireland, came to America when he was nineteen years old, became a distinguished preacher and divine, and, before he was called to the presidency of Nassau Hall, he had been the teacher of pupils whose names are familiar in American history. Among them were Benjamin Rush, Ebenezer Hazard, James Waddell, D. D., John Bayard, and many others. In 1743 he was invited to preach to the *Second* Society in New Haven, Connecticut, but, as that society was not recognized by the civil authority or the New Haven Association, it was an indictable offence to preach to it! As he was on his way to church, he was seized by a constable and imprisoned. A few days afterward he was indicted by the grand-jury, and judgment was given that he should be carried out of the colony as a VAGRANT. The sentence was executed. He petitioned the Colonial Assembly in the following month to review the case, but his prayer was denied! Twenty years from the time he was carried out of New Haven as a vagrant he was President of Nassau Hall, and the University of Glasgow conferred upon him the degree of Doctor of Divinity, being, it is believed, the first time the degree was conferred by a foreign university upon any Presbyterian clergyman in America. ·

Dr. Finley was a man of great ability and extensive learning, every branch of study that was taught in the college being familiar to him. He died in Philadelphia, and the trustees of the college caused a cenotaph to be placed to his memory, among the monuments of the illustrious presidents whose dust is in the Princeton graveyard.

The wife of Dr. Finley was Sarah Hall, a lady of rare excellence; and their daughter, Rebecca Finley, became the wife of Samuel Breese, whose daughter Elizabeth Ann Breese was married, May 14, 1789, to the Rev. Jedediah Morse, of Charlestown, Massachusetts.

They began house-keeping shortly afterward in a hired house on Main Street, just at the foot of Breed's Hill. Of the simplicity of the times and the circumstances that surrounded the childhood of our subject, something may be inferred from the gifts which the newly-married couple received from their admiring people. Mr. Morse writes to his father:

"The people have been very kind in assisting us to furnish the house. We have had the following presents, viz.:

"An iron bake-pan and tea-kettle; a japanned box for sugar; three iron pots, two iron skillets, a spider, loaf of sugar, mahogany tea-table, price nine dollars; five handsome glass decanters, twelve wine-glasses, two pint-tumblers, a soup-tureen, an elegant tea-set of china, price about ten dollars; two coffee-pots, four bowls, a beautiful lantern, japanned waiter, price five dollars.

"These are quite a help to us at this time, and are manifestations of the affection of the people."

Two persons more unlike in temperament, it is said, could not have been united in love and marriage than the parents of Morse. The husband was sanguine, impulsive, resolute, regardless of difficulties and danger. She was calm, judicious, cautious, and reflecting. And she, too, had a will of her own. One day she was expressing to one of the parish her intense displeasure with the treatment her husband had received, when Dr. Morse gently laid his hand upon her shoulder and said, "My dear, you know we must throw the mantle of charity over the imperfections of others." And she replied, with becoming spirit, "Mr. Morse, charity is not a fool."

Miss Lucy Osgood, daughter of the Rev. Dr. Osgood, of Medford, Massachusetts, knew them well, and in one of her letters gives us this life-like portrait of both:

"His tall, slender form, the head always slightly inclining forward, his extremely neat dress, mild manners, and persuasive tones, aided by the charm of that perfect good-breeding which inspires even the rudest with a sense of respect for the true gentleman, made him in all places a most acceptable guest; while his own house was always celebrated as the very home of hospitality.

"Foreigners very extensively brought letters of introduction to Dr. Morse; and, though his kindness of heart sometimes exposed him to imposition, he often had the opportunity of yielding efficient service to estimable and meritorious characters. In his duties as a host, his admirable wife zealously coöperated, making her home attractive to visitors of every description by her cordial, dignified, and graceful manners, and her animated conversation. She was, indeed, distinguished for possessing, in an eminent degree, both the fascination and the virtues which most adorn a woman."

One of her sons wrote of her :

"Her pleasing manners and remarkable social powers amused and enlivened her husband's guests, while engaged in grave debate. When the Middlesex Canal, the earliest enterprise of the kind in our country, and projected by the Hon. James (afterward Governor) Sullivan, was in process of construction, it met with strong opposition. Dr. Morse, who believed it of great public utility, espoused the enterprise with his accustomed ardor, and at his house the able engineer, Colonel Loammi Baldwin, under whose superintendence the canal was built, repeatedly met the other directors sociably to talk over their difficulties.

"Mrs. Morse was present, not merely as a listener,.but occasionally spoke, and her words elicited from Baldwin, that ' madam's conversation and cup of tea removed mountains in the way of making the canal.' She was a good reader, and delighted to gather around her listeners, to whom she would read aloud from Leighton or other favorite authors. The best portrait of her is an oil painting by her son, in my possession, which represents her reading by candle-light. She was unassuming in her manners, and her remark that she liked the Charlestown people, because ladies could wear calico dresses when making visits, increased her popularity among the good people of the parish. Of her influence in making her home happy, Dr. Todd says : ' An orphan myself, and never having a home, I have gone away from Dr. Morse's house in tears, feeling that such a home must be more like heaven than any thing of which I could conceive.' "

To these parents eleven children were born, of whom only three survived their infancy. These three were sons, who attained old age, and were distinguished for purity, integrity, and great usefulness. The youngest of these brothers died first, then the second, and finally the oldest.

Richard Cary Morse was born on the 18th of June, 1795. He entered Yale College in 1808, when he was in his fourteenth year, and graduated in 1812, the youngest member of his class. The year immediately following his graduation he spent in New Haven, being employed as the amanuensis of President Dwight, and living in his family. In 1814 he entered the Theological Seminary at Andover, and, having passed through the regular three years' course, was licensed to preach in 1817. The winter immediately succeeding his licensure he spent in South Carolina as supply of the Presbyterian Church on John's Island.

On his return to New England, he was associated with his father for some time in a very successful geographical enterprise; and, in the spring of 1823, enlisted with his brother in another enterprise still more important—establishing the *New York Observer*, of which he was associate editor and proprietor for thirty-five years; and during this long period he contributed largely to its columns, especially by translations from the French and German. He became early impressed with the idea that he had not the requisite natural qualifications for the ministry, and therefore silently retired from it—though his whole life was a continued act of devotion to the objects which the ministry contemplates.

He had great aptness for acquiring languages. Not only was he familiar with the Latin, Greek, and Hebrew, but was also well versed in the French and German, and had become, in some degree, a proficient in several other modern languages. His mind was of a highly-inquisitive cast; and, though he moved about so quietly and noiselessly, he was always adding to the stores of his information. Rev. Dr. Sprague said of him: " If I were to designate any particular feature of his mind as more prominent than another, perhaps it would be his literary taste. The productions of his pen, though I believe they rarely if ever appeared before the world in connection with his name, were singularly faultless, and might well challenge the closest criticism." He died in Kissingen, Bavaria, September 23, 1868. His remains were brought home, and buried in Greenwood.

Sidney E. Morse was born February 7, 1794; entered the

Freshman class at Yale in 1805, when but eleven years old, and was graduated in 1811.

When Mr. Morse was only seventeen years old, he wrote a series of articles in the Boston *Centinel*, on the dangers from the undue multiplication of new States, thus early in life connecting himself with the newspaper press. He then studied theology at Andover, and law at Litchfield, Connecticut, in the famous law-school there. His father and Mr. Evarts (father of Hon. William M. Evarts, of this city), and other clergymen and laymen in and near Boston, wishing to establish a religious newspaper, Mr. Sidney E. Morse, at their invitation, undertook it, wrote the prospectus, employed a printer, and, as sole editor and proprietor, issued the Boston *Recorder*, the prototype of that numerous class of journals now known as " religious newspapers." In 1823, in connection with his younger brother, Richard C. Morse, he established the *New York Observer*.

Mr. Morse was the author of a school geography which has had a vast circulation, and his father before him was the pioneer in the same field.

His genius was inventive. In 1817 he and his elder brother patented the flexible piston-pump. In 1839 he produced the new art of cerography, for printing maps on the common printing-press, illustrating his new geography with it, one hundred thousand copies being sold the first year. This art has not been patented, and the process has never been made public. In his later years he engaged with his son, Mr. G. Livingston Morse, in the invention of the bathometer, for rapid explorations of the depths of the sea.

With a thorough theological and legal education, his mind trained to patient thought and cautious investigation, slow in his intellectual operations, and accurate in his statements, he had the highest possible qualifications for the great work of his life. When his mind was "made up," and his position taken, it was next to impossible to dislodge him. The tenacity with which he held his ground was justified by the caution with which it had been chosen; and it was held with conscientious sincerity and herculean ability.

His cast of mind was eminently mathematical and statistical, finding for itself enjoyment in the most abstruse, perplexing, and extended calculations and computations, tracing the peculiarities of numbers and the results of combinations. His memory of figures was extraordinary, and for hours he would descant in general converse upon the results obtained, with the same accuracy as if the figures were before him. To *discourse* upon the discoveries in art and science, and still more upon the moral progress of the age, and the great agencies in the past that had brought on the present, was the recreation and enjoyment of his life. His physical health was remarkable, as he never was laid aside a day in his life by illness, until the final blow fell on him. Of large frame and of very sedentary habits, he yet retained so great muscular power that he could, and sometimes did perform, from choice, the severest manual labor for an entire day, without exhaustion. No one ever saw him unduly excited, or heard from his lips a severe and unkind expression; while kindness, gentleness, and grace, pervaded his spirit and life. With great intellectual force, and energy that suffered no weariness or relaxation, there was also this evenness of temperament and perfect self-control, that never suffered him to be betrayed into a rash, hasty, or ill-advised word or deed. He died in the city of New York, December 23, 1871, in the seventy-eighth year of his age, and was buried in Greenwood.

SAMUEL FINLEY BREESE MORSE, the oldest of these brothers, and the inventor of the Telegraph, was born at the foot of Breed's Hill, in Charlestown, Massachusetts, April 27, 1791.

Dr. Belknap, of Boston, writing to Postmaster-General Hazard, in New York, says: "Congratulate the Monmouth Judge" (Mr. Breese, the grandfather) "on the birth of a grandson. Next Sunday he is to be loaded with names, not quite so many as the Spanish ambassador who signed the treaty of peace of 1783, but only four! As to the child, I saw him asleep, so can say nothing of his eye, or his genius peeping through it. He may have the sagacity of a Jewish rabbi, or the profundity of a Calvin, or the sublimity of a Homer, for aught I know. But time will bring forth all things."

This was a very curious prognostication on the birth of a child who became as widely known to the world as Calvin or Homer.

Dr. Witherspoon, the successor of Dr. Finley in the presi-

dency of Princeton College, visited Mr. Morse a few days after
the birth of his son, and, many years afterward, the father, writing of Dr. Witherspoon, said : " With that great and good man
I was well acquainted.   When my eldest son was an infant of a
few days old, the doctor paid us his last visit.   It will never be
forgotten ; for, deeply affected with this interview with the
granddaughter of his revered predecessor in office, he took her
infant son into his arms, and, after the manner of the ancient
patriarchs, with great solemnity gave him his blessing."

CHAPTER II.

1791–1811.

EARLY EDUCATION—HIS SCHOOL-MISTRESS—DRAWING WITH A PIN—AT GRAM-
MAR-SCHOOL—YALE COLLEGE—PRESIDENT DWIGHT—PROFESSORS DAY AND
SILLIMAN—STUDIES IN ELECTRICITY—GERMS OF THE TELEGRAPH—POR-
TRAIT-PAINTING—RECOLLECTIONS BY FELLOW-STUDENTS.

ON the father's and the mother's side, from an early period in the history of the Morse family, we have discovered traits of character which were developed in a remarkable manner in the inventor of the Telegraph. His brothers and his ancestors were distinguished for intelligence, energy, original thinking, perseverance, and unbending integrity.

The boy was trained in the school of the Puritans, by a father who was in advance of the age in which he lived. Parental discipline was not severe, but religious principles were inculcated as the source of the highest enjoyment, as well as the basis of right action. Although the son never broke away from the restraints of early instruction, he manifested in early childhood and in youth a beautiful playfulness, and fondness for amusements, that were never checked by his parents, however unlike the school in which he was trained they may now appear.

The boy was sent, when he was four years of age, to an old lady's school within a few hundred yards of the parsonage. She was an invalid, and unable to leave her chair. She was known as "Old Ma'am Rand." Her school was in a small building opposite the public-school house. She governed her unruly little flock with a long rattan, which reached across the small room in which they were gathered. One of her punishments was pinning the young culprit to her own dress. The first essays at painting or rather drawing of the young artist were quite discouraging; for he, unfortunately, had selected the old lady's face as his model, a chest of drawers for his canvas, and a pin for his pencil. We do not know now successful he was in this his first attempt, but his reward was an attachment by a large pin to the old lady's dress. In his struggles to get free the dress parted, and was dragged to a distant part of the room, but not out of reach of the terrible rattan, which descended vigorously on his devoted head.

At seven years of age he was sent to the preparatory school of Mr. Foster, at Andover, where he was fitted for entering Phillips Academy, in the same place, then under the direction of Mark Newman, the predecessor of John Adams. Here for several years he pursued the studies preparatory to entering Yale College.

Among the letters addressed to him at this early period in his life by his father, is one that incidentally shows the style of boy, who was capable of appreciating such instructions before he was ten years old.

From Rev. Dr. Morse to his Son Finley.

"CHARLESTOWN, *February* 21, 1801.

"MY DEAR SON: You do not write me as often as you ought. In your next, you must assign some reason for this neglect. Possibly I have not received all your letters. Nothing will improve you so much in epistolary writing as practice. Take great pains with your letters. Avoid vulgar phrases. Study to have your ideas pertinent and correct, and clothe them in an easy and grammatical dress. Pay attention to your spelling, pointing, the use of capitals, to your handwriting. After a little practice, these things will become natural, and you will thus acquire a habit of writing correctly and well. General Washington was a remarkable instance of what I have now recommended to you. His letters are a perfect model for epistolary writers. They are written with great uniformity in respect to the handwriting and disposition of the several parts of the letter. I will show you some of his letters when I have the pleasure of seeing you next vacation, and when I shall expect to find you much improved.

" Your natural disposition, my dear son, renders it proper for me earnestly to recommend to you to *attend to one thing at a time ;* it is impossible that you can do two things well at the same time, and I would therefore never have you attempt it. Never undertake to do what ought not to be done, and then, whatever you undertake, endeavor to do it in the best manner. It is said of De Witt, a celebrated statesman in Holland, who was torn to pieces, in the year 1672, that he did the whole business of the republic, and yet had time left to go to assemblies in the evening, and sup in company. Being asked how he could possibly find time to go through so much business, and yet amuse himself in the evenings as he did, he answered : 'There was nothing so easy, for that it was only doing one thing at a time, and never putting off any thing till to-morrow, that could be done to-day.' This steady and undissipated attention to one object, is a sure mark of a superior genius; as hurry, bustle, and agitation, are the never-failing symptoms of a weak and frivolous mind. I expect you will read this letter over several times, that you may retain its contents in your memory. Give me your opinion on the advice I have given you. If you improve this well, I shall be encouraged to give you more, as you may need it. Your mamma is very well, as are your brothers Edward, Richard Cary, and James Russell; the last named you have never seen; your brothers are very fond of him, as we all are, for he is a fine little boy.

"We all unite in love to you and Mr. Brown. Tell Mr. Brown that I have a little pain in my breast, which renders writing hurtful to me, else I would write to him.

"Your affectionate parent,
"J. MORSE."

The reply to this letter has not been preserved, but the judicious counsel of the father, repeated often, was not lost on his son. He studied, read, and wrote, at this early age, as if he were conscious that man's work was expected of him. Even at this period of life, before habits could have been formed, or character developed, he showed a tendency to turn away from the routine studies of the school, to think and act for himself.

He roved among books, but books that were not in the course. He pored over Plutarch's "Lives of Illustrious Men," and his ambition was fired by the records of their deeds and fame. When he was only thirteen years of age, and at this preparatory school in Andover, he wrote a sketch of the " Life of Demosthenes," and sent it to his father; among whose papers it is preserved, as a mark of the genius, learning, and taste of the child!

He dreamed while he was awake. He grew rapidly in stature. His attainments in general scholarship were remarkable, and in the regular studies of the school his proficiency was such that, at the age of fourteen, he was thoroughly qualified to enter college, and was admitted to the Freshman class in Yale.

Domestic reasons induced his father to detain him from college another year, and he joined the class in 1807.

Timothy Dwight, D. D., was then the President of Yale College, and at his feet, and under the forming power of this great man, Finley Morse sat four years. Dr. Dwight was the warm personal friend, correspondent, and counselor of Dr. Morse, Finley's father, and at his expressed desire, as well as from the promptings of his own feelings of friendship, Dr. Dwight took the deepest personal interest in the young student confided to his special care. The president was a man of vast and varied learning, and of strong original powers of mind. He was a master of inductive philosophy. Few men have ever lived possessing such command of facts, having them arranged in such order, in his wonderful memory, as to be able to bring them always and instantly to his use. Professor Olmstead says:

"He combined, in a remarkable degree, the dignity that commands respect, the accuracy that inspires confidence, the ardor that kindles animation, and the kindness that wins affection. He urged upon his students the importance of observing and retaining facts; he explained the principles of association, and the various acts which would contribute to fix them in the mind, and also displayed, in the reasonings and illustrations, both the efficacy of his rules and the utility of the practice which he earnestly recommended.

"In theology and ethics, in natural philosophy and geography, in history and statistics, in poetry and philosophy, in husbandry and domestic economy, his treasures seemed alike inexhaustible. Interesting narration, vivid description, and sallies of humor; anecdotes of the just, the good, the generous, the brave, the eccentric—these all were blended in fine proportions to form the bright and varied tissues of his discourse. Alive to all the sympathies of friendship, faithful to its claims, and sedulous in performing its duties, he was beloved by many from early life with whom he entered on the stage, and whom, as Shakespeare says, he ' grappled to his soul with hooks of steel.'

"I think it may safely be said that those who gained the most intimate access to him, whether associates, or pupils, or amanuenses, admired, revered, and loved him most."

Before Finley Morse finished his collegiate course his two brothers entered Yale, and, Dr. Dwight's eyesight having been impaired, these young men became his amanuenses. Thus, their relations to the president being intimate and confidential, they were in a situation to feel the full influence of his almost magical power. When Finley Morse was a sophomore in college he wrote in one of his letters to his parents, dated December 23, 1807:

"A remarkable phenomenon appeared here a few days ago. A meteor passed some distance from the town and burst in Fairfield County; large pieces of stone were contained in it, and lay scattered round a number of miles. Mr. Silliman went with Mr. Kingsley to see a piece of this stone; he applied a magnet to it, and by its attraction found it to contain iron. The explosion was very loud; it was heard here in New Haven while the students were in at prayers; I heard it at the same time. I will try and obtain a piece of the stone of Mr. Silliman, and keep it to bring home for a curiosity."

And in his next he gives a report of a scene which shows that boys in college were, two generations ago, about the same as now. He was boarding in commons, and thus he writes:

"*December* 28, 1807.

" We had a new affair here a few days ago. The college cooks were arraigned before the tribunal of the students, consisting of a committee of four from each class in college; I was chosen as one of the committee from the Sophomore class. We sent for two of the worst cooks, and were all Saturday afternoon in trying them; found them guilty of several charges, such as being insolent to the students, not exerting themselves to cook clean for us, in concealing pies which belonged to the students, having suppers at midnight, and inviting all their neighbors and friends to sup with them at the expense of the students · and this not once in a while, but almost

2

every night. We extorted this from one of them, that the reason
they were so neglectful toward us was, because there had been no
disturbance in college for seven years; that the students, and the
authority, not taking much notice of their conduct, they meant to
do as they please. The committee, after arranging the charges in
their proper order, presented them to the president; he has had
the authorities together, and they are now considering the subject.
This afternoon, Tuesday, December 29th, they have been together,
and I, with many others, have been with them all the afternoon;
there was no recitation at four o'clock, they were so busily engaged.
I know not how this affair will end, but I expect in the expulsion of
some, if not all, of the cooks. It is now three weeks since the students convened to appoint their committee, and since that we have
lived extremely well; indeed, for my part, I think we have lived
very well this term. The fault is not so much in the food as in the
cooking, for our bill of fare has generally been in the following
way: Chocolate, coffee, and hashed meat, every morning; at noon,
various; roast-beef twice a week, pudding three times, and turkeys
and geese upon an average once a fortnight; baked beans occasionally; Christmas, and other merry days, turkeys, pies, and puddings,
many as we wish for; at night for supper we have, chocolate and
tea in general, pies once a week; I ought to have added that in future we are to have beefsteaks and toast twice a week; before this
the cooks were too lazy to cook them. I will inform you of the
result of this affair as soon as it is completed.

"I have just now as much as I can do; my leisure moments are
employed in composing, reviewing geometry, and reading history;
I am now reading Winterbottom's "China." I have read Cave's
"Stranger in Ireland," and intend soon to read his "Northern Summer," I am very much pleased with him as an author. I began to
read Robertson's "Charles V.," but, finding several leaves in the
book missing, I have deferred it till another time."

                                        "*January* 25, 1808.

"The result of the cooks' trial is: one has been dismissed, two
remain on trial for good behavior, the rest are in their former
standing."

Jeremiah Day was at this time the Professor of Natural
Philosophy in Yale College. Under his instructions Mr. Morse
began the study of electricity, and received those impressions
which were destined to produce so great an influence upon him

personally, and upon the business, the intercourse, and the happiness of the human race. Dr. Dwight was the man who prepared his naturally susceptible mind to receive, retain, and utilize those impressions. Professor Day was then young and ardent in his pursuit of science, kindling readily the enthusiasm of his students by the fire of his own. Afterward he became the president of the college, and his name is identified with its subsequent renown. Forty years after Morse had left the institution, Dr. Day, ex-president of the college, bore this testimony:

"In my lectures on Natural Philosophy, the subject of electricity was specially illustrated and experimented upon. Enfield's work was the text-book.

"The terms of the 21st Proposition of Book V. of 'Enfield's Philosophy,' are these: 'If the circuit be interrupted, the fluid will become visible, and when it passes it will leave an impression upon any intermediate body.'

"I lectured upon and illustrated the first two experiments propounded by the 21st Proposition, and I recollect the fact with certainty, by memoranda now in my possession. The experiments referred to are in terms as follows:

"Experiment. 1st. Let the fluid pass through a chain, or through any metallic bodies, placed at small distances from each other, the fluid in a dark room will be visible between the links of the chain, or between the metallic bodies.

"Experiment 2d. If the circuit be interrupted by several folds of paper, a perforation will be made through it, and each of the leaves will be protruded by the stroke from the middle to the outward leaves."

This was the germ of the great invention that now daily and hourly astonishes the world, and has given immortality of fame to the student who, twenty-two years afterward, conceived the idea of making this experiment of practical value to mankind. Writing on the subject in 1867, Mr. Morse said: "The fact that the presence of electricity can be made visible in any desired part of the circuit was the crude seed which took root in my mind, and grew up into form, and ripened into the invention of the Telegraph."

But there was at the same time, in the faculty of Yale Col-

lege, another illustrious man, to whom, more than to Dr. Dwight
or Dr. Day, Mr. Morse was indebted for those impressions
which resulted finally in his great invention. Benjamin Silliman long held front rank among men of science. His contributions made rich the journal that was known by his name, and
his lectures, letters, and travels, rendered his name familiar
throughout the bounds of civilization and learning. Silliman
was Professor of Chemistry while Morse was a student in Yale,
and was at once his teacher and friend. When his testimony
was required, to show when and how the mind of Morse was
first turned to the study of electricity, and in what stage of
advancement the science was at the time of Morse's attention to
it in college, Professor Silliman said: " S. F. B. Morse was an
attendant on my lectures in the years 1808, 1809, and 1810.
I delivered lectures on chemistry and *galvanic electricity.* The
batteries then in use were the *pile of Volta,* the battery of
Cruikshanks, and the *Couronne des tasses,* well known to the
cultivators of that branch of science. *I always exhibited these
batteries to my classes ; they were dissected before them, and
their members and the arrangement of the parts, and the mode
of exciting them, were always shown."*

And the professor went on to show that, when Mr. Morse
came to reside in New Haven, ten years after his graduation,
he resumed his inquiries in the same direction, with lively interest in the pursuit of electrical science. He says : " Mr.
Morse resided near me for several years, from 1821–'22 onward.
The families were on terms of intimacy, and Mr. Morse was in
the habit of frequent communication with me. About this time
Dr. Hare's splendid galvanic calorimoter, and his galvanic defla-
grator, were invented, and were in my possession, and many
interesting and beautiful results were exhibited by them, as, for
example, the fusion of charcoal, and the combustion of metals.
*Mr. Morse was often present in my laboratory during my pre-
paratory arrangements and experiments,* and was thus made
acquainted with them."

In the year 1809, while Mr. Morse was yet a student in
Yale, a work was published, entitled an " Epitome of Electricity
and Galvanism," by two gentlemen of Philadelphia. The work
excited interest beyond the city where it was published, and

arrested the attention of the Rev. Dr. Morse, the father of Finley Morse, still residing in Charlestown, Massachusetts. Dr. Morse wrote to Dr. John McLean, Professor of Natural Philosophy in Princeton College, asking him to write a review of the work for the *Panoplist*, a magazine then published in Boston. The subject was at that time commanding marked attention, and the Morses, father and sons, were the men to be intelligently interested in the developments of the science. We shall find the son, Finley Morse, renewing his studies in the same direction with Professor Dana, of the University of New York, five years before the invention, and, at a still later date, with Professor Renwick, of Columbia College, becoming charged with all the principles and phenomena of the science, as if, even then, in his own mind, as in the recesses of providential design, the grand result was maturing.

The testimony of Professors Day and Silliman was given in court, when it was important, in the defence of his claim to priority in the invention of the Telegraph, for Mr. Morse to be able to show that his mind was early interested in the study of chemistry and electricity. While he was collecting testimony from his instructors, at whose feet he sat while a boy in college, he was not aware that, among the letters and papers of his venerable father, long since deceased, there were quietly reposing some of the letters that the young student wrote to his parents while he was in college, and in which he refers to the studies that specially interested him, and made a lasting impression upon his mind. These letters were found among the old papers of his father, Dr. Morse, after the death of the son, and it is quite probable they have never been read from the year of their date to the present time, a term of sixty-five years. Certainly if Mr. Morse had known of their existence, he would have brought them from their hiding-place, and by their evidence proved what he was in the habit of asserting, that while in college these subjects engaged his special attention. Writing to his parents, and dating, Yale College, New Haven, January 1, 1809, he says :

"I am very much pleased with chemistry. It is very amusing, as well as instructive. There are many very beautiful and surprising experiments performed, which are likewise very useful. I intend, with your leave, getting me 'a chemical trough' and small apparatus when I come home, Ward" (a classmate) "and I to bear the expense together. You will find our experiments very entertaining. There will be a number of articles which we shall want, which we shall be obliged to get here, on account of their being obtained here cheaper, such as gun-barrels, retorts, etc., the use of which I will explain to you hereafter."

January 9, 1809, he writes again as to the manner in which he would pass an approaching vacation, when he was not going home on account of the expense of travel; he says: "Please to write often, as it will serve to heighten our spirits; they are a little depressed at the approach of a vacation, which we are not destined to enjoy. I find it a difficult task to do nothing. I shall be employed in the vacation in the 'Philosophical Chamber' with Mr. Dwight, who is going to prepare a number of experiments in electricity."

February 27, 1809, he writes: "My studies are, at present, optics in philosophy, dialing, Homer, besides attending lectures, etc., all of which I find very interesting, and especially Mr. Day's lectures, who is now lecturing on electricity." Still more explicit and emphatic are his words, in a letter of March 8, 1809:

"My studies are quite easy to what they were last term. Homer is quite easy; optics in philosophy are in some degree hard, but interesting; and spherics, in the second volume of Webber, is very hard. Our disputes and compositions require a great deal of hard thinking and close application, which I hope they do not want from me. Our chemical lectures at present are not very interesting. Mr. Silliman is now lecturing on the earths, and this part has always been considered very dry. Mr. Day's lectures are very interesting, they are upon electricity; he has given us some very fine experiments, the whole class taking hold of hands, form the circuit of communication, and we all received the shock apparently at the same moment. I never took an electric shock before; it felt as if some person had struck me a slight blow across the arms. Mr. Day has given us two lectures on this subject, and I believe there are two more remaining; I will give you some account of them as soon as they are delivered, which will probably be in the course of this week."

These passages are taken from the very few of his college letters which have been found. Scores have been lost, and it is extraordinary that so many have survived the half of a century.

The Rev. Dr. Barstow, of Keene, N. H., a great student and a distinguished divine, was in college with Finley Morse, and his two brothers, who entered before Finley completed his course. Dr. Barstow writes of the three brothers:

" All three were exceedingly reputable, studious, and conformed to the laws of the college, holding an honorable rank in the curriculum of branches pursued in their several classes. But, beyond all this, they accomplished much in pursuit of branches agreeable to their respective tastes, talents, and inclinations; exhibiting as wonderful a variety as we ever see in the members of the same household. Richard, with all the sedateness and gravity of a young theologue, studied and pondered the deep mysteries of theology, and the deeds and doctrines of the Reformers. Sidney E. pursued with avidity those branches of learning that prepared him so admirably to perform the important duties of a religious journalist, to the great satisfaction and benefit of the Christian public; and the Professor, Samuel Finley Breese, inquired with enthusiasm into those physical sciences that prepared him for his distinguished career as an electrician, together with the æsthetics of a self-taught artist and painter.

" The lectures of Professor Silliman, upon chemistry and mineralogy, were then exciting great interest upon those subjects among the students; and in them Finley Morse exhibited ESPECIAL ENTHUSIASM. Finley was the most companionable and genial of the three; he was ever ready to welcome to his rooms those college friends that loved to associate with him; always gentlemanly; always having a kind word for others, and always ready to do kind offices to all.

" On a certain occasion, the writer of this note was admiring his pictures, and the inquiry was made, 'Why can you not paint my likeness?' The answer immediately was, 'I will do it;' and the result was a most *perfect likeness*, though the coloring was not so perfect as Mr. Morse accomplished after attending upon the instruction of others. But he would receive no compensation for the portrait, delighting to do a favor to those he esteemed."

Dr. John W. Sterling, of Port Richmond, Staten Island, in a letter dated January 10, 1872, about three months before the death of Professor Morse, incidentally gives some pleasant recollections of the college-life of the young Morses :

"It so happened that, in the year 1809, when I was of the Freshman class of Yale College, Mr. S. F. B. Morse was a member of the Senior, Sidney E. Morse of the Junior, and Richard Morse of the Sophomore classes. Among the reminiscences of those early days, I recall to mind the portraits painted on the walls of his room by the celebrated S. F. B. Morse, and also an amusing sketch, by this gentleman, of 'Freshmen climbing the Hill of Science,' representing these poor fellows scrambling upon their hands and knees in order to reach the pinnacle of eminence. But what remains most vividly in my memory is, the balloon which they constructed of letter-paper, purchased, I think, at the paper-mill at Humphreysville, styled Rock of Rimmon by its poetic proprietor, Colonel Humphreys.

"This balloon was eighteen feet in length, was suspended from the tower of the Lyceum of Yale College, inflated with rarefied air, and sent aloft with its blazing tail, rising most gloriously until it vanished in the distance. This balloon was recovered, and another effort was made to raise it. In rising, however, it lurched, driven by the wind against the middle college-building, took fire, ascended in a blaze, but was soon reduced to black ashes."

When four years old, the boy began to scratch the portrait of his teacher with a pin upon a chest of drawers, and this early tendency manifested itself as he grew. In college it contributed to his support. Dr. Barstow recollects that he would not take pay for the picture made of *him*, but Morse was glad to get what he could in this way, to aid him in the payment of expenses, which were exceedingly heavy upon a clergyman having three sons in college at the same time.

He tried his hand upon some of his classmates. The imperfect likenesses, and worse paintings, appeared marvelous, when produced by an untaught boy. The young men were willing to pay moderate prices for rude pictures of themselves, which were a surprise and delight to their friends at home. But he made no great attainments in the art while in college. As yet no master had given him a lesson. He was feeling his own way along, with dreams of future distinction, even at this early period.

August 9, 1809, he writes to his parents :

" I employ my leisure time in painting. I have a large number of persons engaged already to be drawn on ivory, no less than seven. They obtain the ivories for themselves. I have taken Professor Kingsley's *profile* for him. It is a good likeness, and he is pleased with it. I think I shall take his likeness on ivory, and present it to him at the end of the term."

"*June* 25, 1810.

" Mr. Nettleton is better, and is willing I shall take his likeness as part pay (for board). I shall take it on ivory. My price is five dollars for a miniature on ivory, and I have engaged three or four at that price. My price for profiles is one dollar, and everybody is ready to engage me at that price."

His college course was drawing near its close. He had no profession in view, but to be an artist, a painter, was his ambition. Had not his father been a man of large views and generous feelings, he could not have yielded to his son's desires to turn away from the learned professions, for which he had given him a liberal education. But the bent of his genius was already clearly indicated. July 22, 1810, he writes to his parents as to his future :

" I am now released from college, and am attending to painting. As to my choice of a profession, I still think that I was made for a painter, and I would be obliged to you to make such arrangements with Mr. Allston, for my studying with him, as you shall think expedient. I should desire to study with him during the winter, and, as he expects to return to England in the spring, I should admire to be able to go with him, but of this we will talk when we meet at home."

This was written in the Senior recess, before commencement, when he was to be graduated.

His mother writes to him and gives directions as to the making of his coat in which to appear at commencement when he graduates, and his father gives his consent that he should be one of the managers of the commencement ball.

The first group that he ever painted was executed while he was a student in college. It is a family scene, and is still preserved, having an interest far beyond that which attaches to the first effort of one who afterward reached the heights of fame. The painting represents Rev. Dr. Morse, the father, standing by the side of a globe, on which he is discoursing to his three sons, while the mother sits by. A copy of this picture is here given.

When Dr. Morse was in Charleston, South Carolina, in 1810, he was intrusted with the care of the son of a friend, and brought him to the North to enter Yale College. Having been admitted, he was confided to the special attention of Finley Morse, then in his senior year. The recollections of this Southern student, now the venerable Joseph M. Dulles, Esq., of Philadelphia, are fresh and vivid, and are given in his own words, from a letter written October 16, 1872:

" I first became acquainted with him at New Haven, when about to graduate with the class of 1810, and had such association as a boy preparing for college might have with a senior who was just finishing his course. Having come to New Haven under the care of Rev. Jedediah Morse, the venerable father of the three Morses, all distinguished men, I was commended to the protection of Finley, as he was then commonly designated, and therefore saw him frequently during the brief period we were together. The father I regarded as the gravest man I ever knew. He was a fine exemplar of the gentler type of the Puritan, courteous in manner, but stern in conduct and in aspect. He was a man of conflict, and a leader in the theological contests in New England in the early part of this century. Finley, on the contrary, bore the expression of gentleness entirely. In person rather above the ordinary height, well formed, graceful in demeanor, with a complexion, if I remember right, slightly ruddy, features duly proportioned, and often lightened with a genial and expressive smile. He was, altogether, a handsome young man, with manners unusually bland. It is needless to add that with intelligence, high culture, and general information, and with a strong bent to the fine arts, Mr. Morse was in 1810 an attractive young man. During the last year of his college-life he occupied his leisure hours, with a view also to his self-support, in taking the likenesses of his fellow-students on ivory, and no doubt with success, as he obtained afterward a very respectable rank as a portrait-painter. Many pieces of his skill were afterward executed in Charleston, South Carolina. I met him there, and in his genial manner he said to me: 'I am so glad to see you. You remember that miniature; it was unfinished when I left New Haven.

THE FAMILY OF REV. DR. MORSE.

I have carried it with me ever since, and over Europe, and thought a hundred times that I would wash it out and put the ivory to some other use. Come to my studio and I will be glad to give it to you.' This memorial of our former intimacy is still in my possession."

His college course being terminated at commencement in the year 1810, he returned to his father's house in Charlestown, Massachusetts, with a settled purpose to pursue the art of painting. His mind was busy with something besides books. Writing to his brothers who were still in college, he uses "sympathetic" ink, invisible until exposed to heat, and in their reply they tell him they cannot read it; he answers, and announces his devotion to his chosen art

"BOSTON, *December* 8, 1810.

"MY DEAR BROTHERS: You wanted to know how you should read what I had written with the sympathetic ink. It was written on the paper which covered the newspaper. It appears to me, if you hold it to the fire so as to warm it till it is quite hot, the writing will appear. I can hardly believe that it should lose its effect in going between this and New Haven; what was written was not of much consequence, and now can be but entirely useless as it was new then, but now must be quite stale. There is nothing new here now; I have almost completed my landscape; it is 'proper handsome' so they say, and they want to make me believe it is so, too, but I sha'n't yet a while.

"I am going to begin, as soon as I have finished this, a piece, the subject of which will be 'Marius on the Ruins of Carthage.' Mr. Allston is very kind and attentive to me, and tries every way to be serviceable to me.

"I am attending a course of anatomical and surgical lectures in Boston, under Dr. Warren. He is an excellent lecturer, and knows anatomy as well as any man, if not better, in the United States. The lectures, contrary to my expectations, are extremely interesting. One would suppose at first they would be rather disagreeable and disgusting on account of the dissections, but it is not at all so. They have just begun. They are delivered every day at one o'clock, and are in length about an hour."

CHAPTER III.

1811–1815.

WASHINGTON ALLSTON—MORSE GOES TO LONDON UNDER HIS TUITION—THE VOYAGE—LONGINGS FOR A TELEGRAPH—BENJAMIN WEST—MORSE'S LETTERS TO HIS PARENTS—TO A FRIEND AT HOME—IMPRESSIONS OF WEST—LESLIE THE PAINTER—HE AND MORSE BECOME ROOM-MATES—SAMUEL TAYLOR COLERIDGE—TRIUMPHS OF THE YOUNG ARTIST—MEETS WITH WILLIAM WILBERFORCE, HENRY THORNTON, ZACHARY MACAULAY, LORD GLENELG, AND OTHERS—VISIT AT MR. THORNTON'S—INTERCOURSE WITH COLERIDGE — TRAVELS TO OXFORD, AND INCIDENTS — FIRST PORTRAIT ABROAD—LESLIE AND MORSE—LETTERS TO HIS PARENTS—ZERAH COLBURN—DARTMOOR PRISONERS—ATTEMPTS TO SERVE THEM—DUNLAP'S ACCOUNT OF MORSE—DYING HERCULES—JUDGMENT OF JUPITER—GOLD MEDAL—MRS. ALLSTON'S DEATH—SCENE AT MR. WILBERFORCE'S—RETURN HOME.

WASHINGTON ALLSTON returned from Europe in 1809, and spent two years in Boston, where he was married to the sister of the Rev. Dr. Channing. Just from college, and burning with ambition to be a painter, young Morse sought the acquaintance of Allston, who was then the greatest artist in this country. Morse saw him and loved him. The affection grew into reverence, continued through life, and when the great master, Allston, died, more than thirty years after this first meeting, his favorite pupil, Morse, begged the brush, still fresh with paint, as it dropped from the dying artist's hand, and kept it as a sacred memorial of his teacher and friend. He deposited it in the New York Academy of Design, which he founded, and it is there preserved as a sacred memorial of Allston, and of the veneration of Morse for his first master in art.

If the youth would be a painter, his father was disposed to give him such advantages as were necessary to his success. Allston was about returning to Europe, and to his care Mr. Morse was committed. More than to any, or all other teachers, Morse was indebted to Allston for his rapid triumphs in art.

Washington Allston was born in Charleston, South Carolina, November 5, 1779, and was graduated at Harvard College in the year 1800, having already developed a love for music, poetry, and painting. With tastes the most delicate and pure, ardent in his feelings, delighting in the heroic, romantic, and ideal, he was one of the most noble and beautiful characters of the age which he adorned. He went to London in 1801, and studied under Benjamin West, with whom he formed an intimate friendship. Then he studied in Paris. In Italy he spent four years. Here he found Samuel Taylor Coleridge, of whom he said, in one of his letters, " To no other man do I owe so much intellectually as to Mr. Coleridge, who has honored me with his friendship for more than five-and-twenty years." In England Mr. Allston was also the friend of Wordsworth, Southey, Lamb, Reynolds, and other brilliant and distinguished men. After a brief visit of two years in his own country, he returned to London, and divided his time between poetry and painting. He was a deeply religious man. A Christian by conviction, his whole nature was filled with adoration of Him whom not having seen he loved, an ever-present Being in whom he lived and moved. Having passed seven years abroad in this second visit, he came home to America, where his name was already illustrious as the greatest artist the country had produced. His works commanded the highest prices that had ever been paid in America for paintings. A rare impersonation of the virtues that adorn humanity, with fine intellectual powers, and a spirit attuned to the love of his fellow-men, such was the man to whom Finley Morse was confided at the outset of his career in the art of painting.

Mr. Morse began to write a journal on the voyage from New York to Liverpool. He wrote daily till the voyage was ended, then ceased; resumed it again on the return-voyage, four years afterward; and, with the exception of a few notes during one of his journeys in Europe, no diary remains. We are therefore left to recollections of others, letters to and from him, and records of the public press, for the material of his biography. Happily these materials are so abundant as to enable us to follow him through every step of his life.

Extracts from his Journal.

"After being wind-bound in New York harbor for several days, I embarked on board the ship Lydia, Captain Waite, for Liverpool, on Saturday, July 13, 1811; went only as far as the quarantine ground on Staten Island, where we lay over Sunday. We have fourteen very agreeable passengers, collected from all quarters of the globe : Mr. Amberger, a Russian; Mr. Neupaner, a Prussian; Mr. Minshall, the *famous dramatist*, an Englishman; Mr. Gray and Mr. Parmer, Scotchmen; Captain Visscher and lady, Mr. Allston and lady, Mrs. Waite, the wife of the captain, and a woman-servant of Captain and Mrs. Visscher, Mr. Searl, and Mr. Lord, Americans."

He beguiled the hours of the voyage by making notes upon the passengers, the crew, the ship, and the sea, with pencil-sketches, for he was young and buoyant, and every thing was fresh and new. The *famous dramatist* was the occasion of infinite amusement, for everybody laughed *at* him, while he imagined that his wit and humor were entertaining others. The journal says:

"Mr. Minshall is the author of several plays, as he calls them, though no one can make head or tail of them; he will receive flattery of the grossest kind, and is so puffed up by it as to make himself a laughing-stock to the whole ship's company. He has been repeating to us this evening an epilogue to one of his plays, with such out-of-the-way gestures as to make us almost burst our sides with laughing, he supposing all this time that we were laughing at the wit of the composition, and joining with us in our mirth with his whole soul."

Nothing unusual occurred to make the passage memorable, and in twenty days from port the land beyond was in sight. In six days more they made the harbor of Liverpool, where, says the journal:

"We prepared to go ashore among hundreds of people who had assembled on the wharf. Some had come to hear the news; some

to receive letters from friends in America ; some from mere curiosity. But by far the greater part of the crowd had hastened to
see us dashed against the head of the wharf by the fury of the
tide. About a quarter-past eleven o'clock I placed my foot upon
terra firma, not a little rejoiced on the occasion, although in a land
of strangers. My fellow-passengers with me walked up into town
to find lodgings. We established ourselves at the Liverpool Arms
Hotel, the same at which Professor Silliman staid when in this
place a number of years since.

"*Friday, August 9th.* I went to the mayor to get leave to go
to London. He gave me ten days to get there, and told me if he
found me in Liverpool after that time he should put me in prison,
at which I could not help smiling. His name is Drinkwater, but,
from the appearance of his face, I should judge it might be Drink-
brandy."

Thus hurried out of town by the mayor, with a degree of
severity only to be accounted for by the excitements of the day,
which then indicated hostilities between the United States and
England, Mr. Morse set off in a post-chaise for London with Mr.
and Mrs. Allston. The journey of two hundred miles was extended through a week, as the health of Mrs. Allston required
slow stages and frequent rest.

He found lodgings in London at No. 67 Great Titchfield
Street, and immediately wrote to his parents announcing his arrival. In this *first* letter he expresses a longing that seems
prophetic of his great invention. He says, after mentioning his
safety :

"I only wish you had this letter now to relieve your minds from
anxiety, for while I am writing I can imagine mother wishing that
she could hear of my arrival, and thinking of thousands of accidents which may have befallen me. *I wish that in an instant I
could communicate the information : but three thousand miles are
not passed over in an instant, and we must wait four long weeks
before we can hear from each other.*"

On the outside of this letter, yellow with age, is written in
his own hand with pencil, but at what date is not known, probably toward the end of his life, these words : "LONGING FOR A
TELEGRAPH EVEN IN THIS LETTER."

The letter continues :

"I long to begin to paint. Mr. Allston has just returned from Mr. West, who will be very glad to see me to-morrow. His great picture" (Christ Healing the Sick) "is much talked of, and is pronounced by connoisseurs the best ever painted in England. Mr. West told Mr. Allston that its exhibition had produced to the British Institution, for whose benefit it was exhibited, upward of nine thousand pounds, although it was open only a few weeks.

"Not being well to-day, I sent my letter of introduction to Dr. Lettsom, with a request that he would call on me, which he did, and prescribed a medicine which cured me in an hour or two. Dr. Lettsom is a very singular man. He looks considerably like the print you have of him : he is a moderate Quaker, but not precise and stiff like the Quakers of Philadelphia. He is very pleasant and sociable, and withal very blunt in his address ; he is a man of excellent information, and is considered among the greatest literary characters here. There is one peculiarity, however, which he has in conversation, that of using the verb in the third person singular with the pronoun in the first person, as, instead of *I show*, he says *I shows*, etc., upon which peculiarity the famous Mr. Sheridan made the following lines in ridicule of him :

> 'If patients call, both one and all,
> I bleeds 'em, and I sweats 'em ;
> And if they die, why, what cares I ?
> I Letts'om.' "

On the following day Mr. Allston introduced the young student to the great master Mr. West.

That was a memorable moment in the history of Finley Morse. The fame of Benjamin West was at that time as wide as the world of art ; and his history was familiar to every American who aspired to eminence in that world. Mr. West was an American, and now at the head of the Royal Academy of England—his time and genius in the employ of the king. Morse, a young pilgrim from the United States, slender, fair-haired, modest, and gentle, with his foot not yet on the first round of the ladder of fame, stood before his illustrious countryman, and the distance between them appeared all but infinite. Yet the career of West was the guide and stimulus to the youthful student.

Benjamin West was born in Springfield, Pennsylvania,

where his father kept a country store. The boy was only seven years old when he made with a pen and ink the likeness of his little sister in a cradle, and so life-like that the mother, who caught him at it, exclaimed, "I declare, he has made a likeness of our Sally!" A party of wild Indians taught him the use of their colors, and he made hair-brushes from the back and tail of a cat. A friend sent him a box of paints and brushes when he was eight years old. The reputation of the artist-boy reached Philadelphia. He was encouraged to study. His portrait of a beautiful woman in Lancaster made him famous in that region, and sitters thronged him. The provost of the University of the State invited him to Philadelphia, with a promise of patronage. The family were Quakers, and to the Society of Friends the question of the boy's future was referred. They very wisely decided that "a man-child has been born, to whom God has given some remarkable gifts, and we shall do God's will by giving him our sanction to use them." Very wise these good Quakers were in their decision. They said: "Genius is given of God for some high purpose. What that purpose is, let us not inquire; it will be manifested in his own good time and way. He hath in this remote wilderness endowed with rich gifts this youth, who has now our consent to cultivate his talents for art." Then all the women came forward and kissed the handsome young artist, and the men laid their hands upon his head. Thus, with the kisses of women and the benedictions of men, the young Benjamin was consecrated to the work of his life. He painted in Philadelphia and then in New York, and, when his portraits and other pictures had brought him money enough to warrant the expense, he went to Italy in 1760. He was then only twenty-two years old. His career was upward, steadily and rapidly. He visited all the chief cities of Italy, copied the greatest works of the old masters, then went to Paris, and, arriving in London in 1763, was welcomed by Sir Joshua Reynolds, who encouraged him to exhibit his pictures there. They commanded recognition, and established his reputation at once. He determined to remain in London. Two years after his arrival the king sent for him, and gave him a commission, took him into his favor, afterward gave him a salary, and required his whole time to be devoted to his service. During the

3

War of American Independence, West remaining true to his native country, enjoyed the continued confidence of the king, and was actually engaged upon his portrait when the Declaration of Independence was handed to him. Mr. Morse received the facts from the lips of Mr. West himself, and communicated them to me in these words:

"I called upon Mr. West, at his house in Newman Street, one morning, and in conformity with the order given to his servant Robert, always to admit Mr. Leslie and myself, even if he was engaged in his private studies, I was shown into his studio. As I entered, a half-length portrait of George III. stood before me upon an easel, and Mr. West was sitting with his back toward me, copying from it upon canvas. My name having been mentioned to him, he did not turn, but, pointing with the pencil he had in his hand to the portrait from which he was copying, he said:

"'Do you see that picture, Mr. Morse?'

"'Yes, sir,' I said; 'I perceive it is the portrait of the king.'

"'Well,' said Mr. West, 'the king was sitting to me for that portrait when the box containing the American Declaration of Independence was handed to him.'

"'Indeed,' I answered; 'and what appeared to be the emotions of the king? what did he say?'

"'Well, sir,' said Mr. West, 'he made a reply characteristic of the goodness of his heart,' or words to that effect. 'Well, if they can be happier under the government they have chosen, than under mine, I shall be happy.'"

As the king became superannuated, the work on which West was engaged for the royal chapel was suspended, and his salary discontinued. But his position as the great master of the age was secure. And as President of the Royal Academy, the painter of "Christ Healing the Sick," and of "Christ Rejected by the Jews," the presence of the venerable man, now seventy-three years old, excited, in the mind of the student standing before him, emotions of admiration rising into reverential awe.

West received young Morse as a father and a friend. The introduction by Allston would have been sufficient, and he had letters to Mr. West, which secured his attention and awakened his interest at once.

In a very few days Mr. Morse was hard at work, and the

impressions made upon him by the great master, at whose feet
he had come to sit, and the inspiration which had already taken
possession of his soul, will appear in a letter written within a
fortnight:

To his Parents.

"LONDON, *August* 24, 1811.

"I have begun my studies, the first part of which is drawing;
I am drawing from the head of Demosthenes at present, to get accustomed to handling black and white chalk; I shall then commence
a drawing, for the purpose of trying to enter the Royal Academy.
It is a much harder task to enter now than when Mr. Allston was
here before, as they now require a pretty accurate knowledge of
anatomy before they suffer one to enter, and I shall find the advantage of my anatomical lectures.   I feel rather encouraged from this
circumstance, since the harder it is to gain admittance the greater
the honor it will be should I enter.   I have likewise begun a large
landscape, which at a bold push I intend for the exhibition, though
I run the risk of being refused.   I am admitted a student in the
British Institution, an establishment having the same views with
the Royal Academy, the improvement of artists; but it only requiring the introduction of some one of the directors, Mr. West was
so good as to introduce me there.

"I was introduced to Mr. West by Mr. Allston, and likewise
gave him your letter.   He was very glad to see me, and said he
would render me every assistance in his power.   At the British
Institution I saw his famous piece of 'Christ Healing the Sick.'   He
said to me, 'This is the piece I intended for America, but the British
would have it themselves; but I shall give America the better one.'
He has begun a copy, which I likewise saw; and there are several
alterations for the better, if it is possible to be better.   A sight of
that piece is worth a voyage to England of itself.   The encomiums
which Mr. West has received on account of that piece has given
him new life, and some say he is at least ten years younger.   He
is now likewise about another piece, which will probably be superior
to the other; he favored me with a sight of the sketch, which he
said he granted to me because I was an American.   He had not
shown it to anybody else.   Mr. Allston was with me, and told me
afterward that, however superior his last piece was, this would far
exceed it.   The subject is, 'Christ before Pilate.'   It will contain
about fifty or sixty figures the size of life.

"Mr. West is in his seventy-fourth year (I think), but to see him you would suppose him only about five-and-forty. He is very active; a flight of steps at the British Gallery he ran up as nimbly as I could. He was particular in his inquiry respecting the arts in the United States, and appeared very zealous that they should flourish there. He expressed great attachment to his native country, and he told me, as a proof of it, he presented them with this large picture. I walked through his gallery of paintings of his own productions. There were upward of two hundred, consisting principally of the original sketches of his large pieces. He has painted in all upward of six hundred pictures, which is more than any artist ever did, with the exception of Rubens. Mr. West is so industrious now that it is hard to get access to him, and then only between the hours of nine and ten in the morning. He is working on eight or nine different pieces at present, and seems to be more enthusiastic than he ever was before.

"I was surprised, on entering the Gallery of Paintings in the British Institution, at seeing eight or ten ladies, as well as gentlemen, with their easels and pallets, and oil-colors, employed in copying some of the pictures. You can see, from this circumstance, in what estimation the art is held here, since ladies of distinction, without hesitation or reserve, are willing to draw in public.

"I have seen but little of London as yet, being more desirous of commencing my studies at present, than to gratify my curiosity. I, however, in going to and from dinner, generally make a little circuit to see what is to be seen. If you have a plan of London I will direct you where to find me. I am on the west side of Great or Upper Titchfield Street, near the corner of that street and Mary-le-bone Street. The place where I dine is in Wardour Street, at the corner of that street and Knaves Acre. I pass down Titchfield Street, by Oxford Market into Oxford Street, and go a short distance eastward, and Wardour Street is on the south side. I have not felt any of those disagreeable feelings which I expected to experience on my first arrival here; on the contrary, I have been in very good spirits, and felt more enthusiastic and determined than ever in the pursuit of my profession. I rise at seven, and breakfast, and by half-past seven get to work; these two or three days past I have sat over my drawing from half-past seven until five o'clock in the afternoon, which is my dining-hour. After dinner I generally walk a little, and visit Mr. and Mrs. Allston, who live but about three minutes' walk from me, at 49 London Street. He is very sociable and pleasant with me, and visits me every day to talk and smoke his cigar with me. . . . I am very anxious at present to get into the Royal Academy; I have begun a drawing for the purpose from the Gladiator statue, and will tell you the issue in my next."

After he had studied a year with Mr. West, and was better able to judge of the man and the artist, Mr. Morse writes to an intimate personal friend in his own country:

"Mr. West has been so long at the head of his profession, and is so well known to the world, that I could relate little of his history that would be new to you. As a painter he has as few faults as any artist of ancient or modern times. In his studies he has been indefatigable, and the result is a perfect knowledge of the philosophy of his art. There is not a line or a touch in his pictures which he cannot account for on philosophical principles; they are not the productions of accident, but of study. His forte is in composition, design, and elegant grouping; his faults are said to be a harsh and hard outline, and bad coloring. These faults he has in a great degree amended; his outline is softer, and his coloring, in some pictures in which he has attempted truth of color, is not surpassed by any artist now living, and some have even said that Titian himself did not surpass it. He has just completed an historical landscape which, for clearness of coloring, combined with grandeur of composition, has never been excelled. In his private character he is unimpeachable; a man of tender feelings; with a mind so noble that it soars above the slanders of his enemies, and he expresses pity rather than revenge toward those who through wantonness or malice plan to undermine him. No man, perhaps, ever passed through so much abuse, and I am confident no one ever bore up against its insolence with more nobleness of spirit. With a steady perseverance in the pursuit of the sublimest profession, he has traveled on, heedless of his enemies, till he is sure of immortality.

"Excuse my fervor in the praise of this extraordinary man. He is not such a one as can be met with in every age. And I think there can be no stronger proof that human nature is the same always, than that men of genius in all ages have been compelled to undergo the same disappointments, and to pass through the same storms of calumny and abuse, doomed in their lifetime to endure the ridicule or neglect of the world, and to wait for justice till they were dead."

The artist-life of Mr. Morse in London was brightened by the companionship of one who rose to great eminence in his profession, and whose memory is cherished with pride in our country as well as in England.

Charles R. Leslie was born in London, in 1794, three years after the birth of his friend, room-mate, and fellow-student, Morse. His parents were Americans, residing temporarily in London at the time of his birth. When the boy was six years old his parents returned to the United States with him, and, giving him an ordinary school education, apprenticed him to a bookseller in Philadelphia. But the genius of painting was in him, and asserted itself early. He was sent to London to be a pupil of Benjamin West, and, thus being brought into immediate acquaintance with Mr. Morse, the two young men became warm personal friends, had their studios together, and were soon bound by an affection that continued unabated till they were separated by death. Leslie was the soul of humor. It brims over in his letters, and pictures, and conversation. He selected subjects for its display in the pages of Shakespeare, Cervantes, Molière, and others. His success was great, and he was soon elected an associate and member of the Royal Academy. In the year 1833 he came to the United States to enter upon the professorship of Drawing in the United States Military Academy at West Point. He was not contented there, and in the course of a few months returned to England. In 1847 he became Professor of Painting in the Royal Academy, and his lectures in that chair have been published as a hand-book for young painters.

His associations with men of genius were intimate and beautiful, making his Autobiography one of the most delightful volumes, bringing us into living converse with Coleridge and Charles Lamb, Rogers, Washington Irving, and scores of men whose names are part of the ideal life of every lover of art and letters. He speaks of his introduction to London and Morse :

"For a few days I was at the London Coffee-House, on Ludgate Hill, with Mr. Inskip and other Americans. I delivered my letters to Mr. West, and was kindly received by him. I visited the galleries of artists, the theatres, and the other principal objects of attraction to strangers, and

'Such sober certainty of waking bliss
I never knew till now.'

But these enjoyments were soon interrupted by a severe illness, which confined me to my room in the hotel. I was solitary, and began to find that even in London it was possible to be unhappy. I did not, however, feel this in its full force until I was settled in lodgings, consisting of two desolate-looking rooms up two pair of stairs in Warren Street, Fitzroy Square. My new acquaintances, Allston, King, and Morse, were very kind, but still they were *new acquaintances*. I thought of the happy circle round my mother's fireside, and there were moments in which, but for my obligations to Mr. Bradford and my other kind patrons, I could have been content to forfeit all the advantages I expected from my visit to England, and return immediately to America. The two years I was to remain in London seemed, in prospect, an age.

"Mr. Morse, who was but a year or two older than myself, and who had been in London but six months when I arrived, felt very much as I did, and we agreed to take apartments together. For some time we painted in the same room, he at one window and I at the other. We drew at the Royal Academy in the evening, and worked at home in the day. Our mentors were Allston and King; nor could we have been better provided: Allston, a most amiable and polished gentleman, and a painter of the purest taste; and King, warm-hearted, sincere, sensible, prudent, and the strictest of economists.

"When Allston was suffering extreme depression of spirits, immediately after the loss of his wife, he was haunted during sleepless nights by horrid thoughts; and he told me that diabolical imprecations forced themselves into his mind. The distress of this to a man so sincerely religious as Allston, may be imagined. He wished to consult Coleridge, but could not summon resolution. He desired, therefore, that I should do it; and I went to Highgate, where Coleridge was at that time living with Mr. Gillman. I found him walking in the garden, his hat in his hand (as it generally was in the open air), for he told me that, having been one of the Bluecoat Boys, among whom it is the fashion to go bareheaded, he had acquired a dislike to any covering of the head. I explained the cause of my visit, and he said: 'Allston should say to himself, *" Nothing is me but my will.* These thoughts, therefore, that force themselves on my mind are no part of *me*, and there can be no guilt in them." If he will make a strong effort to become indifferent to their recurrence, they will either cease, or cease to trouble him.' He said much more, but this was the substance, and after it was repeated to Allston I did not hear him again complain of the same kind of disturbance."

Morse had made decided progress in his studies before Leslie joined him, but the companionship of such a man was a constant refreshment and stimulus. Before the first month of his residence in London was spent, he writes to his parents :

"London, *September* 3, 1811.

"I have finished a drawing which I intended to offer at the Academy for admission. Mr. Allston told me it would undoubtedly admit me, as it was better than two-thirds of those generally offered, but advised me to draw another, and remedy some defects in handling the chalks (to which I am not at all accustomed), and he says I shall enter with some *éclat*. I showed it to Mr. West ; he told me it was an extraordinary production, that I had talents, and only wanted knowledge of the art to make a great painter. Since giving him your last letter and Dr. Waterhouse's, he has been very friendly and liberal to me, and says, if in any way he can benefit me, he will do it with pleasure. For the first, to economize, he told me a way of preparing common paper to paint on, instead of canvas, which will be a great saving of expense to me."

The scene that occurred on the presentation of this drawing Mr. Morse was fond of describing in after-years, and it furnishes an invaluable lesson.

Anxious to appear in the most favorable light before West, he had occupied himself for two weeks in making a finished drawing from a small cast of the Farnese Hercules. Mr. West, after strict scrutiny for some minutes, and giving the young artist many commendations, handed it again to him, saying, "Very well, sir, very well ; go on and finish it."

"It *is* finished," replied Morse.

"Oh, no," said Mr. West ; "look here, and here, and here," pointing to many unfinished places which had escaped the untutored eye of the young student. No sooner were they pointed out, however, than they were felt, and a week longer was devoted to a more careful finishing of the drawing, until, full of confidence, he again presented it to the critical eyes of West. Still more encouraging and flattering expressions were lavished upon the drawing, but on returning it the advice was again given, " Very well, indeed, sir; go on and finish it."

" Is it not finished ? " asked Morse, almost discouraged.

" Not yet," replied West; " see, you have not marked that muscle, nor the articulations of the finger-joints."

Determined not to be answered by the constant " Go and finish it " of Mr. West, Morse again diligently spent three or four days retouching and renewing his drawing, resolved, if possible, to elicit from his severe critic an acknowledgment that it was at length finished. He was not, however, more successful than before; the drawing was acknowledged to be exceedingly good, " very clever, indeed ; " but all its praises were closed by the repetition of the advice—

" Well, sir, go and finish it."

" I cannot finish it," said Morse, almost in despair.

" Well," answered West, " I have tried you long enough. Now, sir, you have learned more by this drawing than you would have accomplished in double the time by a dozen half-finished beginnings. It is not numerous drawings, but the *character of one*, which makes a thorough draughtsman. *Finish* one picture, sir, and you are a painter."

When Mr. West was painting his " Christ Rejected," Morse calling on him, the old gentleman began a critical examination of his hands, and at length said, " Let me tie you with this cord, and take that place while I paint in the hands of our Saviour." Morse of course complied ; West finished his work, and releasing him said, " You may say now, if you please, you had a hand in this picture."

Allston was as severe a teacher and critic as West. In one of his early letters to his parents, Morse writes:

" My room-mate is Leslie, the young man who is so much talked of in Philadelphia; we have lived together since December, and have not as yet had a falling out. I find his thoughts of the art agree perfectly with my own; he is enthusiastic, and so am I, and we have not time to think scarcely of any thing else. Every thing we do has a reference to the art, and all our plans are for our mutual advancement in it. We enjoy much of the company of Mr. Allston, and a few other gentlemen, consisting of three or four painters and poets. We meet by turns at each other's rooms. Mr. Allston is our most intimate friend and companion. I can't feel too grateful to him for his attentions to me; he calls every day, and superintends all we are doing. When I am at a stand and perplexed in some parts of the picture, he puts me right, and encourages me to proceed, by praising those parts which he thinks good; but he is faithful, and always tells me when any thing is bad. It is mortifying, sometimes, when I have been painting all day very hard, and begin to be pleased with what I have done, on showing it to Mr. Allston, with the expectation of praise, and not only of praise, but a score of 'excellents, well-dones, and admirables'—I say, it is mortifying to hear him after a long silence say: '*Very bad, sir; that is not flesh, it is mud, sir; it is painted with brick-dust and clay.*' I have felt, sometimes, ready to dash my palette-knife through it, and to feel at the moment quite angry with him; but a little reflection restores me. I see that Mr. Allston is not a *flatterer*, but a *friend*, and that, really to improve, I must see my *faults*. What he says after this always puts me in good-humor again. He tells me to *put a few flesh-tints here, a few gray ones there, and to clear up such and such a part, by such and such colors;* and not only that, but takes the palette and brushes, and shows me how. In this way he assists me; I think it one of the greatest blessings that I am under his eyes. I don't know how many errors I might have fallen into if it had not been for his attentions."

Speedily admitted to the Royal Academy, and pursuing his art with enthusiasm, Morse begins to be a critic in the first years of his pupilage. He writes to his parents:

"London, *January* 30, 1812.

"I called, a day or two since, on Sir William Beechy, an artist of great eminence, to see his paintings. They are beautiful beyond any thing I ever imagined; his principal excellence is in coloring, which to the many is the most attractive part of the art. Sir William is considered the best colorist now living. You may be apt to ask 'If Sir William is so great, and even the best, what is Mr. West's great excellence?' Mr. West is a *bad colorist* in general, but he excels in the grandeur of his thought; Mr. West is to painting what Milton is to poetry, and Sir William Beechy to Mr. West, as Pope to Milton; so that by comparing with, or rather illustrating, the one art by the other, I can give you a better idea of the art of painting, than in any other way; for, as some poets excel in the different species of poetry, and stand at the head of their different kinds, in the same manner do painters have their particular branch of their art: and as epic poetry excels all other kind of poetry, because it addresses itself to the sublimer feelings of our nature, so does historical painting stand preëminent in our art, because it calls forth the same feelings. For poets' and painters' minds are the same, and I infer that painting is superior to poetry, from this: that the painter possesses, with the poet, a vigorous imagination, where the poet stops; while the painter exceeds him in the mechanical and very difficult part of the art, *that of handling the pencil.*"

The years 1811–1815, which were passed by Mr. Morse in London, were eventful in the political world, including, as they did, the period of the war between Great Britain and the United States (1812–1814), and the war between France and the allied European powers, terminating in the battle of Waterloo and the Treaty of Paris in 1815. Mr. Morse was in constant correspondence with his friends at home, and intensely interested in the great events of the age. In the spring of 1812, within the first year of his life in London, he writes to his parents of—

The Assassination of the Prime-Minister.

"LONDON, *May* 17, 1812.

"I write in great haste, just to inform you of a dreadful event which happened here last evening, and rumors of which will probably reach you before this; it is no less than the *assassination of Mr. Perceval,* the Prime-Minister of Great Britain. As he was entering the *House of Commons* last evening, a little past five o'clock, he was shot directly through the heart, by a man from behind the door; he staggered forward and fell, and expired in about ten minutes. The mention of this shocking affair is but to remove any doubts you might have of the fact; I heard of it last evening, about three hours after it was perpetrated, but could not believe it, until the particulars related in the morning papers and *my own eyes* confirmed it. I have just returned from the *House of Commons;* there was an immense crowd assembled, and very riotous: in the hall was written in large letters, '*Peace, or the Head of the Regent!*' This country is in a very alarming state, and there is no doubt but great quantities of blood will be spilled before it is restored to order; even while I am writing, a party of Life Guards are patrolling the streets. London must soon be the scene of dreadful events. Last night I had an opportunity of studying the public mind; it was at the *theatre;* the play was ' *Venice preserved, or the Plot discovered.*' If you will take the trouble just to read the first act, you will see what relation it has to the present state of affairs. When *Pierre* says to *Jaffier,* ' Canst thou kill a senator ? ' there were three cheers, and so through the whole; whenever any thing was said concerning conspiracy, and in favor of it, the audience applauded; and when any thing was said against it they hissed. When Pierre asked the conspirators if *Brutus was not a good man,* the audience were in a great uproar, applauding so as to prevent for some minutes the progress of the performance. This, I think, shows the public mind to be in great agitation. You must not feel anxious respecting me; I can take care of myself, for, although London will probably be the scene of much bloodshed, I hope I shall have prudence enough to keep clear from danger. If I follow my pursuits without meddling with the affairs of others, I shall remain unmolested ; so don't feel anxious. This is written in haste. The papers will give you more particulars. . . .

" *May 17th.*—The assassin, Bellingham, was immediately taken into custody. He was tried on Friday, and condemned to be executed to-morrow morning (Monday, 18th). I shall go to the place to see the concourse of people. I should not be surprised if an attempt were made to rescue him.

" *Monday Morning, 18th.*—I went this morning to the execution; a very violent rain prevented so great a crowd as was expected. A few minutes before eight o'clock Bellingham ascended the scaffold. He was very genteelly dressed. He bowed to the crowd, who cried out, ' God bless you ! ' repeatedly. I saw him draw the cap over his face and shake hands with the clergyman. I staid no longer ; but immediately turned my back and was returning home. I had taken but a few steps before the clock struck eight, and on turning back I saw the crowd beginning to disperse. I have felt the effects of this sight all day, and shall probably not get over it for weeks. There were no accidents."

In a postscript to one of his letters of the same date, he says :

" Mr. West is very kind to me; I visit him occasionally of a morning to hear him converse on the art. He appears quite attached to me, as he is, indeed, to all young American artists ; it seems to give him the greatest pleasure to think that one day the arts will flourish in America. He says that Philadelphia will be the Athens of the world."

In a playful letter to one of his brothers, Morse describes— as he perhaps would not to his parents—

His Amusements

" LONDON, *June* 15, 1812.

" I have only a few moments to write you, as to-day the gallery of the Marquis of Stafford is open to artists; and, as it is but one day in the week for two months in the year, I cannot well miss it.

" The queen held a drawing-room a short time since, and I went to St. James's Palace to see those who attended.   It was a singular sight to see the ladies and gentlemen in their court dresses ; the gentlemen were dressed in buckram-skirted coats without capes, long waistcoats, cocked-hats, bag-wigs, swords, and large buckles in their shoes ; the ladies in monstrous hoops, so that in getting into their carriages they were obliged to go edgewise.   Their dresses were very rich.   Some ladies, I suppose, had about them, to adorn them, twenty or thirty thousand pounds' worth of diamonds. I had a sight of the prince regent as he passed in his splendid state carriage, drawn by six horses; he is very corpulent; his pictures are good, but he is very red and considerably bloated.   I likewise saw the Princess Charlotte of Wales—she is handsome—the Dukes of Kent, Cambridge, Clarence, and Cumberland, Admiral Duckworth, and many others.   The prince held a levee a few days since, at which Mr. Van Rensselaer was presented.

" I went out to Epsom races with Mr. Van Rensselaer in his carriage a short time ago, rather for the ride than to see the running.   Epsom is about nine or ten miles from London.   I saw a great many splendid equipages and a great deal of company; most of the neighboring nobility were there ; there was very good racing.   I was on a hill in the centre of the course, so that I could see nearly the whole course, which was a mile and a half in length.

" I occasionally attend the theatres.   At Covent Garden there is the best acting in the world.   Mr. Kemble is the first tragic actor now in England ; Cook was a rival, and excelled him in some characters.   Mrs. Siddons is the best tragic actress perhaps that ever lived.   She is now advanced in life, and is about to retire from the stage.   On the 29th of this month she makes her last appearance.   I must say I admire her acting very much.   She is rather corpulent, but has a remarkably fine face; the Grecian character is portrayed in it. She excels in deep tragedy. In *Mrs. Beverly*, in the play of 'The Gamesters,' a few nights ago, she so arrested the attention of the house, that you might hear your watch tick in your fob, and at the close of the play, when she utters an hysteric laugh for joy that her husband was not a murderer, there were three different ladies in the boxes who actually went into hysterics, and were obliged to be carried out of the theatre. Mrs. Siddons is a woman of irreproachable character, and moves in the first circles. The stage will never again see her equal. You mustn't think, because I praise the acting, that I am partial to theatres; I think in a certain degree they are harmless, but too much attended they dissipate the mind. There is no danger of my loving them too much.

"Last night, as I was passing through Tottenham Court Road, I saw a large collection of people of the lower class making a most terrible noise by beating on something of the sounding genus. Upon going nearer and inquiring the cause, I found that a butcher had just been married, and that it is always the custom on such occasions for his brethren by trade to serenade the couple with 'marrow-bones and cleavers.' Perhaps you have heard of the phrase 'musical as marrow-bones and cleavers.' This is the origin of it. If you wish to experience the sound, let each one in the family take a pair of tongs and a shovel, and then standing all together let each one try to outdo the other in noise, and this will give you some idea of it. How this custom originated I don't know; I hope it is not symbolical of the harmony which is to exist between the parties married."

In another letter to his parents, in the beginning of his second year, he

Dreams of Greatness.

"LONDON, *September* 20, 1812.

"I have removed from 82 Titchfield Street to No. 8 Buckingham Place, Fitzroy Square. . . .

"I have just finished a model in clay of a figure ('The Dying Hercules'), my first attempt at sculpture. Mr. Allston is extremely pleased with it; he says it is better than all the things I have done since I have been in England, put together, and says I must send a cast of it home to you, and that it will convince you that I shall make a painter. He says also he shall write to his friends in Boston, to call on you and see it when I send it.

"Mr. West, also, was extremely delighted with it. He said it was not merely an academical figure, but displayed *thought*. He could not have paid me a higher compliment. Mr. West would write you, but he has been disabled from painting or writing, for a long time, with the gout in his right hand. This is a great trial to him. I am anxious to send you something to show you that I have not been idle since I have been here. My passion for my art is so firmly rooted that I am confident no human power could destroy it. The more I study, the greater I think is its claim to the appellation of *divine ;* and I never shall be able sufficiently to show my gratitude to my parents for enabling me to pursue that profession, without which I am sure I should be miserable. And if it is my destiny to become GREAT, *and worthy of a biographical memoir*, my biographer will never be able to charge upon my parents that bigoted attachment to any individual profession the exercise of which spirit by parents toward their children has been the ruin of some of the greatest geniuses ; and the biography of men of genius has too often contained that reflection on their parents. If ever the contrary spirit was evident, it has certainly been shown by my parents toward me. Indeed, they have been almost too indulgent. They have watched every change of my capricious inclinations, and seem to have made it an object to study them with the greatest fondness ; but I think they will say that, when my desire for change did cease, it always settled on painting. I hope that one day my success in my profession will reward you in some measure for the trouble and inconvenience I have so long put you to.

" I am now going to begin a picture of the death of Hercules, this figure to be as large as life. I shall send it to you as soon as practicable, and also one of the same to the Philadelphia Exhibition, if possible, in season for the next in May."

Mr. Morse had brought with him from his distinguished father and his father's eminent friends, letters of introduction to some of the best men in England. Among them were William Wilberforce and Henry Thornton, both of them illustrious philanthropists, and at that time members of Parliament; Zachary Macaulay, editor of the *Christian Observer*, and father of the historian ; the two Grants, one of whom was afterward Lord Glenelg; and many others. The young artist was warmly received by these distinguished and excellent men. He was, however, so absorbed in his studies, and so firmly resolved to permit nothing to interfere with his progress, that he declined to deliver these letters for several months. His father reproves him for his neglect, and he justifies himself by showing that social duties would occupy more time than he could spare from his work, and that mingling in society was inconsistent with devotion to study. But in the course of the year he ventured upon making himself known ; and his letters frequently mention the delightful intercourse with public men which these letters secured.

To his Parents.

"LONDON, *December* 22, 1812.

"Last Thursday week I received a very polite invitation from Henry Thornton, Esq, to dine with him, which I accepted. Hearing that your son was in the country, he found me out, and has shown me every attention ; he is a very pleasant, sensible man; but his character is too well known to you to need any eulogium from me. At his table was a son of Mr. Stephen, who was the author of the odious Orders in Council. Mr. Thornton asked me at table, if I thought that ' if the Orders in Council had been repealed a month or two sooner, it would have prevented the war.' I told him I thought it would, at which he was much pleased, and, turning to Mr. Stephen, he said: 'Do you hear that, Mr. Stephen? I always told you so.' Last Wednesday I dined at Mr. Wilberforce's ; I was extremely pleased with him ; at his house I met Mr. Thornton and Mr. Grant, members of Parliament. In the course of conversation, they introduced America. Mr. Wilberforce regretted the war extremely ; he said it was like two of the same family quarreling ; that he thought it a judgment on this country for their wickedness, and that they had been *justly* punished for their arrogance and insolence at sea, as well as the Americans for their vaunting on land. As Mr. Thornton was going, he invited me to spend a day or two at his seat at Clapham, a few miles out of town. I accordingly went, and was very civilly treated; the *reserve* which I mentioned in a former letter was evident, however, here, and I felt a degree of embarrassment arising from it which I never felt in America. The second day I was a little more at my ease. At dinner were two sons of the Mr. Grant I mentioned above; they are, perhaps, the most promising young men in the country, and you may possibly one day hear of them as at the head of this nation. After dinner I got into conversation with them and Mr. Thornton. When America again became the topic of conversation, they asked me a great many questions, which I answered to the best of my ability. They at length asked me if I did not think that the ruling party in America were very much under French influence. I replied no; that I believed, on the contrary, that nine-tenths of the American people were prepossessed strongly in favor of this country; as a proof, I urged the universal prevalence of English fashions in preference to French; English manners and customs; the universal rejoicings on the success of the English over the French; the marked attention shown to English travelers and visitors; the neglect with which they treated their own literary productions, on account of the strong prejudice in favor of English works; that every thing, in short, was enhanced in its value by having attached to it the name English. They were very much pleased with what I told them, and acknowledged that America, and American visitors generally, had been treated with too much contempt and neglect. In the course of the day I asked Mr. Thornton what were the objects that the English Government had in view when they laid the Orders in Council. He told me, in direct terms ' *The universal monopoly of commerce ;* ' that they had long desired an excuse for such measures as the Orders in Council, and that the French decrees were exactly what they wished, and the opportunity was seized with avidity the moment it was offered; they knew that the Orders in Council bore hard upon the Americans, but they considered that as merely *incidental.* To this I replied, if such was the case as he represented it, what blame could be attached to the American Government for declaring war? He said that it was urged that America ought to have considered the circumstances of the case, and that Great Britain was fighting for the liberties of the world; that America was in a great degree interested in the decision of the contest, and that she ought to be content to suffer a little. I told him that England had no right whatsoever to infringe on the *neutrality* of America, or to expect, because she (England) supposed herself to have justice on her side in the contest with France, that of course the Americans should think the same. The moment America declared this opinion, her neutrality ceased. 'Besides,' said I, ' how can they have the face to make such a declaration, when you just now said that their object was universal monopoly, and they longed for an excuse to adopt measures for that end? ' I told him that ' it showed that all the noise about England's fighting for the liberties of mankind proved to be but a thirst, a selfish desire for *universal monopoly.*' This, he said, seemed to be the case; he could not deny it. He was going on to

4

observe something respecting the French decrees, when we were interrupted, and I have not been able again to resume the conversation, as I returned to town with him shortly after in his carriage, where, as there were strangers, I could not introduce it again. I shall take the opportunity some time to pursue the subject with him. The prince's declaration, vindicating the English Government from blame in the war with America, has been published some time. It is a flimsy thing, and by the friends of the administration thought to be but a weak defence."

Among the autographs which Mr. Morse preserved to the end of his life is the following note from Mr. Wilberforce, to whom he had neglected to deliver his letters of introduction, notwithstanding his father's urgency that he should make the acquaintance of that remarkable man :

"KENSINGTON GORE, *January* 4, 1813.

" SIR : I cannot help entertaining some apprehension of my not having received some letter or some card, which you may have done me the favor of leaving at my house. Be this, however, as it may, I gladly avail myself of the sanction of a letter from your father, for introducing myself to you ; and as many calls are mere matters of form, instead of knocking at your door, I take the liberty of begging the favor of your company at dinner on Wednesday next, at a quarter before five o'clock, at Kensington Gore (one mile from Hyde Park corner), and of thereby securing the pleasure of an acquaintance with you. The high respect which I have long entertained for your father, in addition to the many obliging marks of attention which I have received from him, render me desirous of becoming personally known to you, and enable me with truth to assure you I am, with good-will, sir,

" Your faithful servant,

" W. WILBERFORCE.

"MORSE, *Esq.*"

This was the beginning of an acquaintance which proved to be of great value to the young artist ; the recollections of it and of the men with whom it brought him into contact being among the pleasantest of his life.

Professor Morse was very fond of repeating to his friends his pleasant recollections of intercourse with Benjamin West, Allston, Coleridge, Rogers, and other celebrated men of the day. Some of these reminiscences were preserved by Mr. James Wynne:

West averred that the Revolutionary war was carried on and troops sent in direct opposition to the judgment and wishes of the king, who only yielded to the strong representations of his ministry, that he had no right to dismember so large and important a part of the British Empire. As an evidence of this, he cited the case of Lord Mansfield, who, on the occasion of a question as to the propriety of sending more troops to America, in the House of Peers, remarked that "it was now time for the government to throw off the mask." The king, who could be aroused on certain occasions, became exceedingly angry with Lord Mansfield for the manner in which he had procured his sanction to send troops, and directed him never to see his face again—an order which was never relaxed.

It may be that West's partiality for the king induced him to overlook his own part in the American war, and disposed him to place on the shoulders of others the blame which should in part, at least, have been borne by him. Be this as it may, the friendship subsisting between them continued unabated, although occasions were not wanting in which those who were jealous of the influence of an American over the mind of their king strove to alienate their friendship. West was fully aware of this, and, while he seldom paid attention to these attempts, could not fail occasionally to be annoyed at them. As an illustration of this feeling he narrated to Morse the following:

" ' While,' remarked West, 'the king was on a visit to me, news was brought of an important victory of his troops over the rebels. Not finding him at the palace, the messenger immediately traced him to my studio, and communicated the intelligence. After this was accomplished, turning to me, the messenger said:

" ' And are you not gratified at the success of his majesty's troops ? '

" ' No,' I replied ; ' I can never rejoice in the misfortunes of my countrymen.'

" ' Right,' replied the king, rising and placing his hand approvingly on my shoulder. ' If you did, you would not long be a fit subject for any government.' "

Among the members of the Royal Academy with whom Morse was in the habit of frequent association, was Fuseli, whose erratic genius is perpetuated in the remarkable productions of his pencil, which at that time had great currency. Fuseli, who was a profound thinker and an agreeable companion, was on one occasion debating the question of the immortality of the soul with a disbeliever.

"I do not know that your soul is immortal," said Fuseli to his companion—"perhaps it is not; but I know that mine is."

"Why so?" demanded his companion, greatly astonished at the comparison.

"Because," said Fuseli, "I can conceive more in one minute than I can execute in a lifetime."

No stronger illustration than this can be given of the soul's immortality.

Another of these was Northcote, who did not affect to conceal his jealousy of other artists. On one occasion Coleridge attempted to take him to task for this unfortunate trait in his character. "Nonsense!" replied Northcote. "You possess, all men of genius possess, the same quality. As a test, are you willing to admit that Southey is as great a poet as yourself?"

"To be sure I am," replied Coleridge.

"Will you confess," continued Northcote, "that if you saw Southey standing under that beam"—pointing to the one above his head—"you would not secretly wish it to fall on and crush him?"

It must be admitted that Northcote's envy was inveterate and incurable.

Coleridge, who was a visitor at the rooms of Leslie and Morse, frequently made his appearance under the influence of those fits of despondency to which he was subject. On these occasions, by a preconcerted plan, they often drew him from this state of despondency to one of brilliant imagination. "I was just wishing to see you," said Morse, on one of these occasions, when he entered with a hesitating step, and replied to their frank salutations with a gloomy aspect and deep-drawn sighs. "Leslie and myself have had a dispute about certain lines of beauty; which is right?" And then each argued with the other for a few moments, until Coleridge became interested, and, rousing from his fit of despondency, spoke with an eloquence and depth of metaphysical reasoning on the subject far beyond the comprehension of his auditors. Their point, however, was gained, and Coleridge was again the eloquent, the profound, the gifted being which his remarkable productions show him to be.

"On one occasion," says Morse, "I heard him improvise, for half an hour, in blank verse, what he stated to be a strange dream, which was full of those wonderful creations that glitter like diamonds in his poetical productions."

"All of which," remarked I, "is undoubtedly lost to the world."

"Not all," replied Mr. Morse, "for I recognize in the 'Ancient Mariner' some of the thoughts of that evening; but doubtless the greater part, which would have made the reputation of any other man, perished with the moment of inspiration, never again to be recalled."

When his tragedy of "Remorse," which had a run of twenty-one nights, was first brought out, Washington Allston, Charles King, Leslie, Lamb, Morse, and Coleridge, went together to witness its performance. They occupied a box near the stage, and each of the party was as much interested in its success as Coleridge himself.

The effect of the frequent applauses upon Coleridge was very manifest; but when, at the end of the piece, he was called for by the audience, the intensity of his emotions was such as none but one gifted with the fine sensibilities of a poet could experience. Fortunately, the audience was satisfied with a mere presentation of himself. His emotions would have precluded the idea of his speaking on such an occasion.

Allston, soon after this, became so much out of health that he thought a change of air, and a short residence in the country, might relieve him. He accordingly set out on this journey, accompanied by Leslie and Morse. When he reached Salt Hill, near Oxford, he became so ill as to be unable to proceed, and requested Morse to return to town for his medical attendant, Dr. Tuthill, and Coleridge, to whom he was ardently attached. Morse accordingly returned, and, procuring a post-chaise, immediately set out for Salt Hill, a distance of twenty-two miles, accompanied by Coleridge and Dr. Tuthill. They arrived late in the evening, and were busied with Allston until midnight, when he became easier, and Morse and Coleridge left him for the night. Upon repairing to the sitting-room of the hotel, Morse opened Knickerbocker's "History of New York," which he had thrown into the carriage before leaving town. Coleridge asked him what work he had.

"Oh," replied he, "it is only an American book!"

"Let me see it," said Coleridge. He accordingly handed it to him, and he was soon buried in its pages. Mr. Morse, overcome by the fatigues of the day, soon after retired to his chamber and fell asleep. On awakening the next morning, he repaired to the sitting-room, when what his astonishment to find it still closed, with the lights burning, and Coleridge busy with the book he had lent him the previous night!

"Why, Coleridge," said he, approaching him, "have you been reading the whole night?"

"Why," remarked Coleridge, abstractedly, "it is not late."

He replied by throwing open the blinds and permitting the broad daylight, for it was now ten o'clock, to stream in upon them.

"Indeed," said Coleridge, "I had no conception of this; but the work has pleased me exceedingly. It is admirably written; pray, who is its author?"

He was informed that it was the production of Washington Irving. It is needless to say that, during the long residence of Irving in London, they became warm friends.

Among the literary acquaintances formed by Morse in London at this period was Rogers, the poet, whose breakfasts attained so wide a celebrity. At one of these, at which Leslie and Morse were the only guests, Rogers waggishly remarked to Morse that his friend Leslie was a very clever artist, but that it was a great pity that he did not throw more grace and beauty into his female figures.

Now, if Leslie prided himself upon any thing, it was precisely upon the grace and symmetry of his female figures, in which he particularly excelled, and so Morse informed him.

"You think so," said Rogers, quietly indulging in a pleasant laugh at his own waggery, and changed the conversation, without explanation, to another subject.

It is well known that Rogers's house was literally made up of choice gems, and among these was a sketch of the "Miracle of the Slain" by Tintoretto, which Rogers informed Morse was executed by that great artist preparatory to the execution of the painting itself.

Morse asked Rogers where the original now was, as he had an order to paint a copy of it, and supposed, as it had been captured by Napoleon I., it was in Paris. Rogers informed him that it had been returned to Venice, where Morse afterward found it in the Academy of Fine Arts, immediately opposite Titian's "Assumption of the Virgin." The copy he then made, and which upon the death of its owner fell again into his hands, was among his own pictures as long as he lived. Fuseli, who at the time of Mr.

Morse's residence in London was at the zenith of his fame, considered the original the finest picture in the world.

At this period Abernethy was in the full tide of his popularity as a surgeon, and Allston, who had for some little time had a grumbling pain in his thigh, proposed to Morse to accompany him to the house of the distinguished surgeon to consult him on the cause of the ailment. As Allston had his hand on the bell-pull, the door was opened and a visitor passed out, immediately followed by a coarse-looking person with a large, shaggy head of hair, whom Allston at once took for a domestic. He accordingly inquired if Mr. Abernethy was in.

"What do you want of Mr. Abernethy?" demanded this uncouth-looking person, with the harshest possible Scotch accent.

"I wished to see him," gently replied Allston, somewhat shocked by the coarseness of his reception; "Is he at home?"

"Come in, come in, mon," said the same uncouth personage.

"But he may be engaged," responded Allston; "perhaps I had better call another time."

"Come in, mon, I say," replied the person addressed, and partly by persuasion and partly by force, Allston, followed by Morse, was induced to enter the hall, which they had no sooner done than the person who admitted them closed the street-door, and, placing his back against it, said, "Now tell me what is your business with Mr. Abernethy. I am Mr. Abernethy."

"I have come to consult you," replied Allston, "about an affection—"

"What the de'il hae I to do with your affections?" bluntly interposed Abernethy.

"Perhaps, Mr. Abernethy," said Allston, by this time so completely overcome by the apparent rudeness of the eminent surgeon as to regret calling on him at all, "you are engaged at present, and I had better call again."

"De'il the bit, de'il the bit, mon," said Abernethy. "Come in, come in," and he preceded them to his office, and examined his case, which proved to be a slight one, with such gentleness as almost to lead them to doubt whether Abernethy within his consulting-room, and Abernethy whom they had encountered in the passage, was really the same personage.

The first portrait Mr. Morse painted in London was that of his friend Leslie, and Leslie at the same time made a portrait of

Morse. His mother received a letter in the spring of 1812, from a lady in Philadelphia, in which these portraits are alluded to:

"I have this moment received a letter from Miss Vaughan in London, dated February 20th, and knowing the passage below would be interesting to you, I transcribe it with pleasure, and add my very sincere wish that all your hopes may be realized:

"'Dr. Morse's son is considered a young man of very promising talents by Mr. Allston and Mr. West, and by those who have seen his paintings. We have seen him, and think his modesty and apparent amiableness promise as much happiness to his friends as his talents may procure distinction for himself. He is peculiarly fortunate, not only in having Mr. Allston for his adviser and friend, but in his companion in painting, Mr. Leslie, a young man from Philadelphia, highly recommended, and whose extreme diffidence adds to the most promising talents, the patient industry, and desire of improvement, which are necessary to bring them to perfection. They have been drawing each other's pictures. Mr. Leslie is in the Spanish costume, and Mr. Morse in a Highland dress. They are in a very unfinished state, but striking likenesses.' This Highland lad, I hope, my dear friend, you will see, and in due time be again blessed with the original."

Samuel F. B. Morse to his Parents.

"LONDON, *March* 24, 1813.

"With regard to my expenses, I got through the first year with two hundred pounds, and hope the same sum will carry me through the second. If you knew the manner in which we live, you would wonder how it was possible I could have made so great a change in my habits. I am obliged to screw and pinch myself in a thousand things in which I used to indulge myself at home. I am treated with no dainties, no fruit, no nice dinners (except once in an age, when invited to a party at an American table), no fine tea-parties, as at home. All is changed; I breakfast on simple bread-and-butter and two cups of coffee; I dine on either beef, mutton, or pork (*veal* being out of the question, as it is one shilling and sixpence per pound), baked with potatoes, warm perhaps twice a week, all the rest of the week cold. My drink is *water*, porter being too expensive. At tea, bread-and-butter, with two cups of tea. This is my daily round. I have had no new clothes for nearly a year; my best are threadbare, and my shoes out at the toes, my stockings all want to see *my mother*, and my hat is growing hoary with age. This is my picture in London, do you think you would know it? 'But,' you will say, 'what do you do with the money if you live thus sparingly?' Why, I will tell you the whole. When I first came to London, I was told, if I meant to support the character of a gentleman, I must take especial care of my personal appearance; so I thought it a matter of course that I must spare no expense in order to appear well. So, this being first in my mind, I (supposing very wisely that London folks had nothing else to do but to see how I was dressed) laid out a considerable part of my money on myself; meanwhile, picture-galleries and collections, with many other places which I ought constantly to have visited, and which cost some money, were neglected; and why? because *I could not afford it!* Well, in process of time, I found no very particular advantage to be gained by supporting the character of a gentleman, for these reasons: in the first place, *nobody saw me;* in the second place, if they *had seen me,* they would not *have known me;* and, thirdly, if they had *known* me, they would not have *cared* a farthing about me. So I thought within myself what I came to England for, and I found that it was not to please English folks, but to study painting; and, as I found I must sacrifice painting to dress and visiting, or dress and visiting to painting, I determined on the latter, and ever since have lived accordingly, and now the tables are turned: I visit galleries and collections, purchase prints, etc., and, when I am asked why I don't pay more attention to my dress, I reply that I *cannot afford it.* Provision of every kind is excessively high here, and is increasingly so. A pair of fowls, such as we could get in America for about three shillings per pair, are eighteen shillings sterling; a turkey, from ten shillings sixpence to a guinea; beef is thirteen pence per pound; pork, fourteen pence; mutton, one shilling; and veal, as I said before, one shilling and sixpence; bread is one shilling and eightpence the quartern loaf, half of one of which we eat in a day. Everything seems to be in proportion: shoes are from fifteen shillings to a guinea per pair, boots three pounds, and so on. By this you can form a slight estimate how much it costs to live in this country. It is known by the experience of two or three Americans, whom I know, that a pound goes no farther in England than a dollar in America. My greatest expense, next to *living,* is for canvas, frames, colors, etc., and visiting galleries. The frame of my large picture which I have just finished cost nearly twenty pounds, besides the canvas and colors, which cost nearly eight pounds more, and the frame was the cheapest I could possibly get. Mr. Allston's frame cost him sixty guineas. Frames are very expensive things, and on that account I shall not attempt another large picture for some time, although Mr. West advises me to paint *large* as much as possible. The picture which I have finished is ' The Death of Hercules ; ' the size is eight feet by six feet and six inches. This picture I showed to Mr. West a few weeks ago, and he was extremely pleased with it, and paid me many very high compliments ; but, as praise comes better from another than from one's self, I shall send you a complimentary note which Mr. West has promised to send me on the occasion. I sent the picture to the *Exhibition* at *Somerset House*, which opens on the 3d of May, and have the satisfaction, not only of having it *received*, but of having the praises of the *council* who decide on the admission of pictures. Six hundred pictures were refused admission this year, so you may suppose that a picture (of the size, too, of which mine was) must possess some merit to be received in preference to six hundred ! A small picture may be received, even if it is not very good, because it will serve to fill up some little space which would otherwise be empty, but a large picture, from its excluding many small ones, must possess a great deal in its favor in order to be received.

" If you recollect, I told you I had completed a model of a single figure of the same subject; this I sent to the Society of Arts at the Adelphi, to stand for the prize (which is offered every year for the best performance in painting, sculpture, and architecture), and is a *gold medal ;* yesterday I received the note accompanying this, by which you will see that it is adjudged to me in sculpture this year; it will be delivered to me in public on the 13th of May or June, I don't know which, but I shall give you a particular account of the whole process as soon as I have received it. By knowing these facts, you will perceive that I have not been idle since my residence here. I wish I could send you some specimen of my painting, but captains and passengers absolutely refuse carrying any thing larger than a small package of letters; and indeed, if there were opportunities, I could at present send nothing very interesting to you, my works consisting merely of drawings of heads, hands, and feet, and now and then a portrait for improvement. I shall soon commence some of papa's friends ; Dr. Lettsom I shall ask first, Mr. Wilberforce I shall also ask, but do not know whether he will have time to sit to me. Sir Joshua Banks is now very ill indeed, and I doubt whether he will recover, and, even if he does, there is so much ceremony necessary, and it is considered so great a favor for a man of his rank to sit to an obscure artist, that I doubt very much whether I should be able to obtain his consent; he might consent, however, if I mentioned that it was my father's request; and, if he recovers, I shall at least ask him.

"I cannot close this letter without telling you how much I am indebted to that excellent man Mr. Allston; he is extremely partial to me, and has often told me that he is proud of calling me his pupil; he visits me every evening, and our conversation is generally upon the inexhaustible topic of our *divine* art, and upon *home*, which is next in our thoughts. I know not in what terms to speak of Mr Allston. I can truly say I do not know the slightest imperfection in him; he is amiable, affectionate, learned, possessed of the greatest powers of mind and genius, modest, unassuming, and, above all, a *religious* man. You may perhaps suppose that my partiality for him blinds me to his faults, but no man could conceal, on so long an acquaintance, every little foible from one constantly in his company; and, during the whole of my acquaintance with Mr. Allston, I never heard him speak a peevish word, or utter a single inconsiderate sentence; he is a man in praise of whom I cannot speak sufficiently, and my love for him I can only compare to that love which ought to subsist between brothers. He is a man for whose genius I have the highest veneration, for whose principles I have the greatest respect, and for whose amiable qualities I have an increasing love. I could write a quire of paper in his praise, but all I could say of him would give you but a very imperfect idea of him. To learn all his excellences, you must be acquainted with him. Do not think this mere fulsome compliment; what I write I write sincerely; you know I am not in the habit of writing what I don't think. You must recollect, when you tell friends that I am studying in England, that I am a pupil of Mr. Allston, and not Mr. West; they will not long ask who Mr. Allston is; he will very soon astonish the world. He claims me as his pupil, and told me a day or two since, in a jocose manner, that he should have a battle with Mr. West unless he gave up all pretension to me. It is said, by the greatest connoisseurs in England, who have seen some of Mr. Allston's works, that he is destined to revive the art of painting in all its splendor, and that no age ever boasted of so great a genius. It might be deemed invidious (and therefore I should not wish it mentioned as coming from me), were I to make public another opinion of the first men in this country:

it is, that Mr. Allston will almost as far surpass Mr. West as Mr. West has other artists, and this is saying a great deal, considering the very high standing which Mr. West holds at present."

Samuel F. B. Morse to his Parents.

"LONDON, *May* 2, 1814.

"You will probably, before this reaches you, hear of the splendid *entrée* of Louis XVIII. into London. I was a spectator of this scene. On the morning of the day, about ten o'clock, I went into Piccadilly, through which the procession was to pass; I did not find any great concourse of people at that hour, except before the Poultney Hotel, where the sister of the Emperor Alexander resides, on a visit to this country, the Grand-duchess of Oldenburg. I thought it probable that, as the procession would pass this place, there would be some uncommon occurrence taking place before it, so I took my situation directly opposite, determined at any rate to secure a good view of what happened. I waited four or five hours, during which time the people began to collect from all quarters; the carriages began to thicken, the windows and fronts of the houses began to be decorated with the white flag, white ribbons, and laurel. Temporary seats were fitted up on all sides, which began to be filled, and all seemed to be in preparation. About this time the king's splendid band of music made its appearance, consisting, I suppose, of more than fifty musicians, and to my great gratification placed themselves directly before the hotel; they began to play, and soon after the grand-duchess, attended by several Russian noblemen, made her appearance on the balcony, followed by *the Queen of England*, the Princess Charlotte of Wales, the Princess Mary, Princess Elizabeth, and all the female part of the royal family. From this fortunate circumstance, you will see that I had an excellent opportunity of observing their persons and countenances. The Duchess of Oldenburg is a common-sized woman, of about four or five-and-twenty; she has rather a pleasant countenance, blue eyes, pale complexion, regular features, her cheek-bones high but not disagreeably so. She resembles very much her brother the emperor, judging from his portrait. She has with her her little nephew, Prince Alexander, a boy of about three or four years old. He was a lively little fellow, playing about, and was the principal object of the attention of the royal family. The queen, if I was truly directed to her, is an old woman of very sallow complexion, and nothing agreeable either in her countenance or deportment; and, if she was not called a queen, she might as well be any ugly old woman. The Princess Charlotte of Wales I thought pretty; she has small features, regular, pale complexion, great amiability of expression, and condescension of manners; the Princess Elizabeth is extremely corpulent, and from what I could see of her face was agreeable, though nothing remarkable. One of the others, I think it was the Princess Mary, appeared to have considerable vivacity in her manners; she was without any covering to her head; her hair was sandy, which she wore cropped; her complexion was probably fair originally, but was rather red now; her features were agreeable.

"It now began to grow late, the people were beginning to be tired, wanting their dinners, and the crowd to thicken, when a universal commotion, and murmur through the crowd and from the house-tops, indicated that the procession was at hand. This was followed by the thunder of artillery, and the huzzas of the people toward the head of the street, where the houses seemed to be alive with the twirling of hats and shaking of handkerchiefs. This seemed to mark the progress of the king; for, as he came opposite each house, these actions became most violent, with cries of '*Vivent les Bourbons!*' '*Vive le roi!*' '*Vive Louis!*' etc. I now grew several inches taller; I stretched my neck, and opened my eyes. One carriage appeared, drawn by six horses, decorated with ribbons, and containing some of the French noblesse; another, of the same description, with some of the French royal family. At length came a carriage drawn by eight beautiful Arabian cream-colored horses; in this were seated Louis XVIII., King of France, the Prince Regent of England, the Duchess d'Angoulême, daughter of Louis XVI., and the Prince of Condé. They passed rather quickly, so that I had but a glance at them, though a distinct one. The prince regent I had often seen before; the King of France I had a better sight of afterward, as I will presently relate. The Duchess d'Angoulême had a fine expression of countenance, owing probably to the occasion, but a melancholy cast was also visible through it; she was pale. The Prince of Condé I have no recollection of. After this part of the procession had passed, the crowd became exceedingly oppressive, rushing down the street to keep pace with the king's carriage. As the king passed the royal family, he bowed, which they returned by kissing their hands to him and shaking their handkerchiefs with great enthusiasm. After they had gone by, the royal family left the balcony, where they had been between two and three hours. My only object now was to get clear of the crowd. I waited nearly three-quarters of an hour, and at length, by main strength, worked myself edgewise across the street, where I pushed down through stables and houses, and by-lanes, to get thoroughly clear, not caring where I went, as I knew I could easily find my way when I got into a street. This I at last gained, and, to my no small astonishment, found myself by mere chance directly opposite the hotel where Louis and his suite were. The prince regent had just left the place; and with his carriage went a great part of the mob, which left the space before the house comparatively clear. It soon filled again. I took advantage, however, and got directly before the windows of the hotel, as I expected the king would show himself, for the people were calling for him very clamorously. I was not disappointed; for, in less than half a minute, he came to the window, which was open, before which I was. I was so near him I could have touched him; he staid nearly ten minutes, during which time I observed him carefully. He is very corpulent—a round face, dark eyes, prominent features; the character of countenance much like portraits of the other Louises; a pleasant face, but, above all, such an expression of the moment as I shall never forget, and in vain attempt to describe. His eyes were suffused with tears, his mouth slightly open, with an unaffected smile full of gratitude, and seemed to say to every one, ' Bless you! ' His hands were a little extended sometimes, as if in adoration to heaven, at others as if blessing the people. I entered into his feelings. I saw a monarch, who for five-and-twenty years had been an exile from his country, deprived of his throne; and, until within a few months, not the shadow of a hope remaining of ever returning to it again. I saw him raised as if by magic from a private station in an instant to his throne, to reign over a nation which has made itself the most conspicuous of any nation on the globe. I tried to think as he did, and, in the heat of my enthusiasm, I joined with heart and soul in the cries of ' *Vive le roi!* ' ' *Vive Louis!* ' which rent the air from the mouths of thousands. As soon as he left the window, I returned home much fatigued, but well satisfied that my labor had not been for naught.

" Mr. Wilberforce is an excellent man; his whole soul is bent on doing good to his fellow-men. Not a moment of his time is lost. He is always planning some benevolent scheme or other; and not only planning but executing. He is made up altogether of affectionate feeling. What I saw of him in private gave me the most exalted opinion of him as a Christian. Oh, that such men as Mr. Wilberforce were more common in this world. So much human blood would not then be shed to gratify the malice and revenge of a few wicked, interested men.

"I hope Cousin Samuel Breese will distinguish himself under so gallant a commander as Captain Perry. I shall look with anxiety for the sailing of the Guerriere; there will be plenty of opportunities for him, for peace with us is deprecated by the people here, and it only remains for us to fight it out gallantly, as we are able to do, or submit slavishly to any terms which they please to offer us; a number of humane schemes are under contemplation, such as burning New London, for the sake of the frigates there, arming the blacks in the Southern States, burning all of our principal cities, and such like plans; which, from the supineness of the New-England people, may be easily carried into effect. But no, the *humane*, *generous* English cannot do such base things—I hope not; let the event show it. It is, perhaps, well I am here, for, with my present opinions, if I were at home, I should most certainly be in the army or navy: my mite is small, but when my country's honor demands it, it might help to sustain it. There can now be no French party. I wish to know very much what effect this series of good news will have at home. I congratulate you as well as all other good people on the providential events which have lately happened; they must produce great changes with us; I hope it will be for the best.

"I am in excellent health, and am painting away; I am making studies for the large picture I contemplate for next year. It will be as large, I think, as Mr. Allston's famous one, which was ten feet by fourteen."

Samuel F. B. Morse to a Friend.

"LONDON, *May* 30, 1813.

"You ask in your letter what books I read, and what I am painting. The little time that I can spare from painting, I employ in reading and studying the old poets—Spenser, Chaucer, Dante, Tasso, etc., etc.; these are necessary to a painter. As to painting, I have just finished a large picture, eight feet by six and a half, the 'Death of Hercules,' which is now in the Royal Academy exhibition at Somerset House. I have been flattered by the newspapers, which seldom praise young artists, and they do me the honor to say that my picture, with the pictures of another young man by the name of Monroe, form a distinguished trait in this year's exhibition; and, in enumerating about fifty of the preëminent works of the exhibition, they have placed mine in the list.   There were exhibited this year nearly one thousand pictures; and about two thousand were offered, but the rest were rejected.   This praise I consider much exaggerated.   Mr. West, however, who saw it as soon as I had finished it, paid me many compliments, and told me that, were I to live to his age, I should never make a better composition—this I consider but a *compliment*, and as meant only to encourage me; as such I receive it.   A few days since I had the honor of receiving the prize gold medal offered for the best piece of sculpture at the Adelphi Society of Arts this year, which was presented me by the Duke of Norfolk.   I mention these circumstances merely to show that I am getting along as well as can be expected, and, if any credit attaches to me, I willingly resign it to my country, and feel happy that I can contribute a mite to her honor."

Samuel F. B. Morse to his Parents.

"LONDON, *June* 13, 1813.

"I send by this opportunity (Mr. Elisha Goddard) the little cast of the 'Hercules' which obtained the prize this year at the Adelphi, and also the gold medal which was the premium presented to me before a large assembly of the nobility and gentry of the country, by the Duke of Norfolk, who also paid me a handsome compliment at the same time.   There were present Lord Percy, the Margravine of Anspach, the Turkish, Sardinian, and Russian ambassadors, who were pointed out to me, and many noblemen whom I do not now recollect.   My large picture also has not only been received at the Royal Academy, but has one of the finest places in the rooms.   It has been spoken of in the papers.   They not only praise me, but place my picture among the most attractive in the exhibitiou.   This I know will give you pleasure, and I write it with great pleasure.   I also send a catalogue of the exhibition, with one of the papers which criticises my picture, that you may see for yourselves."

The early triumphs of men are more highly valued than successes in after-life.   Among the papers that Mr. Morse preserved to the day of his death is a copy of the *British Press*, May 4, 1813, in which his picture "The Dying Hercules" is placed among the *nine* best paintings in a gallery of nearly one thousand, and among them the works of Turner, Northcote, Lawrence, and Wilkie.

Samuel F. B. Morse to his Parents.

"LONDON, *June* 15, 1814.

"I expected at this time to have been in Bristol, with Mr. and Mrs. Allston, who are now there, but the great *fêtes* in honor of the peace, and the visit of the allied sovereigns, have kept me in London till all is over. There are now in London upward of twenty foreign princes, also the great Emperor Alexander, and the King of Prussia. A week ago yesterday they arrived in town, and, contrary to expectation, came in a very private manner. I went to see their *entrée*, but was disappointed, with the rest of the people, for the Emperor Alexander, disliking all show and parade, came in a private carriage, and took an indirect route here. The next and following day I spent in endeavoring to get a sight of them. I have been very fortunate, having seen the Emperor Alexander no less than fourteen times, so that I am quite familiar with his face; the King of Prussia I have seen once; Marshal Blucher five or six times; Count Platoff three or four times; besides Generals de Yorck, Bulow, etc.—all whose names must be perfectly familiar to you, and the distinguished parts they have all acted in the great scenes just past. The Emperor Alexander I am quite in love with; he has every mark of a great mind. His countenance is an uncommonly fine one; he has a fair complexion, hair rather light, and a stout, well-made figure; he has a very cheerful, benevolent expression, and his conduct has everywhere evinced that his face is the index of his mind. When I first saw him he was dressed in a green uniform, with two epaulets and stars of different orders; he was conversing at the window of his hotel with his sister, the Duchess of Oldenburg; I saw him again soon after, in the superb coach of the prince regent, with the duchess his sister, going to the court of the queen. In a few hours after I saw him again, on the balcony of the Poultney Hotel; he came forward and bowed to the people. He was then dressed in a red uniform, with a broad blue sash over the right shoulder; he appeared to great advantage. He staid about five minutes. I saw him again five or six times through the day, but got only indifferent views of him. The following day, however, I was determined to get a better and nearer view of him than before. I went down to his hotel about ten o'clock, the time when I supposed he would leave it; I saw one of the prince's carriages drawn up, which opened at the top, and was thrown back before and behind. In a few minutes the emperor with his sister made their appearance and got into it. As the carriage started, I pressed

5

forward and got hold of the ring of the coach-door and kept pace
with it for about a quarter of a mile. I was so near that I could
have touched him; he was in a plain dress, a brown coat, and altogether like any other gentleman. His sister, the duchess, also was
dressed in a very plain, unattractive manner, and, if it had not been
for the crowd which followed, they would have been taken for any
lady and gentleman taking an airing. In this unostentatious manner does he conduct himself, despising all pomp, and seems rather
more intent upon inspecting the charitable, useful, and ornamental
establishments of the country, with a view, probably, of benefiting
his own dominions by his observations, than of displaying his rank
by the splendor of dress and equipage. His condescension also is
no less remarkable; an instance or two will exemplify it : On the
morning after his arrival, he was up at six o'clock, and while the
lazy inhabitants of this great city were fast asleep in their beds, he
was walking with his sister the duchess in Kensington Gardens;
as he came across Hyde Park, he observed a corporal drilling some
recruits, upon which he went up to him and entered into familiar
conversation with him, asking him a variety of questions, and, when
he had seen the end of the exercise, shook him heartily by the hand
and left him. As he was riding on horseback, he shook hands with
all who came round him.

"A few days ago, as he was coming out of the gate of the London
Docks, on foot, after having inspected them, a great crowd was
waiting to see him, among whom was an old woman of about
seventy years of age, who seemed very anxious to get near him,
but, the crowd pressing very much, she exclaimed 'Oh, if I could
but touch his clothes!' The emperor overheard her, and, turning round, advanced to her, and, pulling off his glove, gave her his
hand, and, at the same time dropping a guinea into it, said to
her, 'Perhaps this will do as well.' The old woman was quite
overcome, and cried 'God bless your majesty!' till he was out of
sight.

"An old woman in her ninetieth year sent a couple of pair of
warm woolen stockings to the emperor, and with them a letter stating that she had knit them with her own hands expressly for him,
and, as she could not afford to send him silk, she thought that wool-
en would be much more acceptable, and would also be more useful
in his climate. The emperor was very much pleased, and determined
on giving her his miniature set in gold and diamonds, but, upon
learning that her situation in life was such that money would be

more acceptable, he wrote her an answer, and, thanking her heartily for her present, inclosed her one hundred pounds.

"These anecdotes speak more than volumes in praise of the Emperor Alexander. He is truly a great man. He is a great conqueror, for he has subdued the greatest country in the world, and overthrown the most alarming despotism that ever threatened mankind. He is great also because he is good; his whole time seems spent in distributing good to all around him; and wherever he goes he makes every heart rejoice. He is very active, and is all his time on the alert in viewing every thing that is worth seeing. The emperor is also extremely partial to the United States; every thing American pleases him, and he seems uncommonly interested in the welfare of our country. I was introduced to-day to Mr. Harris, our *chargé d'affaires* to the court of Russia. He is a very intelligent, fine man, and is a great favorite with Alexander. From a conversation with him, I have a scheme in view which, when I have matured, I will submit to you for your approbation.

"The King of Prussia I have seen but once, and then had but an imperfect view of him. He came to the window with the prince regent, and bowed to the people (at St. James's Palace). He is tall and thin, has an agreeable countenance, but rather dejected in consequence of the late loss of his queen, to whom he was very much attached.

"General Blucher, now Prince Blucher, I have seen five or six times. I saw him on his entrance into London, all covered with dust, and in a very ordinary kind of vehicle. On the day after, I saw him several times in his carriage, drawn about wherever he wished by the *mob*. He is *John's* greatest favorite, and they have almost pulled the brave general and his companion, Count Platoff, to pieces, out of pure affection. Platoff had his coat actually torn off him, and divided into a thousand pieces as *relics*, by the good people—their kindness knows no bounds; and I think, in all the battles which they have fought, they never have run so much risk of losing their limbs as in encountering their friends in England. Blucher is a veteran-looking soldier; a very fine head, monstrous mustaches. His head is bald, like papa's; his hair gray, and he wears powder. Understanding that he was to be at Covent Garden Theatre, I went, as the best place to see him; and I was not disappointed. He was in the prince's box, and I had a good view of him during the whole entertainment, being directly before him for three or four hours. A few nights since I also went to the theatre to see *Platoff*, the *hetman* (*chief*) *of the Cossacks*. He has also a very fine countenance, a high and broad forehead, dark complexion, and dark hair. He is tall and well made, as I think the Cossacks are generally; he was very much applauded by a very crowded house, the most part collected to see him."

A very noted youth fell into the hands of Morse while in London, and is thus mentioned in a letter from a friend of his:

"Morse and I intend going to Hampton Court as soon as we have sent our pictures to the exhibition, and, Allston having promised to accompany us, we shall have a very pleasant little jaunt.

"Zerah Colburn, the little calculator, has called on us two or three times, as Morse is painting his portrait. He is a fine, lively little fellow, and the most inquisitive child I ever saw. He has excited much astonishment here, and, as they are very unwilling just at this time to allow any cleverness to the Americans, it was said in some of the papers that he was a Russian. There was some great arithmetical question, I do not exactly know what, which he solved almost as soon as it was put to him, though it for several years baffled the skill of some of the first professors. His father expects soon to return to America, and says he has collected money sufficient to educate his son there, and that he now has power to prove to the world how much he has been injured by the accusations of avarice and selfishness that have appeared against him in the public prints."

The war between England and the United States (1812–'14) naturally imposed delicate and oftentimes responsible duties upon American residents in London. Their kind offices were constantly sought by parties whose misfortunes had brought them into trouble, or by those who did not wish to run the risk of being detained in a hostile country. Of such applications as are answered in this letter, Mr. Morse had many:

"LONDON, *March* 15, 1814.

"MY DEAR FRIEND : Your letter with Dr. Hayward's came to hand, some time ago, at Bristol. The moment I came to London I presented your letter to Mr. Cooper, and he very politely gave me a note to the Alien Office, which I presented. I have called since about a dozen times to inquire the result of Mr. Cooper's application, and to-day received for answer that '*England would not become the medium of communication between France and the*

United States.' Please inform Dr. Cushing that, by the request of Mr. Thornton, I made application to Mr. Cooper for him at the same time, and Mr. Cooper's application was for both of you."

" Believe me sincerely yours,

"S. F. B. MORSE."

Samuel F. B. Morse to Henry Thornton.

"BRISTOL, *December* 30, 1813.

"RESPECTED SIR: I take the liberty of addressing you in behalf of an American prisoner of war now in the Stapleton depot, and I address you, sir, under the conviction that a petition in the cause of humanity will not be considered by you as obtrusive. The prisoner I allude to is a gentleman of the name of Burritt, a native of New Haven, in the State of Connecticut; his connections are of the highest respectability in that city, which is notorious for its adherence to Federal principles. His friends and relations are among my father's friends, and although I was not, until now, personally acquainted with him, yet his face is familiar to me, and many of his relatives were my particular friends while I was receiving my education at Yale College, in New Haven. From that college he graduated in the year ——. A classmate of his was the Rev. Mr. Stuart, who is one of the professors of the Andover Theological Institution, and of whom I think my father has spoken in some of his letters to Mr. Wilberforce. Mr. Burritt, after he left college, applied himself to study, so much so as to injure his health, and, by the advice of his physicians, he took to the sea as the only remedy left for him. This had the desired effect, and he was restored to health in a considerable degree. Upon the breaking out of the war with-this country, all the American coasting-trade being destroyed, he took a situation as second-mate in the schooner Revenge, bound to France, and was captured on the 10th of May, 1813. Since that time he has been a prisoner, and from the inclosed certificates you will ascertain what has been his conduct since. He is a man of excellent religious principles, and (I firmly believe) of the strictest integrity. So well assured am I of this, that, in case it should be required, *I will hold myself bound to answer for him in my own person.* His health is suffering by his confinement, and the unprincipled society which he is obliged to endure is peculiarly disagreeable to a man of his education. My object in stating these particulars to you, sir, is (if possible and consistent with the laws of the country), to obtain for him, through your influence, his liberty on his parole of honor. By so doing you will probably be the means of preserving the life of a good man, and will lay his friends, my father and myself, under the greatest obligations.

"Trusting to your goodness to pardon this intrusion upon your time, I am, sir, with the highest consideration, your most obedient, humble servant,

"SAMUEL F. B. MORSE."

Henry Thornton, Esq., to Samuel F. B. Morse.

"DEAR SIR: You will perceive by the inclosed that there is, unhappily, no prospect of our effecting our wishes in respect to your poor friend at Bristol. I shall be glad to know whether you have had any success in obtaining a passport for Dr. Cushing.

"I am, dear sir, yours, etc.,

"H. THORNTON.

"BATAKIN, *February* 17, 1814."

Lord Melville to Mr. Thornton.

"ADMIRALTY, *February* 7, 1814.

"SIR: Mr. Hay having communicated to me a letter which he received from you on the subject of Benjamin Burritt, an American prisoner of war in the depot at Stapleton, I regret much that, after consulting on this case with Sir Rupert George, and ascertaining the usual course of proceeding in similar instances, I cannot discover any circumstances that would justify a departure from the rules observed toward other prisoners of the same description. There can be no question that his case is a hard one; but I am afraid that it is inseparable from a state of war. It is not only not a solitary instance among the French and American prisoners, but, unless we were prepared to adopt the system of releasing all others of the same description, we should find that the number who might justly complain of undue partiality to this man would be very considerable.

"I have the honor to be, sir, your most obedient and very humble servant,

"MELVILLE."

S. E. Tyler to Samuel F. B. Morse.

"STAPLETON DEPOT, *February* 24, 1814.

"MR. SAMUEL F. B. MORSE—

"DEAR SIR: Having some knowledge of your family and friends in Boston and Charlestown, I have taken the liberty to address this communication to you, hoping that my unhappy situation will be a sufficient apology for the liberty I have taken. I was captured in April, 1813, bound from Charleston, South Carolina, to Bordeaux, and have been confined as a prisoner of war ever since. During my confinement I have written several times to my friends in Boston (of which place I am a native), but as yet have been without advices from them, which I can attribute to nothing but the obstacles in the communication between the two nations. I was entirely ignorant of your having been at the prison until to-day, when I received the information from Mr. Burritt, and I regret exceedingly that it was not in my power to have had an interview with you. I am a son of Mr. William Tyler, who, before his decease, carried on the rope-making business in West Boston, near the almshouse. I also have a brother-in-law, Mr. John Andrews, who carries on the sail-making business at the head of India Wharf, who is my guardian, and agent for me, as it respects my father's estate.

"For reasons above stated I have been induced to make an application to you for pecuniary assistance, which, if you should be disposed to grant, I will give you an order on my brother for the amount, or will request him to repay it immediately to your correspondent either in Boston or Charlestown. Let me assure you, sir, that I would not make this application to you unless strongly prompted by most poignant suffering. Should you comply with my request, you will have the satisfaction of relieving an unfortunate fellow-creature, and you will confer lasting obligations on me.

"If you would be good enough to inform me if there is any prospect of peace, or the probability of the exchange of prisoners being resumed, you will greatly oblige me. In the hope of shortly hearing from you,

"I remain respectfully your obedient servant,

"SAMUEL E. TYLER."

Mr. Morse had some warm friends and fellow-countrymen residing at Bristol, and they encouraged him to believe that he would find several willing to sit to him for their portraits if he would visit that city. He did so, and found friends with whom his time was pleasantly spent, but very little in the line of his profession to reward him for leaving his studies and seeking employment. A letter from Washington Allston, in London, gives us insight into the life of artists:

Allston to Morse.

"LONDON, *January* 2, 1814.

"MY DEAR SIR: In the first place, I wish you and all of Mr. Visscher's family a happy New-Year. Last week I wrote you a letter that must have been vastly *entertaining—as how?* because it was altogether about my *own affairs.* Now, for the sake of symmetry, I send you another of the same kind.

"Since my return I have had the courage to examine the state of my finances at my banker's, and found the balance in my favor to have been reduced to so small a sum as makes me think 'tis time to look about me; and to endeavor, as soon as possible, after the proper *ways and means* for increasing it. On considering the subject, I was naturally led to the landscape in Bristol, when it occurred to me that *perhaps* the price I had fixed for it (viz., six hundred guineas) might be too high for that market; and that I should stand a better chance of selling it by reducing it to five hundred. I would thank you to consult with Mr. Visscher on this point; for I depend so much on his judgment, that I should not hesitate a moment to put it at five hundred guineas, provided he should think *that* a more salable price. Will you write me immediately and let me know his opinion?

"I gave the finishing touch to my picture yesterday, and shall send it to the gallery to-morrow. Leslie's picture will do him great honor; he has improved it very much since his return. As to my ' *own beautiful self,*' Mrs. A. says I am a *picture* of health. At any rate I find my health every day improving, and promise myself the pleasure of sending Mr. King a very favorable bulletin. Pray be particular in letting us know how his two patients in Mr. Visscher's family bear this cold fog. We have had it so thick and brown here, that it might well have passed for Shakespeare's ' *blanket of the dark* ' that Macbeth speaks of. Mrs. A. unites with me in best regards to our friends in Portland Square, and yourself.

"Sincerely yours,

"W. ALLSTON."

In the autumn of the same year, while Allston was at Bristol with Morse, Leslie wrote:

Leslie to Morse.

"LONDON, *November* 29, 1814.

"MOST POTENT, GRAVE, AND REVEREND DOCTOR: I take up my pencil to make ten thousand apologies to you for addressing you in humble black-lead. Deeply impressed as I am with the full conviction that you deserve the very best Japan ink, the only ex-cuse I can make to you is the following : it is perhaps needless to remind you that the tools to which ink is applied to paper, in order to produce writing, are made from goose-quills, which quills I am goose enough not to keep a supply of ; and, not having so much money at present in my breeches-pocket as will purchase one, I am forced to betake to my *pencil,* an instrument which, without paying myself any compliment, I am sure I can wield better than a *pen.* I am glad to hear that you are so industrious, and that Mr. A. is succeeding so well with portraits. I hope he will bring all he has painted to London. I am looking out for you every day. I think we form a kind of family here, and I feel, in an absence from Mr. and Mrs. A. and yourself, as I used to do when away from my mother and sisters. By-the-by, I have not had any letters from home for more than a month. It seems the Americans are all united, and we shall now have war in earnest. I am glad of it for many reasons. I think it will not only get us a more speedy and permanent peace, but may tend to crush the demon of party-spirit and strengthen our government.

"I am done painting the gallery, and have finished my drawings for the prize : thank you for your good wishes.

" I thought Mr. Allston knew how proud I am of being consid-ered his student. Tell him, if he thinks it worth while to mention me at all in his letter to Delaplaine, I shall consider it a great honor to be called so.

" Yours most truly,
" C. B. L."

Leslie to Morse.

" Mr. Allston and I have sent our pictures to the gallery. He has made good interest to get his large one placed at the end of one of the rooms. As to mine, it is of small consequence where they put it. Mr. Allston, after finishing his ' Diana,' showed it to Mr. West, who was (to speak even moderately) in raptures with it. He immediately called his son Raphael, ' There,' says the old gen-tleman, ' there, why there is nobody who does any thing like this.' Raphael exclaimed, ' It looks like a bit of Titian.' ' Oh yes,' an-swered his father, ' that's Titian's flesh, that's Titian's flesh.' After this shower of compliments, Mr. Allston said, ' I am very highly gratified, sir, to find it meets your approbation.' ' Sir,' said Mr.

West, ' I cannot find words to express what I think of it.' He then proceeded to point out the beauties of the parts, and praised the composition, drawing, etc., as he had done the color. He seemed particularly pleased with the landscape. He told Mr. Allston to follow this up, adding, ' Sir, you will find thousands of people who will give you *two hundred guineas* for a picture of this size, who have not room in their houses for larger ones.' He said he could have sold all the small sketches in his gallery many times over, but he chose to keep them himself. Several he has sold, and painted duplicates of them. Mr. Allston mentioned his subject of ' Venus and Adonis,' and Mr. West advised him by all means to paint it, but not to have the figures the size of life. Mr. Allston is going to begin the old gentleman's portrait very soon. He promises himself much pleasure in the execution of it."

" Mr. Morse has related to me," says Dunlap, " some particulars of a ramble he took in company with Earle, when they both were students of the Royal Academy in 1813. With their sketch-books and drawing apparatus, they visited the sea-shore and the towns adjacent, making pedestrian excursions into the country in search of scenery, and sometimes meeting an adventure. On one occasion, their aim after a day's ramble was to reach Deal, and there put up for the night; but they found, when about five miles from the town, that they had to cross a dreary moor, and the sun was about to withdraw his light from them. As they mounted a stile they were met by a farmer, who accosted them with :

"' Gentlemen, are you going to cross the moor so late ? '

"' Yes. We can't lose our way, can we ? '

"' No ; but you may lose your lives.'

"' How so ? '

"' Why there be always a power of shipping at Deal, and the sailors be sad chaps; they come ashore and rob and murder on the moor; without your leave or by your leave.'

"' Has any thing of the kind taken place lately ? '

"' Why, yes, a young woman was murdered not long ago by two sailors. You will see the spot on your way, *if you will go :* there is a pile of stones where she was killed. The fellows were taken, and I saw them hanged.'

"' So there is no danger from them, then.'

"' About a mile farther on you will see bushes on your left hand—there a man was murdered not long ago; but the worst place is farther on. You will come to a narrow lane with a hedge on each side; it will be dark before you get there, and in that lane you will come to a stile, and just beyond you will see a white stone set up, and on it is written all the circumstances of the murder of a young woman, a neighbor of mine, who was coming home from town all dressed in white, with a bundle in her hand, tied in a dark-red handkerchief. But, gentlemen, you had better turn back and stop the night at my house, and you shall be heartily welcome.'

" They thanked him, but saying they were two, and a match for two, they full of confidence pursued their route. It soon became twilight. They found the heap of stones, and a slight shudder occurred when looking on the dreary scene, and the mark by which murder was designated. They passed on rather tired, and striving to keep up each other's courage until they came to the bushes. Here was another spot where foul murder had been committed. They quickened their pace as they found darkness increase; and now they came to the lane with the high hedge-row on each side, which rendered their way almost a path of utter darkness. They became silent, and with no pleasant feelings expected to see the stile, and, if not too dark, the stone erected to commemorate the murder of the young girl in white with the dark-red handkerchief.

" ' What's that ? ' said Earle, stopping.

" ' I see nothing,' said Morse—' yes—now, that I stoop down, I see the stile.'

" ' Don't you see something white beyond the stile ? '

" ' That, I suppose, is the white stone.'

" ' Stones do not move,' said Earle.

" Morse stooped again, so as to bring the stile against the sky as a background, and whispered: ' I see some one on the stile— hush ! '

" A figure now approached, and, as they stood aside to give ample room for it to pass, they perceived a tall female dressed in white, with a dark-red bundle in her hand. On came the figure, and the lads gazed with a full recollection of the farmer's story of murder, and some feelings allied to awe. On she came, and without noticing them passed to go over the moor.

" ' It will not do to let it go without speaking to it,' thought Morse, and he called out, ' Young woman ! are you not afraid to pass over the moor so late ? '

" ' Oh no, sir,' said the ghost, ' I live hard by, and when I've done work I am used to crossing the moor in the eve—good-night,' and on she tripped.

"The young painters laughed at each other, and pursued their way without further thought of ghosts or murderers. They saw, indeed, the murder-marking monument, but it was too dark to read the tale, and they soon found themselves in comfortable quarters, after their long day's ramble, and forgot their fears and their fatigues together.

"Eighteen years or more after, Mr. Morse inquired of Leslie for their old companion, Earle, and learned that he had been rambling far beyond Deal. 'He had visited every part of the Mediterranean,' said Leslie, 'roamed in Africa, rambled in the United States, sketched in South America, attempted to go to the Cape of Good Hope in a worn-out Margate hoy, and was shipwrecked on Tristan d'Acunha, where he passed six months with some old tars, who hutted there. At length a vessel touched the desolate place and released him. He then visited Van Diemen's Land, New South Wales, and New Zealand, where he drew from the naked figure, and saw the finest forms in the world addicted to cannibalism.

"Returning to Sydney, he, by way of variety, proceeded to the Caroline Islands, stopped at the Ladrones, looked in upon Manila, and finally settled himself at Madras, and made money as a portrait-painter. Not content, he went to Pondicherry, and there embarked for France, but stopped at the Mauritius, and, after some few more calls at various places, found his way home. Here his sister had married a Mr. Murray, a relative of the Duke of Athol, and, being left a widow, he found a home as *chargé d'affaires* for his grace, who, you know, is a harmless madman, thinks himself overwhelmed with business, and shuts himself up with books and papers, which he cannot understand, and then calls for his coach, and, riding out on some important errand, which forgotten, he returns again.

"Earle wrote and published his travels, and attracted some attention. One day he came to me with delight painted on his face.

"'I am anchored for life; I have an offer of two hundred pounds a year, and every thing found me, only to reside under the roof of the Duke of Athol, and ride out with him when he takes it in his head to call his coach. I am settled at last!'

"I congratulated him.

"'You can write and draw at your leisure, and give us all your adventures?'

"'Yes, nothing could be happier.'

" A few weeks after Earle came again.

" ' Congratulate me, Leslie ! '

" ' What has happened ? '

" ' I have been offered a berth on a ship bound to the south pole ! I have accepted it; it is- just what I wish.'

" And he is now in his element again; for rove he must as long as he lives."

Mr. Dunlap gives other incidents in the life of Morse, while in London :

" The first portraits painted in London both by Morse and Leslie were portraits of each other, in fancy costume. Morse was painted by Leslie in a Scotch costume, with black-plumed bonnet, and tartan plaid ; and Leslie by Morse in a Spanish cavalier's dress, a Vandyck-ruff, black cloak, and slashed sleeves. Both these portraits are at the house of their ancient hostess, who retains mementos of the like character—some product of the pencil of each of her American inmates. ¹

" It was about the year 1812 that Allston commenced his celebrated picture of the ' *Dead Man restored to Life by touching the Bones of Elisha*,' which is now in the Pennsylvania Academy of Arts. In the study of this picture he made a model in clay of the head of the dead man, to assist him in painting the expression. This was the practice of the most eminent old masters. Morse had begun a large picture to come out before the British public at the Royal Academy exhibition. The subject was the ' Dying Hercules,' and, in order to paint it with the more effect, he followed the example of Allston, and determined to model the figure in clay. It was his first attempt at modeling. His original intention was simply to complete such parts of the figure as were useful in the single view necessary for the purpose of painting ; but, having done this, he was encouraged, by the approbation of Allston and other artists, to finish the entire figure.

" After completing it, he had it cast in plaster of Paris, and carried it to show to West. West seemed more than pleased with it. After surveying it all round critically, with many exclamations of surprise, he sent his servant to call his son Raphael. As soon as Raphael made his appearance, he pointed to the figure, and said:

" ' Look there, sir; I have always told you any painter can make a sculptor.'

"From this model, Morse painted his picture of the 'Dying Hercules,' of colossal size, and sent it, in May, 1813, to the Royal Academy exhibition at Somerset House.

"The picture was well received. A critic of one of the journals of that day, in speaking of the Royal Academy, thus notices Morse: 'Of the *academicians*, two or three have distinguished themselves in a preëminent degree; besides, few have added much to their fame, perhaps they have hardly sustained it. But the great feature in this exhibition is, that it presents several works of very high merit by artists with whose performances, and even with whose names, we were hitherto unacquainted. At the head of this class are Messrs. *Monro* and *Morse*. The prize of History may be contended for by Mr. *Northcote* and Mr. Stothard. We should award it to the former. After these gentlemen, Messrs. *Hilton*, *Turner*, *Lane*, *Monro*, and *Morse*, follow in the same class.'—(*London Globe*, May 14, 1813.)

"In commemorating the 'preëminent works of this exhibition,' out of nearly two thousand pictures, this critic places the 'Dying Hercules' among the first twelve. This success of his first picture was highly encouraging to Morse, but it was not confined to the picture. Upon showing the plaster model to an artist of eminence, he was advised by him to send it to the Society of Arts to take its chance for the prize in sculpture, offered by that society, for an *original cast of a single figure.* Finding that the figure he had modeled came within the rules of the society, he sent it to their rooms, and was not a little astonished a few days after at receiving a notice to appear on the 13th of May, in the great room of the Adelphi, to receive in public the *gold medal,* which had been adjudged to his model of the 'Hercules.' On that day there were assembled the principal nobility of Britain, the foreign ambassadors, and distinguished strangers; among them but two Americans. The Duke of Norfolk presided, and from his hands Morse received the gold medal, with many complimentary remarks. It is worthy of notice that at this period Great Britain and the United States were at war. We see in this another instance of the impartiality with which the English treated our artists. Allston and Leslie were treated in the same manner during this period of national hostility. Allston says England made no distinction between Americans and her own artists; yet Trumbull attributed his failure, at this time, to the enmity of the English. We are glad to bear testimony to the good feeling of the enlightened public of Great

Britain, which placed them above a mean jealousy or a barbaric warfare upon the arts.

"Encouraged by this flattering reception of his first works in painting and in sculpture, the young artist redoubled his energies in his studies, and determined to contend for the highest premium in historical composition, offered by the Royal Academy at the beginning of the year 1814. The subject was 'The Judgment of Jupiter in the Case of Apollo, Marpessa, and Idas.' The premium offered was *a gold medal and fifty guineas.* The decision was to take place in December of 1815. The composition, containing four figures, required much study; but by the exercise of great diligence the picture was completed by the middle of July. Our young painter had now been in England four years, one year longer than the time allowed him by his parents, and he had to return immediately home; but he had finished his picture under the conviction, strengthened by the opinion of West, that it would be allowed to remain and compete with those of the other candidates. To his regret, the petition to the council of the Royal Academy for this favor, handed in to them by *West*, and advocated strongly by him and Fuseli, was not granted. He was told that it was necessary, according to the rules of the Academy, that the artist should be present to receive the premium; it could not be received by proxy. Fuseli expressed himself in very indignant terms at the narrowness of this decision.

"Thus disappointed, the artist had but one mode of consolation. He invited West to see his picture before he packed it up, at the same time requesting Mr. West to inform him, through Mr. Leslie, after the premiums should be adjudged in December, what chance he would have had if he had remained. Mr. West, after sitting before the picture for a long time, promised to comply with the request; but added, 'You had better remain, sir.' "

The subsequent history of the plaster casts that were made of the "Dying Hercules" is interesting. One of them found its way into the basement of the Capitol of the United States, and was there discovered by Mr. Morse under very extraordinary circumstances, which will be stated hereafter. This cast he gave to a friend, Rev. E. G. Smith, who wrote to Mr. Morse in 1860, asking a brief statement of the circumstances of its execution and its successful competition for the gold medal.

To this note Mr. Morse replied:

"You ask if the cast of the 'Hercules' is the original cast or a copy. A mould was made from the original clay model, from which were cast some five or six. I brought the mould with me from England, but, through ignorance of its character, a man, in cleaning house, supposed the parts to be broken plaster, and threw them into the street during my absence at the South, so that the original mould, is destroyed. A copy, or rather one of the casts from the original mould, was in the Pennsylvania Academy of Fine Arts, but was destroyed in the fire which consumed the Academy building. A mutilated fragment of another is, or was, in the National Academy collection in New York. Yours is the only perfect (so far as it is perfect) cast I know, the others having passed out of my knowledge. A fresh mould was made from the cast in Philadelphia many years ago by some moulders there, from which some casts (how many I don't know) were made, and sold by them as *antique!* So old Paff, an eccentric picture-dealer of olden time once told me. But you want to know something of its early history; this I give you in brief:

"In the year 1812 I had so far advanced in my studies as to attempt a large picture of a single figure. The subject I chose was 'The Death of Hercules.' My friend and master at this time was Washington Allston, who was then painting his picture of the 'Dead Man restored to Life by touching the Bones of Elisha.' He had modeled in clay the head of the 'dead man,' for the purpose of aiding him in the painting, explaining to me that this was often the practice of the most celebrated old masters. From this example I determined to model the figure of the 'Hercules' to aid me in my painting of the 'Dying Hercules.' It was my first attempt at modeling, and as the model, so far as it was to be of use in my picture, required only correctness and finish in *one view of it*, to wit, the view chosen for the painting, I at first only completed it in that view. At this point Mr. Allston expressed himself so pleased with it, that he advised me to finish it in *every view ;* in other words, to make a complete statue, alleging, among other reasons, that I should thus become familiar with the human figure more readily than in any other way. Hence, I completed the whole figure, and, on showing it to Mr. West, was much flattered by his praise of it. I was advised by friends that a premium of a gold medal was offered for just such an original model, and was recommended to send it to the Adelphi Society of Arts to compete for this prize. I accordingly sent it to the rooms of the society, and, to my surprise, a few days after, received the summons to appear on a certain day at the rooms of the society in full meeting, to receive the gold medal from the president, the Duke of Norfolk. This was during the war of 1812 ; and I have often spoken of it as a pleasing inci- dent, that, while a fierce strife was going on without between the two nations as nations, yet, in the Department of Fine Arts at least, there was a neutral peaceful ground on which artists and their encouragers could stand and be in perfect harmony with each other."

Death of Mrs. Allston.

On the 2d day of February, 1815, Mrs. Allston died sud- denly in London. The blow was so fearful and unexpected, that for a time it threatened to be fatal to the reason, if not to the life, of the surviving husband. The next morning Mr. Morse writes to his father :

" I write in great haste and much agitation. Mrs. Allston, the wife of our beloved friend, died last evening, and the event over- whelmed us all in the utmost sorrow. As for Mr. Allston, for sev- eral hours after the death of his wife he was almost bereft of his reason. Mr. Leslie and I are applying our whole attention to him, and we have so far succeeded as to see him more composed."

Mr. Morse wrote also to Mr. Channing, and, sending the letter to Dr. Morse, requested him to communicate the distress- ing intelligence to Mr. Allston's friends. Mr. Leslie, in his au- tobiography, describes the scene of Mrs. Allston's death, and its terrible effect upon the mind of the sensitive and devoted artist and poet.

The sympathy of Mr. Allston's friends, and their great grief with him in his sorrow, may be learned from this letter to Mr. Morse from a gentleman in England to whom the intelligence was sent :

Mr. J. J. Morgan to Mr. Morse.

"CALNE, WILTSHIRE, *February*, 1815.

" MY DEAR SIR : I received your letter only yesterday; the news it conveyed has literally stupefied us with affliction. It was not possible for me to write yesterday, so completely was I terror- stricken. It is with difficulty, and doubtless with incoherence, that I now write. Mrs. Morgan and Miss Brent most bitterly lament that you did not send for one or both of them. To have seen their

6

friend, their more than sister, though but for her last departing
hour, would have been some consolation. Their distress is very
great. The only thought which now promises the least comfort is,
that so innocent, so excellent a woman is removed from this world
of trial and trouble to that of perfect happiness, and to a union
with her Creator.

"But what is now to be done with Allston? Comfort it were
a mockery to attempt offering. Religion, and the impression of
time, are his only hope. But, pray, write to us, and say whether
we (any of us) can now be of any service. Mrs. M., or Charlotte,
or I, will come to town instantly, to be of the slightest service.
For Heaven's sake, write us! Tell us every thing concerning
Allston; tell us every thing concerning our excellent friend departed—the pain, during her illness; the burial, where; what comfort, what female friend or companion, had she? I fear and tremble
while anticipating the particulars; yet we must know them.

"Gracious God! unsearchable indeed are Thy ways! The insensible, the brutish, the wicked, are powerful; and everywhere, in
every thing, successful—while Allston, who is every thing that is
amiable, kind, and good, has been bruised, blow after blow; and
now, indeed, his cup is full!

"I am too unwell, too little recovered from the effect of your
letter to write much. Coleridge intends writing to-day. I hope he
will. Allston may derive some little relief from knowing how
much his friends partake of his grief.

"Once more I entreat you to let us know if any of us can be
of the slightest service. Perhaps our excellent Allston would be
somewhat relieved by an excursion down here. With us he shall
meet with every attention possible. I will come up and fetch him,
upon your slightest hint of its usefulness. At any rate, I beg you
to write soon, and say every thing for us all to Allston, every
thing kind you can think of. You cannot say more than we feel."

In the month following, Mr. Morse wrote to his parents a
very full account of his temporary residence at Bristol, his
struggles to support himself, and the disappointments to which
he was subjected. In his letter dated March 10, 1815, he says:

"My jaunt to Bristol, *in quest of money*, completely failed.
When I was first there I expected, from the little connection I got
into, I should be able to support myself. I was obliged to come to
town on account of the exhibitions, and staid longer than I ex-

pected, intending to return to Bristol. During this time I received two pressing letters from Mr. Visscher (which I will show you), inviting me to come down, saying that I should have plenty of business. I accordingly hurried off. A gentleman, for whom I had before painted two portraits, had promised, if I would let him have them for ten guineas apiece, twelve being my price, he would procure me five sitters. This I acceded to. I received twenty guineas, and have heard nothing from the man since, though I particularly requested Mr. Visscher to inquire, and remind him of his promise. Yet he never did any thing more on the subject. I was there three months, gaining nothing in my art, and without a single commission. Mr. Breed, of Liverpool, then came to Bristol. He took two landscapes, which I had been *amusing myself with* (for I can say nothing more of them), at ten guineas each. I painted two more landscapes, which are unsold. Mr. Visscher, a man worth about a hundred thousand pounds, and whose annual expenses, with a large family of seven children, are not one thousand, had a little frame, for which he repeatedly desired me to paint a picture. I told him I would, as soon as I had finished one of my landscapes. I began it immediately, without his knowing it, and determined to surprise him with it. I also had two frames which fitted Mr. Breed's pictures, and which I was going to give to Mr. Breed, with his pictures. But Mr. Visscher was particularly pleased with the frames, as they were a pair, and told me not to send them to Mr. Breed, as he should like to have them himself, and wished I would paint him pictures to fit them (the two other landscapes before mentioned). I accordingly was employed three months longer in painting these three pictures. I finished them; he was very much pleased with them; all his family were very much pleased with them; all who saw them were pleased with them. But he *declined taking them*, without even asking my price, and said that he had more pictures than he knew what to do with. Mr. and Mrs. Allston heard him say twenty times he wished I would paint him a picture for the frame. Mr. A——n, who knew what I was about, told him, no doubt, I would do it for him, and, in a week after, I had completed it. I had told Mr. Visscher, also, that I was considerably in debt, and that, when he had paid me for these pictures, I should be something in pocket, and, by his not objecting to what I said, I took it for granted (and from his requesting me to paint the pictures) that the thing was certain. But thus it was, without giving any reason in the world, except that he had pictures enough, he declined taking them, making me spend three months longer in Bristol than I otherwise should have done, standing still in my art, if not actually going back, and run in debt for some necessary expenses of clothing in Bristol, and my passage from and back to London. During all this time not a single commission for a portrait, *many* of which were promised me, nor a single call from any one to look at my pictures. Thus ended my jaunt *in quest of money.* Do not think that this disappointment is in consequence of any misconduct of mine. Mr. Allston, who was with me, experienced the same treatment, and had it not been for his uncle, the *American* consul, he might have starved, for the Bristol people; his uncle was the only one who purchased any of his pictures. Since I have been in London, I have been endeavoring to regain what I lost in Bristol, and I hope I have so far succeeded as to say, *I have not gone back in my art.* In order to retrench my expenses, I have taken a painting-room out of the house, at about half of the expense of my former room; though inconvenient in many respects, yet my circumstances require it, and I willingly put up with it. As for *economy*, do not be at any more pains in introducing that *personage* to me. We have long been friends and necessary companions. If you could look in on me and see me through a day, I think you would not tell me in every letter *to economize more.* It is impossible; I cannot economize more. I live on as plain food, and as little, as is for my health; less and plainer would make me ill, for I have given it a fair experiment. As for clothes, I have been decent, and that is all. If I visited a great deal, this would be a heavy expense; but, the less I go out, the less need I care for clothes, except for cleanliness. My only heavy expenses are colors, canvas, frames, etc., and these are heavy."

On the back of the last page of the letter he adds, as a postscript: "The seal of my letter is worth noticing. It is a celebrated antique gem, set in Michael Angelo's ring, which he always used as a seal. I have the seal—an impression from the original."

In a note to Mrs. Morse, his friend Leslie says: "I am very glad to see that Mr. Coleridge is writing again, and, of course, talking also. I hope he is near Mr. Allston."

Mr. Morse speaks of Mr. Allston in one of his letters, after mentioning an attack of illness: "I never felt so low-spirited as when he was ill. I often thought, if he should be taken away at this time, what an irreparable loss it would be, not only to me, but to America, and to the world. Oh! he is an angel on earth. I cannot love him too much. Excuse my warmth; I never can speak of Mr. Allston but in raptures."

And Mr. Allston, writing to Mr. Morse, at Bristol, makes the following suggestions:

"I write to thank you for the very agreeable intelligence contained in your letter to Leslie [the expected sale of one of Mr. A.'s paintings]; but, in a particular manner to request, or rather to advise, you not to take a share in the intended raffle. For this I can offer two reasons: 1. That the price of a share is too much for you to risk upon an uncertainty; 2. That I much fear, should you win, the world may suspect, on account of our connection, that I was in some way interested in it. I think, upon the whole, you had better not take one, but wait until you can paint a landscape equal to it yourself; which I make no doubt you will ere long be able to do, if you are industrious. I shall follow your advice in not being too sanguine respecting its success. But hope is pleasant, and I shall therefore indulge it until I hear from you again. I am quite satisfied that it should go at five hundred guineas, and, as soon as it is sold, I shall, according to my promise, bespeak an elegant frame for it. I have at last the satisfaction to inform you that my large picture is in the British Gallery, and, moreover, hung in the place where Mr. West's was."

Mr. Morse, during the latter part of his residence in London, denied himself in great measure the pleasures of society, which were pressed upon him. In the second year of his life there, he had received the following note from Zachary Macaulay, which is copied here as an illustration of the mode of getting about in London sixty years ago:

"Mr. Macaulay presents his compliments to Mr. Morse, and begs to express his regret at not having yet been so fortunate as to meet him. Mr. Macaulay will be particularly happy, if it should suit Mr. Morse to dine with him at his house at Clapham, on Saturday next at five o'clock. Mr. M.'s house is five doors beyond the Plough, at the entrance of Clapham Common. A coach goes daily to Clapham from the Ship at Charing Cross, at a quarter-past three, and several leave Grace-Church Street, in the City, every day at four. The distance from London Bridge to Mr. Macaulay's house is about four miles."

"26 BIRCHIR LANE, *June* 23, 1812."

But Mr. Morse assures his parents that visiting costs too much time. He writes to them:

"James Russell, Esq., has been extremely attentive to me. He has a very fine family, consisting of four daughters, and, I think, a son, who is absent in the East Indies. The daughters are very beautiful, accomplished, and amiable, especially the youngest, Lucy. I came very near being at my old game of falling in love; but I find that *love* and *painting* are quarrelsome companions, and that the house of my heart was too small for both of them; so I have turned *Mrs. Love* out-of-doors. 'Time enough,' thought I (with true old-bachelor complacency), 'time enough for you these ten years to come.' Mr. Russell's portrait I have painted as a present to Miss Russell, and will send it to her as soon as I can get an opportunity. It is an excellent likeness of him. I should be very happy to send also the portraits of the rest of the family to her, but, as I am obliged to support myself now, every thing must be turned to account.

"You wish me to keep up my acquaintance with Mr. Burder, Messrs. Macaulay, Taylor, and others. Mr. Burder has never shown me the slightest attention. I never have seen him, to speak to him, but once; and then, when I delivered my letter of introduction to him, he said he hoped he should have the pleasure of my company to dine *soon*, and he would let me know when it would be , convenient. I have not heard from him from that time to this. There is no blame attached to him. He is a man full of business, like papa, and I suppose it has slipped his memory, and it is perhaps better for both of us, for I should only hinder him, and he me. It is utterly impossible for me to keep up an acquaintance in England, and I therefore do not attempt it. My studies absorb all my time, and I wish no other *employment* or *pastime*. 'Tis not in London, as in Boston, or one of our cities, where you have your friends in a *little* circle round you. But a visit in London is a serious undertaking, probably a walk of two or three miles, if not five or six. Mr. Taylor lives two miles from me, Mr. Burder six, Mr. Macaulay seven, Mr. Thornton seven, Mr. Wilberforce five, Dr. Lettsom three; Mr. Allston *two streets*, Mr. West *two streets*. So you see by this who are most likely to be my intimates, and what time I must spend just to *step* in and make a call; and, what makes the matter worse, I seem to live in the centre of a great circle, as it respects them."

Mr. Wilberforce speaks, in one of his letters to Dr. Morse, of his deep interest in his son, and his desire that he would be more at home in his house. And, among the autographs which the son preserved to the end of his life, was a pleasant note from Mr. Wilberforce, dated

"KENSINGTON GROVE, *June* 1, 1815.

"MY DEAR SIR: Till I heard, three or four days ago, from Mr. Sanders the Black School-master, that you were in London, I had conceived, from the contents of a letter I received some little time ago from your father, that you were on the Continent, and not likely to be in England again till the middle or end of July. It is long since I had the pleasure of seeing you, and I need not assure you that you are always an acceptable visitor; but I did not return to the neighborhood of London till Parliament reassembled, and during its sittings I am always so much occupied and engaged that I am forced to give up almost all social intercourse. The consequence is, that toward the end of the session, as just now, I have a large arrear of social debts to pay to my friends, and the few days I have at command are preëngaged. But at breakfast, at about ten or half-past ten, I should be happy to see you any day, and let me beg you to come some fine morning, and say you are come to breakfast. I have a parcel of newspapers and pamphlets to send you. In haste, but with real regard, and taking, for your good father's sake, a real interest in your welfare, I remain, my dear sir,

"Yours sincerely,

"W. WILBERFORCE.

"S. F. B. MORSE, *Esq.*"

This friendly note is dated June 1, 1815. On the 18th day of the same month the battle of Waterloo was fought, and on the 6th day of the month following the allied armies entered Paris. There was no electric Telegraph at that time to carry news across channels, continents, and oceans; but the future inventor of such an agent relates an interesting incident of the reception of these tidings in London. Mr. Morse says:

"It was at one of my visits, in the year 1815, that an incident occurred which well illustrates the character of the great philan-

thropist. As I passed through Hyde Park on my way to Kensington Grove, I observed that great crowds had gathered, and rumors
were rife that the allied armies had entered Paris, that Napoleon
was a prisoner, and that the war was virtually at an end; and it
was momentarily expected that the park guns would announce the
good news to the people. On entering the drawing-room at Mr.
Wilberforce's, I found the company, consisting of Mr. Thornton,
Mr. Macaulay, Mr. Grant the father, and his two sons Robert and
Charles, and Robert Owen, of Lanark, in quite excited conversation
respecting the rumors that prevailed. Mr. Wilberforce expatiated
largely on the prospects of a universal peace in consequence of the
probable overthrow of Napoleon, whom naturally he considered the
great disturber of the nations. At every period, however, he exclaimed, 'It is too good to be true, it cannot be true.' He was altogether skeptical in regard to the rumors. The general subject,
however, was the absorbing topic at the dinner-table; after dinner
the company joined the ladies in the drawing-room. I sat near a
window which looked out in the direction of the distant park.
Presently a flash and a distant dull report of a gun attracted my
attention, but was unnoticed by the rest of the company. Presently another flash and report assured me that the park guns were
firing, and at once I called Mr. Wilberforce's attention to the fact.
Running to the window, he threw it up in time to see the next flash
and hear the next report. Clasping his hands in silence, with the
tears rolling down his cheeks, he stood for a few moments perfectly
absorbed in thought, and, before uttering a word, embraced his wife
and daughter, and shook hands with every one in the room. The
scene was one not to be forgotten."

A few days after this scene Mr. Morse left England for his
native land.

CHAPTER IV.

1815-1823.

RETURN TO AMERICA—OPENS A STUDIO IN BOSTON—NO SUCCESS—INVENTS
IMPROVEMENT IN PUMP—TRAVELS IN VERMONT AND NEW HAMPSHIRE
AS PORTRAIT-PAINTER—MEETS HIS FUTURE BRIDE—PURSUES HIS IN-
VENTION—GOES TO CHARLESTON, SOUTH CAROLINA—DR. FINLEY—SUC-
CESS—ALLSTON'S ENCOURAGEMENT—RETURNS NORTH—MARRIAGE—
CHARLESTON AGAIN—THE PUMP—W. ALLSTON—MORSE PAINTS THE POR-
TRAIT OF PRESIDENT MONROE—THIRD WINTER IN CHARLESTON—NEW
HAVEN—PAINTING "HOUSE OF REPRESENTATIVES"—HISTORY OF THE
PICTURE.

AFTER waiting fourteen days in Liverpool for a fair wind,
Mr. Morse set sail August 21, 1815, in the ship Ceres, Captain Webber, for Boston. Two hundred vessels sailed in company.
"We gradually lost sight of our companions," he writes, "as
night approached, and at sunset they were dispersed all over the
horizon." The passage was long and boisterous. His sea-diary
is but a record of head-winds, rain, gales, tempests, sea-sickness,
and every thing disagreeable. They sighted the signal of a ship
in distress. The captain refused to go to the rescue, on the
ground that he had enough to do to look out for his own. The
passengers entreated him to have mercy, but he was obstinate.
Mr. Morse then assured him that, as soon as they landed in Boston, he would expose his inhumanity by stating the facts in the
public journals. This brought him to, and he bore down for
the dismasted ship whose signal-guns and signs of distress called
two other ships to its aid.

One gale followed another. "Obliged," he says, "to keep
our berths, cabin dark, dead lights on. Oh, who would go to
sea who can stay at home." A few days after this despairing
groan, the sea is calm : " A serene and delightful night; the full
moon rose in a cloudless sky. The sea is like a mirror, with not
a ripple on its surface, and the ship is as still as if we were at
anchor in the harbor : nothing is in sight but sky and water,
and the color of the water is so like the sky that we seem to be
suspended in the midst of space."

He arrived in Boston on the 18th day of October, after a
passage of fifty-eight days, and an absence from his country of
more than four years. His profession he had pursued with ardor and great success ; his ambition was stimulated, and he was
buoyant with hope ; and the impelling power of necessity was
upon him, for his profession was to be his only source of support.

The year 1816 was spent in Boston and in Charlestown,
where he lodged at his father's house. His father had engaged
a studio for him in the city. His great picture was opened for
exhibition. The fame of the young artist had preceded him,
and hundreds of people went to see a picture by the favorite
pupil of Allston and West. He was constantly invited to the
entertainments of the cultivated and wealthy families of the city
of Boston. The " Judgment of Jupiter " was admired by the
critics and the multitude. He set up his easel with the confident expectation that his fame and his work would bring him
orders and money. But an entire year dragged itself along,
without an offer for his picture, or an order for an historical
work. His mind was too active and earnest for such a life as
this. In the evenings at home he meditated an invention by
which a great improvement would be made in the common
pump and, one that could be adapted to the forcing-pump in the
fire-engine. His brother, Sidney E. Morse, two years younger
than he, entered into the project with him, and they completed
the invention and secured a patent. In the autumn the following notice was published:

"NEW INVENTIONS.—A new-constructed *patent pump* is in operation on Gray's Wharf, in Charlestown, where any who feel de-

sirous of seeing it may see it on any day during ONE WEEK from this date, from half ebb to half flood-tide. Four men can work it with ease and deliver three hundred and sixty gallons in one minute. The pump-bore is five inches in diameter; a wooden ball four and three-fourth inches, entered at the bottom of the log, will pass freely through and be delivered at the nose."

His friends in London did not forget him. Leslie writes:

"LONDON, *November* 17, 1815.

"MY DEAR MORSE: I have just received your very welcome letter announcing your arrival. Our sorrow for the length and unpleasantness of your voyage is entirely swallowed up in joy for your safety, about which we were extremely anxious, from accounts we have had of the hurricanes off Boston.

"We continue pretty much as when you left us, excepting that our good old landlady, Mrs. Bridgen, has been very dangerously ill with a violent attack of the rheumatic gout. She is now, thank Heaven, nearly recovered, and I am sure your letter did her more good than any thing the doctor has given her for some time. When she was first taken ill, she refused to have a physician. I used every argument in my power to persuade her to it, but she would not consent, saying it would go off of itself. Knowing too well the fatal effects of this dread of the doctor, I went without her knowledge to an eminent one (Dr. Blackburn), and sent him to her, and I am by no means sure that he did not save her life. During her illness I had opportunities of discovering more of the real character of Mr. Bridgen than I had ever known before. He showed a most affectionate disposition, and I am sure it was merely his testy manner that had before obscured it. He was unceasingly assiduous in his attentions to her, and, though in bad health himself, sat up with her, and did every thing in his power to alleviate her sufferings in the kindest manner possible. He was describing to me one night how indefatigable he had formerly been in his occupation: 'For' (said he with tears in his eyes), 'I loved my *missus*, sir, and thought I could never do enough for her.' He spoke in the highest terms of her excellent temper, at the same time reproaching himself for having tormented her so much by his bad one, of which he seemed perfectly sensible.

"Soon after you left London, Mr. McMurtrie arrived from Philadelphia. He is one of our few men of taste. He was highly delighted with Allston's pictures, and persuaded him to send out his

'Dead Man' to Philadelphia for exhibition, which I suppose is there by this time. McMurtrie introduced us to the great General Scott, and his aide-de-camp Major Mercer, who were fellow-passengers with him. They are both most gentlemanly men. Scott is six feet four inches high, well made, and has a fine face. His eyes are remarkably expressive. I regretted exceedingly you were not here; you would have been so delighted with them. I painted a portrait of Mercer, and am making a copy of Mr. West's pictures (the Cupid with a lion, sea-horse, etc.) for the general, for which I am to have sixty guineas. They are now in France, and when they return I am to have the honor of painting a portrait of the general. Mr. Ogden, who commanded a regiment of volunteers in the battle of New Orleans, has lately been here. He brought a letter of introduction to me from Jarvis, the painter, and a portrait of Jackson, painted in the true Italian touch, by the immortal Wheeler, which he is having engraved here. General Jackson is by no means handsome, having very much the physiognomy of a dried shad, with the complexion of a pair of leather breeches; nevertheless, he was the man that did John's business for him. Ogden told me that the battle was gained principally by the volunteers, who were composed of the wealthiest citizens of New Orleans.

"I have very little information to give you in the arts, excepting that Holland was not elected an associate, and that Jackson and Mulready were. Haydon gets on slowly with his picture. Collins has improved wonderfully, and made some of the most exquisite sketches from Nature I have ever seen. Kukup is likely to get the prize, I believe; he has but one antagonist (Williehass). Allston is more than half through his 'Peter,' and a glorious picture it will be. I am painting a half-length of a beautiful actress (Mrs. Mardyn) for exhibition. She has just appeared at Drury Lane in Mrs. Jordan's characters. Her beauty, however, is her greatest attraction. Collard, Lonsdale, Haydon, Hewling, desire their regards to you.

"Your sincere friend,
"LESLIE."

The state of the arts in America at this juncture is shown in a letter from the Rev. Samuel F. Jarvis to S. F. B. Morse:

"NEW YORK, *January* 29, 1816.

"You are now, I suppose, unremittingly engaged in the pursuits of your profession. It will gratify me much to hear what you are doing. Portrait-painting alone is profitable in this country—our rich men not having yet obtained that relish for the fine arts which would lead them to admire a painting for its own sake, or to patronize genius from the noble principles of love for excellence, and love for country. The Bostonians probably will patronize you, however, because you are their fellow-citizen, and, though the thought of being indebted to that motive cannot be a very pleasing one to you, yet it may in time lead to juster views. You know, I presume, that Colonel Trumbull has seated himself down in this city, and his collection you are probably well acquainted with. Our Academy of Arts is at present in rather a languishing state; but I trust we shall soon be able to make it worth attention. The corporation of this city have given, or are about giving, a large lot near the new City Hall in Broadway, where it is proposed to erect a building to correspond with that noble edifice (not to vie with it, of course, but as a sort of appendage), which is to be devoted to our literary, scientific, and elegant institutions. We are to have in it the City Library, Scudder's Museum, the Academy of Fine Arts, a chemical laboratory, and apartments for the several learned societies—the New York Historical Society, the New York Literary and Philosophical Society, etc. I hope that we shall institute an Academy of Painting; and it would give me great pleasure to see you one of the professors of it. Why will you not let us have the pleasure of seeing you, when we can talk over these matters at our leisure? I am reserving the painting of my phiz for your pencil; and as they tell me I look best in the winter, because fattest, you see it is of great importance that I see you at this season. Have you attended at all to architecture? That is with me a favorite science, though I know but little about it. I hope some time or other to see a Gothic church erected here, and I must consult your taste concerning the plans. There has been a Gothic church erected at New Haven since you were there, and it is my intention to put up a monument in it to the memory of my father, the decorations of which I wish to have correspondent with the style of the building. As you have probably noticed the principal monuments in England, it may be in your power to furnish me with a design."

His thoughts were much with those friends he had left. Allston he loved and revered. He pours out his heart to him in letters, some of which have been found among Mr. Allston's papers. The passage in the following letter, where the pupil implores his master's forgiveness for possible errors, beautifully illustrates the feeling that subsisted between them.

" MY DEAR SIR : I have but one moment to write you by a vessel which sails to-morrow morning : I wrote Leslie by New Packet some months since, and am hourly expecting an answer. I congratulate you, my dear sir, on the sale of your picture of the '*Dead Man.*' I suppose you will have received notice before this reaches you, that the Philadelphia Academy of Arts have purchased it for the sum of thirty-five hundred dollars. Bravo for our country ! I am sincerely rejoiced for you, and for the disposition which it shows of future encouragement. I really think the time is not far distant when we shall all be able to settle in our native land with profit as well as pleasure. . . . I long to spend my evenings again with you and Leslie ; I shall certainly visit Italy (should I live and no unforeseen event take place) in the course of a year or eighteen months. Could there not be some arrangement made to meet you and Leslie there ? You will now be in funds, and perhaps would not dislike to visit again the scenes of your early studies. Do write me, if it is but a line, and say if it cannot be so arranged. . . . My conscience accuses me, and hardly too, of many instances of pettishness and ill-humor toward you, which make me almost hate myself, that I could offend a temper like yours ; I need not ask you to forgive it, I know you cannot harbor anger a minute, and perhaps have forgotten the instances ; but I cannot forget them. If you had failings of the same kind, and I could recollect any instances where you had spoken pettishly or ill-natured to me, our accounts would then have been balanced, they would have called for mutual forgetfulness and forgiveness ; but when on reflection I find nothing of the kind to charge you with, my conscience severely upbraids me with ingratitude to you, to whom (under Heaven) I owe all the little knowledge of my art which I possess ; but I hope still I shall prove grateful to you ; at any rate, I feel my errors and must mend them.

" I was at a large party at William Walter Channing's a few evenings since ; I there saw your '*Katherine and Petruchio.*' It reminded me of old times.

" I have just completed a Kitcat landscape, a sea-piece on a common half-length upright, a ship in distress on the top of a small piece of a single wave which occupies the whole foreground ; she comes out against a bright bank of clouds, *such as you like*, is scudding directly toward you under a close-reefed foresail. I bought a famous model of a seventy-four a week or two since, seven feet long and five feet high, completely rigged and perfect in every part; all the blocks traverse, so that I can brace or square the yards at pleasure, or place that in what state of dishabille I please. I gave twenty dollars for it, and it was sold a few weeks before for one hundred. I shall keep it to paint from always. Please write me soon and tell me all about yourself and Leslie. Remember me most particularly to Leslie, Collard, Lonsdale, Collins, Haydon, Mr. and Mrs. Hewlings, Cregan, Martin, Lane (if in London), and *the Bridges.*

" Yours most sincerely,

" SAMUEL F. B. MORSE."

To this letter Mr. Allston replied in these words:

" MY DEAR SIR : I will not apologize for having so long delayed answering your kind letter, being, as you well know, privileged by my friends to be a lazy correspondent. I was sorry to find that you should have suffered the recollection of any hasty expressions you might have uttered to give you uneasiness. Be assured that they never were remembered by me a moment after; nor did they ever in the slightest degree diminish my regard or weaken my confidence in the sincerity of your friendship or the goodness of your heart. Besides, the consciousness of warmth in my own temper would have made me inexcusable had I suffered myself to dwell on an inadvertent word from another. I therefore beg you will no longer suffer any such unpleasant reflections to disturb your mind; but that you will rest assured of my unaltered and sincere esteem.

" Your letter, and one I had about the same time from my sister Mary, brought the first intelligence of the sale of my picture, it being near three weeks later when I received the account from Philadelphia. When you recollect that I considered the 'Dead Man' (from the untoward fate he had hitherto experienced) almost literally as a *caput mortuum*, you may easily believe that I was most agreeably surprised to hear of the sale. But, pleased as I was, on account of the very seasonable pecuniary supply it would soon afford me, I must say that I was still more gratified at the encouragement it seemed to hold out for my return to America—not that I expect as ready a sale for every large picture I might paint; but from the growing interest in the arts, which the present purchase appears to indicate among our countrymen, I think I may reasonably reckon on a *quantum sufficit* of taste in them to calculate on at least a decent support from future exhibitions. The 'St. Peter' has been long since finished, exhibited, and sent home to Sir G. I worked on it for three weeks after it came out of the Gallery; repainted the angel's head, and made other alterations. Sir G. and Lady Beaumont expressed themselves highly pleased with it. The Gil Blas was bought by Lieutenant Drayton, of South Carolina. 'Tis now, I believe, at Philadelphia. In Somerset House I exhibited a landscape. You saw the dead color of it last summer. I inclose a short notice of it from the *Examiner.* I don't remember whether Leslie had begun his 'Death of Rutland' before you left London. He has made a fine picture of it. The head of Rutland is very beautiful, and yet full of expression. Indeed, the whole picture is firmly and well painted. By-the-by, I have given up the subject of '*Christ Healing the Sick,*' and have made a sketch of another much finer, which I think by all odds my best composition; it is both picturesque and *highly* impassioned. When I have begun it *in large* (which will be as soon as I shall have found a good painting-room) I will tell you what it is, and more about it. You find I have not been sparing about my own concerns; so, if you don't tell me *more* about yourself and your pursuits in your next than you have done in your first letter, I shall become modest, and write more in future about *matters and things in general.* . . .

" Very truly yours,
" W. ALLSTON."

Two lively letters from Leslie, in London, cheered him during this year of discouragement and fear:

"LONDON, *January* 30, 1816.

"DEAR MORSE: I have as yet received but one letter from you, which was written the day after your arrival. I suppose by this time you have been duly and truly welcomed by all your friends; have had each of your arms shaken into a sort of demi-dislocation, and have had your health drunk till you are an insured man, wind and limb, these thousand years at least, to say nothing of the turkeys, geese, and all other good things, that have been eaten in honor of your arrival. I say, now that all these ceremonies are settled and passed, I hope and expect that you will allow the recollection of your friends on this side of the water to occupy some of your thoughts. Be assured that those friends think of you very often, and that your image is deeply engraven on their hearts, associated with many past scenes of enjoyment. Since you left us we have been going on much in the old way, 'living from hand to mouth' (as it is vulgarly expressed). Mr. Allston has finished his 'Peter,' of which he has made a glorious picture, and which will be seen by the public at the British Gallery in a few days. There is but one opinion of it among his friends. But what seems to please him most is the very high opinion Haydon has of it. Punishment seems at last likely to overtake the members of the British Institution for their various misdemeanors. They narrowly escaped this year having no exhibition at all, by reason of no pictures being sent. Allston intended his for Spring Gardens; but a very tempting offer being made to him by Young, that of allowing him to work on it for three weeks at the Gallery, induced him to send it there. Notwithstanding, however, that they had succeeded in getting his great picture, which fills the end of one of their great rooms, their ranks were so scanty that they were obliged to apply to Mr. West for assistance, who undertook to fill a whole side of a room with old works of his own. I understood they also applied to Hayter, who was finishing a large picture of three children (portraits), and have taken that in under the appellation of 'The Garland.' The rest of the collection consists principally of the paltry sketches for which they were to give premiums, and the fragments and refuse of Somerset House. It is generally anticipated that this same British Institution will die a natural death one of these days.

"I am going on with my 'Clifford and Rutta,' and a copy from Mrs. West's picture of 'Cupid commanding the Elements,' for General Scott, and now and then making the pot boil with a portrait or so. I am admitted to the life at the Academy, where I draw very regularly. They have instituted a painting school at the Academy, which they have begun to supply with pictures from the Dulwich collection, which formerly belonged to Sir Francis Bourgeois. The academicians are visitors by turns the same as in the life, and the school is in the inner room. I made a few sketches this year at the Gallery, and I shall attend the school at the Academy when Turner is visitor, as I am persuaded I can learn more from him than any one of the R. A.'s. I believe there is no doubt but that government will buy the Elgin Marbles, and it is said they will be removed to the British Museum next summer. The Academy are going to have a new set of casts in the spring, and England will present far more advantages to the students in arts, as

7

indeed it does already, than any other part of the world. I hope you will be able to realize your plan of returning in a year.

"There was no gold medal given the last year at Somerset House: Kukup and Williehass were the only candidates. Mr. West told me that he thought, had you been allowed to try, your picture would have stood a better chance than either of them. Mr. Allston has sold his 'Gil Blas' (which is at the Gallery) to Colonel Drayton of the U. S. Army. I am very glad to see our heroes take an interest in the arts."

"LONDON, *September* 6, 1816.

"DEAR MORSE: I have just received your letter by Mr. Peyson. I am sorry to hear that the arts are advancing so slowly in America; but as to encouragment there is very little anywhere, I apprehend, just at present. There is a general stagnation of business in England, and the artists are as much affected by it as any other class of men. I hope, however, your prospects may not be really so dull in America as you imagine. As you were before a little too sanguine of success, it is possible you may now be more depressed than there is really cause to be. I am glad to hear that you are going on a tour into Vermont and New Hampshire; it will be a pleasant relaxation to you, and I hope you will return well loaded with sketches. I sincerely hope that you will be able to revisit Europe; but, by all means, come to London, instead of Rome. I am convinced there are greater advantages here than anywhere. You will find a great deal that will be new to you, and the Elgin Marbles will be placed in a building erected for them at the Museum, where it is to be hoped we shall be able to study them in good lights. I never thought of preserving catalogues of the exhibition to send you, as I did not suppose the *mere names* of pictures would give you any pleasure. And as to critiques, they (you know) are so bad that it is impossible to form any idea of the pictures they describe. The Somerset House show was not so good as usual. Turner has two small pictures, by no means his best. Hilton's great picture of the 'Raising of Lazarus' disappointed every one. Lawrence had some fine portraits, among which was one of Canova, the Italian sculptor, a very intelligent and agreeable head.

"Your humble servant exhibited a beautiful landscape of a sunrise, which, I believe, he had outlined before you went away. Mr. A. is at present painting a picture of 'Rebecca at the Well,' for

Mr. Van Schaick. He has lately painted a head of Dante's Beatrice, which is extremely beautiful, and has a chastity and refinement of expression equal to Raphael. I am at present painting portraits of Mr. and Mrs. Adams, and studying at the Gallery. The exhibition of old masters was the finest I have seen by far. They had two of the cartoons, the 'Miraculous Draught of Fishes,' and the 'Paul preaching at Athens.' The 'Bacchus and Ariadne,' by Titian, and the most beautiful little Paul Veronese (of the 'Adoration of the Shepherds') I ever saw, which I am now making a finished copy of. There were two large Paulos, 'Wisdom and Strength,' and 'The Painter between Virtue and Vice,' of which you may have seen prints. There was also a glorious portrait of Lorenzo de Medicis, by Sab. del Piombo, the most intellectual and grand head I ever saw for a portrait; and there was a beautiful little picture, by Raphael, of St. Catherine. The *Catalogue Raisonné* appeared according to promise, but is not near so good as the one last year. At the conclusion the author says that Mr. Payne Knight told the directors it was the custom of the Greek nobility to strip and exhibit themselves naked to the artists in various attitudes, that they might have an opportunity of studying fine form. Accordingly, those public-spirited men, the directors, have determined to adopt the plan, and are all practising like mad to prepare themselves for the ensuing exhibition, when they are to be placed on pedestals. It is supposed that Sir G. Beaumont, Mr. Long, Mr. Knight, etc., will occupy the principal lights. The Marquis of Stafford, unfortunately, could not recollect the attitude of any one antique figure, but was found practising, having the head of the dying gladiator, the body of the Hercules, one leg of the Apollo, and the other of the dancing Faun, turned the wrong way. Lord Mulgrave, having a small head, thought of representing the Torso, but he did not know what to do with his legs, and was afraid that as Master of the Ordnance he could not dispense with his *arms*. In another part of the catalogue there is a quotation from one of Leigh Hunt's poems, where one angel says to another—

> 'If your cloud holds two,
> I'll get up and ride with you.' "

Disappointed in his expectations of encouragement in historical painting, Mr. Morse resolved to go into the country, and earn his bread by painting the portraits of the people. In the rural districts of New England he would find ready introduction to the most respectable families, as his father's name was a household word in every town. With letters to the pastors and others, he took his way into the world to seek his fortune; fame did not tempt him now. During the autumn of 1816, and the winter of 1816–'17, he visited several towns in New Hampshire and Vermont. He painted portraits in Walpole, Hanover, Windsor, Portsmouth, and Concord, meeting with moderate success, and receiving the modest sum of fifteen dollars for each portrait. At Concord, New Hampshire, the sun shone brightly upon him. He writes from this place to his parents: "I am still here (August 16th), and am passing my time very agreeably. I have painted five portraits at fifteen dollars each, and have two more engaged, and many more talked of. I think I shall get along well. I believe I could make an independent fortune in a few years if I devoted myself exclusively to portraits, so great is the desire for good portraits in the different country towns."

He doubtless was candid when he wrote that he was "passing his time in Concord very agreeably." In his history of Concord, Dr. Bouton says: "At a party given by Mr. Sparhawk, in 1818, among the invited guests was Samuel F. B. Morse, now distinguished as the inventor of the electric Telegraph, who was that evening introduced to Miss Lucretia P. Walker, daughter of Charles Walker, who was accounted the most beautiful and accomplished young lady of the town, whom Mr. Morse subsequently married."

She was a young lady of great personal loveliness and rare good sense. The eye of the artist was attracted by her beauty, her sweetness of temper, and high intellectual culture, which fitted her to be his companion. Her sound judgment and prudence made her a counselor and friend. All the letters that she wrote to him, before and after their marriage, he carefully preserved, and they are witnesses to her intelligence, education, tenderness of feeling, and admirable fitness to be the wife of such a man as Mr. Morse.

Before an engagement of marriage was made, their correspondence was so frequent and voluminous that the artist must have been rapid with pen and brush to have been able to satisfy the demands of his patrons and his love. Early in the year

1817 the engagement was concluded. He imparted a knowledge of the fact at once to his parents, having received the cordial approbation of the parents of Miss Walker. To them Rev. Dr. Morse addressed a letter inviting their daughter to visit Charlestown, that he and Mrs. Morse might form the acquaintance of one who was to stand to them in this new and near relation. The letter was in these stately but affectionate terms:

Rev. Dr. Morse to Mr. and Mrs. Walker.

"CHARLESTOWN, *January* 13, 1817.

"DEAR SIR AND MADAM: The mutual attachment subsisting between our eldest son and your daughter, and the matrimonial engagement which in consequence has been entered into by them, with the consent of their parents, respectively, render it proper and desirable, in prospect of such a connection in our families, that an acquaintance should be formed between us. As this cannot now be done personally, with convenience, I take the liberty to commence it by letter. From this acquaintance, and future intercourse, Mrs. Morse and myself anticipate much pleasure and satisfaction. We are very anxious to become *personally* acquainted with your daughter, who is much endeared to us by the amiable dispositions and virtues which she is reported to possess, as well as from the consideration that she shares so largely in the affections of a beloved son. And I accordingly write this for the purpose of requesting your permission that your daughter should make us a visit with our son, of such length as may suit her convenience.

"We hope you will not deny us this request, a compliance with which will afford us much gratification. If it can be made convenient, we should be obliged particularly if they could be here in the course of the *next* week. It will, be assured, give us much pleasure to see you, or any of your family, at our house, whenever it may be convenient to you, or to them.

"Mrs. Morse unites in kind regards to you both, with, dear sir, and madam, your affectionate and obedient servant,

"JED. MORSE."

The visit was made, to the delight of all parties. The young lady returned to her parents in Concord, and the artist continued his travels and painting. The congratulations of friends poured in upon him when his engagement became known. Leslie, the friend of his youth, in London; his companion in study and in many a gay and festive hour—the humorist alike with pen and pencil, and in conversation more than with either —wrote to him when he heard of it :

"So, you are over head and ears in love ? Happy fellow ! You have described her in such delicious terms that your pen should have flowed with honey instead of ink. Excuse my saying one serious word to you, my dear Morse, on this serious subject, though I have little doubt your own excellent judgment has already dictated it to you. Take care to ascertain, before the knot is tied, whether she has a deep sense of true religion. Do not, on any account, marry unless you are satisfied that she has, and be not contented with a mere outward profession ; she must *delight* in it. Her religion must be practical, or she will not make the kind of wife I should wish a friend to have. You and I have seen how very greatly true Christianity conduces to domestic comfort in the instance of Mr. and Mrs. Allston."

Such counsel from such a rare genius as Leslie reveals the inner life in a light at once unexpected and beautiful. Leslie proceeds in the next paragraph to describe the paintings in the annual exhibition then open in the British Gallery, among them some just finished, which are now famous, Wilkie's "Sheepshearing" and others ; and, after cheering his friend with words of hope, he adds : "Believe that you are destined to do something great, and you will do it. I write this with the hope of rousing your spirits. You will be pleased to hear that Collins, who was a Deist, has become a sincere Christian. I find there are more artists religious than I was aware of ; Wilkie and Haydon are, and so are Ward, and Jackson, and Linnell. Willes you knew was a Christian, and Starke and Severn are both Christians, and very amiable young men."

As Morse pursued his wandering life among the cities and rural towns of Vermont and New Hampshire, the letters to and from him keep us acquainted with his progress, and with the peculiar bent of his mind, even in the midst of his labors, as a painter of portraits. We would not look among letters of love to find notices of useful inventions in the arts ; yet, in the midst of these effusions of the heart, put away more than half a century ago, we discover the young lover, while making declarations of his affection, mingling his hopes and fears with calculations about the prospective profits of his "flexible piston-pump." He writes to Miss Walker, in June, 1817: "I am preparing for a journey to Washington, to take out our PATENTS FOR THREE MACHINES, which, in the opinion of judicious, philosophical, and practical men, will be of great value. I would not be too sanguine. It is best to be always prepared for disappointment." Finding that the business at Washington could be attended to by an agent, he did not go, and in the month of July writes to Miss Walker:

"We are in daily expectation of hearing of the arrival of our models of machinery at Washington, and of receiving our letters-patent. We have just tried our fire-engine on a large scale, and it succeeds to our utmost expectation. We have shown it in operation to several friends, who have given it their entire approbation, and think that it will not only be profitable to us, but beneficial to the community. From its cheapness, it will be within the reach of every village. But good-by, dearest; I hope to talk over all these things shortly with you."

His brother, Sidney E., was at work diligently upon improvements in the new engine, their joint production, and, in a letter to Finley, the brother writes, closing with a mock-heroic name which he had *invented:*

"Since you left us I have been employed in newly modifying and improving the pump-machine. I have got it now exactly to my mind. The valves will be on a new plan, far superior to any thing ever before thought of. The bag-piston, I find, is no new thing. The 'Cyclopædia' states that one Benjamin Martin, an Englishman, invented the same thing more than fifty years ago. His pump, they say, worked admirably, but was never introduced into common use, because the leathers, when dry, were continually *cracking.* I have invented a remedy for all difficulties, and have got a pump in every respect to my liking. Particulars when you return. I think of calling it 'Morse's Patent Metallic Double-Headed OCEAN-DRINKER and DELUGE-SPOUTER VALVE *Pump-Boxes.*' "

And Finley himself writes to his father, from Concord, in August, 1817:

"When in Andover, I conversed with Mr. Farrar and others on

the subject of our *engines*. Mr. F. was highly delighted, and said he should certainly wait to know the result of our experiment, and would take ours, in preference to any others, for their college engine, and, instead of one, would probably want *two*. He said that the town, also, had long had an idea of procuring an engine; but, on account of the expense, had not yet obtained one. He said he believed they had subscribed about *three hundred dollars*, but it was not sufficient, and they had given up the idea at present; but he thought they would have *one of ours, without doubt*.

"In Concord, also, all that I have conversed with seem highly pleased. Mr. Sparhawk, the Secretary of State (who is very much my friend), carried me to see the Concord engine, which is a miserable affair, and which cost four hundred and fifty dollars. He said it was always out of order, and they did not like it. He also said if ours succeeded, and cost only half or even two-thirds of the price, they would have two or three in Concord.

"I wish much to know how Dearborn proceeds with the engine and bellows. I think the prospect brightens with respect to our inventions, if our smallest can be made so as to be afforded at one hundred and fifty dollars, and so that our patent-fee should be on it fifty dollars. I think we should make something handsome."

The *New Hampshire Patriot*, of April 14, 1818, has this notice:

"An additional fire-engine has been purchased by the inhabitants of this town. It is a new invention of Mr. Morse, the celebrated painter, and is procured for about half the usual expense— say one hundred and fifty to two hundred dollars. It requires much less manual labor, and throws the water to as great a distance and in as large quantities. As yet we have seen only the operation of Mr. Morse's miniature model. Should his invention succeed equal to expectation and appearance, every village of any considerable extent will be a gainer to purchase one or more of these engines."

To Miss Walker he writes from his father's house in Charlestown:

"*November* 20, 1817.

"Our inventions are in a prosperous way; it takes a deal of time and patience to attend to them, but I hope they will be a handsome property to us ere long. All is in God's hands; in his own time and his own way, all things shall work for good to us if we love Him."

And in the same letter he mentions sending a curious gift to a young lady, and such a present as could have come only from a young man of an ingenious turn of mind. It illustrates the mechanical tendencies of his intellect at this period of his life. He writes:

"I send by Mr. Ambrose with the book the lock which I once mentioned to you; it may amuse you. I think it will puzzle the ingenuity of Mr. J. to find it out. I will tell you how it opens by the annexed figure: the word that opens it must be spelt in a line between the two marks on the end-pieces, and when spelt the right-hand end pulls out about a quarter of an inch, and the ketch can be lifted up. You must not tell Mr. J. the key-word; it is the name of some one you know. I must leave it for your ingenuity to find out whose it is."

And, again, a week later:

"Our inventions are slowly progressing. Surely an inventor earns his money hard. It appears to me I would not go through the vexations, and delays, and disappointments, I have gone through, for double what I expect to obtain from them. They, however, promise very well, and I hope to realize something handsome from them. Our engine has been proved. Tell Mr. Sparhawk (with my best respects to him and Mrs. Sparhawk) that we can order one made for Concord, if they please, for one hundred and fifty dollars, which shall throw three barrels eighty feet in five seconds, by the power of eight men. I wish the Concord people would give us an order for such a one, which shall be warranted, and thus encourage the new invention. An advertisement is preparing for the papers, which will be ready in a day or two."

Little did the perplexed and anxious artist, then bewailing the vexatious delays and disappointments of the inventor, imagine that, within twenty short years from that time, his bride to whom he was then writing would be in her grave, their children homeless, he living in a solitary garret, carrying in the darkness to his comfortless chamber the simple food which he prepared with his own hands, while toiling to produce an invention that was to electrify the world! And in another letter, after filling three pages with details of his inventions, he says: " But good-by, Lucrece; I am bothering you with engines and *machinations*, and I am sure they can't be pleasant to you; so I will stop."

The Allstons, of South Carolina, were frequently at the North, and among the friends of their relative, Washington Allston, Mr. Morse became acquainted with Hon. John A. Allston of Charleston, who assured him that a far more hopeful field for his professional labors would be found in the South than in the rural towns of New England. Rev. Dr. Morse had written to his son, while in Walpole, New Hampshire, saying:

" Mr. Legare, cousin to the Legares you know, a young man of genius and taste, says he prefers your prize picture to Mr. Allston's great picture. He returns to Carolina next month, and speaks favorably of your spending the winter there, and will do what he can to prepare the way for you, should you go. Mr. Gallaudet was here yesterday with a young Frenchman [Le Clerc] deaf and dumb, a most interesting character. I showed him, and Dr. Coggswell, of Hartford, with Mr. G., your paintings. They were highly gratified. The remarks of the Frenchman were very sensible and shrewd. He understood the subjects perfectly, and appeared to have fine taste."

Dr. Morse's large acquaintance in the South, where he had spent several months at different times, .and where relatives of his were residing, encouraged his son Finley to contemplate with favor the suggestions of Mr. Allston and Mr. Legare. Dr. Finley, his uncle, was at this time a resident of Charleston, and to him he wrote on the subject. The answer to his inquiries was a cordial invitation to come on and find a home in his uncle's house. While making preparations to go to the South, he writes to his Lucretia: " I am over head and ears in business, so much so that I am at a loss which thing to commence first. Portraits and engines, and pumps and bellows, and various models of various things, letters to write, and visits to pay, and preparations for voyages by sea and land, all crowd upon me. Tell Mr. Sparhawk that the engine is commenced, and will be finished with all expedition. I hope the Pembroke people will wait until they see ours before they order their engine."

His arrangements being completed, he went to New Haven, and there laid before the professors of the college, and others, the inventions which he and his brother had patented. From New York he writes to his parents:

"CITY HOTEL, NEW YORK, *January* 10, 1818.

"MY DEAR PARENTS: I arrived here safely last evening, from New Haven. Commodore Perry was a fellow-passenger. I was much pleased with him. I left the machine business in a prosperous way in New Haven. I showed the models to President Day, Professor Silliman, Mr. Whitney, Mr. Porter, and others; from Mr. Day and Mr. Whitney I obtained recommendations which I will transcribe. Mr. Silliman was so much pleased that he requested me to let him take the model of the engine to show it to the class, and wishes me to make a set of drawings, with an abstract of the specifications, for the first number of a periodical publication, devoted to the arts and sciences, he is about to commence, to be out in May next; he to be at the expense of engravings. The models I left with Mr. Porter, who is our agent at New Haven; with him I made the following agreement, viz.:

"'I authorize John E. Porter, Esq., of New Haven, to contract with any mechanic that he may think proper, to construct and sell at his own expense any number of Morse's patent fire-engines, he paying or securing to be paid, to the satisfaction of said Porter the sum of thirty dollars for each one he shall so construct and sell, which sum said Porter is authorized to receive and hold for our benefit, and for his compensation we will allow him twelve and a half per cent. on the sum so secured and paid to us. "'SAMUEL F. B. MORSE.

"'For { SIDNEY E. MORSE, and
{ SAMUEL F. B. MORSE.

"'NEW HAVEN, *January* 8, 1818.'

"By this contract we make it for the interest of Mr. Porter to exert himself in behalf of the machines, and we are secured twenty-five dollars on each one. Mr. Day's recommendations run thus:

"'Having seen an improved pump-piston, contrived by Mr. Morse for the purpose of playing without friction, and an application of it to the fire-engine and other instruments, I take the liberty of stating that it appears to me to be calculated to answer a useful purpose; as it unites simplicity in the construction, with effectual security against friction.

"'JEREMIAH DAY.

'"YALE COLLEGE, *January* 8, 1818.'

" Mr. Whitney's runs thus:

" 'Having examined the model of a fire-engine, invented by Mr. Morse, with pistons of a new construction, I am of opinion that an engine may be made on that principle (being more simple and much less expensive), which would have a preference to those in common use.

" 'ELI WHITNEY.

" 'NEW HAVEN, *January* 8, 1818.'

" I am unfortunate in not finding, in New York, either George Clinton or Mr. Moses Rogers. The former resides in Albany, the latter is in England. I called on Mr. Van Schaick, and on Monday we shall endeavor to find some one to arrange the business of the inventions with."

With his mind quite as full of the pump as of painting, Mr. Morse sailed from New York in a packet, and arrived in Charleston, January 27, 1818. A cordial welcome greeted him at Dr. Finley's. He wrote to his parents the next day, expressing his resolution to put the pump aside, and devote himself wholly to his chosen art. He says:

" I find myself in a new climate, the weather warm as our May. I have been introduced to a number of friends. I think my prospects are favorable. I did nothing about the machine in New York. The absence of Governor Clinton entirely deranged my plans. Rev. Dr. Spring advised me to leave it until my return to New York, after the subject had been noticed in *Silliman's Journal*. He thought it would then be revived with better effect. The street commissioner, Mr. Macomb, was very much pleased with the model, and said it promised to be extensively useful. The machine business (between ourselves) I am heartily sick of. It yields much vexation, labor, and expense, and no profit. Yet I will not abandon it. I will do as well as I can with it, but I will make it subservient to my painting, as I am sure of a support, and even independence, if I pursue it diligently, and I am sure I am disposed to do it."

Bright as his prospects appeared when he entered under the most favorable auspices the charmed circles of society in the hospitable city of Charleston, the weeks wore slowly away, and no sitters presented themselves at the door of his solitary studio. Weary with waiting, and drawn northward by a magnet more powerful than that which he afterward employed, he resolved to return to his Lucretia, and portraits at fifteen dollars. These, and a pump that would throw three barrels of water in a minute, began to appear more likely to yield to the young people the income needed to render it prudent to marry, than the generous hospitalities of Charleston, with no orders for the artist's pencil. He implored his uncle, Dr. Finley, to sit to him for his portrait, that he might leave a memorial of his visit, and make some return for the kindness he had received. Then he would turn his back upon Charleston, and seek his native New England. This decision was evidently prompted by feeling rather than judgment, though it must be admitted there was nothing else for him to do. Dr. Finley consented to sit. The artist summoned to the work before him all the energies and resources of his youth and manhood. Never, in his anxious contests for prizes in the Royal Academy, had he made a more heroic effort than in this attempt to produce a perfect picture of his relative and friend. The studies of the past were invoked to aid him, and hopes of the future nerved him. If it were the last, as it was the first, work in the South, and far from the home of his childhood, it should be a memento of what the neglected and despairing artist could do. It was done, and to this day it is valued as one of the best productions of his master-hand. As he advanced in its execution, and intelligent critics were invited by Dr. Finley to see the coming portrait, three applications were filed by persons who now desired to be portrayed on canvas. The clouds began to break away. The wonderful skill of the artist became the talk of the town. In a few weeks his list of patrons to be painted amounted to one hundred and fifty. His price was sixty dollars a portrait! His success was assured. He toiled unceasingly, literally day and night, and even then he could not meet the demand for his work. Drawings were made of many who would permit him to finish the painting at greater leisure in the ensuing summer.

In the distance he saw, and not very far off, the vision of wife and home. He would go North in the early summer, and return in the autumn with his bride, and make a home in that genial clime, among friends to whom he had become strongly attached. Mr. John A. Allston, who had advised Mr. Morse to come to Charleston, continued to give him encouragement and material aid.   Writing to him, on learning that Mr. Morse wished to paint a portrait of his daughter, Mr. Allston says:

"GEORGETOWN, *March* 29, 1818.

" SIR: I have lately received a letter from my brother Motte, in which he tells me you have authorized him to communicate your intention of shortly commencing the *full-sized, half*-portrait of my daughter.   Upon your application to my brother, and to Mrs. Colcock, at whose boarding-school my daughter is, she will attend to you for that purpose.

" I am unwilling that a painter of your reputation should pass me without gratifying myself completely, and therefore beg the favor of you to answer the following question, with the least possible delay: What is your price for a full-length portrait of my daughter executed *nearly* in miniature, say from twelve to twenty-four inches in length, with as superb a landscape as you are capable of *designing* and painting?   It would be a convenient opportunity to make out this painting, while my daughter is attending you for her full-sized, *half*-portrait.   I would be very glad to have a painting of her in the way described.   You need not take any steps toward it until you write and receive my answer.   I am, sir, most respectfully, your obedient and humble servant,

" JOHN A. ALLSTON.

"SAMUEL F. B. MORSE, *Esq.*"

And the patron's idea of the art will be gathered from a subsequent letter written by Mr. Allston, on receiving Mr. Morse's reply to his inquiries.

"GEORGETOWN, *April* 7, 1818.

" SIR: I have just received your favor, of the 30th ultimo, and thank you very cordially for your goodness in consenting to take my daughter's full-length likeness in the manner I described, say, twenty-four inches in length.   I will pay you most willingly the two hundred dollars you require for it, and will consider myself a gainer by the bargain.   I shall expect you to decorate this picture with the most superb landscape you are capable of designing, and that you will produce a masterpiece of painting.   I agree to your taking it with you to the northward to finish it.   Be pleased to represent my daughter in the finest attitude you can conceive.   I wish the drapery to be white, but if you think some light color would be handsomer, you can adopt it.   I cannot refrain from assuring you that your letter has delighted me beyond measure, particularly that part of it which proposes your taking this picture with you to the North to finish, as I know from sad experience the difference between pictures executed at leisure and those done under a pressure of business. In the short space of twelve months I have paid much more than two thousand dollars for pictures of my family, not one of which can be said to be even a tolerable likeness, though two of them are certainly beautifully painted. As the season has far advanced, and my brother Motte writes me that you have already seventy portraits on your list to be finished in rotation, I must relinquish for the present my application to you for the several portraits I had intended, until your return to Charleston in November next.

"The full-sized half-length portrait of my daughter I hope you will have time to do justice to, and to finish before you leave Charleston, as my brother informs me it is now at the head of your list. If, however, you would prefer to take this picture also with you to the northward to finish, I would have no objection, but I could never consent to it unless you will agree to receive payment for it immediately. If you think your time will permit you to finish this picture in your best style before your departure from Charleston, I would of course greatly prefer it, and only make use of the above observation in case you might prefer taking it with you.

"I am, sir, with great respect,

"Your most obedient and humble servant,

"JOHN A. ALLSTON.

"SAMUEL F. B. MORSE, *Esq.*"

Mr. Allston paid the artist handsomely for these pictures of his children, and Mr. Morse begged him afterward to accept as a present his great picture, "The Judgment of Jupiter." It was accepted in terms as honorable to the writer as to the artist who so handsomely had expressed his sense of obligation. Mr. Allston writes to Mr. Morse:

"GEORGETOWN, *April* 18, 1820.

"MY DEAR SIR: I thank you very sincerely for your kind letter of the 14th inst., which has just reached me. I am unable to express to you sufficiently the sense of the obligation I entertain, for the very splendid present you have been pleased to make me. Much less am I able to convey to you the value I set upon the friendly sentiments you must have experienced and which have induced you to make me a present so highly flattering to me. The painting is of inestimable value, and, though I am delighted in being the owner of it, yet I cannot refrain from saying (however undeserving I am of it) that I value your regard even more than the picture. This present is an exhibition of exalted sentiments. It may be my lot to view it for a number of years. I shall never pass it but with mingled emotions of admiration for ˙ your talents, and of unfeigned homage to your superior feelings. I will direct Messrs. Kershaw and Lewis to forward it to me.

"I wish you, my dear sir, a safe voyage to the North, and that we may live to meet again—and to accept the unfeigned assurance of the regard of your much obliged and most obedient servant,

"JOHN A. ALLSTON.

"SAMUEL F. B. MORSE, *Esq.*"

The subsequent history of this picture is remarkable. While Mr. Allston lived, it was the most attractive picture in his gallery. At his death, his paintings were sold and scattered, and this one was lost to the knowledge of the artist and his friends. Many years after, an American collector of pictures bought it in England, and presented it to Mrs. Parmalee, a niece of Prof. Morse, without the slightest suspicion of his being the author. He recognized it instantly on seeing it, and it is now in the possession of the family.

In May of 1818, having spent less than five months in Charleston, and having painted fifty-three portraits, and commenced nine, to be finished in the summer, Mr. Morse returned to Boston. Not many days after his arrival he received a letter from Dr. Finley, in Charleston, rallying him playfully on his having met his Lucretia; and then the uncle says:

"Finley, I am afraid you will be too happy; you ought to meet a little rub or two, or you will be too much in the clouds, and forget that you are among mortals. Let us see if I cannot give you a friendly hoist downward. Your pictures; ay, suppose I should speak of them, and what is said of them during your absence. I will perform the office of him who was placed on the triumphal car of the conqueror to abuse him lest he should be elated. Well, 'His pictures,' say people, 'are undoubtedly good likenesses, but he paints carelessly, and in too much haste, and his draperies are not well done; he must be more attentive, or he will lose his reputation.' 'See,' say others, 'how he flatters!' 'Oh,' says another, 'he has not flattered me,' etc., etc. By-the-by, I saw old General C. C. Pinckney yesterday, and he told me in his laughing, humorous way, that he had requested you to draw his brother Thomas' twenty years younger than he really was, so as to be a companion to his own when he was twenty years older than at this time, and to flatter him, as he had directed Stuart to do so to him. Here you have a nice little anecdote to amuse yourself and friends with."

Resuming his labors at home, Mr. Morse spent the summer in completing the portraits he had brought with him in an unfinished state, and executing such orders as now came to his hand. On the 6th of October, 1818, the *New Hampshire Patriot* had the following notice:

"Married in this town, October 1st, by Rev. Dr. McFarland, Mr. Samuel F. B. Morse (the celebrated painter) to Miss Lucretia Walker, daughter of Charles Walker, Esq."

His bridal tour, with horse and gig, after the fashion of the day, is portrayed in a letter to his parents:

"Concord, N. H., *October* 5, 1818.

"My dear Parents: I was married, as I wrote you I should be, on Tuesday morning last. We set out at nine o'clock, and reached Amherst, over bad roads, at night. The next day we continued our journey through Wilton to New Ipswich, eighteen miles, over one of the worst roads I ever traveled; all up hill and down, and very rocky, and no tavern on the road. We inquired at New Ipswich our best route to Northampton, where we intended to go to meet Mr. and Mrs. Cornelius; but we found, on inquiry, that there were nothing but cross-roads, and these very bad, and no tavern where we could be comfortably accommodated. Our horse was also tired; so we thought our best way would be to return. Accordingly, the next day we started for Concord, and arrived on Friday evening safe home again. Lucretia wishes to spend this week with her friends, so that I shall return (Providence permitting) on this day week, and reach home by Tuesday noon; probably to dinner. We are both well, and send a great deal of love to you all. Mr. and Mrs. Walker wish me to present their best respects to you.

"Your affectionate son,

"Samuel F. B. Morse."

On the 12th of the next month, Mr. Morse, with his young wife, sailed in the schooner Tontine, Captain Fanning, from New York, for Charleston, S. C. They were welcomed with great hospitality by the many friends that Mr. Morse had made the previous winter, and their residence was rendered peculiarly pleasant by the many attentions they received. Mrs. Morse won general admiration and love. Several other artists had established themselves at Charleston, attracted, doubtless, by the fame of his great success, and with them he had to divide the business. One man, whom he had employed as a waiter in his studio, suddenly assumed the proportions of a painter of portraits, and announced himself in the papers as an artist. He did not fail altogether in finding patrons, who discovered rare merit in the painter. But Mr. Morse's old patrons returned with new friends, and he soon had as much work upon his hands as he could possibly accomplish. Yet he could not dismiss the *inventions* from his thoughts. He was experimenting upon improvements in the engine. His letters to his brother are not preserved, but one, in reply to his suggestions, shows how pertinaciously his mind was at work:

From Sidney E. Morse.

"ANDOVER, *January* 17, 1819.

"DEAR BROTHER: For various reasons, which it is not necessary to mention, I do not think your experiment a fair test of the principle. The friction of the potato plug against the sides of the tube might have been sufficient to destroy the whole force. In experiments on so small a scale, the friction is very great compared with the force exerted. I would not advise you to try the full experiment, as you propose, with oil and valves, etc., because there will be a great deal of perplexity and expense which you do not anticipate; and, in trying the experiment on so small a scale, there will be a great many little causes of failure not affecting the truth of the principle. Besides, the principle can be much more satisfactorily tested by a simple experiment than by a complicated one. I have thought of the following method

"Procure a cylindrical vessel of tin, of any dimensions, according to the size of the boat you employ (the larger the better, if it is not inconveniently large). Let it be divided into two apartments by a perpendicular partition, as in the following diagram:

" *A B* represents the cylinder, *c d* the partition running from the top nearly to the bottom; *e* is a little tube ¼ of an inch in diameter or less, capable of being stopped perfectly tight with a plug (and therefore I think should not be of tin). *f* is a tube ½ an inch in diameter, and capable also of being completely closed with a plug, or with the hand. Take care that there is no leakage, especially in the partition between the two apartments. To 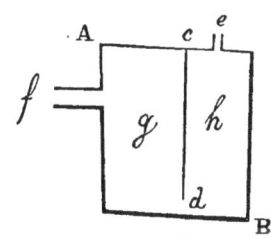 prepare for the experiment: First, let the tube *e* be carefully stopped. Then turn the cylinder over so that the line *c d* shall be parallel with the horizon, and then pour in water at the orifice *f*, till you have filled the apartment *h*. Then let the cylinder assume its original position, and if every thing is tight the water will remain in the apartment *h*, while the apartment *g* is empty. The next step is to close the orifice *f*, either with your hand or a plug—while some one unstops the tube *e*, and pours in a dozen or twenty drops of ether, which will float on the top of the water in the apartment *h*. Then let the tube *e* be closed again. Let the cylinder now be placed in the boat with the orifice *f* toward the stern, and apply heat to the water in the apartment *h* in any convenient way. When the water becomes blood-warm the ether will be converted into vapor, and force the water from the apartment *h* into the apartment *g*, and, if my theory is correct, will propel the boat forward. If you can conveniently apply heat enough to make the water boil, you may simplify the apparatus still further, for then you might use the steam of the water, instead of the steam of ether, to force the water out of the apartment *h*, and so dispense with the tube *e*. Two or three days since, I saw the *National Intelligencer*, for Wednesday and Thursday, January 27th and 28th, and noticed an article headed 'Antiquity of Steamboats.' I want you to get the paper, and read that article. You will find that they are now actually building a steamboat on the very principle of the experiment which we tried in the navy-yard.

"I am much rejoiced to hear that you are going on so prosperously in your business. Don't let the experiment take up your time or your thoughts, so as to interfere with your business.

"Your affectionate brother,

"SIDNEY E. MORSE."

To Mr. Washington Allston, having now returned from London, and established himself in Boston, Mr. Morse wrote, proposing to exhibit and sell some of the pictures, in Charleston, of his distinguished friend. Mr. Allston's mother was living at that time in Charleston. To the letter of Morse, Mr. Allston replied as follows:

From Washington Allston.

"BOSTON, *January* 27, 1819.

"MY DEAR SIR: Before this reaches you, you will probably receive the landscape, which you were so good as to undertake the disposal of in Charleston, or at least to give house-room to there; I mean the landscape I painted in Italy, and which has been for a year or two past in Mr. Sully's room, in Philadelphia. The price I have set on it is two hundred and fifty guineas; not a farthing less. If it is worth any thing, I think it worth three hundred; but I am content to get two hundred and fifty. At any rate, however, I beg you to observe that I would on no account sell it for more than three hundred, even if it should be offered. The price is two hundred and fifty; ask that, and with that I shall be content. I have directed the case containing the picture to be addressed to you, to the care of Mr. Hugh Paterson, who was formerly my agent; and I must beg the favor of you to pay the freight and other charges that may be incident to the landing of it, as I have no longer any account standing with 'Mr. Paterson, which I will repay you when we meet; or you may deduct the sum from the sale, if it should be so fortunate as to meet with a purchaser. I will make no apology for giving this trouble, since I know you would not consider it other than a pleasure to render me a service.

"Now the business part of my letter is over, I suppose you will expect something like news concerning the art. Sargent is going on with his second picture of the 'Landing of our Forefathers,' and I think will make it better than that of the 'Entrance into Jerusalem.' He is a worthy and liberal man, and I hope he may meet with that praise for it which his love of the art, under so many unexciting, not to say discouraging circumstances, may fairly entitle him to; and under which his perseverance is no small proof that he cultivates it solely for itself. Mr. Stuart has lately painted a fine head of Commodore Perry. Fisher left this for Charleston some time since, and I suppose is now there. Leslie, from whom I lately had a letter, does not contemplate returning to America before the next autumn. John Payne has written a tragedy on the subject of 'Junius Brutus,' which is now acting with great applause at the Drury Lane. Kean plays the principal part in it. This is all the news I have to tell about others. Now concerning myself: I yesterday received an official communication from Mr. Howard, the secretary of the Royal Academy, informing me that on the 2d of November last I was elected an associate of that body. I had received intelligence of it about three weeks ago, both from Leslie and Collins. I must own this is very pleasing to me, and I am sure it will be very gratifying to you; I am the more pleased too with the distinction, inasmuch as I never would nor did solicit a vote from any academician. And this is a proof that the report of candidates being expected to canvass, or in other words to beg votes, is without foundation. I wish you could see Collins's letter. I suppose you know he was made an associate before you left England. He says I must come back. But that I have no thoughts of —at least for many good years, if it should please God to grant me them.

"Something like encouragement seems to appear in our horizon; and if we have any talents we owe something to our country when she is disposed to foster them. One of the gentlemen concerned told me two days ago that he was appointed one of a committee for engaging me to paint a picture for the hospital here. As yet I have had no formal notice of it; but do not doubt that the communication will soon be made. This, however, is between ourselves. I expect, in your answer to this, a full and particular account of all that you are doing. You cannot be too minute. Remember me most cordially to your wife. And pray present my respects to Mrs. Heyward, Mrs. and Miss Rutledge, and Colonel Drayton and his lady. Remember me also to White, Racot, Frazer, and Cogdell. Believe me sincerely your friend,

"WASHINGTON ALLSTON."

This letter was post-marked January 29th, and, before it could have been received in Charleston, Mr. Morse writes to his friend and teacher:

"CHARLESTON, S. C., *February* 4, 1819.

"WASHINGTON ALLSTON, Esq.

"My DEAR SIR : Excuse my neglect in not having written you before this, according to my promise before I left Boston. I can only plead an apology (what I know will gratify you), a *multiplicity* of *business.* I am painting from morning till night, and have continual applications ; I have added to my list, *this season* only, to the amount of three thousand dollars ; that is, since I left you. Among them are three full-lengths to be finished at the North, I hope in Boston, where I shall once more enjoy the advantages of your criticisms. I am exerting my utmost to improve; every picture I try to make my best ; and in the evening I draw two hours from the antique, as I did in London, for I ought to inform you that I fortunately found a fine *Venus de Medicis* without a blemish, imported from Paris some time since by a gentleman of this city, who wished to dispose of it ; also a *young Apollo*, which was so broken that he gave it to me, saying that it was useless. I have, however, after a great deal of trouble, put it together entirely, and these two figures, with some fragments, hands, feet, etc., make a very good academy. Mr. Fraser, Mr. Cogdell, Mr. Fisher, of Boston, and myself, meet here of an evening to improve ourselves. I feel as much enthusiasm as ever in my art, and love it more than ever. A few years, at the rate I am now going on, will place me independent of public patronage ; thus much for myself, for you told me in one of your letters from London that I must be more of an egotist, or you should be less of one in your letters to me, which I should greatly regret. And now permit me, my dear sir, to congratulate you on your election to the Royal Academy. I know you will believe me when I say I jumped for joy when I heard it : though it cannot add to your merit, yet it will extend the knowledge of it, especially in our own country, where we are still influenced by foreign opinion, and more justly perhaps in regard to taste in the fine arts than in any other thing.

"I have been using a compound, or rather mixture, in flesh, on which I wish your opinion. Yellow-ochre has heretofore been the best yellow that I could use, but it always appeared to me to want *brilliancy ;* *chrome*-yellow, on the contrary, is too bright, or *eggy ;* but these two I have mixed *half-and-half,* and find it excellent flesh-yellow. I find this mixture also excellent in the shadows of white drapery, and in reflected lights, when properly tempered with blue and red. A very strong tint of this yellow, laid on boldly in a shadow, gives a clearness and liquidness to it which no other yellow that I have used can give; and gives a warmth and glow to the picture, without being hot. I should like to know the result of your experiment with it.

"How does your great picture progress ? I hope to see it, when

I return, entirely finished. Have you got a good room? How are your Boston friends disposed toward you now? Are they still desirous of keeping you with them, and of giving you something to paint for them? Do write me, dear sir, all about yourself, as you used to wish me to do of myself. I long to see you, and talk over every thing. Do write me, dear sir, soon. You know what a gratification it will be to one who is proud in calling himself your pupil. May God bless you, dear sir, and believe me your affectionate pupil,

"S. F. B. Morse."

The Common Council of Charleston paid Mr. Morse the compliment of requesting him to paint the portrait of James Monroe, then the President of the United States. And after spending the summer at the North, and leaving his wife and their infant daughter in Concord, with Mrs. Morse's parents for the winter, he returned South, taking Washington in his way, that he might execute the commission for the city. He was alarmed at the price of board, as he writes to his wife, finding it to be two dollars a day in New York City, and equally high in Washington. I began," he says, in a letter, " on Monday to paint the President, and have almost completed the head"—this was on Thursday—" I am thus far pleased with it, but I find it very perplexing, for he cannot sit more than ten or twenty minutes at a time; so that, the moment I feel engaged, he is called away again. I set my palette to-day at ten o'clock, and waited until four o'clock this afternoon before he came in. He then sat ten minutes, and we were called to dinner. Is not this trying to one's patience? My room is at his house, next to his cabinet-room, for his convenience. When he has a moment's leisure he comes in to sit to me. He is very agreeable and affable, as are also his family. I drank tea with them on Saturday, and dined with them on Monday and to-day." When his work was completed, the family were so delighted with it that he was obliged to remain and make a copy for them. The portrait was considered, by all who saw it at the time, a great triumph of art. It remains in the City Hall of Charleston.

Another winter was spent in Charleston, South Carolina. His brother Richard having become a preacher, came down, and was employed on John's Island, where the artist frequently vis-

ited him.   Speaking of one of these visits in a letter to his wife,
April 8, 1820, he says:

"My visit to John's Island was a very agreeable one.   I staid
at Mr. James Legare's, and painted Mrs. Legare, at my leisure.   In
the intermediate time we went—I say *we*—there was Prof. Porter,
of Andover, and brother Richard, and Mr. Wilson, and Thos. Legare, and his sons, and the sons of Mr. James Legare, and two or
three others—we spent a week upon the island.   On Monday, we
all dined with Mr. Wilson, and in the afternoon I mounted a horse
(the first time for ten years), and with a Mr. Hart, and Richard, and
Mr. John Legare, set out with six hounds in search of a fox.   We
had not proceeded half a mile when the dogs opened their cry, and
the chase commenced.   Owing to my want of skill in riding, I was
unable to keep up with the rest of the company, over ditches, and
fences, and cotton-fields, and old logs, so that I did not enjoy the
sport so much as the rest; but I was, fortunately, *in at the death*,
as the huntsmen say; for, after a chase of about half an hour, the
fox took to a cotton-field, and after *doubling* two or three times
was caught by the dogs.   As this field was near where I was left
by the rest, I rode in, in time to see him caught.

"On Tuesday was our great hunting-day.   The Legares, Wil-
sons, Prof. Porter, Richard, and myself, with two or three others,
set out at nine o'clock in the morning, on a deer-hunt, with eleven
hounds, and a negro, to *drive the woods.*   We were all well mounted
and with guns.   I have drawn a little figure below, to explain our
proceedings.   The triangular piece is a piece of woods; the negro,

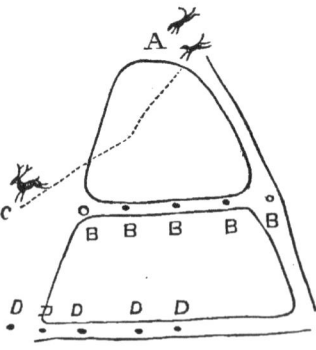

with the dogs, was put into the
woods at *A*, while we galloped brisk-
ly along the road, and took our different *stands* at *B, B*, etc.   The dogs
soon *opened*, but, to our mortification,
the deer took the course *C*, and
avoided us.   When we found the
dogs had passed the road, we all galloped off again, and took stands at
D, in hopes of heading the deer, but
he again avoided us in the same way;
so we lost the deer.   The dogs soon,
however, opened again, and we found they had scented a fox.   We
had a fine chase of an hour after him, in which time we saw him

often, and I was enabled to keep up with the rest of the company all the time. We lost him, however, in the end; but I was very much amused at the sagacity of the fox and the hounds. I arrived at Mr. Legare's in the evening at eight o'clock, having been on horseback eleven hours, much fatigued, but very much benefited in my health by this fine exercise."

A list of the names of all the persons whose portraits he painted in Charleston during the successive winters of his residence in that city he preserved with care to the end of his life. It includes Dr. Finley, the Allstons, Mrs. Porter, Dr. Mitchill, Mrs. Hitchborn, Dr. Baron, Mr. Perroneau, Judge Desausure, Mr. Simmons, Mrs. Stiles, Mrs. Heyward, Mrs. Bentham, Bishop Smith, Major Theus, Major-General Pinckney, Mrs. Smilie, Mr. John Axson, Dr. Poyas, Colonel Drayton, Judge and Mrs. Cheves, Mr. Legaré, Mrs. Dr. Grimkie, Mrs. Colcock, Lady Nesbit, Mr. and Mrs. Huger, and scores of others. Mr. Cogdell furnishes Mr. Dunlap with this record of one of Mr. Morse's last works in Charleston :

"In January, 1821, my friend Morse had several conversations with me about the practicability of establishing an academy. We agreed to have a meeting; we solicited the main hall of the city. Mr. Morse moved that the Hon. Joel R. Poinsett take the chair; Mr. Jay that Mr. Cogdell act as secretary. Mr. Morse then submitted a resolution asking of the council a site in the public square for the building, and we adjourned. A number of artists and amateurs were requested to meet at my office, where the first organization was made of the Academy of Fine Arts. Gentlemen were named officers and directors; on my writing to them, they accepted. Thus was brought into existence the South Carolina Academy of Fine Arts.

"JOEL R. POINSETT, *President.*

Directors:

Samuel F. B. Morse,	Charles Frazer,
Joshua Cantir,	John S. Cogdell,
John B. White,	Wm. Jay, architect,
Charles C. Wright, die-sinker,	Wm. Shields,
James Wood, engraver,	Chs. Simmons, engraver.

"The Legislature granted a charter, but, my good sir, as they possessed no powers under the constitution to confer taste or talent, and possessed none of those feelings which prompt to patronage; they gave none to the infant academy. We have had as splendid exhibitions as I have ever seen in any other city. On the presentation of my bust of Dr. J. E. Holbrook, I received from the directors, under the eleventh rule, the title of academician; but, *cui bono?* The institution was allowed, from apathy and opposition, to die, and the property has been sold recently to pay its debts; but Mr. Poinsett and myself, with a few others, have purchased, with a hope of reviving, the establishment."

In the month of February, 1820, the Rev. Dr. Morse resigned his charge as pastor in Charlestown, Massachusetts, and removed to New Haven, Connecticut, with the family of his son. Mr. Morse joined his family there in the spring, when he came from South Carolina, and passed the summer in that city. He had constant employment for his pencil in completing, the paintings he had commenced in Charleston, and he found great delight in renewing his studies of electricity and galvanism in the laboratory of Yale College. To this spot he resorted while Prof. Silliman was preparing his experiments, and gratified his tastes for philosophical and chemical studies, in the midst of his profession as an artist. The painting of portraits was to him, as to all painters of original power, a weariness, and Mr. Morse resolved to attempt something in which it might be raised to the dignity of history. He conceived the idea of making a large picture of the "House of Representatives" at Washington, presenting a view of the chamber, and portraits of individual members. For this purpose he went to Washington in November, 1821, and was kindly received by the President of the United States, who encouraged his grand undertaking, and gave him every facility for its execution. The architect of the House, Mr. Bullfinch, and all the officers of the House, entered cordially into the work, and encouraged him with their efficient aid.

"The President," Mr. Morse writes to his wife, "asked me, in the course of conversation, whether he could obtain from New Haven some small elms for his estate in Virginia. He seemed desirous of having some. Now, I should like very much if father could procure a dozen at my expense (they will be but a trifle) and bring them on with him when he comes to

Washington. They will not take up any room if the roots are wound round with mats, and the whole done up as apple or other trees are transplanted. I should like very much to make this little acknowledgment to the President for his civilities, and I think he would be pleased with the attention."

Mr. Morse obtained the use of one of the lower rooms of the Capitol, and there established his studio, to make it convenient for the members to sit to him for their portraits; and while they were not with him he could work upon the interior of the chamber. He writes to Mrs. Morse:

"I am up at daylight, have my breakfast and prayers over, and commence the labors of the day long before the workmen are called to work on the Capitol by the bell. This I continue unremittingly till one o'clock, when I dine in about fifteen minutes, and then pursue my labors until tea, which scarcely interrupts me, as I often have my cup of tea in one hand and pencil in the other. Between ten and eleven o'clock I retire to rest. This has been my course every day (Sundays, of course, excepted) since I have been here, making about fourteen hours' study out of the twenty-four. This, you will say, is too hard, and that I shall injure my health. I can say that I never enjoyed better health, and my body, by the simple fare I live on, is disciplined to this course. As it will not be necessary to continue long so assiduously, I shall not fear to pursue it till this work is done.

"I receive every possible facility from all about the Capitol. The door-keeper, a venerable man, has offered to light the great chandelier expressly for me to take my sketches in the evening, for two hours together, for I shall have it a candle-light effect, when the room, already very splendid, will appear ten times more so."

His absorption in the picture was so great that once he arose in the night mistaking the light of the moon for day, and went to his task, and at another time lost the reckoning of the days of the week, and attempted to enter the Hall on Sunday to pursue his work, and could hardly be persuaded to admit that he had lost a day. By the middle of December he was working sixteen hours a day. "I never enjoyed better health; the moment I feel unwell I shall desist, but I am in the vein now, and must have my way. I have had a great deal of difficulty with the perspective of my picture. But I have conquered, and have accomplished my purpose. After having drawn in the greater part three times, I have as many times rubbed it all out again. I have been, several times, from daylight until eleven o'clock at night, solving a single problem." And then he turns away from his " vexations " and " disappointments" to his anxieties for his little family in New Haven, and says : " How I do long to see that dear little girl of mine, and to hear her sweet prattle ! Instruct her early, my dear wife, in the most important of all concerns ; teach her that there is a great Father above, her obligations to Him and to her Saviour. Kiss her often for papa, and tell her he will come back one of these days."

The work required far more time than he anticipated. December was gone before the portraits of the members were begun. On the 2d of January, 1822, he writes :

" I have commenced to-day taking the likenesses of the members. I find them not only willing to sit, but apparently esteeming it an honor. I shall take seventy of them, and perhaps more; all, if possible. I find the picture is becoming the subject of conversation, and every day gives me greater encouragement. I shall paint it on part of the great canvas when I return home. It will be eleven feet by seven and a half feet; that will divide the great canvas exactly into two equal parts, on one of which I paint the House of Representatives, and the other the Senate. It will take me until October next to complete it."

He painted eighty portraits on the great picture, and on the 10th of February left Washington. By steady travel in the stage he performed the journey from Washington to New Haven in six days, reaching his home and family on Saturday the 16th of the month.

As a work of art this picture was admirable, but it failed to attract the attention of the public. The artist's expectations of deriving profit from its exhibition were disappointed. It proved a loss to him pecuniarily, and was at length sold to an English gentleman, who took it to his own country, where it remained for several years. The artist lost trace and knowledge of it. While abroad in after-years he made inquiries for it in vain. After the lapse of a quarter of a century he received the following letter from an artist friend :

F. W. Edmonds, Esq., to Prof. Morse.

"NEW YORK, *December* 7, 1847.

"MY DEAR SIR: I was applied to by a gentleman a few days since to call and see your picture of the 'House of Representatives' which has been sent to this city from London by a house who had advanced a sum of money upon it while in England. I called upon Mr. Durand, and he accompanied me on visiting it. We found it at the store of Coates & Co., No. 54 Exchange Place, nailed against a board partition in the third story, almost invisible from the dirt and dust upon it. It has evidently been rolled up, and, having no strainer, its surface is as uneven as the waves of the sea. In one place where it has been rolled the paint has pealed off in a narrow but long seam, but this is above the heads of the figures, and I think can be easily repaired. Otherwise the picture seems in a good condition if washed, stretched, and varnished. They (Coates & Co.) hold it for sale, but in its present condition few, except those very familiar with pictures, would look at with a view of purchasing it. I suggested to them to wait till I could write to you before they showed it, as you would probably desire that it should be cleaned and varnished, and, if you were likely soon to be in the city, would perhaps prefer doing it yourself. I think it would not cost over ten dollars to put it in good order. Excuse me for troubling you in this matter, but, believing it to be one of the best works ever painted by you, and knowing it to be invaluable as containing portraits of many eminent statesmen of this country, I could not patiently be silent while in its present condition.

"Respectfully and truly yours,

"SAMUEL F. B. MORSE, Esq."   "F. W. EDMONDS.

The picture was rescued from its confinement, and became the property of the distinguished artist Daniel Huntington, Esq., in whose private gallery it is preserved.

In the winter of 1822, notwithstanding the great expenses to which Mr. Morse had been subjected in producing this picture, and before he had realized any thing from its exhibition, he made a donation of five hundred dollars to the library fund of Yale College, probably the largest donation, in proportion to the means of the giver, which that institution ever received. The corporation, by vote, presented the thanks of the board in the following letter:

"YALE COLLEGE, *December* 4, 1822.

"DEAR SIR: I am directed, by the corporation of this college, to present to you the thanks of the board for your subscription of five hundred dollars for the enlargement of the library. Should this example of liberality be generally imitated by the friends of the institution, we should soon have a library creditable to the college, and invaluable to men of literary and philosophic research.

"With respectful and grateful acknowledgments,

"Your obedient servant,

"JEREMIAH DAY.

"Mr. SAMUEL F. B. MORSE."

CHAPTER V.

1823–1828.

INVENTS A MACHINE FOR CUTTING MARBLE—GOES TO ALBANY—LITTLE SUCCESS—RETURNS TO NEW YORK—PORTRAIT OF CHANCELLOR KENT—ICHABOD CRANE—ARRANGEMENTS TO GO TO MEXICO AS ATTACHÉ TO THE LEGATION—LETTER FROM HON. ROBERT Y. HAYNE—THE SCHEME ABANDONED—IN NEW HAVEN—TRAVELS IN NEW ENGLAND—SETTLES IN NEW YORK—COMMISSIONED TO PAINT PORTRAIT OF GENERAL LAFAYETTE —GOES TO WASHINGTON—SUDDEN DEATH OF HIS WIFE—DEATH OF HIS FATHER—FOUNDS THE NATIONAL ACADEMY OF DESIGN—SKETCH-CLUB—LETTER FROM GENERAL T. S. CUMMINGS—LORD LYNDHURST'S LETTER—STUDIES IN ELECTRO-MAGNETISM—PROFESSOR DANA'S LECTURES—HIS OWN LECTURES—ESCAPE FROM DEATH.

THE inventive faculty, so characteristic of the family to which Mr. Morse belonged, we have already seen developed in him. While struggling in his profession, and having far less to do than he desired, he turned his attention to the invention of a machine for carving marble, and by which he hoped to be able to produce statues—perfect copies of any model. Others have attempted machines for similar purposes, and perhaps with no better success than crowned his efforts.

On the 6th of August, 1823, while in New Haven, he sent to the Secretary of State at Washington a letter in the form of a *caveat*, in which he describes the machine he had invented, and his intention to secure a patent for the same. Mr. Augur, an ingenious mechanic of New Haven, was employed to construct a working machine. Afterward he used it successfully in cutting statues from the solid marble. This machine is frequently alluded to in his correspondence, and he looked to it as a source of great pecuniary profit. Early in February of this same year

Mr. Morse went to Boston with his picture of the House of Representatives, and placed it there upon exhibition.

On the first day the receipts were forty dollars and fifty-five cents, which sum was sufficient to encourage him that it would be successful. Mr. Allston called to see it, and Mr. Morse, in a letter to his wife, remarks that " Mr. Allston says it is a magnificent picture. He has suggested some small improvements, which I can make in two days." But it failed to excite public attention; and, leaving it there on exhibition, he went, in the month of August, to the city of Albany, N. Y., where he had been encouraged to hope for patronage from the public men. He had formed a pleasant acquaintance with the Patroon, the Hon. Stephen Van Rensselaer, of Albany, who was a member of Congress while Mr. Morse was engaged in painting his picture of the House of Representatives. He immediately commenced the portrait of the Patroon, which he designed to exhibit in Albany as a specimen of his art. Day after day he waited patiently in hopes of winning, by the exhibition of the portrait, a few at least who might be tempted to employ him. He writes to his wife :

"I have found lodgings—a large front room on the second story, twenty-five by eighteen feet, and twelve feet high—a fine room for painting, with a neat little bedroom, and every convenience, and board, all for six dollars a week, which I think is very reasonable. My landlord is an elderly Irish gentleman, with three daughters, once in independent circumstances, but now reduced. Every thing bears the appearance of old-fashioned gentility, which you know I always liked. Every thing is neat and clean and genteel. The family reside at No. 94 North Pearl Street. They are well acquainted with Bishop Brownell and his lady, and say that they always call when they come to Albany. Colonel Baldwin has been very kind and obliging to me. He is in high estimation in this city, and deservedly so. Elkanah Watson is not in town. I called on Rev. Dr. Chester, and heard him preach to-day. Bishop Hobart and a great many acquaintances were on board of the boat upon which I came up to this city. I can form no idea as yet of the prospect of success in my profession here. If I get enough to employ me, I shall go no farther; if not, I may visit some of the smaller towns in the interior of the State. I await with some anxiety the *result of experiments with my machine.* I hope the invention may enable me to remain at home."

On the 16th of August he writes:

"I have not as yet received any application for a portrait. Many tell me I have come at the wrong time—the same tune that has been rung in my ears so long! I hope the right time will come by-and-by. The winter, it is said, is the proper season; but, as it is better in the South in that season, and it will be more profitable to be there, I shall give Albany a thorough trial and do my best. If I should not find enough to employ me here, I think I shall return to New York and settle there. This I had rather not do at present, but it may be the best that I can do. Roaming becomes more and more irksome. Imperious necessity alone drives me to this course. Don't think by this I am faint-hearted. I shall persevere in this course, painful as is the separation from my family, until Providence clearly points out my duty to return."

August 22d.—"I have something to do. I have one portrait in progress, and the promise of more. One hundred dollars will pay all my expenses here for three months, so that the two I am now painting will clear me in that respect, and all that comes after will be clear gain. I am, therefore, easier in my mind as to this. The portrait now painting is Judge Moss Kent, brother of the Chancellor. He says that I shall paint the Chancellor when he returns to Albany, and his niece also; and, from these particulars, you may infer that I shall be here for some little time longer, just so long as my good prospects continue; but, should they fail, I am determined to try New York City, and sit down there in my profession permanently. I believe I have now attained sufficient proficiency to venture there. My progress may be slow at first, but I believe it will be sure. I do not like going South, and I have given up the idea of New Orleans or any Southern city, at least for the present. Circumstances may vary this determination, but I think a settlement in New York is more feasible now than ever before. I shall be near you and home in cases of emergency, and in the summer and sickly season can visit you at New Haven, while you can do the same to me in New York, until we live again at New Haven altogether. I leave out of this calculation the *machine for sculpture.* If that should entirely succeed, my plans would be materially varied; but I speak of my present plan as if that had failed. I hope Mr. Augur will not be discouraged by the little minutiæ of

9

the machine, but carry it through. I should like to have a letter from him on the subject, putting down a list of questions respecting marble and marble-cutting which he wishes me to ask of stone-cutters, as there are some here, and I can gain much from them.

"With respect to young Longworth, I should have no objection to take him as a pupil, if I go to New York, on what terms I am hardly prepared now to say. I may find it to be an advantage to take a number of pupils."

August 24*th.*—"I finished Mr. Kent's picture yesterday, and received the money for it. Mr. Kent is very polite to me, and has introduced me to a number of persons and families; among others to the Kanes—very wealthy people—to Governor Yates, etc. Mr. Clinton's son called on me and invited me to their house. I have been introduced to Señor Rocafuerto, the Spaniard, who made so excellent a speech before the Bible Society last May. He is a very handsome man, very intelligent, full of wit and vivacity. He is a great favorite with the ladies, and is a man of wealth and a zealous patriot, studying our manners, customs, and improvements, with a view of benefiting his own countrymen in Peru."

August 27th, he writes again to his wife:

"My last two letters have held out to you some encouraging prospects of success here, but now they seem darkened again. I have had nothing to do this week thus far but to wait patiently. I have advertised in both of the city papers that I should remain one week to receive applications, but as yet it has produced no effect. Mr. Kent's niece has not arrived as expected, so that it is doubtful whether I shall paint her; but, as she lives in New York, and as it is to be for Mr. Kent, I can make arrangements to paint it for him there. Chancellor Kent is out of town, and will not be in until the end of next month. It is hardly worth while to stay solely for that; many have been talking of having their portraits painted, but there it has thus far ended. I find nothing in Albany which can profitably employ my leisure hours. If there were any pictures or statuary where I could sketch and draw, it would be different. I have visited several families who have been very kind to me, for which I am thankful. I shall leave Albany and return to New York a week from to-day, if there is no change in my prospects. The more I think of making a push at New York as a permanent place of residence in my profession, the more proper it seems that it should be at once. New York does not yet feel the influx of wealth from the Western canals, but in a year or two she will feel it, and it will be advantageous to me to be previously identified among her citizens as a painter. It requires some little time to become renowned in such a city."

All his hopes of patronage in Albany were dissipated; and on the 3d of September he writes to his wife:

"I have nothing to do, and shall pack up on the morrow for New York, unless appearances change again. I have not had full employment since I have been in Albany, and I feel miserable in doing nothing."

After a brief visit with his family at New Haven, he went to New York, to carry out his purpose of making a permanent settlement in that city in the pursuit of his profession as an artist. He made the passage from New Haven to New York by water; was driven in by a gale into Black Rock Harbor, and there detained, and the next day completed the journey to New York by land. Writing home the next day, he says:

"I have obtained a place to board at friend Coolidge's, at two dollars and twenty-five cents a week, and have taken for my studio a fine room in Broadway, opposite Trinity Churchyard, for which I am to pay six dollars and fifty cents a week, being fifty cents less than I expected to pay. I shall go to work in a few days vigorously. It is a half-mile from my room to the place where I board, so that I am obliged to walk more than three miles every day. It is good exercise for me, and I feel better for it. I sleep in my room on the floor, and put my bed out of sight during the day, as at Washington. I feel in the spirit of 'buckling down to it,' and am determined to paint and study with all my might this winter."

The first portrait which he painted, after his coming to New York, was that of the distinguished Chancellor Kent. He says of the Chancellor:

"He is not a good sitter; he scarcely presents the same view twice; he is very impatient, and you well know that I cannot paint an impatient person; I must have my mind at ease or I cannot paint. I have no more applications as yet, but it is not time to expect them. All the artists are complaining, and there are many of them, and they are all poor. The arts are as low as they can be.

It is no better at the South, and all the accounts of the arts or artists are of the most discouraging nature."

And in successive letters to his wife he says:

"I waited many days in the hope of some application in my profession, but have been disappointed, until last evening I called and spent the evening with my friend Mr. Van Schaick, and told him I had thought of painting some little design from the 'Sketch-Book,' so as not .to be idle, and mentioned the subject of 'Ichabod Crane.discovering the headless horseman.' He said: 'Paint it for me, and another picture of the same size, and I will take them of you.' So I am now employed. I shall want immediately the little plaster cast of the horse, which is at my painting-room. I have received Mr. Augur's letter. It is a very encouraging one. All the difficulties that he complains of are unconnected with the invention, and those which we apprehended have not been realized, so that here is. fresh cause for gratitude. *My secret scheme* is not yet disclosable, but I shall let you know as soon as I hear any thing definite."

"You will be anxious to know what I am doing. The answer is very simple—'*Nothing.*' I am waiting for applications, but none offer. The chancellor's picture and Mr. Dewey's have been finished about a week; and, as far as painting is concerned, I am completely idle, and of course a little low-spirited. I have been active in calling on my friends and inviting them to my room; they have promised to come, but as yet few have called. As far as human foresight can perceive, my prospects seem gloomy indeed. The only gleam of hope—and I cannot underrate it—is from confidence in God. When I look upward, it calms my apprehensions for the future, and I seem to hear a voice saying: 'If I clothe the lilies of the field, shall I not also clothe you?' Here is my strong confidence, and I will wait patiently for the direction of Providence. I have seen many of the artists; they all agree that little is doing in the city of New York. It seems wholly given to commerce. Every man is driving at one object — the making of money—not the spending of it.

"What is Mr. Augur doing with the machine? Is he still sanguine? I should be glad to hear from him."

"*My secret scheme* looks promising, but I am still in suspense; you shall know the moment it is decided one way or the other. I met with a singular accident to-day. You recollect I complained of a little bone being out of place in my left hand, which pained me when I touched it. To-day in coming out of the house I slipped down, and came with my whole weight upon my left hand. I felt something snap, and experienced a good deal of pain in it for a few moments; upon examining my hand, I found, to my surprise, that this bone had snapped into its place, and in about half an hour the pain left me, and my hand is as well as it ever was."

The straits to which he was reduced, and his plans for the future, are developed in the following letter:

"New York, *December* 21, 1823.

"My dear Wife : . . . Last Saturday we had a meeting at a private house. Dr. Milnor was present, and made an address. While engaged there, a thief slipped into the entry where were our hats and coats, but, being discovered, he made a precipitate retreat, and carried with him my hat. The circumstance was not known to us till we were ready to go; no other gentleman lost any thing. Had they taken Edward's surtout, they would have deranged his whole business, as all his memoranda and accounts were in the pocket of it. The act was a very audacious one, and to me a serious loss, as I had to purchase immediately another hat, which cost four dollars, and obliged me to break the last five-dollar bill I have.

" My cash is almost gone, and I begin to feel some anxiety and perplexity to know what to do. I have advertised, and visited, and hinted, and pleaded, and even asked one man to sit, but all to no purpose. I have been stopped, too, in the pictures for Mr. Van S., by the delay of the packet having the little horse on board; the Paragon has not yet arrived. My expenses, with the most rigid economy too, are necessarily great; my rent to-morrow will amount to thirty-three dollars, and I have nothing to pay it with. What can I do? I have been here five weeks, and there is not the smallest prospect *now* of any difference as to business. I am willing to stay, and wish to stay, if there is any thing to do. The pictures that I am painting for Mr. V. S. will not pay my expenses if painted here; my rent and board would eat it all up. I have thought of various plans, but what to decide upon I am completely at a loss, nor can I decide, until I hear definitely from Washington in regard to my Mexico expedition. Since brother Sidney has hinted it to you, I will tell you the state of it. I wrote to General Van Rensselaer, Mr. Poinsett, and Colonel Hayne of the Senate, applying for some situation in the legation to Mexico soon to be sent thither. I stated my

object in going, and my wish to go free of expense, and under government protection.   I received a letter a few days ago from General Van Rensselaer, in which he says: ' I immediately laid your request before the President, and seconded it with my warmest recommendations.   It is impossible to predict the result at present.
If our friend Mr. Poinsett is appointed minister, which his friends
are pressing, he will no doubt be happy to have you in his suite.'

"Thus the case rests at present: if Mr. Poinsett is appointed, I
shall probably go to Mexico; if not, it will be more doubtful.   I
have placed it on this ground, that I am to be at no expense in
getting there, and back again; so that, if I fail in the objects of my
visit there, I am at no expense, and I am also under government
protection, should the country be in a revolutionary state and un-
safe for other strangers.   If I go, I should take my picture of the
House of Representatives, which, in the present state of favorable
feeling toward our country, I should probably dispose of to advantage.   All accounts that I hear from Mexico are in the highest degree favorable to my enterprise, and I hear much from various
quarters."

December 29th.—" I am waiting with some anxiety for news
from Washington.   There is no guessing when the President will
make his appointment.   It rests with him.   My way, however, is
plain: I see present duty, and that is as much as I ought to desire."

In the midst of his discouragements he had determined to
go if possible, to Mexico, and establish himself in his profession
in the capital.   Having met Mr. Poinsett, the former American
minister to that country, and formed with him a pleasant acquaintance, he had learned much from him in relation to Mexico, and had been encouraged to believe that he might succeed
in that comparatively untried field of professional labor.

He submitted to Mr. Poinsett a series of written questions,
and had received from him written answers, giving the most
minute information in relation to the prospects of success in
that country, and the preparation which it would be necessary
for him to make for the journey.   Through his friend General
Stephen Van Rensselaer, of Albany, and others, he hoped, and
with good reason, to be able to procure an appointment to Mexico on the legation about to be sent to that country.   Strong
hopes were entertained that Mr. Poinsett himself would be ap-

pointed minister; but, after great delay, the mission was given to the Hon. Ninian Edwards, of Illinois.

These negotiations in relation to the appointment occupied several months, during which time Mr. Morse was kept in a state of the greatest anxiety; and, not until the middle of March, was it finally settled that he should be attached to the legation. A note from the Hon. Robert Y. Hayne, the distinguished Senator from South Carolina, whose name is associated in history with that of Webster and the great debate on State rights in the Senate, informed Mr. Morse of his appointment. He says: "Governor Edwards's suite consists of Mr. Mason, of Georgetown, District of Columbia, secretary of the legation; Mr. Hodgson, of Virginia, private secretary, and yourself *attaché*." Mr. Hayne addressed to Mr. Morse the following letter, which contains material of interest in connection with the politics of that day:

Hon. R. Y. Hayne to S. F. B. Morse.

"WASHINGTON, *March* 15, 1824.

"DEAR SIR: Having a few moments at command, I hasten to answer yours of the 9th inst. The movement in Pennsylvania took place without the knowledge or concurrence of Mr. Calhoun or of his friends here. The first step was as unexpected to us as it could have been to you. It was a spontaneous movement of Mr. Calhoun's friends in Pennsylvania, founded on a conviction that they could not successfully oppose General Jackson, and believing that it was necessary to concentrate on him, in order to defeat Crawford. Pennsylvania was the foundation of Mr. Calhoun's hopes— and, that being taken away, it is the duty of Mr. Calhoun's friends to admit that his prospects of the presidency are destroyed; those who supported him, therefore, will have to decide for themselves what is next to be done. In South Carolina, Jackson is by far the most popular man, and will doubtless be supported. I think the great object ought to be to defeat Crawford. If Adams be the only man who can accomplish that in New England, he ought, I think, to be supported there. A friendly feeling should be cherished by the friends of all the anti-caucus candidates; the common cause must not be jeopardized by disputes among them. I will confess that I prefer Jackson to any candidate except Calhoun. I think you have a very mistaken impression of him in New England.

I am satisfied that, in good sense, practical knowledge, and even in temper, he is decidedly superior to Adams or Crawford. The general's conduct and deportment here have secured him many friends, and when his conduct is examined in those respects in which it has been censured, I feel assured that it will be found that in many instances facts have been mistaken, and in others that he can be fully justified. I think he will be a safe President, surrounded by an able cabinet. I think his prospect for the presidency is at present decidedly the best.

"I will with great pleasure see Mr. Edwards on the subject of your application, and will exert any influence I may possess in your behalf. Remember me to your venerable father and Mrs. Morse, and for yourself receive the assurance of the great respect and esteem of yours,

"ROBERT Y. HAYNE."

General Van Rensselaer, in Washington, wrote to him:

"I congratulate you on your prospect of visiting Mexico, and I hope you will meet with success in your enterprise. The minister is absent on a visit to Philadelphia. I will endeavor to procure a letter from Colonel Gometz or Colonel Polilatie; Mr. Poinsett thinks it, however, unnecessary. If you could send me, without much trouble, a seed of the *arbor de las manitas*, or 'hand-tree,' you would oblige me. I wish you a pleasant voyage and journey, and safe return."

One of his relatives writes to him, in reference to his proposed expedition to Mexico: "I think the experiment worth making; there is everything to gain and nothing to lose," which happily presents the desperate condition of his affairs.

He continues the story:

"I left home on the 5th of April, 1824, for Washington and Mexico, accompanied by my father, wife, and sister, as far as New York. On the 7th they returned to New Haven, and I proceeded on my way to Philadelphia, with my heart too full of the various saddening emotions which naturally occur to one who has parted with his dearest friends for a long and uncertain period, to enjoy either the country through which I passed or the society of my fellow-passengers. A thousand affecting incidents of separation from my beloved family crowded upon my recollection. The unconscious gayety of my dear children as they frolicked in all their wonted playfulness, too young to sympathize in the pangs that agitated their distressed parents; their artless request to bring home some trifling toy, the parting kiss, not understood as meaning more than usual; the tears and sad farewells of father, mother, wife, sister, family, friends; the desolateness of every room, as the parting glance is thrown on each familiar object, and farewell, farewell, seemed written on the very walls—all these things bear upon my memory; and I realize the declaration that 'the places which now know us shall know us no more.'"

With these sorrowful reflections, Mr. Morse pursued his journey, only to find in Washington that political reasons, long since forgotten, prevented Mr. Edwards from going to Mexico, and the expedition was abandoned. Disappointment was thus far the rule rather than the exception of his life. He writes to his wife from Washington, April 22, 1824:

"I hardly know what to say, or think, or do. I went to the House of Representatives this morning, to hear the report of the committee in the case of Mr. Edwards. They stated it was necessary to a full investigation, to have Mr. Edwards present, who is now absent in Illinois. Mr. Randolph, one of the committee, informed the House that a warrant was already issued to detain him, and that a messenger was on the way to serve it. Thus am I placed in a most unpleasant state; one which no human foresight could predict or provide against. Some say that I shall be detained for more than a month, and advise me to go home and wait; others advise me to give up going; and others to go on without the legation. Among the latter is Mr. Poinsett." The next day he writes: "I have seen the President and the Secretary of State, and had a conversation with them on the subject of the detention of the legation. The President told me explicitly that there would be a delay of five or six weeks at least, and perhaps of some months. It was intimated that it might be necessary to send the secretary of the legation without the minister for the present. In that case we should sail from New York."

But it was finally determined that the legation should not be sent, and Mr. Morse returned to his family in New Haven. The summer was spent there, and in Concord, Portsmouth, and Portland, whither he went for the purpose of painting portraits of particular individuals, who applied to him to come for that purpose. In the autumn of that year he resumed his professional labors in the city of New York, and for a time had his family with him there. His studio was at number 96 Broadway. He lodged in his studio, and boarded at Mrs. Thompson's. He received as his pupils some young men, who afterward attained distinction in their professions, among them were Field and Agate. In December, he writes:

"I am going on prosperously, through the kindness of Providence in raising up many friends, who are exerting themselves in my favor. My storms are partly over, and a clear and pleasant day is dawning upon me.

"Mr. Auger's bust of the 'Apollo,' made with my machine, is very much admired; and, in the *Statesman* of this evening, there is a handsome notice of it by Mr. Carter, who called to see it. I hope I may be able to sell it for Mr. Auger. I have put the price at three hundred dollars; but I think, although it is worth that and more, that, in consequence of the defects in the marble, it cannot be sold for so much. This work does him the greatest credit."

These expectations, so cheerfully expressed in this letter to his wife, were still further heightened by his receiving a commission from the corporation of the city of New York to paint a portrait of General Lafayette, who was at this time on a visit to the United States. Lafayette was in Washington, and thither Mr. Morse resorted, after having, by correspondence, arranged for the time which could be given to him by the General for the purpose of taking his portrait. Mr. Morse was received by him with great kindness, and the acquaintance then commenced was continued until the death of Lafayette.

Mr. Morse's letters to Mrs. Morse furnish the best account of his struggles and success at this critical period in his history:

"NEW YORK, *January* 4, 1825.

"You will rejoice with me, I know, in my continued and increasing success. I have just learned in confidence from one of the members of the committee of the corporation appointed to procure a full-length portrait of Lafayette, that they have designated me as the painter of it, and that a sub-committee was appointed to wait on me with the information. They will probably call to-morrow; but, until it is thus officially announced to me, I wish the thing kept secret, except to the family, until I write you more definitely on the subject, which I will do the moment the terms, etc., are settled with the committee. I shall probably be under the necessity of going to Washington to take it immediately (the corporation, of course, paying my expenses), but of this in my next. If I go on to Washington, I shall not probably be in New Haven till the 1st of February, but shall make a great effort to be there before. I shall write you fully of my determination and plans the moment they are formed.

"NEW YORK, *January* 6, 1825.

"I have been officially notified of my appointment to paint the full-length portrait of Lafayette, for the city of New York, so that you may make it as public as you please. The terms are not definitely settled; the committee are disposed to be very liberal. I shall have at least seven hundred dollars—probably one thousand. I have to wait until an answer can be received from Washington from Lafayette to know when he can see me; the answer will arrive, probably, on Wednesday morning; after that I can determine what to do about going on; the only thing I fear is, that it is going to deprive me of my dear Lucretia. Recollect the old lady's saying, often quoted by mother, 'There is never a convenience but there ain't one.' I long to see you.

"Mr. Auger's bust is exciting great attention and admiration, as will be seen by the New York papers. I cannot but hope I shall be able to dispose of it for him. Tell him I shall hold it at three hundred dollars, and he ought not to let it go for one cent less.

"I have made an arrangement with Mr. Durand to have an engraving of Lafayette's portrait; I receive half the profits. Vanderlyn, Sully, Peale, Jarvis, Waldo, Inman, Ingham, and some others, were my competitors in the application for this picture."

"NEW YORK, *January* 8, 1825.

"Your letter of the 5th I have just received, and one from the committee of medical students, engaging me to paint Dr. Smith's portrait for them when I come to New Haven. They are to give me one hundred dollars. I have written them that I should be in New Haven by the 1st of February, or, at farthest, by the 6th. So that it is only prolonging for a little longer, my dear wife, the happy meeting which I anticipated by the 25th of this month. Events are not under our own control. When I consider how

wonderfully things are working for the promotion of the great and
long-desired event—that of being constantly with my dear family—
all unpleasant feelings are absorbed in this joyful anticipation, and
I look forward to the spring of the year with delightful prospects
of seeing my dear family permanently settled with me in our own
hired house here.   There are more encouraging prospects than I
can trust to paper at present, which must be left for your private
ear, and which in magnitude are far more valuable than any encouragement yet made known to you.   Let us look with thankful
hearts to the Giver of all these blessings."

" WASHINGTON, February 8, 1825.

" I arrived safely in this city last evening.   I find I have no time
to lose, as the marquis will leave here the 23d.   I have seen him,
and am to breakfast with him to-morrow, and to commence his portrait.   If he allows me time sufficient, I have no fear as to the result.   He has a noble face.   In this I am disappointed, for I had
heard that his features were not good.   On the contrary if there is
any truth in expression or character, there never was a more perfect
example of accordance between the face and the character.   He
has all that noble firmness and consistency, for which he has been
so distinguished strongly indicated in his whole face.   While he
was reading my letters I could not but call to mind the leading
events of his truly eventful life.   'This is the man now before me,
the very man,' thought I, ' who suffered in the dungeon of Olmutz;
the very man who took the oaths of the new constitution for so
many millions, while the eyes of thousands were fixed upon him
(and which is so admirably described in the life which I read to
you just before I left home) ; the very man who spent his youth,
his fortune, and his time, to bring about (under Providence) our
happy Revolution ; the friend and companion of Washington, the
terror of tyrants, the firm and consistent supporter of liberty ; the
man whose beloved name has rung from one end of this continent
to the other, whom all flock to see, whom all delight to honor; this
is the man, the very identical man !'   My feelings were almost too
powerful for me, as I shook him by the hand, and received the
greeting of, ' Sir, I am exceedingly happy in your acquaintance, and
especially on such an occasion.'

" I attended the debates to-day.   The House was principally, if
not wholly, occupied in discussing the measures for balloting for
President.   The next day after to-morrow will be the great day.

From all I can learn there is scarcely a doubt but the choice will fall on Mr. Adams."

[No choice having been made by the people, the election went to the House of Representatives, and John Quincy Adams was elected.]

"WASHINGTON, *February* 10, 1825.

"I went last evening to the President's levee, the last which Mr. Monroe will hold as President of the United States. There was a great crowd, and a great number of distinguished characters, among whom were General Lafayette, the President-elect, J. Q. Adams, Mr. Calhoun, the Vice-President-elect, General Jackson, etc. I paid my respects to Mr. Adams, and congratulated him on his election. He seemed, in some degree, to shake off his habitual reserve, and, although he endeavored to suppress his feelings of gratification at his success, it was not difficult to perceive that he felt in high spirits on the occasion. General Jackson went up to him, and, shaking him by the hand, congratulated him cordially on his election. The general bears his defeat like a man, and has shown, I think, by this act, a nobleness of mind which will command the respect of those who have been most opposed to him. The excitement (if it may be called such) on this great question, in Washington, is over, and every thing is moving on in its accustomed channel again. All seem to speak in the highest terms of the order and decorum preserved through the whole of this imposing ceremony, and the good feeling which seems to prevail, with but trivial exceptions, is thought to augur well in behalf of the new administration.

"I went, last night, in a carriage with four others—Captain Chauncey, of the Navy; Mr. Cooper, the celebrated author of the popular American novels; Mr. Causici (pronounced Cau-see-chee), the sculptor; and Mr. Owen, of Lanark, the celebrated philanthropist. Mr. Cooper remarked that we had on board a more singularly-selected company, he believed, than any carriage at the door of the President's, viz. : a *misanthropist* (such he called Captain Chauncey, brother of the commodore), a *philanthropist* (Mr. Owen), a *painter* (myself), a *sculptor* (Mr. Causici), and an *author* (himself).

"The Mr. Owen mentioned above is the very man I sometimes met at Mr. Wilberforce's in London, and who was present at the interesting scene I have often related that occurred at Mr. Wilberforce's. He recollected the circumstance, and recognized me, as I did him, instantly, although it is twelve years ago.

"I am making progress with the general, but am much perplexed for want of time; I mean *his time*.   He is so harassed by
visitors, and has so many letters to write, that I find it exceedingly
difficult to do the subject justice.   *I give him the last sitting in
Washington to-morrow*, reserving another sitting or two when he
visits New York in July next.   I have gone on thus far to my satisfaction, and do not doubt but I shall succeed entirely, if I am
allowed the requisite number of sittings.   The general is very
agreeable.   He introduced me to his son, by saying: 'This is Mr.
Morse, the painter; the son of the geographer; he has come to
Washington to take the *topography* of my face.'   He thinks of
visiting New Haven again, when he returns from Boston.   He regretted not having seen more of it when he was there, as he was
much pleased with the place.   He remembers Prof. Silliman and
others, with great affection.   I have left but little room in this letter to express my affection for my dearly-loved wife and children;
but, of that, I need not assure them.   I long to hear from you;
but direct your letters next to New York, as I shall probably be
there by the end of next week, or the beginning of the succeeding
one.   Love to all the family, and friends and neighbors.   Your
affectionate husband, as ever."

Alas, for all human hopes!   One more sitting, and the
proud artist was to return to his beloved wife.   A letter from
his father brings to him the overwhelming intelligence of her
sudden death!

Rev. Dr. Morse to his Son.

"NEW HAVEN, *February* 8, 1825.

"MY AFFECTIONATELY-BELOVED SON: Mysterious are the ways
of Providence.   My heart is in pain and deeply sorrowful, while I
announce to you the sudden and unexpected death of your dear
and deservedly-loved wife.   Her disease proved to be an *affection
of the heart—incurable*, had it been known.   Dr. Smith's letter,
accompanying this, will explain all you will desire to know on this
subject.   I wrote you yesterday that she was *convalescent*.   So
she then appeared, and so the doctor pronounced.   She was up
about five o'clock yesterday afternoon, to have her bed made, as
usual; was unusually cheerful and social; spoke of the pleasure of
being with her dear husband in New York, ere long; stepped into
bed herself; fell back, with a momentary struggle, on her pillow;
her eyes were immediately fixed, the paleness of death over-

spread her countenance, and in five minutes more, without the slightest motion, her mortal life terminated. It happened that, just at this moment I was entering her chamber-door with Charles in my arms, to pay her my usual visit, and to pray with her. The nurse met me affrighted, calling for help. Your mother, the family, and neighbors, full of the tenderest sympathy and kindness, and the doctors, thronged the house in a few minutes; every thing was done that could be done, to save her life. But her 'appointed time' had come, and no earthly skill or power could stay the hand of death. It was the Lord who gave her to you, the chiefest of all your earthly blessings, and it is He that has taken her away; and may you be enabled, my son, from the heart to say, 'Blessed be the name of the Lord!' Go directly to Him who alone can give you effectual help in time of need. Think of Jesus at the house of Martha and Mary, on the death of their brother—whom Jesus loved—how he pitied them, wept with them, and comforted them. This same Jesus, with the like feelings which he manifested on this occasion, still lives at the right hand of his Father, is touched with the feelings of his afflicted children, and pleads effectually with his Father in their behalf. When the disciples had buried John the Baptist, 'they went and told Jesus.' Go, my afflicted son, and tell him your sorrow, of the loss you have sustained. He loves to have his disciples manifest this affectionate confidence in him, and to come and tell him all their troubles. He will direct and comfort you. Pursuing this course, you will surely find the most solid support, and in no other is it to be found. Our neighbors are full of sympathy for us, and manifest it in all ways best adapted to comfort us. For you they express the tenderest feelings, with many tears, and they cheerfully promise to remember you in their prayers. I have no doubt these prayers will be heard, and that you will have the comfort of them. The shock to the whole family is far beyond, in point of severity, that of any we have ever before felt; but we are becoming composed, we hope, on grounds which will prove solid and lasting.

"I expect this will reach you on Saturday, the day after the one we have appointed for the funeral, when you will have been in Washington a week, and I hope will have made so much progress in your business as that you will soon be able to return.

"All join in tenderest sympathy and love for you, with your afflicted and affectionate father,

"JED. MORSE."

His brother Sidney also wrote to him:

"NEW YORK, *February* 9, 1825.

"MY DEAR BROTHER: Father has doubtless informed you of the melancholy event which has filled all our hearts with unspeakable sorrow. May God support you under this most afflicting stroke of his providence! He has seen fit to deprive us of her, who was so eminently lovely, at a moment when our earthly prospects had put on their most smiling aspect, and when we were fondly looking forward to long years of enjoyment; and she was to have been a partaker in every pleasure; but God has taken her to himself, to that world where we must all soon follow, and where separation and sorrow are unknown. Let us bow before the will of him who does all things right."

He was at Gadsby's Hotel, when this blow fell upon him. Unable to keep his appointment to proceed that day with his painting, and having sent a message to General Lafayette, explaining his absence, he received immediately from the General a few lines of generous sympathy:

"I have feared to intrude upon you, my dear sir, but want to tell you how deeply I sympathize in your grief—a grief of which nobody can better than me appreciate the cruel feelings. You will hear from me, as soon as I find myself again near you, to finish the work you have so well begun. Accept my affectionate and mournful sentiment. "LAFAYETTE.

"*February* 11, 1825."

He left Washington the day after the news reached him, and stopped in Baltimore over Sunday, with a friend, from whose house he writes to his parents:

"BALTIMORE, *Sunday, February* 13, 1825.

"MY DEAR FATHER: The heart-rending tidings which you communicated reached me, in Washington, on Friday evening. I left yesterday morning, spend this day here at Mr. Cushing's, and set out on my return home, to-morrow. I shall reach Philadelphia on Monday night, New York on Tuesday night, and New Haven on Wednesday night. Oh, is it possible—is it possible? shall I never see my dear wife again? But, I cannot trust myself to write on the subject. I need your prayers, and those of Christian friends, to God for support. I fear I shall sink under it.

"Oh, take good care of her dear children!

"Your agonized son, "FINLEY."

He did not reach New Haven, traveling by stage, until nearly a week after his wife had been consigned to the grave. A month after the death of his wife he writes to a friend:

"NEW YORK, *March* 20, 1825.

"MY DEAR MADAM: Though late in performing the promise I made you, of writing you when I arrived home, I hope you will attribute it to any thing but forgetfulness of that promise. The confusion and derangement consequent on such an afflicting bereavement as I have suffered, have rendered it necessary for me to devote the first moments of composure to looking about me, and to collecting and arranging the fragments of the ruin which has spread such desolation over all my earthly prospects. Oh, what a blow! I dare not yet give myself up to the full survey of its desolating effects; every day brings to my mind a thousand new and fond connections with dear Lucretia, all now ruptured. I feel a dreadful void, a heart-sickness, which time does not seem to heal, but rather to aggravate. You know the intensity of the attachment which existed between dear L. and me, never for a moment interrupted by the smallest cloud; an attachment founded, I trust, in the purest love, and daily strengthening by all the motives which the ties of *nature*, and more especially of *religion*, furnish.

"I found in dear L. every thing I could wish. Such ardor of affection, so uniform, so unaffected, I never saw nor read of, but in her. My fear with regard to the measure of my affection toward her, was not that I might fail of 'loving her as my own flesh,' but that I should put her in the place of him who has said, 'Thou shalt have no other gods but me.' I felt this to be my greatest danger, and to be saved from this *idolatry* was often the subject of my earnest prayers. If I had desired any thing in my dear L. different from what she was, it would have been that she had been *less lovely*. My whole soul seemed wrapped up in her; with her was connected all that I expected of happiness on earth. Is it strange, then, that I now feel this void, this desolateness, this loneliness, this heart-sickness; that I should feel as if my very heart itself had been torn from me? To any one but those who knew dear L., what I have said might seem to be but the extravagance of an excited imagination; but to you, who knew the dear object I lament, all that I have said must but feebly shadow her to your memory."

The death of his Lucretia was the great calamity of Mr. Morse's early life. Her virtues, her charms of mind and of per-

10

son are celebrated by those who knew her; so that we have no reason to doubt that she was one of the most lovely of women. The late Prof. Benjamin Silliman, Sr., who knew her well, composed the following epitaph, which is now upon her tombstone in the beautiful cemetery in New Haven:

IN MEMORY OF

LUCRETIA PICKERING,

WIFE OF

SAMUEL F. B. MORSE,

WHO DIED 7TH OF FEBRUARY, A. D. 1825,

AGED 25 YEARS.

SHE COMBINED, IN HER CHARACTER AND PERSON,
A RARE ASSEMBLAGE OF EXCELLENCES:
BEAUTIFUL IN FORM, FEATURES, AND EXPRESSION,
PECULIARLY BLAND IN HER MANNERS,
HIGHLY CULTIVATED IN MIND,
SHE IRRESISTIBLY DREW ATTENTION, LOVE,
AND RESPECT;
DIGNIFIED WITHOUT HAUGHTINESS,
AMIABLE WITHOUT TAMENESS,
FIRM WITHOUT SEVERITY, AND
CHEERFUL WITHOUT LEVITY,
HER UNIFORM SWEETNESS OF TEMPER
SPREAD PERPETUAL SUNSHINE AROUND
EVERY CIRCLE IN WHICH
SHE MOVED.
" WHEN THE EAR HEARD HER IT BLESSED HER,
WHEN THE EYE SAW HER IT GAVE
WITNESS TO HER."
IN SUFFERINGS THE MOST KEEN,
HER SERENITY OF MIND NEVER FAILED HER :
DEATH TO HER HAD NO TERRORS,
THE GRAVE NO GLOOM.
THOUGH SUDDENLY CALLED FROM EARTH,
ETERNITY WAS NO STRANGER TO HER THOUGHTS,
BUT A WELCOME THEME OF
CONTEMPLATION.
RELIGION WAS THE SUN
THAT ILLUMINED EVERY VIRTUE,
AND UNITED ALL IN ONE
BOW OF BEAUTY.
HERS WAS THE RELIGION OF THE GOSPEL;
JESUS CHRIST HER FOUNDATION,
THE AUTHOR AND FINISHER OF HER FAITH.
IN HIM SHE RESTS, IN SURE
EXPECTATION OF A GLORIOUS
RESURRECTION.

More than thirty years after the death of Mrs. Morse a gentleman in Boston addressed to Mr. Morse a letter of inquiry respecting the portrait of General Lafayette, and, in the midst of his telegraphic success and fame, he returned the following reply:

"POUGHKEEPSIE, *June* 11, 1858.

"MY DEAR SIR: In answer to yours of the 8th instant, just received, I can only say it is so long since I have seen the portrait I painted of General Lafayette for the city of New York, that, strange to say, I find it difficult to recall even its general characteristics. That portrait has a melancholy interest for me, for it was just as I had commenced the second sitting of the General at Washington that I received the stunning intelligence of Mrs. Morse's death, and was compelled abruptly to suspend the work. I preserve, as a gratifying memorial, the letter of condolence and sympathy sent in to me at the moment by the General, and in which he speaks in flattering terms of the promise of the portrait as a likeness. I must be frank, however, in my judgment of my own works of that day. This portrait was begun under the sad auspices to which I have alluded, and, up to the close of the work, I had a series of constant interruptions of the same sad character. A picture painted under such circumstances can scarcely be expected to do the artist justice, and, as a work of art, I cannot praise it. Still, it is a good likeness, was very satisfactory to the General, and he several. times alluded to it in my presence in after-years (when I was a frequent visitor to him in Paris) in terms of praise.

"It is a full-length, standing figure, the size of life. He is represented as standing at the top of a flight of steps, which he has just ascended upon a terrace, the figure coming against a glowing sunset sky, indicative of the glory of his own evening of life. Upon his right, if I remember, are three pedestals, one of which is vacant, as if waiting for his bust, while the two others are surmounted by the busts of Washington and Franklin—the two associated eminent historical characters of his own time. In a vase, on the other side, is a flower—the *heliotrope*—with its face toward the sun, in allusion to the characteristic, stern, uncompromising consistency of Lafayette—a trait of character which I then considered and still consider the great prominent trait of that distinguished man."

Heart-broken, Mr. Morse went on with his work in the city of New York. His position as an artist was established, and other men would have been content with the bright prospects which his profession opened before him. But he was constantly

aiming at something higher and better for the advancement of
the arts and the honor of his country.   April 8, 1825, he writes
to his parents from New York :

"I have as much as I can do, but, after being fatigued at night,
and having my thoughts turned to my irreparable loss, I am ready
almost to give up.   The thought of seeing my dear Lucretia, and
returning home to her, served always to give me fresh courage and
spirits whenever I felt worn down by the labors of the day, and now
I hardly know what to substitute in her place.   To my friends here
I know I seem to be cheerful and happy, but a cheerful countenance
with me covers an aching heart, and often have I feigned a more
than ordinary cheerfulness to hide a more than ordinary anguish.

"I am blessed with prosperity in my profession.   I have just
received another commission, from the corporation of the city, to
paint a common-sized portrait of Rev. Mr. Stanford for them, to be
placed in the almshouse."

May 26, 1825.—"I have at length become comfortably settled,
and begin to feel at home in my new establishment.   All things at
present go on smoothly.   Brother Charles Walker and Mr. Agate
join with me in breakfast and tea, and we find it best for convenience, economy, and time, to dine from home—it saves the perplexity of providing marketing and the care of stores, and, besides,
we think it will be more economical, and the walk will be beneficial."

The death of his wife was followed, with no great interval,
by the death of his venerable father.   No man who has attained
distinguished position in life has been more indebted for early
culture to his parents than Mr. Morse.   A clergyman, with no
means of support but such as he derived from his people and
from his literary labors, Dr. Morse had given to his children the
highest advantages of education which the country would afford ;
and, when this son had manifested a desire to pursue art as his
profession, his father, at a great personal sacrifice, gave him the
advantages of education under the best masters in the world in
a foreign country, sustaining him there for successive years,
when it was necessary for him (the father) to exercise great
self-denial in order to command the means to give such advantages to his son.   These sacrifices were always appreciated and
gratefully acknowledged in the letters which he so frequently

wrote to his parents; and now, when he was continuing his struggles in New York as an artist, his family were still, in a great measure, dependent upon his father for their support.

His brothers, Sidney and Richard, established themselves in New York, in the year 1823. Having founded the *New York Observer*, they were now engaged in building it up with great industry, perseverance, and ability, finally crowned with complete success. During its earlier years they were unable to do more than to sustain themselves and their paper; and Finley Morse, the artist, was obliged to look oftentimes to his father for assistance. Dr. Morse died June 9, 1826, in the city of New Haven.

"There he had resided during the latter part of his life, in the midst of a highly-cultivated and Christian community, the leading members of which, men of world-wide literary and scientific fame, and of religious sentiments in harmony with his own, were his daily companions; while all, of all classes, loved and honored him for the services he had rendered to his country and to mankind."

NATIONAL ACADEMY OF DESIGN.

Colonel Trumbull, celebrated as one of the earliest and most successful of American painters, and whose works portray some of the most important scenes of the American Revolution, was at this time at the head of the American Academy of Arts, in the city of New York. His administration was not popular with the artists who had occasion to study their profession with the works collected and possessed by the Academy. The artists complained of being denied facilities which they required for the successful prosecution of their studies; and especially that the hours when they could obtain access to the works which they desired to copy were not convenient for them; and that no attention was paid to their remonstrances.

Mr. Dunlap reports that, on one occasion, Messrs. Cummings and Agate (both of whom afterward became distinguished in their profession) came to the door of the Academy, and, finding it closed, were turning away, when he, Mr. Dunlap, spoke to them, and advised them to make their complaint to the directors of the Academy. They replied that it would be useless; and Mr. Dunlap says: "At that moment one of the directors appeared, coming from Broadway toward them. I urged the young gentlemen to speak to him, but they declined, saying, 'they had so often been disappointed, that they gave it up.' The director came and sat down by the writer, who mentioned the subject of the recent disappointment, pointing to the two young men who were still in sight. The conduct of the person whose duty it was to open the doors was promptly condemned by that gentleman; and, while speaking, the president appeared, coming to his painting-room, which was one of the apartments of the Academy. It was unusually early for him, although near eight o'clock. Before he reached the door, the curator of the Academy opened it and remained.

" On Mr. Trumbull's arrival, the director mentioned the disappointment of the students. The curator stoutly asserted that 'he would open the doors when it suited him.' The president observed, in reply to the director: 'When I commenced the study of painting, there were no casts in the country. I was obliged to do as well as I could.' These young gentlemen should remember that *the gentlemen* have gone to a great expense in importing casts, and that they' (the students) 'have no property in them;' concluding with these memorable words, in the encouragement of the curator's conduct, 'They must remember that BEGGARS are not to be CHOOSERS.'" Dunlap continues, "We may consider this the condemnatory sentence of the American Academy of Fine Arts." It was so, as it afterward appeared.

When these facts came to be known, the indignation of the artists was general, and a strong desire was expressed that some measures might be taken to secure for the artists the privileges of the Academy; or, if that were not possible, that some new association should be formed to procure for them the advantages which they felt to be indispensable to their progress. Mr. Morse was called on to concentrate these efforts. He invited a few of the artists to his rooms, and there the propriety of further endeavors to conciliate the directors by petition was discussed. Mr. Morse suggested that an association might be formed "for the Promotion of the Arts, and the Assistance of Students"—simply a union for improvement in drawing.

On the 8th of November, 1825, a meeting of the artists,

probably the first ever held in the city, took place in the rooms of the Historical Society (generously loaned them on that occasion), for the purpose of taking into consideration "the formation of a Society for Improvement in Drawing." Mr. Durand was called to the chair, and Mr. Morse was appointed secretary.

The question of organization was put, and carried unanimously; and the so-associated artists were thenceforth to be known as the "New York Drawing Association." Samuel F. B. Morse was chosen to preside over its meetings. The members were:

Samuel F. B. Morse, Henry Inman, A. B. Durand, Thomas S. S. Cummings, Ambrose Andrews, Frederick S. Agate, William G. Wall, William Dunlap, James Coyle, Charles C. Wright, Mosley J. Danforth, Robert Norris, Edward C. Potter, Albert Durand, John W. Paradise, Gerlando Marsiglia, Ithiel Town, Thomas Grinnell, George W. Hatch, John R. Murray, Jr., John Neilson, John L. Morton, Henry J. Morton, C. C. Ingham, Thomas Cole, Hugh Reinagle, Peter Maverick, D. W. Wilson, Alexander G. Davis, John Frazee.

By its few and simple rules it was provided "that its members should meet in the evenings, three times a week, for drawing; that each member furnish his own drawing-materials; that the expense of light, fuel, etc., be paid by equal contributions; that new members should be admitted on a majority of votes—paying five dollars entrance-fee; that the lamp should be lighted at six, and extinguished at nine o'clock, P. M." The lamp was a can, containing about half a gallon of oil, into which was inserted a wick of some four inches in diameter; it was set upon an upright post, about ten feet high. To give sufficient light, the wick was necessarily considerably out of the oil, and caused smoke. There was no chimney, and lamp-black was abundant; added to that, some forty draftsmen had an oil-lamp each. The reader may easily imagine the condition of the room!

At a meeting of the New York Drawing Association, held on the evening of the 14th of January, 1826, Mr. Morse, the president, stated that he had certain resolutions to offer the Association, which he would preface with the following remarks:

"We have this evening assumed a new attitude in the community: our negotiations with the Academy are at an end; our union with it has been frustrated, after every proper effort on our part to accomplish it. The two who were elected as directors from our ticket have signified their non-acceptance of the office. We are, therefore, left to organize ourselves on a plan that shall meet the wishes of us all. A plan of an institution which shall be truly liberal, which shall be mutually beneficial, which shall really encourage our respective arts, cannot be devised in a moment; it ought to be the work of great caution and deliberation, and as simple as possible in its machinery.

"Time will be required for the purpose. We must hear from distant countries to obtain their experience, and it must necessarily be perhaps many months before it can be matured. In the mean time, however, a preparatory simple organization can be made, and should be made as soon as possible, to prevent dismemberment, which may be attempted by out-door influence. On this subject let us all be on our guard; let us point to our public documents to any who ask what we have done, and why we have done it; while we go forward, minding only our own concerns, leaving the Academy of Fine Arts as much of our thoughts as they will permit us, and, bending our attention to our own affairs, act as if no such institution existed.

"One of our dangers at present is division and anarchy, from a want of organization suited to the present exigency. We are now composed of artists in the four arts of design, viz., painting, sculpture, architecture, and engraving. Some of us are professional artists, others amateurs, others students. To the professed and practical artist belongs the management of all things relating to schools, premiums, and lectures, so that amateur and student may be most profited. The amateurs and students are those alone who can contend for the premiums, while the body of professional artists exclusively judge of their rights to premiums, and award them. How shall we first make the separation has been a question which is a little perplexing. There are none of us who can assume to be the body of artists without giving offense to others; and still every one must perceive that, to organize an Academy, there must be the distinction between professional artists, amateurs who are students, and professional students. The first great division should be the body of professional artists from the amateurs and students constituting the body, who are to manage the entire concerns of the institution, who shall be its officers, etc. There is a method which strikes me as obviating the difficulty : place it on the broad principle of the formation of any society—universal suffrage. We are now a mixed body; it is necessary for the benefit of all that a separation into classes be made. Who shall make it? Why, obviously the body itself. Let every member of this association take home with him a list of all the members of it. Let each one select for himself from the whole list *fifteen*, whom he would call professional artists, to be the ticket which he will give in at the next meeting. These fifteen thus chosen shall elect not less than *ten*, nor more than *fifteen*, professional artists, in or out of the association, who shall (with the previously-elected fifteen) constitute the body to be called the National Academy of the Arts of Design. To these shall be delegated the power to regulate its entire concerns, choose its members, select its students, etc. Thus will the germ be formed to grow up into an institution, which we trust will be put on such principles as to encourage—not to depress—the arts. When this is done, our body will be no longer the Drawing Association, but the National Academy of the Arts of Design, still including all the present association, but in different capacities.

"One word as to the name 'National Academy of the Arts of Design.' Any less name than National would be taking one below the American Academy, and therefore is not desirable. If we were simply the Associated Artists, their name would swallow us up ; therefore, National seems a proper one as to the arts of design : these are painting, sculpture, architecture, and engraving, while the fine arts include poetry, music, landscape gardening, and the histrionic arts. Our name, therefore, expresses the entire character of our institution, and that only."

This arrangement was unanimously adopted, and a list of the members of the association was immediately furnished to each member, who, from it, was requested to select, by the next meeting, fifteen professional artists to form his ticket, the fifteen "having the highest number of votes to constitute a 'Body of Artists,' who shall, before Wednesday evening next, elect not less than ten nor more than fifteen others, from professional artists resident in the city of New York, the whole body thus chosen to be called the 'National Academy of the Arts of Design.'" And, by resolution, those remaining in the association after such election, and wishing to belong to the new institution, were to be declared students of the new institution, and a certificate of membership to be given to them.

On the 15th of January, 1826, in conformity with the resolution, the association proceeded to ballot. Whereupon the following gentlemen were chosen: S. F. B. Morse, Henry Inman, A. B. Durand, John Frazee, William Wall, Charles C. Ingham, William Dunlap, Peter Maverick, Ithiel Town, Thomas S. Cummings, Edward Potter, Charles C. Wright, Mosley J. Danforth, Hugh Reinagle, Gerlando Marsiglia.

And between the 15th and the 18th of the month the above-named artists assembled for the performance of their part of the task; for, on the 18th of January, 1826, the president stated that "the professional artists chosen at the last meeting of the association had balloted for *ten* professional artists on one ticket, and five subsequently on separate tickets, and that the following gentlemen were those elected: Samuel Waldo, William Jewett, John W. Paradise, Frederick S. Agate, Rembrandt Peale, James Coyle, Nathaniel Rogers, J. Parisen, William Main, John Evers, Martin E. Thompson, Thomas Cole, John Vanderlyn (who declined), Alexander Anderson, D. W. Wilson. By this method was formed the National Academy of the Arts of Design. Samuel F. B. Morse and John L. Morton were chosen to act as president and secretary until the adoption of a constitution.

The National Academy of Design, thus ushered into the world, was composed of members and professional artists, and thus divided in the four arts of design :

In painting: Samuel F. B. Morse, Henry Inman, Thomas S. Cummings, William Dunlap, Rembrandt Peale, Charles C. Ingham, Thomas Cole, John Evers, Signor Marsiglia, Frederick S. Agate, Edward C. Potter, Hugh Reinagle, James Coyle, D. W. Wilson, J. Parisen, John W. Paradise, Nathaniel Rogers, William Wall. *In sculpture:* John Frazee. *In architecture:* Ithiel Town, Martin E. Thompson. *In engraving:* A. B. Durand, William Main, Mosley J. Danforth, Peter Maverick, Charles C. Wright.

The following were students in the Antique School of the first grade: John L. Morton, amateur; Henry J. Morton, amateur; John J. Neilson, amateur; George W. Hatch, Thomas Grinnell, Ambrose Andrews, Robert Norris, Albert Durand, John W. Paradise, Alexander G. Davis, John R. Murray, Jr.

Mr. Morse was requested to prepare a short address to the

public, setting forth the views and general intentions of the institution, from which the following is an extract :

"An institution with this name has recently been organized by the artists of this city, founded on principles which, it is believed, will elevate the character and condition of the arts of design in our country.

"The want of such an institution has long been felt by those interested in the advancement of the liberal arts, especially by artists themselves; and to its establishment, accordingly, almost the whole body of the profession in this city have concentrated their efforts.

"The National Academy of the Arts of Design is founded on the common-sense principle *that every profession in society knows best what measures are necessary for its own improvement.* Its success is no more problematical than the success of many societies that might be named where the members are exclusively of one profession. *To others* shall be left the discussion of the question *whether the common method of raising funds for the support of institutions for the encouragement of literature* and the arts, by connecting a large body of stockholders with them, be on the whole advisable or not.

"It may be observed, however, that the little experience had on this subject does not seem favorable to such a mode of procedure. In the *permanent formation of this institution* a DIFFERENT COURSE WILL BE PURSUED—a course sanctioned by the experience of academies of arts in Europe, especially the Royal Academy of London."

Almost coeval with the National Academy, was founded the "Sketch Club"—"'*The Old' Sketch Club:*"

"The second exhibition of the National Academy was held in the room over Tylee's Baths, in Chambers Street. After the exhibition the room was fitted up with plaster casts and drawing-boards, and there the students of the Antique School met to receive instruction from the founders of the Academy. One night the teachers were as usual assembled. Previous to the opening of the school, seated in a corner, were Morse, Durand, Cummings, and Ingham. The subject of conversation was the recent breaking up of that most agreeable club, the 'Lunch.' Mr. Ingham remarked that now there was an opportunity for the artists to establish a club. All agreed that such a thing was feasible. Mr. Ingham proposed that those present should consider themselves the nucleus of one, which, when established, should be called the *Sketch Club*—to consist of artists, authors, men of science, and lovers of art; and that Morse should be the first president. Mr. Morse highly approved of the idea, but declined being the president, saying that it was enough for him to be president of the Academy; that the person best entitled to the honor of being president of the proposed association was Mr. Ingham, who had originated the scheme. Mr. Cummings coincided, and, after some further conversation on the rules to be adopted, it was agreed to postpone the further consideration of the subject to Wednesday in the following week, and that a meeting should be called at Mr. Ingham's. A meeting of the principal artists was held there, and the rules of the proposed club discussed and adopted.

"The plan had been for the members to meet at an hotel, to be entertained at the cost of the host of the evening. This arrangement was supposed to have caused a rivalry in expense, which led to the breaking up of the club. To avoid a like result, the artists determined to have their club as inexpensive as possible; and, to attain this end, it was agreed that the 'Sketch Club' should meet at the houses of the members, in rotation, and that the entertainment should be confined to dried fruit, crackers, milk, and honey. Mr. Ingham was elected president, and Mr. John Inman secretary.

"The first regular meeting took place at the rooms of Thomas Cole. It was a decided success. All the members exerted themselves to please, and every thing was agreeable—even the figs, milk, and honey. But on the day after the feast, came the pangs of repentance, and many a vow was made that the refreshments of the club should be changed. . . .

"It may be regretted that its early *minutes*, witticisms, essays, drawings, verses, papers, etc., have been neglected or destroyed. Not a vestige to be found of that, one of the oldest and most interesting of clubs. It was formed for the promotion of mutual intercourse and improvement in impromptu sketching. Drawing for *one* hour from a subject proposed by the *host*, whose property the drawings remained, was part of the programme positive; the poets and others frequently amusing themselves during *that* hour by passing round a subject, on which each, in turn, furnished four lines—no more, no less; and some truly amusing mongrels were the result. Its members comprised, in a high degree, the talent of the country. In its organization *over*-great care had been taken to guard against destruction by *extravagance* in its entertainments in eating, and

'*milk and honey, raisins, apples, and crackers*' were the limitation,
the prescribed bill-of-fare. The medicinal qualities of the one were
appreciated on the first dose, and the dryness of the other was not
relished.

" 'The rule' was more observed in the breach than in the
observance. The first great outbreak, however, occurred at Member J——s H——'s, at his *then* up-town residence, viz., east side
Broadway, between Broome and Spring Streets. On that evening,
at the appointed hour for refreshments, the drawing-room doors
were thrown open, and an elegant supper appeared before the
astonished guests. A general revolt took place. *Protests* were
entered, remonstrances made; a compromise *finally*, or, it rather
should be said, *speedily* ensued. It was decided that the supper
should be eaten, but that it should be done '*standing.*'

" '*Sitting down* to supper,' it was said, was prohibited by '*the
rules.*' The distinction was a very *nice* one; so was the supper.

" Members did not long '*stand out;*' chairs were in demand,
and in less than fifteen minutes the whole were as comfortably
seated as if no such *prohibition* had ever in the rules existed, and
looked as innocently unconscious as if nothing had occurred contrary thereto. More ample justice could not have been done to a
feast. Milk and honey never again appeared at the festive board.
Many, very many happy meetings had that CLUB."

In 1873, almost half a century from this date, a reunion of
the old Sketch Club was held at the house of Jonathan Sturgis,
Esq., and a splendid entertainment in defiance of all the
" rules " was given by the liberal and hospitable host. Only two
of the *original* members were present, Cummings and Durand.
Morse, the founder and president, had been laid with the dead
but a few months before.

During the years from 1826 to 1829, Mr. Morse resided in
the city of New York, pursuing, with great industry, his profession as a painter; but oftentimes discouraged to the very
last degree, by a want of success commensurate with his ambition. Poverty, so often the lot of men of genius and of
the highest desert, pressed him continually; preparing him,
doubtless, for the still greater hardships which he was to pass
through. Still struggling to accomplish the great work for
which he was trained, he was now both a teacher and a pupil.
A large part of his time was necessarily given to the Acad-

emy of Design, over which he was called to preside, by reëlection, from year to year, from its origin down to the year 1845, and he would have been continued in the presidency during the whole of his protracted life, had he not considered it essential to the interests of the institution that he should retire from it after he became absorbed in the scientific pursuits which his invention of the Telegraph required. The industry with which he pursued his profession may be inferred from the catalogue of some of the principal paintings which were exhibited in the annual expositions of the Academy of Design. But, in addition to these, he painted a great number of portraits and other pictures which were never placed on public exhibition. This catalogue, prepared by General T. S. Cummings (whose history of the National Academy of Design has furnished the facts in regard to Mr. Morse's connection with that institution), is worthy of being preserved.

Ichabod Crane discovers the Headless Horseman, S. H.	1826
A family picture	1826
Portrait of the late Mayor W. Paulding	1826
Portrait of Rev. Dr. Stanford. New York Corporation	1826
Portrait of De Witt Clinton, Governor State of New York	1826
Full-length portrait of General Lafayette. New York Corporation	1827
Portrait of Judge Mitchell, Connecticut	1827
House of Representatives in the Capitol: 88 portraits	1827
Una and the Dwarf. Relating adventure of the Red Cross Knight.	1828
Portrait of Fitz-Greene Halleck	1828
Portrait of F. G. King, Professor of Anatomy, N. A. D., and his academician picture	1828
View of Cazenovia Lake	1828
View of Parapet Falls, at Trenton Falls	1828
Portrait of William Cullen Bryant	1829
Landscape Figures	1830
Review Exhibition (Rome)	1831
Portrait of the late Thomas Addis Emmet	1831
Portrait of Thorwalsden	1832
Amalfi, from the Grotto of the Capuchin Convent	1833
The Wetterhorn and Falls of the Reichenbach	1833
The Brigand alarmed	1833
Pifferari, or Calabrian Minstrels	1833
Full-length portrait of a lady	1834
The Gold-Fish, etc. A family group	1835
Portrait of Major-General Stark	1835
Portrait of Rev. Dr. Sprague, of Albany	1835

Portrait of Rev. Dr. Nott, of Connecticut . . . 1835
Portrait of Euchee Billy. A sketch of an Indian chief taken in
    1820. (New York University) 1836
Portrait of Dr. Augustus Smith 1836
Landscape Composition. Helicon and Aganippe . . 1836
Sunset View of St. Peter's, Rome 1836
Full-length portrait of a young lady. (New York University) . 1837
Nothing exhibited 1838–1863

In the second winter exhibition was exhibited Mr. Morse's Interior of the House of Representatives.

General Cummings, who has retired from the city (where he held high rank as an artist and teacher of art) to the repose of rural life, has kindly furnished the following sketch of Mr. Morse's professional life in New York, and an estimate of his ability:

"MANSFIELD CENTRE, TOLLAND COUNTY, CONN., *April* 21, 1873.

"My acquaintance with Mr. Morse commenced in the fall of 1824 or spring of 1825, and continued until his decease. It opened immediately on the meeting of the artists after the rudeness I had received at the American Academy of Fine Arts, as described by Dunlap and by myself in my 'Records of the National Academy of Design.' In the controversy which followed, Mr. Morse took a very deep and leading interest, the full particulars of which are given in the Annals. Ultimately, and on the formation of the National Academy of Design, he became its president, and so continued for years, namely, from 1827 to 1845, and, at my especial invitation and request, to serve the interests of the institution, from 1861 to 1862, and, I may add, was beloved by all.

"At the time of our first acquaintance Mr. Morse was in the enjoyment of lucrative and prosperous practice, as a portrait-painter, in the city. His studio was crowded with works in progress, and the demands on his pencil unceasing from the talent, wealth, and fashion of the city, daily refusing commissions, and sending the applicants to other artists for execution. As a portrait-painter Mr. Morse was very unequal; yet many of his works there are which will stand favorable competition with the best produced to the present day, and none more preëminently so that I can at present call to mind than the portrait of the Rev. Dr. Stanford—a half-length, now on the possession of the Commissioners of Charities, in the public building in Third Avenue, in the neighborhood of Twentieth Street. Mr. Morse's connection with the Academy was doubtless unfavorable in a pecuniary point of view. His interest in it interfering with professional practice, and the time taken to enable him to prepare his course of lectures, materially contributed to favor a distribution of his labors in art to other hands, and it never fully returned to him. His 'Discourse on Academies of Art,' delivered in the chapel of Columbia College, May, 1827, will long stand as a monument of his ability in the line of art-literature. As an historical painter Mr. Morse, after Allston, was probably the best-prepared and most fully-educated artist of his day, and should have received the attention of the Government, and a share of its distributions in art-commissions. There political influence was brought to bear against him; and, on the selection of the artists to fill the four panels in the Rotunda in the Capitol, Mr. Morse was found to be not one of the number. That was to him a source of great unhappiness and professional disappointment. The 'Signing of the First Compact by the Pilgrims on board the May Flower' had always been his favorite subject, and he had spent years of thought on the *then* leading subject of his heart. Hence the reasons especially for the artists coming to his rescue, to employ him to paint an historical picture. That picture, it was hoped, might occupy one of the panels in the Rotunda; and, had it been painted, it probably would have done so. Certain it is, the artist contributors never intended to take it from Mr. Morse."

A brilliant assembly was gathered in the chapel of Columbia College, May 3, 1827. The college was then in what is now the lower part of the city, in College Place, below the City Hall. The occasion that had called together the most cultivated and refined ladies and gentlemen, was the first anniversary of the National Academy of Design, and the president, Samuel F. B. Morse, delivered an address which was published in pamphlet form, at the request of the Academy, through a committee, consisting of Dunlap, Ingham, and Wright. The address is remarkable for the extent of learning it displays, and the ripe thought of the author.

The Academy being in its infancy, and some eminent artists being hostile to its establishment and its plans, this address of Mr. Morse was honored by a severe review in the *North American*, which had then reached its fifty-eighth number, and had justly acquired a national reputation. It was contended by the reviewer that the new Academy was presumptuous in assuming the title of "National," as it had no claim to national recognition, or to the countenance of the artists of the whole country. To this attack Mr. Morse replied with great ability in a paper first published in the *Journal of Commerce*, and afterward in pamphlet form.

The reply revealed the lofty spirit of independence and the high sense of the dignity of his profession, which then controlled the purposes of the president of the Academy. Mr. Morse sent a copy of his address to Lord Lyndhurst, son of the celebrated painter Copley, and to some inquiries in his letter received the following reply:

"GEORGE STREET (LONDON), *December* 28, 1827.

"DEAR SIR: I beg you will accept my best thanks for your discourse delivered before the National Academy at New York, which has been handed to me by Mr. Ward. The tenor of my father's life was so uniform as to afford fine materials for the biographer. He was entirely devoted to his art, which he pursued with unremitting assiduity to the last hour of his life. The result is before the public, in his works, which must speak for themselves; and considering that he was entirely self-taught, and never saw a decent picture, with the exception of his own, until he was nearly thirty years of age, the circumstance is, I think, worthy of admiration, and affords a striking proof of what natural genius, aided by determined perseverance, can under almost any circumstances accomplish.

"I remain, dear sir, your faithful servant,

"LYNDHURST."

STUDY OF ELECTRO-MAGNETISM.

We now leave Mr. Morse's artistic pursuits for the present, and find him once more a student of science, and of that department which had particularly interested him while in college under Professors Day and Silliman.

In the year 1827 Mr. Morse became interested in the study of electricity, and particularly in electro-magnetism. At that time he was intimately associated with James Freeman Dana, of Columbia College, who delivered a course of lectures on the subject, before the New York Athenæum. Mr. Morse attended these lectures, and the lecturer was in the habit of frequently visiting him at his studio, where subjects of mutual interest

11

were freely discussed. Professor Dana was an enthusiast in the science of electro-magnetism, and his wife relates that it so possessed his mind that she frequently heard him talk of it in his sleep. Subsequently, when it became important for Mr. Morse to establish by positive evidence the simple fact that he was taught by Professor Dana at this time, that promising scholar was dead. His wife survived him, and, on being applied to for her recollections, she testified as follows:

Deposition of Matilda W. Dana, of Boston, in the State of Massachusetts, taken at the Office of George S. Hillard.

"I am the widow of Professor James Freeman Dana; my husband and myself resided in the city of New York in the years 1826–1827; my husband died on the 15th day of April, 1827, in the city of New York. In the year 1827 he delivered a course of lectures upon the subject of electro-magnetism, and also upon the subject of electricity, before the New York Athenæum, in the chapel of Columbia College. I attended several of these lectures; his mind was most intensely interested in the subject of electro-magnetism —so much so, indeed, that I frequently heard him talk of it in his sleep. I know that my husband, in the years 1826–1827, and up to the time of his death, was on terms of intimacy with Professor Samuel F. B. Morse, and was in the habit of frequently visiting in Professor Morse's painting-room, which, at that time, was at the corner of Broadway and Pine Street, in the city of New York. I have a distinct recollection of visiting Professor Morse's room in 1827, in company with my husband, and of examining some of Professor Morse's paintings. My husband had a very keen perception of the beautiful, and was a great admirer of the fine arts, and took particular delight and interest in the art in which Professor Morse was at that time engaged. I have no doubt that this circumstance led him to cultivate an intimacy and friendship with Professor Morse, and I know that such intimacy and friendship did exist up to the time of my husband's death. I frequently heard my husband speak of his having been on visits to Professor Morse's rooms, and he frequently told me he had been on such visits. From what he said to me, and from what I saw, I know that he must have spent much time at Professor Morse's rooms. I frequently heard him speak of Professor Morse's pictures; there was one I know, he much admired, that was the picture entitled 'Una, the Dwarf, and

Arthur,' from Spenser's 'Faerie Queene.' My husband took me with
him to Professor Morse's room, to see that picture, and I recollect
seeing it at his room, and it was much admired both by me and by
my husband; and my husband was so much interested at that time
with electro-magnetism, that it was a favorite theme in his conversations with all his associates and friends. He was in the habit
of dwelling much upon it, and of explaining to his friends the
results of his experiments in that science. From the terms of intimacy existing between him and Professor Morse, I can scarcely conceive it possible that he and Professor Morse should not have had
frequent and repeated conversations on the subject of electro-magnetism. I knew that my husband at that time was in the constant
habit of stating to his friends and associates his views of that
wonderful science, which then was regarded as, in a great measure,
new in this country, and little understood. He was unusually frank
and communicative in his social intercourse with his friends; that
was a distinguishing trait in his character. He seemed anxious to
induce, in the minds of others, an interest in the science of electro-
magnetism, as he entertained the idea that, ultimately, it would be
an instrument of wonderful and highly-beneficial results to the
world, when it should be more fully understood, its principles developed and applied to practical purposes. On the death of my husband I received from Professor Morse a very kind note of condolence, to which I have often recurred with grateful remembrance,
as a token of kind regard from an intimate friend and associate of
my deceased husband. I have often spoken of it, and shown it to
my daughter, as coming from an intimate friend of her father. I
cannot now state positively that I saw Professor Morse at these
lectures before the Athenæum; but from the intimacy that existed
between them, and the professional relations to each other, I have
no doubt that he did attend those lectures. I should have thought
it very singular if he had not, and presume that his absence would
have been a subject of remark if he were absent. I recollect Professor Morse at that time delivered lectures before the Athenæum
upon the fine arts, and that my husband and myself attended them.
I am very sure that Professor Morse, in his letter of condolence,
expressed the pleasure he had had in attending my husband's lectures. And I further depose and say that the two papers now produced and made an exhibit in this cause, and upon the first page
of which I have written my name, and the date of taking of this
deposition—one headed '1st, 2d. On Electro-Magnetism before

the New York Athenæum;' the other headed '2d, 3d, 4th. On Electro-Magnetism, before the New York Athenæum'—are the original lectures delivered by my husband James Freeman Dana, before the New York Athenæum, in the year 1827; that said original lectures and the drawings therein, as well as the heading to each, above quoted, are in the handwriting of my said husband, and the same have been in my possession since the death of my said husband; and that my husband, at the time of the delivery, *exhibited to his audience various experiments with an electro-magnet*, illustrative of the subject-matter of said lectures, and *then had and exhibited to his audience an electro-magnet in a horseshoe form. After his death that identical magnet was sold to his successor, Professor John Torrey.* Since the funeral of my husband I have not seen Mr. Morse, until the 19th of September, instant. He then, before seeing said lectures, or before I told him what they contained, stated to me several of the experiments which were exhibited by my husband at the time he delivered the same before the Athenæum.

(Signed)   " MATILDA W. DANA.

" Sworn to before me, the 24th day of September, A. D. 1849.
                    " GEORGE S. HILLARD,
                    " Commissioner, etc., etc., etc."

The first words that fell from the lips of Professor Dana in his course of lectures, and which reached the ear of Mr. Morse, were these, and the last lines of the first paragraph have wonderful significance in connection with the results:

" The discovery of the voltaic pile by the illustrious philosopher whose name the instrument bears, is emphatically the most important discovery of the age. It will ever render memorable in the annals of science the first year of the present century. Its influence on the progress of philosophy has been viewed with astonishment, even by the most ardent and sanguine imaginations. It has multiplied discoveries with a rapidity and to an extent without parallel in the history of physics. It has given to us new powers over the material world, and has presented us with new substances possessing almost magical properties. The tide of discovery has rolled over us like a flood, and yet new results are daily offered, and new relations and connections of its influence are hourly developed.

" The year 1819 witnessed the discovery, by means of the voltaic apparatus, of a mysterious connection between the electric power and the magnetic influence, which has afforded phenomena of a most engaging and unexpected nature; has presented experiments and results which have been witnessed but with admiration, and laid the foundation upon which a new science, electro-magnetism, has been erected.

"The principles of this new science have been subjected to a rigorous mathematical analysis, which place them on a basis no less firm than that of the theory of gravitation, and gives them a charm which renders the subject highly attractive from the perfect coincidence of geometrical deductions with physical facts; but, divesting them of mathematical considerations, I shall attempt, in a popular manner, to elucidate the laws of electro-magnetism, by experiments, in the lectures which I have the honor this season to offer to the Athenæum."

And he closed the lecture by saying:

"Conductors of electricity receive and transmit the electric influence instantly to every part of their substance; metals, alloys, well-burnt charcoal: non-conductors receive the influence only at the point of contact, but do not transmit it; glass, resin, silk, etc. There are many bodies which hold an intermediate station between conductors and non-conductors; they are called imperfect conductors.

"When a connection is made between the positive and negative poles of a voltaic apparatus by means of conductors, the battery is *discharged;* the electric tension is destroyed; that is, the instruments which indicate the presence of electricity cease to be affected. But the apparatus possesses within itself the power of renewing its first state of electric tension in imperceptible intervals of time, and consequently the connecting substance between the two poles is continually performing the same office during its whole time of contact that it did at the first moment. While the connecting wire is performing this function, it is evident that it must be in a state different from that in which it exists when separated from the instrument. Now, since a small wire may be employed to discharge a powerful apparatus, it follows that the principle which is active in it is condensed and concentrated into a very small space. A wire, while it is performing this function, we shall call the *conjunctive wire.*

"In the hypothetical language of electricians, a current of electricity flows through the conjunctive wire, but whether a material substance be conceived to pass through the wire or not, it certainly suffers some peculiar changes, and acquires some peculiar properties which it retains while it is made the medium of communication between the poles of the voltaic instruments in a state of activity. If the wire be small, it is heated, and it produces effects on the magnetic needle which are constant and invariable."

In his second lecture Professor Dana said :

" The effect of the conjunctive wire in impressing the magnetic state is uniform and constant, and we can infer with absolute certainty the kind of magnetism which will be exhibited by either end of a needle, by reference to its position with regard to the wire. We are led to this by our previous knowledge of the positions assumed by a magnetic needle under the influence of the wire. Thus, if the electric current flow from the right hand to the left, and the needle to be magnetized be placed over the wire, the end pointing from us will acquire the austral magnetism, or a north polarity, etc. We have seen that the pole of the magnetic needle, *over* which the positive electricity enters, turns to the east, but the pole *under* which it enters, turns to the west. If, therefore, a needle be placed between two conjunctive wires situated in the same vertical plane, and transmitting the electric current in opposite directions, it is evident that both will conspire to produce the same effect, which will, consequently, be much more considerable than that produced by either of them alone; but a wire bent so as to have its ends connected with the opposite poles of the voltaic instrument, will evidently have the electric current passing in opposite directions in its upper and lower portions, and consequently it will produce on a needle between them an effect similar to that produced by the two wires. Wires thus situated produce a more prompt development of magnetism in steel than a single wire does, because both tend to turn the same kind of magnetism in the same direction, and the opposite magnetisms in opposite directions, and hence we have one method of measuring the action of a battery on steel bars. Again, two parallel wires, having the electric current moving through them, in the same direction, will evidently produce a greater effect on a steel bar than either of them alone, for the effect of the whole must be greater than that of a part.

" Where several conjunctive wires are placed together, side by side, the power is apparently diminished in the central wires, and concentrated in the extreme portion; the magnetic state of the latter seems to be augmented by induction or by position.

" When such an assemblage of wires acts on the magnetism of a piece of steel, they decompose it, and each individual wire acts with most force on the magnetism nearest to it. Each conspires in its action to produce the same effect as the others; and hence, in addition to the effects of currents in opposite directions, we have another method of increasing the power of a battery in magnetizing needles. We shall probably render steel strongly magnetic, if we combine these two methods of increasing the effect. *This is effected by forming the conjunctive wire into a spiral around the steel bar to be magnetized;* for, at the opposite extremities of any diameter of this spiral, it is evident that the electric current moves in opposite directions. Suppose the spiral to be placed horizontally, east and west, the current on its upper part to move from north to south, it will at its lower part move from south to north; and the spiral thus gives us the combined influence of currents in opposite directions. Moreover, the different coils of the spiral are nearly at right angles with the axis of *the included bar;* and they are parallel to each other. Hence, at any given portion of the bar the effect of many currents passing in the same direction is produced, *and the included bar becomes strongly magnetic; and a spiral placed round a piece of soft iron bent into the form of a horseshoe magnet, renders it strongly and powerfully magnetic when the electric current is passing through it.*" . . . [And this, be it remembered, was said in 1827.] "The opposite sides of a conjunctive wire exhibit the opposite magnetisms; and we have seen that, by placing the wires parallel to each other, and connecting them with a battery so that they may transmit the current in the same direction, the magnetisms seem to be concentrated in the extreme wires, and that we can thus separate them in a degree from each other. Now, when we consider that the direction of the magnetic power is at right angles to the conjunctive wire it is evident that in a helix this direction must nearly coincide with that of the axis of the helix, and the one kind of magnetism be found concentrated at one extremity, and the other kind at the opposite end. . . . Iron filings adhering to dissimilarly electro-magnetic wires, repel each other; and to similarly electro-magnetic wires, attract each other.

" In the course of our reasoning, by which we were led from step to step to the adoption of a spiral or helix in powerfully developing magnetism in bars, we inferred that two or more parallel and similarly electro-magnetic wires acted with greater energy than one, and that the magnetisms were accumulated in the extreme wires by a species of induction between them all. A ribbon of metal substituted for these wires exerts a stronger influence on the needle at its edges than at its sides, for a similar reason. So, also, if *a series of concentric wires* be used, and the electric current sent through them in the same direction, we infer that they will have the power of the corresponding sides of the different rings concentrated and accumulated in their common centre, and will, on the same side of their centre, act as parallel similarly electro-magnetic wires. A *flat spiral or volute*, having two ends connected with the opposite poles of a battery, will correctly represent concentric rings under the condition we have proposed; and the great quantity of iron filings which such a spiral or volute takes up, and the accumulation of them in the centre, fully evinces the concentration of power there, and the correctness of the reasoning by which we have been led to this modification of the conjunctive wire."

This was the second step which Morse took toward the great invention. The first was in Yale College. The second was under a professor of Columbia College.

He learned from Professor Dana, in 1827, the elementary facts that lie at the basis of the electro-magnet, to wit:

The effect of a *single straight conjunctive wire* in producing magnetism. (Oersted's discovery.)

The effect of a conjunctive wire, *bent into the form of a ring*, for the purpose of increasing the magnetism. (Schweigger's experiment.)

The effect of *a series of these conjunctive wire rings*, forming a *spiral*, for the purpose of increasing still further the magnetism. (Arago's experiment, at the suggestion of Ampère.)

The effect of a *flat spiral* or *volute*, the conjunctive wire *superposed* upon itself, for still further increasing the magnetism. Schweigger discovered the principle of this modification, and embodied it in his *multiplier*, while Dana applied it to the magnetizing of iron filings in demonstrating its magnetic power, and suggested it for the electro-magnet.

He learned from Professor Dana, in 1827, the *rationale* of the *electro-magnet*, which latter was exhibited in action. He witnessed the effects of the conjunctive wire in the different

forms described by him in his lectures, and exhibited to his audience. The electro-magnet was put in action by an *intensity battery ;* it was made to sustain the weight of its armature, when
the conjunctive wire was connected with the poles of the battery
or the circuit was *closed ;* and it was made " to drop its load "
upon *opening* the circuit. These, with many other principles of
electro-magnetism, were all illustrated, experimentally, to his
audience. Mr. Morse afterward, in writing on the subject, pays
a noble tribute to his teacher, Professor Dana, of whom he said :

" The *volute modification* of the helix, to show the concentration
of magnetism at its centre, adapted to the electro-magnet, the modification since universally adopted in the construction of the *electro-magnet,* is justly due, I think, to the inventive mind of Professor
James Freeman Dana. Death, in striking him down at the threshold of his fame, not only extinguished a brilliant light in science,
one which gave the highest promise of future distinction, but, by
the suddenness of the stroke, put to peril the just credit due to him
for discoveries he had already made. Dana had not only mastered
all of the science of *electro-magnetism* then given to the world—a
science in which he was an enthusiast ; but, standing on the confines
that separate the known from the unknown, was, at the time of his
decease, preparing for new explorations and new discoveries. I
could not mention his name, in this connection, without at least rendering this slight but inadequate homage to one of the most liberal
of men and amiable of friends, as well as promising philosophers of
his age. Dana, in 1827, publicly exhibited the electro-magnet, with
its spiral conjunctive wire. He also exhibited, at the same time,
and directly in the same connection with the electro-magnet, the 'flat
spiral,' or '*volute modification* of the conjunctive wire ; ' showing
its increased power over the single spiral, demonstrating this effect
with iron filings, and directly suggesting its application to the soft-
iron horseshoe bar."

The year following Mr. Morse devoted to his profession, in
which he was now eminently successful. His sitters were so
numerous that he was unable to meet the demands of all who
sought him, and his brother artists remember with gratitude his
kindness in sending to them many persons whom he could not
find time to paint.

He employed his evenings in preparing a series of lectures

on "The Fine Arts," which he delivered before the New York Athenæum. This is said to have been the first series of lectures on the subject ever delivered in the United States. Writing to his mother, March 1st, he says: "My lectures at the Athenæum closed on Thursday evening to a 'most fashionable and crowded house,' as the phrase is." Visiting his relatives at Utica, in the summer, he wrote to his brother:

"In coming from Whitesboro', on Friday, I met with an accident, and a most narrow escape with my life: the horse which had been tackled into the wagon was a vicious horse, and had several times run away, to the danger of Mr. Dexter's life and others of the family. I was not aware of this, or I should not have consented to go with him, much less to drive him myself. I was alone in the wagon, with my baggage, and the horse went very well for about a mile; when he gradually quickened his pace, and then set out, in spite of all check, on the full run. I kept him in the road, determined to let him run himself tired, as the only safe alternative; but, just as I came in sight of a piece of the road which had been concealed by an angle, there was a heavy wagon, which I must meet so soon that, in order to avoid it, I must give it the whole road; this being very narrow, and the ditches and banks on each side very rough, I instantly made up my mind to a serious accident. As well as the velocity of the horse would allow me, however, I kept him on the side, rough as it was, for about a quarter of a mile pretty steadily, expecting, however, to be upset every minute, when all at once I saw before me an abrupt, narrow, deep gully, into which the wheels on one side were just upon the point of going down, when it flashed across me in an instant that if I could throw the horse down into the ditch, the wheels of the wagon might perhaps rest equipoised on each side, and perhaps break the horse loose from the wagon. I pulled the rein and accomplished the object in part; the sudden plunge of the horse into the gully broke him loose from the wagon, but it at the same time turned one of the fore-wheels into the gully, which upset the wagon, and threw me forward at the moment when the horse threw up his neck, just taking off my hat, and leaving me in the bottom of the gully. I fell on my left shoulder, and, although muddied from head to foot, I escaped without any injury whatever; I was not even jarred painfully. I found my shoulder a little bruised, my wrist very slightly scratched, and yesterday was a little, and but very little, stiffened in my limbs, and to-day have not the slightest feeling of bruise about me, but think I feel better than I have for a long time. Indeed, my health is entirely restored; the riding and country air have been the means of restoring me. I have great cause of thankfulness for so much mercy, and for such special preserving care."

Returning to the city of New York, his children being scattered among his relatives in different parts of the country, Mr. Morse resumed his labors. Business increased. The most eminent citizens became his personal friends and gave him commissions. Success, however, served only to stimulate him to higher efforts; and he resolved that he would seek, by study in Italy, to perfect himself in the art to which he had now fully devoted his life.

CHAPTER VI.

1829–1832.

COMMISSIONS TO PAINT IN ITALY — JOURNEY TO ROME — LETTER TO HIS COUSIN — ENGLAND — PARIS — AVIGNON — MARSEILLES — NICE — THE CORNICE ROAD — GENEVA — PISA — ROME — THE VATICAN — GALLERIES OF ART — NOTES — THORWALDSEN — PORTRAIT — JAMES FENIMORE COOPER — H. GREENOUGH — LETTERS — RETURN TO PARIS — FRIENDSHIP WITH LAFAYETTE — SYMPATHY WITH POLAND — IMPRISONMENT OF DR. HOWE — FALL OF WARSAW — LETTERS TO HIS BROTHER — SUGGESTS LIGHTNING-TELEGRAPH — HUMBOLDT — PRESIDES AT FOURTH-OF-JULY DINNER — LETTERS OF LAFAYETTE — INTERIOR OF THE LOUVRE — HUMBOLDT AND MORSE — DUNLAP'S NOTICES OF MORSE IN PARIS AND LONDON.

PRESIDENT of the National Academy, and among the first in his profession in the United States, Mr. Morse had never been in Italy. He had a profound consciousness that whatever attainments in art he had already made, or could yet make, until he had studied under the old masters, who being dead yet speak, there was much to be learned, and he must sit as a learner in the presence of their works. Having received the following commissions for pictures, he resolved to go abroad again :

"We, the subscribers, having learned that Samuel F. B. Morse is about to embark for Europe, for the purpose of study and practice in his profession, in Rome, Paris, and London, do commission said Morse to execute the orders severally placed against our names, and do agree to advance the money for the same, at such time and in such proportions as shall be specified in a written order from the said Morse, the holder of such order to be considered as duly authorized to receive the same, and the money to be paid to him, and his receipt taken in discharge of said subscription, or the several parts thereof.

"NEW YORK, *September* 25, 1829.

Philip Hone, $100—to be disposed of in such way as may be most agreeable to Mr. Morse. A picture not larger than Newton's or Leslie's—say twenty-five by thirty.

· M. Van Schaick, $200—paid for two cabinet pictures, copies or originals—twenty-four by eighteen. Either landscapes or heads.

Chas. Carvill, $100. Like A. P. & Slender, belonging to Haggerty.

DeWitt Bloodgood, $100 (copy or copies). Some small, high-finished picture; heads from Titian.

Dr. David Hosack—two cabinet pictures, not over twenty-five by thirty inches, at $150 each—$300.

Jona. Goodhue, $100—to be at the disposal of Mr. Morse. Wishes two pictures at $50 each.

Benj. L. Swan, $100. To be one picture, as Mr. Morse may select, twenty-five by thirty inches, as a companion to one painting in Rome, by Mr. Peale.

John B. Van Schaick, $50—à la discrétion.

R. V. DeWitt, $100. One or two pictures; if one, a landscape ; if two, one landscape and one figure.

Stephen Van Rensselaer, Albany. Two or more pictures. (See accompanying letter.)

Robert Donaldson (15 State Street, New York)—school of Athens—$100; size, say thirty inches by thirty-eight or forty.

Frederick Sheldon, $100. To be at the disposal of Mr. Morse; say a landscape of Claude or Poussin, twenty-five by thirty.

G. G. Howland, $150—two landscapes—Mr. Morse's taste—good size, twenty-five by thirty inches, or thereabout, of Poussin or Claude.

Moss Kent, $100—at my discretion.

Charles Walker, $500: 'Miracolo del Servo' of Tintoretto, or some picture of that class.

Moses H. Grinnell, $100. His brother thinks of the picture by Carlo Dolce in the Borghese Palace.

P. and C., a picture each, for $60 each.

J. L. Morton, $30.

Mr. Donaldson's subscription is only in part payment for the copy to be painted for him.

S. Salisbury, a view of the Fountain of Egeria, with figures antique, for $200, twenty-five by thirty inches.

Wm. H. Russell, Esq., of New York, copy of 'The Fine Arts,' by Alessandro Turchi, in the Colonna Palace. Fifty-four by thirty-six inches, $250.

Leaving his children in the care of his relatives, Mr. Morse sailed from New York November 8, 1829, and landed in Liverpool on the 4th day of December. He was lodged at the Liverpool Arms Hotel, where he put up eighteen years before, when he arrived as a student in England. He came on the same errand now, though he had long since become a teacher and master. The few days that he passed in England are recalled by a letter he wrote in Dover to a favorite cousin, on Christmas-day, 1829:

"When I left Liverpool, I took my seat upon the outside of the coach, in order to see as much as possible of the country through which I was to pass. Unfortunately, the fog and smoke were so dense that I could see objects but a few yards from the road. Occasionally, indeed, the fog would become less dense, and we could see the fine lawns of the seats of the nobility and gentry which were scattered on our route, and which still retained their verdure. Now and then the spire and towers of some ancient village church rose out of the leafless trees, beautifully simple in their forms, and sometimes clothed to the very tops with the evergreen ivy. It was severely cold; my eyebrows, hair, cap, and the fur of my cloak, were soon coated with frost, but I determined to keep my seat, though I suffered some from the cold. Their fine natural health, or the frosty weather, gave to the complexions of the peasantry, particularly the females and children, a beautiful rosy bloom. Through all the villages there was the appearance of great comfort and neatness—a neatness, however, very different from ours. Their nicely-thatched cottages bore all the marks of great antiquity, covered with brilliant green moss like velvet, and round the doors and windows were trained some of the many kinds of evergreen vines which abound here. Most of them, also, had a trim court-yard before their doors, planted with laurel, and holly, and box, and sometimes a yew, cut into some fantastic shape. The streets of all the villages were uniformly clean. The whole appearance of the villages was neat and venerable, like some aged matron, who, with all her wrinkles, her stooping form, and gray locks, preserves the dignity of cleanliness in her ancient but becoming costume. At *Trentham*, we passed one of the seats of the Marquis of Stafford, ' *Trentham Hall*.' Here the marquis has a fine gallery of pictures, and among them *Allston's* famous picture of '*Uriel in the Sun*.' I slept the first night in Birmingham, which I had no time to see, on account of darkness, smoke, and fog, three most inveterate enemies to the seekers of the picturesque and of antiquities. In the morning, before daylight, I resumed my journey toward *London*. At ' *Stratford on Avon*,' I breakfasted, but in such haste, as not to be able to visit again the house of *Shakespeare's* birth, or his tomb; this house, however, I visited when in England before. At *Oxford*, the city of so many classical recollections, I stopped but a few moments to dine. I was here, also, when before in England. It is a most splendid city; its spires, and domes, and towers, and pinnacles, rising from amid the trees, give it a magnificent appearance as you approach it. Before we reached *Oxford*, we passed through Woodstock and Blenheim, the seat of the Duke of Marlborough, whose splendid estates are at present suffering from the embarrassment of the present duke, who has ruined his fortunes by his fondness for play. Darkness came on after leaving Oxford. I saw nothing until arriving in the vicinity of the great metropolis, which has, for many miles before you enter it, the appearance of a continuous village. We saw the brilliant gas-lights of its streets, and our coach soon joined the throng of vehicles that rattled over its pavements. I could scarcely realize that I was once more in London, after fourteen years' absence.

"My first visit was to my old friend and fellow-pupil Leslie, who seemed overjoyed to see me, and has been unremitting in his attentions during my stay in London. Leslie I found, as I expected, in high favor with the highest classes of England's noblemen and literary characters. His reputation is well deserved, and will not be ephemeral. I received an invitation to breakfast from Samuel Rogers, Esq., the celebrated poet, which I accepted with my friend Leslie. Mr. Rogers is the author of 'Pleasures of Memory,' of 'Italy,' and other poems. He has not the proverbial lot of the poet—that of being poor—for he is one of the wealthiest bankers, and lives in splendid style. His collection of pictures is very select, chosen by himself, with great taste.

"I attended, a few evenings since, the lecture on anatomy at the Royal Academy, where I was introduced to some of the most distinguished artists; to Mr. Shee, the poet and author as well as painter; to Mr. Howard, the secretary of the Academy; to Mr. Hilton, the keeper; to Mr. Stothard, the librarian, and several others. I expected to have met and been introduced to Sir Thomas Lawrence, the president, but he was absent, and I have not had the pleasure of seeing him. I was invited to a seat with the academicians, as was also Mr. Cole, a member of our Academy in New York. I was gratified in seeing America so well represented in the painters Leslie and Newton. The lecturer also paid, in his lecture, a high compliment to Allston, by a deserved panegyric, and by several quotations from his poems, illustrative of principles which he advanced.

"After the lecture I went home to tea with Newton, accompanied by Leslie, where I found our distinguished countryman, Washington Irving, our secretary of legation, and W. E. West, another American painter, whose portrait of Lord Byron gave him much celebrity. I passed a very pleasant evening, of course. The next day I visited the National Gallery of Pictures, as yet but small, but containing some of the finest paintings in England. Among them is the celebrated 'Raising of Lazarus,' by Sebastian del Piombo, for which a nobleman of this country offered to the late proprietor sixteen thousand pounds sterling, which sum was refused. I visited also Mr. Turner, the best landscape-painter living, and was introduced to him. I went also, a few days since, to the British Museum, which has undergone many improvements since I was last in England, particularly in the addition of a splendid wing, nearly five hundred feet long, containing a noble addition of books—the late king's library of seventy thousand volumes. This museum now contains all the royal libraries, from Henry VIII. down to the present time. The whole number of volumes, I was told by the Rev. Mr. Horne, the librarian (who politely accompanied me through the rooms), was over three hundred thousand. I asked him whether it was accessible to any who wished to consult it, and I learned that the utmost liberality, consistent with the preservation of the books and manuscripts, is observed. He generously offered to procure me admission at all times, when I returned to reside for some time in London. In one part of the museum is the place for consulting books. Here perfect silence is preserved, not a whisper being allowed. If a book is wanted, the name is written on a piece of paper, and handed to one of the librarians or his assistants, of which there are a great many in attendance, who procures it. There were, perhaps, thirty individuals thus seated in the midst of books piled up around them, and, with their eyebrows knit intently searching for some desired information, they looked like so many school-boys hard at work at their lessons. The room containing the king's library is one of the most splendid I ever saw. The columns are of polished granite and marble, and the floors, inlaid with oak and mahogany, were kept as highly polished with wax and are as carefully rubbed as our mahogany furniture. In the room for antiquities are many brought from Egypt by Belzoni, sphinxes, sarcophagi, portions of obelisks, and many inscribed stones. Here also is the celebrated 'Rosetta stone,' with the triple inscription on it, which was captured in Egypt by the English from the French, and is the source of the discovery of a key to the hieroglyphics of Egypt, which is now used to such advantage by Champollion. I did not see so much of London or its curiosities as I should have done at another season of the year. The greater part of the time was night—literally night; for, besides being the shortest days of the year (it not being light until eight o'clock and dark again at four), the smoke and fog have been most of the time so dense that darkness has for many days occupied the hours of daylight. On one day in particular I was writing at the window at two o'clock in the day, and was obliged to desist, not being able to see, while in houses on the opposite side of the street candles were seen in various rooms.

"On the 22d inst., Tuesday, I left London, after having obtained in due form my passports for the Continent, in company with J. Town, Esq., and N. Jocelyn, Esq. (American friends), intending to pass the night at Canterbury, thirty-six miles from London. The day was very unpleasant, very cold, and snowing most of the time. At Blackheath we saw the palace at which the late unfortunate queen of George IV. resided. On the heath, among the bushes, is a low furze, with which it is in part covered; there were encamped in their miserable blanket-huts a gang of gypsies; no wigwams of the Oneidas ever looked so comfortless. On the road we overtook a gypsy girl with a child in her arms, both having the stamp of that singular race strongly marked upon their features: black hair and sparkling black eyes, with a nut-brown complexion, and cheeks of russet red, and not without a shrewd intelligence in their expression. At night about nine o'clock we arrived at the Guildhall Tavern in the celebrated and ancient city of Canterbury. Early in the morning, as soon as we had breakfasted, we visited the superb cathedral. This stupendous pile is one of the most distinguished Gothic structures in the world; it is not only interesting from its imposing style of architecture, but from its numerous historical associations. The first glimpse we caught of it was through and over a rich decayed gate-way to the inclosure of the cathedral-grounds. After passing the gate, the vast pile—with its three great towers, and innumerable turrets, and pinnacles, and buttresses, and arches, and painted windows—rose in majesty before us; the grand centre tower, covered with a gray moss, seemed like an immense mass of the Palisades, struck out with all its regular irregularity, and placed above the surrounding masses of the same gray rocks. The bell of the great tower was tolling for morning service, and yet so distant, from its height, that it was scarcely heard upon the pavement below; we entered the door of one of the towers and came immediately into the nave of the church. The effect of the long aisles and towering clustered pillars and richly-carved screens of a Gothic church upon

12

the imagination can scarely be described—the emotion is that of awe. A short procession was quickly passing up the steps of the choir, consisting of the beadle, or some such officer, with his wand of office, followed by ten boys in white surplices; behind these were the prebends and other officers of the church; the one thin and pale, the other portly and round, with powdered hair, and sleepy, dull, heavy expression of face, much like the face that Hogarth has chosen for the 'Preacher to his Sleepy Congregation.' This personage we afterward heard was Lord Nelson, the brother of the celebrated Nelson, and the heir to his title. The service was read in a hurried and commonplace manner to about thirty individuals, most of whom seemed to be the necessary assistants at the *ceremonies*.

" The effect of the voices in the responses, and the chanting of the boys, reverberating through the aisles and arches and recesses of the church, was peculiarly imposing, but, when the great organ struck in, the emotion of grandeur was carried to its height—I say nothing of devotion; I did not pretend on this occasion to join in it. I own that my thoughts as well as my eyes were roaming to other objects, and gathering around me the thousand recollections of scenes of splendor, and of terror, of bigotry and superstition, which were acted in sight of the very walls by which I was surrounded. Here the murder of Thomas à Becket was perpetrated, there was his miracle-working shrine, visited by pilgrims from all parts of Christendom, and enriched with the most costly jewels that the wealth of princes could purchase and lavish upon it; the very steps worn into deep cavities by the knees of the *devotees*, as they approached the shrine, were ascended by us. There stood the tomb of Henry IV. and his queen, and here was the tomb of Edward, the Black Prince, with a bronze figure of the prince richly embossed and enameled reclining upon the top, and over the canopy were suspended the surcoat and casque, the gloves of mail and shield with which he was accoutred when he fought the famous battle of Cressy; there also stood the marble chair in which the Saxon kings were crowned, and in which, with the natural desire that all seemed to have in such cases, I could not avoid seating myself; from this chair, placed at one end of the nave, is seen to the best advantage the length of the church, five hundred feet in extent. After the service I visited more at leisure the tombs and other curiosities of the church. The precise spot on which Archbishop Becket was murdered is shown, for the spot upon which his head fell on the pavement was cut out as a relic and sent to Rome, and the placed filled in with a fresh piece of stone about four inches square. The cloisters of the church, in ruins, are very splendid in their architecture. The crypt, under the church, is a fine specimen of Saxon architecture, and contains the ruins of the Virgin Mary's chapel, which once was enriched with a silver image of the Virgin, constantly lighted with silver lamps suspended from the ceiling, which was profusely studded with jewels and enameled.

"After leaving the cathedral we visited a part of the ancient walls (Roman remains) of the city; they are very high, with round and square towers at intervals of perhaps two hundred feet; they were coated with a cement filled with flints of all sizes, from the smallest to the bigness of a *cocoa-nut*. We next visited the remains of the monastery of St. Augustin; here stood till within a few years 'Ethelbert's Tower,' a beautiful Saxon ruin, which fell by natural decay, and is entirely gone; the north gate of the monastery is an exquisite piece of Gothic architecture, fast going to decay; a large and annually widening crack in each of the towers gives ominous notice of a fall, and, unless some public spirit is manifested to preserve it, this beautiful gate will speedily share the fate of Ethelbert's Tower. But it is idle to talk of public spirit, as you will agree, when I tell you that the gate is now 'Beer's Brewery,' the room over the gate-way a 'cockpit,' over the door leading into the church is seen the sign of 'Fives and Tennis Court'—the great courtyard is now a 'bowling-green.'

"In the afternoon we left Canterbury and proceeded to Dover, intending to embark the next morning (Thursday, December 24th) for Calais or Boulogne in the steamer. The weather, however, was very unpromising in the morning, being thick and foggy and apparently preparing for a storm; we therefore made up our minds to stay, hoping the next day would be more favorable—but Friday, Christmas-day came with a most violent northeast gale and snow-storm—Saturday the 26th, Sunday the 27th, and at this moment, Monday 28th, the storm is more violent than ever, the streets are clogged with snow, and we are thus embargoed completely for we know not how long a time to come.

"Notwithstanding the severity of the weather on Thursday, we all ventured out through the wind and snow to visit Dover Castle, situated upon the bleak cliffs to the north of the town. After ascending the hill by numerous flights of steps, we crossed the moat which encircles the castle, upon a modern drawbridge. Here, we were accosted by the warder of the castle, a veteran soldier, who with great garrulousness offered his services to conduct us through the works, which cover more than thirty acres. We acccepted his offer and commenced the circuit. 'Queen Elizabeth's Pocket-pistol' was the first object that was shown us—it is a beautiful piece of ordnance of brass, a present to that queen from Holland. It has erroneously been called 'Queen Anne's Pocket-pistol,' and the following motto was said to be upon it:

> 'Keep me bright and rub me clean,
> I'll carry a ball to Calais Green.'

This is not the motto; I copied the following true motto from it on the spot, which some of our Dutch friends must translate for you:

> 'Breck scuret al muer ende wal.
> Bin ic geheten
> Doer berch en dal boert minen bal.
> Van mi gesmeten.'

It is twenty-four feet long, and has date of 1544 upon it; it has lately been mounted upon a splendid bronze carriage, by the order of the Duke of Wellington. The castle, with its various towers and walls, and outworks, has been the constant care of the government for ages. Here are the remains of every age, from the time of the Romans to the present. About the centre of the inclosure stand two ancient ruins—the one, a tower built by the Romans, thirty-six years after Christ; and the other, a rude church built by the Saxons in the sixth century. Other remains of towers and walls indicate the various kinds of defensive and offensive war in different ages, from the time when the round or square tower with its loopholes for the archers and cross-bowmen, and gates secured by heavy portcullis, were a substantial defense, down to the present time, when the bastion of regular sides advances from the glacis, mounted with modern ordnance, keeping at a greater distance the hostile besiegers. Through the glacis in various parts are sally-ports, from one of which, opening toward the road to Ramsgate, I well remember seeing a corporal's guard issue, about fifteen years ago, to take possession of me and my sketch-book, as I sat under a hedge at some distance to sketch the picturesque towers of this castle. Somewhat suspicious of their intentions, I left my retreat, and, by a circuitous route into the town, made my escape, not, however, without ascertaining from behind a distant hedge that I was actually the object of their expedition. They went to the spot where I had been sitting, made a short search, and then returned to the castle through the same sally-port. At that time (a time of war not only with France, but America also), the strictest watch was kept, and to have been caught making the slightest sketch of a fortification would have subjected me to much trouble. Times are now changed, and, had 'Jack Frost' (the only commander of rigor now at the castle) permitted, I might have sketched any part of the interior or exterior. In the interior of the inclosure rises the donjon-keep, higher than any other part of the buildings or fortifications. It is now a magazine of powder. We did not go into any of the excavations underneath the castle, which are very extensive; they are now filled with military stores. After leaving the castle, we visited the shaft which is on the hill back of the tower, and is a passage for facilitating the forming of troops upon the top of the hill; it is a kind of well sunk upon the top of the heights, and met at the bottom by a horizontal tunnel on a level with the streets of the town.

"BOULOGNE-SUR-MER, FRANCE, *December* 29, 1829.

"This morning at ten o'clock, after our tedious detention, we embarked from Dover in a steamer for this place, instead of Calais. I mentioned the steamer; but, cousin, if you have formed any idea of elegance, or comfort, or speed, in connection with the name of steamer, from seeing our fine steamboats, and have imagined that English or French boats are superior to ours, you may as well be undeceived—I know of no description of packet-boats in our waters bad enough to convey the idea. They are small, black, dirty, confined things, which would be suffered to rot at the wharves for want of the least custom from the lowest in our country. You may judge of the extent of the accommodations, when I tell you that there is in them but one cabin—six feet six inches high, fourteen feet long, eleven feet wide, containing eight berths. Our passage was fortunately short, and we arrived in the dominions of 'His most Christian Majesty' Charles X., at five o'clock. The transition from a country where one's own language is spoken, to one where the accents are strange—from a country where the manners and habits are somewhat allied to our own, to one where every thing is different, even to the most trifling article of dress—is very striking on landing, after so short an interval from England to France. The pier-head at our landing was filled with human beings in strange costume, from the gray *surtout* and belt of the *gendarmes*, to the broad twilled and curiously plaited caps of the mas-

culine women, which latter beings, by-the-by, are the licensed porters
of baggage to the custom-house.

"PARIS, *January* 7, 1830.

"Here have I been, in this great capital of the Continent, since
the first day of the year. I shall remember my first visit to Paris
from the circumstance that, at the dawn of day of the new year, we
passed the 'Porte St.-Denis' into the narrow and dirty streets of
this great metropolis.

"The Louvre was the first object we visited. Our passports
obtained us ready admittance; and, although our fingers and feet
were almost frozen, we yet lingered three hours in the grand 'gallery of pictures.' Indeed, it is a long walk simply to pass up and
down the long hall, the end of which, from the opposite end, is
scarcely visible, but is lost in the mist of distance. On the walls
are twelve hundred and fifty of some of the *chefs-d'œuvre* of painting. Here I have marked out several which I shall copy on my
return from Italy. I have my residence at present at the Hôtel de
Lille, which is situated very commodiously in the midst of all the
most interesting objects of curiosity to a stranger in Paris—the
palace of the Tuileries, the Palais Royal, the Bibliothèque Royale,
or royal library, and numerous other places, all within a few paces
of us. On New-Year's day the equipages of the nobility and foreign ambassadors, etc., who paid their respects to the king and the
Duke of Orleans, made considerable display in the Place du Carrou-
sel and in the court of the Tuileries.

"At an exhibition of manufactures of porcelain, tapestry, etc., in
the Louvre, where were some of the most superb specimens of art
in the world in these articles, we also saw the Duchesse de Berri.
She is the mother of the little Duc de Bordeaux, who, you know, is
the heir-apparent to the crown of France. She was simply habited
in a blue pelisse and blue bonnet, and would not be distinguished
in her appearance from the crowd except by her attendants in livery. I cannot close, however, without telling you what a delightful evening I passed evening before last at General Lafayette's. He
had a *soirée* on that night, at which there were a number of Americans. When I went in, he instantly recognized me, took me by
both hands, said he was expecting to see me in France, having
read in the American papers that I had embarked. He met me
apparently with great cordiality, then introduced me to each of his
family, to his daughters, to Madame Lasterie and her two daughters
(very pretty girls), and to Madame Ramousal, and two daughters

of his son, G. W. Lafayette, also very accomplished and beautiful girls. The General inquired how long I intended to stay in France, and pressed me to come and pass some time at La Grange, when I return from Italy. General Lafayette looks very well, and seems to have the respect of all the best men in France. At his *soirée* I saw the celebrated Benjamin Constant, one of the most distinguished of the liberal party in France. He is tall and thin, with a very fair, white complexion, and long white silken hair, moving with all the vigor of a young man."

The three years that Mr. Morse passed in Europe at this time are reflected in such letters to his friends, and in fragments of diaries kept in tiny "scratch-books." These little books, which he made and could easily carry in his vest pocket, he filled with drawings of objects that met his eye—often pictures of peculiar people, and added brief notes with pencil. Before he left New York, he was offered pecuniary inducements to become the foreign correspondent of newspapers, but he made no positive engagements, and he says in an early letter : "I fear it will consume more of my time than the thing is worth ; my time here is worth a guinea a minute in the way of my profession. I find my pen and pencil are enemies to each other. I must write less and paint more."

Leaving Paris, on his journey to Italy, he rested a few days at Lyons, in the study of the antiquities and architecture of that interesting city. His note-book has a pencil-drawing of a "Sister of Charity" whom he met in a hospital, and whose face suggests to him a picture of Mercy. The gold-works and the silver-factories being explored, he continues his course southward, mentioning a "telegraph making signals" on a hill which he passed. The olive and orange trees soon tell him that he is in a warmer clime. He spent Sunday, January 24, 1830, in Avignon, the ancient city of the popes in the time of the exile, and worshiped in the cathedral-church of St.-Agricol, as there was not a Protestant place of worship in the city. Here, for the first time in his life, he saw a military pageant contribute to the effect of divine service. " A superb military band of music, followed by troops, entered the church ; the nave was filled with people, principally women ; drums were beating and fifes playing ; the troops formed two lines from the altar to the great door, and their officers marched up through the lines and took seats within the railing of the altar. On each side of the altar fierce-looking soldiers stood, with long beards, and armed with battle-axes, their high, cylindrical, bear-skin caps giving them a height almost gigantic. The church seemed to be a military garrison. At the word of command drums and trumpets were sounded, and a little bell announced the priest, a venerable man, in a green, embroidered dress, who performed the service. The band of twenty-seven performers in the transept on the left commenced playing, and produced the most thrilling music." He did not enjoy the service, with the exception of the music, of which he heard more in the evening, and expressed himself "enchanted" with it. The beauty of the women draws from him this remark : "We have observed more beautiful faces among the women in a single day at Avignon, than we saw during two weeks at Paris."

"*Monday, January 25th.*—We ascended the hill of the Dons, upon which the palace of the popes is built. The hill is terraced, and is ascended in many places by flights of rude stone steps. The staircase to the terrace of the palace is peculiarly grand. The interior of the chapel, which we entered, has been much abused, but had evidently been splendidly decorated. The paintings and statuary are not of a high order. The altars, of variously-colored marbles, are very rich. The votive offerings were amusing—execrable paintings, representing scenes of deliverance : a man has a stone falling on his head, another jumping from a tower, waxen legs and arms—a curious assemblage. From the top of the great tower we had a magnificent prospect—the mountains in the far distance, and the Rhone winding through an immense plain studded with hamlets, and dividing into two branches, uniting again. To the west rose the picturesque castle and towers of Villeneuve, having for a background the mountains toward Nismes. To the south a river is seen sparkling through the plain, and rushing to meet the Durance. From the hill I made several sketches. The museum, where are some fine pictures, was, unfortunately, closed. Our landlord told me that Napoleon I. often stopped with him, and his officers said that he was so much pleased with his fare, that he was accustomed to say, when his fare was bad in distant places, 'This is not so comfortable as at Madame Pierrori's, in Avignon.' "

"*January 26th.*—At six o'clock last evening left Avignon on the *diligence*. At precisely twelve o'clock to-day the Mediterranean opened, with its blue expanse, before us; the castellated islands in the harbor of Marseilles, and the lug-sailed boats, like birds, resting on the bosom of the waters; the high, fortified mountain beyond the harbor—made a scene of exceeding beauty as we approached the town. Halting to be searched for wine, we entered and found comfortable quarters at the Hôtel Beauvau. One or two days in the city and he went to Toulon, the gates of which had to be opened before the diligence could enter; and then we passed through a row of sentinels and over a drawbridge, again through files of sentinels, and the arched passages of the walls into the streets of the city."

Having explored this great naval station, and critically examined the vessels-of-war, and noticed the five hundred galley-slaves, with dresses to mark the degree of crime for which they were condemned to this service, Mr. Morse remarks:

"The stone-houses for covering the ships while they are building, are substantial, having a Gothic arched roof, supported by stone arches, resting upon eight solid piers of stone, about twenty feet apart, and perhaps fifty feet high. In the model-room are models of vessels of all classes, methods of drawing up ships on railways, plans of dry-docks, and other marine machinery, exceedingly beautiful. The city is just now agitated by a most melancholy incident. A sergeant had formed the intention of killing his captain, in resentment for some supposed injury. The *colonel* of the regiment, universally popular with his troops and with the inhabitants of the city, ignorant altogether of the feelings of this man toward him, beckoned him to come to him after the parade. The sergeant, supposing that by some means the colonel had obtained knowledge of his intentions, leveled his gun and shot him dead upon the spot. The colonel is lying in his house, which I passed, and the wretched culprit I saw under guard marched to prison. He will be shot in a few days."

Mr. Morse pursued his journey, by private carriage, with a pleasant party of friends, stopping at every place of interest on the road. Nice, at that time, was in the territory of Italy, and the King of Sardinia, Charles Felix, was making a royal visit in the city when Mr. Morse arrived:

"Entering the cathedral, we saw the king seated on a throne, under a splendid canopy of crimson and gold, on the right of the altar. Mass was celebrated, and the king then rose, bowed toward the altar, crossed himself, and retired."

Mr. Morse delayed a day or two in this delightful city, which has become the great winter resort of invalids and pleasure-seekers, and then, by the famous Cornice road, went on to Genoa. The railway now carries the traveler through mountains that were then slowly traversed by coach and horses; the romantic passes that were then the marvel and delight of passengers with steady nerves, are only matters of history. He says:

"At eleven we had attained a height of at least two thousand feet, and the precipices became frightful, sweeping down into long ravines to the very edge of the sea, and then the road would wind at the very edge of the precipice two or three thousand feet deep. Such scenes pass so rapidly it is impossible to make note of them. From the heights on which La Turbia stands, with its dilapidated walls, we see the beautiful city of Monaco, on a tongue of land extending into the sea."

Now the road began to descend along the most frightful precipices and ravines; the slopes of the mountains were terraced and covered with vines, where it would seem almost impossible to climb. Mr. Morse rested at Mentone, "a beautiful place for an artist," and then went to San Remo, where he spent the night. Porto Maurice and Oniglia, familiar names to travelers, he mentions, and he makes a sketch of the cupola of a little church in Oniglia, and of some ruins in the rear of the inn at which he dined. His path lay along rugged precipices, dizzy heights, lofty arches, and dangerous passes; he lodged at Albenza, and the next day passed over some of the most stupendous parts of the road, admiring the engineering skill that accomplished it, and the enterprise that attempted it. Having spent the next night at Savona, he reached Genoa on the 6th of February, and was permitted to enter, after being searched for "powder and tobacco." Its palaces and churches astonished and delighted him, and, after a few days of sight-seeing, he posted to Pisa, where he studied and sketched the Duomo, the Baptistry, the Leaning Tower, and the Campo Santo. He did not linger in Florence, as he would return to study the treasures of art in that city at his leisure. He arrived in Rome, February 20, 1830. Taking lodgings at No. 17 Via de Prefetti, he entered at once upon the· work for which he had come. He writes, March 7th:

"I have begun to copy the 'School of Athens,' from Raffaelle, for Mr. R. Donaldson. The original is on the walls of one of the celebrated Camera of Raffaelle in the Vatican; it is in fresco, and occupies one entire side of ·the room. It is a difficult picture to copy, and will occupy five or six weeks, certainly. Every moment of my time, from early in the morning until late at night, when not in the Vatican, is occupied in seeing the exhaustless stores of curiosities in art and antiquities with which this wonderful city abounds. I find I can endure great fatigue, and my spirits are good, and I feel strong for the pleasant duties of my profession. I feel particularly anxious that every gentleman who has given me a commission shall be more than satisfied that he has received an equivalent for the sum generously advanced to me. But I find that to accomplish this, I shall need all my strength and time for more than a year to come, and that will be little enough to do myself and them justice. I am delighted with my situation, and more than ever convinced of the wisdom of my course in coming to Italy.

"*March* 17*th*.—Mr. Fenimore Cooper and family are here. I have passed many pleasant hours with them, particularly one beautiful moonlight evening, visiting the Coliseum. After the Holy Week, I shall visit Naples, probably with Mr. Theodore Woolsey, who is now in Rome.

"*March* 18*th*.—Ceremonies at the Consistory; delivery of the cardinals' hats; at nine o'clock went to the Vatican." (Here is a picture of what he saw.) "Two large fantails, with ostrich-feathers; ladies penned up; pope; cardinals kiss his hand ·in rotation; address in Latin, tinkling, like water gurgling from a bottle; the English cardinal first appeared, went up, and was embraced and kissed on each cheek by the pope; then followed the others in the same manner; then each new cardinal embraced in succession all the other cardinals; after this, beginning with the English cardinal, each went to the pope, and he, putting on their heads the cardinal's hat, blessed them in the name of the Trinity. They then kissed the ring on his hand, and his toe, and retired from the throne. The pope then rose, blessed the assembly, by making the sign of the cross three times in the air, with his two fingers, and left the room. His dress was a plain mitre of gold tissue, a rich garment of gold and crimson, embroidered, a splendid clasp of gold, about six inches long by four wide, set with precious stones, upon his breast. He is very decrepit, limping or tottering along, has a defect in one eye, and his countenance has an expression of pain, especially as the new cardinals approached his toe. The cardinals followed the pope, two and two, with their train-bearers. After a few minutes the doors opened again, and a procession headed by singers entered, chanting as they went; the cardinals followed them with their train-bearers. They passed through the Consistory, and thus closed the ceremony of presenting the cardinals' hats. A multitude of attendants, in various costumes, surrounded the pontiff's throne, during the ceremony, among whom was Bishop Dubois, of New York."

Mr. Morse's note-books are filled with mere mention of pictures in the several rooms of the various palaces and galleries that he explored, and of incidents that marked his daily life in Rome. A few days—in the abrupt and abbreviated terms of his diary—will show the habit of the man:

" *Thursday, March* 18, 1830.—Colonna Palace; Earl Shrewsbury occupies it. *First Room.*—' Death of Cleopatra,' by Muratori, pupil of Guido, well composed; head of Cleopatra, good. ' Rebecca at the Well,' by the same; good parts, but much mannered. *Second Room.* —' The Colonna Family rising from the Tomb,' by Pietro da Cortona; sky, good. A beautiful piece of still-life, by Castiglione; spoils. *Third Room.* —' The Audience Chambers,' exceedingly splendid in tapestry, etc. *Fourth Room.*—' Calvin and Luther,' by Titian. Portrait of one of the Colonna family, called the ' Green Picture,' by Paul Veronese, proves that harmony may be produced in one color; curtain in the background, *hot* green, middle tint; sleeves of the arms, *cool;* vest, which is in the mass of light, as well as the lights of the curtain, WARM; white collar, which is the highest light, cool!!! ' Holy Family, etc., resting on their Flight to Egypt,' by Bonifacio, fine for color, supports my theory. *Fifth Room.*—A most splendid hall. ' St. John preaching in the Wilderness,' by M. Angelo Battaglia; splendid for color, and light and shade; the dove over the head of John is full of light.

It is a picture that bears examination; it has a fine depth of *chiaro-oscuro*. Four pictures by Orizonti, good, but mannered. Several good landscapes, in temper, by Gaspar Poussin. A strange picture by Nicolo Lunno, the master of Pietro Perugino, 'The Devil seizing a Child,' the mother praying to the Madonna, who with a club is beating off the devil. 'St. Sebastian,' by Guido; fine for *chiaro-oscuro*. A grand full-length of 'Lucretia Colonna,' by Vandyck; shining like a diamond. 'Holy Family,' etc., by Titian; splendid for color.

ACADEMY OF ST. LUKE'S.

" ' Raphael's Skull; ' Harlow's picture of the making of a cardinal. Said to have been painted in twelve days. I don't believe it. 'The Angels appearing to the Shepherds,' by Bassan; good for color—much trash in the way of portraits. Lower rooms contain the pictures for the premiums; some good, all badly colored. *Third Room.*—Bass-reliefs for the premiums. *Fourth Room.*—Smaller premium pictures; bad. *Fifth Room.*—Drawings; the oldest best, modern bad.

" Church of St. Peter, interior of the prison, etc. St. Andrew's Church, too dark when we went in to see the famous frescos of Domenichino.

" *Friday, March 19th.*—We went to St. Peter's to see the procession of cardinals; singing in the capella. Cardinals walked two and two through St. Peter's, knelt on purple-velvet cushions before the capella in prayer, then successively kissed the toe of the bronze image of St. Peter, as they walked past it. This statue of St. Peter as a work of art is as execrable as possible; part of the toe and foot is worn away and polished, not by the kisses, but by the wiping of the foot after the kisses by the next comer, preparatory to kissing it, sometimes with the coat-sleeve by a beggar, with the corner of the cloak by the gentlemen, the shawl by the females, and with a nice cambric handkerchief by the attendant at the ceremony, who wiped the toe after each cardinal's performance. This ceremony is variously performed; some give it a single kiss and go away, others kiss the toe and then touch the forehead to it, others again kiss the toe, touch the forehead to it, and kiss the toe again, repeating the operation sometimes three times. This day is one of the numerous festivals of the Church; it is St. Joseph's day; the shops are shut, and before many of them, on the side pavement, are tables decorated with evergreens and flowers, on which are large pans of fried cakes, hot from the kettle of oil in which they are fried, and which is in the centre of a group of cooks busily engaged in preparing these cakes for their customers, who perform a meritorious act doubtless in eating them this day—St. Joseph being very fond of these doughnuts, as we should call them in New England. Women with enormous buckles.

" *Saturday, March 20th.— Giustiniani Palazzo.*—Bass-reliefs in the yard, stucco; nothing good. *Braschi Palace.*—A most splendid staircase; the richest in Rome that I have seen in the palaces. An assortment of St. Sebastians by the dozen; two in the hall, one in the second room. *Third Room.*—A Titian, ' Woman taken in Adultery;' fine for arrangement of color. A Murillo, 'The Assumption of the Virgin.' 'Angel Boys' Heads;' good. 'Marriage of Cana,' by Garofalo; some of the costumes, fine. In the large hall is a very fine statue of ' Antinous,' colossal in size and of the purest form. A sweet portrait in Lely's style of a female like N. R.

" *Palazzo Massino.*—An exquisite statue of a Discobolus, and some good pictures.

" *Palazzo Mattei.*—Fine bass-reliefs in the court-yard and exquisitely sculptured ornaments exposed to the weather. On the box, ' *Scritture par. la Sacra Rota.*' Ancient seats in the stairway. View from the top of the Campidoglio : to the east, Albano, Frascato, and, more toward the north, Preneste, and in the valley, at a great distance, Cercello; went to the very top and stood by the statue on the pinnacle.

" *Sunday, March 21st.— Chiesa d' Orsoline.*—Nun taking the veil. Illustrissima Signori Anna Mazzetti, to assume the name of S. Maria Clementina di S. Camillo. Church small, altar rich; cardinal enters; nun enters splendidly dressed, lace over blue; kneels before the cardinal; a companion; dress of cardinal, a gold-tissue mitre, robes of white, fringed with gold lace; two attendants hold up the skirts of his robe while he addresses them; nun's hair much dressed with curls and silver and diamond ornaments of wheat-ears, necklace, and ear-rings; attendant of nun in rich blue, silk turban embroidered with gold; address long; music; cardinal puts on a splendid mitre and takes the rood or crozier. First act closes by a procession out of the church, headed by the cardinal and nun. Music as an interlude. Cardinal enters without nun for a few minutes, during which music plays rapid airs; nuns' voices in another room; kissing the other nuns. Could not see for a large pillar and bonnet.

" Chiesa Nuova, at seven o'clock in the evening; a sacred opera called ' The Death of Aaron ; ' church dark, women not admitted ; bell rings, and a priest before the altar chants a prayer, after which a boy about twelve years old apparently addresses the assembly from the pulpit ; I know not the drift of his discourse, but his utterance was like the same gurgling process which I noticed in the orator who addressed the pope ; it was precisely like the fitful tone of the Oneida interpreter.

" *Tuesday, March 23d.*—At the Vatican all the morning. While preparing my palette, a monk, decently habited for a monk, who seemed to have come to the Vatican for the purpose of viewing the pictures, after a little time approached me, and, with a very polite bow, offered me a pinch of snuff, which of course I took, bowing in return, when he instantly asked me alms. I gave him a *bajocco*, for which he seemed very grateful. Truly this is a nation of beggars.

" *Wednesday, March 24th.*—Vatican all the morning ; saw in returning a great number of priests, with a white bag over the left shoulder, and begging of the persons they met. This is another instance of begging and robbing confined to one class.

" *Thursday, March 25th.*—Festa of the Annunciation, Vatican shut. Doors open at eight of the Chiesa di Minerva ; obtained a good place for seeing the ceremony ; at half-past nine the cardinals began to assemble ; Cardinal Barberini officiated in robes, white, embroidered with gold ; singing ; taking off and putting on mitres, etc. ; jumping up and bowing, kissing the ring on the finger of the cardinal ; putting incense into censers ; monotonous reading or rather whining of a few lines of prayer in Latin ; flirting censers at each cardinal in succession ; cardinals bowing to one another ; many attendants at the altar ; cardinals embrace one another. After mass a contribution among the cardinals in rich silver plate. Enter the virgins in white, with· crowns, two and two, and candles ; they kiss the hem of the garment of one of the cardinals ; they are accompanied by three officers, and exit. Cardinals' dresses exquisitely plaited (sixty-two cardinals in attendance).

" CAMPIDOGLIO EXPOSITION OF THE WORKS OF THE LIVING ARTISTS IN ROME.

" *First Room.*—Portrait of female at the toilet, by Geddes, English ; for effect, *chiaro-oscuro*, and coloring, good. Deluge by Schnelz, French ; faults of the French school. Large picture of a sick child brought to the Virgin by her relative, by the same artist ;

parts full of feeling, particularly the boy himself, and the sister of the boy; parts well painted, but bad in general effect, and badly colored. A great picture of the assassination of Vitellius, by Quecy, a Roman artist; bad throughout. A sweet picture of Italian peasant at a fountain, by Weller of Mannheim; the costumes and indeed all beautifully painted. Two flower-pieces, by Senff, a Prussian; good. Statuary—a fine bass-relief of Christians about to be torn in pieces by a tiger, by Tenerrani, of Carrara. Statue, female playing on a guitar, by Scolari; good.

"PALAZZO SINIBALDI.—At half-past eight, the company began to assemble in the splendid saloon of this palace, to which I was invited; the singers, about forty in number, were upon a stage erected at the end of the room; white drapery hung behind festoons with laurel-wreaths (the walls were painted in fresco); four female statues standing on globes upheld seven long wax-lights; the instrumental musicians, about forty, were arranged at the foot of these statues. Sala was lighted principally by six glass chandeliers. Much female beauty in the room, dresses very various. Signora Luigia Tardi sung with much judgment, and was received with great applause. A little girl, apparently about twelve years old, played upon the harp in a most exquisite manner, and called forth *bravas* of the Italians, and of the foreigners bountifully. The manners of the audience were the same as those of fashionable society in our own country, and indeed in any other country. The display in dress, however, less tasteful than I have seen in New York; but, in truth, I have not seen more beauty and taste in any country, combined with cultivation of mind and delicacy of manner, than in our own. At one o'clock in the morning, or half-past six, Italian time, the concert was over.

" *Friday, March* 26*th.*—I have observed almost every morning at the *caffè* beggars of some description, and different every morning. This morning, a tall priest with a tin box; a few mornings ago, friar with white mask, and his hat hung on his back. While waiting to enter the Sinibaldi Palace last evening, being too early, I walked with Mr. S. in a direction where we heard some chanting in the street. Proceeding down a back street or two, we came to the portico of a church illuminated by a multitude of wax-candles burning before the Virgin; a crowd filled the portico, and had assembled in great numbers about the railing. We stood at a little distance looking on. The officiating priest in the proper time held up the Host, at which all the people knelt, far and near.

"*Saturday, March 27th.* — SCIARRA PALACE, *First Room.*— Copy·'Transfiguration,' by Carlo Napolitano, not G. Romana, as erroneously said; two deep-toned pictures, by Valentin; an exquisite little picture, 'Mother and Child,' by Titian; mother's dress, warm crimson, warm flesh, principal light; deep-blue ultra under the child and back of the mother; green curtain in background.

"*Second Room.*—Two small Claudes—one 'Lake of Bracino,' on silver—the other, 'Flight into Egypt,' on copper; landscapes by Both, very good; 'Castle Nuovo,' in Naples,.by Canelletti.

"*Third Room.*—Voucts's picture of the 'Present, Past, and Future.'

"*Fourth Room.*—'The Minstrels' of Titian; Raphael's portrait of himself; Leonardo da Vinci's 'Modesty and Vanity;' 'The Three Card-Players,' by Caravaggio.

EXPOSITION AT THE CAMPIDOGLIO (CONTINUED).

"*Second Room.*—Wyatt's statue of a female entering the bath, an exquisite work.

"*Third Room.*—Gibson's statue of a female untying her sandal; 'Judith and Holofernes,' by Cav. Vernet; finely conceived, especially the character and figure of Judith; the color is generally bad, but the lower part is well painted and well toned; there is a masterly precision throughout, every thing is firmly and correctly expressed; the head of Holofernes is French, too strongly charged, but well meant. Portrait of the Pope, by Vernet; very rich, and parts well painted, but is too much cut up. 'Nun taking the Veil,' by Roger, French painter; good in parts, especially the background. 'Greek Girl,' by Adkins, English, and a female portrait by the same artist; both rich for color. 'Warrior preparing for Battle, taking Leave of his Mistress,' by Levern, English; sweet, rich-toned little picture 'Albanese Female,' nearly full length, by Vernet; parts well expressed,.but chalky in color. 'Friar in the Catacombs, frightened to Death,' a story well told, but too brown, by Diofabi, a Russian. Portraits, full length, in St. Peter's, by Cavalleri, of Turin, well drawn in the architecture. A 'Mountebank Exhibition,' by Weller, of Mannheim, contains great variety of character and costume, and is carefully and beautifully finished; the Amphitheatre Marcellus forms the greater part of the background. A landscape by Karezewski, a Pole; parts, good. 'The Vintage,' by Levern, English; an exquisite picture, golden in tone, and well composed. A good landscape, by Desoulavy, English. A fine landscape, well colored, and in fine keeping, by Wilson, a Scotch painter. 'Interior of an Italian Kitchen,' by Bravo, a Dane.

" Went to the Coliseum. Cross in the centre of the arena has upon it this inscription, on a little white board nailed on it: 'Baciando la Santa Croce si acouistono due cente geomo d'indulgenza.' The rooks were chattering about the tops of the ruined arches, and the smaller birds were singing in the bushes that covered the dilapidated walls. Went to the baths of Titus, which are near the Coliseum. Here are the fine arabesques, from which it is said Raphael copied his 'Logge.' It is a mistake; he may have taken some few detached parts, but his ' Logge ' are original. He has caught, indeed, the spirit of those arabesques, all which is perfectly fair. They are exquisitely beautiful, but going fast to decay.

" *Monday, March 29th.*—Early this morning was introduced to the cavalier Horace Vernet, Principal of the French Academy. Found him in the beautiful gardens of the Academy. He came in a *négligé* dress—a cap, or rather turban, of various colors, a party-colored belt, and a cloak. He received me kindly; walked through the antique gallery of casts, a long room, and a splendid collection, selected with great judgment; the collection, also, of architectural casts was splendid.

" Visited Mr. Gibson's studio, and Mr. Wyatt's. Mr. Gibson is a man of real genius. He is not far behind Thorwaldsen. His groups of the ' Seizure of Hylas,' and of ' Psyche borne by Zephyrs,' are quite antique in their character and feeling. Mr. Wyatt's are also excellent. His ' Nymph entering the Bath ' is as chaste in sentiment, and as beautiful for character, as I have ever seen of a nude figure.

" *Tuesday, March 30th.*—Went to the Vatican in the morning. While recreating, took a lounge in the upper *logge* of the Vatican, which contain some curious maps of the world, and its various parts, painted in fresco on the walls. The first map has on it the Island of S. Brandani, mentioned by Irving in his ' Columbus;' the second is New Spain, on which North America is represented, the whole northern part, from a parallel about Cape Hatteras, as ' Terra sive Mare Incognitum;' the third is Japan; the fourth, America, or Peru; the fifth, ' Tartarorum regiones;' sixth, India beyond the Ganges, or China; seventh, India this side the Ganges; eighth, Persia; ninth, Turkey beyond Europe; tenth, Africa; eleventh, Africa, eastern part; twelfth and thirteenth, the world, on the first of which is America, Terra Labrador, and C. del Labrado; and from them to C. della Florida, nearly all the way high ridges of mountains are made to extend from the coast far into the interior. A little south of Labrador is 'Terra de Baccalaos;' Canada is down, and but one of the lakes, which is not named; all beyond is 'terra incognita;' fourteenth, is Greenland, and congelations, with houses and Indians on the ice, and reindeer; fifteenth, much injured, appears to be Russia; sixteenth, Moscovia; seventeenth, Finland, Lapland, etc.; eighteenth, Hungary, and Poland, etc.; nineteenth, Denmark, Holland, Germany; twentieth, India, Canaan, and Palestine, more beautifully executed than the rest, the Holy Land in gold; twenty-first, Asia Minor; twenty-second, Greece; twenty-third, Italy; twenty-fourth, France; twenty-fifth, Spain; twenty-sixth, Great Britain.

" *Wednesday, March* 31*st.*—Early this morning was waked by the roar of cannon. Learned that it was the anniversary of the present pope's election. Went to the Vatican; the colonnade was filled with the carriages of the cardinals; that of the new English cardinal, Weld, was the most showy.

"There is a corporal's guard of soldiers stationed before the Castle of St. Angelo, and another at the entrance of the colonnade to St. Peter's. Their principal duty seems to be to shoulder arms at a certain signal, and present arms when a cardinal's carriage passes.

" *Thursday Morning, April* 1*st.*—At the Vatican all day. Open to the public. Went with Mr. Cooper into the room of the mosaics, which I had never visited before. There are ten thousand three hundred and sixteen different tints in glass, each in separate boxes, occupying a hall of great length. The street leading to the Vatican is very narrow, and filled with the meanest shops.

"Went in the evening to the *soirée* of the Chevalier Vernet, Director of the French Academy. He is a gentleman of elegant manners, and sees, at his *soirées*, the first society in Rome. His wife is highly accomplished, and his daughter is a beautiful girl, full of vivacity, and speaks English fluently. Books of plates were on the table, among them an interesting work by Williman, published in Paris, on costume, etc. During the evening there was music. His daughter played on the piano, and others sang. There was chess, and, at a sideboard, a few played cards. The style was simple; every one at ease, like our *soirées* in America. Several noblemen and dignitaries of the Church were present.

"*Friday, April 2d.*—Vatican all day.   In the evening went to
the Church of the Trinita di Monte, and heard the exquisite singing
of the nuns.   After vespers witnessed a ceremony in which two
boys, of eight and ten years of age, were brought to the altar before
the officiating cardinal.   They knelt before him while he read from
a book held by an attendant.   Assistants were on either side ; some
held lighted wax-candles, others held up the robes of the cardinal,
and others prompted the boys in the parts they were to act.   During
the ceremony a white band was tied round the heads of each of the
boys.   In conclusion, the cardinal and attendants retired and the
boys knelt on each side of a man at the altar, who appeared to be
their parent.

"*Sunday, April 4th.*—Palm Sunday.   Sistine Chapel, half-past
nine o'clock.   Cardinals ; rich dresses, purple and gold ; Cardinal
Weld's the most splendid.   Pass through files of guards ; ladies outside the bar ; ambassadors' boxes ; royal box ; cardinal, attendants
in white, gentlemen of the cardinal.   Ten o'clock, commence.   Cardinals put on mitre and received palms, which are of straw, with
crosses, etc., upon them.   They retire to their seats, give palms to
attendants, who, at a signal, prostrate them on the floor, like ground
arms.   (Cardinal Barberini officiated instead of the pope.)   In receiving the palm from the cardinal, each recipient kisses the two
hands of the cardinal.   Procession commences at half-past ten.   A
cross, with two candles on each side.   Cardinals return during
chanting from the choir.   Cardinals divested of their finery, and appear as ordinary, in purple and ermine.   Putting incense into censers.   Prayer-book.   Many attendants to assist in the ceremony of
opening a book.   Cardinal says three or four words in a drawling
tone.   One, in a drawling, school-boy tone, reads from a book in the
middle of the room.   Great work made in bringing .back the book.
Chanting ; which, for the most part, is a monotonous brawling.
Some good singing, and then a long, tedious tone of recitation in
Latin.   History of the crucifixion from the Testament, of more than
three-quarters of an hour.   (Attendants of the cardinals have olive-
branches instead of palms.)   A pause, and all the cardinals kneel.
One next takes the book, shows it to cardinal, bows, turns round,
bows each side, advances one side of the altar, and kneels ; advances
to the altar, bows, and kneels again ; lays the book on the altar,
bows, and kneels again.   It remains a few seconds, and is removed
again in the same manner.   A few words are again read from it ;
the cardinals stand, and all together appear talking in the most rapid

manner to each other. They all sit, and chanting commences, which lasts a few minutes. Twenty-two cardinals present. Robing and disrobing officiating cardinals. Incense is now puffed four times before ·each cardinal; the attendant bows, puffs four times, and goes to the next, and so on. A little reading by the officiating cardinal at the altar. Count Ferroneye among the spectators, with the three highest orders in Europe on his breast—the Golden Fleece, the Holy Ghost, and the Grand Cross of St.-Louis. Cardinal Giulio Maria della Somaglia in state, on an elevated bed of cloth-of-gold and black, embroidered with gold; his head on a black-velvet cushion, embroided with gold; dressed in his robes as when alive. He officiated, I was told, on Ash Wednesday. Four wax-lights, two on each side of the bed; room, crimson and gold; three guards at the foot of the bed; great throng of people of all grades through the suite of apartments—the Cancellerie—in which he lived. They were very splendid, chiefly of crimson velvet, and damask, and gold. The cardinal has died unpopular, for he has left nothing to his servants by his will; he directed, however, that no expense should be spared in his funeral, wishing that it might be splendid; but, unfortunately for him, he has died precisely at that season of the year (the Holy Week) when alone it is impossible, according to the Church customs, to give him a splendid burial.

" *Monday, April 5th.*—Visited the Sapienza; the museum is very creditable; the collection of butterflies very complete; the skeletons of horse, cow, ram, etc., beautifully prepared; also the birds; a *lusus naturœ*, two children preserved in spirits, united somewhat similar to the Siamese boys.

" Cabinets of mineralogy and chemistry very good; the professor exceedingly polite and attentive. Campidoglio; part of it a prison; prisoners with little bags on the end of rod, like fishing-lines from the windows. Palatine Hill. Gardens of the Villa Spada, which are built upon the ruins of the palace of the Cæsars; the gardens are now neatly laid out in walks, arched over with trees and flowering shrubs.

" *Tuesday, April 6th.*—I amused myself before going into the Vatican by a walk in St. Peter's; the various and strange actions and scenes that are here witnessed strike a stranger with wonder. In one of the chapels there is the monotonous chanting of the priests at their prayers; all kinds of costumes were seen in various parts of the church, kneeling in acts of devotion, or in conversation in groups; boys were carrying candlesticks larger than themselves to furnish some of the numerous altars; and at the confessionals were motley groups, some in the act of confession, others waiting their turn; there were ragged beggars and gentlemen, the simply-dressed nun, with her white-muslin veil, and the gay-colored dames of the villages of the Sabine Hills.

"Went to the Vatican, and learned that it is shut for ten days. Took my picture to my room.

"*Wednesday, April 7th.*—This morning the beggar at the *café* was an old, gray-bearded man, with a brass box about as large as a pocket-lantern, and which might easily be mistaken for one; it was battered and bright, with the crucifix embossed in front. The old man sat on one of the seats of the *café* for a moment, opened his box and counted his receipts; the largest piece was a one-half *biocchi*, and these were few; he muttered a prayer over them as he put them back, and tottered out of the house. Went to the Piazza Navone, being market-day, in search of prints; the scene here is very amusing, from the variety of wares exposed, and the confusion of noises and tongues, and now and then a jackass swelling the chorus with his most exquisite tones.

"At three o'clock went to St. Peter's to see ceremonies at the Sistine Chapel. Cardinal asleep; monotonous bawling, long and tedious; candles put out one by one, fourteen in number; no ceremonies at the altar; cardinals present, nineteen; seven yawns from the cardinals; tiresome and monotonous beyond description. After three hours of this most tiresome chant, all the candles having been extinguished, the celebrated '*Miserere*' commenced. It is indeed sublime, but I think loses much of its effect from the fatigue of body, and mind, too, in which it is heard by the auditors; the '*Miserere*' is the composition of the celebrated Allegri, and, for giving the effect of wailing and lamentation, without injury to harmony, is one of the most perfect of compositions. The manner of sustaining a strain of concord by new voices, now swelling high, now gradually decaying away, now sliding imperceptibly into discord, and suddenly breaking into harmony, is admirable; the imagination is alive, and fancies thousands of people in the deepest contrition; it closed by the cardinals clapping their hands for the earthquake.

"*Thursday Morning, April 8th.*—Holy Thursday; rose early, and at eight o'clock rode to St. Peter's and ascended the long flight of steps to the Vatican; placed ourselves in the crowd of ladies and gentlemen, ready to rush into the Sistine Chapel the moment it should open. The Swiss Guards were this day dressed in bright hel-

mets of steel, with breastplates of the same material, and some of
their officers with the ancient armor upon their shoulders and arms.
After waiting some time, the door of the chapel was opened, and,
after a few privileged persons were admitted, all were allowed to pass,
that is to say, if they had on a black coat and white cravat and
black pantaloons; a brown coat or a frock coat found very little
favor; sometimes they passed, if it was accompanied with a German voice, that language being the language of the Swiss Guards.
A few gentlemen were allowed to go into the strangers' box, within
the grating, where, on former occasions, I fortunately got, but to-
day was too late. I therefore, with Mr. C——, of Alexandria, and
Mr. Salisbury, took my stand in that part of the chapel which is
nearest the door; here, on the right where you enter, the ladies are
permitted to see the ceremonies. We waited long, and at length
ascertained there would be a tedious chant, after which there would
be a procession of the Host into the Pauline Chapel to be buried.
We left the crowded Sistine Chapel and took our places behind the
line of guards extending through the hall between two doors—one
of the Pauline Chapel, the other leading into apartments along the
front of St. Peter's. Here, having waited a long time—it being after
eleven o'clock—a bustle was made in the hall, and the head of a procession made its appearance from one of the doors of the great
hall; a cross and candles were borne before, and, soon after, a rich
crimson-damask sedan-chair, borne by bearers dressed in the same
materials and colors, in which his Holiness the Pope was seated; he
passed close to us, and as he passed moved his hand as usual in the
act of blessing. Finding some who were near us had got between
the guards into the procession of ambassadors, etc., and who were
suffering no obstruction, Mr. Cooper and I successfully attempted
the same manœuvre and mounted the staircase directly after the
pope, and as far as the crimson-and-velvet and gold-furnished cham
ber, temporarily built for the ceremony of the benediction; here we
were stopped by the guards, but were permitted to stand without
the line, or be in the balcony with the ambassadors, etc., which was
next to and on the left of that at which the pope was to appear.
Having examined the splendid chair on which he was to be borne,
and while he was robing in another apartment, we found that, although we might have a complete view of the pope and the ceremonies before and after the benediction, yet the principal effect
was to be seen below; we therefore left our place at the balcony,
where we could see nothing but the crowd, and hastened below.

On passing into the hall we were so fortunate as just to be in season for the procession from the Sistine Chapel to the Pauline; the
cardinals walked in procession two and two, and one bore the Host,
while eight bearers held over him a rich canopy of silver tissue
embroidered with gold. Thence we hastened to the front of St.
Peter's, where in the centre, upon the highest step, we had an
excellent view of the balcony, and, turning round, could see the immense crowd which had assembled in the piazza, and the splendid
square of troops which were drawn up before the steps of the church.
Here I had scarcely time to make a hasty sketch, in the broiling sun,
of the window and its decorations, before the precursors of the pope,
the two large feather fans, made their appearance on each side of the
balcony, which was decorated with crimson and gold; and immediately after the Pope, with his mitre of gold tissue and his splendid
robes of gold and jewels, was borne forward, relieving finely from
the deep crimson darkness behind him. He made the usual sign of
blessing with his two fingers raised; a book was then held before
him, in which he read, with much motion of his head, for a minute.
He then rose, extending both his arms—this was the benediction—
while at the same moment the soldiers and crowd all knelt, the cannon from the Castle of St. Angelo was discharged, and the bells in
all the churches rung a simultaneous peal; the effect was exceedingly grand, the most imposing of all the ceremonies I have witnessed. The pope was then borne back again. Two papers were
thrown from the balcony, for which there was a great scramble
among the crowd.

"From this ceremony we went into the chapel to witness the
washing of feet of the pilgrims. Thirteen persons dressed in white,
with white caps, some with long beards, were seated upon a high
seat on one side of the chapel. After the usual pushing and squeez-
ing for places I got near enough to see the ceremony. A chant
commenced, during which the pope (or it might have been a cardinal, for his face being in profile I could not discern accurately) began by washing, or rather touching with water, the foot of the first
pilgrim, wiping it with the towel which an attendant bore, and then,
kissing the foot, presented a large bouquet of flowers to that pilgrim, and so on through the whole; it lasted but a few minutes.
From this place, which was opposite the Sistine Chapel, we went
into the Pauline Chapel to see the Holy Sepulchre; this was splendidly illuminated with hundreds of wax-candles disposed in a most
effective manner. Thence we came down into St. Peter's, and

upon the steps found a procession of pilgrims, male and female, of all ranks, and kinds, and countries, about to enter the church; we looked into the church; the great altar was dismantled, and all the lamps out before it; most if not all the candles of the other altars, being collected in one of the side chapels, were brilliantly illuminating a dark part of the church.

"From these ceremonies we took some rest by walking through the splendid galleries of the Vatican, which are thrown open to the public throughout, into the garden of the Vatican, rich with flowers and orange-trees, and lemon-trees, and other tropical fruits; a large copper pineapple, upon a pedestal in front of a high, deep niche, makes a distinguished figure, and an ancient ship as a fountain is a large toy on the other side of the Vatican.

"After dinner went again to St. Peter's to hear the music; the 'Miserere' was exquisitely performed in the side-chapel, quite equal, I thought, to that in the Sistine Chapel the evening before.

"We next went to the Convent of the Trinita di Pellegrini to see the pilgrims having their feet washed and eating their supper. A long hall, perhaps two hundred feet in length, was set out on each side with a row of tables, which were to be served by cardinals and nobles, who were to wait on the pilgrims. In another apartment, into which we were too late to enter, there were about three hundred pilgrims, who had their feet washed and were waiting for their supper. They were soon after ushered into the supper-room; they were a most strange company, ragged, and dirty, and unshaven; their food was plentifully and indeed I may say luxuriously prepared for them—a thick, apparently nice soup, fish and salad, wine, figs, apples, etc. Before eating they all rose, and a blessing appeared to be asked by some one of the cardinals, and while they were eating a man from a box at one side of the room, like an orchestra-box, read what seemed to be a sermon. Each end of the table was decorated with flowers. I asked one from one of the princely waiters, and he politely gave me two, which I preserved.

"We went into the church; an altar was splendidly illuminated, and at a side-altar the crucifix was laid upon the ground on cushions. Before it hundreds knelt to kiss it, and there was a plate to receive money. In returning home, visited the Pantheon and the Church of St. Andrea de la Valle, where were similar ceremonies. Saw also the shops of the bacon and cheese venders illuminated; in one was a small fountain playing. The bacon was tastily arranged, the flitches looking like large leaves of books and gilt. A recess, with looking-glasses at the end, gave the appearance of an almost endless vista of lights.

"In the Via Portugese is a house which always has at night a lamp in the corner of the eves, from the following occurrence: A gentleman, who lived in the house some years ago, had an orang-outang, which one day got loose, and, finding the child of the gentleman, seized it and rushed to the top of the house with it before he was discovered; when first seen he was with the child on the corner of the house, and threatening every moment to throw the child into the street. He was, however, arrested in his intention, and the child was saved. In commemoration of the event he during his life kept a light burning on the corner, and left by his will a sufficient sum to maintain it after his decease.

"*Friday, April 9th.*—All the morning was spent in endeavoring to find places where we had been informed were the most interesting ceremonies of the day, but we were disappointed. At one o'clock we went to the church of St. Sylvestro in Capite, to witness the service of the *tre ore* of agony. As its name indicates, it was three hours in length; the church was hung with black. A temporary pulpit was erected at one side, from which a fleshy friar harangued the people with much gesticulation; opposite him was the orchestra, which at intervals gave good music, but the harangue of the priest in the intermission was so long and monotonous, relieved by a priest in another pulpit, who read in a dull, school-boy tone, that I was glad to make my retreat—I had seen enough. The priest's eloquence was of the same kind I had before heard, his words coming forth like water from a narrow-necked flask. We went in search of the Greek church; finding no service, went to St. Peter's, passing a long procession of monks, in black hoods, with staves surmounted by death's heads, and a girdle of beads and a cross, also surmounted with death's heads; they had on the hood, or mask, having all the face covered but the eyes; they sang or rather croaked as they went, 'with solemn step and slow.' When we arrived at St. Peter's, the ceremonies were performing in the choir; the tiresome chant, which had been in continuation for nearly the three hours, rightly called the three hours of agony, was nearly drawing to a conclusion, three lights, of the fifteen, alone remaining unextinguished. These fifteen lights, by-the-by, represent the twelve Apostles and the three Marys (in brown wax-candles, to signify mourning); their extinguishment, the desertion of all, one after another, but Mary the Virgin; this is the centre candle, and, when all are extinguished but this, it is removed, still burning, behind the altar; the '*Miserere*' then commences. We heard the exquisite '*Miserere*,' and afterward went toward the high altar, with the crowd, to witness the showing of the sacred relics, from a balcony some sixty or seventy feet above the crowd. A priest with two attendants made his appearance; a row of seven or eight waxcandles was upon the balustrade, and presently he held up a glittering mass of something that looked like a jeweled cap or crown. This was the spear, the very spear which pierced the side of our Saviour; the priest walked backward and forward in the balcony with it, for a moment, and then retired; he then came forth with a small cross also jeweled, and paced up and down in the same manner; this was a piece of the genuine cross. Next he brought out a splendidly jeweled frame containing the portrait of a head; this was St. Veronica's handkerchief with which she wiped the Saviour's face in going to the cross, and which received the impression of his features upon it. The distance, from any one in the crowd, of these relics of course prevented any examination or inquiry. This being ended, we returned home, and, after dinner, went again to the Trinita di Pelligrini to see what I omitted seeing last evening—the washing of the pilgrims' feet. This was in a room near the supper-hall. We arrived in season, and found that this was a *bona-fide* washing of feet, tubs being provided for each pilgrim, and cardinals and others were literally performing the ceremony of washing their feet for them. On our way to St. Peter's I ought to have noticed our visit to a palace in which another cardinal (the third who has died within a few days) was lying in state—Cardinal Bertazzoli. The apartments of this cardinal seemed to be very bare of furniture—whether usually so, or stripped for the occasion, I know not. The room in which he lay was very splendid—of crimson and gold—as were also the other rooms; he was upon a high bed of cloth-of-gold tissue, under a rich canopy of crimson velvet embroidered with flowers of gold, and with gold lace at the side; candles of wax were in high candlesticks, at his feet a crucifix, and basin of holy water with a little brush to sprinkle it. Priests were just about to engage in chanting a requiem when we left. Ever since the benediction, all the bells in the city have been silent, and all the guards have their muskets reversed. In returning from the Trinita di Pellegrini, the shops of those that sell bacon, cheese, and lard, struck us with the splendor and ingenuity of their decorations; besides innumerable lamps, and candles, and tinsel and gilding of the bacon

and hams, there was in the Piazza Pallarola a shop, which had in
the window a group of sculpture, made entirely of lard, and of
the size of life, representing a child riding upon a goat, while another child is pulling back the goat by the tail. The action of the
whole was very spirited, and the figures, and animal, and all things
considered, exceedingly well done, especially the struggling of the
goat to go forward, and the determined effort of the child to prevent him.

"*Friday, April* 16*th.*—At the Vatican all day. I went to the
soirée of the sister Persianis in the evening. There I had the pleasure of meeting, for the first time, with THORWALDSEN, the great
Danish sculptor, the first now living. He is an old man in appearance, having a profusion of gray hair, wildly hanging over his
forehead and ears. His face has a strong northern character, his
eyes are light gray, and his complexion sandy. He is a large man,
of perfectly unassuming manners and of most amiable deportment.
Daily receiving homage from all the potentates of Europe, he is
still without the least appearance of ostentation. He readily assented to a request to sit for his portrait, which I hope soon to take.
The *soirée* this evening had several other distinguished persons
from various countries present.' From Sweden, from England, from
France, from Switzerland, and from America, there were representatives. The young ladies sang and played beautifully on the harp
and piano; the older people of the party played cards, as stupidly
as card-players in all other countries.

"*Monday, April* 19*th.*—Went to the Vatican. In passing
through the Via del' Orso, near the Ponte St. Angelo, I saw quite a
romantic scene, if it had been at a more romantic hour. A young
man with his guitar was sitting near a window playing, while a
very pretty girl was with the greatest vivacity singing to him. The
old people were listening, while they were employed in their domestic engagements, spinning and ironing.

"Visited Thorwaldsen at his house, in the Via Sistina, on the
Pincian Hill. He was at home, and showed me his private collection of pictures, some ancient, but mostly modern, and very fine, in
landscape particularly, for I was unprepared to find so good land-
scape-painters among the moderns in Italy—they were not Italians,
however. I was shown three rooms; the last was the private study
of Thorwaldsen, where I found a bass-relief in progress in the clay.

"*Tuesday, April* 27*th.*—My birthday. How time flies, and to
how little purpose have I lived! Engaged at home in painting.

of men playing at *mora*, wh... consists in two p...
down the hand together, with an... number of the fin...
and each calling out in the same ... with the number
to make the whole number of fingers of both their
together; he that guesses right is the winner.

"*Friday, April 30th.*—A funeral procession pa...
to-day. On the bier, exposed, as is customary here,
young girl, apparently of fifteen, dressed in rich lac...
embroidered with gold, and silver, and flowers ...
and sprinkled also with real flowers, and at her ...
coronet of flowers. She had more the appearance ...
death. No relative appeared near her; the who...
conducted by the priests and monks, and those ...
white hoods, with faces covered, except two holes t...

"*Monday, September 20th.*—Began the port...
brated sculptor, Thorwaldsen. He is a most amiab...
universally respected. He is the greatest sculpto...
have studied his works; they are distinguished for ...
...t expression, and truth in character and design; t...
...re characterized by simplicity. These qualities
...with that beauty which we so much admi...
...in literature or art. Thorwal...
...he rather seems to be ...
...imbued with the spirit ...
...kindred works. ...
...The Triumph of Alexa...
...a noblemen, ... for his splendid ...

In going to dinner, observed what I have often before seen, a group of men playing at *moro*, which consists in two persons striking down the hand together, with any number of the fingers extended, and each calling out in the same breath the number they suppose to make the whole number of fingers of both their hands added together; he that guesses right is the winner.

"*Friday, April 30th.*—A funeral procession passed the house to-day. On the bier, exposed, as is customary here, was a beautiful young girl, apparently of fifteen, dressed in rich laces and satins, embroidered with gold, and silver, and flowers, tastefully arranged, and sprinkled also with real flowers, and at her head was placed a coronet of flowers. She had more the appearance of sleep than of death. No relative appeared near her; the whole seemed to be conducted by the priests and monks, and those hideous objects in white hoods, with faces covered, except two holes for the eyes.

"*Monday, September 20th.*—Began the portrait of the celebrated sculptor, Thorwaldsen. He is a most amiable man, and is universally respected. He is the greatest sculptor of the age. I have studied his works; they are distinguished for simple dignity, just expression, and truth in character and design; the composition is also characterized by simplicity. These qualities combined endow them with that beauty which we so much admire in the works of Greece, whether in literature or art. Thorwaldsen cannot be said to imitate the antique; he rather seems to be one born in the best age of Grecian art, imbued with the spirit of that age, and producing from his own resources kindred works. One of his principal works is a bass-relief of 'The Triumph of Alexander,' executed for a nobleman, who intended it for his splendid mansion on the Lago di Como. Before the work was completed, however, the marquis died, and his son, the present marquis, not inheriting the taste or disposition of his father, has offered it for sale.

"Thorwaldsen has just completed the monument of Pope Pius VII., which is now erecting in St. Peter's. It consists of a mausoleum in the Egyptian order, on the top of which is a colossal figure of the pope, seated in the papal chair, and with his right hand raised in the attitude of giving the benediction; on each side of the great door of the tomb is a colossal female figure, the one Fortitude and the other Wisdom. His studios are in the Palazzo Barberini; they are very extensive, and are literally filled with the works of this great man. He has executed many colossal works: a statue of Copernicus, of the Emperor Alexander of Russia, several colossal horses. Next to his 'Triumph of Alexander,' which is, perhaps, his most colossal work, his 'St. John preaching,' which is a series of nine statues and groups, is the most beautiful. The dignity and earnest zeal of the preacher, the various listeners, admirably selected from nature, the group of children observing a dog, alone inattentive among the audience, are all well conceived, and make the series one of the most interesting pieces of sculpture in the world."

This portrait of Thorwaldsen was completed by Morse, and sent by the painter to Philip Hone, Esq., of New York, who had commissioned him to paint him a picture for one hundred dollars. It remained in Mr. Hone's gallery until the sale of his pictures, after his death. Mr. Wright then became its owner, and, on the sale of his pictures, in 1868, John Taylor Johnston, Esq., President of the Metropolitan Museum of Art, bought it for four hundred dollars. When he learned that Mr. Morse was very desirous of possessing it again, that he might present it to the King of Denmark, Mr. Johnston with great cheerfulness and generosity begged Mr. Morse to accept it. Mr. Morse was exceedingly grateful, and immediately forwarded it to the Danish monarch, in whose gallery it now hangs. To Mr. Johnston, on hearing of his great generosity, Mr. Morse wrote the following letter:

"DRESDEN, SAXONY, *January* 23, 1868.

"MY DEAR SIR: Your letter of the 6th instant is this moment received, in which I have been startled by your most generous offer, presenting me with my portrait of the renowned Thorwaldsen, for which he sat to me in Rome in 1831. I know not in what terms, my dear sir, to express to you my thanks for this most acceptable gift. I made an excursion to Copenhagen in the summer of 1856, as a sort of devout pilgrimage to the tombs of two renowned Danes, whose labors in their respective departments—the one, *Oersted*, of Science, the other, *Thorwaldsen*, of Art—have so greatly enriched the world. The personal kindness of the late King Frederick VII., who courteously received me at his castle of Fredericksborg, through the special presentation of Colonel Rastoff, more recently the Danish minister at Washington; the hospitalities of many of the principal citizens of Copenhagen; the visits to the tomb and museum of the works of Thorwaldsen, and to the room in which the immortal Oersted made his brilliant electro-magnetic discovery; the casual and accidental introduction and interview with a daughter of Oersted—all created a train of reflections which prompted me to devise some suitable mode of showing to these hospitable people my appreciation of their friendly attentions, and I proposed to myself the presentation to his majesty the King of Denmark of this portrait of Thorwaldsen, for which he sat to me in Rome, and with which I knew he was specially pleased. My desire to accomplish this purpose was further strengthened by the additional attention of the king, at a later period, in sending me the decoration of his order of the Danebrog. From the moment this purpose was formed, twelve years ago, I have been desirous of obtaining this portrait, and watching for the opportunity of possessing it again.

"Its history, in brief, is this: Among the commissions given me on my professional visit of study to Europe, in 1829, prolonged to the autumn of 1832, was one from the then Mayor of the city of New York, the late liberal-minded Philip Hone. He put into my hands *one hundred* dollars, with the request to paint him a picture for his gallery, leaving to me the choice of the subject. In Rome, I became personally acquainted with Thorwaldsen, who not merely treated me with his usual kindness, but seemed to take unusual pains to show me little attentions, and specially to seek my companionship in his evening walks for recreation on the Pincian Hill. I ventured to ask him to give me sittings for his portrait, a request which he promptly granted. The portrait in question is the result. It was sent to Mr. Hone, and occupied a place in his gallery during his life. When the gallery, in consequence of his decease, was dispersed, I was absent from the city, and ignorant of the fact, and the time of sale, or I should then have competed for its possession.

"For some time I was unable even to ascertain its new possessor. But at length, from my worthy friend and pupil, D. Huntington, Esq., I learned that it was in the collection of Mr. Wright, and that he valued it too highly for the indulgence of any hope that he would part with it. When, in March of last year, Mr. Wright's collection was brought to the hammer, I was here in Europe, but was apprised by my brother, after the sale, that the portrait of Thorwaldsen was sold for over *four hundred* dollars, but the name of the purchaser was not mentioned. In my reply to my brother, I find this passage: 'I don't know whether to be glad or sorry that my portrait of Thorwaldsen brought so much, for I was watching an opportunity of possessing it for myself, and, although rejoiced to find my picture valued so highly, yet it would seem hard that a picture for which I received but one hundred dollars could not be possessed again by its author without paying more than three times the sum he received for it.'

"This brief history will show you, my dear sir, what a boon you have conferred upon me. Indeed, it seems like a dream. And if my most cordial thanks, not merely for the *gift*, but for the graceful and generous manner in which it has been offered, is any compensation, you may be sure they are yours. These are no conventional words, but they come from a heart that can gratefully appreciate the noble sentiments which have prompted your generous act. I have written my brother Sidney E. Morse, and requested him to receive for me the portrait. Again thanking you, my dear sir, I am with gratitude and esteem your friend and servant,

"SAMUEL F. B. MORSE.

"To JOHN TAYLOR JOHNSTON, Esq."

When Mr. Morse writes to his brothers from Italy, we find him occasionally breaking away from the charmed circle of art:

"ROME, *January* 5, 1831.

"MY DEAR BROTHERS: A short time ago, I asked an Italian friend of mine to get for me some cuttings of two kinds of grapes which are celebrated here, that I might send them to the United States. He has been so obliging as to present me with six vines, with their roots carefully packed in their natural earth (which, by-the-by is the Vale of Tempe, Adrian's Villa, Tivoli), and they are in such fine order, and the season so favorable to send them, that I have ventured to incur the expense of transmission as they are, to such of my horticultural friends as I know will take good care of them, and distribute cuttings (if they should be successful in cultivating them) to others, so that these two fine varieties of grapes may be introduced into the country. They are packed in one parcel, all their roots being in a tub with earth, moss, etc. But you will find, after unwinding the cloth which envelops them, the two kinds separated by being tied round, each three of a kind, with a separate band. One is the *Pergolese* grape, the other the *Pizzutello*. I know not which of each parcel is the *Pergolese*, or which is the *Pizzutello*, but, in separating them, take one from each bunch, making three pairs, and oblige me by delivering to each of the following persons one pair : one to Dr. Ives, of New Haven; one to Dr. Hosack; and one to R. V. De Witt, Esq., of Albany."

"*April* 15, 1831.

"We have recently heard of the disasters of the Poles. What noble people; how deserving of their freedom! I must tell you of an interesting circumstance that occurred to me in relation to Poland. It was in the latter part of June of last year, just as I was completing my arrangements for my journey to Naples, that I was tempted by one of those splendid moonlight evenings, so common in Italy, to visit once more the ruins of the Coliseum. I had frequently been to the Coliseum in company, but now I had the curiosity to go alone—I wished to enjoy, if possible, its solitude, and its solemn grandeur, unannoyed by the presence of any one. It was eleven o'clock when I left my lodgings, and no one was walking at that hour in the solitary streets of Rome. From the Corso to the Forum, all was as still as in a deserted city. The ruins of the Forum, the temples and pillars, the Arch of Titus, and the gigantic arcade of the Temple of Peace, seemed to sleep in the grave-like stillness of the air. The only sound that reached my ears was that of my own footsteps. I slowly proceeded, stopping occasionally and listening, and enjoying the profound repose, and the solemn, pure light, so suited to the ruined magnificence around me. As I approached the Coliseum, the shriek of an owl and the answering echo broke the silence for a moment, and all was still again. I reached the entrance, before which paced a lonely sentinel, his arms flashing in the moonbeams. He abruptly stopped me, and told me I could not enter. I asked him why. He replied that his orders were to let no one pass. I told him I knew better, that he had no such orders, that he was placed there to protect visitors, and not to prevent their entrance, and that I should pass. Finding me resolute (for I knew by experience his motive was merely to extort money), he softened in his tone, and wished me to wait until he could speak to the sergeant of the guard. To this I assented, and, while he was gone, a party of gentlemen approached also to the entrance. One of them, having heard the discourse between the sentinel and myself, addressed me. Perceiving that he was a foreigner, I asked him if he spoke English. He replied, with a slight accent, 'Yes, a little; you are an Englishman, sir.' 'No,' I replied, 'I am an American, from the United States.' 'Indeed!' said he, 'that is much better,' and, extending

14

his hand, he shook me cordially by the hand, adding, 'I have a
great respect for your country, and I know many of your countrymen.' He then mentioned Dr. Jarvis, and Mr. Cooper, the novelist,
the latter of whom he said was held in the greatest estimation in
Europe, and nowhere more so than in his country, Poland, where
his works were more sought after than those of Scott, and his mind
was esteemed of an equal, if not of a superior cast. This casual
introduction of literary topics furnished us with ample matter for
conversation while we were not engaged in contemplating the sublime ruins over which, when the sentinel returned, we climbed. I
asked him respecting the literature of Poland, and particularly if
there were now any living poets of eminence. He observed, 'Yes,
sir, I am happily traveling in company with the most celebrated
of our poets, Meinenvitch;' and who as I understood him was one
of the party walking in another part of the ruins. Engaged in
conversation, we left the Coliseum together, and slowly proceeded
into the city. I told him of the deep interest with which Poland
was regarded in the United States, and that her heroes were spoken
of with the same veneration as our own. As some evidence of this
estimation, I informed him of the monuments erected by the cadets
of West Point, our Polytechnic School, to the memory of Kos-
ciusko. With this intelligence he was evidently much affected; he
took my hand, and exclaimed with great enthusiasm, and emphatically, 'We, too, sir, shall be free; the time is coming; we too shall
be free, my unhappy country will be free.' (This was before the
revolution in France.) As I came to the street where we were
to part, he took out his note-book, and, going under the lamp of a
Madonna, near the Piazza Colonna, he wished me to write my name
for him, among the other names of Americans which he had treas-
ured in his book. I complied with his request. In bidding me
adieu, he said, ' It will be one of my happiest recollections of Rome,
that the last night which I passed in this city was passed in the
Coliseum, and with an American, a citizen of a free country. If you
should ever visit Warsaw, pray inquire for Prince ——; I shall be
exceedingly glad to see you!' Thus I parted with this interesting
Pole. That I should have forgotten a Polish name, pronounced but
once, you will not think extraordinary. The sequel remains to be
told. When the Polish Revolution broke out, what was my surprise
to find the poet Meinenvitch, and a prince whose name seemed like
that which he pronounced to me, and to which was added, ' just
returned from Italy,' among the first members of the provisional

government! When the first news of the revolution in Poland reached Rome, it was in the highest degree interesting to witness the strong feeling and enthusiasm which animated the Poles who were on a visit to Italy. When they met each other, they embraced, and the tears would flow down their cheeks, while they vowed to each other to return home immediately to fight for their country. Some English friends of mine called to see two Polish gentlemen, one an artist, who were both packing up to go home, full of nothing but zeal for the cause of their beloved country. In taking leave, the Englishmen expressed a hope that they should meet again. ' No, no,' said they, ' never on earth, we go to die for our country; we shall meet in heaven.' "

The studies of Mr. Morse in public and private galleries, minutely described in his sketch-books, were continued with industry and zeal in several cities of Italy. His letters to his brothers, and to other relatives in the United States, contained detailed accounts of his work with the brush, and his studies among the old masters wherever he found them; denying himself society in which he would have indulged with the greatest enjoyment, had not time appeared to him too precious to spend on any thing but the acquisition of knowledge that should be useful in his art, he made himself thoroughly acquainted with every department of his profession.

In the autumn of 1831 he went to Paris, and, having established himself in very modest quarters, No. 29 Rue de Turenne, near the Madeleine, he began to copy in the Louvre. His friends Greenough and Cooper often wrote to him, and their letters give glimpses of life abroad. From Florence, Mr. Greenough writes:

" As for the commission from Government, I don't speak of it yet. After about a fortnight I shall be calm, I think. Morse, I have made up my mind on one score, viz., that this order shall not be fruitless to the greater men who are in our rear. They are sucking now and rocking in cradles, but I can hear the pung! pung! puffetty! of their hammers, and I am prophetic, too! We'll see if Yankee-land can't muster some ten or a dozen of them in the course of as many years! If you go home, you will be married; if you are married, you will stay there. Pray, advertise for me when you get there: *Wanted.*—A young woman of knowledge without being

aware of it; very humble at finding herself proud; a blond, and inclining to the *petite*, not slothful in business, fervent in spirit, serving the Lord.—My love to Mr. Cooper, and my respectful regards
to the family.   Ever thine,   HORATIO G——."

.   .   .   .

"Accept my warmest thanks for your sympathy—the interest
you express in my welfare fills no small portion of the void which
my troubles may have made in my heart.   As for my kind friends
in the Rue St. Dominique, may the Disposer of events send them
thousands of such sensations as I experienced when I read what you
say of their regret at my difficulties!   But I will hope that by exertion I may reach a point where to feel interest in me shall not be
to suffer.   You mention a certain plan, but you roll it under your
tongue again in the most tantalizing way.   Why won't you, in your
next, sketch with your pen the plan of your picture, for I'm not sure
I understand it; that is, if indeed you meant I should?   I don't wish
to beg a secret.

"You were right, I had heard of the resolution submitted to
Congress, etc.; Mr. Cooper wrote me about it.   I have not much
faith in Congress, however.   I will confess that, when the spectre
Debt has leaned over my pillow of late, and, smiling ghastlily, has
asked me if she and I were not intended as companions through life, ·
I snap my fingers at her and tell her that Brother Jonathan talks of
adopting me, and that he won't have her of his household.   'Go to
London, you hag,' says I, 'where they say you're handsome and
wholesome; don't grind your long teeth at me, or I'll read the
Declaration of Independence to ye!'   So you see I make uncertain
hopes fight certain fear, and borrow from the generous, good-natured
Future the motives for content which are denied me by the stinted
Present.   I still continue to think that another year will find me
somewhere in Germany.   I must cut through the snarl into which
four years have wound my relations, and come smack on my feet.
I'm afraid of a habit, and the habit of being assisted is one of the
most ruinous.

"In the mean while I'm trying to mix a little with the world, and
to learn how to behave myself.   I have hitherto read my Dante, etc.,
and when thrown into contact with folk have gotten through as
quick as possible, with the idea that every word spared was so much
clear gain; but I now find that a man needs a circle of acquaintance,
and have already made several pleasant acquisitions in this way.

"What shall I say in answer to your remarks on my opinions?

Shall I go all over the ground again? It were useless. That my heart is wrong in a thousand ways I daily feel, but 'tis my stubborn head which refuses to comprehend the creation as you comprehend it. That we should be grateful for all we have, I feel—for all we have is given us; nor do I think we have little; for my part I would be blessed in mere existence were I not goaded by a wish to make my one talent two; and we have Scripture for the rectitude of such a wish. I don't think the stubborn resistance of the tide of ill-fortune can be called rebellion against Providence. 'Help yourself, and Heaven will help you,' says the proverb. When Leonidas stood with his three hundred in the gap against the tide of Persian tyranny, was his a rebellion against the decree that doomed his country to defeat? No, he stood there to see it done, and to decimate his conquerors according to the decree of the Disposer of all. I suppose you have Brisbane with you by this time with several new German syllogisms. If the truth were known, that fellow went to Berlin to refit after the battering his metaphysics had received at your hands. Hateful word that same metaphysics. Let's have reasoning till all's blue, but let's have *hold* of something. Let's have Poetry, too; for she raises our motives instead of poisoning them; she makes another world, instead of topsy-turvying this.

"There hangs before me a print of the Bunker-Hill Monument. Pray, be judge between me and the building committee of that monument. (See illustration on page 214.)

"There you observe that my model was founded solidly, and on each of its square plinths were trophies, or groups, or cannon, as might be thought fit. (No. 1.) Well, they have taken away the foundation, made the shaft start sheer from the dirt like a spear of asparagus, and, instead of an acute angle, by which I hoped to show the work was done, and lead off the eye, they have made an obtuse one, producing the broken-chimney-like effects, which your eye will not fail to condemn in No. 2. Then they have inclosed theirs with a light, elegant fence, *à la Parigina*, as though the austere forms of Egypt were compatible with the decorative flummery of the Boulevards. Let 'em go for dunderheads, as they are!

"I'm remodeling Washington; the old model was made too long since to repeat any more. Harry is painting, and is quite a favorite with his master. The boy grows fast; I have great hopes of him. Gore is painting his mud portrait very well; he may be found at any time of the day with one of the mud-beavers of the Arno for a model; a red-headed, long-bearded, fiery-faced, green-eyed fellow, that has killed his man and cuts all his bread with a pointed knife two inches longer than the law directs. Gore has imagination; he feels character. I have the promise of certain drawings for the Academy; your bust and Cole's have both gone, directed to Mr. Morton. Cole is probably in Naples. My 'Lafayette' is boxed without a stain. I congratulate you on your sound

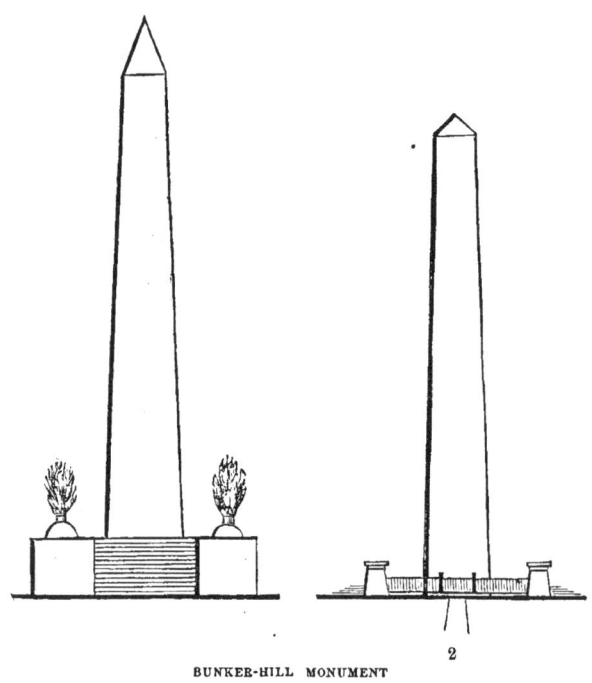

BUNKER-HILL MONUMENT

conscience with regard to the affair that you wot of. As for your remaining free, that's all very well to think during the interregnum; but a man without a true love is a ship without ballast, a one-tined fork, half a pair of scissors, an utter flash in the pan. Will you give my love to the Coopers, and say to Mr. C. that I have received his note, and am awaiting his letter, of which he speaks!

"HORATIO GREENOUGH."

"FLORENCE, *July* 19, 1832.

"Yours of the 9th reached me yesterday and stopped my grumbling. I could find but one excuse for your silence, and that was too painful to be admitted, even as a conjecture, viz., that you had been drawn by the crowd into some tremendous row, and made a revolutionary figure at the expense of all your friends. I don't doubt you will profit by your exhibition, and I have every hope of your receiving some handsome commission. I have written to the Government my terms; if they are accepted I shall have a proposition to make. We will have a knot of us here, which shall form an epoch, by the beard of Jupiter Flaminius! I see by the papers that some fellow has attacked me; says I'm an educated man, allied with *literati*, and possess every means of doing myself honor; it's a heavy charge, is it not? I suppose he hints I have not made use of these advantages; but he's too quick, let him wait a little. All this is as it should be; let 'em spare my character, and they may call me dunce to doomsday, and I'll be half ready to say, amen! As to going home in October, I'd give my little finger to do so, but I don't think it possible.

"If I can muster the cash I'll come to say good-by to ye as far as Paris; but I'll say beforehand that I shall be a blockhead, for I know I shall come moping back with a face as long as an ox-bow. So Cooper is gone to take another pull at Johannisberg; much good may it do him; God bless him! I begin to doubt if ever I shall leave Italy; they write me that artists stand as ignorantly with the public as ever. If I return it will be to marry and become citizen, and I won't do that unless I can stand on fair ground. I've just modeled a statue half the size of life. Here he is: 'The Genius of America' holding out the bud of promise and pointing to posterity. I made such a mess with the head in small that I have done it larger, to give you a little notion of the expression. I must close this. Crank is in Venice, with W. and Alexander; W. is not a man after my heart; he is corrupt, depend on it; I have been obliged to haul off, for he assumed intimacy of the closest kind. Cole is painting away up-stairs; Gore is recovered. My love to Cooper, and my respectful salutation to the lilies of his household. Thine till the Dr. has had his wicked will of me.

" Horatio Greenough."

"Florence, August 20, 1832.

"My eyes have been opened painfully, within a year, to the perception of the light in which artists are held, *all the world over.* In Italy they deserve it. You can speak of France and England better than myself; but, in America, they do not deserve it. They are quite equal in knowledge, and light, and character, to the mass of the most refined classes, and are totally above the rabble. You

have had a proof, in your own experience, how completely the title
of artist throws into the shade the qualities and the virtues which
ought to have secured your pride from any wound. Your experience, then, will make you (as you are a man) safe in future. I
know Congress too well to think much better of the prospects of art
now than I did formerly. 'Tis not the money we want, 'tis the
consideration and weight. The money comes then, of course, as it
does to men of other respectable callings. Now, I choose to reside
in old Europe, and live secluded, and try to respect myself, rather
than be waiting at the doors of the rich, at home, for the vain, or
patronizing, or pitying proofs of their superabundance. If I am
disappointed of my statue, off I go to Germany. If I do not get
the order, good-by to the drudgery of the trade. I will make one
statue, and go about my business, i. e., provided the country remains as ignorant ·on this point as now. Let me beg of you to
hang on to the conception of the *departure* and *return* of Columbus.
You are perfectly qualified to do honor to the country in such works,
and should never give up the plan. Hang on like Columbus himself. You could make the first a grand picture in character and
effect of composition; you would embody in the second all your
scheme of color and *chiaro-oscuro*. These subjects are yours, you
are theirs; have faith, and fear not. Cole is driving through, to get
ready to go home, next month, *via* Leghorn. He intended to have
remained here another year, had commissions in abundance, and
was under full sail, when he got news of sad domestic affliction,
sickness, and (you know the other word), so, like the glorious fellow
he is, he sent home his spare cash, and is getting ready to follow it,
to struggle with all your difficulties, and mine, with a family on his
shoulders. He has painted several things of high merit, and a
'*Campagna di Roma*,' which is a master-piece in the middle and
back grounds. Cole knows as well the value and power of art as
any man, and only wants the *pou sto* to be a great man in art.
Will he ever get it? I hope so; but, if he does, Fortune will give
it him, without raising her bandage from her eyes.

"So you are going home, my dear Morse, and God knows if
ever I shall see you again. Pardon, I pray you, any thing of levity
which you may have been offended at in me. Believe me, it arose
from my so rarely finding one to whom I could be natural, and give
loose, without fear of good faith or good-nature ever failing.
Wherever I am, your approbation will be dearer to me than the
hurrah of a world.

"I shall write to glorious Fenimore in a few days.   My love to Allston and Dana.   God bless you!   H. GREENOUGH."

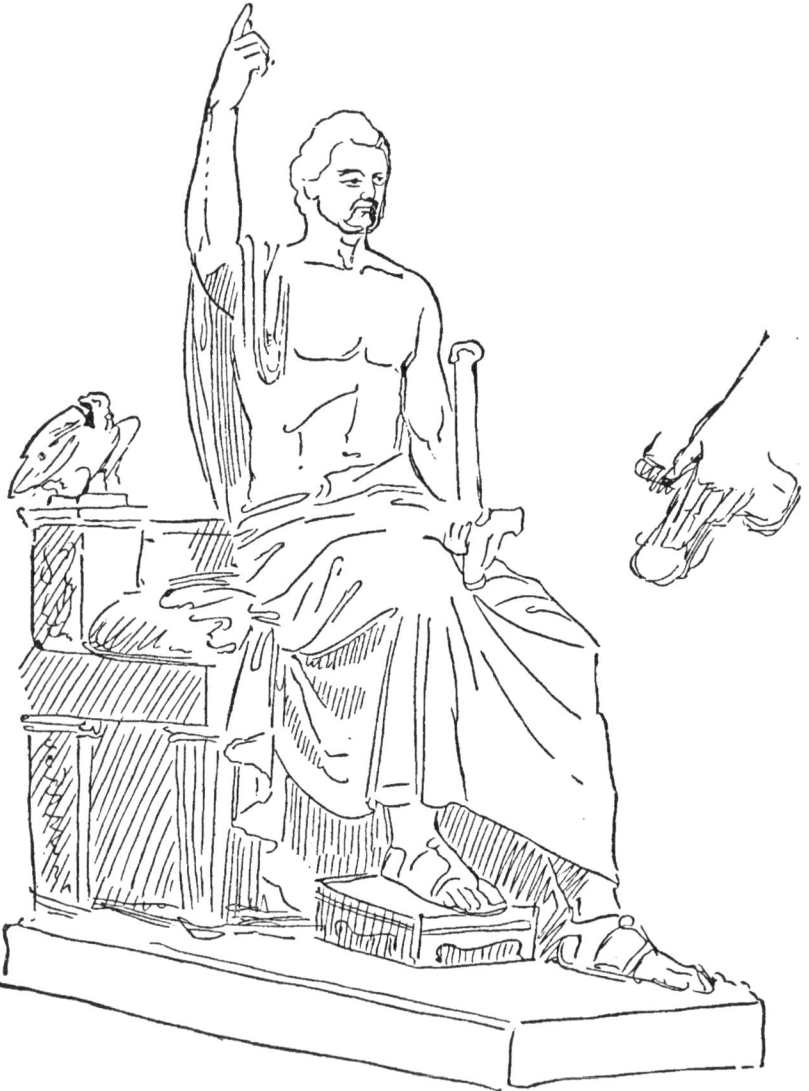

GREENOUGH'S WASHINGTON.

"FLORENCE, *November* 18, 1832.

. . . . "I have finished my design for the statue in clay, half size of life, and the drawing will in a few days be ready to send to

Washington. I have had the greatest difficulty in finding a place big enough to do the work in. At one time I feared I should be obliged to go to Rome; however, I am at length suited, and shall have my man-mountain up by the close of February, if not sooner. I will give you a scratch to convey a general notion of the composition. I can't say I have fixed any thing, still it will require strong reasons to change the general action it has seemed to me characteristic of the man. I had and still have the notion of making him hold the sword, as (*see* p. 218) in the sketch on the other leaf, but I fear it will not be so distinct as I made it in the first sketch; the arm would almost entirely hide it, you observe, as seen in front. We shall see how it pleases at headquarters. I suppose Mr. Cooper is with you before this : God bless him ! Pray, ask him to write me, if it were only a few words; I should be so happy to see his hand once more. . . . H. G."

James Fenimore Cooper, the American novelist, was at this time in Europe, with his family ; and, between him and Mr. Morse a friendship was then formed, which was continued, without interruption, until the death of Mr. Cooper. We find a large number of letters from the novelist to Mr. Morse, rich in themselves, and the more interesting and entertaining, as they develop peculiar traits of character in Mr. Cooper, such as would not be inferred from his published works alone. Some of the brief notes, too trivial in themselves to be inserted, have a humor peculiarly beautiful in the intercourse of the men.

James Fenimore Cooper to Mr. Morse.

"*July* 31, 1832.

"MY DEAR MORSE: Here we are at Spa—the famous hard-drinking, dissipated, gambling, intriguing Spa—where so much folly has been committed, so many fortunes squandered, and so many women ruined ! How are the mighty fallen ! We have just returned from a ramble in the environs, among deserted reception-houses, and along silent roads. The country is not unlike Ballston, though less wooded, more cultivated, and perhaps a little more varied. The town is irregular, small, consisting almost entirely of lodging-houses (I mean for single families), and infinitely clean. The water is a tonic, and the air (we are at an elevation of twelve hundred feet) so light and bracing that I have determined to stay a week, on account of my wife—perhaps a fortnight. I have got a comfortable house, with every requisite, consisting of nine bed-rooms, four parlors, stable, etc., for fifteen francs a day. The piano is strumming down-stairs, and I am writing up, just as if we were in the Rue St.-Dominique, and we only arrived last night. Our quarantine will be up to-night at twelve, and yet we are in no hurry to improve it. We lost three days at Liége (always in quar-antine) that had much better been passed here.

"I have had a great compliment paid me, Master Samuel, and, as it is nearly the only compliment I have received in traveling over Europe, I am the more proud of it. Here are the facts: You must know there is a great painter in Bruxelles of the name of Ver-bœck-oven (which, translated into the vernacular, means a *bull and a book baked in an oven!*), who is another Paul Potter. He out-does all other men in drawing cattle, etc., with a suitable landscape. In his way, he is truly admirable. Well, sir, this artist did me the favor to call at Bruxelles with the request that I would let him sketch my face. He came after the horses were ordered, and, know-ing the difficulty of the task, I thanked him, but was compelled to refuse. On our arrival at Liége, we were told that a messenger from the governor had been to inquire for us, and I began to bethink me of my sins. There was no great cause for fear, how-ever, for it proved Mr. Bull-and-book-baked had placed himself in the *diligence*, come down to Liége (sixty-three miles), and got the governor to give him notice, by means of my passport, when we came. Of course I sat. I cannot say the likeness is good, for it has a vastly live-like look, and is like all the other pictures you have seen of my chameleon face. Let that be as it will, the com-pliment is none the less, and, provided the artist does not mean to serve me up as a specimen of American wild beasts, I shall thank him for it. To be followed twelve posts by a first-rate artist, who is in favor with the king, is so unusual, that I was curious to know how far our minds were in unison, and so I probed him a little. I found him well skilled in his art, of course, but ignorant on most subjects. As respects our general views of men and things, there was scarcely a point in common, for he has few salient qualities, though he is liberal; but his gusto for natural subjects is strong, and his favorite among all my books is 'The Prairie,' which you know is filled with wild beasts. Here the secret was out. That picture of animal nature had so caught his fancy, that he followed me sixty miles to paint a sketch. He sent me a beautiful pencil-sketch of the Belgian hind, as a memorial of our achievement,

which I hope to show you at my return.   Wappero is in high re-
pute.   Mr. Verbœckhoven spoke of him as one would speak of a
master, and with sincere respect.   Others did the same.

"King Leopold was at Liége during our stay, as was his brother,
the reigning Duke of Saxe-Coburg-Gotha, with his two sons.   It is
said they all go off together to Campiègne to celebrate the approaching marriage.   We had the town illuminated, and a salute
that sounded fearfully like minute-guns.

"*August 1st.*—We have just made the tour of the springs, for
there are four of them, in a circuit of about five miles, each having,
it is said, a different property, and all tasting as much alike as if it
had been drawn from the two ends of the same barrel.   Well, faith
is a comfortable ingredient in a traveler's mind.   For my part, I
believe all I hear, which is much the least troublesome mood.   As
for the contradictions, I endeavor to forget them.

"We have a delicious air, and rather pretty environs, but the
place is dull as a desert.   There are a few English, who pass you
as if they were afraid some tailor had broke loose, and always look
the other way until you are past, and then they are always staring
after you to see if you are somebody.   Our indifferent manner never
fails to deceive them, for their quality always give a certain amount
of trust and assume a certain genteel *hauteur;* none escape these
two rocks in good-breeding but those who are at the top of the
ladder, and these are commonly known by means of fame, which
never fails to blow a trumpet beforehand.   'Tis a thousand pities
that people who have so many really good points, and so much good
sense in general, should be such fools, in these points, as to make
themselves uncomfortable, and everybody else who will submit to
their dictation.

"NONNENWERTH, *August* 15, 1832.

"MY DEAR MORSE: Here we are, on an island of the Rhine,
about half-way between Cologne and Coblentz, and in a deserted
convent of Benedictine nuns.   I am writing to you, you rogue, in
the ancient refectory, which is now the *salle à manger* of half a
dozen Fenimore Coopers, with the Rhine rippling beneath my windows, the Drachenfels in full view, by pale moonlight, a dozen
feet sounding distant and hollow in the cloisters, and with a bottle
of Liebfrauenmilch at my elbow.   The old convent is degraded to
the occupation of a tavern.   Our island, if not as important and well
defended as that of Barataria, has some hundred acres, and is altogether a willowish, serpentine, wildish place.   Our candles are

farthing rush-lights, and these, in rooms that need fifty bougies, leave a sombre and appropriate gloom, so that, with one exception, I do not remember a more romantic nightfall in all our pilgrimage, than this. Your friends the Hawkers told us of the place, though I believe they had never visited it, and we left the carriage on the main, this afternoon, to come over here for the night. We are quite alone, which adds to the pleasure, unless we could choose our companions. Mrs. C., the girls, Master Paul, and myself, each equipped with a candle, have just returned from a pilgrimage to the chapel, where we find most of the necessary ingredients for a funeral or a marriage, even at this hour; indeed, it is only ten years since the last nuns (eight in number) dispersed, so that every thing is quite fresh and ecclesiastical. To add to the satisfaction, the Benedictines were not a rigid order, and all is genteel and nice, as they say in London. I have this moment quitted the window, and there was a footstep beneath it. My sight was a little dimmed by rushlights, and fancy was left to supply the functions of observation. This might be the soul of the last lady abbess, who no doubt was fat, and had a solid step, or it might have been some truant nun scratching at the convent-walls, in a sort of habitual kicking against the pricks. Alas! it was only an old horse that appeared to range at free commons over the isle. Well for the horse, he is not more than half flesh at the best.

"I am summoned to my cell. Mrs. Cooper has sent her maid to say I must quit the refectory, where I have tarried an indecent period already, and I obey. The cloister looks gloomy. A distant door opens, and a man issues into their vaults. It is my Swiss, who looks twice, and takes off his traveling cap with academic air, and the maid skims along with the light. I follow. A door, half open, gives me a glimpse of four men. They may be banditti, though they are in the Prussian uniform. A grinning crone meets us on the flight of heavy steps. And here I am in a cell converted into a parlor, with a round table under my elbows, and a sofa under my seat. The adjoining room was formerly the parlor of the lady abbess, and indeed there is a suite of very respectable apartments, that show the good woman was well lodged. The voice of Master Paul is sounding through them irreverent and gay. The wind begins to murmur, casements to close, and we may have thunder next. This opinion has proved prophetic, there has arisen a sudden gust, with lightning. I take a candle and go through the corridors in quest of a sensation. A door communicating with the gallery of the chapel is open and I enter, shutting myself in. Here was what I wanted—images of saints, crucifixes, a dim light, rattling windows, and solitude. Every thing was so fresh that the stuffed velvet chair of the lady abbess was near the railing and a *prie-dieu* at its side. I took a seat. In few moments the door slowly opened, and a hag thrust her wrinkled face into the gallery. I groaned, whether it was with fear or fun I leave you to guess, and away the old woman went as if the —— was after her. I withdrew like a well-bred ghost that has delivered his message. 'But how came you in the convent?' you may be disposed to inquire.

"We found that the water of Spa did so much good to Mrs. Cooper, that we remained until last Monday; we then came to Aix —next day to Cologne, and to-day here. We are on our way to Switzerland. If you want change of air, jump into the *diligence*, and come to Berne, where we will give you rooms for the last of the month. I do not expect to see Paris before this day month.

"'Tis near midnight, Mr. Morse, all but Nature is asleep, and I have been walking in the long and empty corridors. Strange thoughts come uppermost in such a place, and at such a time, Master Samuel; the rustling of the wind seems as the murmuring of uneasy sisters, the pattering of the rain like floods of tears, and the thunder sounds as so many *gémissements* at the sins of man. I seek my pillow.

" *Thursday Morning.—Laus Deo!* a peaceable night, and a refreshing morn, birds singing beneath my window, the Rhine glittering between islands, the arch of Rolandseck tottering on a mountain near, and the tower of the Drachenfels on another. We dress and perambulate. I have been pacing the dimensions of our abode. The abbey pile extends six hundred feet in one direction, and about three hundred in another. The cloisters are about six hundred feet round. There are offices to a goodly extent, and cow-yard and granaries; on the whole it is a capital thing, for one night, taking Drachenfels and Rhine into the count. The Liebfrauen-milch is but questionable, though the fruits are excellent for the latitude.

"RUDESHEIM, IN THE DUCHY OF NASSAU, *Friday, 17th.*— Here I am finishing this letter in a tower, actually built by the Goths, at least so says tradition. It is an appendage of the inn, and forms part of our apartment, giving two or three stories of very romantic-looking little round rooms. We left the convent on Thursday and went to Coblentz, and to-day we came to Bingen, and crossed the Rhine in boats to this tower. We are in the midst of good wine. Johannisberg is in plain view from my window, Steinberg a league or two off, Geisenheim and other notabilities, all within call. My landlord has given me a bottle of cordial that he tells me he has from his own vines. In short, this is the country for your lover of the true Rhenish, which you know means me.

"There is mention made, in the introduction of 'Heidenmauer,' of a castle belonging to a Prince of ——. Well, we passed it to-day, and ascended the mountain. The prince had just gone to Cologne, and we had a clear field. Really the spot is bewitching ; he has repaired an old baronial castle, and equipped it completely in baronial style. The buildings are several hundred feet above the river, and as irregular as heart could wish. One high tower has the beacon-light swung off, as in the middle ages, and there are balconies and outside staircases in them to turn the head of even a sailor. The furniture is either many hundred years old, or made to imitate articles of that age—chiefly the former; plenty of old armor, and the knights' hall is really a curiosity. The fireplace is as big as a Paris bedroom, and in one corner is a very ancient vessel to hold water, with a trough of stone to catch the drippings; most of the wood is oak. In short, the whole thing is in keeping—stained glass, casements, and other niceties—I wish you had been with us. I have never seen any thing in its way to equal it. The prince had been passing several weeks in this aerie. You can look down perpendicularly, from various terraces, balconies, and towers, three or four hundred feet.

"Yours truly,
"J. FENIMORE COOPER.

"Master MORSE."

On the 18th of September, 1831, Mr. Morse wrote to his brothers from Paris:

"I arrived safely in this city on Monday noon in excellent health and spirits; my last letter to you was from Venice, just as I was about to leave it, quite debilitated and unwell from application to my painting, but more, I believe, from the climate, from the perpetual sirocco which reigned uninterrupted for weeks. I have not time now to give you an account of my most interesting journey through Lombardy, Switzerland, part of Germany, and through the eastern part of France. I found, on my arrival here, my friend Mr. Greenough, the sculptor, who had come from Florence to model the bust of General Lafayette, and we are in excellent, convenient rooms together, within a few doors of the good general.

" I called yesterday on General Lafayette early in the morning. The servant told me that he was obliged to meet the Polish committee at an early hour, and feared he could not see me. I sent in my card, however, and the servant returned immediately, saying that the General wished to see me in his chamber. I followed him through several rooms and entered the chamber. The General was in dishabille, but, with his characteristic kindness, he ran forward, and, seizing both my hands, expressed with great warmth how glad he was to see me safely returned from Italy, and appearing in such good health. He then told me to be seated, and without any ceremony began familiarly to question me about my travels, etc. The conversation, however, soon turned upon the absorbing topic of the day, the fate of Poland, the news of the fall of Warsaw having just been received by telegraphic dispatch. I asked him if there was now any hope for Poland. He replied, 'Oh, yes! their cause is not yet desperate; their army is safe; but the conduct of France, and more especially of England, has been most pusillanimous and culpable. Had the English Government shown the least disposition to coalesce in vigorous measures with France for the assistance of the Poles, they would have achieved their independence.' The General looks better and younger than ever. There is a healthy freshness of complexion, like that of a young man in full vigor, and his frame and step (allowing for his lameness) are as firm and strong as when he was our nation's guest. I sat with him ten or fifteen minutes, and then took my leave, for I felt it a sin to consume any more of the time of a man engaged as he is in great plans of benevolence, and whose every moment is therefore invaluable.

" The news of the fall of Warsaw is now agitating Paris to a degree not known since the trial of the ex-ministers. About three o'clock our servant told us that there was fighting at the Palais Royal, and we determined to go as far as we prudently could, to see the tumult, we proceeded down the Rue St.-Honoré. There was evident agitation in the multitudes that filled the sidewalks—an apprehension of something to be dreaded. There were groups at the corners; the windows were filled, persons looking out as if in expectation of a procession or of some *fête*. The shops began to be shut, and every now and then the drum was heard beating to arms. The troops were assembling, and bodies of infantry and cavalry were moving through the various streets. During this time no

15

noise was heard from the people—a mysterious silence was observed, but they were moved by the slightest breath. If one walked quicker than the rest, or suddenly stopped, thither the inquiring look and step were directed, and a group instantly assembled. At the Palais Royal a larger crowd had collected, and a greater body of troops were marching and countermarching in the Place du Palais Royal. The Palais Royal itself had the interior cleared and all the courts. Every thing in this place of perpetual gayety was now desolate; even the fountains had ceased to play, and the seared autumnal leaves of the trees, some already fallen, seemed congruous with the sentiment of the hour. Most of the shops were also shut and the stalls deserted. Still there was no outcry, and no disturbance. Passing through the Rue Vivienne, the same collections of crowds and of troops were seen; some were reading a police notice just posted on the walls, designed to prevent the riotous assembling of the people, and advising them to retire when the riot act should be read. The notice was read with murmurs and groans, and I had scarcely ascertained its contents before it was torn from the walls with acclamations.

"As night approached we struck into the Boulevard de la Madeleine. At the corner of this Boulevard and the Rue des Capucines is the hotel of General Sebastiani. We found before the gates a great and increasing crowd. We took a position on the opposite corner, in such a place as secured a safe retreat in case of need, but allowed us to observe all that passed. Here there was an evident intention in the crowd of doing some violence; nor was it at all doubtful what would be the object of their attack. They seemed to wait only for the darkness and for a leader. The sight of such a crowd is fearful, and its movements, as it was swayed by the incidents of the moment, were in the highest decree exciting. A body of troops of the line would pass: the crowd would silently open for their passage, and close immediately behind them. A body of the National Guard would succeed, and these would be received with loud cheers and gratulations. A soldier on guard would exercise a little more severity than was perhaps necessary for the occasion; yells and execrations and hisses would be his reward. Night had now set in. Heavy dark clouds, with a misty rain, had made the heavens above more dark and gloomy. A man rushed forward toward the gate, hurling his hat in the air and followed by the crowd, which suddenly formed into long lines behind him. I now looked for something serious. A body of troops were in line before the gate. At this moment two police-officers, on horseback, in citizen's dress, but with a tricolored belt around their bodies, rode through the crowd and up to the gate, and in a moment after I perceived the multitude from one of the streets rushing in wild confusion into the boulevard, and the current of the people setting back in all directions. While wondering at the cause of this sudden movement I heard the trampling of horses; and a large body of carabiniers, with their bright helmets glittering in the light of the lamps, dashed down the street and drew up before the gate. The police-officers put themselves at their head, and harangued the people. The address was received with groans. The carabiniers drew their swords, orders were given for the charge, and in an instant they dashed down the street, the people dispersing like the mist before the wind. The charge was made down the opposite sidewalk from that where we had placed ourselves, so I kept my station, and, when they returned up the middle of the street to charge on the other side, I crossed over behind them and avoided them."

Mr. Morse soon began a great work which, after consultation with Mr. Cooper and other friends, he had determined to undertake. This was no less than painting the interior of the Louvre, including copies of the most celebrated pictures in the gallery. To this work he devoted himself with all the ardor of his nature, expending upon it months of labor. Writing to his brother, May 6, 1832, he says:

" My anxiety to finish my picture and to return drives me, I fear, to too great application and too little exercise; and my health has, in consequence, been so deranged that I have been prevented from the speedy completion of my picture. From nine o'clock until four daily I paint uninterruptedly at the Louvre; and, with the closest application, I shall not be able to finish it before the close of the gallery, on the 10th of August, and the time each morning before going to the gallery is wholly employed in preparation for the day; and, after the gallery closes at four, dinner and exercise are necessary; so that I have no time for any thing else. The cholera is raging here, and I can compare the state of mind in each man of us only to that of soldiers in the heat of battle : all the usual securities of life seem to be gone. Apprehension and anxiety make the stoutest hearts quail. Any one feels, when he lays himself down at night, that he will, in all probability, be attacked before daybreak, for the disease is a pestilence that walketh in darkness, and seizes the greatest number of its victims at the most helpless hour of the night.   Fifteen hundred were seized in a day, and fifteen thousand at least have already perished, although the official accounts will not give so great a number.

"*May* 14*th.*—My picture makes progress, and I am sanguine of success if nothing interferes to prevent its completion   I shall take no more commissions here, and shall only complete my large picture and a few unfinished works.

"General Lafayette told me a few weeks ago, when I was returning with him in his carriage, that the financial condition of the United States was a subject of great importance, and he wished that I would write you and others, who were known as statistical men, and get your views on the subject.   There never was a better time for demonstrating the principles of our free institutions by showing a result favorable to our country."

The most of Mr. Morse's evenings were occupied with labor in behalf of the Poles, whose sufferings at that time excited the sympathy of the friends of liberty throughout the world.   A committee was organized for the purpose of devising ways and means to alleviate their condition; General Lafayette was one of the members of this committee, and consequently Mr. Morse, who was also a member, was brought frequently into his society. In the month of March Mr. Morse writes to his brother:

"Information has been received by Mr. Rives, our minister from Berlin, that Dr. S. G. Howe was seized and thrown into prison in that city by the Prussian Government, charged with a charitable mission from our committee.   Dr. Howe had been intrusted with twenty thousand francs for the relief of the distressed Poles; and his intentions and motives were in no degree political, but in furtherance of the benevolent designs of the contributors in the United States.   A letter from Berlin, written by A. Brisbane, Esq., and which Mr. Rives has just read to me, says that Dr. Howe is in close confinement, and no one is permitted to have communication with him.   Mr. Brisbane waited on the Minister of Justice, and found him uncompromising, and manifesting great irritation on the subject. Mr. Cooper and myself have just been to Mr. Rives, who has promptly put measures in train for causing Dr. Howe to be set at liberty.   We have put into the hands of Mr. Rives a record of our proceedings in committee to lay before Baron Werther, the Prussian minister here; embracing a copy of Dr. Howe's commission, in order to show him that the doctor's mission was not political, and we are in hopes that such representations will be forwarded to Berlin without delay as will cause him to be at once released."

" *March* 17th.—Last night we held a special meeting of our committee to consider what could be done to release Dr. Howe. The Prussian authorities here, I am happy to say, have behaved courteously and acted promptly. A courier has been dispatched to Berlin, and from the representations of the mission here we hope for a speedy and happy termination and explanation of the affair."

" *April* 6th.—Dr. Howe, we learn, is liberated at Berlin, but is to be escorted by the police to the frontier of France. The proceedings against him have been outrageous, and that Government would not have dared to treat a citizen of any other country in so cavalier a manner."

SUGGESTIONS OF A TELEGRAPH.

Among the artist friends of Mr. Morse in Paris, at this time, was R. W. Habersham, of Augusta, Georgia, whose statements in relation to Mr. Morse's first suggestion of a Telegraph are confirmed by the recollections of Mr. Cooper. Mr. Morse, however, was never able to call to mind the conversations which are so minutely related in the following statement by Mr. Habersham :

"In the year 1831 I went to Paris, to study art in the *atelier* of Baron Gros. In the autumn of that year, I became acquainted with the moralist Jouffroy, who was already famous as a thinker, but who seemed to feel a want that all his brilliant speculations could not supply, and to be in pursuit of something which constantly eluded him. Soon after, I met Professor Morse, who was copying in the Louvre Rembrandt's famous picture of 'Tobit and the Angel,' and soon formed so satisfactory an opinion of him that, in the spring of 1832, when the cholera broke out in Paris, and I found that he had resolved to remain, I determined to remain also. I lived near the Odeon, he near the Madeleine, No. 29 Rue de Surenne; so, not liking the thought of his being alone, with strangers, unfamiliar with the language, and liable to be stricken down in a moment, with no friend near, I proposed to find lodgings nearer him. Fortunately, he lived in a private house, in which two rooms could

be hired.   I took them, and, perceiving that his were low and confined, while mine were large and airy, I offered to give him my bedroom, and convert my parlor into a dormitory for myself, taking one
of his as a sitting-room.   He kindly acceded to this, and we soon
found it convenient to have one room in common, and to take our
meals together.   It was then that I gradually brought before him
the questions discussed with Jouffroy, without giving his name or
authority, and in conversations carried on often through the open
door of our sleeping-apartments, after we had retired, got an insight into the vast superiority of the Christian's faith, even as a
working-power, over the philosophy of such men as Cousin and
Jouffroy.

"In 1832, the longest railroad in the world was between
Charleston, South Carolina, and Augusta, Georgia, one hundred
and thirty-five miles; the next, between Liverpool and Manchester,
thirty miles; the third, from the Quincy granite-quarries to Boston,
ten miles; and the mails were carried by coach, overland, in preference to the sailing-vessels, which were then solely used for marine
navigation.   In consequence of this, letters reached me from Savan-
nah a month later than those of the same date from New York.
Art students twenty years of age are not apt to be models of patience, and my *forte* did not lie in quiet submission to the irreme-
diable; whence from me much discontent, made audible, and considerable imprecation on Uncle Sam's mails, smothered from respect
to my mentor.   But, on one occasion, the attempt at smothering
failed, and I consigned the whole post-office department to a place
so warm that the letters would have been, in those days of sealing-
wax and wafers, soon beyond assorting.   This led to a conversation
which showed that Morse's mind was already in the matter, and
explained certain visits, at which I had not been 'invited to assist.'
It came out that he was inquiring into the French Semaphore Telegraph system, with a view to its introduction into America, although
I believe he dismissed it, as being *too slow for us*, and inapplicable to
our wants, in spite of our very clear atmosphere.   It was then that
he used this expression: 'The French system would do better in
our clear atmosphere than here; but it is too slow; *lightning will
scarcely be too fast.*'   There was, on one occasion, another reference
made to the conveyance of sound under water, and to the length of
time taken to communicate the letting in of the water into the Erie
Canal, by cannon shots, to New York, and other means, during which
the suggestion of using keys and wires, like the piano, was rejected

as requiring too many wires, if other things were available. I recollect, also, that in our frequent visits to Mr. J. Fenimore Cooper's, in the Rue St.-Dominique, these subjects, so interesting to Americans, were often introduced, and that Morse seemed to harp on them, constantly referring to Franklin and Lord Bacon. Now I, while recognizing the intellectual grandeur of both these men, had contracted a small opinion of their moral strength; but Morse would uphold and excuse, or rather deny, the faults attributed; Lord Bacon, especially, he held to have *sacrificed himself to serve the queen in her aberrations ;* while of Franklin, the 'great American' recognized by the French, he was particularly proud."

Mr. Cooper, in his novel entitled " The Sea Lions," on page 140, says: ·

" We pretend to no knowledge on the subject of the dates of discoveries in the arts and sciences, but well do we remember the earnestness, and single-minded devotion to a laudable purpose, with which our worthy friend first communicated to us his ideas on the subject of using the electric spark by way of a telegraph. It was in Paris, and during the winter of 1831–'32, and the succeeding spring, a time when we were daily together, and we have a satisfaction in recording this date, that others may prove better claims if they can."

Mr. Morse's own recollection of the time of the first conception of the Telegraph dates only from October, 1832, on board the ship Sully, and in a letter to Mr. Cooper he suggested that he must be mistaken. In reply, however, under date of " May 18, 1849, Hall, Cooperstown," Mr. Cooper said:

" For the time, I still stick to Paris, so does my wife, so does my eldest daughter: you did no more than to throw out the general idea, but I feel quite confident this occurred in Paris. I confess I thought the notion evidently chimerical, and as such spoke of it in my family. I always set you down as a sober-minded, common-sense sort of a fellow, and thought it a high flight for a painter to make, to go off on the wings of the lightning. We may be mistaken, but you will remember that the priority of the invention was a question early started, and my impressions were the same, much nearer to the time than it is to-day."

These conversations, so accurately attested by independent

witnesses, are of value, inasmuch as they show the familiarity of Mr. Morse with the powers of electricity, and the tendency of his mind toward original investigation and invention. To him these thoughts were so familiar that he soon forgot he had ever expressed them before others. That he did, we have the best reasons for believing.

While at work upon his picture in the Louvre the great naturalist, already known throughout the civilized world, Baron Humboldt, became interested in Mr. Morse. They had met at the house of Baron Gerard, who was in the habit of drawing around him the artists and men of science, and whose *salon* was a favored resort of genius and taste. Humboldt conceived a great fondness for Morse, and, often coming to him in the gallery, would take him away from his immediate work, to stroll among the works of art, and converse upon topics congenial to their inquiring minds. This acquaintance was afterward revived in Paris, when Morse returned with his great invention, and again in Potsdam, where the humble artist, crowned with honors, visited his illustrious friend.

The American residents in Paris celebrated the "Fourth of July," in the year 1832, with a banquet, at which Mr. Morse presided, with Mr. Cooper as vice-president. Among the guests on that occasion were General Lafayette, and Hon. William C. Rives, United States minister. After the blessing had been asked by Professor Hovey, of Amherst College, the president gave the toasts in their order, and, on offering one in honor of Lafayette, Mr. Morse said:

"1 cannot propose the next toast, gentlemen, so intimately connected with the last, without adverting to the distinguished honor and pleasure we this day enjoy above the thousands, and I may say hundreds of thousands, of our countrymen who are at this moment celebrating this great national festival—the honor and pleasure of having at our board our venerable guest on my right hand, the hero whom two worlds claim as their own. Yes, gentlemen, he belongs to America as well as to Europe. He is our fellow-citizen, and the universal voice of our country would cry out against us, did we not manifest our nation's interest in his person and his character. With the mazes of European politics we have nothing to do; to changing schemes, of good or bad government, we cannot make ourselves a party; with the success or defeat of this or that faction we can have no sympathy. But with the great principles of rational liberty, of civil and religious liberty, those principles for which our guest fought by the side of our fathers, and which he has steadily maintained for a long life 'through good report, and evil report,' we do sympathize; we should not be Americans if we did not sympathize with them, nor can we compromise one of these principles, and preserve our self-respect as loyal American citizens. They are the principles of order and good government, of obedience to law, the principles which under Providence have made our country unparalleled in prosperity, principles which rest not in visionary theory, but are made palpable by the sure test of experiment and time.

" But, gentlemen, we honor our guest as the stanch, undeviating defender of these principles, of our principles, of American principles. Has he ever deserted them? Has he ever been known to waver? Gentlemen, there are some men, some too who would wish to direct public opinion, who are like the buoys upon tidewater—they float up and down as the current sets this way or that. If you ask at an emergency where they are, we cannot tell you; we must first consult the almanac, we must know the quarter of the moon, the way of the wind, the time of the tide, and then we may guess where you will find them. But, gentlemen, our guest is not of this fickle class. He is a tower amid the waters, his foundation is upon a rock, he moves not with the ebb and flow of the stream; the storm may gather, the waters may rise and even dash above his head, or they may subside at his feet, still he stands unmoved. We know his site and his bearings, and with the fullest confidence we point to where he stood six-and-fifty years ago. He stands there now. The winds have swept by him, the waves have dashed around him, the snows of winter have lighted upon him, but still he is there.

" I ask you therefore, gentlemen, to drink with me in honor of General Lafayette."

Then followed a large number of volunteer toasts by G. W. Haven, of New Hampshire; John Biddle Chapman, of Pennsylvania; Major W. T. Poussin, W. P. Dwight, Mr. Cooper, Mr. Rives, Mr. Niles, and many others.

From time to time Mr. Morse was in the receipt of friendly notes from General Lafayette; some of them are found among his papers, and many of them were given away, as autographs, to friends. We copy at this point all that are preserved, whether received in Paris or after his return to the United States:

" PARIS, *September* 11, 1832.

"MY DEAR SIR: I have seen the Poles who mean to go to the United States. They are twenty, and hope to find a ship which will carry them for three hundred francs each. They flatter themselves to get that sum, or the greatest part of it, from the French committee; but, should they go to New York, do you think that they will find means to be supported until they have found a place to form their colony upon? Do you think, also, that lands in the State of Ohio, or elsewhere, could be granted to them, or that they will find in the sympathy of the United States a little capital to form. their settlement? We must have a strong hope of it before we encourage their emigration, which they have much at heart.

"Most truly and affectionately,
"Your friend,
"LAFAYETTE."

"I would be very sorry, my dear friend, to let you depart before you have received my affectionate good wishes. You will find me to-morrow at nine.

"Most truly, your friend,
"*Monday, September*, 1832."   "LAFAYETTE.

"LA GRANGE, *September* 27, 1832.

"MY DEAR SIR: I am sorry to see you will not take Paris and La Grange in your way to Havre, unless you were to wait for the packet of the 10th, in company with General Cadwalader, Commodore Biddle, and those young, amiable Philadelphians who contemplate sailing on that day. But, if you persist to go by the next packet, I beg you here to receive my best wishes and those of my family for your happy voyage. Upon you, my dear sir, I much depend to give our friends of the United States a proper explanation of the state of things in Europe. You have been very attentive to what has past since the Revolution of 1830. Much has been obtained here and other parts of Europe in this whirlwind of a week. Further consequences here and in other countries—Great Britain and Ireland included—will be the certain result, though they have been mauled and betrayed, where they ought to have received encouragement. But it will not be so short and so cheap as we had a right to anticipate it might be. I think it useful, on both sides of the water, to dispel the cloud which ignorance or design may throw over the real state of European and French politics. In the mean while, I believe it to be the duty of every American returned home to let his fellow-citizens know what wretched handle is made of the violent collisions, threats of a separation, and reciprocal abuse, to injure the character and question the stability of republican institutions. I too much depend upon the patriotism and good sense of the several parties in the United States, to be afraid that those dissensions may terminate in a final dissolution of the Union; and should such an event be destined in future to take place, deprecated as it has been by the best wishes of the departed founders of the Revolution—Washington at their head—it ought at least in charity not to take place before the not remote period when every one of those who have fought and bled in the cause shall have joined their contemporaries. What is to be said of Poland, and the situation of her heroic, unhappy sons, you well know, having been a constant and zealous member of our committee. You know what sort of mental perturbation among the ignorant part of every European nation has accompanied the visit of the cholera in Russia, Germany, Hungary, and several parts of Great Britain and France—suspicions of poison, prejudices against the politicians, and so forth. I would like to know whether the population of the United States has been quite free of those aberrations, as it would be an additional argument in behalf of republican institutions and superior civilization resulting from them.

" Most truly and affectionately,

" Your friend,

" LAFAYETTE."

"I have just now good news from ——, dated 15th. My grandson says that five attacks from the Miguelists have been most gallantly repelled; it is to be hoped the infamous Miguels will ultimately be overthrown. I hope you are arrived in good health, my dear sir, and, referring you to the European papers, inclose two special little speeches of your friend,   LAFAYETTE.

' PARIS, *December* 8, 1832."

"PARIS, *February* 28, 1833.

" MY DEAR SIR : I am highly obliged to you for your kind letter, and for your publication of my observations on the present melancholy affairs in the United States. I see with pleasure that they have been repeated in all the American papers, namely, at

Charleston; so they have been in the papers of this country. Inclosed you will find some late observations of mine in the House;
they will give you an account of political matters on this side of
the Atlantic.

Most truly and affectionately,

" Your friend,

" LAFAYETTE."

"LA GRANGE, November 5, 1833.

" MY DEAR SIR: The particular accounts I can give you of the
family at La Grange are almost the only addition to be made to your
investigation of European papers. You well know the divisions in
the public opinion, so that, by comparing together their several expressions, you may form a correct judgment of the actual situation
and progress of affairs on this side of the Atlantic. You will not
therefore suppose that the constitutionality of the *Juste-Milieu* and
its royal chief is so far, as their followers pretend to be, from the
principle and wishes of anti-liberal governments, nor will you think
that the patriotism and republicanism of France is all confined within
the formula marked out in the name of a society. Under the invo-
cation of Robespierre, that society itself, chiefly composed of
honest citizens and devoted patriots, has been unfortunately and
designedly led into errors, to which the police agents have not been
strangers. The best account that has been given of that publication is, agreeably to my opinion, to be found in the *Comique Français* of the 28th of October, and the inclosed. The eyes of Jules
Lasteyrie are not yet recovered, and require a long management,
but the sight of both of them will be preserved. Oscar Lafayette
has been, by the scientific examination jury, admitted to the Polytechnic School. The greater part of the family are at La Grange,
and request their best compliments to you. We shall leave here
for the session of the House—that is to be opened for the 23d of
December. I don't hear from our excellent friend Mr. Cooper and
family. He must be in New York before this letter reaches you.
I intend writing to him, namely, on the subject of one of his letters,
by the next packet; in the mean while tell him that Chodiko, having
been prevented to leave us and repair to Montauban, has anticipated his predictions by asking a passport to quit France for England. I don't know where he now is. I have several times spoken,
and lately written, to Dwernicki. What remains of the French
debt to the American committee is not yet settled and paid.

Chodiko must be very forlorn. I shall know more in a few days, on a trip to town. My grandson is arrived from the south. He goes the day after to-morrow to Paris, with Mr. Gallatin's, Mr. Rives's, Mr. Cooper's, and your own long letter, and an introduction to Mr. Livingston, who has notes very similar, I think, to our notions, and will frame an article for the *Revue des Deux Mondes.* I shall send it as soon as it comes out. I will be much obliged to you, my dear sir, if you are pleased to call upon Mr. Prince, Long Island, and request him to send me grafts of the fine North River Spitzenberg red apple, of the bloody peach, the inside of which is red, and some mock-orange trees—they are tall, and handsomer than the European varieties; you would recommend them, with a bill of the costs, to the captain of a packet, so as to have time to place them. Pay my compliments to Mr. Prince, who has been so very kind in his invoices to me.

" Most truly and affectionately,

" Your old friend,

" LAFAYETTE."

To this letter Mr. Morse replied as follows:

To General Lafayette.

" NEW YORK, *January 6, 1834.*

" MY DEAR GENERAL : Your obliging letter of the 5th of November, just received, finds me confined to the house by temporary lameness. I owe you an apology, my dear General, for I am in your debt since your last interesting letter introducing to me the *amiable,* and, I am happy to add, *popular* Maroncelli. I thank you for making him known to me, although I feel that I am not so situated in my domestic establishment—being alone—as to show him all the attentions I could wish, or he deserves. Yet I have had the pleasure of introducing him to our club, who meet weekly, of which Mr. Gallatin, Mr. Jay, Chancellor Kent, the professors of Columbia College, etc., are members, and we have been highly gratified in his society. The ten years' imprisonment of Silvio Pellico has been published here, and has excited great interest for Mr. Maroncelli, so that I believe he finds himself very agreeably engaged. He is about publishing, he tells me, his own history of that imprisonment.

" I am rejoiced to know that your grandson, Jules Lasteyrie, will not lose his sight, although I regret to learn that his recovery will be tedious; what a melancholy event would the loss of his eyes have been to him and to all your dear family! I am glad to learn, also, that your other grandson, Oscar Lafayette, has entered the Polytechnic School. I incerely pray that France and the world may see in the grandson the same enlarged benevolence, the same love of true liberty, the same persevering consistency, the same self-devotion to the happiness of mankind, as have distinguished and immortalized the grandfather. Tell him, my dear General, that the world will have its eye on him; his name cannot be hid, he must sustain it in all its glory; and I pray that God's strength may be given him, that he may be able to sustain it unsullied.

"You will have learned before this of the arrival of our excellent and distinguished friend Cooper and his charming family; they arrived on the very day of the date of your letter, the 5th of November, and are now well. I dined with them on New-Year's day. Mr. Cooper is about replying to the attacks made upon him while absent, and in his pamphlet will make an *exposé* of the finance discussion in Paris, which will create a little disturbance probably in the minds of some Americans who were aiding and abetting the attacks on you, my dear General, and on their country's institutions, in that discussion.

"I have this moment written a line to Mr. Prince, of Long Island, inclosing your request respecting the grafts and trees, and desiring him to have them prepared immediately. I hope you will receive them by the same packet which takes this letter.

"As to political affairs in this country, my dear General, I am conscious there are others better informed than myself, who will keep you advised of their various changes. I have been too long absent from my country to retain any thing of mere party feeling; I cannot identify myself with any of the present parties. I read, as far as I have the time, the statements of all, till I have become quite familiar with the general character of party strife. I find the usual quantity of denunciations of the outs against the ins, and of charges of tyranny and usurpation, and the usual forebodings of anarchy and ruin from the measures of the existing Administration; and I can trace, or think I can trace, most of the asperity and bitter revilings which disfigure and disgrace our press, to the fears of office-holders, or the disappointments of office-seekers. Some of our orators declaim loudly on the danger to our institutions of certain measures, and others threaten a separation of the Union. Yet the solid, substantial, enterprising, active majority of the people are not moved by verbiage or rhetorical figures; they read and calmly digest those dashing arguments *pro* and *con.*; the wordy war rages in the halls of Congress, and the echoes of the strife ring through the land, but it is mere sound, until an evil truly presses upon the people, until they feel their freedom actually invaded, and their interests suffering in earnest from bad legislation, and then the voice of the people is heard in its might, and the strife of party is hushed; the troubles of the land are put into retirement by our bloodless weapon of revolution, the ballot-box, and the evil is remedied. This seems to be the natural operation, my dear General, of our beautiful institutions, nor can I be excited to alarm for their safety except in the supposable case of a general demoralization comprised in an absence of religious principle, and a prevalence of ignorance; and of such a state of things there is little prospect, while the benevolent are so active in their various societies for the diffusion of religious and scientific knowledge. No, my dear General; you have lived to see your favorite principles triumphant in one country, at least. They have withstood many a storm that has threatened them; they have been severely tried in the furnace, and are yet to be tried, but like gold they have hitherto come out, and, I am persuaded, will ever come out, purified; and you have the glorious anticipation that they must and will eventually triumph throughout the world, though all the tyrants of the earth league together to crush them."

General Lafayette to Mr. Morse.

"PARIS, *February* 27, 1834.

"MY DEAR SIR: Permit me to send you a letter for Mr. Maroncelli, relative to a little money transaction, which I much wish to be put into his own hands. You may have heard of an indisposition which still detains me in my room; and, as reports about it have been aggravated, I have the pleasure to assure you that I am much better, and shall soon have got rid of it. Remember me most affectionately to the Cooper family, and other friends, and believe me,   "Your affectionate friend,

"LAFAYETTE."

His last year in Paris had been made very pleasant to Mr. Morse by the kind attentions of General Lafayette, at whose house in the city, and at La Grange, the artist was a frequent and welcome guest. When the sad intelligence reached the United States of the death of Lafayette, in 1834, Mr. Morse addressed the following note to the son of his illustrious friend:

To George Washington Lafayette, Member of Chamber of Deputies, etc.

"I scarcely know in what language to express to you, and to all your family, the feelings of unfeigned sorrow with which the intelligence of the death of your great and good father, the illustrious General Lafayette, oppressed me. The announcement was the more sudden to me, as I had received a letter from him but a short time before this, in which he expressed a confidence of his speedy recovery. Allow me, my dear sir, to mingle my tears with yours for the irreparable loss you have suffered. In common with this whole country, now clad in mourning, with the lovers of true liberty and of exalted philanthropy throughout the world, I bemoan the departure from earth of your immortal parent; yet I may be permitted to indulge in additional feelings of more private sorrow at the loss of one who honored me with his friendship, and had not ceased, till within a few days of his death, to send to me occasional marks of his affectionate remembrance. Be assured, my dear sir, that the memory of your father will be especially endeared to me and mine.

"Accept for yourself, my dear sir, and for all the bereaved family, the assurance of my heart-felt condolence, and believe me, with the sincerest respect and esteem, your obedient servant and friend,

"S. F. B. MORSE."

Having proceeded so far with his picture that he was able to finish it at home, Mr. Morse left Paris, and made a visit to London, for the purpose of renewing the associations of his earlier art-life.

To his Brothers.

"LONDON, September 21, 1824.

"Here I am, once more, in England, and on the wing home. I shall probably sail from Havre in the packet of October 1st (the Sully), and I shall leave London for Southampton and Havre on the 26th inst., to be prepared for sailing.

"I am visiting old friends, and renewing old associations in London. Twenty years make a vast difference, as well in the aspect of this great city as in the faces of old acquaintances. London may be said literally to have gone into the country. Where I once was accustomed to walk in the fields, so far out of town as even to shoot at a target against the trees with impunity, now there are spacious streets, and splendid houses, and gardens. I spend a good deal of my spare time with Leslie. He is the same amiable, intelligent, unassuming gentleman that I left in 1815. He is painting a little picture, 'Sterne recovering his Manuscripts from the Curls of his Hostess at Lyons.' I have been sitting to him for the head of Sterne, whom he thinks I resemble very strongly. At any rate, he has made no alteration in the character of the face from the one he had drawn from Sterne's portrait, and has simply attended to the expression.

"When I left Paris, I was feeble in health, so much so, that I was fearful of the effects of the journey to London, especially as I passed through villages suffering severely from the cholera. But I proceeded moderately, lodged the first night at Boulogne-sur-Mer, crossed to Dover in a severe southwest gale, and passed the next night at Canterbury, and the next day came to London. I think the ride did me good, and I have been exercising a great deal, riding and walking since, and my general health is certainly improving. I am in hopes that the voyage will completely set me up again."

Mr. Dunlap records some interesting incidents in the visit of Mr. Morse to London and Paris, both on his journey to Italy, and his return :

"In 1829 Mr. Morse found himself in circumstances to visit, not only England again, but to reside for a sufficient time in Italy to study the works of art, copy many of the best pictures, and to improve in every branch of painting, to a degree which has surprised me, as much as it has given me pleasure. On his arrival from America, he found his friends Newton and Leslie in London, and with them attended two lectures at the Royal Academy, both remarkable for circumstances of very different natures. Leslie introduced Morse to the academicians, who received the president of the National Academy of Design with peculiar honor. The first of these lectures was remarkable, as being the last time Sir Thomas Lawrence was out of his house; the second, for a compliment paid by the lecturer to Washington Allston.

"Martin Archer Shee, the successor of Lawrence, was, on this occasion, requested to take the presidential chair; Morse, Leslie, and Newton, sat at his right hand. Mr. Greene, the lecturer, remarked, that he was glad Mr. Morse was present, as he had had occasion to mention an American gentleman who was an honor to the Royal Academy, Mr. Allston; and in the course of his lecture he quoted two of Allston's sonnets.

16

"Returning homeward he made a stop in Paris, and pursued his studies in the Louvre. He there made a picture of that celebrated gallery, copying in miniature the most valuable paintings as hanging on the walls. Of this splendid work my friend James Fenimore Cooper speaks thus, in a letter to me, dated Paris, March 16, 1832 : ' Morse is painting an exhibition picture that I feel certain must take. He copies admirably, and this is a drawing of the Louvre, with copies of some fifty of its best pictures.' The picture of the gallery of the Louvre was not finished until Morse returned to New York ; but, when nearly finished and removed from the gallery, the Chevalier Alexandre Le Noir, conservateur of the Museum of France (a celebrated antiquary, who is now engaged in arranging the papers on the ruins of Palenque in Mexico), wished to see the painting, and made an appointment for the purpose. He sat long before it, and complimented the artist highly, who received the praise as the effusion of politeness ; but the next day he had a proof of the learned critic's good opinion, for he received from him two folios and a quarto, published by him, containing several hundred plates, descriptive of the ancient monuments of France and their history.

"On leaving Paris," continues Mr. Dunlap, "he returned to London, and had the satisfaction of renewing former recollections and acquaintances, and particularly of enjoying the society of his friend Leslie. His good old friend and master, West, was no more, and his younger friend and instructor, Allston, was in America ; but he had recollections of the latter brought to his mind very unexpectedly. Morse had brought a letter to a gentleman from Italy, whose direction was No. 11 Tinny Street, London. After an absence of sixteen or seventeen years he had no remembrance of the street, or thought that it was connected with any transaction of interest to him. He sought the street, and, on entering it, he saw objects which appeared familiar to him, but which might only have reminded him of those dreamy sensations we experience through life, when, entering a strange place, we feel as if all the scene was merely a renewal of former impressions, made we know not how or when. He inquired for No. 11, of a gentleman passing, who exclaimed, ' Surely I know you, sir.' ' My name is Morse.' ' And have you forgotten that house ? ' pointing to it, ' that is No. 11 ; my name is Collard, and there, with you and your friend Allston, and his friends Coleridge and Lonsdale, I have passed many hours in time past.' The reality now flashed upon Morse ; he entered the house, and found himself in the apartment where he had witnessed such poignant scenes of distress in former days—the chamber in which his dear friend and mentor's wife had expired.

"Mr. Morse acquired a vast fund of knowledge in his European tour, having familiarized himself with the best models in the world; and he quitted England, in 1832, with every prospect of winning, in a few years, a splendid fame.

"Mr. Morse has told me that he formed a theory for the distribution of colors in a picture many years since, when standing before a picture of Paul Veronese, which has been confirmed by all his subsequent studies of the works of the great masters. This picture is now in the National Gallery, London. He saw in it that the highest light was cold; the mass of light, warm; the middle tint, cool; the shadow, negative; and the reflections, hot. He says he has tried this theory by placing a white ball in a box, lined with white, and convinced himself that the system of Paul Veronese is the order of Nature. Balls of orange or of blue, so placed, give the same relative result. The high light of the ball is uniformly cold, in comparison with the local color of the ball. 'I have observed in a picture by Rubens that it had a foxy tone, and on examination I found that the shadow (which according to my theory ought to be negative) was hot. Whenever I found this to be the case, I found the picture foxy.' On one occasion his friend Allston said to him, while standing before an unfinished painting, 'I have painted that piece of drapery of every color, and it will not harmonize with the rest of the picture.' Morse found the drapery belonged to the mass of light, and said, 'According to my theory, it must be warm; paint it flesh-color.' 'What do you mean by your theory?' Morse explained as above. Allston immediately said: 'It is so; it is in nature;' and has since said, 'Your theory has saved me many an hour's labor.'"

General James Grant Wilson, of New York, has kindly furnished pleasant recollections of conversations with Morse and Leslie.

"Professor Morse, some twenty years ago, as we were riding together in the cars, said to me: 'Shall I tell you about some of the great painters living in London when I was studying and starving with Leslie in a London garret?' The answer was, of course, 'Yes;' and he began a charming monologue concerning West, Allston, Haydon, Fuseli, and other great heirs of fame, fragments of which I jotted down the day following. . . . 'Among other artists with whom I was intimate was poor Haydon, who was so vain that he confessed he was uneasy at a funeral unless he was first in the procession. Going in company with a friend, in 1842, to call on him, my companion, on our entering the room, said: "Haydon, I have brought an old friend to see you. Do you remember him?" Looking at me intently for a few seconds he broke forth with, "Why, Morse; my friend Morse, how are you? Still painting and starving, eh?" . . . Tom Thumb killed Haydon!' Observing the surprised and inquiring looks of his listener, Morse continued: 'At the time or soon after that Haydon opened an exhibition of his greatest works, including "Christ's Entry into Jerusalem," Tom Thumb made his appearance in London, when his (Haydon's) gallery was immediately deserted, while all London flocked to see the diminutive dwarf. 'Twas too much for the poor painter; he became desperate at the failure of his exhibition, for which he had anticipated such great success, and put an end to his existence.' In answer to the inquiry as to Haydon's character and the causes that led to so distinguished an artist's being constantly in debt and harassed almost to death by creditors, the professor replied: 'Haydon was a person of inordinate vanity; he thought the eyes of the whole earth were upon him. He was improvident and reckless in expenditures, incurring the most extravagant expenses for the furtherance of high art; i. e., any thing to assist him in his painting, such as the purchase of expensive works of art, employing living models, etc.'

"'Another distinguished painter, with whom I was well acquainted, was Fuseli, a friend of Sir Joshua Reynolds, by whose advice he abandoned literature for art. Fuseli could speak with fluency nine languages, and enjoyed annoying certain of his literary companions with the display of antique lore. He on one occasion repeated half a dozen sonorous and well-sounding lines to Professor Porson, one of the best Greek scholars of his time, and said, "With all your learning you cannot tell me who wrote them." The Cambridge professor was compelled to admit that he did not know the author. "I should think not," chuckled Fuseli; "I made them this moment!" He would sometimes, when in a passion, give vent to his fury by swearing in half a dozen languages. I once accompanied the Swiss painter to the house of a wealthy amateur artist, where we were invited to dine. He wished to obtain Fuseli's opinion of a large picture which he had just completed, and accordingly after dinner it was inspected by all the party. "Extraordinary! *ex-traordinary!* EXTRAORDINARY!" exclaimed Fuseli. "Do you ad-mire my picture?" asked the delighted amateur. "Oh, extraor-dinary!" again exclaimed Fuseli. On our way home, accompanied by another artist named Lamb, he said, "Why, Mr. Fuseli, how could you possibly admire such a paltry picture—so out of drawing, and the coloring so wretched!" "Oh!" was the reply, "I said ex-traordinary, but I meant extraordinary BAD!" That word has often since done duty for me under similar circumstances,' added Morse, with a merry laugh. 'On another occasion an American artist, named B——, a great quack, who, by advertising, puffery, and toady-ism, managed to obtain considerable business, took a fine residence in a fashionable quarter of London, and invited a large number of artists, authors, and fashionable people, to a house-warming. B——, walking with Fuseli in one of the largest apartments, remarked, "I intend to have the walls whitewashed, and then paint on them a series of magnificent historical pictures. What do you think of it?" "*Better paint the pictures first, and then whitewash them!*" was Fuseli's reply.'

"My conversation with Leslie, which occurred some sixteen months later, was chiefly in regard to his early artist-life in London, when he and Morse shared a room together in Warren Street, and their most familiar friends were Washington Allston and a young American artist named King. 'In those days,' he remarked, 'the Allstons, Morse, and myself, spent our evenings together, and happy evenings they were, I can assure you. Of course, we often went to the theatre, and I remember one famous occasion when we saw Mrs. Siddons and her brothers, John and Charles, in "Henry VIII." The author of "Home, Sweet Home" was with us that night. About that time (1812 or 1813) we all spent a delightful day together at Hampton Court. Allston had a measureless admiration of Turner. He thought him the greatest painter since the days of Claude. It was reported that Turner had declared his intention of being buried in his "Carthage," which you have seen in the National Gallery. I was told that he said to Chantrey: "I have appointed you one of my executors; will you promise to see me rolled up in it?" "Yes," said the sculptor, "and I promise you also that as soon as you are buried I will have you taken up and unrolled!" This story was so generally circulated and credited that, when Dean Milman heard that Turner was to be buried in St. Paul's Cathedral, he said, "I will not read the service over him if he is wrapped up

in that picture."' . . . Such was the sparkling *commensalia* of Leslie
that much of its brilliancy and interest is lost in the attempt to
transfer it to paper, and I cannot but regret that I did not at the
time jot down more of his conversation concerning his gifted friends,
particularly that portion of it referring to Sir Walter Scott, Irving,
and Morse."

As the career of Mr. Morse as a painter closed here, and the
remainder of his life was devoted to the Telegraph, this is the
appropriate place in which to present a critical notice prepared
for this work by D. Huntington, Esq., the distinguished artist,
and President of the National Academy of Design:

"My acquaintance with Professor Morse began in the spring of
1835, when I was placed under his care by my father as a pupil.
He then lived in Greenwich Lane (now Greenwich Avenue), and
several young men were studying art under his instruction. He
was actively engaged in painting, though he devoted a part of his
time to experiments connected with his Telegraph. He gave a
short time every day to each pupil, carefully pointing out our errors,
and explaining the principles of art. After drawing for some time
from casts, with the crayon, he allowed us to begin the use of the
brush, and we practised painting our studies from the casts, using
black, white, and raw umber. I believe this method was of great
use in enabling us early to acquire a good habit of painting. I
only regret that he did not insist on our sticking to this kind of
study a longer time, and drill us more severely in it, but he indulged our hankering for color too soon; and, when once we had
tasted the luxury of a full palette of colors, it was a dry business
to go back to plain black and white. In the autumn of that year,
1835, he removed to spacious rooms in the New-York University,
on Washington Square.

" In the large studio in the north wing, he painted several fine
portraits, among them the beautiful full length of his daughter,
Mrs. Lind. He also lectured before the students, and a general
audience, illustrating his subject by painted diagrams.

" During this winter he was much occupied with the telegraphic
experiments, and exhibited to his pupils one of the earliest, if not
the first successful operation of the instrument. Though charmed
with the success of the experiment, we had no faith in its practical
results, and mourned over this sad infatuation (as we thought it) of
our master, which consumed so much of the time which we thought

he ought to devote to his art. Over his pupils he exercised a kind, paternal influence, and we held him in esteem and reverence.

"His friends and brother artists were disappointed that he did not obtain one of the Government orders at that time, given for historical paintings, to fill the vacant panels of the Rotunda. To compensate him for this neglect, they made up a purse, and gave him a commission for an historical picture. He chose for his subject 'The Compact of the Pilgrims on board the Mayflower,' which he considered as the germ of our free government. He made many studies for this proposed picture, and drew the outline of the composition on a canvas of a large cabinet size. I remember it as a well-arranged group, simple and dignified in its general lines, and promising to be a successful work. I inquired of him, a few years ago, what had become of this canvas. He told me it had been lost, with many other sketches, during one of his visits to Europe. The money which had been advanced he returned to the subscribers.

"Professor Morse's love of scientific experiments was shown in his artist-life. He formed theories of color, tried experiments with various vehicles, oils, varnishes, and pigments. His studio was a kind of laboratory.

"A beautiful picture of his wife and two children was painted, he told me, with colors ground in milk, and the effect was juicy, creamy, and pearly, to a remarkable degree. Another picture was commenced with colors mixed with beer, afterward solidly impasted and glazed with rich, transparent tints in varnish. His theory of color is fully explained in the account of his life in Dunlap's 'Arts of Design.' He proved its truth by boxes and balls of various colors. He had an honest, solid, vigorous *impasto*, which he strongly insisted on in his instructions—a method which was like the great masters of the Venetian school. This method was modified in his practice by his studies under West, in England, and by his intimacy with Allston, for whose genius he had a great reverence, and by whose way of painting he was strongly influenced. He was a lover of simple, unaffected truth, and this trait is shown in his works as an artist; he had a passion for color, and rich, harmonious tints run through his pictures, which are glowing and mellow, and yet pearly and delicate. He had a true painter's eye, but he was hindered from reaching the fame his genius promised as a painter by various distractions; such as the early battles of the Academy of Design in its struggle for life, domestic afflictions, and, more than all, the engrossing cares of his invention. The 'Hercules,' with its colossal proportions and daring attitude is evidence of the zeal and courage of his early studies. An interesting account of this work, and of the model in plaster, which he made for it, is given in 'Dunlap,' vol. ii., p. 311. It is now placed for safe-keeping in the Academy of Design, and is worthy of being carefully preserved in a public gallery, not only as an instance of successful study in a young artist (Morse was in his twenty-first year), but as possessing high artistic merit, and a force and richness which plainly show that, if his energies had not been diverted, he might have achieved a name in art equal to the greatest of his contemporaries.

"His 'Gallery of the Louvre' I know only from the studies made for it; but they indicate a great mastery of perspective, of grouping, and coloring. His large picture of 'The House of Representatives,' for many years owned in England, was brought to this country by an amateur, taken to San Francisco for exhibition, returned to New York, and is now in my studio. It has those traits of truthfulness, simplicity, and a subdued, mellow richness, which characterize many of his works, but which are preëminent in this. The architecture is well drawn, the accessories rendered with accuracy, the flesh-color is deep and luminous, and the general effect harmonious and agreeable. The rich, solid, impasted execution is like some great old Venetian painter, and the hue and texture remind one of the works of Tintoretto.

"The following account of this picture is taken from the *Daily Graphic*, of May 26, 1873 : 'In the studio of D. Huntington is a most interesting historical painting by Professor Morse, which bears the date of 1822. The canvas is eight feet by eleven feet, and represents the old House of Representatives at the hour of lighting. In the centre hangs the great chandelier, and on a high step-ladder a negro is turning up the Argand burners, which are evidently of interest, as the group on the platform, among whom are Story and Marshall, are regarding the operation. Scattered among the seats and around the room, are the members talking together, and one with his back toward the light is endeavoring to read. In the half gloom of the gallery are several persons, one of whom is Morse, the geographer, and father of the professor, also Professor Silliman and an Indian princess. There is the greatest fidelity in the painting of the room, and what renders the picture still more valuable is the fact that the faces are all portraits. The key to the picture cannot be found, but the faces of a number have been recognized by the likenesses as those of Chief-Justices Marshall and Story; Stephen

Van Rensselaer; Governor Tomlinson, of Connecticut; Gales and Seaton, of the *National Intelligencer,* and several others. The studies for these heads were made by Professor Morse in Washington, and afterward were stolen, some of them finally finding their way into private collections, where they now are. The aim of the artist seems to have been to present a true picture of the House at that time, rather than to attempt any thing picturesque. The whole work has an honest air, which adds to its historical interest. The costumes are those of that time, when gentlemen wore ruffled shirts and white ties. There is but little attempt at composition. The groups are arranged in broken lines, but the effect of the whole is a little stiff. The low rich tones, the crimsons, and warm grays, are very agreeable. The perspective is good, and the painting, especially of the columns, is very solidly done. For its historical accuracy, its portraits, its representations of the costumes, and the appearance of the old House of Representatives; for its rendering of a phase of our national life now passed away, as well as from the fact that it is the work of one of the fathers of American art, and one of the most illustrious of Americans, it deserves a place in the national Capitol, and none could be more appropriate than that same room it pictures, which is now fitted for a public gallery.'

"Professor Morse's world-wide fame rests, of course, on his invention of the Electric Telegraph; but it should be remembered that the qualities of mind which led to it, were developed in the progress of his art-studies, and if his paintings, in the various fields of history, portrait, and landscape, could be brought together, it would be found that he deserved an honored place among the foremost American artists."

The picture of the Louvre, which Mr. Morse began in Paris, he finished after his return to New York, and it was purchased by George Clark, Esq., of Otsego, and removed to Hyde Hall, on Otsego Lake.

We have now followed Mr. Morse through what may be called his art-life. After his return to the city of New York, he pursued his profession as a means of support; but, during the voyage across the ocean in the autumn of 1832, a vision broke upon him, which produced a revolution in his life, and on the commerce and intercourse of mankind. We have seen that his genius was inventive. From early youth he had displayed the inventive faculty—a distinctive feature of the family to

which he belonged. He was stimulated by an ardent desire
for usefulness and fame. The honor of his country was always
very near his heart. His desire for distinction as a painter, as
we gather from letters to his most intimate associates, had in it
more of patriotism than selfishness. He longed to distinguish
his country by his own distinction ; and, in the future controversies in which his great invention involved him, the honor of
America was uppermost in his mind. Encouraged and excited
by the associations of the past three years in Europe, laden with
the riches which he had amassed in the galleries of Italy, and
flushed with the highest hopes of future success, he embarked
at Havre on the 1st day of October, 1832, for the city of New
York.

Minister of the United States; Mr. J. F. Fisher, of Philadelphia; Dr. Charles T. Jackson, of Boston; Mr. S. F. B. Morse of New York; Mrs. T. Palmer, Miss E. Palmer, Mr. C. Palmer, Mr. F.

CHAPTER VII.

1832.

PACKET-SHIP SULLY—ELECTRO-MAGNETISM—DINNER-TABLE CONVERSATION—
IDEA OF THE TELEGRAPH—FIRST MARKS MADE—THE INVENTION AN-
NOUNCED TO PASSENGERS—DRAWINGS EXHIBITED—PREDICTION TO CAP-
TAIN PELL—PROF. E. N. HORSFORD'S HISTORY OF THE SCIENCE—STEPHEN
GREY— LEYDEN JAR—FRANKLIN'S EXPERIMENTS—CHARLES MARSHALL —
LE SAGE—LOMOND—REUSSER—CAVALLO—WEDGEWOOD—RONALDS—DYAR
—GALVANISM, OR VOLTAISM—VOLTA—SCHWEIGGER—COXE—MAGNETISM—
ELECTRO-MAGNETISM—AMPÈRE—SCHILLING—COOKE AND WHEATSTONE—
OERSTED — SPIRAL COIL, 1821 — ARAGO — STURGEON — JAMES FREEMAN
DANA — JOSEPH HENRY—FECHNER—OHM'S LAW—STEINHEIL—DANIEL—
SOEMMERING—SAMUEL FINLEY BREESE MORSE—INVENTION AND DISCOV-
ERY—CLAIMS OF DISCOVERERS AND INVENTORS—SUCCESSIVE STEPS IN
TELEGRAPHIC INVENTION.

THE packet-ship Sully, Captain Pell, sailed from Havre on the 1st day of October, 1832, for New York. Among the cabin-passengers were the Hon. William C. Rives, of Virginia, returning with his family from Paris, where he had been as Minister of the United States; Mr. J. F. Fisher, of Philadelphia; Dr. Charles T. Jackson, of Boston; Mr. S. F. B. Morse, of New York; Mrs. T. Palmer, Miss E. Palmer, Mr. C. Palmer, Mr. F. Palmer, Mr. W. Palmer, Mr. J. Haslett, Charleston, S C.; Mr. Lewis Rogers, Virginia; Mr. W. Post, New York; Mr. Constable, New York; Mons. de la Cande, Mons. J. P. Chazel, Charleston; Mr. A. Scheidler, Frankfort, Germany; Mr. and Mrs. Burgy, and others.

In the early part of the voyage conversation at the dinner-table turned upon recent discoveries in electro-magnetism, and the experiments of Ampère with the electro-magnet. Dr. Jackson spoke of the length of wire in the coil of a magnet, and the question was asked by some one of the company, "If the velocity of electricity was retarded by the length of the wire?" Dr. Jackson replied that electricity passes instantaneously over any known length of wire. He referred to experiments made by Dr. Franklin with several miles of wire in circuit, to ascertain the velocity of electricity; the result being that he could observe no difference of time between the touch at one extremity and the spark at the other. At this point Mr. Morse interposed the remark, "If the presence of electricity can be made visible in any part of the circuit, I see no reason why intelligence may not be transmitted instantaneously by electricity." The conversation went on. But the one new idea had taken complete possession of the mind of Mr. Morse. It was as sudden and pervading as if he had received at that moment an electric shock. All that he had learned in former years, the experiments he had seen in his boyhood, his studies with Professors Day and Silliman, the later and significant discourses of Professor Dana, and conversations with Professor Renwick, were revived, and began to form themselves into means and ways to the accomplishment of a grand result. He withdrew from the table and went upon deck. He was in mid-ocean, *undique cœlum, undique pontus.* As the lightning cometh out of the east and shineth unto the west, so swift and far was the instrument to work that was taking shape in his creative mind.

Lightning and electricity had long been known as one and the same. Signals had been made at a distance by electricity, and intelligence thus transmitted, as beacon-fires on hill-tops had from time immemorial flashed the knowledge of events across continents. But this was not *the* conception of that moment in the brain of Morse. His was a thought that, so far as he knew, had never entered the mind of man before! He would transmit intelligence and record it at a distance. That is a telegraph. Nothing else is a telegraph; an instrument to write at a distance. The purpose instantly formed absorbed his mind, and to its perfection his life from that moment was devoted. He was the man to do the work. His mind was eminently inventive and mechanical. In his early youth and riper manhood he had sought out many inventions. His name had long been enrolled among inventors in the Patent-Office of the United States. Patience, perseverance, and faith, were hereditary traits of his character. He was now forty-one years old.

The mechanism by which the result would be reached was to be wrought out by slow and laborious thought and experiment, but the grandeur of that result broke upon him as clearly and fully as if it had been a vision from heaven. Difficulties afterward arose in his path, to be surmounted or removed by toilsome and painful processes; for it is the order of Nature that birth-throes should bear some proportion to the greatness of the birth. But in that first hour of conception, when his soul was all aglow with the discovery, he saw the end from the beginning. The current of electricity passes instantaneously to any distance along a wire; the current being interrupted, a spark appears. The spark shall be one sign; its absence another; the time of its absence another. Here are three signs to be combined into the representation of figures or letters. They can be made to form an alphabet. Words may thus be indicated. A telegraph, an instrument to record at a distance, will be the result. Continents shall be crossed. This great and wide sea shall be no barrier. "If it will go ten miles without stopping," he said, "I can make it go around the globe."

Of all the great inventions that have made their authors immortal, and conferred enduring benefit upon mankind, no one was so completely grasped at its inception as this. His little note or scratch book was always at hand, in which he made sketches of objects that met his eye, or of images formed in his mind. Scores of these books are now in existence, in which his early and later pencilings are preserved. As he sat upon the deck after the conversation at dinner, he drew from his pocket one of these books, and began to make marks to represent letters and figures to be produced by the agency of electricity at a distance from the place of action. First, he arranged ten dots and lines so as to represent figures referring to words. Next, he drew the wires in tubes. Then came the magnets, and by-and-by cog-rules, to be used in regulating the power. In the course of a few days his book presented several pages, which are here reproduced, showing the first marks ever made in the invention of the Telegraph:

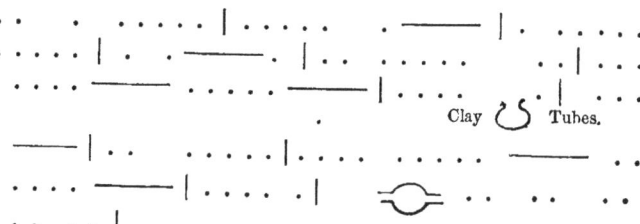

Clay 〜 Tubes.

Close Tubes.

215 War.	56 Holland.	15 Belgium.	5 Alliance.	
161 France.	252 England.	300 against	41 Russia.	35 Prussia.
25 Austria.	4030 Wednesday.	141 6th Aug.		
222 Naturalist,	32 died.		Cuvier. 1.6.8.5.4.3	

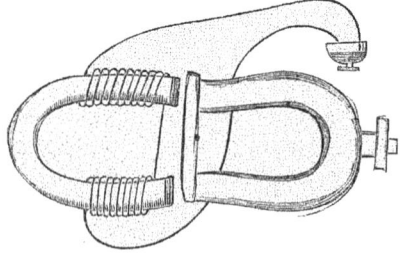

Magnet lifting sixty pounds.

A single space separates each of the first five figures.
Two spaces separate each of the last five.
Three spaces separate each number completed.

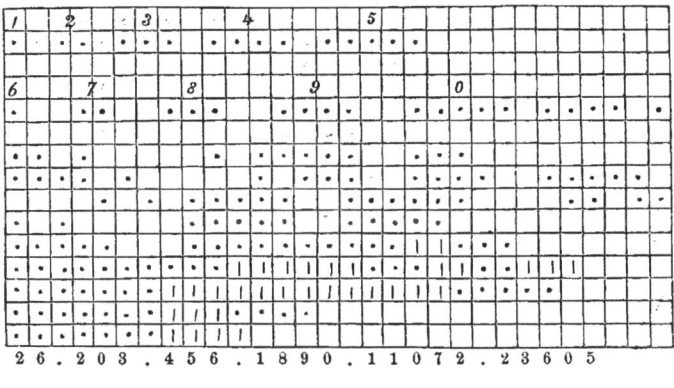

2 6 . 2 0 3 . 4 5 6 . 1 8 9 0 . 1 1 0 7 2 . 2 3 6 0 5

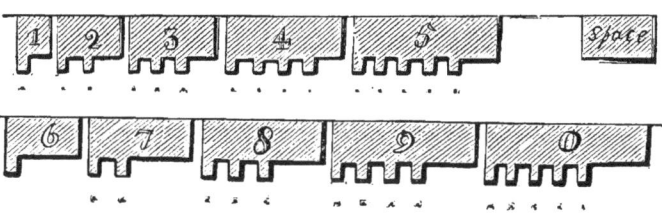

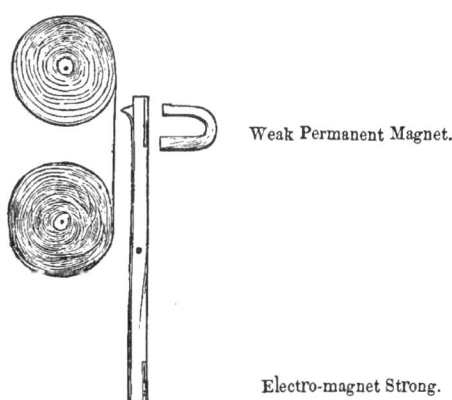

Weak Permanent Magnet.

Electro-magnet Strong.

He wrought incessantly that day, and sleep forsook him in his berth that night. His mind was on fire. In a few days he submitted these rough drafts to Mr. Rives, who suggested various difficulties. But Mr. Morse was ready with a solution. Mr. Fisher states that Mr. Morse illustrated to him his system of signs for letters, to be indicated by a quick succession of strokes or shocks of the galvanic current, to be carried along upon a single wire. After several sleepless nights, while his mind was in labor with the subject, he announced it at the breakfast-table, and explained the process by which he proposed to accomplish it. He then exhibited the drawing of the instrument, by which he would do the work, and so completely had he mastered all the details, that five years afterward, when a model of this instrument was constructed, it was instantly recognized as the one he had devised and ‚drawn in his sketch-book, and exhibited to his fellow-passengers on the ship. J. Francis Fisher, Esq., counselor-at-law of Philadelphia, stated, when his testimony was required:

"In the fall of the year 1832 I returned from Europe as a passenger with Mr. Morse, in the ship Sully, Captain Pell, master; during the voyage the subject of an electric telegraph was one of frequent conversation; Mr. Morse was most constant in pursuing it, and *alone* the one who seemed disposed to reduce it to a practical test; and I recollect that for this purpose he devised *a system of signs for letters*, to be indicated and marked by a quick succession of *strokes*, or shocks of the galvanic current; and I am sure of the fact that it was deemed by Mr. Morse perfectly competent to effect the result stated; I did not suppose that any other person on board the ship claimed any merit in the invention, or was in fact interested to pursue it to maturity, as Mr. Morse then seemed to be; nor have I been able since that time to recall any fact or circumstance to justify the claim of any person other than Mr. Morse to the invention."

And Captain Pell stated, under oath, that when he saw the instrument, September 27, 1837, he recognized in it the same mechanical principles and arrangements which he had heard Mr. Morse explain on board of the Sully in 1832. Captain Pell says:

"Before the vessel was in port, Mr. Morse addressed me in these words: 'Well, captain, should you hear of the telegraph, one of these days, as the wonder of the world, remember the discovery was made on board the good ship Sully.'"

Thus it appears from his own records, and the recollections of the captain and passengers, gentlemen of the highest respectability and intelligence, that on shipboard Mr. Morse had actually drawn out and recorded a system of signs, composed of a combination of dots and spaces, to indicate letters, figures, and words, and a mode of applying the electric or galvanic current so as to make these signs permanent upon paper, to be passed along in the instrument which he had invented. The INVENTION was accomplished and announced ere the inventor set foot on his native shore. While the Sully is pursuing her way across the sea, and the inventor is thinking out his great conception, we will review the progress of electrical science, and learn the material he had with which to make his idea real: [1]

The knowledge that certain substances, like amber, would, when rubbed with dry silk, or woolen, or fur, attract light bodies, like pith-balls, or feathers, and which is at the foundation of *electricity*, was known centuries before the Christian era. The knowledge that a certain iron-ore was endowed with the property of attracting pieces of iron, lay at the foundation of *magnetism*, and was also of very early origin. *Galvanism*, at the farthest, scarcely goes back beyond 1790, and, for application to the invention of the recording telegraph, not beyond the beginning of this century.

ELECTRICITY.—The second step in electricity must have been the discovery that, under certain circumstances, instead of attracting light bodies, the amber repelled them; and the third step, that the peculiar quality or force was something that could be transmitted along what is called a *conductor*.

As early as 1729 Stephen Grey employed as conductor packthread or twine, six hundred and fifty feet long, suspended by silk threads.[2] He also discovered that electricity could be conducted through metallic wires.

The Leyden jar dates soon after 1745. This discovery, by which the electric force might be stored up, made it possible to

---

[1] The history that occupies the remainder of the chapter was prepared expressly for this volume by Professor E. N. Horsford, of Cambridge, Massachusetts.

[2] Lecture by Dr. B. W. Richardson, F. R. S., before the Brethren of the Charter House.—*Illustrated London News*, February 21, 1874.

intensify its action. The accumulation of force in the interior, and its corresponding diminution on the outside, was restored by the interposition of a conductor, connecting the outside with the inside. This conductor might be of great length. The velocity of the current traversing the wire seemed instantaneous, and numerous attempts to determine it were made almost immediately after.

Winkler,[1] of Leipsic, made an experiment July 28, 1746, including the river Pleisse in his circuit. Experiments were made in Paris, including the water of the basin of the Tuileries in the circuit.[2] Le Monnier made an experiment with a wire thirteen hundred and nineteen feet in length, which seemed to show that the velocity was instantaneous.[3] Watson, of England, in 1747, made an experiment, employing two miles of wire in the air and two of earth in its circuit, with a like result.[4]

Dr. Franklin performed a similar experiment in 1748.[5]

Franklin says: "Two iron rods about three feet long were planted just within the margin of the river, on opposite sides. A thick piece of wire with a small round knob at its end was fixed on the top of one of the rods, bending downward so as to deliver commodiously the spark upon the surface of the spirit. A small wire fastened by one end to a handle of the spoon containing the spirit was carried across the river, and supported in the air by the rope commonly used to hold by in drawing ferry-boats over. The other end of this wire was tied round the coating of the bottle, which being charged, the spark was delivered from the hook to the top of the rod standing in the water on that side. At the same instant the rod on the other side delivered a spark into the spoon, and fired the spirit, the electric fire returning to the coating of the bottle, through the handle of the spoon and the supporting wire connected with them."

POSSIBILITY OF AN ELECTRIC TELEGRAPH.—The existence of a force that might be stored up and transmitted through great lengths of wire, and through circuits of great length, of which the earth formed a part, was demonstrated before the middle of the eighteenth century. As both Watson and Franklin fired gunpowder and spirits with the electric force through great lengths of wire and earth introduced into their circuits, it is interesting to note how long ago electricity was employed, using the earth as a part of the circuit, for the transmission of signals.

---

[1] Priestley's "History of Electricity," p. 59.

[2] "Encyclopædia Britannica," edition of 1810, p. 736.

[3] Ibid.   [4] Ibid.   [5] Parton's "Life of Franklin."

Yet these brilliant results do not seem to have been followed by any immediate effort to produce a practical telegraph for the transmission of intelligence.

FIRST PROPOSED ELECTRIC TELEGRAPH.—The first person to propose the use of friction electricity as a medium for transmitting intelligence was a contributor to the *Scots Magazine*, in 1753. The communication was signed " C. M.," and it is believed to have been written by Charles Marshall, of Paisley, who was at the time sojourning at Renfrew, from which place the letter was written:[1]

> " *To the Editor of the Scots Magazine.*
>
> "RENFREW, *February* 1, 1753.

"SIR: It is well known to all who are conversant in electrical experiments, that the electric power may be propagated along a small wire, from one place to another, without being sensibly abated by the length of its progress. Let, then, a set of wires, equal in number to the letters of the alphabet, be extended horizontally between two given places, parallel to one another, and each of them about an inch distant from that next to it. At every twenty yards' end let them be fixed in glass or jewelers' cement to some firm body, both to prevent them from touching the earth or any other non-electric, and from breaking by their own gravity. Let the electric gun-barrel be placed at right angles with the extremities of the wires, and about one inch below them; also let the wires be fixed in a solid piece of glass at six inches from the end, and let that part of them which reaches from the glass to the machine have sufficient spring and stiffness to recover its situation after' having been brought in contact with the barrel. Close by the supporting glass let a ball be suspended from every wire; and about a sixth or an eighth of an inch below the balls place the letters of the alphabet, marked on bits of paper, or any other substance that may be light enough to rise to the electrified ball, and at the same time let it be so continued that each of them may reassume its proper place when dropped. All things constructed as above, and the minute previously fixed, I begin the conversation with my distant friend in this manner: Having set the electrical machine agoing, as in ordinary experiments, suppose I am to pronounce the word *sir:* with a piece of glass, or any other *electric per se*, I strike the wire *s* so as to bring it in contact with the barrel, then *i*, then *r ;* all in the same way; and my correspondent, almost in the same instant, observes these several characters rise in-order to the electrified balls at his end of the wires. Thus I spell away as long as I think fit; and my correspondent, for the sake of memory, writes the characters as they

---

[1] " Angewandten Electrikitäts-Lehre." Kuhn, pp. 798, 822.

rise, and may join and read them as often as he inclines. Upon a signal given, or from choice, I stop the machine, and, taking up the pen in my turn, I write down whatever my friend at the other end strikes out. If anybody should think this way tiresome, let him, instead of the balls, suspend a range of bells from the roof, equal in number to the letters of the alphabet, gradually decreasing in size from the bell *A* to *Z ;* and from the horizontal wires let there be another set reaching to the several bells; one, viz., from the horizontal wire *A* to the bell *A*, another from the horizontal wire *B* to the bell *B*, etc. Then let him who begins the discourse bring the wires in contact with the barrel as before; and the electric spark, breaking on bells of different size, will inform his correspondent by the sound what wires have been touched, and thus, by some practice, they may come to understand the language of the chimes in whole words, without being put to the trouble of noting down every letter. The same thing may be otherwise effected: Let the balls be suspended over the characters as before, but, instead of bringing the ends of the horizontal wires in contact with the barrel, let a second set reach from the electrified cable, so as to be in contact with the horizontal ones, and let it be so contrived, at the same time, that any of them may be removed from its corresponding horizontal by the slightest touch, and may bring itself again into contact when set at liberty. This may be done by the help of a small spring and slides, or twenty other methods, which the least ingenuity will discover. In this way the characters will always adhere to the balls, excepting when any one of the secondaries is removed from contact with its horizontal; and then the letter at the other end of the horizontal will immediately drop from its ball. But I mention this only by way of variety. Some may, perhaps, think that, although the electric fire has not been observed to diminish sensibly in its progress through any length of wire that has been tried hitherto, yet, as that has never exceeded some thirty or forty yards, it may be reasonably supposed that in a far greater length it would be remarkably diminished, and probably would be entirely drained off in a few miles by the surrounding air. To prevent the objection, and save longer argument, lay over the wires from one end to the other with a thin coat of jeweler's cement. This may be done for a trifle of additional expense; and, as it is an *electric per se*, will effectually secure any part of the fire from mixing with the atmosphere.

"I am, etc.,   C. M."

The method proposed by Marshall seems to have contained the essential elements of telegraphy.

Le Sage, at Geneva, in 1774, devised a plan of electric telegraphy and put it in operation. It was strikingly like that of Marshall, employing a wire for each letter, and producing repulsion between the pith-balls by an electric discharge for each wire.[1]

[1] Moigno's "Télégraphie Électrique," p. 59.

Lomond, in 1787, devised an instrument which, operated in one room, gave intelligent signals in an adjoining apartment.[1]

Reusser, of Geneva, in 1794, employed the electric spark to transmit intelligence, using an arrangement of lines and spaces, with stripes of tin-foil so contrived that, when these spaces were illuminated by the sparks, the form of the letter or figure was exhibited. The illumination of each letter or figure required a direct and return wire, and, as his plan employed thirty-seven characters, there were required seventy-four wires between each two stations. Similar telegraphs were devised by Salva, and Betancourt, at Madrid, operating many miles in length, in 1797 and 1798 (Humboldt).

Böckmann, in 1795, proposed the use of sparks, one, two, or more, to indicate the letters of the alphabet; and Cavallo, in 1797, successfully tested the project through a wire two hundred and fifty feet long. Lullin, about the same time, made a like suggestion.[2]

In "The Wedgwoods, being a Life of Josiah Wedgwood," by Llewellynn Jewett, London, 1865, is the following notice (p. 178) of a proposed telegraph:

"This Thomas Wedgwood was, I believe, cousin to Josiah, being son of Aaron Wedgwood, etc., etc. . . . He was a man of high scientific attainments, and has the reputation of being the first inventor of the electric telegraph (afterward so ably carried out by his son Ralph), and of many other valuable works."

Page 180: "In 1806, Ralph Wedgwood established himself at Charing Cross, and soon afterward his whole attention began to be engrossed with his scheme of the electric telegraph, which in the then unsettled state of the kingdom—in the midst of war, it must be remembered—he considered would be of the utmost importance to the Government. In 1814, having perfected his scheme, he submitted his proposal to Lord Castlereagh, and most anxiously waited the result. His son Ralph, having waited on his worship

---

[1] It is thus described by Arthur Young, in his "Travels in France," vol. i., p. 979, fourth edition, 1787: ' M. Lomond has made a remarkable discovery in electricity. You write two or three words on a paper; he takes it into a room, and turns a machine inclosed in a cylindrical case, at the top of which is an electrometer, a small pine pith-ball; a wire connects with a similar cylinder and electrometer in a distant apartment; and his wife, by remarking the corresponding motions of the ball, writes down the words they indicate, from which it appears that he has formed an alphabet of motion. As the length of the wire makes no difference in the effect, a correspondence might be carried on at any distance, within or without a besieged town, for instance, or for objects much more worthy of attention, and a thousand times more harmless."

[2] "Vollst. Abh. d. theor. und prak. Lehre v. d. Electr.," Leipzig, 1797, Bd. ii., pp. 337–388.

for a decision, as to whether Government would accept the plan or not, was informed that 'the war being at an end, the old system was sufficient for the country.' The plan therefore fell to the ground, until Professor Wheatstone, in happier and more enlightened times, again brought the subject forward with such eminent success. The plan thus brought forward by Ralph Wedgwood, in 1814, and of which, as I have stated, he received the first idea from his father, was thus described by him in a pamphlet, entitled, 'An Address to the Public on the Advantages of a Proposed Introduction of the Stylographic Principle of Writing into General Use; and also of an Improved Species of Telegraphy, calculated for the Use of the Public, as well as for the Government.'"

The pamphlet is dated, May 29, 1815.

Extract from the Pamphlet.

"A modification of the stylographic principle, proposed for the adoption of Parliament, in lieu of telegraphs, viz.:

"The Fulguric-Polygraph, which admits of writing in several distant places at one and the same time, by the agency of two persons only.

"This invention is founded on the capacity of electricity to produce motion in the act of acquiring an equilibrium:

"Which motion by the aid of machinery is made to distribute matter at the extremities of any given course. And the matter so distributed being variously modified in correspondence with the letters of the alphabet, and communicable in rapid succession at the will of the operator, it is obvious that writing at immense distances hereby becomes practicable; and further, as lines of communication can be multiplied from any given point, and those lines affected by one and the same application of the electric matter, it is evident from hence, also, that fac-similes of a dispatch, written as for instance in London, may with facility be written also in Plymouth, Dover, Hull, Leith, Liverpool, and Bristol, or any other place, by the same person, and by one and the same act."

He goes on to speak of the advantages to the public, and says:

"To the seat of her Government (England), therefore, it must be highly desirable to effect the most speedy and certain *communication from every quarter of the world.*"

All these employed friction electricity, as did Ronalds, of England, in 1816, on a line eight miles in length, operating with pith-balls on the faces of synchronous clocks, and Harrison Gray Dyar, on the Long-Island race-course,[1] near New York, in 1827, on a line of two miles, using the current to discolor prepared paper.

---

[1] Dyar's (defendant's) testimony, "Bain's Case," pp. 13, 327.

Up to this time the elements out of which to produce a success-ful telegraph had not been brought to light. The agent at command —friction electricity—was fitful, influenced by the weather, and, at a distance, liable at times to be feeble.

GALVANISM, OR VOLTAISM.—The discovery of the voltaic pile, in 1800, opened up a new era for invention in telegraphy. It gave the advantage of the constant current of a battery over the intermitted shocks of the electrical apparatus. Sömmering, in 1809-'11, em-ployed the electric current developed by the voltaic pile to produce chemical decompositions with the evolution of visible gas; he em-ployed thirty-five wires, each wire having the same letter or figure at either end, and an additional wire for producing an alarum, by causing an augmentation of gas in a manner to release a detent and set in motion clock-work to ring a bell. It would of course be pos-sible to transmit words by producing gas-bubbles at the ends of the wires, bearing in their order of succession the letters of which the words were composed. Each of the thirty-five wires had its return-wire, making seventy in all.

This was not, strictly speaking, a telegraph—a *writing* at a dis-tance; it was a *signal* apparatus—a voltaic semaphore. But it was cumbrous, time-consuming, and interesting chiefly as illustrat-ing how early the projectile force of the voltaic battery was ap-plied to the production of visible chemical effects at a distance.

Schweigger proposed to reduce the great number of wires in Sömmering's apparatus to two, and instead of a tube for the evo-lution of gas for each letter, a single tube only, and the letter to be indicated by the number of seconds through which the evolution of hydrogen should continue. This apparatus so simplified was to be used in connection with a signal-book.

Dr. John Redman Coxe, of Philadelphia, in 1810-'11, proposed a plan similar to that of Sömmering, which, however, was not carried out to practical testing.[1] He communicated an account of it, which was published in "Thomson's Annals of Philosophy" (February, 1816).

MAGNETISM.—The date of the discovery of the magnetic needle was in remote antiquity. The Chinese were familiar with its use before its introduction into Europe. This instrument, so indispen-sable to the navigation of the ocean and to numerous uses on land, consists of a slender bar of hardened iron or steel resting at its centre upon a sharply-pointed support. When this piece of iron was

---

[1] Coxe's deposition, p. 63, defendant's testimony, Morse *vs.* Bain Telegraph Case.

rubbed in a certain way with a natural loadstone, or an artificial magnet, it acquired the property when free to move on its support of pointing with one extremity to the north, and the other, of course, to the south. These extremities were respectively called the north and south poles.

ELECTRO-MAGNETISM.—It was early known that the position of the needle might be changed by electric discharges in its neighborhood, but its susceptibility to the influence of the galvanic current was the discovery of Oersted, of Copenhagen, in 1819. He found that when the electric current passes in a direction, north or south, through a wire, it causes a free magnetic needle immediately above or below it to assume or tend to assume a position at right angles to the direction of the current, and that by reversing the direction of the current the movement of the needle may be alike reversed.

This observation, usually ascribed to Oersted, seems to have been first made by Romagnési, a physicist of Trent. In a work entitled "Manuel du Galvanisme," par Joseph Lyarn, Paris, 1864, under the heading, "Appareil pour reconnaître l'action du galvanisme, sur la polarité d'une aiguille aimantée," after explaining the way to prepare the apparatus, which consists simply in putting a freely suspended magnetic needle parallel and close to a straight metallic conductor, through which a galvanic current is circulating, he described the effects in the following words : "D'après les observations de Romagnési, physicien de Trente, l'aiguille déjà aimantée, et que l'on soumet ainsi au courant galvanique, éprouve une déclinaison ; et d'après celles de J. Mojon, savant chimiste de Gènes, les aiguilles non aimantées acquièrent, par ce moyen, une sorte de polarité magnétique."

In the next year Schweigger, of Halle,[1] discovered that the deflection of the needle may be increased by coiling an insulated wire in a series of ovals or flat rings, compactly disposed, in a loop, and conducting the current around the needle from end to end; and produced the "galvanic multiplier," by which the deflection of the needle was much greater and more prompt. This discovery was the basis of the galvanometer, invented and first used by Professor Joseph Henry, of the United States.

Ampère, following up the discovery of Schweigger, developed the theory of electro-magnetism, which has since been universally adopted. He proposed to the French Academy at its session, October 2, 1820 ("Comptes Rendus"), a plan for a telegraph, in which

---

[1] Kuhn, "Ang. Elek.-Lehre," p. 514.

there was to be a needle for each letter. Ampère ascribes the original suggestion to Laplace.

Ritchie, in 1830, carried out this idea to a model by surrounding each needle with a coil of wire, so arranged as to disclose a letter in connection with the deflection of each needle. Mr. Alexander, of Edinburgh, made another modification in 1837.

The telegraph of Baron Pawel Larrowitsch Schilling, of Cronstadt, was based on the suggestion of Ampère. He had been associated with Sömmering as early as 1810 (Kuhn, p. 836). His plan seems to have been matured and set in practical operation, according to Amyot, in 1832–'33, but he was unable to secure such satisfactory demonstrations as would justify the support of the Russian Government until 1836, and in 1837 this persevering philosopher and inventor died. His instrument, however, exhibited by Moucke to William Fothergill Cooke in 1836, awoke his inventive genius, and he produced in the same year a needle telegraph, and in 1837 Cooke and Wheatstone a still more perfect needle telegraph.

Before Oersted, and Ampère, and Schweigger, the needle telegraph was impossible. After their discoveries reciprocal motion, or alternate right-and-left deflection, needed only a constant battery to render *signal* telegraphy possible. But *recording* telegraphy required a greater amount of force at the receiving station than was needed to move the needle, and another system of device must be brought into service.

The unequal action of the battery was a serious obstacle to progress in the direction of needle telegraphy, and, before research had overcome the difficulties ultimately surmounted by Daniel, the science of electro-magnetism had made great strides in a new direction.

The first step in this direction was taken by Arago immediately after the discovery of Oersted, in the same year with the discovery of the multiplier by Schweigger. He magnetized a straight iron bar or needle by placing it in a long spiral of wire and transmitting the galvanic current through the coil.

De la Rive sent a current through a close circuit of insulated copper wire, showing that the ring produced by the current acquired singular magnetic properties. Barlow, in describing the apparatus, in 1824, says: "A fine copper wire covered with silk thread is coiled five or six times, and tied together so as to form a ring about an inch in diameter, and the ends of the wire are con-

nected one with the zinc and the other with the copper slip above
the cork. When the apparatus is placed in water, slightly acidulated with sulphuric or nitric acid, the ring becomes highly magnetic," etc.

In this year Schweigger produced the flat spiral or volute coil.
In 1824 Barlow gives a diagram of the volute in one plane, invented by Schweigger, and says, page 266: "The best form for
the spiral, however, is that in which the wire lies all in one plane"
(as in Fig. 24). (This figure exhibits a coil like the hair-spring of
a watch.) "This being connected by its two extremities with the
poles of the battery will take up an astonishing quantity of filings,
which, by their reciprocal attraction toward each other, exhibit the
most pleasing appearance."

The discovery of the action of the spiral coil upon the magnetic
needle seems to have been independently made by Ampère, in 1821:
"I showed," he says "that the current which is in the pile acts on
the magnetic needle by the conjunctive wire. I described the instrument, which I proposed to construct, and, among others, the
galvanic spiral. I read a note upon the electro-chemical effects of a
spiral of iron wire, subjected to the action of the earth, directing
an electric current as well as a magnet.

"I announced the new fact of the attraction and repulsion of
two electric currents, without the intermediation of any magnet, a
fact which I had observed in spirals twisted spirally." [1]

Arago's discovery, that soft iron may be rendered a temporary
magnet by placing it within a helix of wire, through which is circulating a galvanic current, dates 1821. He says: "A piece of soft
iron, when surrounded by a helix of wire and a current of galvanic
electricity passed through it, becomes a temporary magnet." [2]

Sir Humphrey Davy arrived at the same discovery of electrical
induction in soft iron in 1821. "Simultaneously with Arago's experiments, Davy arrived at the same facts." [3]

THE HORSESHOE ELECTRO-MAGNET.—The next step was taken
by Mr. William Sturgeon, of London, in 1825. He found that by
coiling copper wire loosely around a varnished piece of insulated
soft iron, bent into the form of a horseshoe; the successive coils out
of contact with each other, he could convert the non-magnetic soft

---

[1] *Yelloch's Journal of Science*, vol. lvii. p. 47, 1821.

[2] *Yelloch's Journal of Science*, vol. lvii., p. 42, 1821. Also, "Encyclopædia Britannica," vol. viii , p. 662.

[3] "Encyclopædia Britannica," vol. viii., p. 662.

iron into an electro-magnet. When the current was interrupted, the soft iron ceased to be magnetic; when the current was restored, the iron became again magnetic. This gave the possibility of producing reciprocal motion. The capacity, thus imparted to the iron to attract other iron, and to release it when the current was interrupted, was, in two particulars, not suited to be used in telegraphy. It employed a quantity battery, consisting of a single pair, and the length of wire connecting the battery with the magnet was inconsiderable.

The researches of these philosophers reached America in due time. The first to discuss them in public lectures was Professor James Freeman Dana, brother of the late distinguished Dr. Samuel L. Dana, of Lowell. In a course of lectures before the New York Athenæum, in the months of January and February, 1827, Professor Dana exhibited and experimented with Sturgeon's magnet, and used the following suggestive language, which is to be found in the manuscript copy of his lectures now in the Harvard University Library:

" The effect of the conjunctive wire in impressing the magnetic state is uniform and constant, and we can infer with absolute certainty the kind of magnetism which will be exhibited by either end of the needle, by reference to its position with regard to the wire. We are led to this by our previous knowledge of the positions assumed by a magnetic needle under the influence of the wire. Thus if the electric current flow from the right hand to the left, and the needle to be magnetized be placed over the wire, the end pointing from us will acquire the austral magnetism, or a north polarity, etc. We have seen that the pole of the magnetic needle, *over* which the positive electricity enters, turns to the east, but the pole *under* which it enters turns to the west. If, therefore, a needle be placed between two conjunctive wires situated in the same vertical plane, and transmitting the electric current in opposite directions, it is evident that both will conspire to produce the same effect, which will consequently be much more considerable than that produced by either of them alone; but a wire bent in this

form, having its two ends connected with the opposite poles of the voltaic instrument, will evidently have the electric current passing in opposite directions in its upper and lower portions, and consequently it will produce on a needle, between them, an effect similar to that produced by the two wires. Wires thus situated produce a more prompt development of magnetism in steel than a single wire does, because both tend to turn the same kind of magnetism in the same direction, and the opposite magnetisms in opposite directions, and hence we have one method of measuring the action of a battery on steel bars. Again, two parallel wires, having the electric current moving through them, in the same direction, will evidently produce a greater effect on a steel bar than either of them alone, for the effect of the whole must be greater than that of a part.

"When several conjunctive wires are placed together, side by side, the force is apparently diminished in the central wires, and concentrated in the extreme portions; the magnetic state of the latter seems to be augmented by induction or by position.

"When such an assemblage of wires act on the magnetism of a piece of steel, they decompose it, and each individual wire acts with more force on the magnetism nearest to it. Each conspires, in its action, to produce the same effect as the others; and hence, in addition to the effects of currents in opposite directions, we have another method of increasing the power of a battery in magnetizing needles. We shall probably render steel strongly magnetic, if we continue these two methods of increasing the effect. This is effected by forming the conjunctive wire into a spiral around the steel bar to be magnetized; for, at the opposite extremities of any diameter of this spiral, it is evident that the electric current moves in opposite directions. Suppose the spiral to be placed horizontally, east and west, the current in its upper part to move from north to south, it will, at its lower part move from south to north, and the spiral thus gives us the combined influence of currents in opposite directions. Moreover, the different coils of the spiral are nearly at right angles with the axis of the included bar, and they are parallel to each other. Hence, at any given portion of the bar, the effect of many currents passing in the same direction is produced, and the included bar becomes magnetic; and a spiral placed round a piece of soft iron bent into the form of a horseshoe magnet, renders it strongly and powerfully magnetic when the electric current is passing through it. . . .

"The opposite sides of a conjunctive wire exhibit the opposite magnetisms; and we have seen that, by placing the wires parallel to each other and connecting them with a battery so that they may transmit the current in the same direction, the magnetisms seem to be concentrated in the extreme wires, and that we can thus separate them in a degree from each other. Now, when we consider that the direction of the magnetic power is at right angles to the conjunctive wire, it is evident that in a helix, this direction must nearly coincide with that of the axis of the helix, and the one kind of magnetism be found concentrated at one extremity, and the other kind at the opposite end. . . .

"Iron filings adhering to dissimilarly electro-magnetic wires repel each other, and to similarly electro-magnetic wires, attract each other.

"In the course of our reasoning, by which we were led from

step to step to the adoption of a spiral or helix in powerfully developing magnetism in bars, we inferred that two or more parallel and similarly electro-magnetic wires acted with greater energy than one, and that the magnetisms were accumulated in the extreme wires by a species of induction between them all. A ribbon of metal substituted for these wires exerts a stronger influence on the needle at its edge than at its sides, for a similar reason. So, also, if a series of concentric wires be used, and the electric current sent through them in the same direction, we infer that they will have the power of the corresponding sides of the different rings concentrated and accumulated in their common centre, and will on the same side of their centre act as parallel similarly electro-magnetic wires. A flat spiral, or volute, having two ends connected with the opposite poles of the battery, will correctly represent concentric rings under the condition we have proposed; and the great quantity of iron filings which such a spiral or volute takes up, and the accumulation of them in the centre, fully evinces the concentration of power there, and the correctness of the reasoning by which we have been led to the modification of the conjunctive wire."

The next step was taken by Professor Joseph Henry, Secretary of the Smithsonian Institution, then Professor of Physics in the Albany Academy.[1] Reflecting on the increased magnetic effects observed in the compact coils of insulated wire of Schweigger, he first employed the insulated wire of many concentric coils to make an electro-magnet. By a covering of silk or cotton, successive coils of the wire were kept distinct and apart, so that it could be compactly wound in successive layers upon itself, and thus a current could be made to pass an indefinite number of times around an iron bar, and the power of the bar to attract other iron multiplied alike somewhat correspondingly, and this with the use of a comparatively small battery. He also, for the first time, in 1829, employed the battery of many pairs, to send from a distance a current through insulated wire, many times wound up on itself, around a horseshoe-shaped soft-iron bar, and demonstrated the dependence of the projectile force of the current upon the number, instead of the size, of plates. The discovery may be thus stated: He found that a battery of a single pair, the zinc plate four by seven inches, at a distance of eight feet, operating through a coil of insulated wire, eight feet long, wound around a small horseshoe magnet, produced magnetism enough to lift four and one-half pounds. At a distance of one thousand and sixty feet, it lifted but half an ounce, only $\frac{1}{144}$ as much.

[1] "Transactions of the Albany Institute," June, 1828.

By now substituting a Cruikshank's battery, in which was exactly the same amount of zinc surface—but in twenty-five plates instead of one—the magnet, at a distance of one thousand and sixty feet, as before, lifted eight ounces. That is, by dividing the zinc plate into twenty-five plates, and putting each with its fellow of copper into a separate cell, the power to lift at a distance of one thousand and sixty feet was increased sixteen times.[1]

Had this discovery been preceded by the constant battery of Daniel (which was not invented until 1836), practical registering electro-magnetic telegraphy would have been possible in 1828. Barlow, of England, had observed, in 1825, that the power of the galvanic current he employed diminished with the increase of the distance from the battery; but Henry's researches had shown that by employing a battery of many pairs—which he called an intensity battery—and by causing the wire to pass a great number of times concentrically around a bar of iron, it was possible to produce the physical result of motion, with a feeble current, at relatively great distances from its source.

Barlow had employed a *quantity* battery—a battery of a single pair. Henry employed a battery of many pairs—an *intensity* battery.

Professor Henry, in his paper in *Silliman's Journal*, January, 1831, after repeating the results of the paper of 1828, says: "The fact that the magnetic action of a current from a trough is, *at least*, not sensibly diminished by passing through a long wire, is directly applicable to Mr. Barlow's project of forming an electro-magnetic telegraph, and also of material consequence in the construction of the galvanic coil."

The first suggestion contemplating a really practical distance came from Fechner, who says, in 1829 (Kuhn, p. 835): "There is no doubt that if twenty-four different multipliers—the number of the letters—were in Leipsic, for example, and the insulated wire conducted under ground to Dresden, we should have a medium, not very costly, perhaps, through which determined characters could be sent instantaneously from one to the other." He says further, in 1832, that, "by the employment of a very thinly-wound (insulated) copper wire, coated with silver, of which one foot in uncovered condition weighed 1.95 grain, a pile of one hundred and seven small platinum pairs would be adequate for telegraphic communications ten geographical miles. The length of wire for such a dis-

[1] *Silliman's Journal*, January, 1831.

tance, both ways, would require for each letter twenty miles of wire, which would involve no small outlay." Fechner also pointed out that the "telegraphic conduction does not depend on the great thickness of the pairs of plates, and the strength of the conducting fluid (quantity of electricity), but, on the contrary, on the number of the pairs of plates in the pile; and would increase in direct relation to the thickness of the wire."[1]

"Ohm's Law," of 1825, and "Schweigger's Multiplier," of 1820, were here first traced out to their practical end, of a galvanic semaphore. The conditions were expressed on which the success of the needle invention depended—numerous pairs, a large conducting wire, multiplied convolutions of insulated wire. All were wrapped up in these few clear sentences of Fechner, before 1832.

" *Ohm's Formulæ.*—The amount of electric or chemical power developed in the voltaic circuit, or, in other words, the quantity of electricity which passes through a transverse section of the circuit in a unit of time, evidently depends upon two conditions, viz., the power or electro-motive force of the battery, and the resistance offered to the passage of the current by the conductors, liquid or solid, which it has to traverse. With a given amount of resistance, the power of the battery is proportional to the quantity of electricity developed in a given time; and by a double or treble resistance, we mean simply that which, with a given amount of exciting power in the battery, reduces the quantity of electricity developed, or work done, to one-half or one-third. If, then, the electro-motive force of the battery be denoted by E, and the resistance by R, we have, for the quantity of electricity passing through the circuit in a unit of time, the expression:

$$q = \frac{E}{R} \quad \cdots \quad (1).$$

This is called Ohm's law, from the name of the distinguised mathematician who first announced it.

" By means of the formula (1), we may estimate the effect produced on the strength of the current by increasing the number and size of the plates of the battery. The resistance R consists of two parts, viz., that which the current experiences in passing through the cells of the battery itself, and that which is offered by the external conductor which joins the poles; this conductor may consist either wholly of metal, or partly of metal and partly of electrolytic liquids. Let the resistance within the battery be r, and the external resistance r'; then, in the one-celled battery we have:

$$q = \frac{E}{r + r'} \quad \cdots \quad (2).$$

[1] In this he was anticipated by Professor Henry, as above.

Now, suppose the battery to consist of n cells perfectly similar, then the electro-motive force becomes nE, the resistance within the battery nr; if, then, the external resistance remains the same, the strength of the current will be denoted by:

$$q = \frac{nE}{nr + r'} = \frac{E}{r + \dfrac{r'}{n}} \quad \cdots \quad (3).$$

If r' be small, this expression has nearly the same value as $\frac{E}{r+r'}$; that is to say, if the circuit be closed by a good conductor, such as a short thick wire, the quantity of electricity developed by the compound battery of n cells is sensibly the same as that evolved by a single cell of the same dimensions. But if r' is of considerable amount, as when the circuit is closed by a long thin wire, or when an electrolyte is interposed, the strength of the current increases considerably with the number of plates. In fact the expression (3) is always greater than (2); for—

$$\frac{nE}{nr + r'} - \frac{E}{r + r'} = \frac{(n-1)\,Er'}{(nr + r')\,(r + r')}$$

a quantity which is necessarily positive when n is greater than unity.

"Suppose, in the next place, that the size of the plates is increased, while their number remains the same, then, according to the chemical theory, an increase in the surface of metal acted upon must produce a proportionate increase in the quantity of electricity developed, provided the conducting power of the circuit is sufficient to give it passage.

"According to the theory which attributes the development of the electricity to the contact of dissimilar metals, an increase in the size of the plates does not increase the electro-motive force, but it diminishes the resistance within the cells of the battery by offering a wider passage to the electricity. Hence, in the single cell, if the surface of the plates, and therefore the transverse section of the liquid be increased m times, the expression for the strength of the current becomes:

$$\frac{E}{\dfrac{r}{m} + r'} = \frac{mE}{r + mr'}.$$

If r' be small, this expression is nearly the same as $\frac{mE}{r+r'}$; that is to say, the quantity of electricity in the current increases very nearly in the same ratio as the size of the plates; but when the external resistance is considerable, the advantage gained by increasing the size of the plates is much less.

"We may conclude, then, that when the resistance in the circuit is small, as in electro-magnetic experiments, a small number of large plates is the most advantageous form of battery; but in overcoming great resistances, power is gained by increasing the number rather than the size of the plates." [1]

MAGNETO-ELECTRICITY.--The phenomena of electro-dynamic induction, or of magneto-electricity, were first discovered by Faraday in 1831, and published in 1832.

Professor Henry investigated the laws of these phenomena, and discovered induced currents of a second and third order, and so on through a series of five terms (Kuhn, p. 671). Upon these discoveries was based the magneto-electric induction apparatus (as distinguished from hydro-electric induction apparatus) of which Gauss and Weber availed themselves to produce a needle telegraph. "A circuit of wire 7,460 feet long was led across the houses and steeples of Göttingen, from the Observatory to the Cabinet of Natural Philosophy, requiring no especial insulation, which was a fact of great importance. The principle was thereby at once established of bringing the galvanic telegraph to the most convenient form. . . .

"All that was required in addition to this, was to render the signs audible; a task that apparently presented no very great difficulty, inasmuch as in the very scheme itself a mechanical motion, namely, the deflection of a magnetic bar, was given.

"Should it be desired that the indicator should write, it is merely required to adapt to one end of the magnectic bar a small vessel filled with a black color, and terminating in a capillary tube. This tube, instead of striking a bell, thus makes a black spot upon some flat surface held in front of it. If these spots are to compose writing, the surface upon which they are printed must be kept moving in front of the indicator with a uniform velocity; and this is easily brought about, by means of an endless strip of paper, which is rolled off one cylinder on to another by clock-work." [2]

It will be seen that the idea of the acoustic as well as the recording telegraph, which was subsequently developed at the suggestion of Gauss and Weber, by Steinheil, is here foreshadowed.

Steinheil's invention was produced in 1837, and published in 1838. The telegraph was in actual operation through a circuit of six miles—from 1838 to 1844—when Professor Steinheil became fully acquainted with the recording telegraph of Professor Morse, and recommended its adoption in place of his own and of all others,

---

[1] Watt's "Dictionary of Chemistry," vol. ii., p. 459.

[2] "Annals of Electricity," vol. iii., p. 448, No. 17, March, 1839, copied from the "Göttingen Gelehrte Anzeigen," p. 1,272, 1834.

upon the whole system of telegraph-lines of which he was super-intendent. Steinheil's apparatus, which elicited great admiration as a product of inventive genius, produced sounds on bells—an effect achieved ten years before as a result of electro-magnetism, by Professor Henry, at Albany, in 1828, and described in a letter by Professor James Hall[1] as having been witnessed by himself in that year. Steinheil's apparatus also recorded messages in alphabetic characters of ink, consisting of combinations of dots and spaces in two rows.[2]

Steinheil discovered what had been remarked in regard to fric-tional electricity nearly a hundred years before, by Winckler, Le Monnier, Watson, and Franklin, that the galvanic current could be transmitted through the earth as a part of the circuit, and thus re-duced the number of wires necessary for the operation of his telegraph to one.

Wheatstone at a later period enriched this field of invention with his dial magneto-electric telegraph, of such great merit and extensive use.

With the mention of the constant battery of Daniel, produced in 1836, and perhaps the amalgamation of the zinc plate by Stur-geon, the enumeration of the discoveries entering into the invention of the electric telegraph will be complete.

We have glanced at the types of telegraphs resting on friction electricity, those resting on the deflection of the magnetic needle, by Schweigger's multiplier, and those resting on magneto-elec-tricity.

Sömmering had produced a galvanic telegraph, producing sig-nals, by the evolution of gas-bottles in a series of tubes, and em-ploying the chemical powers of the battery. Schilling, Ritchie, Alexander, and Cook and Wheatstone, had employed the electro-magnet to produce signals by deflecting needles. Gauss and Weber, and Steinheil, employed magneto-electric apparatus, without a bat-tery, to deflect needles, or large, straight, permanent magnets. The former proposed, and the latter i nvented, a needle device which produced sounds on bells, and recorded messages in an alphabet of dots and spaces. Professor Henry, before 1832, had rung a bell by operating upon one end of a large needle, or a straight magnet, poised between the two poles of an electro-magnet, while the oppo-site end was made by the transmission of the current from a battery

---

[1] "Smithsonian Report," p. 96, 1857.
[2] H. Schellen, Braunschweig, p. 79, 1864.

to strike a bell. To neither of these types did the *recording electro-magnetic* telegraph belong. *Professor Morse's invention was a new departure.*

CLAIMS OF DISCOVERERS AND INVENTORS.

It is natural and proper, when a great and useful art has been born to civilization, that all persons, and especially the friends of the persons who have had a share in the production and perfection of the art, should feel jealously alive to the just distribution of the honors which follow such an event.

Such honors are sometimes, not infrequently, indeed, unfairly distributed. Adventitious circumstances may cause mistake. The memory is sometimes at fault. The claims of some may be exaggerated. The just claims of others may be overlooked. It will serve to open up the subject, if we consider a little carefully the meaning of some of the words we use.

A *tele-graph* is, literally, a *writing* at a *distance*. Strictly speaking, the earlier forms of signal apparatus were not telegraphs; they were *semaphores*—signal-bearers.

The signal may be addressed to the eye or to the ear. If to the former, it would be a visual; to the latter, an acoustic semaphore. Franklin, Watson, De Luc, Cavallo, and others, employed friction electricity to flash powder and fire alcohol. These experiments heralded an electric *visual* semaphore. They also rang bells by electricity, and in so doing foreshadowed an *acoustic* semaphore.

The plans of Le Sage, Lomond, Reusser, Boeckman, Salva, Betancourt, and Ronalds, were of the class of electric *semaphores*. That of Harrison Gray Dyar approached nearly to that of an electric *telegraph*.

Voltaic semaphores belong necessarily to this century. They were only possible after the recognition of the fact that the current might be made effective at a distance by the use of the pile, or battery of many pairs. Sömmering's, in 1809–'11, was the first of the class, and established the fact that visible effects could be produced at a distance of ten thousand feet.[1] His device was a visual *semaphore*. Bain's so-called electro-chemical plan, of 1846, was a voltaic *telegraph*. He employed a battery, but not a magnet, and wrote and printed with Morse's alphabet.

[1] Kuhn, 1866.

Electro-magnetic *semaphores* were possible only after the discovery of Oersted, in 1819, and the discovery of the multiplier, in 1820, by Schweigger. The first of these was projected by Ampère, but never carried out. It was a needle device. Visible signs were to be made by the deflection of a needle, the voltaic current being sent through a multiplier, or long link-shaped coil of insulated wire, within which a needle was freely suspended or supported. The next seems to have been Schilling's, made some time between 1820 and 1832, a rude copy of which, made by Professor Moucke, of Heidelberg, aroused at a later period (1836) the spirit of invention of Cooke.

The magneto-electric visual semaphore of Gauss and Weber appeared in 1833. The development of this type by Steinheil to an acoustic semaphore and an actual recording telegraph was accomplished in 1837.

Cooke's needle semaphore came in 1836, and Cooke and Wheatstone's in 1837. These were not writing or printing instruments. They made evanescent signs, which could be observed, translated, and recorded.

Electro-magnetic *telegraphs* were not practicable before an intensity battery had been employed in connection with a distant electro-magnet, surrounded with a multiplied insulated coil. This was first actually done through a distance of 1,060 feet, in 1828–'29, by Professor Henry. This experiment demonstrated that with increased power in the battery, with improvements in the magnet, and inventions of special mechanical devices, an electro-magnetic telegraph for registration at distances sufficiently great to meet the wants of the every-day world, might be devised. The invention, however, in its most elementary condition, was not made for four years thereafter, and then without a knowledge of these experiments, nor was it brought into working condition for three more, and then at first without employing either of these essential elements, to wit, the magnet of multiplied coils, the battery of multiplied pairs, and the long conductor; and more than two years additional passed before a caveat was lodged, and three more before a patent was granted, and still four years elapsed before the invention was in successful public service.

This delay between the discovery of a scientific truth, and its application to the useful arts, is not unusual.

After Winkler's experiment with a long conducting wire at
Leipsic, in 1744, and Watson's experiment in 1747–'48, with a circuit of two miles of wire and two of earth; and Franklin's experiments, from 1748 to 1754, exhibiting reciprocal motion, rotation of
wheels, ringing of bells, firing of combustibles, etc., it was possible
to produce electric signals conveying intelligence.

The first that appeared was that of Le Sage, in 1774, after an
interval of twenty years; then Lomond's in 1787, after thirty-
three years; then Reusser's in 1794, after forty years; then Salva's
with a conducting wire of many miles, in 1796, after about forty-
two years; then Betancourt's, of twenty-six miles, in 1797–'98,
after forty-three years ; then Ronald's, in 1816, after sixty-two
years; and then Harrison G. Dyar's, in 1828, after seventy-four
years.

After the discovery of the pile of Volta, in 1800, it was possible
to invent—

Sömmering's electro-chemical semaphore, which did not appear
till 1809–'11, after eleven years. J. Redman Coxe's (of Philadelphia) suggestion dates 1816, after sixteen years. Bain's electro-
chemical recording telegraph, which did not appear till 1846, after
forty-six years.

After Oersted's discoveries of 1819 *and* 1820, and especially of
Schweigger's multiplier, constructed with insulated wire immediately after it was possible to produce Ampère's suggestion (or
invention), which appeared the same year, and of which he remarks that this result had been suggested by Laplace.

Schilling's invention was in progress from 1820 to 1832, a period
of twelve years.

Cooke and Wheatstone's invention in 1836–'37, after sixteen
years.

After Sturgeon's electro-magnet, in 1826, when an electro-magnetic recording telegraph was possible for short distances, Morse's
conception came in 1832, after six years.

After Henry's electro-magnet, wound with insulated wire in
1828, published in 1831, which made electro-magnetic telegraphy
possible for increased distances, came Morse's receiving or relay
battery and recording telegraph, invented in 1832, and in working
condition in 1836, after an interval of five years. It was publicly

exhibited in 1837, after six years; and operated between Baltimore and Washington in 1844, after thirteen years.

After Faraday's and Henry's discoveries in magneto-electricity, *in* 1831, came Gauss and Weber's needle telegraph, in 1833, two years later, and Steinheil's telegraph, in 1837, after six years. Steinheil had demonstrated the practicability of using the earth for a part of the electro-magnetic circuit in 1838. It was not used in this country until 1845.

After the invention of Daniell's constant battery, in 1835, the successful electro-magnetic telegraph was practicable.

As we have now fixed some of the more important dates and intervals, let us put on record two or three more that we need to bear in mind—recalling that, while Sömmering and Bain needed only the voltaic pile or a battery of many pairs, Schilling, Cooke, and Wheatstone needed in addition the galvanic multiplier; Morse the battery and electro-magnet; Gauss, Weber, and Steinheil a magneto-electric machine.

· Sömmering's voltaic semaphore preceded Schilling's needle semaphore by a dozen years and more.

In point of time, Morse's invention on the Sully preceded Cooke's at Heidelberg by four years—1832-'36.

In point of construction and actual working, Morse preceded Cooke by a year—1835-'36.

In point of exhibition to the public, Cooke and Wheatstone were coincident with Morse—1837.

In point of actual use by the public, Cooke and Wheatstone preceded Morse by six years—1838-'44.

These relations of discovery to invention and practical application may be illustrated in tabular form :

Constant battery of Daniell, 1835, without which the electro-magnetic *telegraph* would not have succeeded.	Volta, 1800.	Electro-chemical semaphores Soemmering's, in 1809-'11. Bain's electro-chemical telegraph, in 1846.
	Oersted. 1819. Schweigger, 1820.	Needle semaphores. Ampère's, in 1820 Schilling's, 1820-'32. Cooke's, in 1836 Cooke and Wheatstone's, in 1837.
	Arago, in 1820. Sturgeon, in 1825. Henry, in 1829.	Recording telegraph of Morse, in 1832
	Faraday, in 1831.	Magneto-electric telegraphs Gauss and Weber's, in 1833-'34. Steinheil's, in 1837. Wheatstone's later business alphabet—semaphore.

Having thus before us the great facts in the history of the new art, we are in condition to examine more carefully into the claims to originality and priority of the discoverers and inventors.

Let us have distinct ideas in our assignment of credit. The discovery of a law, or the invention of a device, may be strictly original to two or more persons. It may be made by one in ignorance that it had been made by another before him, or the two may have been coincident in time as well as result. It may have been made and never published or communicated to others.

Volta was alone in the invention of the pile.

Sömmering was alone in observing that the current of the voltaic pile might be projected to. great distances with as effective force to produce *chemical decompositions* as at moderate distances.

Oersted was alone in originality [1] and time in observing the deflection of the needle by the galvanic current.

Schweigger was alone in originality and time in the multiplier of insulated wire.

Arago was alone in magnetizing iron in the axis of a long oblique spiral.

Sturgeon was alone in the electro-magnet with the loose oblique spiral; and later in amalgamating the zinc element of the battery.

Moll and Henry were coincident in the quantity magnet with a single pair.

Henry was alone in the insulated concentric coil and multiplied windings applied to a horseshoe-shaped bar of iron with a single pair and with many pairs.

Henry was alone in the insulated concentric wire of many windings and battery of many pairs at a distance from the electromagnet.

Now, all these discoveries, in so far as the attribute of originality is concerned, were in some degree suggested, somewhat in their order of succession, by the publication of the discoveries which preceded them.

Oersted deflected a needle slowly with a single wire, Schweigger quickly with multiplied coils.

Arago made straight hard iron (steel) magnetic by a single loose long coil.

Sturgeon made a horseshoe of soft iron magnetic with a loose long coil of sixteen turns and lifted nine pounds in 1825–'26. Moll made a closer single coil of eighty-three turns and lifted seven-

---

[1] It seems that, possibly, Oersted was anticipated by Romagnesi. (*See* p. 264)

ty-five pounds, and finally one hundred and thirty-five pounds, in 1828.

Henry, with greatly multiplied concentric coils, lifted more than a ton in 1830. All these operated by a battery of a single pair of plates, and little interval between the battery and the magnet.

Now, Henry started out, before the publication of Moll, with a new combination of *many* pairs, many *concentric* coils, and *distance* between the battery and the magnet, and found, as the experiment seemed to show, that the effect of the current in magnetizing soft iron at this distance was at least not appreciably less at a distance of one thousand and sixty feet than at points near the battery.

WHAT THE INVENTOR OF THE ELECTRO-MAGNETIC RECORDING TELE-GRAPH MUST HAVE KNOWN.

What was needed to the *original conception* of the Morse recording telegraph ?

1. A knowledge that soft iron, bent in the form of a horseshoe, could be magnetized by sending a galvanic current through a coil wound round the iron, and that if would lose its magnetism when the current was suspended.

2. A knowledge that such a magnet had been made to lift and drop masses of iron of considerable weight.

3. A knowledge, or a belief, that the galvanic current could be transmitted through wires of great length.

These were all. Now comes the conception of devices for employing an agent which could produce reciprocal motion to effect registration, and the invention of an alphabet. In order to this invention, it must be seen how up and down—reciprocal—motion could be produced by the opening and closing of the circuit. Into this simple band of vertical tracery of paths in space must be thrown the shuttle of time and a ribbon of paper. It must be seen how a lever-pen, alternately dropping upon, and rising at defined intervals from, a fillet of paper, moved by independent clock-work, would produce the fabric of the alphabet and writing and printing.

Was there any thing required to produce these results which was not known to Morse?

Of the details of scientific research bearing on electro-magnetism, scattered through journals of various languages, Professor Morse knew comparatively little. He was a liberally educated gentleman, devoted to the art of painting. He had somewhat unusual advantages. He had attended the courses of lectures of Professor Silliman and Professor Day, embracing the sciences of galvanism and electricity, when an under-graduate, in 1808–'10, at Yale College. He had been an assistant to Professor Silliman in his laboratory in 1822 and the years following. He had, at a later period, attended the lectures of Professor James Freeman Dana, before the Athenæum in New York, and witnessed an original and brilliant course of experimental lectures, embracing all that was known in 1827 on electro-magnetism, with something of prophetic suggestion.

He knew generally, when he stepped on board the Sully, in 1832, that a soft-iron horseshoe-shaped bar of iron could be rendered magnetic while a current of galvanic electricity was passing through a wire wound round it; and he knew that electricity had been transmitted, apparently instantaneously, through wires of great length, by Franklin and others. In the course of conversation on board that vessel, the topic of the velocity of the electric current arose. In the leisure of ship-life, the idea of a *recording* electric telegraph seized Professor Morse's mind, and he gave expression to his conviction that it was *possible*. As it was possible to *dispatch* and to *arrest* the current, he conceived that some device could be found for compelling it to manifest itself by this intermittent action, and produce a record.

He knew, for he had witnessed it years before, that, by means of a battery and an electro-magnet, reciprocal motion could be produced. He knew that the force which produced it could be transmitted along a wire. He *believed* that the battery current could be made, through an electro-magnet, to produce physical effects at a *distance*. He saw in his mind's eye the existence of an agent and a medium by which reciprocal motion could be not only produced but *controlled* at a *distance*. The question that addressed itself to him at the outset was naturally this: "How can I make use of the simple up-and-down motion of opening and closing a circuit to write an intelligible message at one end of a wire and at the same time print it at the other?"

If we pause a moment to consider that in our ordinary writing with a pen upon paper we must employ at least a hundred differently shaped and proportioned lines, and produce them by many hundred combinations of nerve and muscular effort, and that in printing we must have not less than about thirty-six letters and figures, we shall appreciate the grandeur of Morse's conception, in which any message whatever could be written at one end of the wire and printed with perfect distinctness at the other, for permanent preservation, at the rate of twenty-five words a minute. Like many a kindred work of genius, it was in nothing more wonderful than in its simplicity. First, he caused a continuous ribbon or strip of paper to move under a pencil by clock-work, that could be wound up. The paper moved horizontally. The pencil moved only up and down; when resting on the paper it made a mark—if for an instant only, a dot; if for a longer time, a line. When lifted from the paper it left a blank. Here were three elements—dots, lines, and spaces—which, interwoven with intervals of time, could either of them be repeated, or they could be combined variously with each other to produce groups that should stand for letters.

The grandeur of this wonderful alphabet of dots, lines, and spaces, has not been fully appreciated. It has been translated from one sense to another. In the Morse telegraph it may be used, and is used, by the sight, the touch, the taste, the hearing, and the sense of feeling.[1]

Bain succeeded in using the current of electricity without an electro-magnet, but he had to borrow Morse's alphabet. Thompson's reflecting galvanometer, used by the Atlantic cable, although a visual semaphore, employs the Morse alphabet.

Sir William Thompson has recently succeeded in converting his wonderfully sensitive apparatus into a recording telegraph, with the Morse alphabet.

We are no longer surprised when we find that Steinheil, at the head of German telegraphy, advised the abandonment of his own most ingenious and elaborate apparatus, and the adoption of the Morse system and its alphabet. Nor do we wonder at its general adoption throughout the world.

All concede the conception of the written and recorded alphabet and the mode of printing to Morse on board the Sully. This conception *presupposes* the use of the electrical current, the employ-

---

[1] The taste is occasionally taken advantage of where accidents occur on the line of railroads and telegraphs, where a skillful operator happens to be present. He cuts the wire, establishes metallic communication with the earth, and signals by uniting and separating the end of the severed wire near the station, with the metallic conductor leading to the earth. He receives the message in answer by placing his tongue between the two metallic points, receiving the shocks and observing the intervals between them, which correspond with those produced by the key at the station.

ment of the alternate activity and repose of the current, and an apparatus for breaking and closing the circuit at determined intervals.

THE NEED OF AN INVENTOR.

The indebtedness of Professor Morse, as an inventor, to others may be regarded as of two kinds. There were the results of scientific research and discovery made by men who had gone before him, and with which he was, in general terms, familiar. Then there was the coöperation of assistants whom he took into his confidence and compensated for their services.

He completed the plan of his alphabet, his mode of writing and printing, and committed them to paper, on board the Sully, in 1832, and exhibited a working model of his conception in action in 1835; and a model, but not in action, of the relay to various persons in 1835 and 1836. His alphabet, his new mode of writing and printing, were clear-cut, realized conceptions; but to perfect the apparatus involved resources which he had not. There were no shops at that time to which he might go for the ready purchase of electro-magnets, batteries, insulated wires, etc. A blacksmith must be employed to bend an iron rod to the form of a horseshoe, and the wire must be wound by hand. Nor were there at hand facilities for repairs, or professors accomplished and ready to advise in the science scarcely yet developed enough to meet the wants of the inventor. There was not a constant battery. There was, indeed, the battery of many pairs (Cruikshank's), and Sturgeon had produced his electro-magnet in 1825. But the new art required an inventor.

The substitution by Henry of the concentric multiplier, in place of the loose, oblique coil of Sturgeon, reduced the strength of the battery necessarily required; and his employment of a battery of many pairs in place of a single pair having the same surface, which projected the current through greater length of wire, and so made possible the magnetizing of iron at a distance, revealed the direction in which development was to take place. This disclosed a principle on which the registering apparatus could be worked at a distance. But still there was needed an inventor.

Not one of all the brilliant scientific men who have attached their names to the history of electro-magnetism had brought the means to produce the practical registering telegraph. Some of them had ascended the tower that looked out on the field of conquest. Some of them brought keener vision than others. Some of them stood higher than others. But the genius of invention had not recognized them. There was needed an inventor. Now, what sort of a want is this ?

There was required a rare combination of qualities and conditions. There must be ingenuity in the adaptation of available means to desired ends ; there must be the genius to see through non-essentials to the fundamental principle on which success depends ; there must be a kind of skill in manipulation; great patience and pertinacity; a certain measure of culture; and the inventor of a recording telegraph must be capable of being inspired by the grandeur of the thought of writing, figuratively speaking, with a pen a thousand miles long—with the thought of a postal system without the element of time. Moreover, the person who is to be the inventor must be free from the exactions of well-compensated, every-day absorbing duties—perhaps he must have had the final baptism of poverty.

Now, the inventor of the registering telegraph did not rise from the perusal of any brilliant paper; he happened to be at leisure on shipboard, ready to contribute and share in the after-dinner conversation of a ship's cabin, when the occasion arose.

Morse's electro-magnetic telegraph was mainly an invention employing power and agencies, through mechanical devices, to produce a given end. It involved the combination of the results of the labors of others with a succession of special contrivances and some discoveries of the inventor himself. There was an ideal whole almost at the outset, but involving great thought and labor and patience and invention to produce an art harmonious in its organization and action.

CHAPTER VIII.

1832–1838.

ARRIVAL IN NEW YORK—THE BROTHERS' TESTIMONY—MOULD AND TYPE
THE FIRST THINGS MADE FOR THE TELEGRAPH—CASTINGS PRESERVED—
STRUGGLES OF THE INVENTOR—POVERTY AND DISTRESS—HIS BROTHERS'
SYMPATHY AND AID—MAKING THE TELEGRAPHIC INSTRUMENT—AT THE
LATHE — FAITH IN GOD AND HIMSELF — REJECTED AS ONE OF THE
PAINTERS OF A PICTURE FOR THE CAPITOL — ARTISTS' SYMPATHY —
ELECTED PROFESSOR IN UNIVERSITY OF NEW YORK—ROOMS IN BUILDING
—APPARATUS — COOKS HIS OWN FOOD IN HIS ROOM — ANNOUNCEMENT
OF HIS INVENTION — FRENCH IDEA OF TELEGRAPH — PROFESSOR GALE'S
STATEMENT—DANIEL HUNTINGTON—HAMILTON FISH—REV. MR. SEELYE—
COMMODORE STARBUCK—ROBERT G. RANKIN—REV. DR. H. B. TAPPAN—
ALFRED VAIL BECOMES A PARTNER—LETTER TO SECRETARY OF TREAS-
URY—SECRETARY'S REPORT TO CONGRESS—PROFESSOR GALE A PARTNER
—THE INSTRUMENT AT SPEEDWELL — THREE MILES OF WIRE — EXPERI-
MENTS—EXHIBITION IN NEW YORK — TEN MILES OF WIRE — FIRST DIS-
PATCH PRESERVED—EXHIBITED TO THE FRANKLIN INSTITUTE—REPORT—
THE INSTRUMENT IN WASHINGTON—EXHIBITED TO THE PRESIDENT AND
CABINET—HON. F. O. J. SMITH — PROFESSOR MORSE'S LETTERS TO MR.
SMITH—REPORT OF COMMITTEE OF COMMERCE—PARTNERSHIP WITH MR.
SMITH—LETTERS TO VAIL—PREPARATIONS FOR A JOURNEY TO EUROPE.

THE Sully reached the wharf at the foot of Rector Street, New York, November 15, 1832. The two brothers of Mr. Morse, Sidney E. and Richard C. Morse, were there to meet and welcome him on his arrival. His brother Richard says :

" Hardly had the usual greetings passed between us three broth-ers, and while on our way to my house, before he informed us that he had made, during his voyage, an important invention, which had occupied almost all his attention on shipboard—one that would astonish the world, and of the success of which he was perfectly sanguine; that this invention was a means of communicating intelligence by electricity, so that a message could be written down in a permanent manner, by characters, at a distance from the writer. He took from his pocket and showed from his sketch-book, in which he had drawn them, the kind of characters he proposed to use. These characters were dots and spaces, representing the ten digits or numerals; and in the book were sketched other parts of his electro-magnetic machinery and apparatus, actually drawn out in his sketch-book."

His brother Sidney says:

"He was full of the subject of the Telegraph during the walk from the ship, and for some days afterward could scarcely speak about any thing else. He expressed himself anxious to make apparatus and try experiments, for which he had had no materials or facilities on shipboard. In the course of a few days after his arrival he made a kind of cogged or saw-toothed type, the object of which, I understood, was to regulate the interruptions of the electric current, so as to enable him to make dots, and regulate the length of marks or spaces on the paper upon which the information transmitted by his telegraph was to be recorded. He proposed at that time a single circuit of wire, and only a single circuit, and letters, words, and phrases, were to be indicated by numerals, and these numerals were to be indicated by dots and other marks and spaces on paper. It seemed to me that, as wire was cheap, it would be better to have twenty-four wires, each wire representing a letter of the alphabet, but my brother always insisted upon the superior advantages of his single circuit."

Without delay Mr. Morse proceeded to construct the instrument which was to test the practicability of his invention. He was now an inmate of his brother Richard's house, and there he resided several months. Mrs. Morse states that he was, immediately after his arrival, engaged in melting lead and casting it into moulds, making forms which he called type. She says—and her memory was doubtless sharpened by the unlucky accident she mentions—that "he melted the lead, which he used, over the fire in the grate of my front parlor, and, in his operation of casting the type, he spilled some of the heated metal upon the drugget, or loose carpeting before the fireplace, and upon a flag-bottomed chair, upon which his mould was placed."

This was the first step that Mr. Morse took in the actual construction of his electro-telegraphic instrument. Some of the
first forms or type thus made by casting melted lead into a
mould prepared for receiving them, he presented to the writer
of this memoir, who deposited them with the New York Historical Society, to be preserved in the archives of that institution.

From this hour began a struggle that lasted twelve years,
more severe, heroic, and triumphant, than the annals of any
other invention furnish for the warning and encouragement
of genius. With his mind absorbed in this one idea of a
recording telegraph, and wholly dependent upon his profession
as an artist, it was impossible to pursue his art with the
enthusiasm and industry essential to success. Nor would his
invention have been perfected while he continued his devotion
to his profession as an artist. His situation was forlorn in
the extreme. The father of three little children, now mother-
less, his pecuniary means exhausted by his residence in Europe,
unable to pursue his art without sacrificing his invention,
he was at his wits' ends. He had visions of usefulness, by the
invention of a Telegraph that should bring the ends of the earth
into instant intercourse. Thoughts of fame came to him by day
and night, and a lawful ambition was kindled. He was poor,
and knew that wealth, as well as usefulness and fame, was within his reach. He had long received assistance from his father
and brothers, when his profession did not supply the needed
means of support for himself and family, but it seemed like
robbery to take the money of others to expend upon experiments, the success of which he could not expect them to believe
in until he could give practical evidence that the instrument
could do the work proposed. It was the old story repeated,
and to be repeated, of genius contending with poverty. He
knew what rapid progress was now made in science and art;
the idea which he had started might spread like electricity itself,
far and wide; the danger was great that some one else, with
more time and means, would seize the thought, reduce it to
practice, and present it to the world, while he was brooding
over it in melancholy indecision and helplessness. His letters
to friends in former years very frequently indicated a tendency

to despondency. He was now sinking very low. The apprehension that he might not be able to go on with his work filled
him at times with anguish. His brothers comforted, encouraged,
and cheered him. In the house of his brother Richard he
found a home, and the tender care that he required. Sidney,
the other brother, lent him the resources of a powerful intellect.
With them it was his habit to consult with the greatest freedom, telling them all the difficulties he encountered, and the
steps that he must mount to reach the height of his great conception.

Just before he left Europe to return home, he had written
to his brothers, and these were his sad words : " I have frequently felt melancholy in thinking of my prospects for encouragement when I return, and your letter found me in one of
those moments. You cannot, therefore, conceive with what
feelings I read your offer of a room in your new house. Give me
a resting-place, and I will yet move the country in favor of the
arts. I return with some hopes, but many fears. Will my
country employ me on works which may do it honor ? I want
a commission from Government to execute two pictures from
the life of Columbus, and I want eight thousand dollars for
each, and on these two I will stake my reputation as an artist."

Two or three years were passed in this melancholy mood,
his profession as an artist taking him from place to place, as he
had commissions that required him to reside for a time here
and there. Small opportunity was allowed him to pursue his
vision of the Telegraph. " During this time," he says, " I never
lost faith in the practicability of the invention, nor abandoned
the intention of testing it as soon as I could command the
means."

On the corner of Nassau and Beekman Streets his brothers
afterward erected a building in which were the offices of the
newspaper of which they were the editors and proprietors.
In the fifth story of this building a room was assigned to
him, which for a long time was his study, studio, bedchamber,
parlor, kitchen, drawing-room, and workshop. On one side
of the room stood the little cot on which he slept, when sleep
was kind enough to visit him, in the brief hours which he
allowed himself for repose. On the other side of the room, by

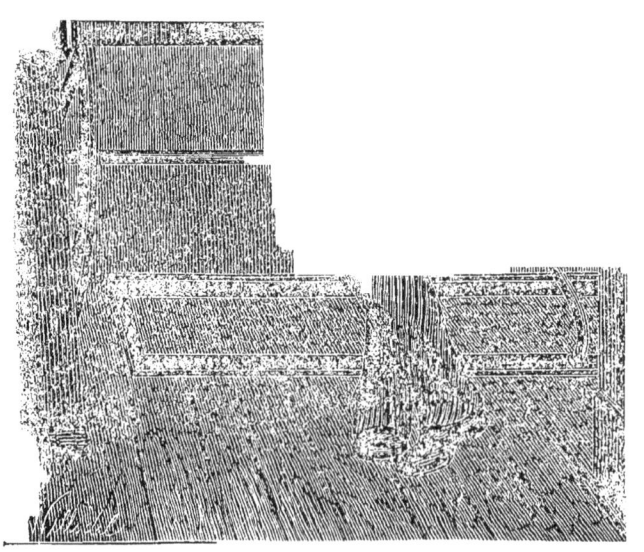

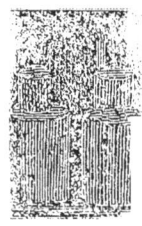

MORSE MAKING HIS OWN INSTRUMENT.

the window, stood his lathe, with which he, his own mechanician and workman, as well as inventor, turned the brass apparatus necessary for him to use in the construction of his instrument. He had, with his own hands, first whittled the models;
then with the models he made the moulds and the castings. In
the lathe, with the graver's tool, he gave them polish and finish.
Into this room were brought to him, from day to day, crackers
and the simplest food, which, with tea, prepared by himself,
sustained his life, while he toiled incessantly to give form and
being to the idea that possessed him.

To mingle with the world in the pursuit of his favorite art,
or to enjoy the pleasures of social life, of which no man was
more fond, would divert his mind from the work in which he
was absorbed, while patiently and believingly he hoped to reach
the grand result. He had faith in God, and strong confidence
in his own ability eventually to make the instrument practically
successful. He knew what he had done before. Nothing appeared to him wanting except the pecuniary means to sustain
him to the hour of accomplishment. If he should die before it
was done, his conception would perish with him. Stimulated
by these anticipations and apprehensions, he studied the strictest
economy in food and dress, dependent now almost exclusively
upon his brothers for the scanty supply which he was willing to
receive while engaged in a work which to all others seemed
visionary.

In the midst of this conflict, the Government was offering to
American artists, to be selected by a committee of Congress,
commissions to paint pictures for the panels in the Rotunda of
the Capitol. Morse was anxious, as we have already seen, to be
employed upon one or more of them. The artists of the country
urged his selection. He was the President of the National
Academy of Design, and there was an eminent fitness in calling
him to this national work. No artist in the United States, except Allston, his teacher and friend, had so high and so wide a
reputation as Morse, and Allston urged the appointment of
Morse, declining to take one of the commissions that was offered
to himself. John Quincy Adams, ex-President of the United
States, and now a member of the House of Representatives,
and on the committee to whom this subject was referred, submit-

19

ted a resolution in the House that foreign artists be allowed to compete for these commissions, and in support of his resolution alleged that there were no American artists competent to execute the paintings. This allegation gave great and just offence to the artists and the public. A severe and masterly reply to the remarks of Mr. Adams appeared in the New York *Evening Post.* This reply was written by James Fenimore Cooper, but it was attributed to Mr. Morse, whose pen was well known to be as skillful as his pencil. So far from being its author, Mr. Morse did not know that Mr. Adams had made the offensive remarks until Mr. Cooper came and read to him the reply in the *Post.* But it was generally understood that Mr. Morse was regarded by Mr. Adams as the author, and that in consequence of that belief the name of Mr. Morse was rejected by the committee. He never recovered from the effects of that blow. Forty years afterward he could not speak of it without emotion. He had consecrated the previous years of his life to preparation for such a work. His brethren of the profession had accorded to him the highest position in their guild. His ambition had fastened upon this as the fitting opportunity to place before his countrymen, in the Capitol, the greatest achievement of his genius and skill. His teacher and friend, Washington Allston, wrote to him these sympathetic lines:

"I have learned the disposition of the 'pictures.' I had hoped to find your name among the commissioned artists; but I was grieved to find that all my efforts in your behalf have proved fruitless. I know what your disappointment must have been at this result, and most sincerely do I sympathize with you. That my efforts were both sincere and conscientious I hope will be some consolation to you. But let not this disappointment cast you down, my friend. You have it still in your power to let the world know what you can do. Dismiss it, then, from your mind, and determine to paint all the better for it. God bless you!

"Your affectionate friend,
"WASHINGTON ALLSTON."

But it was well for him, and his country, and the world, that the artist was disappointed: Morse the painter became Morse the inventor. He had indeed been for some years plodding on with his invention, earning his daily bread with his brush, and by giving lessons in art, but never abandoning the idea that the Telegraph was yet to be accomplished. His brother artists were grieved at the rejection of their President by the Government, and they made an expression of their chagrin and sympathy by such a testimonial as is doubtless without a parallel in the history of the arts. General Cummings, in his "Annals of the Academy," gives the facts in these words:

"The writer called a meeting of artists at his house, March 17th —suggested and arranged an association for the purpose of raising funds, in fifty-dollar shares, for procuring Morse to paint an historical picture—the title, 'A Joint-stock Association of Artists for procuring Morse to paint an Historical Picture.' Certificates were immediately prepared and subscribers solicited. In a few days the writer had the satisfaction of obtaining such to the amount of five hundred dollars. John L. Morton, by his exertions, added another five hundred. The efforts of others in a short time increased that amount to two thousand dollars. At that point a great addition was at once made to the fund. A gentleman *well known*, but who declined to have his name made public, subscribed *one thousand*—thus making a total of *three thousand dollars;* and Mr. ——, of Brooklyn, generously offered to contribute, free of charge, canvas, and all material required in the execution of the work. Thus armed, the writer and John L. Morton waited on Morse, and communicated the result—the first knowledge he had of the undertaking. The effect was electrical —it aroused him from his depression, and he exclaimed, 'that never had he read or known of such an act of professional generosity;' and that he was fully determined to paint the picture—his favorite subject, 'The Signing of the First Compact on board the Mayflower'—not of small size, as requested, but of the size of the panels in the Rotunda. That was immediately assented to by the committee, thinking it possible that one or the other of the pictures so ordered might fail in execution—in which case it would afford favorable inducements to its substitution, and of course much to Mr. Morse's profit—as the artists from the first never contemplated taking possession of the picture so executed; it was to remain with Mr. Morse, and for his use and benefit. Two or three installments were collected and paid him, when his departure for Europe, in the furtherance of his *Telegraph*—the success of which has 'won him world-renowned reputation'—caused a suspension of the painting, and delay was requested and acceded to by the subscribers."

When Mr. Morse determined to go abroad, he wrote to Mr. Cummings as follows:

" Circumstances relating to the Telegraph, invented by me in 1832, will require my attention for an indefinite time, and I am about to visit Europe, principally in reference to matters in connection with this invention. At the same time, indeed, I have in view some studies connected with the picture which the association have commissioned me to paint for them. Yet, I ought not to conceal from the gentlemen who have so generously formed the association, that circumstances may arise, in relation to the Telegraph, which may make it a paramount duty, to myself and my country, to suspend for a season the commission with which they have honored me."

Finding that he could not execute the painting, and wishing to relieve himself of the position in which he then stood, Mr. Morse returned to the stockholders the amount *in full, with interest,* and canceled the obligation.

In the year 1835 Mr. Morse was appointed Professor of the Literature of the Arts of Design in the New York City University. Before the apartments were completly finished he removed from Greenwich Lane to the third floor, front rooms, in the north wing of the University building, looking out upon Washington Square.

" There," he says, " I immediately commenced, with very limited means, to experiment upon my invention.[1] My first instrument was made up of an old picture or canvas frame fastened to a table; the wheels of an old wooden clock, moved by a weight to carry the paper forward; three wooden drums, upon one of which the paper was wound and passed over the other two; a wooden pendulum suspended to the top piece of the picture or stretching frame, and vibrating across the paper as it passes over the centre wooden drum; a pencil at the lower end of the pendulum, in contact with the paper; an electro-magnet fastened to a shelf across the picture or stretching-frame, opposite to an armature made fast to the pendulum; a type rule and type for breaking the circuit, resting on an endless band, composed of carpet-binding, which passed over two wooden rollers, moved by a wooden crank, and carried forward by points projecting

[1] *See* appendix A for illustrated history of the invention.

from the bottom of the rule downward into the carpet-binding; a lever, with a small weight on the upper side, and a tooth projecting downward at one end, operated on by the type, and a metallic fork also projecting downward over two mercury-cups, and a short circuit of wire, embracing the helices of the electro-magnet connected with the positive and negative poles of the battery and terminating in the mercury-cups. When the instrument was at rest the circuit was broken at the mercury-cups; as soon as the first type in the type-rule (put in motion by turning the wooden crank) came in contact with the tooth *on the lever*, it raised that end of the lever and depressed the other, bringing the prongs of the fork down into the mercury, thus closing the circuit; the current passing through the helices of the electro-magnet caused the pendulum to move and the pencil to make an oblique mark upon the paper, which, in the mean time, had been put in motion over the wooden drum. The tooth in the lever falling into the first two cogs of the types, the circuit was broken when the pendulum returned to its former position, the pencil making another mark as it returned across the paper. Thus, as the lever was alternately raised and depressed by the points of the type, the pencil passed to and fro across the slip of paper passing under it, making a mark resembling a succession of V's. The spaces between the types caused the pencil to mark horizontal lines, long or short, in proportion to the length of the spaces. With this apparatus, rude as it was, and completed before the first of the year 1836, I was enabled to and did mark down telegraphic intelligible signs, and to make and did make distinguishable sounds for telegraphing; and, having arrived at that point, I exhibited it to some of my friends early in that year, and among others to Professor Leonard D. Gale, who was a college professor in the university.[1] I also experimented with the *chemical* power of the electric current in 1836, and succeeded in marking my telegraphic signs upon paper dipped in turmeric and a solution of the sulphate of soda (as well as other salts), by passing the current through it. I was soon satisfied, however, that the electro-*magnetic* power was more available for telegraphic purposes and possessed many advantages over any other, and I turned my thoughts in that direction. Early in 1836 I procured forty feet of wire, and putting it in the circuit I found that my battery of one cup was not sufficient to work my instrument. This result suggested to me the probability that the magnetism to be obtained from the electric current would diminish in proportion as the

[1] *See* page 299.

circuit was lengthened, so as to be insufficient for any practical purposes at great distances; and to remove that probable obstacle to
my success I conceived the idea of combining two or more circuits
together in the manner described in my first patent, each with an
independent battery, making use of the magnetism of the current on
the first to close and break the second; the second, the third, and
so on. This contrivance was fully set forth in my patents. My
chief concern, therefore, on my subsequent patents was to ascertain
to what distance from the battery sufficient magnetism could be obtained to vibrate a piece of metal, knowing that, if I could obtain
the least motion at the distance of eight or ten miles, the ultimate
object was within my grasp. A practical mode of communicating
the impulse of one circuit to another, such as that described in my
patent of 1840, was matured as early as the spring of 1837, and exhibited then to Professor Gale, my confidential friend.

"Up to the autumn of 1837 my telegraphic apparatus existed in
so rude a form that I felt a reluctance to have it seen. My means
were very limited—so limited as to preclude the possibility of constructing an apparatus of such mechanical finish as to warrant my
success in venturing upon its public exhibition. I had no wish to
expose to ridicule the representative of so many hours of laborious
thought. Prior to the summer of 1837, at which time Mr. Alfred
Vail's attention became attracted to my Telegraph, I depended upon
my pencil for subsistence. Indeed, so straitened were my circumstances that, in order to save time to carry out my invention and to
economize my scanty means, I had for many months lodged and
eaten in my studio, procuring my food in small quantities from some
grocery, and preparing it myself. To conceal from my friends the
stinted manner in which I lived, I was in the habit of bringing my
food to my room in the evenings, and this was my mode of life for
many years."

In the year 1853, Professor Morse alluded to these days of
trial in some remarks at a meeting of the Association of the
Alumni of the University of New York City:

"Yesternight, on once more entering your chapel, I saw the
same marble staircase and marble floors I once so often trod, and so
often with a heart and head overburdened with almost crushing
anxieties. Separated from the chapel by but a thin partition was
that room I occupied, now your Philomathean Hall, whose walls—
had thoughts and mental struggles, with the alternations of joys

and sorrows, the power of being daguerreotyped upon them—
would show a thickly-studded gallery of evidence that there the
Briarean infant was born who has stretched forth his arms with the
intent to encircle the world.   Yes, that room of the University was
the birthplace of the Recording Telegraph.   Attempts, indeed,
have been made to assign to it other parentage, and to its birthplace other localities.   Personally, I have very little anxiety on this
point, except that the truth should not suffer ; for I have a consciousness which neither sophistry nor ignorance can shake, that
that room is the place of its birth, and a confidence, too, that its
cradle is in hands that will sustain its rightful claim."

"In 1835," says Professor Horsford, "Morse made his discovery
of the *relay*, the most brilliant of all the achievements to which his
name must be forever attached.   It was the discovery of a means by
which the current, which through distance from its source had become feeble, could be reënforced or renewed.   This discovery, according to the different objects for which it is employed, is variously known as the registering magnet, the local circuit, the margi-
nal circuit, the repeater, etc.   It made transmission from one point
on a main line through indefinitely great distances, and through an
indefinite number of branch lines, and to an indefinite number of
way-stations, and registration at all, possible and practicable, from
a single act of a single operator."

Professor Morse also exhibited to Professor Horsford one of
the instruments which illustrated his inventive genius.   It re-
sembled, in external appearance, a small melodeon, having a key-
board, on which were the letters, the figures, periods, commas, etc.
These keys were levers.   The ends of the levers, distant from the
seat of the operator, were in connection with brass circular disks,
upon the rims of which were prominences and depressions of unequal length, so arranged that the prominences would close and the
depressions open the magnetic circuit, and thus magnetize and de-
magnetize a bar of soft iron.   When magnetized, the bar of iron
drew to itself one end of a lever, having an iron armature, to the
other end of which a pencil or pen was attached, the point of which,
by this action of the magnet, was pressed against a moving ribbon
of paper ; when the bar was demagnetized, the lever was restored
to its original position by a spring, and the pencil lifted from the
paper.   It is easy to see that an arrangement of prominences and
depressions, or conductors and non-conductors, on the brass circles
might be so contrived that each key should produce its own partic-

ular set of lines, dots, and spaces. This was the *first practical*
Registering Telegraph. Its invention dates October, 1832, on the
Sully. Its first testing was made in 1835.

The piano key-board of Morse, and its complex devices for interrupting and closing the circuit, gave place, as the result of practical experiment, before the issue of the patent, to the very simple
device of the single key, with which we are all familiar. The pencil
and pen gave place to a stylus—a simple, hard point, resting upon
a ribbon of paper, moving at a uniform rate, immediately over a
groove. His plan, from the outset, contemplated a single current
and circuit. After the discovery of Steinheil, that the earth might
be used for a part of the circuit, Morse adopted the arrangement of
a single line of wire between the stations.

"In 1836, and the early part of 1837," Professor Morse says,
"I directed my experiments mainly to modifications of the marking
apparatus, contrivances for using fountain-pens, marking with a
hard point through pentagraphic or blackened paper, at one time
on a revolving disk, spirally from the centre, at another on a cylinder, by which means a large, ordinary sheet of paper might be so
written upon that it could be read as a commonplace-book, and
bound for reference in volumes, and devising modes of marking
upon chemically-prepared paper. As my means and the duties of
my profession would admit, the spring and autumn of 1837 were
employed in improving the instrument, varying the modes of writing, experimenting with plumbago and various kinds of ink or col-
oring-matter, substituting a pen for a pencil, and devising a mode
of writing on a whole sheet of paper instead of on a strip of ribbon; and, in the latter part of August or the beginning of September of that year, the instrument was shown in the cabinet of
the University to numerous visitors, operating through a circuit of
seventeen hundred feet of wire running back and forth in that
room.

"At this date (early in 1837) the public attention had been
drawn to the subject of telegraphs by rather pompous announce-
ments of marvelous improvements by two French gentlemen of the
names of Gonon and Servell, improvements so ambiguously described and mystified, that I was deceived by them into the belief
that their invention must be an electric telegraph.

"NEWLY-INVENTED TELEGRAPH.—We take the following from
a Washington letter in the *Baltimore Patriot:* 'Mr. Gonon and
his associate, Mr. Servell, have, after many years' application to the

subject, invented an important system of telegraphs, which casts into the shade every thing of the same kind that has yet been attempted. By their admirable plan, they can communicate every kind of information, word by word, and punctuate the same, without using more signals than words, and with as much rapidity as a person can write or even speak! They have received the most flattering encouragement from those literary and scientific gentlemen to whom they have explained the system, and not a doubt is entertained that it will accomplish the purposes of the inventors, and realize all that has been anticipated for it. Mr. Gonon assures me that he will be able to communicate a dispatch of one hundred words from New York to New Orleans in *half an hour!*—and those who are thoroughly acquainted with the system confirm his promises. How elementary does every other system appear, in comparison to that which can accomplish such an object! The imagination is overpowered in contemplating the consequences of such an achievement of human ingenuity. Distance is annihilated. Thousands of miles no longer divide us. We know on the instant, as it were, the actions, the wishes, the determinations of our fellow-beings of other States. Fortunate it is that we live in an age for whose intellectual progress nothing is too ripe.'

"My brother, the editor of the *New York Observer*, copied the above announcement into his paper, and, in a few words, stated the fact of the existence of my invention, and showed how, in one mode, electricity might be made to answer the purpose of telegraphic communication—a mode of his own—not attempting to describe mine; and the following was the first public mention of the Morse Telegraph :

"'We know nothing of the telegraph of Messrs. Gonon and Servell, except what is related in the above paragraph; but we do know that a gentleman of our acquaintance, several years since, suggested that intelligence might be communicated almost instantaneously, hundreds if not thousands of miles, by means of very fine wires, properly coated to protect them from moisture, and extending between places thus widely separated. It is well known that the electric fluid occupies no perceptible time in passing many miles on a wire, and, if it is possible by connecting one end of the wire with an electrical or galvanic battery to produce any *sensible effect whatever* at the other, it is obvious that, if there are *twenty-four* wires, each representing a letter of the alphabet, they may be connected with the battery successively, in any order, and, if so connected in the order of the letters of any word or sentence, that word or sentence could be read or written by a person standing at the other end of the wires. All the letters of a paragraph in a newspaper could thus be touched successively by a man in Philadelphia, and the contents, *verbatim et literatim*, be conveyed to New York as fast as a compositor could set up the type! It is not impossible that the time may be near when speeches in Congress, taken down by reporters, and conveyed by these "electric telegraphs" to New York or New Orleans, may be in type, printed, circulated, and read within a few hours after the voice of the speaker has ceased at Washington. The wires necessary for a distance of a hundred miles need not weigh many pounds, and if inclosed in an India-rubber tube, and supported on high poles erected along the route, at intervals of four or five hundred feet, could be extended through an immense distance at a trifling expense. The feasibility of the project depends entirely upon the practicability of producing any sensible effect at one end of a long wire, by connecting the other end with an electrical or galvanic battery.'

"The improvements of the French gentlemen, promising such miraculous results, proved, on inquiry, to be only some modification of the now almost universally-exploded aërial telegraph, improvements upon Chappe's semaphore, and having no relation to the Electric Telegraphs of modern days."

Whatever it was, the plan of the Frenchmen commanded the attention of Congress; a bill was introduced to refund to its projectors the money they had expended in experiments, but it has passed out of sight, and the "impossible" mode of Professor Morse connects all quarters of the globe.

The recollections of those who were witnesses of Professor Morse's experiments, or of their results, form the most valuable portion of this history, and, though necessarily repetitious, are here recorded.

Professor L. D. Gale gives the minutest account of the birth of the invention. He says: "I was a colleague professor in the University of the City of New York, in January, 1836, with Professor Morse, who had rooms in the University building. During the month of January he invited me into his private room in the University, where I saw for the first time certain apparatus constituting his electro-magnetic telegraph. The invention at that time consisted of the following pieces of apparatus:

"*First.* A train of clock-wheels, being part of a common wooden clock, adapted to regulate the motion of a strip of paper, or ribbon formed of strips of paper pasted together, end to end, about one and a half inch wide.

"*Second.* Three cylinders or drums of wood, arranged as in the accompanying drawings of the apparatus, which drawings represent the apparatus essentially as then constructed, to wit: A, B, C, are

the cylinders; A is the paper cylinder from which the paper is unrolled, passing over cylinder B to cylinder C, which is connected
with and moved by the clock machinery of D, which is the wooden

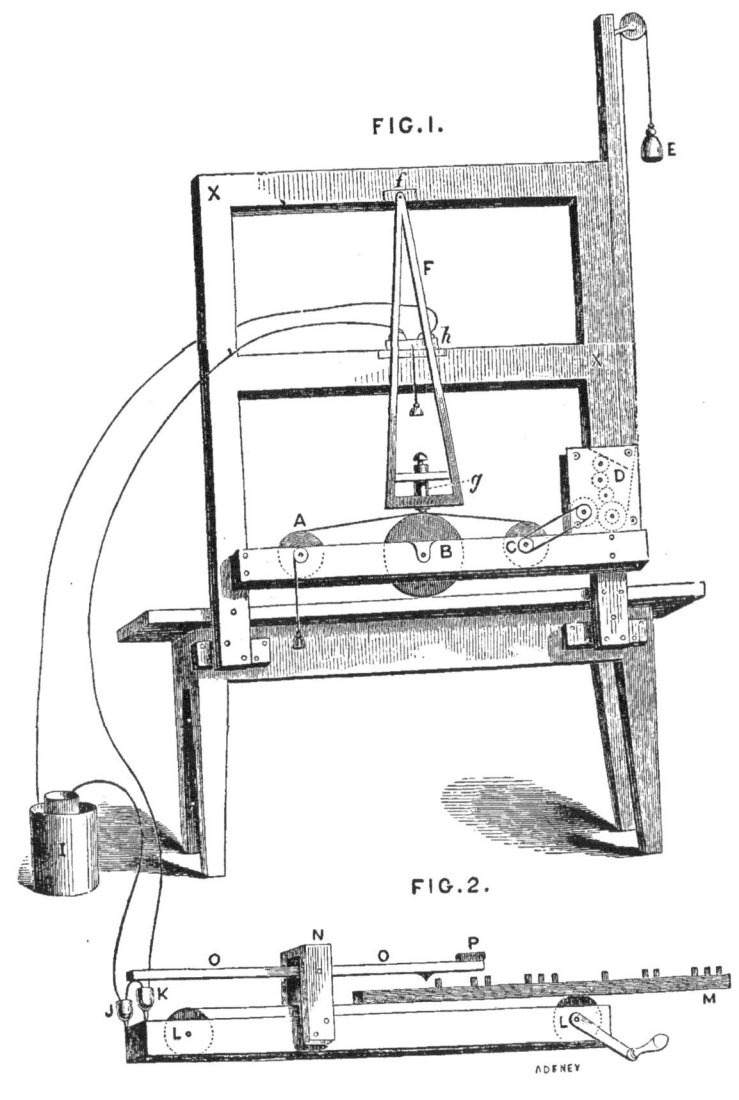

FIG. I.

FIG. 2.

clock of which I spoke, and which was moved by the weight E. A
wooden pendulum, F, of the shape delineated, was suspended over
the centre of cylinder, B having its pivot at *f*. This pendulum had

its motion at right angles or across the paper, when the paper was in motion. In the lower part of the pendulum, through two cross-pieces, was fixed a pencil-case, in which a pencil moved easily up and down, and was kept in constant contact with the paper by a light weight, *g*. At *h* was a projecting shelf from the frame XX, upon which shelf was an electro-magnet fixed, while the armature to be attracted by the said magnet was fixed upon the pendulum. The wires or conductors from the helices of the magnet passed, one to one pole of a single-pair galvanic battery, I, while the other wire passed to a cup of mercury, *k*, at the portrule. The other pole of the battery was connected by a wire to the other cup of mercury, *l*.

" *Third.* The portrule, represented below the table. This portrule was a rude frame, containing two cylinders, LL, about two inches diameter and two inches long; one of them was turned by a crank, and they were connected by a band of green-worsted binding about one and a half inch in diameter; M was the rule or composing-stick; it was made by two small thin rules about two feet long, side by side, but separated about the eighth of an inch from each other, forming a sort of trough in which were set up the type hereafter to be described, the cogs of which type are seen projecting on the top of the rule, M. At N two standards were raised from the sides of the long frame of the portrule and united at the top, in which stand-ards was suspended a lever, OO. At one end of this lever was a fork of copper wire, to be plunged, when the lever was depressed, into the two cups of mercury, *k* and *l ;* the other end of the lever bore a weight to keep that end down, and beneath the weight was a tooth like those upon the keys of a hand-organ.

" *Fourth.* There was a series of pieces of thin type-metal, which Professor Morse called type, and which he showed me also in draw-ings in a sketch-book, which drawings he informed me he had made on board the ship. These are accurately represented in the sub-joined drawing. They consisted of eleven pieces, having from one (1) to five (5) cogs each, except one, which was used as a space; the first five numbers consisted of cogs, from one to five respectively, with a *short* space after; the second five numbers consisted also of cogs from one to five respectively, with a *long* space after, a space double the length of the first.

" The operation of the apparatus when used was this: Suppose that the numbers 456, 320, and 4, were to be the numbers desired to be sent, the type 4, 5, 6, were set up in the rule M; after which a space was put to separate the whole number from the next, and so on. The rule, M, was then placed on the band of the portrule, and by turning the crank the rule was sent gradually forward; the cogs of the type operating the lever, O O, to break and close the circuit of the battery, J. When the circuit was closed, the magnet, *h*, attracted the pendulum, F, causing a movement of the pencil, *g*, of about a fourth of an inch. The pencil being in contact with the paper, if the paper moved in the direction of the arrow, or *vice' versa*, a continuous straight line was marked upon the paper, while the pendulum was stationary either at one end or the other limit of its motion, but when attracted by the magnet from one limit to the other, and suddenly released by the cessation of the magnetic force, it marked a V-shaped point, as in the 'example of imprinting' in the drawing, and the successive breakings and closings of the circuit by the cogs of the type caused the points to be impressed or marked upon the moving paper in the manner there shown. By reading the extremities of the V-shaped point or points the figures intended were readily recognized.

"During the year 1836, and beginning of 1837, the studies of Professor Morse on his telegraph I found much interrupted by his attention to his professional duties. I understood that want of pecuniary means prevented him from procuring to be made such mechanical improvements, and such substantial workmanship, as would make the operation of his invention more exact. In the months of March and April, 1837, the announcement of an extraordinary telegraph on the visual plan (as it afterward proved to be), the invention of two French gentlemen, of the names of Gonon and Servell, was going the rounds of the papers. The thought occurred to me, as well as to Professor Morse and some others of his friends, that the invention of his electro-magnetic telegraph had somehow become known, and was the origin of the new telegraph thus conspicuously announced. This announcement at once aroused Professor Morse to renewed exertions to bring the new invention creditably before the public, and to consent to a public announcement of the existence of his invention. From April to September, 1837, Professor Morse and myself were engaged together in the work of preparing magnets, winding wire, constructing batteries, etc., in the Uuniversity, for an experiment on a larger but still very limited scale, in the little leisure that each had to spare, and being at the same time much cramped for funds. The labors of Professor Morse at this period were mostly directed to modifications of his instruments for marking, contriving the best modes of marking, varying the pencil, the pen, using plumbago, and ink, and varying also the form of the paper, from a slip of paper to a sheet. The latter part of August, 1837, the operation of the instruments was shown to numerous visitors at the University. It was early a question between Professor Morse and myself, where was the limit of the magnetic power to move a lever. I expressed a doubt whether a lever could be moved by this power at a distance of twenty miles, and my settled conviction was that it could not be done with sufficient force to mark characters on paper at one hundred miles' distance. To this Professor Morse was accustomed to reply, '*If I can succeed in working a magnet ten miles, I can go round the globe.*' The chief anxiety, at this stage of the invention, was to ascertain the utmost limits of distance at which Mr. Morse could work or move a lever by magnetic power. He often said to me, '*It matters not how delicate the movement may be, if I can obtain it at all, it is all I want.*' Professor Morse often re·ferred to the number of stations which might be required, and which, he observed, would add to the complication and expense. He al·ways expressed his confidence of success in propagating magnetic power through any distance of electric conductors which circum-stances might render desirable. This plan was thus often explained to me: 'Suppose,' said Professor Morse, 'that in experimenting on twenty miles of wire we should find that the power of magnet-ism is so feeble that it will but move a lever with certainty a hair's breadth; that would be insufficient, it may be, to write or print, yet it would be sufficient to close and break another or a second circuit twenty miles farther, and this second circuit could be made, in the same manner, to break and close a third circuit twenty miles farther; and so on around the globe.'

"This general statement of the means to be resorted to, now embraced in what is called the *receiving magnet* (relays), to render practical writing or printing by telegraph, through long distances, was shown to me more in detail early in the spring of the year 1837.

"The apparatus was arranged on a plan substantially as indi-cated in the drawings. One (1) is a battery at one terminus of a line of conductors representing twenty miles in length, from one pole of which the conductor proceeds to the helix of an electro-magnet at the other terminus (the helix forming part of the conductor); thence it returns to the battery end, terminating in a mercury-cup, *o*. From the contiguous mercury-cup, *p*, a wire proceeds to the other pole of the battery; when the fork of the lever, c, unites the two cups of mercury the circuit is complete, and the magnet, b, is charged, and attracts the armature of the lever, d, which connects the circuit of battery 2 in the same manner, which again operates in turn the

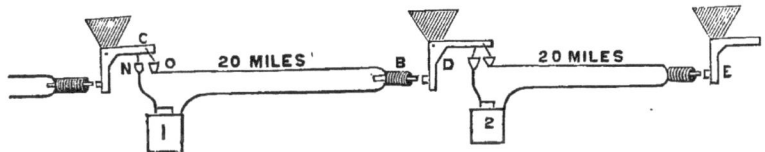

lever, e, twenty miles farther, and so on. This was the plan then and there revealed and shown to me by Professor Morse, and which, so far as I know, has constituted an essential part of his electromagnetic telegraph from that date to the present time.

"On Saturday, the 2d day of September, 1837, Professor Daubeny, of the English Oxford University, being on a visit to this country, was invited with a few friends to see the operation of the telegraph, in its then rude form, in the cabinet of the New York University, where it then had been put up with a circuit of 1,700 feet of copper wire, stretched back and forth in that long room. Professor Daubeny, Professor Torrey, and Mr. Alfred Vail, were present, among others. This exhibition of the telegraph, although of very rude and imperfectly-constructed machinery, demonstrated to all present the practicability of the invention, and it resulted in enlisting the means, the skill, and the zeal of Mr. Alfred Vail, who, early the next week, called at the rooms and had a more perfect explanation from Professor Morse of the character of the invention. The doubt to be dispelled in Mr. Vail's mind was whether the power by magnetism could be propelled to such a distance as to be practically effective. This doubt was dissipated in a few moments' conversation with Professor Morse, and I have ever been under the full conviction that it was the means then disclosed by Professor Morse to Mr. Vail, to wit, the plan of *repeating the power* of magnetism at any distance required, that induced Mr. Alfred Vail, and his brother, Mr. George Vail, at once to interest themselves in the invention, and to furnish Professor Morse with the means, material, and labor, for an experiment on a larger scale."

The writer of this memoir having had an intimate acquaintance of more than thirty years with Robert G. Rankin, Esq., whose residence was formerly on Washington Square, on which also stands the University, and knowing his scientific attainments and early acquaintance with Professor Morse's experiments, addressed to Mr. Rankin a letter of inquiry, to which he sent the following reply:

"NEWBURGH, N. Y., *April* 25, 1873.

"Professor Morse was one of the purest and noblest men of any age. I believe I was among the earliest outside of his family circle to whom he communicated his design to encircle the globe with wire. I was some years since called upon as a witness in the great Louisville suit, but my testimony on that trial was made before a commission from the court, and was confined to technical answers (in the form of an affidavit) to written interrogations, and of course I was restricted in my testimony from testifying to much I might have said, and would have been pleased to say, and I rejoice in the opportunity of giving my recollections. Some time in the fall of 1835 I was passing along the easterly walk of Washington Parade-ground, leading from Waverly Place to Fourth Street, when I heard my name called. On turning round, I saw, over the picket-fence, an outstretched arm, from a person standing in the middle or main entrance-door of the unfinished University building of New York, and immediately recognized the professor, who beckoned me toward him. On meeting and exchanging salutations—and you know how genial his were—he took me by the arm, and said:

"'I wish you to go up into my sanctum and examine a piece of mechanism, which, if you may not believe in, *you*, at least, will not laugh at, as I fear some others will. I want you to give me your frank opinion, as a friend, for I know your interest in and love of the applied sciences.'

"On entering the sanctum in the third story of the finished part of the building, the first thing my eye fell upon was an instrument not dissimilar in outward appearances to one of our modern melodeons, with a sort of key-board, like a movable series of wooden strips. Around the room were placed coils of wire, and many tools and articles generally used for mechanical purposes, besides jars, apparently of chemicals, and implements usually associated with galvanic experiments. My first exclamation was:

"'Well, professor, what are you at now? magnetism, electricity, music' (for I supposed the latter machine was some musical instrument)? •

"His reply was—

"'Well, now, let me do the talking, and you may ask questions after I am through. You see those coils? well, they contain a continuous uninterrupted line of wire of' (so many—I forget how many) 'thousands of feet' (one or more miles in length). 'You see that battery there?—this the positive pole, that the negative pole, all connected with that key-board, and those keys are to connect and interrupt the circuit, and in so doing produce the symbols of letters; although this instrument must be simplified, and is not yet what I want.'

"He made many explanations respecting the process of conductivity and continuity. A long silence on the part of each ensued, which was at length broken by my exclamation—

"'Well, professor, you have a pretty play!—theoretically true, but practically useful only as a mantel ornament, or for a mistress in the parlor to direct the maid in the cellar! But, professor, *cui bono?* In imagination one can make a new earth, and improve all the land communications of our old one; but, my unfortunate practicality stands in the way of my comprehension as yet.'

"We then had a long conversation on the subject of magnetism and its modifications, and, if I do not recollect the very words which clothed his thoughts, they were substantially as follows: He had been long impressed with the belief that God had created the great forces of Nature not only as manifestations of his own infinite power, but as expressions of good-will to man, to do him good, and that every one of God's great forces could yet be utilized for man's welfare; that modern science was constantly evolving from the hitherto hidden secrets of Nature some new development promotive of human welfare, and that at no distant day magnetism would do more for the advancement of human sociology than any of the material forces now known; that he would scarcely dare to compare spiritual with material forces, yet that analogically magnetism would do in the advancement of human welfare what the Spirit of God would do in the moral renovation of man's nature; that it would educate and enlarge the forces of the world. He then went on to say that he believed he had discovered a practical way of using magnetism as a line or means of communication, and interchange of thought in written language, upon every and all pursuits and subjects that engage the human mind, irrespective of distance and time save that required for manipulation, and that it would ultimately become a daily instrumentality in domestic as well as public life. He said he had felt as if he was doing a great work for

20

God's glory as well as for man's welfare; that such had been his long-cherished thought. His whole soul and heart appeared filled with a glow of love and good-will, and his sensitive and impassioned nature seemed almost to transform him in my eyes into a prophet.

"We gradually came back to the practicalities of the matter before us, and after a while I exclaimed:

"'But now, professor, how about rivers, and oceans, and deserts, and bridges, and unpopulated regions, for you know there are a few of such left on this globe of ours?'

"He replied, substantially, that, if his discovery was founded on truth, that truth would find a means of passing under, over, and through all such obstacles.

"We had a prolonged discussion, my own skepticism intensified, perhaps, by his earnestness, and then gradually flickering out like a painter's bow, with the receding sun's rays. Theoretically, I admitted his correctness; but doubts of its practicability had not yet yielded to full belief. Yet there gradually loomed up before my mind a vision, dim, it is true, yet outlined in some great future; a coming magnitude I could not fully comprehend; a sort of mighty handwriting on the surface-walls of this great globe of ours, prophesying the commingling and unification of nations; of the gospel, on some kind of heaven-spread wings, flitting to and fro over the earth, and ignorant and uncivilized humanity brought into subjection to our heaven-born Christianity.

"I had frequent and earnest interviews with the professor for years after, and I need not add that I was a believer in 'Morse's Telegraph.' I recollect well the discussions we had in regard to modes of transmission, in carrying the wires under or over the surface, crossing draw-bridges, and have vivid recollections of (suggested) lofty spars, like ships' masts, and he proposed crossing Hudson River·by wires from Storm King to the east shore; and earnest talk and cipherings on the tensile strength and form of wires, or chains, of sundry self weight-bearing conductors. But the world knows the skepticism that enshrouded even the national wisdom in Congress, continued for years, and the almost heart and soul rending trials the professor passed through, and when he at length showed practically to the world 'what hath God wrought' through him, and the many that endeavored to detract from his well-earned fame. *It will take generations yet to come to commensurate their conditions with his inventions.*

"It is among the most delightful of my 'recollections' of the
Professor—and I have very often related them to friends—that I
scarce recollect a conversation on the great subject—the last at his
own house, not long prior to his death—that he did not in some
way suggest the thought of God's wondrous goodness in enduing
the insensate matter of earth with such an energizing material force
as magnetism, and permitting him to be an instrument of utilizing
it for the welfare of man. '*Si Deus nobiscum, quis contra nos?*'"

This conversation with Mr. Rankin occurred before the inventor had his instrument in working order. His colleague,
Rev. Henry B. Tappan, D. D., LL. D., and subsequently President of the University of Michigan, an eminent philosophical
Divine, having met Professor Morse in Berlin in the year 1868,
referred, in conversation, to the fact that he was one of the
early witnesses of the operation of the Telegraph. In reply to
a note from Professor Morse, Dr. Tappan wrote:

"The University was opened in the autumn of 1832. I was one
of the first professors elected. In the same year you returned from
Europe. Some time after your return, and when you yourself had
been elected a Professor, you related to me, in a free, familiar, and
extended conversation, how your mind had been occupied during
your last voyage with the idea of transmitting and recording words
through distance by means of an electro-magnetic arrangement.
The idea, you said, had haunted you, whether you lay in your berth
or walked the deck, and that you had, at length, arrived at a definite conception of the required arrangement. I cannot recall all
the details of this explanation; I well recollect that it contained
the germ of what you afterward so successfully accomplished.

"In 1835 you had advanced so far that you were prepared to
give, on a small scale, a practical demonstration of the possibility
of transmitting and recording words through distance, by means of
an electro-magnetic arrangement. I was one of the limited circle
whom you invited to witness the first experiments. In a long room
of the University you had wires extended from end to end where
the magnetic apparatus was arranged. It is not necessary for me
to describe particulars which have now become so familiar to every
one. The fact which I now recall with the liveliest interest, and
which I mentioned in conversation at Mr. Bancroft's as one of the
choicest recollections of my life, was that of the first transmission
and recording of a telegraphic dispatch. I suppose, of course, that

you had already made these experiments before the company arrived whom you had invited. But I may claim to have witnessed *the first transmission and recording of words* by lightning ever made public. All who were present were invited to write and send off dispatches from one end of the room to be recorded at the other. I recollect full well my delight at hearing the words which I silently gave in at one end, accurately read off from the strip of paper at the other. The fact was established that words—that the thoughts, of course, expressed by words, could be communicated and recorded with lightning-speed from one place to another. It was one of those startling facts which open to us immeasurable consequences; and justify the imagination in its pictures of the future, and make our dreams but struggles to anticipate surpassing realities.

"Permit me, also, to say that I most sincerely sympathized in the triumph you had won; and that to me it was a reflection full of satisfaction that you, a friend of the philosophic dreamer and poet Coleridge, and the early associate of Leslie and Allston, had, while wandering among the forms of ideal beauty, found a most stupendous practical fact; thus repeating what men are so slow to believe, and yet which so frequently appears, as in Michael Angelo, Milton, and Fulton, that he who pursues the Beautiful may also think the True, and accomplish the Good. The arrangement which you exhibited, on the above-mentioned occasion, as well as the mode of receiving the dispatches, were substantially the same as that which you now employ. I feel certain that you had then already grasped the whole invention, however you may have since perfected the details. I met you, afterward, when you were engaged in making a larger experiment by laying the wires underground between Washington and Baltimore—an experiment whose failure led to a most important result — that of putting into practice your early mode of the elevation of the wires upon poles in the open air; thus escaping the disturbing influences of the earth, and achieving the most economic and rapid execution of the work."

Daniel Huntington, one of the great artists of our country, was at this time a pupil of Mr. Morse, and this is his testimony:

"I studied my profession with Professor Morse, and was his pupil from the month of May, 1833, to the 1st of May, 1835, occupying rooms with him, first in Greenwich Lane, and afterward at the New York City University, where he removed, early in the autumn of 1835, into his newly-prepared rooms in that building, on Washington Square. At the time Professor Morse removed into his new rooms, which were in the third story front, of the north wing, that part of the building was not finished; the lower rooms particularly, and the stairway into the third story, were unfinished. While Professor Morse was in Greenwich Lane he seemed particularly impatient to get into his new rooms, in order to put into operation his plan for an electric telegraph, allusions to which he occasionally made. He had no sooner removed into the rooms in the University than he constructed an instrument which showed how he intended marking characters for letters at a distance; I distinctly remember the general appearance of the instrument and the kind of characters which it marked. The drawing[1] calls to my mind, as a familiar acquaintance, the appearance of the instrument. I am quite sure that I saw the instrument in operation some months previous to the time of my leaving Professor Morse. On the 15th of November, 1835, I took a room at the University by myself, which I hired, and my recollection is, that I saw that instrument in operation at or about the time I took that room. I cannot state the precise date."

This intelligent testimony of Mr. Huntington makes it as certain as human testimony can make any thing, that the instrument was in actual operation in the year 1835.

Hon. Hamilton Fish, Secretary of State, being present at a banquet tendered to Professor Morse, in Paris, in 1858, gave his pleasant recollections:

"It was in early boyhood, under my father's roof, that I made the acquaintance of our guest, then eminent in his profession as an artist, and at the head of the National Academy of Design. I soon learned to appreciate and admire his intelligence, his amiability, and his worth. To a friendly intercourse thus established, and much cherished on my part, I was indebted for *an early explanation* of his discovery, soon after his return from Europe, in 1832. Some time afterward, in the early part of 1836, in a room in the New York University, I witnessed the telegraph in operation, recording messages, transmitted through some mile or more of wire, suspended in successive turns around the walls; there was a small battery in one corner of the room, and a sort of clock-work machinery in another, and the mysterious little click, click, click, of

---

[1] See the drawing in Dr. Gale's statement.

the former produced a simultaneous record on the other. Theory was reduced to practice, and the telegraph demonstrated its efficiency. During the winter of 1844-'45, Professor Morse was a frequent (as he was ever a welcome) visitor in my apartment, in Washington. The practicability of transmitting signs by submerged wires had been then demonstrated; but the distance to which they might be transmitted was of course still a problem. *Mr. Morse, however, unhesitatingly predicted the direct communication between Europe and America; he told me that I would probably live to witness it.*"

Rev. Mr. Seeley, of the American chapel in Paris, said at the same dinner:

"It seems but yesterday that I was a freshman in the New York City University, and our honored guest Professor of the Fine Arts in the institution, and President of the National Academy of Design in the same city. At that time the Professor was reported to be engaged in labors which pertained to science rather than to art; and there was many an ominous shake of the head, accompanied by expressions of apprehension that one of the best artists of our country was sacrificing his genius to a chimera. He persisted, however, *and one afternoon in the spring, or early summer of* 1836, I had the privilege of witnessing an experiment made by him in a large room of the University building. There was present the Professor, with one or two assistants, and several leading gentlemen of the city. A line of slender wire, one mile in length, was stretched around the room in a remarkable manner. . . . To one end of the wire was attached a pen or pencil, which was held over a strip of white paper. . . . The professor proposed to demonstrate the possibility of transmitting and recording messages, *verbatim et literatim*, over any length of wire. Some one whispered a sentence in his ear, and in a few seconds the white paper at the opposite end of the line was covered with broken lines. Time passed over, when one day in 1842 I entered one of the upper lofts of the building in which the *New York Observer* was published, and found our Professor of the Fine Arts superintending experiments in the manufacture of *submarine cables. For he had already projected the extension of telegraphic lines under water.*"

Commodore Shubrick, of the United States Navy, in a letter dated Washington, D. C., October 5, 1860, writes to Professor Morse:

"I have a distinct recollection that in the winter of 1835, being in the city of New York, I was walking with our lamented friend, the late Fenimore Cooper, when we met you, and you invited us to your room in the University, and that you then and there showed us the operation of your telegraphic instrument. The fact is impressed on my mind by the remarks made by Mr. Cooper on the wonderful effects which would grow out of the discovery, if successful (of which he seemed to have no doubt), on the intercommunication of the world. I have frequently seen Mr. Paul F. Cooper, son of our late friend, who recollects having seen the operation of your instrument during the same winter, though he was then a small boy."

The Professor took possession of his rooms in the University in the year 1835, where he set up his rude apparatus, and called in his friends to see its operation. There he wrought through the year 1836, probably the darkest and longest year of his life, giving lessons to pupils in the art of painting while his mind was in the throes of the great invention. He needed only the means to demonstrate, on a scale to command attention, that he had reached a result of incalculable interest and advantage to the human race. Professor Gale has told us of the struggles of Professor Morse during that year; of the necessary occupation of his mind with the instruction of students, and his utter inability, from the want of money, to bring his invention before the public. In 1835 Dr. Tappan and others had seen the apparatus at work and WRITING substantially in the same manner as it writes now. "The words which I silently gave at one end were accurately read off from the strip of paper at the other," says Dr. Tappan. Up to this hour no human aid had been rendered to the solitary inventor. The instrument was constructed. The alphabet was formed. The writing at a distance was done. The TELEGRAPH was made. It was susceptible of vast improvements; they have been in progress up to this time, and will be continued so long as art and science advance. But as the invention was ORIGINAL with Professor Morse, so the execution was *his*, and *his only*. This declaration deserves the more emphasis because every thing essential to the completeness of the Telegraph was afterward claimed by or for others! But we have seen, and proved by the most competent witnesses, that when the Telegraph was first exhibited by Professor Morse, and before he had called in the aid of any other hand or mind, it was a complete instrument, with a complete alphabet, doing the same work that is done with the Morse instrument to-day.

Among the spectators of the successful operation of the instrument on the 2d day of September, 1837, was Alfred Vail. He was born in Morris County, New Jersey, in 1807, and was graduated at the University of the City of New York in 1836. When he first saw the experiments of the Telegraph in the rooms of Professor Morse he grasped the idea, and formed an instant resolution to pursue the subject. The only point on which he desired satisfaction, and at the same point all appeared to hesitate, was the possibility of no limit to the distance through which the current of electricity would flow. This was the link to connect experiment with success. If this link failed, the whole thing was a failure.

It was plain enough that the *Telegraph* was a completed fact. Morse had made an instrument by which words were written at a distance, in characters intelligible to himself and easily learned by others. Such an instrument was now in operation. Men of science and men of business had seen it and wondered. Before their eyes had been stretched a wire 1,700 feet in length, and, with the instrument which Morse had constructed and was now using, words were silently but evidently written down at one extremity of the wire, when communicated at the other. The semaphores or signals of other electricians required watching, and the signals were slowly interpreted. Morse wrote and registered his messages. The work was done and recorded. It was a writing-at-a-distance machine; a Telegraph; the only Telegraph! But the grand question to be decided by experiment, as Morse had already demonstrated to his own satisfaction and that of others, was the possibility of indefinite propagation. Here came in his relay—a conception and production scarcely less important than the instrument itself. Mr. Vail would have this point clearly illustrated and settled, and he would then cheerfully adopt the professor's favorite remark, that, " if he could succeed in working it ten miles, he could make it go around the globe."

"The *relay*," says Professor Horsford, "is a *discovery* as well as a device or a series of devices or inventions. It had its birth in the effort to answer the question, How can the current, which has become feeble through distance from the battery, be *reënforced?* There was need of some principle akin to that which supplies a locomotive and train with fuel, water, and oil, without stopping. The stopping consumes time. To be obliged to repeat the message every few miles would be to abandon it. It would be expensive as well as time-consuming. Now, the reënforcement of the current at a distance from the prime station, through the very instrumentality of the message sent, is an absolute new departure. It is a grand *idea* primarily, and secondarily it involves inventions of mechanical devices to effect several things. In the first place, there is wanted an electro-magnet at the second station, operated through the battery at the primary station. This magnet must draw its armature not to the face of the magnet, but only very near it, and in so doing close the circuit. This takes place with the closing of the first circuit. In opening the first circuit, the second circuit is opened at the same instant, and the magnet at the second station with the arrest of the current loses its magnetism. Now a self-acting, adjustable spring draws the armature away from the face of the magnet, through a space very narrow, but adequate to break the circuit at the second station. Here are the fewest elements of the *relay*. It involves the opening and *closing* of the circuit, by an act going out from the primary station. The *relay* of Professor Morse opens and *closes* in connection with a conductor of an intensity battery, operating through a long conductor upon a distant magnet." This was the invention of Professor Morse described by Professor Gale in his statement already recited in this chapter.

Mr. Vail, having become thoroughly satisfied on this point, embarked in the enterprise. His father, Judge Stephen Vail, and his brother, George Vail, were proprietors of extensive iron and brass works at Speedwell, Morris County, New Jersey. The fact that the family were engaged in such manufactures, led the young man to entertain the idea of engaging in the construction of instruments to be used in the development of the Telegraph. Before going to the University he had taken deep interest in the business of his father and brother: the making of steam-engines and machinery that required the use of both iron and brass; he had been specially engaged in the brass-foundery, and had become noted for his skill in working in that metal. With mechanical genius and fondness also for study, with a taste alike for art and science, he was emphatically the man to be associated with the professor, himself an illustrious example of art and science combined. The young man, ardent, hopeful, and sincere, was not long in bringing both his father and brother to see with him the magnificent possibilities of the electric telegraph for usefulness in the commerce and inter-course of mankind. They not only approved and encouraged the resolution of their son and brother to identify himself with the Telegraph, and to devote his life to its service, but they, with enterprise and faith in its ultimate fruits, promised the necessary funds to make the experiments which were essential to insure confidence in the public mind. Many years afterward Professor Morse, in the height of his success, and crowned with the honors of his country and of distant nations, spoke of this young man in these words:

"Alfred Vail, then a student in the University, and a young man of great ingenuity, having heard of my invention, came to my rooms and I explained it to him, and from that moment he has taken the deepest interest in the Telegraph. Finding that I was unable to command the means to bring my invention properly before the public, and believing that he could com-mand those means through his father and brother, he expressed the belief to me, and I at once made such an arrangement with him as to procure the pecuniary means and the skill of these gentlemen. It is to their joint liberality, but especially to the attention, and skill, and faith in the final success of the enter-prise maintained by Alfred Vail, that is due the success of my endeavors to bring the Telegraph at that time creditably before the public."

With this young and ingenious student Professor Morse entered into partnership, assigning to him one-fourth interest in the patent-right to be secured for the invention.

On the 10th of March, 1837, the Honorable Levi Woodbury, Secretary of the Treasury of the United States, in consequence of the reports that had reached the country of various schemes of telegraphing proposed in Europe, had issued the following:

"Circular to certain Collectors of the Customs, Commanders of Revenue Cutters, and other Persons.

"TREASURY DEPARTMENT, *March* 10, 1837.

" With the view of obtaining information in regard ' to the propriety of establishing a system of telegraphs for the United States,' in compliance with the request contained in the annexed resolution of the House of Representatives, adopted at its last session, I will thank you to furnish the Department with your opinion upon the subject. If leisure permits, you would oblige me by pointing out the manner, and the various particulars, in which the system may be rendered most useful to the Government of the United States and the public generally. It would be desirable, if in your power, to present a detailed statement as to the proper points for the location, and distance of the stations from each other, with general rules for the regulation of the system, together with your sentiments as to the propriety of connecting it with any existing department of the Government, and some definite idea of the rapidity with which intelligence could ordinarily, and also in urgent cases, be communicated between distant places. I wish you to estimate the probable expense of establishing and supporting telegraphs, upon the most approved system, for any given distance, during any specified period.

"It would add to the interest of the subject if you would offer views as to the practicability of uniting, with a system of telegraphs for communication in clear weather and in the daytime, another for communication in fogs, by cannon, or otherwise; and, in the night, by the same mode, or by rockets, fires, etc.

"I should be gratified by receiving your reply by the 1st of October next.

"LEVI WOODBURY,
" *Secretary of the Treasury.*"

To this circular Professor Morse replied four days before his partnership was formed with Mr. Vail:

S. F. B. Morse to the Secretary of the Treasury.

"NEW YORK CITY UNIVERSITY, *September* 27, 1837.

"DEAR SIR: In reply to the inquiries which you have done me the honor to make, in asking my opinion ' of the propriety of establishing a system of telegraphs for the United States,' I would say, in regard to the general question, that I believe there can scarcely be two opinions, in such a community as ours, in regard to the advantage which would result, both to the Government and the public generally, from the establishment of a system of communication by which the most speedy intercourse may be had between the most distant parts of the country. The *mail system*, it seems to me, is founded on the universally admitted principle that the greater the speed with which intelligence can be transmitted from point to point, the greater is the benefit derived to the whole community. The only question that remains, therefore, is, what system is best calculated, from its completenesss and cheapness, to effect this desirable end?

"With regard to telegraphs constructed on the ordinary principles, however perfected within the limits in which they are necessarily confined, the most perfect of them are liable to one insurmountable objection—*they are useless the greater part of the time.* In foggy weather, and ordinarily during the night, no intelligence can be transmitted. Even when they can transmit, much time is consumed in communicating but little, and that little not always precise.

"Having invented an entirely new mode of telegraphic communication, which, so far as experiments have yet been made with it, promises results of almost marvelous character, I beg leave to present to the Department a brief account of its chief characteristics.

"About five years ago, on my voyage from Europe, the electrical experiment of Franklin, upon a wire some four miles in length, was casually recalled to my mind in conversation with one of the passengers, in which experiment it was ascertained that the electricity traveled through the whole circuit in a time not appreciable, but apparently instantaneous. *It immediately occurred to me that, if the presence of electricity could be made* VISIBLE *in any desired part of this circuit, it would not be difficult to construct a* SYSTEM OF SIGNS *by which intelligence could be instantaneously transmitted.* The thought, thus conceived, took strong hold of my mind in the leisure which the voyage afforded, and I planned a system of signs, and an apparatus to carry it into effect. I cast a species of type, which I had devised for this purpose, the first week after my arrival home; and, although the rest of the machinery was planned, yet, from the pressure of unavoidable duties, I was compelled to postpone my experiments, and was not able to test the whole plan until within a few weeks. The result has realized my most sanguine expectations.

" As I have contracted with Mr. Alfred Vail to have a complete apparatus made to demonstrate at Washington by the 1st of January, 1838, the practicability and superiority of my mode of telegraphic communication by means of electro-magnetism (an apparatus which I hope to have the pleasure of exhibiting to you), I will confine myself in this communication to a statement of its peculiar advantages.

" *First.* The *fullest and most precise information* can be almost instantaneously transmitted between any two or more points between which a wire conductor is laid : that is to say, no other time is consumed than is necessary to write the intelligence to be conveyed, and to convert the words into the telegraphic numbers. The numbers are then transmitted nearly instantaneously (or, if I have been rightly informed in regard to some recent experiments in the velocity of electricity, *two hundred thousand miles in a second*) to any distance, where the numbers are immediately recognized, and reconverted into the words of the intelligence.

" *Second.* The same full intelligence can be communicated *at any moment, irrespective of the time of day or night, or state of the weather.* This single point establishes its superiority to all other modes of telegraphic communication now known.

" *Third.* The whole apparatus will occupy but *little space* (scarcely six cubic feet, probably not more than four) ; [1] and it may, therefore, be placed, without inconvenience, in any house.

" *Fourth.* The *record of intelligence is made in a permanent manner, and in such a form* that it can be at once bound up in *volumes,* convenient for reference, if desired.

" *Fifth. Communications are secret* to all but the persons for whom they are intended.

" These are the chief advantages of the electro-magnetic telegraph over other kinds of telegraphs, and which must give it the preference, provided the expense and other circumstances are reasonably favorable.

" The newness of the whole plan makes it not so easy to estimate the expense, but an *approach* to a correct estimate can be made.

" The principal expense will be the first cost of the wire or metallic conductors (consisting of four lengths), and the securing them against injury. The cost of a single copper wire one-sixteenth of an inch diameter (and it should not be of less dimensions), for four

---

[1] It now occupies a space ten inches long, eight inches high, and five wide.

hundred miles, was recently estimated in Scotland to be about one thousand pounds sterling, including the solderings of the wire together; that is, about six dollars per mile for one wire, or twenty-four dollars per mile for the four wires. I have recently contracted for twenty miles of copper wire, No. 18, at forty cents per pound. Each pound, it is estimated, contains ninety-three feet, which gives a result coinciding with the Scotch estimate, if one dollar and sixty cents per mile be added for solderings.

"The preparation of the wire for being laid (if in the ground) comprehends the *clothing of the wires* with an insulating or non-conducting substance; the *encasing them in wood, clay, stone, iron,* or *other metal;* and the *trenching* of the earth to receive them. In this part of the business I have no experience to guide me, the whole being altogether new. I can, therefore, only make at present a rough estimate. Iron tubes inclosing the wires, and filled in with pitch and resin, would probably be the most eligible mode of securing the conductors from injury, while, at the same time, it would be the most costly. Iron tubes of one and one-half inch diameter, I learn, can be obtained, at Baltimore, at twenty-eight cents per foot. The *trenching* will not be more than three cents for two feet, or about seventy-five dollars per mile. This estimate is for a trench three feet deep and one and one-half wide. There is no *grading;* the trench may follow the track of any road, over the highest hills or lowest valleys. Across rivers, with bridges, the circuit may easily be carried, inclosed beneath the bridge. Where the stream is wide, and no bridge, the circuit, inclosed in lead, may be sunk to the bottom.

"If the circuit is laid through the air, the first cost would doubtless be much lessened. This plan of making the circuit has some advantages, but there are also some disadvantages; the chief of which latter is, that, being always in sight, the temptation to injure the circuit to mischievously disposed persons, is greater than if it were buried out of sight beneath their feet. As an offset, however, to this, an injury to the circuit is more easily detected. With regard to danger from wantonness, it may be sufficient to say that the same objection was originally made in the several cases, successively, of water-pipes, gas-pipes, and railroads; and yet we do not hear of wantonness injuring any of these. Stout spars of some thirty feet in height, well planted in the ground, and placed about three hundred and fifty feet apart, would, in this case, be required, along the tops of which the circuit might be stretched. Fifteen such spars would be wanted to a mile. This mode would be as cheap, probably, as any other, unless the laying of the circuit in water should be found to be most eligible. A series of experiments to ascertain the practicability of this mode, I am about to commence with Professor Gale, of our University, a gentleman of great science, and to whose assistance, in many of my late experiments, I am greatly indebted. We are preparing a circuit of twenty miles. The result of our experiments I will have the honor of reporting to you.

"The other machinery, consisting of the apparatus for transmitting and receiving the intelligence, can be made at a very trifling cost. The only parts of the apparatus that waste or consume materials, are the batteries, which consume *acid* and *zinc*, and the register, which consumes *paper* for recording, and *pencils* or *ink* for marking.

"The cost of *printing*, in the first instance, *of a telegraphic dictionary*, should perhaps also be taken into the account, as each officer of the Government, as well as many others, would require a copy, should this mode of telegraphic communication go into effect. This dictionary would contain a vocabulary of all the words in common use in the English language, with the numbers regularly affixed to each word.

"The stations in the case of this telegraph may be as numerous as are desired; the only additional expense for that purpose being the adding of the transmitting and receiving apparatus to each station.

"The cost of supporting a system of telegraphs on this plan (when a circuit is once established) would, in my opinion, be much less than on the common plans; yet, for want of experience in this mode, I would not affirm it positively.

"As to 'the propriety of connecting the system of telegraphs with any existing department of Government,' it would seem most natural to connect a telegraphic system with the Post-Office Department; for, although it does not carry a mail, yet it is another mode of accomplishing the principal object for which the mail is established, to wit: the rapid and regular transmission of intelligence. If my system of telegraphs should be established, it is evident that the telegraph would have but little rest, day or night. The advantage of communicating intelligence instantaneously, in hundreds of instances of daily occurrence, would warrant such a rate of *postage* (if it may be so called) as would amply defray all expenses of the first cost of establishing the system, and of guarding it, and keeping it in repair.

"As every word is numbered, an obvious mode of rating might be, a *charge of a certain amount on so many numbers.* I presume that five words can certainly be transmitted in a minute; for, with the imperfect machinery I now use, I have recorded at that rate, at the distance of half a mile.

"In conclusion, I would say, that if the perfecting of this 'new system of telegraphs (which may justly be called the American Telegraph, since I can establish my claims to priority in the invention) shall be thought of public utility, and worthy the attention of Government, I shall be ready to make any sacrifice of personal service and of time to aid in its accomplishment.

"In the mean time I remain, sir, with sincere respect and high personal esteem,

"Your most obedient, humble servant,

"SAM'L F. B. MORSE.

"Hon. LEVI WOODBURY,
  "*Secretary of the Treasury.*"

Professor Morse then filed in the Patent-Office at Washington the following PETITION:

That your petitioner has invented a new method of transmitting and recording intelligence by means of electro-magnetism, which he denominates the *American Electro-Magnetic Telegraph,* etc.

Petition dated *September* 28, 1837.

SPECIFICATION OF THE AMERICAN ELECTRO-MAGNETIC TELEGRAPH.

To all whom it may concern: Be it known that I, Samuel F. B. Morse, of the city of New York, in the county and State of New York, have invented a new method of transmitting and recording intelligence by means of electro-magnetism, which I call the *American Electro-Magnetic Telegraph,* and I do hereby declare that the following is a full and exact description of said telegraph, so far as it is at present completed. The nature of my invention consists in laying an electric or galvanic circuit, or conductors, of any length, to any distance. These conductors may be made of any metal, such as copper or iron wire, or strips of copper or iron, or of cord, or twine, or other substances, gilt, silvered, or covered with any thin metal leaf, properly insulated, in the ground, or through or beneath the water, or through the air, and by causing the electric or galvanic current to pass through the circuit by means of any generator of electricity, to make use of the *visible signs* of the presence of electricity in any part of the said circuit to communicate any intelligence from one place to another. To make the said visible signs of electricity available for the purpose aforesaid, I have invented the following apparatus, namely:

1. A *system of signs*, by which numbers, and consequently words and sentences, are signified.

2. A *set of type*, adapted to regulate and communicate the signs, with *cases*, for convenient keeping of the type, and *rules*, in which to set up the type.

3. An apparatus called the *portrule*, for regulating the movement of the type-rules, which rules, by means of the type, in their turn regulate the times and intervals of the passage of electricity.

4. A register which *records* the signs permanently.

5. A *dictionary or vocabulary* of words, numbered and adapted to this system of telegraph.

6. *Modes of laying conductors* to preserve them from injury.

1. *The System of Signs.*

The signs are the representatives first of numerals, and are as follows: The single numerals are represented by ten marks, such as dots, lines, or punctures, varied thus: A single mark signifies the numeral *one;* two marks, *two;* three marks, *three;* four marks, *four;* five marks, *five;* six marks, *six;* seven marks, *seven;* eight marks, *eight;* nine marks, *nine;* and ten marks, *ten*, or *cipher. The cipher is also signified by a single mark differently placed from the rest.* The numerals are separated from each other by *short* intervals, so that they would be represented in the different ways, shown in Example 1, of the annexed drawing. The *compound numbers* are separated from each other by *long* intervals; for example, the compound number 324, compounded of 3, and 2, and 4, and the compound number 516, compounded of 5, and 1, and 6, would be represented as shown in Fig. 1, Example 2.

The sign for cipher ($\lfloor \wedge \rfloor$), or (▰▰▰), or (——), placed before a number, signifies that that number is to be read as a number, and not as the representative of a word, thus: "Send 56 copies," would be thus represented: Suppose the word "send" to be represented by the number 21, and the word "copies" by 34, then the sentence would be written as in Fig. 2, Example 2. Thus all numbers, and consequently all *words*, are easily represented.

2. *The Type.*

A set of *type*, made of thin metal, such as type-metal, brass, iron, or other material, consists of twelve different pieces, of the figure and dimensions represented in Example 3 of the annexed drawing.

The *rest* is for the *lever* (hereinafter described) to rest upon previous to beginning to communicate. Each type has a notch or indentation corresponding to its denomination, and the short space in addition. The number of each type is marked upon that part occupied for the space, or interval; the cipher is either marked by

21

the type with ten notches, or with the type of a single tooth, between two sunken spaces. Two additional pieces, making fourteen
in all, are, *first*, the space, or long interval, placed between separate
and compound numbers; and, *second*, the stop, or long type, which
throws up the lever upon a detent, until wanted again.

The *cases* are of wood, or other suitable material, with small com-
partments of the exact length of each type, for the greater convenience in distributing them.

The *rules* are of wood, metal, or other suitable material, and are
formed about three feet long, and with a groove in which to place
the type as represented in Example 4. The rule is furnished with
cogs, for the purpose of being moved by a pinion-wheel.

3. The Portrule.

The portrule is for the purpose of carrying the rule, when prepared with its type. It consists—1. Of a *small* lever, somewhat
like the levers to the keys of a hand-organ, but with the power between the fulcrum and the weight. The lever is made to rise or
fall by passing the rule with its type beneath the projection or
single cog in the lever, which cog falls into each notch and rises on
each tooth of the type. The lever is made a portion of the circuit
by affixing a small portion of the conductor to it, with a joint at
the hinge-end of the lever, moving in mercury, or otherwise connected, so that the circuit be not interrupted. The other end of
the small portion of the circuit is at the end of the lever, which
has the most motion, and, by the rise and fall of the lever, is
made to break and close the circuit at the desired times. The
movable point of the conductor closes the circuit either by a touch,
either into mercury, which holds the other extremity of the circuit,
or upon a plate of copper, silver, or other metal attached to the said
extremity.

The rule is made to pass with regularity, as to space and time,
beneath the lever, by means of a pinion-wheel fitting into the cogs
of the rule, which wheel is made to revolve either by a crank moved
by the hand, or by other power, in any of the well-known and common
mechanical methods.

The rule is kept in its course by a channel, or ways, made for
that purpose. The portrule sends the intelligence.

4. The Register.

The register, at any distance from the portrule, *receives* and *records* the intelligence, and is thus constructed: 1. An electro-magnet, made in any of the usual modes of forming it, such as winding
insulated copper wire, or strips of copper, or tin-foil, or other metal,
around a bar of soft iron, either straight or bent into a circular
form, has the two extremities of the coils connected with the circuit or conductors, so that the coils round the magnet make part of
the circuit. The power of this magnet is applied—2. To a *lever*, or

pendulum, by affixing to the said lever, or pendulum, the armature of the magnet, or short bar of iron, at such a distance that the electro-magnet will readily attract it. A small weight, or spring, keeps the lever and armature from the magnet when the magnet is not in action. To the lever, or pendulum, is attached—3. A *pencil*, or *fountain* pen, or a small *printing-wheel*, or any other marking material. This pencil, or other marking material, is made to mark upon—4. A light *cylinder* of a size to hold a convenient sheet of paper, which is wrapped around it. The cylinder is made to revolve, as to time and place, slowly and regularly upon its arbor, or shaft, by means of clock-machinery, and to advance a short distance upon the staff every revolution by means of a screw and cog apparatus, so that a line formed by a stationary point above the cylinder describes upon it a spiral or screw line. The point of the pencil, or other marking material, is kept in contact with the surface of the paper upon the cylinder either by its own weight or by a small weight attached to it; or, when the printing-wheel is used, the wheel is brought into contact with the paper by the magnet, when required to mark. 5. A *bascule*, or method of changing the poles of the magnet, after every stroke of the lever, is affixed to the magnet, and regulated by the movement of the lever. 6. An *alarm* apparatus, to give notice that a communication is about to be made, is also affixed, and is made to strike or give notice at the first movement of the lever. To each register are attached *duplicate cylinders*, for the convenience of continued writing, so that when one cylinder is filled, the other cylinder, by a shifting apparatus, begins to receive the marks. The paper, when ready to be removed from the cylinder, forms a regular page, prepared for binding in a volume.

5. *The Dictionary, or Vocabulary.*

The dictionary is a complete vocabulary of words *alphabetically* arranged and *regularly numbered*, beginning with the letters of the alphabet, so that each word in the language has its telegraphic number. The modes which I propose of *laying the circuit*, and of insulating the wires and conductors, are various. The wires may be insulated by winding each wire with silk, cotton, flax, or hemp, and then dipping them into a solution of caoutchouc, or into a solution of shellac, or into pitch or resin and caoutchouc. They may be laid through the air, inclosed above the ground, in the ground, or in the water. When *through the air*, they may be insulated by a covering that shall protect them from the weather, such as cotton, flax, or hemp, and dipped into any solution which is a non-conductor, and elevated upon pillars. When inclosed *above the ground*, they may be laid in tubes of iron or lead, and these again may be inclosed in wood, if desirable. When *laid in the ground*, they may be inclosed in iron, leaden, wooden, or earthen tubes, and buried beneath the surface. *Across rivers* the circuit may be carried beneath the bridges, or, where there are no bridges, inclosed in lead or iron and sunk at the bottom, or stretched across, where the banks are high, upon pillars elevated on each side of the river.

What I claim as my invention, and desire to secure by letters-patent, and to protect for one year, by a caveat, is, *a method of recording permanently, by electrical signs, which, by means of metallic wires, or other good conductors of electricity, convey intelligence between two or more places.*

In testimony whereof, I, the said S. F. B. Morse, hereto subscribe my name, in the presence of the witnesses whose names are hereunto subscribed, on the 3d day of October, A. D. 1837.

SAML. F. B. MORSE.

Signed in our presence:

ALEX. J. DAVIS,
E. O. MARTIN. }

Six days after the partnership with Mr. Vail was formed, Mr. Morse wrote to him: "I have only that which is agreeable to tell you. Since you were here, I have had a most satisfactory letter from Hon. W. C. Rives, and also from Captain Pell, who was the commander of the Sully on my passage home. They both have given me most unqualified· testimony to the priority of my invention on board the ship. We have also had a visit from Dr. Jones, of the Patent-Office, one of the *examiners of patents*, for ·many years, at Washington.

"He expressed great satisfaction at the Telegraph, and seemed highly gratified that I intended to exhibit it at Washington.

"I have dispatched my letter to the Secretary of the Treasury, and have the papers and drawings nearly ready for the Patent-Office. They will be on their way, probably, on Monday, or, at farthest, on Tuesday.

☞ "If you intend to do any thing in England or France, no time is to be lost. ☜

"I hold myself in readiness to execute the commission with re-spect to the portraits, any time after next week, and hope to find the machinery in a state of such advancement that we may have time before the winter session to become perfectly familiar with it, so as to strike conviction at once into the minds of the members of Congress, when we exhibit its *powers* before the *powers that be.*

"Professor Gale's services will be invaluable to us, and I am glad he is disposed to enter into the matter with zeal. The more I think of the whole matter, the more I am convinced that, if it is perseveringly pushed at the moment (so favorable on many ac-counts to its adoption by Government), the result will be all that we ought to wish for. We want the wire. We are ready for some important experiments necessary to establish with certainty some points not yet established by experiment. *The law of the magnetic influence at a distance* is not yet discovered, and your twenty miles of wire may enable us to make this discovery and to keep ahead of our European rivals, as well as to proceed with certainty in our other arrangements."

The preparation of a dictionary of the Telegraph was now a work to which the inventor gave much of his time. This was to contain a list of words to which reference could be made by figures and combinations of figures, so that a message might be transmitted with the least possible labor and in the shortest time, yet perfectly intelligible.

Instantly upon the new Telegraph's becoming a subject of discussion, its importance in commerce suggested itself to the active mercantile mind. Before a wire had been stretched along a line of travel, and while Professor Morse was impatient with the manufacturers, who could not produce wire as fast as he wished, he was approached by speculative men, who would have a *private line*, which they could use for their own purposes. He alludes to their proposals in the first of the letters to Mr. Vail, which follow:

" *October* 11, 1837.—I have been consulted (in confidence), that is (*between us all*), on the subject of a secret communication of some two hundred miles, the particulars of which I must leave till I see you. If our water experiment succeeds, I think we shall have immediately a commission of the kind in question. But be close on the subject, for it is essential to its success that it be secret. *Verbum sat.* I am not idle, I assure you. You can have little conception of the labor of *the dictionary.* I am up early and late, yet its progress is slow; but I shall not now leave it till it is complete. I have received the notice from the Patent-Office that the caveat is regularly filed, and all is right there. . . ."

" *October* 14, 1837.—The dictionary occupies now all my time. It is a most tedious, never-ending work. Yet I find that practice gives me facilities, and I hope soon to complete it. You will be pleased with my plan of the permanent dictionary, which I have drawn out ready to show you when I see you. I bring the whole within the consulting face of *twenty-three by twenty-six inches.*"

" *October* 24, 1837.—The *reels* have arrived safely, and we admire the workmanship of them exceedingly; they are exactly right. We have already wound nearly four miles upon one reel, which will hold five miles. The wire is all wound with cotton, and is all in our room. The wire proves to be *not good;* it is made of bad copper, and is brittle, and in short lengths; we have much trouble and consume much time in soldering it, etc. The spark passes freely as yet—*three and a half miles*—and magnetizes well at that distance, though evidently with diminished strength, which would seem to indicate that there is a limit somewhere. We have just heard that Professor Wheatstone has tried an experiment with his method—twenty miles—with success; we have therefore nothing to fear. We also learn that he has sent, to take out a patent, to this country. My *caveat* will be in his way. Professor Locke, of Cincinnati, who has just returned, tells us all this, and he knows Wheatstone and his whole plan, and says there are no less than *six* disputants for the priority of the invention in England. He also says that no one of the European plans pretends to *record permanently;* that mine is decidedly superior in that respect, and *peculiar. . . .*

"The dictionary is at last done. You cannot conceive how much labor there has been in it; but it is accomplished, and we can now talk or write any thing by numbers."

Professor Morse went over to Morristown, and on his return wrote to Mr. Vail that Professor Gale was sending the current through TEN miles of wire:

"*November* 13, 1837.—I arrived just in time to see the experiment Professor Gale was making with the entire *ten miles,* and you will be gratified and agreeably surprised when I inform you that the result now is, that with a little addition of wire to the coils of the small magnet, which I had all along used, the power *was as great apparently* through *ten* as through three miles. This result has surprised us all, yet there is no mistake, and I conceive settles the whole matter. The battery of large plates is, however, absolutely needed; for now the small plates burn the mercury, which must be remedied by using larger plates. If we had the remaining ten miles, it would doubtless be much more satisfactory to the committee of Congress.

"With respect to an experiment at Speedwell, Dr. Gale thinks there will be no difficulty in transporting a couple of miles of wire, wound off on one of the other reels; with this we could perform all that is necessary to show the efficiency of the Telegraph, and the Doctor is willing to accompany me out, or to come out when all things are ready. So the new room may be prepared if you think best, and we will talk from your father's to your brother's house; I can bring out the dictionary when I come, or when you come in.

" The plan of casting the zinc on the copper, the doctor says, is just the thing. The trough I have rudely drawn on the other leaf; its size must be regulated by the size and number of the plates. The *troughs* (there should be two for fifty plates each) ought to be of mahogany, and you will require some tar and rosin to put the plates and trough in order. The plates may be one-quarter of an inch from each other. I am going down-town to inquire about copper, zinc, etc. The connection at the portrule I shall make with mercury. Leave that part till I see you."

In November Professor Morse wrote again to the Secretary of the Treasury:

"NEW YORK, *November* 28, 1837.

" MY DEAR SIR : In my letter to you in answer to the circular respecting telegraphs, which you did me the honor to send me, I promised to advise you of the result of some experiments about to be tried with my electro-magnetic telegraph. I informed you that I had succeeded in marking permanently and intelligibly at the distance of *half a mile.*

" Professor Gale, of our University, and Mr. Alfred Vail, of the Speedwell Iron-Works, near Morristown, New Jersey, are now associated with me in the scientific and mechanical parts of the invention. We have procured several miles of wire, and I am happy to announce to you that our success has, thus far, been complete. At a distance of *five miles,* with a common Cruikshank's battery of eighty-seven plates (four by three and a half inches each plate), the marking was as perfect on the register as in the first instance of half a mile. We have recently added *five miles more,* making in all *ten miles,* with the *same result ;* and we have now no doubt of its effecting a *similar result* at *any distance.* I also stated to you, sir, that machinery was in progress of making, with which, so soon as it should be completed, I intended to proceed to Washington, to exhibit the powers of the invention before you and other members of the Government. I had hoped to be in Washington before the session of Congress, but I find that the execution of new machinery is so uncertain in its time of completion that I shall be delayed, probably, until the beginning of the year. What I wish to learn from you, sir, is, *How late in the session can I delay my visit, and yet be in season to meet the subject of telegraphs, when it shall be presented by your report to Congress?* I am anxious, of course, to show as perfect an instrument as possible, and would wish as much time for the purpose of perfecting it as can be allowed without detriment to my interests as an applicant for the attention of Government to the best plan of a telegraph. I am, my dear sir, with the greatest respect and personal esteem, your most obedient servant, SAM'L F. B. MORSE.

"Hon. LEVI WOODBURY, *Secretary of the Treasury.*"

THE FIRST COMMUNICATION TO CONGRESS.

The Secretary of the Treasury, December 11, 1837, submitted the following report to the Speaker of the House of Representatives:

"TREASURY DEPARTMENT, *December* 6, 1837.

" SIR: I have the honor to present this report in compliance with the following resolution, which passed the House of Representatives on the 3d of February last, viz.: ' *Resolved*, That the Secretary of the Treasury be requested to report to the House of Representatives, at its next session, upon the propriety of establishing a system of telegraphs for the United States.' ' Immediately after its passage I prepared a circular, with the view of procuring, from the most intelligent sources, such information as would enable Congress, as well as the Department, to decide upon the propriety of establishing a system of telegraphs. It seemed also important to unite with the inquiry the procurement of such facts as might show the expense attending different systems; the celerity of communication by each; and the useful objects to be accomplished by their adoption. A copy of the circular is annexed (1).

" The replies have been numerous, and many of them are very full and interesting. Those deemed material are annexed, numbered two to eighteen, inclusive. From these communications, and such other investigations as the pressure of business has enabled me to make, I am satisfied that the establishment of a system of telegraphs for the United States would be useful to commerce as well as the Government. It might most properly be made appurtenant to the Post-Office Department, and, during war, would prove a most essential aid to the military operations of the country. The expense attending it is estimated carefully in some of the documents annexed; but it will depend much upon the kind of system adopted; upon the extent and location of the lines first established; and the charges made to individuals for communicating information through it which may not be of a public character. On these points, as the Department has not been requested to make a report, no opinion is expressed; but information concerning them was deemed useful as a guide in deciding on the propriety of establishing telegraphs, and was, therefore, requested in the circular before mentioned. Many useful suggestions in relation to the subject will be found in the correspondence annexed, and in the books there referred to. The Department would take this occasion to express, in respect to the numerous gentlemen whose views are now submitted to Congress, its high appreciation and sincere acknowledgments for the valuable contributions they have made on a subject of so much interest. I remain, very respectfully, your obedient servant,

"LEVI WOODBURY,
"*Secretary of the Treasury.*

"Hon. J. K. POLK,
"*Speaker of the House of Representatives.*"

Professor L. D. Gale was now made a partner with Professor Morse and Mr. Vail, and a series of experiments was entered upon at the Speedwell Iron-Works, for the purpose of still further improving and testing the system and the machinery essential for success. While here, in the midst of the factories and engaged with Mr. Vail in the perfection of his instruments, the Professor's old love for his pencil is strong upon him, and he is employed in painting the portraits of the family. An extensive building, originally designed for a cotton-factory, furnished a convenient place for the extension of the wires. Young Alfred Vail, fired with the same enthusiasm that had sustained the inventor through so many years of discouragement and struggle, wrought night and day upon the instrument to bring it as nearly as possible to perfection. The instrument thus produced is still in existence, and was exhibited near the close of the life of Professor Morse, when, in the presence of applauding thousands, he sat on the platform in the Academy of Music, in the city of New York, on the evening of the day when his statue had been inaugurated in the Central Park, and with his own fingers sent telegraphic messages across the continent and the ocean to the ends of the earth. The instrument being completed with the aid of Judge Stephen Vail, Hon. George Vail, M. C., and Mr. Alfred Vail, the first experiment was made with three miles of coated copper wire, stretched around a room of the factory in Speedwell, on the 6th day of January, 1838.

The *Morristown Journal* made a report of the experiment in these words:

"It is with some degree of pride, we confess, that it falls to our lot first to announce the complete success of this wonderful piece of mechanism, and that hundreds of our citizens were the first to witness its surprising results. No place could have been found more suitable to pursue the course of experiments necessary to perfecting the detail of machinery than the quiet retirement of the Speedwell works, replete as they are with every kind of convenience which capital and mechanical skill can supply. Professor Morse has quietly pursued the great object which for a considerable time has engaged his attention, and has finally succeeded in carrying it out into sucessful practice, aided by the ingenuity of Mr. Alfred Vail. Others may have suggested the possibility of conveying intelligence by electricity, but this is the first instance of its actual transmission and permanent record.

"The Telegraph consists of four parts:

"1. *The Battery*—A Cruikshank's galvanic trough of sixty pair of plates, seven by eight and a half inches each.

"2. *The Portrule*—An instrument which regulates the motion of the rule. The rule answers to the *stick* of the printers, and in it the *type* representing the numbers to be transmitted are passed beneath the lever, which closes and breaks the circuit.

"3. *The Register*—An instrument which receives and records the numbers sent by the portrule from any distant station.

"4. *A Dictionary*—Containing a complete vocabulary of all the words in the English language, regularly numbered.

"The communication which we saw, made through a distance of two miles, was the following sentence: ' *Railroad cars just ar rived*, 345 *passengers*.'

"These words were put into numbers through the dictionary; the numbers were set up in the telegraph type in about the same time ordinarily occupied in setting up the same in a printing-office. They were then all passed, complete, by the portrule in about half a minute, each stroke of the lever of the portrule at one extremity marking on the register at the other, a distance of two miles, instantaneously. We watched the spark at one end, and the mark of the pencil at the other, and they were as simultaneous as if the lever itself had struck the mark. The marks or numbers were easily legible, and by means of the dictionary were resolved again into words."

The instrument was now ready to be submitted to the public. Professor Morse would show it first to a few intelligent and appreciating friends in New York. With this object in view, he issued invitations, of which the following, to General Cummings, is a copy:

"Professor Morse requests the honor of Thomas S. Cummings, Esq., and family's company in the Geological Cabinet of the University, Washington Square, to witness the operation of the electro-magnetic Telegraph, at a private exhibition of it to a few friends, previous to its leaving the city for Washington.

"The apparatus will be prepared at precisely twelve o'clock, on Wednesday, 24th instant. The time being limited, punctuality is specially requested.

"NEW YORK UNIVERSITY, *January* 22, 1838."

A large and intelligent company, including many of the most learned and influential citizens attended, in response to similar invitations. Some, who were present, have given their recollections of that eventful day; of the modest, quiet self-possession of the inventor, now submitting to the scrutiny of skeptics and objectors the result of his patient years of toil. Gentlemen were requested to give brief dispatches, which were sent over the coil of wire, and read by one who had no knowledge of the words that had been given to the operator. Astonishment was the sensation of the hour. The work bordered upon the miraculous. "To see is to believe," but this result staggered the faith of spectators. General Cummings had recently been promoted to a military command, and, in allusion perhaps to that fact, one of his friends present wrote, and Professor Morse manipulated the instrument to transmit, a sentence, which was produced in telegraphic characters, and read:

" ATTENTION, THE UNIVERSE !
BY KINGDOMS, RIGHT WHEEL !"

Letter by letter, word by word, the sentence was written with the four fingers of the telegraph, so that it was produced four times, on the strip of paper that was moved by the clock-work to receive the impression.

As this is the first sentence that was ever recorded by the Telegraph, and preserved, a fac-simile is here given of the original, now in the possession of General Cummings. It is upon one strip of paper just thirty-six inches in length.:

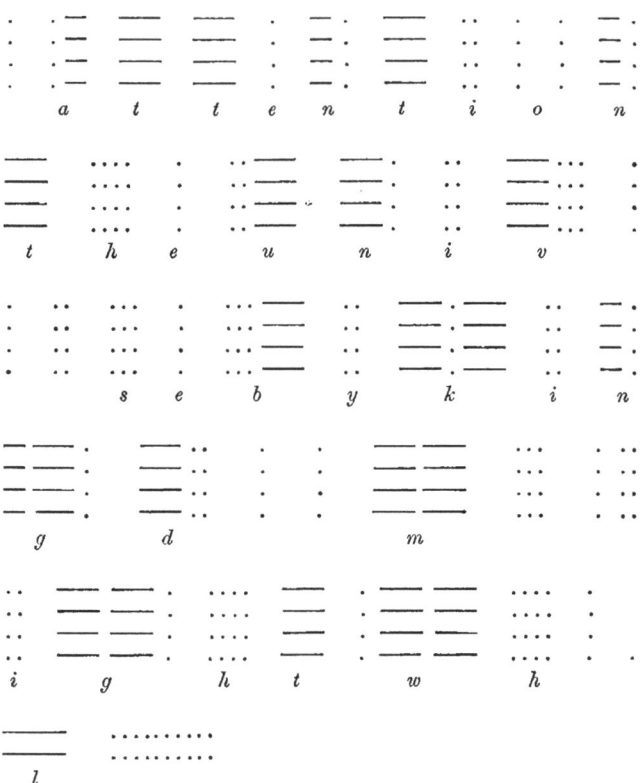

The words were chosen, perhaps playfully, with no thought of their significance beyond the momentary impression, but the one who suggested them was undoubtedly under the influence of the feeling then pervading the minds of all present, that they were standing on the threshold of an event that would command the attention of the world. And they were not mistaken.

The admiration of the company was unbounded. They cheered the inventor with their warm and loud congratulations. Doubt was dispelled. The triumph was complete. The *Journal of Commerce* of January 29, 1838, had the following notice of the exhibition :

"THE TELEGRAPH.—We did not witness the operation of Professor Morse's Electro-Magnetic Telegraph on Wednesday last, but we learn that the numerous company of scientific persons who were present pronounced it entirely successful. Intelligence was instantaneously transmitted through a circuit of TEN MILES, and legibly written on a cylinder at the extremity of the circuit. The great advantages which must result to the public from this invention will warrant an outlay on the part of the Government sufficient to test its practicability, as a general means of transmitting intelligence. Professor Morse has recently improved on his mode of marking, by which he can dispense altogether with the telegraphic dictionary, using *letters* instead of *numbers*, and he can transmit ten words per minute, which is more than double the number which can be transmitted by means of the dictionary."

The *New York Observer* copied the above, and remarked:

"The primitive Telegraph was doubtless that mentioned by Homer—the lighting of a fire on a hill, to give notice of the arrival of a fleet, or of any other expected event, of which that had been made, by previous agreement, the signal. As an improvement upon this, one of the Greek writers recommends a square vessel, filled in part with water, with a large cork floating upon it. Upon the side of this cork should be written various sentences, conveying expected intelligence. At a given signal the water should be drawn from this vessel, till the sentence to be conveyed should be just visible at the top of the vessel, which should be announced by another signal. An observer on a distant hill, furnished with a similar apparatus, by drawing water from his vessel for the same length of time, would ascertain the sentence intended to be conveyed. This he could in the same manner transmit to another, and so on, as far as the time should extend. The great defect of the method is, that no intelligence could be conveyed by it, except such as is anticipated and provided for. To remedy this defect has been the great object of inventors of Telegraphs to this day. The most perfect system yet in operation consists of signals representing the nine digits with the cipher, by the use of which all numbers can be transmitted; a numbered dictionary of sentences, conveying all items of information that can be anticipated; a numbered dictionary of words; and finally, we believe, but are not sure, the designation of the letters of the alphabet by numbers. Much study has been expended and great ingenuity displayed in bringing this system to perfection.

Its great and obvious defect is, that it can be used only in fair weather.

"Some two or three years since an officer in the British Navy announced the invention of a code of signals which should be intelligible to all nations. The details of his plan, we think, have never been made public. The object might be accomplished by a telegraphic or numbered dictionary, translated into all languages, so that in all languages the same number should stand against a word or sentence of the same meaning. These numbers would then resemble the Chinese characters, in which persons of different nations may correspond without understanding each other's spoken language. On this plan all idiomatic expressions must be avoided, and the various inflections of words, to express number, case, tense, etc., must be gathered from the connection; for, if all derived forms of words were inserted in the dictionary, it would make a book of monstrous and unmanageable dimensions.

"The Electro-Magnetic Telegraph, it will be seen, possesses the following important advantages over any previously in use:

"1. *It is wholly independent of the weather.* Clouds, fogs, or the darkness of midnight, are no impediment to its operation. It is often most necessary to announce the arrival, situation, and wants of ships, when, from the state of the weather, or the darkness of night, other telegraphs are wholly useless. Even in the best weather, by working at night as well as by day, twice as much can be done in the twenty-four hours.

"2. *It conveys intelligence with greater rapidity.* There is no reason to doubt, from any facts or principles yet discovered, that intelligence may be conveyed from New York to Washington, or even to New Orleans, without any appreciable loss of time. It is not necessary to have an observatory every few miles, at which time is lost by observing the signals and repeating them, that they may be seen at the next observatory. Time is saved, too, by dispensing with the dictionary.

"3. *It conveys intelligence more perfectly.* It can spell any word correctly. It can give us number and person, mood and tense. If thought best, it can give us the punctuation, and, in short, furnish the *copy*, ready for the hands of any printer who understands the telegraphic alphabet.

"4. *It conveys intelligence with greater certainty.* It does not, like other telegraphs, merely hoist up signals, which may be seen, if any one is looking for them; but it records its message permauently on paper, where it will remain, and may be read at leisure. It will be seen at once that intelligence thus recorded will be much more sure to reach him to whom it is sent, and to be correctly interpreted.

"Nothing but an actual trial, on an extensive scale, and for several years, can show with certainty the full advantages of this invention. We think it evident, however, from what has already been shown, that its value cannot fail to be great."

The next step of the inventor was to bring the instrument to the notice of the Government of the United States. With boldness that speaks well for his candor as well as for his confidence in his invention, he went to Philadelphia and submitted it to the Franklin Institute of that city. This society was composed of men eminent in science, and deeply imbued with the philosophic spirit of inquiry of the illustrious man whose name it bears. There was great fitness in first submitting to a *Franklin* Institute the first invention which proposed to reduce lightning to the service of man. Robert M. Patterson, Esq., of Philadelphia, an active member of the Franklin Institute, having heard of the wonderful invention, wrote to Professor Morse, January 19, 1838, and said to him:

"I am pleased to hear that you have brought your scheme for an electro-magnetic telegraph to such a degree of perfection that you are prepared to exhibit its action, and propose to show it at Washington. Will you permit me to ask you whether it would be convenient to you, and consistent with your views, to stop for a short time at Philadelphia on your way, and let it be seen by the Committee of Science and Arts of the Franklin Institute? This committee has taken an interest in the subject of telegraphs, and has reported upon it to the Secretary of the Treasury. They would be gratified to examine a scheme so eligible and plausible as that which you propose."

The invitation was promptly accepted, and the exhibition was made by Professor Morse on the 8th of February, 1838. The committee reported their high gratification with Professor Morse's Telegraph, and their hope that the Government would give him the means to test it upon an extensive scale. The report was signed by gentlemen whose names and position justly commanded the respect of the public. The signers were : R. M. Patterson, chairman; Roswell Park, Sears C. Walker, Isaiah Lukens, Franklin Peale, and Joseph Saxton.

Robert M. Patterson filled with eminent ability the professor-ships of Natural Philosophy, Chemistry, and Mathematics in the University of Pennsylvania; afterward the professorship of Natural Philosophy in the University of Virginia; and from 1835 to 1851 was Director of the Mint at Philadelphia. He was president of the American Philosophical Society, and a leading member and officer of the Franklin Institute. He was a strong believer in the future of science, and ever ready to welcome with enthusiasm the novelties of inventors.

Roswell Park was Professor of Natural Philosophy in the Uni-versity of Pennsylvania. He was a man of varied information, and wrote a work called "Pantology," a classification of the branches of human knowledge.

Sears C. Walker was Actuary of the Pennsylvania Life Insur-ance Company; Professor of Mathematics in the Philadelphia High School, and eminent in that branch of science.

Isaiah Lukens was a famous clock-maker of Philadelphia, the constructor of the present Independence-Hall (State-House) clock, and an extremely ingenious mechanician. He once, for amusement, constructed a 'perpetual-motion' machine, the secret motive power of which was a mystery that for a time baffled the wise even.

Franklin Peale was another master in mechanics. He was for over twenty-one years connected with the Philadelphia Mint, as melter and refiner and chief coiner, and devised and put into opera-tion the greater part of the machinery still in successful use there.

Joseph Saxton was also eminent as a mechanician. At the time of the Morse experiment he was at the head of the machinists of the mint, but was soon after transferred to Washington, where he was placed at the head of the Department of Weights and Measures, under the Superintendent of the Coast Survey.

Professor Morse wrote with great enthusiasm to his brothers in New York, announcing his success in Philadelphia, and re-ceived a letter from Sidney, who said :

"Your invention, measuring it by the power which it will give man to accomplish his plans, is not only the greatest invention of this age, but the greatest invention of any age. I see, as an almost immediate effect, that the surface of the earth will be net-worked with wire, and every wire will be a nerve, conveying to every part intelligence of what is doing in every other part. The earth will become a huge animal with ten million hands, and in every hand a pen to record whatever the directing soul may dictate. No limit can be assigned to the value of the invention."

From Philadelphia Mr. Morse went to Washington, to challenge the attention of the Government. It was late in the session of Congress, and every day was precious. He obtained the use of the room of the Committee on Commerce, in the Capitol, and into it introduced the apparatus, clumsy and rude indeed, but amply adequate to demonstrate to all comers that it could *write at a distance;* that is, that he had a real *Telegraph.* To this room he invited members of Congress, foreign ministers, and men of science. They came and saw and wondered, but went away with little faith. Mr. Morse received the following note, on the day of its date, from the Secretary of the Navy :

"M. Dickerson presents his respects to Dr. Morse, and informs him that the President and heads of department propose to witness the experiments upon the Galvano-Magnetic Telegraph, to-morrow at one o'clock, February 20, 1838."

It was directed to "Dr. Morse, room of the Committee of Commerce, H. R." The next day, February 21st, Mr. Van Buren, President of the United States, and the entire Cabinet, including John Forsyth, Secretary of State, Levi Woodbury, Secretary of the Treasury, J. R. Poinsett, Secretary of War, and M. Dickerson, Secretary of the Navy, visited the room, and saw the experiments. The chairman of the Committee on Commerce, Hon. F. O. J. Smith, had apprehended the greatness of the coming event, and had encouraged Mr. Morse to hope for success. The inventor, nervously excited, as the eyes of the Government and country were now fixed upon him and his invention, rose to the grandeur of the occasion, and with steady hand, and modest but intelligent words, demonstrated to the President of the United States and the company, that a Telegraph was an accomplished fact. The huge coil of wire on the reels contained a circuit of ten miles, and, as sentence after sen-

22

tence was spoken at one extremity and written down at the other, it was plain enough that it would work just as well on a straight line in the open air.

Mr. Smith, the chairman of the Committee on Commerce, · was in a position to forward the views of the inventor, and, happily for him, appreciated its vast capabilities, and lent his great energies to its advancement. Before the experiments were publicly made in Washington, Mr. Smith had brought Professor Morse before the committee, and inspired him with so much confidence, that he wrote the following letter:

S. F. B. Morse to Hon. F. O. J. Smith.

"WASHINGTON, *February* 15, 1838.

"DEAR SIR: In consequence of the conversation had with the committee on the subject of my Telegraph, I would state that I think it desirable that an experiment, on a somewhat extended scale, should first be made to test both the practicability and the facility of communicating intelligence for at least one hundred miles. The experiment may proceed, as to cost, with perfect safety to the Government: 1. The wire for this distance, consisting of four lengths, making a total of four hundred miles of wire, might be obtained, and receive its covering of cotton and other insulation. This length would amply suffice to ascertain the law of the propulsive power of voltaic electricity, and previous to any measures being taken for burying it in the earth. So that, if any unforeseen difficulty should occur fatal to its practicability, the wire is not consumed or lost. If the expected success is realized, then, 2. The preparation of the wire might be commenced for burying in the earth, and being found complete through the whole route, the several portrules, registers, batteries, etc., might be provided to put the Telegraph into complete action. This experiment of one hundred miles would furnish the data from which to make the estimates of a more general extension of the system. If no insurmountable obstacles present themselves in a distance of one hundred miles, none may be expected in one thousand or in ten thousand miles; and then will be presented for the consideration of the Government the propriety of completely organizing this *new telegraphic system as a part of the Government*, attaching it to some department already existing, or creating a new one, which may be called for by the accumulating duties of the present departments.

"It is obvious, at the slightest glance, that this mode of instantaneous communication must inevitably become an instrument of immense power, to be wielded for good or for evil, as it shall be properly or improperly directed. In the hands of a company of speculators, who should monopolize it for themselves, it might be the means of enriching the corporation at the expense of the bankruptcy of thousands ; and even in the hands of Government alone, it might become a means of working vast mischief to the republic. In considering these prospective evils, I would respectfully suggest a remedy which offers itself to my mind. Let the sole right of using the Telegraph belong, in the first place, to the Government, who should grant, for a specified sum or bonus, to any individual or company of individuals who may apply for it, and under such restrictions and regulations as the Government may think proper, the right to lay down a communication between any two points, for the purpose of transmitting intelligence ; and thus would be promoted a general competition. The Government would have a Telegraph of its own, and have its modes of communicating with its own officers and agents independent of private permission, or interference with and interruption to the ordinary transmissions on the private telegraphs. Thus there would be a system of checks and preventives of abuse, operating to restrain the action of this otherwise dangerous power, within those bounds which will permit only the good and neutralize the evil. Should the Government thus take the Telegraph solely under its own control, the revenue derived from the bonuses alone, it must be plain, will be of vast amount.

"From the enterprising character of our countrymen, shown in the manner in which they carry forward any new project which promises private or public advantage, it is not visionary to suppose that it would not be long ere the whole surface of this country would be channeled for those *nerves* which are to diffuse, with the speed of thought, a knowledge of all that is occurring throughout the land ; making, in fact, *one neighborhood* of the whole country.

"If the Government is disposed to test this mode of telegraphic communication by enabling me to give it a fair trial for one hundred miles, I will engage to enter into no arrangement to dispose of my rights, as the inventor and patentee for the United States, to any individual or company of individuals, previous to offering it to the Government for such a just and reasonable compensation as shall be

mutually agreed upon. I remain, sir, respectfully, your most obedient servant,

"SAMUEL F. B. MORSE.

"To the Hon. F. O. J. SMITH, Chairman of the Committee on Commerce of the
House of Representatives."

And again he wrote:

S. F. B. Morse to Hon. F. O. J. Smith.

"WASHINGTON, *February* 22, 1838.

"DEAR SIR: I have endeavored to approach a proper estimate
of the expense attendant on preparing a complete telegraphic communication for some distance; and, taking into consideration the
possibility that the experiment may be conclusively tried before the
close of the present session of Congress, I have thought that an
appropriation for fifty miles of distance would test the practicability
of the Telegraph quite as satisfactorily as one hundred, because the
obstacles necessary to be overcome would not be more proportion-
ally in fifty than in one hundred; while at the same time the
double circuit necessary in the fifty miles would give a *single circuit*
of one hundred for the purpose of testing the effect of distance upon
the passage of electricity. Fifty miles would require a less amount
of appropriation, and the experiment could also be sooner brought
to a result:

Two hundred miles of wire, or wire for two circuits for fifty miles of distance, including the covering of the wire with cotton, at $100 per
 mile $20,000
Other expenses of preparation of the wire, such as caoutchouc, wax, resin,
 tar, with reels for winding, soldering, etc., say $6 per mile   .   1,200
Batteries and registers, with type, etc., for two stations, and materials
 for experimenting on the best modes of magnets at long distances .   800
Services of Professor Gale in the chemical department; services of Mr.
 Alfred Vail in the mechanical department; services of assistants in
 different departments; my own services in superintending and directing the whole—total   4,000
                                                    ————
         Total .   .   .   . [1] $26,000

"This estimate is exclusive of expense necessary to lay down
the wire beneath the ground. This is unnecessary until the previous preparations are found satisfactory. I cannot say what time
will be required for the completion of the circuits for fifty miles.

[1] This line could now be constructed for less than half the sum.

If the order could be immediately given for the wire, I think all the other matter connected with it might be completed so that every thing could be in readiness in *three months*. Much will depend on the punctuality with which contractors fulfill their engagements in furnishing the wire and other apparatus. I remain, sir, very respectfully, your obedient servant,

"SAMUEL F. B. MORSE.

"To the Hon. F. O. J. SMITH, Chairman of the Committee on Commerce."

Professor Morse now submitted to Congress a respectful memorial, asking an appropriation to defray the expense of subjecting the Telegraph to actual experiment over a length sufficient to establish its feasibility, and demonstrate its value. This petition, its substance being embraced in the foregoing letters to the Hon F. O. J. Smith, was referred to the Committee on Commerce. On the 6th of April, 1838, Mr. Smith made the following

REPORT.

On the 3d of February, 1837, the House of Representatives passed a resolution requesting the Secretary of the Treasury to report to the House, at its present session, upon the propriety of establishing a system of telegraphs for the United States. In pursuance of this request, the Secretary of the Treasury, at an early day after the passage of said resolution, addressed a circular of inquiry to numerous scientific and practical individuals in different parts of the Union; and, on the 6th of December last, reported the result of this proceeding to the House. This report of the Secretary embodies many useful suggestions on the necessity and practicability of a system of telegraphic dispatches, both for public and individual purposes; and the committee cannot doubt that the American public is fully prepared, and even desirous, that every requisite effort be made on the part of Congress to consummate an object of so deep interest to the purposes of Government in peace and in war, and to the enterprise of the age. Amid the suggestions thus elicited from various sources, and embodied in the before-mentioned report of the Secretary of the Treasury, a plan for an electro-magnetic telegraph is communicated by Professor Morse, of the University of the City of New York, preëminently interesting, and even wonderful.

This invention consists in the application, by mechanism, of galvanic electricity to telegraphic purposes, and is claimed by Professor Morse and his associates as original with them; and being so, in fact, as the committee believe, letters-patent have been secured under the authority of the United States for the invention. It has, moreover, been subjected to the test of experiment, upon a scale of ten miles' distance, by a select committee of the Franklin Institute of the city of Philadelphia, and reported upon by that eminently high tribunal in the most favorable and confident terms. An extract from the report thus made is hereunto annexed.

In additional confirmation of the merits of his proposed system of telegraphs, Professor Morse has exhibited it in operation (by a coil of metallic wire measuring about ten miles in length, rendering the action equal to a telegraph of half that distance) to the Committee on Commerce of the House of Representatives, to the President of the United States, and the several heads of departments, to members of Congress generally, who have taken interest in the examination, and to a vast number of scientific and practical individuals from various parts of the Union; and all concur, it is believed, and without a dissenting doubt, in admiration of the ingenious and scientific character of the invention, and in the opinion that it is successfully adapted to the purposes of telegraphic dispatches, and in a conviction of its great and incalculable practical importance and usefulness to the country, and ultimately to the whole world. But it would be presumptuous in any one (and the inventor himself is most sensible of this) to attempt, at this stage of the invention, to calculate in anticipation, or to hold out promises of what its whole extent of capacity for usefulness may be, in either a political, commercial, or social point of view, if the electrical power upon which it depends for successful action shall prove to be efficient, as is now supposed it will, to carry intelligence through any of the distances of fifty, one hundred, five hundred, or more miles, now contemplated. No such attempt, therefore, will be indulged in this report. It is obvious, however, that the influence of this invention over the political, commercial, and social relations of the people of this widely-extended country, looking to nothing beyond, will, in the event of success, of itself amount to a revolution unsurpassed in moral grandeur by any discovery that has been made in the arts and sciences, from the most distant period to which authentic history extends to the present day. With the means of almost instantaneous communication of intelligence between the most distant points of the country, and simultaneously between any given number of intermediate points which this invention contemplates, space will be, to all practical purposes of information, completely annihilated between the States of the Union, as also between the individual citizens thereof. The citizen will be invested with, and reduce to daily and familiar use, an approach to the HIGH ATTRIBUTE OF UBIQUITY, in a degree that the human mind, until recently, has hardly dared to contemplate seriously as belonging to human agency, from an instinctive feeling of religious reverence and reserve on a power of such awful grandeur.

Referring to the annexed report of the Franklin Institute, already adverted to, and also to the letters of Professor Morse, marked two, eight, and nine, for other details of the superiority of this system of telegraphs over all other methods heretofore reduced to practice by any individual or government, the committee agree, unanimously, that it is worthy to engross the attention and means of the Federal Government, to the full extent that may be necessary to put the invention to the most decisive test that can be desirable. The power of the invention, if successful, is so extensive for good and for evil, that the Government alone should possess the right to control and regulate it. The mode of proceeding to test it, as suggested, as also the relations which the inventor and his associates are willing to recognize with the Government on the subject of the future ownership, use, and control of the invention, are succinctly set forth in the annexed letters of Professor Morse, marked eight and nine. The probable outlay of an experiment upon a scale equal to fifty miles of telegraph, and equal to a circuit of double that distance, is estimated at thirty thousand dollars. Two-thirds of this expenditure will be for material which, whether the experiment shall succeed or fail, will remain uninjured, and of very little diminished value below the price that will be paid for it. The estimates of Professor Morse, as will be seen by his letter marked nine, amount to twenty-six thousand dollars; but, to meet any contingency not anticipated, and to guard against any want of requisite funds in an enterprise of such moment to the Government, to the people, and to the scientific world, the committee recommend an appropriation of thirty thousand dollars, to be expended under the direction of the Secretary of the Treasury; and to this end submit herewith a bill.

It is believed by the committee that the subject is one of such universal interest and importance, that an early action upon it will be deemed desirable by Congress, to enable the inventor to complete his trial of the invention upon the extended scale contemplated, in season to furnish Congress with a full report of the result during its present session, if that shall be practicable.

All which is respectfully submitted:

FRANCIS O. J. SMITH,	JAS. M. MASON,
S. C. PHILLIPS,	JOHN T. H. WORTHINGTON,
SAMUEL CUSHMAN,	WM. H. HUNTER,
JOHN I. DE GRAFF,	GEORGE W. TOLAND,
EDWARD CURTIS,
Committee on Commerce, U. S. H. R.

At this stage of the work, Mr. Smith intimated to Mr. Morse his willingness to take a pecuniary interest and responsibility in the enterprise. With commendable delicacy, it was made a condition of such an arrangement that Mr. Smith should obtain leave of absence from Congress, for the remainder of his term then closing, and that he should not be a candidate for reelection. With this understanding, a partnership was formed between Professor Morse, Professor Gale, Mr. Alfred Vail, and Hon. F. O. J. Smith, by the terms of which it was stipulated that Mr. Smith should go to Europe with Professor Morse and secure patents for the telegraph in such countries as it should be practicable for him to do so. The property in the invention was divided into sixteen shares, of which Mr. Morse held nine, Mr. Smith four, Mr. Vail two, and Professor Gale one. In the patents to be obtained in foreign countries the proportions were not the same: Professor Morse was to hold eight, Mr. Smith five, Mr. Vail two, and Professor Gale one.

Professor Morse returned to New York, and made arrangements necessary for his journey to Europe. It was important to secure a patent for the great invention in foreign countries, and every day's delay increased the difficulties of success. Mr. Vail went to Speedwell to prepare an instrument which Professor Morse would take with him to Europe. He wrote to Mr. Vail, March 15th:

"Every thing looks encouraging, but I need not say to you that in this world a continued course of prosperity is not a rational expectation. We shall doubtless find troubles and difficulties in store for us, and it is the part of true wisdom to be prepared for whatever may await us. If our hearts are right, we shall not be taken by surprise. I see nothing now but an unclouded prospect, for which let us pay to Him who shows it us the homage of grateful and obedient hearts, with most earnest prayers for grace to use prosperity aright.

"The wire, and battery, and dictionary, have safely arrived, and are now in the cabinet, where Professor Gale is preparing immediately to institute some experiments important to the invention. As soon as Mr. S. returns from the eastward I shall proceed with him to Washington, arranging matters there in relation to the patent, and then I am ready for Europe."

March 19th Mr. Vail replied : "I feel, Professor Morse, that if I am ever worth any thing, it will be wholly attributable to your kindness—I now should have no *earthly* prospect of happiness and domestic bliss had it not been for what you have done, for which I shall ever remember with the liveliest emotions of gratitude, whether it is eventually successful or not. I can appreciate your reasonable and appropriate remark that·there is nothing certain in this life; that it is a world of care, anxiety, and trouble, and that our dependence must be placed upon a higher power than of earth.[1]

"I am, yours truly, ALFRED VAIL."

From the city of Washington, March 31st, Professor Morse wrote to Mr. Vail: "I write you a hasty line to say, in the first place, that I have overcome all difficulties in regard to a portrule, and have invented one which will be perfect. It is very simple, and will not take much time or expense to make it. Mr. S. has incorporated it into the specification for the patent. Please, therefore, not to pro-

---

[1] These expressions of gratitude by Mr. Vail to Mr. Morse were honorable to Mr. V., and Mr. Morse cherished to the day of his death a tender regard for his young friend. At a banquet given to Mr. Morse more than thirty years after this letter was written, Mr. Morse, then at the height of human glory, spoke of Mr. Vail in such terms of grateful recognition as to call out the following note from a son of Mr. Vail, who was not born when the letter above was written:

"NEW YORK, *June* 13, 1871.

"RESPECTED SIR: Allow me, for myself, to thank you for the kind, generous manner in which you alluded to my father's share in your early labors and struggles, during the babyhood of the now giant Telegraph. I have always felt that you would freely recognize and acknowledge his assistance, and it was therefore exceedingly gratifying to me when, being absent when you spoke them, I read them in the published account of Saturday's evening meeting in your honor. Accept my many wishes for your continued health and honor, and believe me,

"Yours, respectfully, J. CUMMINGS VAIL."

ceed with the type or portrule as now constructed.   I will see you
on my return, and explain it in season for you to get one ready for
us.   I find it a most arduous and tedious process to adjust the
specification; I have been engaged steadily for three days with Mr.
S., and have not yet got half through, but there is one consolation,
when done it will be well done.   The drawings, I find on inquiry,
would cost you from forty to fifty dollars, if procured from the
draughtsman about the Patent-Office.   I have therefore determined
to do them myself, and save you that sum."

During the few weeks spent in completing the instrument
to be taken to Europe, and preparing for an expedition which
promised the most important results, the fertile mind of Mr.
Morse was constantly devising improvements, removing difficulties, and making assurance doubly sure.

CHAPTER IX.

1838-1839.

PROFESSOR MORSE GOES TO ENGLAND—APPLICATION FOR PATENT — REFUSAL —REASONS—FALSE STATEMENT OF AN OFFICIAL—GOES TO PARIS—LETTERS TO HIS DAUGHTER—DR. KIRK'S RECOLLECTIONS—ARAGO—HIS GREAT KINDNESS — EXHIBITION BEFORE ACADEMY OF SCIENCE — BARON HUMBOLDT'S CONGRATULATIONS—REPORT UPON IT—LETTERS TO FRIENDS— HON. H. L. ELLSWORTH'S LETTER—PATENT IN FRANCE—COUNT MONTALIVET—PROFESSOR MORSE'S LETTERS TO MR. SMITH—LORD LINCOLN'S AND LORD ELGIN'S INTEREST IN THE TELEGRAPH—PROFESSOR MORSE GOES TO LONDON—EXHIBITS THE TELEGRAPH AT THE HOUSE OF LORD LINCOLN.

PROFESSOR MORSE left on record a minute account of his attempt and failure to procure a patent in England.

"On May 16, 1838, I left the United States and arrived in London in June, for the purpose of obtaining letters-patent for my Electro-Magnetic Telegraph System. I learned before leaving the United States that Professor Wheatstone and Mr. Cooke, of London, had obtained letters-patent in England for a '*Magnetic-Needle Telegraph*,' based, as the name implies, on the *deflection* of the *magnetic needle*. Their telegraph at that time required *six conductors* between the two points of intercommunication *for a single instrument* at each of the two termini. Their mode of indicating signs for communicating intelligence was by deflecting *five magnetic needles* in various directions in such a way as to point to the required letter upon a diamond-shaped dial-plate. It was necessary that the signal should be *observed at the instant*, or it was lost, and vanished forever.

"I applied for letters-patent for my system of communicating intelligence at a distance by electricity, differing in all respects from

Messrs. Wheatstone and Cooke's system, invented five years before
theirs, and having nothing in common in the whole system but the
use of *electricity* on *metallic conductors*, for which use no one could
obtain an exclusive privilege, since this much had been used for
nearly one hundred years. My system is peculiar in the employment of *electro-magnetism*, or the *motive* power of electricity, *to
imprint permanent signs at a distance.* I made no use of the deflections of the magnetic needle as *signs.* I required but *one conductor*
between the two termini, or any number of intermediate points of
intercommunication. I used *paper moved by clock-work*, upon
which I caused a *lever* moved by *magnetism* to *imprint the letters* and
words of any required dispatch, having also invented and adapted
to telegraph writing a *new and peculiar alphabetic character* for
that purpose; a *conventional alphabet*, easily acquired, and easily
made, and used by the operator. It is obvious, at once, from a
simple statement of these facts, that the system of Messrs. Wheatstone and Cooke, and my system, were wholly unlike each other.
As I have just observed, there was *nothing in common in the two
systems* but the use of electricity upon metallic conductors, for
which no one could obtain an exclusive privilege.

"The various steps required by the English law were taken by
me to procure a patent for my mode, and the fees were paid at the
Clerk's office, June 22d, and at the Home Department, June 25,
1838; also June 26th, caveats were entered at the Attorney and
Solicitor General's—and I had reached that part of the process
which required the sanction of the Attorney-General. At this point
I met the opposition of Messrs. Wheatstone and Cooke, and also of
Mr. Davy, and a hearing was ordered before the Attorney-General,
Sir John Campbell, on July 12, 1838. I attended at the Attorney-
General's residence on the morning of that day, carrying with me
my telegraphic apparatus, for the purpose of explaining to him the
total dissimilarity between my system and those of my opponents.
But, contrary to my expectation, the similarity or dissimilarity of
my mode from that of my opponents was not considered by the
Attorney-General. He neither examined my instrument, which I
had brought for that purpose, nor did he ask any questions bearing
upon its resemblance to my opponents' system. I was met by the
single declaration that my '*invention had been published*,' and in
proof a copy of the *London Mechanics' Magazine*, No. 757, for
February 10, 1838, was produced, and I was told that 'in consequence of said publication I could not proceed.'

" At this summary decision I was certainly surprised, being conscious that there had been no such publication of my method as the law required to invalidate a patent; and, even if there had been, I ventured to hint to the Attorney-General that, if I was rightly informed in regard to the British law, it was the province of a court and jury, and not of the Attorney-General, to try and to decide that point. I conceived that if I had merely offered a substantially *different mode* of doing the same thing, this, according to British law, was sufficient to entitle me to a patent for MY MODE; but if, after having obtained a patent, my opponents could prove before a court and jury that my mode had been previously published, then it was for that court and jury to declare my patent void. I therefore considered myself unjustly dealt with by the Attorney-General, who, it appeared to me, had stepped out of the sphere of his proper duties, assuming the power of a court and jury, to forbid me to proceed.

" Unwilling to yield to such manifest injustice, without attempting to correct what might possibly have arisen from some misapprehension, I, immediately on my return to my lodgings, with the assistance of a legal friend, F. O. J. Smith, Esq., drew up and sent a letter to the Attorney-General, in which I requested a review of his decision, stating the essential differences between my system and that of my opponents, and concluding in these terms:

" ' I forbear to advert to other differences, now clear to my own mind, through fear of too far intruding upon your valuable time and patience. I will at once proceed to obviate the grand objection which I understand to have been regarded as in my way, viz. :

" ' While it is conceded that all my claim rightly attaches to myself by priority of invention, the *publicity* that has been given it (it is contended) divests me of the legal right· to an exclusive property in it. Here, will the Hon. Attorney-General indulge me in the inquiry—

" ' 1. What is the nature of the publication that can operate thus to deprive an inventor of his right to a patent?

" ' 2. What is the nature of the publication in the present case that stands in the way ?

" ' May I not presume the English law to be what the American law is, and what the French law is, *in principle*, upon the subject of publication ? A publication of results—even a minute published description of *mere results* produced by an invention—cannot invalidate a posterior patent in either of those countries, if the *means*, the *modus operandi* producing those results, are not described in the publication to an extent that a clever workman would be enabled to make the same means and to produce the same results.

" 'Suppose it were published that I had invented a gun that would shoot accurately at right angles, beyond any given point; surely, this would not prejudice my claim to a patent subsequently. Suppose I exhibited in the market-place the gun actually made, and yet no one, from such exhibition, could understand its structure, it is respectfully submitted that even such a publication both of means and results could not invalidate my patent subsequently obtained, because the publication did not convey information up to the point that could enable any person to make use of my invention. Such I would with great deference presume to be the *rationale* of the law of England. And, if in the foregoing construction I am correct, the question recurs, What is the nature of the publication in my case?

" 'I send you all that has come within my knowledge as published in this country, all that has been presented to the Hon. Attorney-General as published (*see Mechanic's Magazine*, page 332). Will the Hon. Attorney-General be good enough to analyze this document with me, and compare it even with all the information the opposing claimants in my case possess relative to my invention up to this date?

" 'The magazine article describes:

" '1. The fact that my invention is reduced " *to the use of one wire*," one circuit only.

" 'I believe it will not be contended in any quarter that I am not the first inventor of this reduction of an Electric Telegraph to a *single circuit*. But this is only publishing a result, not the mode in which it is produced. It furnishes no description of the mechanism which I employ, and which enables me successfully to dispense with all wires except one. It would not suggest any *mode* as *my mode* of accomplishing this, to any mind. And yet, it might suggest to *many minds* many modes of doing it, and some one of them might or might not resemble mine; and the several inventors would each be entitled to a patent for their respective modes.

" '2. The publication discloses the fact that my invention contains a register which permanently records, and in characters easily legible, the fullest communication, etc. But this is only a statement of a result. It is no description of the means of recording, or the manner in which my means of recording operate in producing the result. It is as indefinite a description of means as it would be to say, " A has invented a gun which will shoot accurately at right angles."

" ' 3. The publication discloses a specimen of the writing produced by my invention, and an explanation of what the characters thus produced indicate by aid of a dictionary. But the how—by what description of mechanism, or by what sort of type or pen, pencil, or marking instruments, this specimen of characters was produced, is not described, nor published, nor explained. No reader learns this from the publication here exhibited. He learns from it how to read the characters—what they mean—how they connect themselves with a dictionary—but he is no wiser from it as to the mode producing these characters ; and with this ends all the description of either means or results which the publication contains.

" ' I respectfully submit to the Attorney-General, whether such a publication of *results* is to be construed into a description of *means*, or can bring my invention within the meaning of the principle of law heretofore adverted to, invalidating in the slightest degree my claim to a patent.

" ' But, further : If it were even admitted that such publicity has been given to portions of my invention as to preclude me from a valid patent for *those* portions, it will not surely be contended that I am thereby precluded from a patent for the *undisclosed and unpublished portions*, which I take at my risk. For such portions I desire a patient.

" ' In conclusion, allow me to remark that I am quite persuaded that no configuration of the type I use, or of the mechanism by which I bring them into use, has ever to this day come to the knowledge of my opposing claimants : and that they cannot describe any of these particulars of my invention to the Hon. Attorney-General, upon his request, nor even inform him whether I do or do not employ the magnetic needle in the invention, nor how the type make their impression on the paper. And if, with all the assumed publicity of my invention before them, they cannot do this much with accuracy and promptness, I feel confident the Hon. Attorney-General will dismiss all doubt as to the injustice that would be done to me, and to my representatives and estate, by withholding from me the patent for which I have petitioned.

" ' I have written at more length than I intended, but I wish my case to be clearly understood, and in a shape not to be misunderstood. If I have presumed too much in this, I hope to find an apology in the importance, to myself and others associated with me, of the result of much anxious labor, and much expense incurred in years of devotedness to this invention.

   " ' With high consideration, I have the honor to be your obedient servant,   (Signed)

   " ' LONDON, 14 BEDFORD PLACE,   S. F. B. MORSE.
                July 12, 1838.'

"In consequence of my request in this letter, I was allowed a second hearing. I attended accordingly; but, to my chagrin, the Attorney-General remarked that he had not had time to examine the letter. He carelessly took it up, and turned over the leaves without reading it, and then asked me if I had not taken measures for a patent in my own country. And, upon my reply in the affirmative, he remarked that ' America was a large country, and I ought to be satisfied with a patent there.' I replied that, with all due deference, I did not consider that as a point submitted for the Attorney-General's decision ; that the question submitted was, whether there was any legal obstacle in the way of my obtaining letters-patent for my Telegraph in England. He observed that he considered my invention as having been *published*, and that he must *therefore* forbid me to proceed.

"Thus forbidden to proceed by an authority from which there was no appeal, as I afterward learned, but to Parliament, and this at great cost of time and money, I immediately left England for France, where I found no difficulty in securing a patent. My invention there not only attracted the regards of the distinguished *savants* of Paris, but in a marked degree the admiration of many of the English nobility and gentry at that time in the French capital. To several of these, while explaining the operation of my telegraphic system, I related the history of my treatment by the English Attorney-General. The celebrated Earl of Elgin took a deep interest in the matter, and was intent on my obtaining a special act of Parliament to secure to me my just rights as the inventor of the Electro-Magnetic Telegraph. He repeatedly visited me, bringing with him many of his distinguished friends, and among them on one occasion the noble Earl of Lincoln, since one of her Majesty's Privy Council. The Hon. Henry Drummond also interested himself for me, and, through his kindness and Lord Elgin's, I received letters of introduction to Lord Brougham and to the Marquis of Northamptom, the President of the Royal Society, and several other distinguished persons in England. The Earl of Lincoln showed me special kindness; in taking leave of me in Paris, he gave me his card, and, requesting me to bring my telegraphic instruments with me to London, pressed me to give him the earliest notice of my arrival in London.

"I must here say that for weeks in Paris I had been engaged in negotiation with the Russian Counselor of State, the Baron Alexander de Meyendorff, arranging measures for putting the telegraph in operation in Russia. The terms of a contract had been mutually agreed upon, and all was concluded but the signature of the emperor to legalize it. In order to take advantage of the ensuing summer season for my operations in Russia, I determined to proceed immediately to the United States to make some necessary preparations for the enterprise, without waiting for the formal completion of the contract papers, being led to believe that the signature of the emperor was sure, a matter of mere form. Under these circumstances, I left Paris on the 13th of March, 1839, and arrived in London on the 15th of the same month. The next day, I sent my card to the Earl of Lincoln and my letter and card to the Marquis of Northampton, and in two or three hours received a visit from both. By Earl Lincoln, I was at once invited to send my Telegraph to his house in Park Lane, and on the 19th of March I exhibited its operation to members of both Houses of Parliament, of the Royal Society, and the Lords of the Admiralty, invited to meet me by the Earl of Lincoln. From the circumstances mentioned, my time in London was necessarily short, my passage having been secured in the Great Western, to sail on the 23d of March. Although solicited to remain a while in London, both by the Earl of Lincoln and the Hon. Henry Drummond, with a view to obtaining a special act of Parliament for a patent, I was compelled by the circumstances of the case to defer, till some more favorable opportunity, on my expected return to England, any attempt of the kind. The Emperor of Russia, however, refused to ratify the contract made with me by his Counselor of State, and my design of returning to Europe was frustrated; and I have not to this hour had the means to prosecute this enterprise to a result in England. All my exertions were needed to establish my telegraphic system in my own country.

"Time has shown conclusively the essential difference of my telegraphic system from those of my opponents; *time* has also shown that my system *was not published* in England, as alleged by

23

the Attorney-General; for, to this day, no work in England has published any thing that does not show that, as yet, it is perfectly misunderstood.   Professor Wheatstone has even pronounced lately (within three years), in Paris, my system USELESS and IMPRACTI-CABLE, or words to that effect, as I learn from the highest authority. Surely, after the results before the world of the practical operation of my system for so long a time, and over hundreds of miles of country (in 1846), furnishing daily to the press, in cities five or six hundred miles apart, whole columns of news simultaneously, Pro-fessor Wheatstone *could not have understood* my system, and thus risk his reputation as a man of science by such a hasty opinion.   If my system had been published in England, Professor Wheatstone's sagacity would certainly have comprehended its superior simplicity and efficiency, and he never would have hazarded such a remark. I consider this fact conclusive on the point of publication.   But, as this was the ground, the sole ground, of not allowing me to proceed in taking out letters patent, I will not leave the settlement of the question to inference; I will show that there was not even the *shadow of a publication,* in the legal sense of the term.   The sole document upon which my opponents rested to prove a publication, is that referred to in the *Mechanic's Magazine,* page 332.[1]   Let any one read that paper, and see whether my invention is there any-where described.   It is there stated that 'five years before' (in 1832), 'I had invented an Electric Telegraph;' that 'the distin-guishing features of my telegraph' are a *register* which *permanent-ly records in characters* easily legible the fullest communication, and the use of but *one wire* as a conductor; it speaks of 'points or marks' to be read, and of ' a pencil' that marks.   It will scarcely be believed, and yet it is true, that *this is all the description or pub-lication of my invention at that time made in England,* or shown by my opponents; and yet, on such a pretended publication as this, was I forbidden to proceed to obtain letters patent.

   " At that time, I had with me drawings of an instrument called the *receiving magnet,* constructed and put in operation in the spring of 1837, connected with a relay or local battery, a provision against the *reduction of the magnetic power* of the main battery as the length of the conductor increased.   By means of a local *battery* and local *magnet,* any quantity of power could be obtained, accord-ing to the size of said local magnet or local battery.

---

[1] This article in the *Mechanic's Magazine* to which I refer, was copied without alteration from *Silliman's Journal of Science* of October, 1837.

"The *receiving magnet* was a provision devised for an exigency which at that time I conceived only to be possible, but was to be used and would be effective in case the exigency occurred. This instrument was unnecessary in any of the then attempted systems of Electric Telegraphs, nor was it then necessary, nor is it now necessary, in the exhibition of my main instrument called the register, while confined to a few miles of conductors. But it is essential to the efficiency of my system when a circuit connects two points a great distance from each other. Although devised as long ago as 1836, and constructed in the spring of 1837, while providing against a possible exigency, it was not necessary to bring it into actual practical use till the first line of conductors for my Telegraph was prepared. This exigency occurred in trying the power of the register magnet through a circuit of *one hundred and sixty miles* of wire. The magnetism even from a powerful battery was found to be too feeble for the purpose of directly marking mechanically my characters, but the application of the *receiving magnet* which *had been prepared*, in reserve, and was at hand, effectually and immediately relieved the difficulty.

" Now, under what pretence of justice was I denied a patent for this receiving magnet ? It was secured to me in France but a few weeks after the rejection of my application in England.

" This is the statement of the case. The refusal to grant me a patent was at that period very disastrous. It was especially discouraging to have made a long voyage across the Atlantic in vain, incurring great expenditure, and loss of time, which in their consequence also produced years of delay in the prosecution of my enterprise in the United States.

"SAMUEL F. B. MORSE.

"NEW YORK, *April* 2, 1847."

" At the time of preparing this statement, I lacked one item of evidence which it was desirable to have, aside from my own assertion, viz., evidence that the refusal of the Attorney-General was on the ground '*that a publication of the invention had been made.*'— I deemed it advisable rather to suffer from the delay, and endure the taunts which my unscrupulous opponents have not been slow to lavish upon me in consequence, if I could but obtain this evidence in proper shape. I accordingly wrote to my brother, then in London, to procure, if possible, from Lord Campbell or his secretary, an acknowledgment of the ground on which he refused my application for a patent in 1838, since no public report or record in such cases is made. My brother, in connection with Mr. Carpmael, one of the most distinguished patent agents in England, addressed a note to Mr. H. Cooper, the Attorney-General's secretary at the time, and the only official person besides Lord Campbell connected with the matter. The following is Mr. Cooper's reply:

" ' WILMINGTON SQUARE, *May* 23, 1843.

" ' GENTLEMEN : In answer to yours of the 20th inst., I beg to state that I have a distinct recollection of Professor Morse's application for a patent, strengthened by the fact of *his not having paid the fees for the hearing, etc., and their being now owing.* I understood at the time that the patent was stopped on the ground *that a publication of the invention had been made,* but I cannot procure Lord Campbell's certificate of that fact.

" ' I am, gentlemen, your obedient servant,

" ' H. COOPER.'

" I thus have obtained the evidence I desired in the most authentic form, but accompanied with as gross an insult as could well be conceived. On the receipt of this letter, I immediately wrote to F. O. J. Smith, Esq., at Portland, who accompanied me to England, and at whose sole expense, according to agreement, all proceedings in taking out patents in Europe were to be borne, to know if this charge of the Attorney-General's secretary could possibly be true, not knowing but, through some inadvertence on his (Mr. Smith's) part, this bill might have been overlooked. Mr. Smith writes me in answer, sending me a copy *verbatim* of the following receipt, which he holds and which speaks for itself:

" ' Mr. Morse to the Attorney-General,   Dr.

	£	s.	d.
Hearing on a patent.............................	3	10	0
Giving notice on the same.............................	1	1	0
	£4	11	0

Settled the 13th of August, 1838.

(Signed)   H. COOPER.'

" This receipt is signed, as will be perceived, by the same individual H. Cooper, who, nearly ten years after his acknowledgment of the money, has the impudence to charge me with leaving my fees unpaid. I now leave the public to make their own comments both on the character of the whole transaction in England, and on the character and motives of those in this country who have espoused

Lord Campbell's course, making it an occasion to charge me with having '*invented nothing.*'

"SAMUEL F. B. MORSE.

"POUGHKEEPSIE, *December* 11, 1848."

This refusal of a patent in England is a fact of such great importance in the history of Telegraphs, that the letters referred to from Mr. Smith and Mr. Sidney E. Morse, showing clearly the gross wrong that was done, are carefully preserved to substantiate the statements made by Professor Morse.

June 19, 1838, Professor Morse wrote to his daughter, Mrs. Lind: "London is filling fast with crowds of all characters, from ambassadors and princes to pickpockets and beggars, all brought together by the coronation of the queen, which takes place in a few days (the 28th of June). Every thing in London now is colored by the coming pageant. In the shop-windows are the robes of the nobility, the crimson and ermine, dresses, coronets, etc. Preparations for illuminations are making all over the city.

"I have scarcely entered upon the business of the Telegraph, but have examined (tell Dr. Gale) the specification of Wheatstone at the Patent-Office, and, except the alarum part, he has nothing which interferes with mine. His invention is ingenious and beautiful, but very complicated, and he must use twelve wires where I use but four. I have seen also a Telegraph exhibiting at Exeter Hall, invented by Davy, something like Wheatstone's, but still complicated. I find mine is yet the simplest, and hope to accomplish something, but always keep myself prepared for disappointment. Your affectionate father,

"SAMUEL F. B. MORSE."

While attending the ceremonies of the coronation, to which Professor Morse was invited by the courtesy of the American Minister, the Hon. Andrew Stevenson, he learned a pleasing incident illustrating the beautiful character of the maiden queen. He related it in these words:

"I was in London in 1838, and was present with my excellent friend the late Charles R. Leslie, R. A., at the imposing ceremonies of the coronation of the queen in Westminster Abbey. He then related to me the following incident, which I think may truly be said to have been the first act of her Majesty's reign: When her predecessor, William IV., died, a messenger was immediately dispatched by his queen (then become by his death queen-dowager) to Victoria, apprising her of the event. She immediately called for paper, and indicted a letter of condolence to the widow. Folding it, she directed it ' To the Queen of England.' Her maid of honor in attendance, noticing the inscription, said, ' Your Majesty, you are Queen of England.' ' Yes,' she replied, ' but the widowed queen is not to be reminded of that fact first by me.'"

Although the exhibition of the Telegraph must have carried conviction to the minds of all who saw its actual operation, the inventor gained nothing by remaining in London. He determined to " seek his fortune " in Paris. Writing to his daughter on his way thither, he says:

"HAVRE, IN FRANCE, *July* 26, 1838.

" After having been delayed seven weeks in England, endeavoring to obtain a patent, and having had two hearings before the Attorney-General, he decided against us, and (as we can make to appear) *most unjustly.* The ground of objection was not that my invention was not original, and better than others, but that it had been published in England from the American journals, and therefore belonged to the public. The whole matter will be laid before the world in due time, and, so far as most gross injustice is charged on his decision, the charge will be made out. We have, however, by this act of the Attorney-General, been shut out from any expectation of pecuniary advantage in Great Britain, and yet the history of the whole transaction clearly proves me the original inventor of the *first practicable* and the simplest Electric Telegraph, and I am persuaded that eventually the English themselves will do me that justice. Professor Wheatstone and Mr. Davy were my opposers. They have each very ingenious inventions of their own, particularly the former, who is a man of genius, and one with whom I was personally much pleased; he has invented *his,* I believe, without knowing that I was engaged in an invention to produce a similar result, for, although he dates back into 1832, yet, as no publication of our thoughts was made by either, we are evidently independent of each other. My time has not been lost, however, for I have ascertained with certainty that the *Telegraph of a single circuit* and a *recording apparatus* is mine, and I learned from the Attorney-General that Professor Steinheil, of Munich, who has invented his, of a single circuit, subsequent to mine, has, as he observed, ' without doubt taken it from mine.' I found, also, that both Mr. Wheatstone and Mr. Davy were endeavoring to simplify theirs by adding a recording apparatus and reducing theirs to a single circuit. The latter showed to the Attorney-General a drawing, which I obtained sight of, of a method by which he proposed a bungling imitation of my first characters, those that were printed in our journals, and one, however plausible on paper, and sufficiently so to deceive the Attorney-General, was perfectly impracticable. Partiality, from *national or other motives*, aside from the justice of the case, I am persuaded, influenced the decision against me.

"We are now on our way to Paris, to try what we can do with the French Government. I confess I am not sanguine as to any favorable pecuniary result in Europe, but we shall try; and at any rate we have seen enough to know that the matter is viewed with great interest here, and the plan of such telegraphs will be adopted, and of course the United States is secured to us, and I do hope something from them. Be economical, my dear child, and keep your wants within bounds, for I am preparing myself for an unsuccessful result here, yet every proper effort will be made. I am in excellent health and spirits, and leave to-morrow morning for Paris."

"PARIS, *August* 29, 1838.

"I have obtained a patent here, and it is exciting some attention. The prospects of future benefit from the invention are good, but I shall not probably realize much or even any thing *immediately*. I saw by the papers, before I got your letter, that Congress had not passed the appropriation bill for the Telegraph; on some accounts I regret it, but it is only delayed, and it will probably be passed early in the winter. You will be glad to learn, my dear daughter, that your father's health was never so good, and, probably before this reaches you, he will be on the ocean on his return. I think of leaving Paris in a very few days. I am only waiting to show the Telegraph to the king, from whom I expect a message hourly. The birth of a prince occupies the whole attention just now of the royal family and the court; he was born on the 24th inst., the son of the Duke and Duchess of Orleans. My rooms are as delightfully situated, perhaps, as any in Paris; they are close to the palace of the Tuileries, and overlook the gardens, and are within half a stone's-throw of the rooms of the Duke and Duchess of Orleans. From my balcony I look directly into their rooms. I saw the company that were there assembled on the birthday of the little prince, and saw him in his nurse's arms at the window the next day after his birth. He looked very much like any other baby, and not half so handsome as little Hugh Peters. I received from the Minister of War, General Bernard, who has been very polite to me, a ticket to be present at the *Te Deum* performed yesterday in the great cathedral of Paris, Notre-Dame, on account of the birth of the prince. The king and all the royal family and the court, with all the officers of state, were present. The cathedral was crowded with all the fashion of Paris. Along the ways, and around the church, were soldiers without number, almost—a proof that some danger was apprehended to the king; and yet he ought to be popular, for he is the best ruler they have had for years. The ceremonies were imposing, appealing to the senses and the imagination, and not at all to the reason or the heart."

"PARIS, *September* 29, 1838.

" Since my last, matters have assumed a totally different aspect. At the request of Monsieur Arago, the most distinguished astronomer of the day, I submitted the Telegraph to the Institute at one of their meetings, at which some of the most celebrated philosophers of France and of Germany, and of other countries, were present. Its reception was in the highest degree flattering, and the interest which they manifested, by the questions they asked, and the exclamations they used, showed to me then that the invention had obtained their favorable regard. The papers of Paris immediately announced the Telegraph in the most favorable terms, and it has literally been the topic of the day ever since. The Baron Humboldt, the celebrated traveler, a member of the Institute, and who saw its operation before that body, told Mr. Wheaton, our Minister to Prussia, that my Telegraph was the best of all the plans that had been devised. I received a call from the administrator-in-chief of all the Telegraphs of France, Monsieur Alphonse Foy; I explained it to him. He was highly delighted with it, and told me that the Government were about to try an experiment with the view of testing the practicability of the Electric Telegraph, and that he had been requested to see mine and to report upon it; that he should report that ' *mine was the best that had been submitted to him*,' and he added that I had better forthwith get an introduction to the Minister of the Interior, Monsieur the Count Montalivet; I procured a letter from our Minister, and am now waiting the decision of the Government. Every thing looks promising thus far, as much so as I could expect; but it involves the possibility not to say the probability of my remaining in Paris during the winter. If I should be delayed till December, it would be prudent to remain until April. If it be possible without detriment to my affairs to make such arrangements that I may return this autumn, I shall certainly do it; but, if I should not, you must console yourselves that it is in consequence of meeting with success that I am detained, and that I shall be more likely to return with advantage to you all, on account of the delay. I ought to say that the directors of the St. Germain Railroad have seen my Telegraph, and that there is some talk (as yet vague) of establishing a line of my Telegraph upon that road. I mention these, my dear child, to show you that I cannot at this moment leave Paris without detriment to my principal object."

"PARIS, *October* 10, 1838.

" MY DEAR DAUGHTER: You are at an age when a parent's care, and particularly a mother's care, is most needed. You cannot know the depth of the wound that was inflicted when I was deprived of your dear mother, nor in how many ways that wound has been kept open. Yet I know it is all well; I look to God to take care of you; it is his will that you should be almost truly an orphan, for, with all my efforts to have a home for you and to be near you, I have met hitherto only with disappointment. But there are now indications of a change, and, while I prepare for disappointment and wish you to prepare for disappointment, we ought to acknowledge the kind hand of our heavenly Father, in so far prospering me as to put me in the honorable light before the world which is now my lot. With this eminence is connected the prospect of pecuniary prosperity, yet this is not consummated, but only in prospect; it may be a long time before any thing is realized. Study, therefore, prudence and economy in all things; make your wants as few as possible, for the habit thus acquired will be of advantage to you, whether you have much or little."

The Rev. Dr. Kirk, who died in Boston, March 27, 1874, was residing in Paris at the time of Professor Morse's visit, and the two gentlemen, being old friends, took apartments in common for the sake of economy. Dr. Kirk, in a letter written in 1851, alludes to the Telegraph and its inventor:

" On my return to Paris, in the autumn of 1838, I met your brother, and we took rooms at the Hôtel No. 9 Rue Neuve des

Mathurins. Our apartments consisted of a parlor, a bedchamber, and an intervening passage. He put up a table in the bedroom, and placed his galvanic battery upon it. The wires were extended through the passage into the parlor, where the writing apparatus was set up. I remember rallying my friend frequently about the experience of great inventors, who are generally permitted to starve when living, and are canonized after death.

"When the model telegraph had been set up in our rooms, Mr. Morse desired to exhibit it to the *savants* of Paris. But, as he had less of the talking propensity than myself, I was made the grand exhibitor. Our levee-day was Tuesday, and for weeks we received the visits of distinguished citizens and strangers, to whom I explained the principles and operation of the Telegraph. The visitors would agree upon a word among themselves, which I was not to hear. Then the Professor would receive it at the writing end of the wires; while it devolved upon me to interpret the characters which recorded it at the other end. As I explained the hieroglyphics, the announcement of the word, which they saw could have come to me only through the wire, would often create a deep sensation of delighted wonder. And much do I now regret that I did not take notes of those interviews; for it would be an interesting record of distinguished names, and of valuable remarks. As it is, I must merely speak of what memory retains. And what is of chief importance I do distinctly remember.

"1. Men distinguished for their science as well as their social position, and eminent literary men and women, were among the interested spectators of the great invention. They were from England, Spain, Russia, Italy, and America, besides the Parisians and other Frenchmen. I doubt not there were representatives from other nations, because our rooms were full on each exhibition, but I retain no definite recollections beyond what I state. Our own countryman, Robert Walsh, Esq., gave the word 'Immortality,' to be written by the Telegraph.

"2. The impression left on my mind is complete, that, while a few chemists or physicists were familiar with the two great laws of the magnetic fluid which the Telegraph employs (I mean the instantaneousness, or immeasurable rapidity of the current, when the circuit is complete, and the power of making iron attractive), yet I never heard a remark which indicated that the result obtained by Mr. Morse was not NEW, wonderful, and promising immense practical results."

On the 4th day of September, 1838, Professor Morse had the honor and the intense satisfaction of meeting M. ARAGO, the most eminent scientist in France, and of exhibiting to him in private the operation of his Telegraph. Arago was the man of all men then living to comprehend and appreciate the wonderful invention. He gave it a thorough examination, questioned the inventor with great minuteness, and declared himself satisfied with the results, and its capacity to do all that was claimed for it. He instantly proposed to introduce it to the Academy of Science, at their very next meeting, which was to be held on the following Monday. The Telegraph had never been subjected to such an inquisition as it would then undergo. The diffident and anxious inventor prepared himself for the trial with the greatest care. In one of his little note-books of that day are written in a few hints which he jotted down to aid him in the presentation of the case:

" My present instrument is very imperfect in its mechanism, and is only designed to illustrate the principle of my invention. The recording part—all in the box that holds the pen—is made strong and clumsy, for the purpose of safety in traveling. It is all reducible to one-third of the compass here exhibited and without at all impairing its efficiency. It may be made into an ornamental piece of furniture, like a time-piece. My invention was matured by me in 1832, though not announced until the spring of 1837. I have indubitable proof from Mr. Rives, late Minister of the United States to the French Government, as also from other persons of the date of my discovery. My invention differs from that of all others of more recent origin—

" 1. In that it requires but a single circuit of wire by which to communicate all the letters of the alphabet, while the others require several circuits.

" 2. In that I make no use of magnetic needles in conveying intelligence, while the others rely upon numerous needles for that purpose.

" 3. In that mine writes one or any desired copies, simultaneously, of all intelligence sent by it, in permanent characters, while all others carry only momentary signs by motion of needle or by sound, and can furnish no duplicates of them.

" 4. Mine requires no attendance constantly at the place of delivery of intelligence, to render the communications made available

—while others can be operated only by having one or more persons ready at all times to take down every sign transmitted at the time and in the order of their transmission.

" 5. The whole of my invention is worked by mechanism, including type, thereby insuring regularity and precision; others are worked only by hand as an organ or piano is played.

" 6. By my invention I can communicate letters and words in writing more rapidly than any other invention can communicate signs which reach the eye alone.

" The expense of constructing my method of Telegraph, *ready for use*, to and fro, over any given distance, will not exceed thirty-five hundred francs per English mile—and the mechanism at each point will not exceed fifteen hundred. The type will not exceed the expense of one franc per pound. To regulate the passage of the type, a small train of wheels, acted upon by a spring or weight, will be used instead of the hand-crank used for convenience of transportation in the model now presented.

" A small apparatus also belongs to the register, but is not now exhibited, by which the person transmitting intelligence from one point can both set in motion and stop at pleasure the register or recording pen, at any distant point, without the intervention of any person there. This secures to a single individual entire control over the Telegraph at each extremity. To the recording pen now exhibited also belongs a reservoir, sufficiently large to supply the the pen with ink for an indefinite period. My invention, I may add, allows the intelligence sent on any single circuit of wire to be written at any number of intermediate places between any two distant points, and simultaneously with its reception at the most distant points. The other inventions require an entire set of wires for every distinct point of communication."

The anxiously-anticipated day arrived, September 10, 1838. Full of fears of his own ability to do justice to the work, and knowing that he labored under the great disadvantage of speaking through an interpreter, his heart was ready to fail him. He was invited by the secretary to a seat within the pale of the assembled members; around him were gathered all the chiefs of science in that illustrious body to which kings and emperors have sought admission in vain. But near to the unknown American sat one whose fame had already filled the world of science, and at this day is more illustrious as a naturalist than

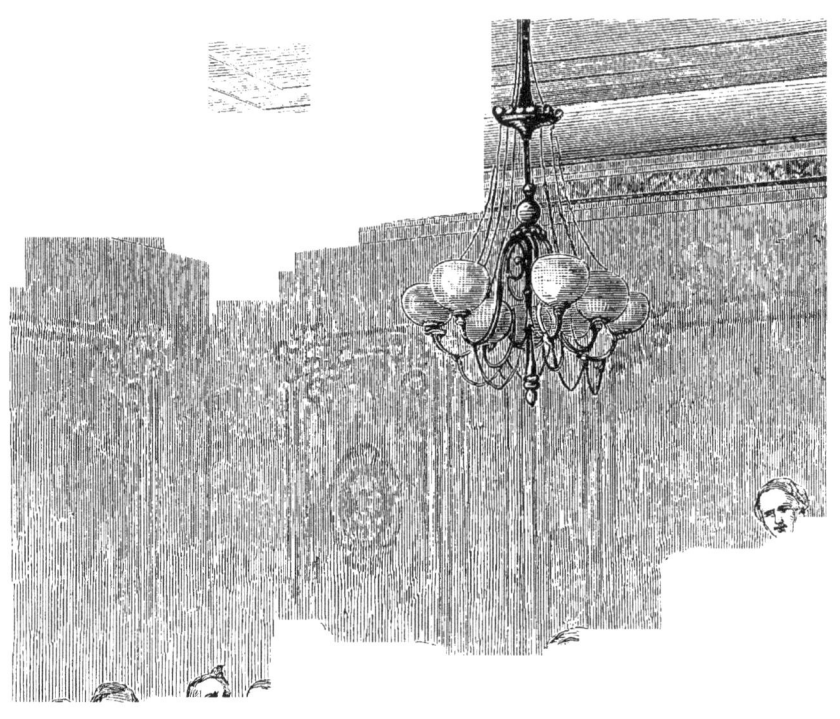

HUMBOLDT, ARAGO, AND MORSE.

any other of the age. This was Baron Humboldt. The secretary, Arago, explained the Telegraph, while Morse stood by to operate upon the instrument, in the presence of this distinguished company. At the conclusion of the explanation by Arago, and in the midst of the plaudits of the Academy, Baron Humboldt arose, and, taking Mr. Morse by the hand, expressed, in strong and hearty terms, his thanks and congratulations. This was the proudest triumph thus far in Morse's life. Still greater triumphs were in store. To his brother Professor Morse wrote:

"At the request of M. Arago I consented to exhibit it to the Institute at one of their sittings. I found myself in the midst of the most celebrated scientific men of the world. M. Arago explained in the most lucid manner the details and actions of the instrument, and I perceived by the expression of face and the exclamations of surprise and gratification which were uttered by the members, as they crowded around the table, that the Telegraph had won their regard."

To Mr. Vail he wrote:

"I exhibited the Telegraph to the Institute, and the sensation produced was as striking as at Washington. It was evident that hitherto the assembled science of Europe had considered the plan of an electric telegraph as ingenious, but visionary, and, like aëronautic navigation, practicable in little more than theory, and destined to be useless.

"I cannot describe to you the scene at the Institute when your box with the registering-machine, just as it left Speedwell, was placed upon the table, and surrounded by the most distinguished men of all Europe, celebrated in the various arts and sciences— Arago, Baron Humboldt, Gay-Lussac, and a host of others whose names are stars that shine in both hemispheres. Arago described it to them, and I showed its action. A buzz of admiration and approbation filled the whole hall, and the exclamations, '*Extraordinaire!*' '*Très-bien!*' '*Très admirable!*' I heard on all sides. The sentiment was universal."

The *Comptes Rendus*, the weekly journal of the Academy, gave the following notice:

"Applied Physics—Electro-Magnetic Telegraph of Mr. Morse, Professor in the University of New York.

" The instrument has been put in operation under the eyes of the Academy; the following is a literal translation of a large portion of the notice delivered by Mr. Morse to the perpetual secretaries :

" Mr. Morse conceives that his instrument is the first practicable application which has been made of electricity to the construction of a telegraph.

" This instrument was invented in October, 1832, while the author was on his way from Europe to America, in the packet-ship Sully. The fact is attested by the captain of the ship and several of the passengers. Among the number of the latter was Mr. Rives, the Minister of the United States near the French Government."

(Here is given the account of Mr. Rives and Captain Pell, after which the account proceeds :)

" The idea of applying galvanism to the construction of telegraphs is not new: Dr. Cone, a distinguished citizen of Philadelphia, makes mention of it in a note inserted by him in February, 1816, in the ' Annals of Dr. Thompson,' page 162, first series; but he did not give any means of effecting it.

" Since the period to which the invention of Mr. Morse's Telegraph goes back, other arrangements, founded on the same principles, have been announced, of which the most celebrated are those of *Mr. Steinheil, of Munich,* and of *Mr. Wheatstone,* of London.

" They differ very much in mechanism. The American Telegraph employs but one circuit;[1] the following is an abridged description :

" At the extremity of the circuit, where the news is to be received, is an apparatus called the *register.* It consists of an electro-magnet, the wire covering of which forms the prolongation of the wire of the circuit. The armature of this magnet is attached to the end of a small lever, which at its opposite extremity holds a pen; under this pen is a ribbon of paper, which moves forward, as required, by means of a certain number of wheels. At the other extremity of the circuit, that is to say, at the station from which

---

[1] " Suppose the places to be put in communication with each other occupy the three angles of a triangle, the four angles of a quadrilateral, or certain points of a line inclosing a space, a single wire passing through all those points would be sufficient, at least according to the theory."

the news is to be sent out, is another apparatus called the *portrule ;* it consists of a battery, or generator of galvanism, at the two poles of which the circuit ends ; near the battery a portion of this circuit is broken; the two extremities, disjoined, are plunged into two cups of mercury near each other. By the aid of a bent wire attached to the extremity of a little lever, the two cups may be, at will, placed in connection with each other, or left separated; thus the circuit is completed and interrupted at pleasure. The movement of the mechanism is as follows : When the circuit is complete, the magnet is charged; it attracts the armature, the movement of which brings the pen into contact with the paper. When the circuit is interrupted, the magnetism of the horseshoe ceases, the armature returns to its first position, and the pen is withdrawn from the paper. When the circuit is completed, and broken rapidly in succession, mere dots are produced upon the moving paper; if, on the contrary, the circuit remain complete for a certain length of time, the pen marks a line, the length of which is in proportion to the time during which the circuit remains complete. This paper presents a long interval of blank if the circuit remain interrupted during some considerable time. These points, lines, and blanks, lead to a great variety of combinations. By means of these elements Professor Morse has constructed an alphabet and the signs of the ciphers. The letters may be written with great rapidity by means of certain types, which the machine causes to move with exactness, and which give the proper movements to the lever bearing the pen. Forty-five of these characters may be traced in one minute.

"The register is under the control of the person who sends the news. In fact, from the extremity called the *portrule*, the mechanism of the register may be set in motion, and stopped, at will. The presence of a person to receive the news is, therefore, not necessary, though the sound of a bell, which is rung by the machine, announces that the writing is about to be begun.

"The distance at which the American telegraph has been tried, is ten miles English, or four post leagues of France. The experiments have been witnessed by a committee appointed by the Congress of the United States. The reports of the committee, which we have not copied, are extremely favorable. The committee of Congress recommended the appropriation of thirty thousand dollars."

Two days after the exhibition, the Hon. H. L. Ellsworth, one of our most intelligent citizens, being at that time in

Paris, wrote the following letter to a friend in the United States :

" I am sure you will be glad to learn that our American friend, Professor Morse, is producing a very great sensation among the learned men of this kingdom, by his ingenious and wonderful Magnetic Telegraph. He submitted it to the examination of the Academy of Sciences of the Royal Institute of France, at their sitting on Monday last, and the deepest interest was excited among the members of that learned body on the subject. Its novelty, beauty, simplicity, and power, were highly commended.

" M. Arago, the learned and eminent principal in the Astronomical Observatory of the French Government, has manifested a very lively interest in relation to it. He addressed the Academy in regard to our countryman's invention in terms that could not but have been most pleasing, as they were certainly most creditable to Mr. Morse. It is understood that a report of the exhibitions will be submitted by M. Arago in the forthcoming number of the published proceedings of the Institute. The favorable consideration and opinion of a man and philosopher so eminent in the scientific world as M. Arago, and so intimately associated with the learned institutions of the French Government, will be in itself a rich reward for American ingenuity to attain in the field of science.

" Other projects for the establishment of a magnetic telegraph have been broached here, especially from Professor Wheatstone, of London, and Professor Steinheil, of Munich. It is said, however, to be very manifest that our Yankee Professor is ahead of them all in the essential requisitions of such an invention, and that he is in the way to bear off the palm. In simplicity of design, cheapness of construction, and efficiency, Professor Morse's Telegraph transcends all yet made known. In each of these qualities, it is admitted, by those who have inspected it closely, there seems to be little else to desire. It is certain, moreover, that in priority of discovery he antedates all others.

" In being abroad, among strangers and foreigners, one's nationality of feeling may be somewhat more excusable than at home. Be this as it may, one cannot but feel gratified, as an American, that our countryman, like Fulton in the practical science of steam, is thus in advance of the learned men of the Old World in this triumphant adaptation to every-day use of the elder sister of Steam-power, *Electricity*. The result of his ingenuity will in a few years impart to the intercourse of man, at points distant from each other, an aspect no less wonderful, free, and influential, than that which the use of steam-power has already imparted to it. In this respect, another revolution is at hand, even more wonderful than its predecessor. I do not doubt that, within the next ten years, you will see this electric power adopted, between all commercial points of magnitude on both sides of the Atlantic, for purposes of correspondence, and men enabled to send their orders or news of events from one point to another with the speed of lightning itself, superseding thereby all the old modes of 'express mails' and of postboy correspondence, in all matters of moment to government and trade. The extremities of nations will be literally *wired* together, and brought, for all purposes of written correspondence, within the compactness of a common centre. In the United States, for instance, you may expect to find, at no very distant day, the Executive messages, and the daily votes of each House of Congress, made known at Philadelphia, New York, Boston, and Portland—at New Orleans, Cincinnati, etc., as soon as they can be known at Baltimore, or even at the opposite extremity of Pennsylvania Avenue! The merchant at Boston, or New York, will yet be able to correspond with his ship-master at New Orleans, on the subject of freights, prices of cotton, sugar, etc., in every hour of the day, and give orders and receive return answers between the same distant points in one and the same hour, and by night as well as by day, amid storms as readily as amid sunshine! To predict this much seems now like a fairy tale; and it is, indeed, overwhelming to contemplate the realities which science and practical skill are pouring in upon our age. It is no longer a proverb, but the saying has risen to the solemnity of a mathematical truth, that '*truth is stranger than fiction.*' Abstract imagination is no longer a match for reality in the race that science has instituted on both sides of the Atlantic."

In a letter to one of his brothers, Professor Morse wrote:

" M. Foy appointed an hour to come and examine my instrument. He examined it minutely, asking many questions, and proposing many objections; after he had seen it sufficiently, he said to me : ' I have been requested by the Minister of the Interior to examine your Telegraph among others, and to report to him ; *I shall report that it is the best I have seen.*' He then advised me to obtain a letter of introduction to the Minister of the Interior, the Count Montalivet, for that the Government intended trying an experiment

24

with the Electric Telegraph, and I should probably be requested to
try mine. Our excellent Minister, General Cass, gave me a most
flattering letter to the Count Montalivet, which I have presented,
and am now waiting further orders. 1 have also received a call
from the directors of the St.-Germain Railroad, which is a course of
about twelve miles out of Paris. They were much pleased, but they
did not wish so complete a telegraph; one circuit and a few signals
were all they wished, but were desirous to know if there could be
any means devised by which they could know at any time where the
cars were on the road."

The services of the distinguished M. Antoine Perpigna were
secured, and under his direction a *brevet d'invention* was
promptly obtained; but no sooner had it been obtained, says
Mr. Morse, "than an unforeseen obstacle was interposed which
has rendered my patent in France of no avail to me. By the
French patent law at the time, one who obtains a patent was
obliged to put into operation his invention within two years
from the issue of his patent, under the penalty of forfeiture if
he does not comply with the law. In pursuance of this requisition of the law, I negotiated with the president (Turneysen)
of the St.-Germain Railroad Company to construct a line of my
Telegraph on their road from Paris to St.-Germain, a distance
of about seven English miles. The company were favorably
disposed toward the project, but upon application (as was necessary) to the Government for permission to have the Telegraph
on their road, they received for answer that telegraphs were a
Government monopoly, and could not therefore be used for
private purpose. I thus found myself crushed between the
conflicting forces of two opposing laws."

His partner, Hon. F. O. J. Smith, who came with him to
the Continent, to aid in securing patents, having returned
to London, on his way to the United States, Mr. Morse wrote
to him frequently and with the greatest freedom, detailing the
minutest incidents in his negotiations, and describing his own
feelings as they were alternately elevated or depressed by the
progress he made. Dating at Paris, September 29, 1838, he says:

"On Monday I received a very flattering letter from our excellent Minister, Governor Cass, introducing me to the Count Monta-

livet, and I accordingly called the next day. I did not see him, but had an interview with the secretary, who told me that the Administrator of the Telegraphs had not yet reported to the Minister; but that he would see him the next day, and that, if I would call on Friday, he would inform me of the result. I called on Friday. The secretary informed me that he had seen Monsieur Foy, and that he had more than confirmed the flattering accounts in the American Minister's letter respecting the Telegraph, but was not yet prepared with his report to the Minister—he wished to make a detailed account of the *differences in favor of mine over all others that had been presented to him,* or words to that effect, and the secretary assured me that the report would be all I could wish. This is certainly flattering, and I am to call on Monday to learn further."

On the 24th of October, 1838, he again wrote from Paris :

"I can only add, in a few words, that every thing here is as encouraging as could be expected. The report of the Administrator of Telegraphs has been made to the Minister of the Interior, and I have been told that I should be notified of the intentions of Government in a few days. I have also shown the railroad Telegraph to the St.-Germain directors, who are delighted with it, and from them I expect a proposition within a few days."

The following letter illustrates the ludicrous manner in which the Professor's patience and temper were tried by the red-tape formalities of officials with whom he was brought into contact in Paris :

"PARIS, *November* 22, 1838.

"Hon. F. O. J. SMITH :

"MY DEAR SIR : I intend sending this letter by the packet of the 24th inst., and am in hopes of sending with it some intelligence from those from whom I have been so long expecting something. Every thing moves at a snail's pace here. I find delay in all things; at least, so it appears to me, who have too strong a development of the American organ of 'go-a-head-ativeness' to feel easy under its tantalizing effects. A Frenchman ought to have as many lives as a cat, to bring to pass, on his dilatory plan of procedure, the same results that a Yankee (a gen-oo-wine Yankee) would accomplish in his single life. Below, I must tell you what has occurred under my own eyes, and, although the matter is small, yet it is but one of thousands in the experience of others, and well illustrates the system of business here, *ex pede Herculem.*

" You will remember that when Mr. Chamberlain went with you to England, he was commissioned by me to obtain some of the clock machinery of the Telegraph, so that by having part executed in England, and part here, the whole machine intended for him to take to the east of Europe, could be completed in less time than if all were done in one place. The object was simply to avoid delay— *to expedite matters.* Well, you know Mr. Chamberlain procured a common brass clock-movement in London; from this he took out all but the wheels of the train, and put in place of them *four* box-wood rollers, which he got turned for one shilling and sixpence sterling. The instrument thus fitted cost about twelve francs. When Mr. Chamberlain arrived at Boulogne, upon searching his trunk this piece of a clock was discovered, and he was told that it must be sent to the administrator at Paris, by the *Douane* at Boulogne, and for the transportation, etc., he was charged and paid at Boulogne eight francs. On his arrival at Paris he called on the administrator, but the little box had not arrived. He called daily for a week, and at length he was told the box had come, but could not be delivered except by order of a certain officer, and some other formalities. This was well enough, but now came the action of the system. A day was consumed in finding the officer, who referred him to a second officer, in another part of the city, who again referred him to a third, and he again to a fourth. It was then discovered that the box was for me. I therefore must make my appearance, to state what the ominous machinery was for. I accordingly, with Mr. Chamberlain and Mr. Lovering, spent a whole day in being sent from office to office, waiting in each to have my turn to speak to the official, and all to no purpose. Another day was spent in like manner, and a third produced this result—I was required to furnish an accurate colored drawing of the machinery, and a minute description with reference to the drawing. I ought to say that two or three times we told them to take the box, that the whole object for which we wanted it was defeated by their vexatious delay, and that I wished no further trouble about it, but this was not allowed. I then went home and spent half a day in drawing accurately the rollers of box-wood, coloring the drawing, and giving a description of these rollers. I did not dream that it was necessary to give them a drawing of a common clock-train. I spent another day in waiting at the Administration of Douanes with the drawing. This at length was compared, with all formality, before four or five officers, with the machinery, and, because the clock-train was not drawn, pronounced incomplete, and the box retained. Again the attempt was made to give them the box, but no, a proper drawing must be made. Mr. Lovering, Mr. Chamber lain, and myself, passed a forenoon in first finding and then explaining to the Chef des Douanes the object of the machine, and the nature of the loss I should suffer by the continuance of this extraordinary procrastination. The chef then wrote a letter, on my promise to furnish the requisite drawing in a month, ordering the box to be delivered to me. We were then sure we were at the end of the matter. Again we went to the Administrator of Douanes; there I was·kept two or three hours, while the papers necessary were drawn up—obligations, receipts, etc. Not less, in printed and written forms, than a quire of foolscap paper was during this affair consumed! The security of a resident in Paris was required for the fulfillment of my engagement. Mr. Lovering was my surety. I was then handed over to an officer, who would give me another paper for another officer, upon paying over again the charge of eight francs to the commissionnaire at Boulogne, whose charge came from the Douane at Boulogne in the official paper. It was in vain they were told that the charge had been paid at Boulogne. Mr. Chamberlain had not the receipt, and it was thought best to pay it, to avoid a fortnight's more delay and loss of time to rectify it. So the money was paid, and with a new paper we went to another officer, who told us there were five francs duties to pay. These were paid, and we then got another paper, which was delivered to another officer, and the box was put into our hands, upon paying a few sous for signing my name to a receipt for the same. I was by no means sure I had got it, until I had put it under my arm, and had run as if I had stolen it, round two or three corners, and even then I fancied that the whole Douane was in commotion to call me back to complete every thing regular. This was all done that every thing should be *according to rule*.

" Well, I got the box home, the original cost of which was twelve francs, having paid to the customs here for it no less than twenty-one francs! But I am by no means sure that the matter is ended yet. I spent a whole day in making the promised new drawing, with all the wheels of the clock-train, and description, and have given it to Mr. Lovering to deposit, to release him from his security. But the object of the drawing is, that it may be presented to the

investigation of a court, who are to decide whether or not more
duty is to be paid, and I am obligated myself to pay any additional
duty they may fix. These are the particulars thus far. You will
exclaim, 'This must be a solitary case.' By no means. At this moment our secretary of legation is waiting this same dilatory, 'regular manner of doing business.' He is entitled by law, in consequence of his official station, to have his parcels from abroad duty
free. He has had a trunk of apparel from America two or three
weeks at Havre, waiting the regular course of a permit for him to receive it, and after dancing attendance on various officials, and notes
and letters passing between the Minister of Finance and the Minister of Marine, the secretary has about made up his mind to send to
Havre and pay the regular duties, and have it sent to him. But even
this will cost him another fortnight, or it may be a month. This
execrable mode of doing things resolves itself into the want of one
simple *principle:* there is no such thing here as *conscience.* This
being the case, no *confidence*, no *discretionary power*, can be given
to any sub-agent, for he will abuse it; and consequently the regular
military muster-roll mode must supply the place of conscience, and
all its circumlocutory, cumbrous powers, etc., etc. But I am not
going to moralize, though there is a fine field for it both morally
and socially. Happy, thrice happy America!

"*Afternoon, November 22d.*—Called on the Ministre de l'Inté-
rieur, no one at home; left card, and will call again to-morrow, and
hope to be in time yet for the packet.

"*November 23d.*—I have again called, but do not find at home
the chief secretary, M. Merlin. I went with Mr. Clark, who gave
me a most amusing account of a case of his, with the Douane, quite
equal to mine. He says that these delays are proverbial here,
every one having to tell of some such case. If regularity is a good,
verily one may have too much of a good thing. I shall miss the
packet of the 24th, but I am told she is a slow ship, and that I
shall probably find the letters reach home quite as soon by the
next. I will leave this open to add, if any thing occurs between
this and next patent-day.

"*November 30th.*—I have been called off from this letter until
the last moment by stirring about and endeavoring to expedite
matters with the Government. I have been to see General Cass
since my last date. I talked over matters with him. He complains
much of their dilatoriness, but sees no way of quickening them. I
have also seen Mr. Anderson, the secretary, and he called with a

M. Ravenant (I think the name is) and another gentleman who had approaches to the Minister of the Interior. They were enthusiastic in their praises of the Telegraph; it excited their wonder at its simplicity and practicability. They will talk about it where it will do service, so I am told. I wait the effects. I called again this morning at the Minister's, and, as usual, the secretary was absent, at the palace, they said. If I could once get them to look at it, I should be sure of them, for I have never shown it to any one who did not seem in raptures. I showed it a few days ago to M. Fremel, the Director of Light-Houses, who came with Mr. Vail and Captain Perry. He was cautious, at first, but afterward became as enthusiastic as any.

" The railroad directors are as dilatory as the Government. But I know they are discussing the matter seriously at their meetings, and I was told that the most influential man among them said they ' must have it.' The railroad directors in England favor the plan of the Telegraph. There is nothing in the least discouraging that has occurred, but, on the contrary, every thing to confirm the practicability of the plan, both on the score of science and expense."

"PARIS, *January* 21, 1839.

" I have shown the Telegraph to a great number of *savants*, and •I still find the same effect produced on all—that of enthusiastic admiration. An officer in the Telegraph-office, M. Moran, after examining the whole operation for some time with apparent incredulity, broke out with an exclamation of his astonishment, and holding up the little fork, with which I closed and broke the circuit, he exclaimed to the company: ' Behold the fork more potent than that of Neptune, destined to greater triumph, although it has one tooth less than his !' and then, addressing me in broken English—

"' Are you not GLORIOUS, sair, to be the author of this wonderful discovery ? '

" I will give you the names of several who called last week: *M. Pazerat*, Engineer and Director of Asphalt Operations; *M. Jormaid*,.member of the Institute and Librarian of the King; M. Clement des Ormes, Professor of Chemistry, etc., etc. ; General Charenon, formerly Governor of Poland ; Baron de Franc, son of the Prince de Salins. There have been many others of the Institute and Chamber of Deputies, whose names I have not recorded. There is some allowance, perhaps, to be made for French manner; but I think I can discover in the most polished manner when there is real or only pretended feeling, for I have now seen all kinds, and

found that often in the commencement there were distrust and caution, and guarded expression of satisfaction, until the operation was
completed, and then all reserve seemed at once broken down, and
the exclamations of ' *Étonnant!*' ' *Très admirable!*' and similar expressions showed that the feeling was sincere. I send you the
Compte Rendu of the *Société Philotechnique*, a committee of which
society, with their president, Baron la Doucette, member of the
Chamber of Deputies, at their head, came to examine it. You see
their report on the tenth and eleventh pages. I learn that the Telegraph is much talked of in all society, and I learn that the *Théâtre
des Variétés*, which is a sort of mirror of the popular topics, has a
piece in which persons are made to converse by means of this Telegraph, some hundreds of miles off. This is a straw which shows
the way of the wind; and, although matters move too slow for my
impatient spirit, yet the Telegraph is evidently gaining on the
popular notice, and in time will demand the attention of governments. I have the promise of a visit from the Count Bondy, Chief
of the Household of the King, and who, I understand, has great
influence with the king, and can induce him to adopt the Telegraph
between some of his palaces. Hopes, you perceive, continue
bright, but they are somewhat unsubstantial to an empty purse. I
look for the first fruits in America. My confidence increases every·
day in the certainty of the eventual adoption of this means of
communication throughout the civilized world. Its practicability,
hitherto doubted by *savants* here, is completely established, and
they do not hesitate to give me the credit of having established
it. I rejoice quite as much for my country's sake as for my own,
that both priority and superiority are awarded to my invention."

In a letter dated Paris, January 28, 1839, the Professor wrote
to Mr. Smith: "I wrote by the Great Western a few days ago.
The event then anticipated in regard to the ministry has occurred.
The ministers have resigned, and it is expected that the new cabinet
will be formed this day, with Marshal Soult at its head. Thus you
perceive new causes of delay in obtaining any answer from the
Government. As soon as I can learn the name of the new Minister
of the Interior, I will address a note to him, or see him, as 1 may be
advised, and see if I can possibly obtain an answer, or at least the
report of the administration of the Telegraphs. Nothing has occurred in other respects but what is agreeable. Every exhibition
of the Telegraph calls forth increased admiration. I have nothing
to complain of on the score of approbation; its simplicity, and su-

periority to all other proposed telegraphs are constantly adverted to by all the *savants*. The Count Remberteau, the Prefect of the Seine, whom I mentioned in a former letter as having been to see me, speaks in terms of admiration of the Telegraph on all occasions. He has doubtless spoken of it to the king, as he said he should; but the king, besides his troubles just now in the formation of a new cabinet, has a domestic affliction which he feels strongly. His daughter, the Duchess of Wurtemberg, whose death has been announced for some time, was buried yesterday, the body having arrived from Italy. This has probably caused some delay. I have need of much patience. . . . I am looking with great interest for intelligence from America, in regard to Telegraph operations there; for I hope more from my own country than from any other. There is more of the 'go-ahead' character with us, suited to the idea of an electric-magnetic Telegraph. Here there are old systems long established to interfere, and at least to make them cautious before adopting a new project, however promising. Their railroad operations are a proof in point. We, on the contrary, have a clear field, and I cannot but hope something from our Government, or our companies, in a speedy establishment of the system. All my leisure (if that may be called leisure which employs nearly all my time) is devoted to perfecting the whole matter. The invention of the correspondent, I think you will all say, is a more essential improvement. It has been my winter's labor, and, to avoid expense, I have been compelled to make it entirely with my own hands. I can now give you its exact dimensions—twelve and a half inches long, six and a half wide, and six and a half deep. It dispenses entirely with boxes of type (one set alone being necessary), and dispenses, also, with the rules, and with all machinery for moving the rules. There is no winding up, and it is ready at all times. You touch the letter, and the letter is written immediately at the other extremity. The instrument will be in operation this week. Before closing, I ought to advert to the most singular winter we have thus far had in Paris. It has been, with the exception of a day or two, like spring. I doubt if it has frozen to the depth of two inches, until yesterday, anywhere in Paris. It is now cold but fine.

" P. S.—I have this moment received official notice from the Academy of Industry, under the presidency of the Duke de Montmorency, that a committee of that society had been appointed to examine my Telegraph; and that to-morrow at three o'clock they will come to see it. Thus progress is slowly made toward the end desired, for the opinion of these societies has great weight with the Government, and the more they can be accumulated the better. I sent you by the last packet the report (favorable) of the committee of the Philotechnique Society. In my next I hope to send you reports of my further progress. One thing seems certain, my Telegraph has driven out of the field all the other plans on the magnetic principle. I hear nothing of them in public or private. No society notices them."

Under date of February 2d he wrote again: "I can compare the state of things here to an April day, at one moment sunshine, at the next cloudy. The Telegraph is evidently growing in favor; testimonials of approbation and compliments multiply; and yesterday I was advised by the secretary of the Académie Industrielle to interest moneyed men in the matter, if I intended to profit by it; and he observed that now was the precise time to do it, in the interval of the Chambers. I am at a loss how to act. I am not a business man, and fear every movement which suggests itself to me. I am thinking of proposing a company on the same plan you last proposed in your letter from Liverpool, and which you intend to create in case the Government shall choose to do nothing; that is to say, a company taking the right at one thousand francs per mile, paying the proprietors fifty per cent. in stocks, and fifty per cent. in cash, raising about fifty thousand francs for a trial some distance. I shall take advice, and let you know the result. I wish you were here; I am sure something could be done by an energetic and business man like yourself. As for poor me, I feel that I am a child in business matters. I can invent and perfect the invention, and demonstrate its uses and practicability; but 'further the deponent saith not.' Perhaps I underrate myself in this case, but that is not a usual fault in human nature.

"I had the committee of the Académie Industrielle to examine the Telegraph last Wednesday, according to appointment. The same effect was produced upon them as usual—skepticism giving way by degrees, and changing to enthusiastic feeling and expression. The Academy will publish their report soon, a copy of which I will send you. It is one of the most distinguished and numerous bodies of *savants* in Europe, numbering between three and four thousand members, in various countries, so that whatever they say will be widely diffused, and I think it will be altogether favorable. I learned, from one of the directors, that my Telegraph is commented on with approbation throughout all Europe, in the scientific and political journals of all the capitals. M. Jobart, the editor of the *Courrier Belge*, of Brussels, particularly, who some time since asserted the possibility of an electric telegraph, has, I understand, commented with enthusiasm on mine.

"With the committee of the Academy came several members of the Chamber of Deputies, one of whom observed to me : ' The Government should by all means own this invention ; it is of vastly more importance than the daguerreotype, which is proposed to the Chambers. Why has it not been offered to the Government ? ' I replied that it had been submitted for several months to the Government, and that my patience had been severely tried in waiting for an answer from the Minister of the Interior. He observed that, if ministers choose to be so dilatory, the Chambers must take it up ; and, says he, ' I will expedite it. Would you have any objection to show the Telegraph in operation before the Chambers ? ' ' None at all,' I replied ; ' on the contrary, I shall be ready at any moment to wait upon them.' ' I will see the questor,' he said, ' and give you notice. M. Arago spoke in the highest commendation of your invention, as being superior to the German invention, but his representations fall short of the reality. I am delighted in the highest degree. The value and importance of this Telegraph are incalculable.'

"This is the substance and nearly the words of the conversation with this member of the Chambers, who spoke English perfectly well. This is the *sunshine*, but the *clouds* are obscuring it, for the cabinet this moment is dissolved by the king (a perilous step), and a new election and assembling will consume two months of time. You will perceive that, in all the disappointments and delays to which the enterprise here has been subjected, there is not one that affects the character of the invention. Every repeated examination of it, by *savants* and committees of scientific societies, only confirms the soundness of its principles and its intrinsic value.

"The labors on the instruments—the correspondent and register, bringing them into one box, in a portable form—you will find are to produce a most interesting change in the whole affair—a change which is not perhaps at first obvious. If made portable, as the improvement I have completed accomplishes, a person traveling, with a box not so large as a writing-desk, can converse on any part of an extended line of thousands of miles with his friends at any other part.

"But its importance, in a military point of view, is incalculable, a hint of which I gave you in a former letter. I have little time and space to add—I expect much from my own 'go-ahead' countrymen. I have received with your letter Dr. Gale's, and am glad he visits Washington with you. Give my respects to him and your lady, whom congratulate from me on your safe return after so many perils. Next Tuesday I have another exhibition of the Telegraph to a room full of *savants* and nobles, the Prince of Rouen (not ruin) at their head, with the Duke de Montmorency, etc., and others, 'too numerous to mention.' I have but two or three weeks here, and hope I shall receive such instructions from you that I can leave matters properly. I must return in the Great Western, on the 25th of March. My family requires my presence, and I cannot neglect them."

The Professor experienced the greatest elevation of hope, followed by the deepest depression of disappointment that at any time befell him, in a negotiation for the invention, and for his own services, that was assumed in the name of the Russian Government by the Baron Meyendorf. His letters will give a correct idea of his feelings. He wrote to Mr. Smith, under date of Paris, July 13, 1839:

"I have been wholly occupied for the last week in copying out the correspondence and other documents, to defend myself against the infamous attack of Dr. Jackson, notice of which my brother sent me. I have sent it this day by Dr. Mitchell, who sails in the Ville de Lyon, on the 16th—the same packet that takes this. I have sent a letter to Dr. Jackson, calling on him to save his character by a total disclaimer of his presumptuous claim, within one week from the receipt of the letter, and giving him the plea of a 'mistake' and 'misconception of my invention,' by which he may retreat. If he fails to do this, I have requested my brother to publish immediately my defense, in which I give a history of the invention, the correspondence between Dr. Jackson and myself, and close with the letters of Hon. Mr. Rives, Mr. Fisher, of Philadelphia, and Captain Pell. I cannot conceive of such infatuation as has possessed this man. He can scarcely be deceived. It must be his consummate self-conceit that deceives him, if he is deceived. But this cannot be ; he knows he has no title whatever to a single hint of any kind in the matter.

"I received your second letter, authorizing me to draw on you

for such moneys as I may want; a closer calculation will oblige
me to draw for two hundred pounds, instead of one hundred and
fifty, as I told you I should in my last, for it is possible that I
shall be compelled to stay a little longer than I anticipated, in
consequence of some prospects favorable from Russia. The Baron
Meyendorf, the Russian Government agent for reporting to the
Emperor all important discoveries, has been to see the Telegraph. He is very much pleased with it, and says he shall report
it to his Government. He introduced to me M. Amyot, who has
proposed also an Electric Telegraph, but upon seeing mine he
could not restrain his gratification, and with his whole soul he is
at work to forward it with all who have influence. He is the
right-hand man of the Baron Meyendorf, and he is exerting all
his powers to have the Russian Government adopt my Telegraph.
To the objections of the various *savants* who were present yesterday at the experiment, that the great difficulty was with the wires,
to prevent their being destroyed by malevolence, he replied that
even this, which was the only plausible objection which would be
urged, was in reality nothing—that, placed beneath a railroad,
they were perfectly secure, for the men that watched the rails
would also watch the wires. I go with him to-morrow, to search
for the drawings of Sömmering's and Steinheil's Telegraph, with
a description of them, at the Institute. He is really a noble-minded
man. The baron told me he had a *large soul*, and I find he has.
I have no claim on him, and yet he seems to take as much interest
in my invention as if it were his own. How different a conduct
from Jackson's! In mentioning obligations, I ought to speak of my
room-mate, Rev. M. Kirk; I am indebted to him mediately for all
the success I have had among the *savants* here. His acquaintance
with M. Julien de Paris, and others, has been of great service,
and his knowledge of the language, of which I am ignorant, enabling him to explain the whole process at my various experiments,
has made him invaluable to me. Indeed, I don't know what I
should have done without him. You will have learned how the
dissolution of the Chambers has created further delay in my business. I was on the very point of having a call to exhibit it to the
Chambers at the moment they were dissolved. I learned through
M. Amyot, that the Government were seriously thinking of establishing a telegraphic line on the electric principle between Paris
and Havre, but that, such was the political state of affairs, nothing would certainly be done this year. But he thought it would

eventually be done, and that mine (if I understood him right) would be the one adopted, or ought to be the one adopted. As to forming a company to take it, I find it impracticable, for this reason: the Telegraph is a Government monopoly, and therefore I am dependent wholly on them. The Government allows no commercial or social use of the Telegraph; and the reason why the railroads have not taken hold is, that Government have not decided whether they can allow it. I get no answer yet from the Minister of the Interior. Do you think your patience would hold out as long? I begin to doubt whether I shall obtain any. Indeed, but for the aspect of things North, the sooner I return home the better. I do not see that I can further benefit the concern at present, here, except by making it known to the various learned men; this obtains honor, to be sure, and spreads its merits; and profit may be a consequence at some future time. I shall, if possible, make this sort of arrangement with the baron, if he should propose any thing from Russia, viz., that I should return to America immediately, and visit Russia, or send an agent, in the summer, for I must return and arrange my affairs for the change which this Telegraph has compelled me to make. He may require an answer from St. Petersburg, and that would delay me; but I had better return and come out again, if necessary, with a more perfected and compact instrument, which I cannot get here, situated as I am.

" I give you a piece of good news in the following article from the *Journal des Débats* of Sunday, February 10th: 'They wrote from Munich the 3d of February, that the Bavarian Government has ordered that the Galvanic Telegraph of the invention of M. de Steinheil, Professor of Chemistry in the University Royal of Munich, will be established on the railroad from Furth to Wurtemberg, and that direction of these telegraphs will be confided to this learned professor.'

" I wish our Government had been the first to adopt the Telegraph; but now the Bavarians have the credit of being the first to establish an Electric Telegraph; but this first adoption gives assurance of their final universal adoption, and if mine is best, as all continue to affirm, mine must supplant all, unless a better (Dr. Jackson's, perhaps) should be found.

" I yesterday paid the balance of patent account, eight hundred and fifty francs, and have the receipt and the patent for the railroad improvement. If I get my correspondence in action satisfactorily, which will no doubt be the case if I can apply myself a few days longer to its completion (having been interrupted so continually, and never allowing the other business of the Telegraph to suffer from any attention to these mechanical improvements, I have been constantly prevented from giving it the finishing touch), I shall venture to add it to the improvements. This will incur an additional expense to you of one hundred and eighty-seven francs. I have these two days past tried the sustaining power of the little batteries, three in number, on Daniel's principle, and to my gratification I find that by simply supplying the top that holds the crystals with them as fast as they dissolve—and this has been but three times in the last forty-eight hours! and of the amount altogether in size of a couple of eggs—the action has been kept up undiminished the whole time, day and night. I intend letting the batteries act themselves out, and will report to you the result.[1] It is a fact of very important bearing, as you see, on the Telegraph. Every day is clearing away all the difficulties that prevent its adoption; the only difficulty that remains, it is universally said, is the protection of the wires from malevolent attack, and this can be prevented by proper police, and secret and deep interment. I have no doubt of its universal adoption; it may take time, but it is certain. I have not yet received the reports in Congress that you say you have sent, but have heard there are packages for me at Havre. I am anxious to know the progress made at home. When is income to take the place of outgo? I wish you could see my brother on the subject of Jackson, and arrange with him. Perhaps you could yourself see Jackson, and see what his design is in this infamous attack of his."

On the 22d of the same month he wrote Mr. Smith from Paris the subjoined exultant letter:

" I have a moment to write to be in time for the packet of the 24th by estafet, and to give you at length a dish of good news respecting the Telegraph. A few days ago at my usual exhibition of the Telegraph on Tuesdays, which I have had for two months past, Monsieur Julien de Paris brought the Baron Meyendorf, the agent of the Emperor of Russia for reporting useful discoveries to the Russian Government. The baron was much struck with the Telegraph, and, learning from me that the administrator-in-chief of Telegraphs in Paris had reported favorably, he wished to know

---

[1] I let the batteries remain fifty-four hours, and they were still powerful enough, but a little enfeebled. There is no difficulty on that score.

if I could procure the report for him, and he would at once transmit it to his Government and recommend the adoption of my Telegraph. I called on the administrator, M. Foy, with your request,
as a member of Congress, to have the report. I did not find him
in, but I left a note requesting a copy of his report. I have just
received an answer from M. Foy, which, although not complying
(from very proper reasons which he assigns) with my request for a
copy of the report, yet gives me all we could wish; I give you a
translation of the letter entire:

"'PARIS, *February* 20, 1839.

"'CABINET OF THE ADMINISTRATOR-IN-CHIEF.

"MY DEAR SIR: I regret sincerely that I was not at home
when you did me the honor to call. I would have fully explained
to you the impossibility of communicating to you my observations
addressed to the Minister of the Interior upon Electric Telegraphs.
These observations make part of my administrative correspondence
with the minister, and I cannot detach them from it with propriety.
I believe, too, my dear sir, that you exaggerate to yourself the importance and extent of it. I had only to submit a summary notice
upon many electric and electro-magnetic Telegraphs which had
been successively put under the eyes of the minister, and my observations were relative only to the projects announced for M. Montalivet to make some essays upon this new kind of telegraphic
communication. You will not then find, my dear sir, as you think,
a detailed and mature report upon your beautiful invention, and
the note that I might address to you would be altogether unworthy the attention of Congress. If, however, I do not believe it of
use to you, sir, nor possible for me to give you a copy of an administrative letter which relates to many personal matters, I take a
true pleasure in confirming to you in writing that which I have already had the honor to say to you *viva voce*, that I have signalized
to monsieur, the Minister of the Interior, your Electro-magnetic
Telegraph, as being the system which presents the best chance of
a practical application, and that I had declared that, if some trials
are to be made with electric Telegraphs, I hesitate not to propose
that they should be made with your apparatus. I thank you, my
dear sir, for the kind offer you have had the goodness to make, of
permitting me to come and see your admirable experiments, of
which I shall avail myself as soon as the recent domestic affliction
which now occupies my mind will allow. Accept, my dear sir,

the assurance of the distinguished consideration of your devoted
servant,   ALPHONSE FOY.'

" This, you perceive, is all that is necessary ; it could not be
more flattering or more favorable. The deficiencies of detail in a
comparison of mine with others will be fully made up in the ' Report of the Académie Industrielle,' which I heard read last evening
at a grand meeting of the Academy at the Place Vendôme ; and in
which both the priority of my invention and its superiority to all
others are fully declared. It was received with acclamation, and I
had the Telegraph there to talk to them. There is truly a liberality in the French scientific classes that I think reflects the greatest credit upon the nation. This report will be published in a few
days, and I will bring a copy, or rather many copies, with me. But
the tidbit of the dish now comes. The Baron Meyendorf did not
write for this note (for I have but this moment received it, and
have not yet shown it to him). He intimated to me that he had
for a long time been in treaty with M. Amyot, who has for some
time been engaged in electric Telegraphs, to establish one in Russia ; that if M. Amyot and I could agree to unite our labors he
would immediately put matters in train for the establishment of a
line of twenty miles from St. Petersburg. I had an interview
with M. Amyot, a noble-hearted, liberal man, and our union was
easily formed. He wished much to accompany me—to take, in fact,
exactly that part in which I needed most the assistance of an experienced scientific man—to make the experiments on the effects of
temperature on the passage of electricity, the size of batteries
necessary, etc. He has philological researches in which he feels also
a deep interest, and on account of which he desires to go to Russia. He wished me merely to state to the baron that I should be
glad to have him (M. Amyot) accompany me. With this understanding I yesterday called on the baron, and so far as he (the
baron) is concerned the whole matter is nearly arranged. I gave
him the estimate of probable expense of establishing a line of
twenty miles, exclusive of ditching, asphalt, and some smaller
items, putting the whole at seven hundred and ninety-four pounds
sterling. He at once said eight hundred pounds, and, add extras,
two hundred pounds more, say one thousand pounds ; and, says he,
' You have omitted the price of your passage from America and back
again,' which he calculated and added. ' Now,' says he, ' what will
you expect of it if it is successful ? ' I said, whatever the emperor

25

may think just.   He answered: ' No, this is not the way we do
business; will you put it on this basis, to receive for five years half
the saving to the Government of your plan over that of the old plan?'
I said yes, if in calculating this saving these points shall be taken
into the account :

"First, the time in which the two Telegraphs are available.
Second, the quantity of information in a given time that each can
transmit under the most favorable circumstances. He said: ' Well,
this I will immediately submit to my Government.   You wish to
return to the United States.   Can you return to Paris by the 1st
of July, so as to be in St. Petersburg by the 15th of July?'   I
told him I thought I could.   ' Well,' said he, ' you will return, then,
I suppose, by the Great Western to New York, on the 23d of March;
arrive, say 10th of April.   You will receive the answer of the Russian Government through its minister in the United States about
the 10th of May.   You will embark from New York about 1st of
June, be in Paris 1st of July, and St. Petersburg 15th of July.   In
fifteen days the trench can be dug, for we have eighty thousand
men at command; and these can be sufficient to dig the trench in
seven days if you desire it.   The emperor will then be in St. Petersburg, which will be favorable to you.'

" Other items I must tell you when I see you in America, for I
feel now that something is likely to be effected; but our whole
energies must be directed to having this first adoption of our system a successful one; all hands must go to work.   What I shall
wish immediately on my return is a clock mechanician, who can
devote himself wholly to making, say six or eight of each of the
machines, the correspondent and. the register, with the simplifica-
tion that a winter's thought and experience have led me to form.
The compensation I have proposed to M. Amyot is one-seventh of
what is received from the Russian Government when the experiment is proved successful.   I hope this will be approved by you.
He appears satisfied with it, and, taking into the account that he
relinquishes his own schemes with the Russian Government, and
strongly advocates with the baron the adoption of mine—that, in
fact, without this arrangement nothing probably would have been
done, for the baron made it conditional; and, moreover, the responsibility he assumes of precisely that part which has not been actually proved by experiment—I think the terms just.   We have nothing to do with his personal expenses; the Russian Government
pay these as well as mine.   I have to close this immediately or I

shall lose the estafet. I have engaged my passage in the Great Western on the 23d of March, and hope to be in New York before 10th of April, perhaps even before this reaches you. I wish I could see you in New York when I arrive. I have just made a proposition to the baron, through M. Amyot, to advance three thousand francs to me in New York so soon as the Government have determined to adopt the system—if it is accepted, well; if not, it will be worth a little risk to seize the present motive to give impulse to the whole business; and funds must be advanced by the company. I have written to Mr. Chamberlain to make new terms in consideration of the change which matters have assumed, and the necessity I am under of personal superintendence in Russia. I hope you will at home also consider this, and arrange justly my proper compensation. On this point I have no fears from those engaged in the enterprise.

"I will write you again, but think I shall probably see you before another letter can reach you by the packet."

"PARIS, *March* 2, 1839.

"By my last letter I informed you of the more favorable prospects of the telegraphic enterprise. These prospects still continue, and I shall return with the gratifying reflection that, after all my anxieties and labors and privations, and yours and my other associates' expenditures and risks, we are all in a fair way of reaping the fruits of our toil. The political troubles of France have been a hinderance hitherto to the attention of the Government to the Telegraph, but in the mean time I have gradually pushed forward the invention into the notice of the most influential individuals of France. I had Colonel Lasalle, aide-de-camp to the king, and his lady, to see the Telegraph a few days ago; he promised that without fail it should be mentioned to the king. You will be surprised to learn, after all the promises hitherto made by the prefect of the Seine, Count Remberteau, and by various other officers of the Government, and after General Cass's letter to the aide on service, four or five months since, requesting it might be brought to the notice of the king, that the king has not yet heard of it. But so things go here. Such dereliction would destroy a man with us in a moment, but here there is a different standard (this, of course, *entre nous*).

"I have just had a visit from the Count de Noe, a peer of France, who brought with him the Duc de Cazes and the Duchess, and the Baron Pasquier, the chancellor of France, with the baroness, to see the Telegraph. The duke was surprised to learn that the Government had had the subject so long under consideration, especially after the administrator of the Telegraphs had reported in its favor, and promised me that he would see immediately the Count de Montalivet on the subject. I told him if any thing was to be done, it was necessary to move quick. I had been in attendance on the Government for an answer the whole winter; that I should leave France in a few days; that Russia had seen the advantage of the invention to her empire, and that I was in treaty to go to St. Petersburg. This seemed to have some effect, and he said there should be no delay. Among the numerous visitors that have thronged to see the Telegraph, there have been a great many of the principal English nobility. Among them, the Lord and Lady Aylmer, formerly Governor of Canada, Lord Elgin and son, the celebrated preserver, not depredator, as he has been most slanderously called, of the Phidian Marbles. Lord Elgin has been twice, and expressed a great interest in the invention. He brought with him yesterday the Earl of Lincoln, a young man of unassuming manners; he was delighted, and gave me his card, with a pressing invitation to call on him when I came to London. I have not failed to let the English know how I was treated in regard to my application for a patent in England, and contrasted the conduct of the French in this respect with theirs. I believe they felt it, and I think it was Lord Aylmer, but am not quite sure, who advised that the subject be brought up in Parliament by some member and made the object of special legislation, which he said might be done, the attorney-general to the contrary notwithstanding. I really believe, if matters were rightly managed in England, something yet might be done there, if not by patent, yet by a parliamentary grant of a proper compensation. It is remarkable that they have not yet made any thing like mine in England. It is evident that neither Wheatstone nor Davy comprehended my mode, after all their assertions that mine was published. If matters move slower here than with us, yet they gain surely. I am told every hour that the two great wonders of Paris just now, about which everybody is conversing, are, Daguerre's wonderful results in fixing permanently the image of the *camera obscura* and Morse's Electro-Magnetic Telegraph; and they do not hesitate to add that, beautiful as are the results of Daguerre's experiments, the invention of the Electro-Magnetic Telegraph is that which will surpass, in the greatness of the revolution to be effected, all other inventions. Robert Walsh, Esq., who has just left me, is beyond measure delighted. I was writing a word from one room to another; he came to me and said, 'The next word you may write is, "IMMORTALITY," for the sublimity of this invention is of surpassing grandeur. *I see now that all physical obstacles which may for a while hinder, will inevitably be overcome ; the problem is solved ;* MAN MAY INSTANTLY CONVERSE WITH HIS FELLOW-MAN IN ANY PART OF THE WORLD.'

"I have sent in to the Baron Meyendorf the details of the engagement between the Russian Government and myself, formed on the basis agreed on in conversation with him, and which I mentioned in my last letter to you. I am anxiously waiting his reply and approval, in order to take my departure from Paris. I have taken my passage in the Great Western, and will give you, when I see you, all the information on this matter which is too long to write. I am glad I had the letters of the captain and passengers of the Sully *with me.* Jackson's impudent assertion of a claim to my invention was talked about much here, and, although disbelieved by my friends without any evidence, but simply from knowing me, it made for a little time an unpleasant state of things. I read these letters to General Cass, to M. Anderson, and to many others, and the antidote has been effectual, and a pretty strong tide of indignation raised against Jackson.... Providentially, I have proof at every point of the futility and baseness of his claim, and, where others could not be witnesses, he is made to witness against *himself.* I am anxious to see you and concert measures for pushing matters, for the iron is hot all over Europe and we must strike now. *A Telegraph Company ought to be formed at once for operations all over the world.* Depend upon it, fifty or a hundred fortunes might be made out of it. It wants only a proper management, and a little capital. Hoping soon to see you, I remain, as ever, truly yours,

"SAMUEL F. B. MORSE."

MORSE AND DAGUERRE.

While in Paris, Professor Morse could not fail to hear of the brilliant and astonishing experiments of M. Daguerre, whose genius and perseverance were then bringing to the birth one of the most beautiful discoveries of this or any age. Professor Morse invited him to examine his Telegraph, and also requested permission to see the results of Daguerre's experiments in the art of painting with sunbeams. As an artist and painter, Morse was naturally anxious to know the meaning of this new art. M. Daguerre promptly acceded to the invitation, and the remarkable results that followed the instructions which Mr. Morse received from the discoverer, the introduction by Mr. Morse of the art into the United States of America, and the identification of his name with Photography as well as with the Telegraph, will be seen in subsequent pages.

Professor Morse alludes, in his letters from Paris, to the interest which some of the British nobility were taking in the Telegraph. . Among them were Lord Lincoln (afterward the Duke of Newcastle) and Lord Elgin. Lord Elgin wrote to him:

" PARIS, *March* 5, 1839.

"You would oblige me greatly if you could allow me to bring my family and some particular friends to have the pleasure of seeing your admirable discovery of the Electric Telegraph, under the great advantage of your exhibition of it, on Thursday next, the 7th inst., at two o'clock—or any other day and hour that would better suit you. I venture to name a private day, because we shall be numerous enough to fill your apartment. Lord Lincoln was extremely sorry that, the departure being quite necessarily fixed for Saturday, he could not have a second opportunity of admiring the beauty and simplicity of your brilliant discovery. I have the honor to be, dear sir, your obedient servant,

" ELGIN."

The visit was made, and a few days afterward Lord Elgin wrote to Professor Morse again :

"I cannot help expressing a very strong desire that, instead of delaying till your return from America your wish to take out a patent in England for your highly scientific and simple mode of communicating intelligence by an Electric Telegraph, you would take measures to that effect at this moment, and for that purpose take your model now with you to London. Your discovery is now much known as well as appreciated, and the ingenuity now afloat is too extensive for one not to apprehend that individuals, even in good faith, may make some addition to qualify them to take out a *first patent* for the principle ; whereas, if you brought it at once, now, before the competent authorities, especially under the advantage of an introduction such as Mr. Drummond can give you to Lord Brougham, a short delay in your proceeding to America may secure this desirable object immediately. With every sincere good wish for your success and the credit you so richly deserve, I am, dear sir, yours faithfully, ELGIN.

"MR. PRESIDENT MORSE."

To Sir Henry Ellis, Lord Elgin wrote:

"DEAR SIR HENRY: I beg leave to make you acquainted with Mr. President Morse, of the National Academy of Design at New York. He has on a former occasion studied the Elgin Marbles; still, if he should wish again to see them, on his present passage through London, I am sure you will have the kindness to give him every facility in your power. He is engaged in perfecting an Electric Telegraph of the highest possible interest; he may possibly not have it with him at this moment, but the beauty and simplicity of his invention, and the ability and clearness with which he explains it, argue much talent and intelligence on his part."

His work in Paris being completed, and nothing more being gained than the positive approbation of his invention by the greatest authorities in the scientific world, Professor Morse went to London, and was immediately invited by Lord Lincoln to make his house the theatre for the exhibition of the Telegraph.

"At the request of the Earl of Lincoln," Professor Morse wrote, "I exhibited at his house my Telegraph to a large company assembled for the purpose; members of the Houses of Parliament, the Lords of the Admiralty, and members of the Royal Society. As a counterpoise to the injustice done me in England in regard to my patent application, I ought to mention the kind interest taken by Lord Elgin, the Earl of Lincoln, Hon. Henry Drummond, and others, in my invention, and their offers of service in procuring for me a patent by a special act of Parliament, which, under other circumstances, might have been procured."

Professor Morse endeavored to secure the attention of Lord Brougham to his invention, and, in reply to his letter requesting an interview, received the following characteristic note:

"Lord Brougham's compliments, and is extremely sorry he is not able to make an appointment to see Mr. Morse; he is engaged every day this week, at the House of Lords, from ten o'clock to dinner-time, and on some days to a later hour. However, if Mr. M.

can come to the House any morning before three, Lord B. will be able to come out to him for a few minutes."

Mr. Morse replied to his lordship:

"Mr. Morse's respects to Lord Brougham, and would say to him that, through the kindness of the Earl of Lincoln, the Telegraph apparatus of Mr. M.'s invention is, for a single day only, at Lord Lincoln's house, 25 Park Lane, where Mr. M. has engaged to show its operation to-morrow (Wednesday), from eleven o'clock until five. Mr. M. scarcely dares hope for the pleasure of Lord Brougham's presence, absorbed as he must be in public affairs; but, if Lord B. could by any means spare a moment for that purpose, Mr. M. need not say how gratified he should be to exhibit his invention to Lord Brougham. Mr. M. will avail himself of Lord B.'s invitation to see him a moment, on Thursday, between ten and eleven, at the House of Lords."

The kindness and consideration shown to Professor Morse by these distinguished men in London made a lasting impression upon his heart. In after years, when the Prince of Wales visited the United States, Professor Morse was invited to address him at the University of the City of New York, and in his remarks recognized the fact that the Duke of Newcastle, who was with the Prince of Wales, was no other than the Earl of Lincoln of 1839. Mr. Morse said:

"An allusion in most flattering terms to me, rendered doubly so in such presence, has been made by our respected Chancellor, which seems to call for at least the expression of my thanks. At the same time it suggests the relation of an incident in the early history of the Telegraph, which may not be inappropriate to this occasion. The infant Telegraph, born and nursed within these walls, had scarcely attained a feeble existence, ere it essayed to make its voice heard on the other side of the Atlantic. I carried it to Paris in 1838. It attracted the warm interest not only of the Continental philosophers, but also of the intelligent and appreciative among the eminent nobles of Britain, then on a visit to the French capital. Foremost among these was the late Marquis of Northampton, then President of the Royal Society, the late distinguished Earl of Elgin, and in a marked degree the noble Earl of Lincoln. The last-named nobleman, in a special manner, gave it his favor; he comprehended its important future, and, in the midst of the skepticism that clouded its cradle, he risked his character for sound judgment in venturing to stand godfather to the friendless child. He took it under his roof in London, invited the statesmen and the philosophers of Britain to see it, and urged forward with kindly words and generous attentions those who had the infant in charge. It is with no ordinary feelings, therefore, that after the lapse of twenty years I have the singular honor this morning of greeting with hearty welcome, in such presence, before such an assemblage, and in the cradle of the Telegraph, this noble Earl of Lincoln, in the person of the present Duke of Newcastle."

CHAPTER X.

1839–1843.

RETURN TO NEW YORK—RUSSIAN CONTRACT—DISAPPOINTMENT AT INACTION
OF CONGRESS—MR. SMITH'S VIEWS OF THE STATE OF THINGS—THE DA-
GUERREOTYPE—INTRODUCED EXPERIMENTS—SUCCESS—TEACHES OTHERS—
SULLY AND ALLSTON—RUSSIA FAILS—DEEP DEPRESSION—LETTER TO HIS
PARTNERS MR. A. VAIL AND HON. F. O. J. SMITH—CONSULTATION WITH
PROFESSOR HENRY—LETTERS OF PROFESSOR HENRY—STRUGGLES OF MORSE
UNDER POVERTY—LETTERS TO MR. VAIL—AN AGENT EMPLOYED AT WASH-
INGTON—FAILURE—AN OLD SORROW—HON. W. W. BOARDMAN, M. C.—
LETTER TO HON. F. O. J. SMITH ON PROFESSOR HENRY'S ENCOURAGE-
MENT—FIRST SUBMARINE CABLE LAID BY PROFESSOR MORSE—REPORT OF
AMERICAN INSTITUTE—HON. C. G. FERRIS—LETTER TO HIM—PROFESSOR
MORSE IN WASHINGTON—FAVORABLE REPORT IN CONGRESS—DEBATE—
PASSAGE OF BILL IN THE HOUSE AND THE SENATE—APPROPRIATING THIRTY
THOUSAND DOLLARS FOR AN EXPERIMENTAL LINE OF TELEGRAPH—DEATH
OF ALLSTON.

PROFESSOR MORSE arrived in New York by the steamship Great Western, on his return from England, April 15, 1839. The next day he wrote to his partner, Hon. F. O. J. Smith:

" I take the first hour of rest, after the fatigues of my boisterous voyage, to apprise you of my arrival yesterday in the Great Western. The day before I left Paris, I concluded the arrangements with the Russian Government, through the Baron Meyendorf, so far as he had power, and shall expect, through the Russian Minister, the answer of the Government at St. Petersburg by the 10th of May. There are some points different from those which I believe I sketched in my letter to you of February 22d. In the second interview, the baron believes he had limited the compensation—'half the economy'—to three years instead of five, as both M. Amyot and myself understood him to say. He seemed a little troubled at this, and reproached himself for not putting it down in writing at the time, for he had written *three years* to his Government, and it was too late to rectify the matter; but he observed that, if I were successful, I might rely on the liberal disposition of the emperor. It is limited also to the route from St. Petersburg to Warsaw, eight hundred miles. I wish much to see you, and with as little delay as possible, for the time is very limited, on account of the season of the year in which it is necessary to be in St. Petersburg, in order to labor at all. I was so unfortunate as to miss Dr. Gale by a single day; he left for the South on Saturday, and I arrrived on Sunday night. I regret this extremely, for I wished much conversation with him on points connected with the scientific parts of the matter. . . .

" I am quite disappointed in finding nothing done by Congress, and nothing accomplished by way of Company. I had hoped to find, on my return home, funds ready for prosecuting with vigor the enterprise which I fear will suffer for this want.

" Think for a moment of my situation! I left New York for Europe to be gone three months, but have been gone eleven months. My only means of support are in my profession, which I have been compelled to abandon entirely for the present, giving my undivided time and efforts to this enterprise. I return without a farthing in my pocket, and have to borrow even for my meals, and, even worse than this, I have incurred a debt of rent by my absence, which I should have avoided had I been at home, or rather if I had been aware that I should have been obliged to stay so long abroad. I do not mention this in the way of complaint, but merely to show that I have also been compelled to make great sacrifices for the common good, and am willing yet to make more, if necessary. If the enterprise is to be pursued, we must all in our various ways put the shoulder to the wheel. I wish much to see you and talk over all matters, for it seems to me that the present state of the enterprise in regard to Russia affects vitally the whole concern."

In communicating these letters from Professor Morse, Mr. Smith makes some observations upon the hesitation of governments and individuals to perceive the splendid capabilities of the invention :

" In the days of the first consulship of Napoleon I., the car of

sovereignty was not so barricaded against all knowledge of reverberating acclamations of distinguished scientists and inventors over
the advances of their respective pursuits for the benefit of mankind,
as it seems to have been in the days of Louis Philippe, liberal as he
was reputed to be, when Professor Morse was visiting Paris, to
make known the wonders of the Electro-Magnetic Telegraph. On
the 20th of March, A. D. 1800, the philosopher named Volta, in a
little village of the Milanese, announced to Sir Joseph Banks,
President of the Royal Society of England, by letter, his beautiful discovery and invention of utilizing the previously miscon-
ceived discovery of Galvani, regardless on his part of any special
application, but as the agent of analyzing the laws of matter and
Nature in general. To the discovery he added a description of his
device for collecting the electric force in greater quantities than
ever before accomplished, and of securing to it all the intensity of
frictional electricity, and also of retaining its action for a longer
time—this by what he designated *La Couronne de Tasses*, or
crown of cups. No sooner had this announcement reached France,
than Napoleon, the First Consul, instead of waiting for Volta to
voluntarily visit Paris, if ever, as a scientist and inventor of eminence, as did Professor Morse in 1838, most flatteringly invited
Volta to make a visit to Paris, and at the Institute explain personally his great invention to the *élite* of European philosophers.
Accordingly, in 1801, Volta attended three meetings of the Academy of Science, where he explained his theory, and the *Voltaic*, or,
as he called it, *electro-motive àction* of different metals. Napoleon
attended in person these meetings; and, when the report of the
committee on the subject was read, Napoleon proposed to suspend
the rules of the Academy, in the formalities required in conferring
honors, and that the gold medal be immediately awarded to Volta,
as a testimony of the gratitude of the philosophers of France for
his discovery; and the proposition was carried by acclamation; and
on the same day Napoleon ordered to be sent to Volta two thousand crowns from the public treasury, to defray the expenses of his
journey. He also founded an annual medal of the value of two
thousand francs to him who should give electricity, or magnetism,
by his researches, an impulse comparable to that which it received
from the discoveries of Franklin and Volta.

"The long stride which Volta laid the foundation for, though
not dreamed of for the purpose by him at the time, in the use of
electricity for telegraphic purposes in after-years, forms an interest-

ing epoch in the history of the Telegraph, though not particularly
germane to the biography of Professor Morse.

"The contrast, however, presented in this experience of the liberality of Napoleon toward Volta, and in the eight months' ignorance by King Louis Philippe of both the invention of the Electro-
magnetic Telegraph and of Professor Morse's stay in Paris, under
illusory promises of the king's cabinet ministers, and his other
many and immediate official attendants, to bring the invention to
the knowledge of the king, is not without its moral to the American
mind. Had the scientists of France in the latter era been as near
Louis Philippe as those of France were to the First Consul, and
had the former been endowed with the same impulses as was the
latter, in the advancement of his government and people to the
zenith of national glory and greatness, who can doubt that Professor Morse's visit to Paris in 1838 would have been signaled by
the prompt construction of an Electro-magnetic Telegraph upon his
plan, through hundreds of miles of French territory, and even to
every commercial city within the confines of the nation ? In such
a case, who can doubt that France would have been foremost and
the first of governments to adopt the great invention, and to utilize
it in advance of every other people ? And, then, what years of auxious and even agonizing suspense would have been saved to Professor Morse in particular, and to his associates, in the struggle to
advance the invention beyond its swaddling-clothes !

"It is foremost among the incomprehensible fatuities of mankind, and of their varied industrial ambitions and interests, that an
invention so patent to every understanding, in its wonders and
ubiquitous powers, should have lingered on, year after year, upon
the impoverished hands of the acknowledged inventor, without inspiring the cupidity of either capitalists or speculators, and especially in a land of enterprise like the United States. But so it was,
as the sequel of Professor Morse's authenticated experience shows."

Mr. Smith wrote to Professor Morse, April 28, 1839 :

"I see nothing yet of your *exposé* of Jackson. It is a shame
that such malignant envy and groundless pretensions should be
suffered to fatten, in any character or capacity, upon the credu-
lity of the people. I could, with your means, ram him into a ten-
pounder, then discharge the wad against the first mud-wall I could
find ! I am devoting my time wholly with reference to bringing
my loose and unsettled interests and business here to such control

—winding up all that are susceptible of it—as will enable me in a few months at farthest to take hold of the telegraph business in good earnest, and make a business of it. I esteem it far better to suffer it to rest, *sub silentio*, for a season, than to have it move in a halting, hobbling pace. I promise myself success in a little while, in thus putting myself in a shape to ' go ahead.' I pray God that, in the mean time, there may be ' no mistake ' about the Russian embassy."

Professor Morse to Mr. Smith.

"NEW YORK *May* 24, 1839.

" My affairs, in consequence of my protracted absence, and the stagnant state of the Telegraph here at home, have caused me great embarrassment, and my whole energies have been called upon to extricate myself from the confusion in which I have been unhappily placed. You may judge a little of this when I tell you that my absence has deprived me of my usual source of income by my profession ; that the state of the University is such that I shall probably leave, and shall have to remove into new quarters ; that my family are dispersed, requiring my care and anxieties, under every disadvantage ; that my engagements were such with Russia, that every moment of my time was necessary to complete my arrangements, to fulfil the contract in season ; and, instead of finding my associates ready to sustain me with counsel and means, I find them all dispersed, leaving me without the opportunity to consult, or a cent of means, and consequently bringing every thing in relation to the Telegraph to a dead stand. In the midst of this, I am called upon by the state of public opinion to defend myself against the outrageous attempt of Dr. Jackson to pirate from me my invention. The words would be harsh that are properly applicable to this man's conduct. He can no longer be under mistake ; he knows that he has not the shadow of a claim to a single suggestion that belongs to the invention. I send you my letter in the *Boston Post*, and republished in the *Observer*. Besides the evidence of Captain Pell, Mr. Rives, and Mr. Fisher, I have the written testimony of several others of the passengers, which I have obtained since I saw you, and they are all *unanimous* in recognizing me, and *me* only, in the invention on board the Sully. They none of them could guess the individual who pretends to the invention, and expressed utter astonishment when informed that Dr. Jackson pretended to it.

" I have given you the darker side of objects first. This darkness enshrouds the *inventor* only, not the invention. Want of time prevents me from copying out the papers relating to the Russian contract. It may suffice perhaps to say that I engaged to leave Europe in the Great Western on the 23d of March, was expected to arrive by the 5th of April, to commence the apparatus for a line of twenty miles of telegraph, if not already commenced by my associates; I was to receive my advices from St. Petersburg by the '10th of May,' officially recognizing the principles of the contract and negotiating the particulars with the Russian Minister; I engaged then to leave America so as to reach Paris by the 1st of July, and St. Petersburg by the 15th of July, with my French companion, M. Amyot. This was the farthest date that could be allowed, if the Telegraph was to be put in operation this season. You see, therefore, in what a condition I found myself when I returned. I was delayed several days beyond the computed time of my arrival by the long passage of the steamer. Instead of finding funds raised by a vote of Congress, or by a company, and my associates ready to back me, I find not a cent for the purpose, and my associates scattered to the four winds. You can easily conceive that I gave all up as it regarded Russia, and considered the whole enterprise as seriously injured if not completely destroyed. In this state of things I was hourly dreading to hear from the Russian Minister, and devising how I should save myself and the enterprise without implicating my associates in a charge of neglect; and, as it has most fortunately happened for us all, the 10th of May has passed without the receipt of the promised advices, and I took advantage of this, and, by the Liverpool steamer on the 18th, wrote to the Baron Meyendorff and to M. Amyot, that it was impossible to fulfill the engagement this season, since I had not received the promised advices in time to prepare. I have requested immediate advices, and promised to be in St. Petersburg by the beginning of May, next year, to fulfill the contract. This is the state of things in relation to Russia, in brief. I have much to communicate, but cannot by letter. I would come on to see you if I had the means, but I have not a copper. Now, what are immediately wanted are *two complete sets* at least of the apparatus, the register and correspondent, and if possible *twenty miles of wire*, so that every thing may be tested here at home, before I embark. I have a most excellent workman at command, who would execute them well and reasonably. It is at once seen how important it is to have matters immediately under way, if it is intended to take advantage of this Russian engagement. I wish to have every thing in prime order, so as to surprise the czar, and for the purpose the sooner I have the apparatus complete, the better; indeed, if I had five hundred dollars of my own (and it must cost much more), I would commence operations immediately.· We have ten miles of wire already; ten more would cost about three hundred and fifty dollars; and I think the other apparatus cannot cost more than one hundred and fifty dollars. Do think of this matter, and see if means cannot be raised to keep ahead with the American Telegraph. I sometimes am astonished when I reflect how I have been able to take the stand with my Telegraph in competition with my European rivals, backed as they are with the purses of the kings, and the wealth of their countries, while our own Government leaves me to fight the battles for the honor of this invention, fettered hand and foot. Thanks will be to you, not to them, if I am able to maintain the ground occupied by the American Telegraph."

THE DAGUERREOTYPE.

After the interview between Professor Morse and M. Daguerre, mentioned in the previous chapter, the Professor wrote to his brothers under date of March 9, 1839:

"You have perhaps heard of the Daguerreotype, so called from the discoverer, M. Daguerre. It is one of the most beautiful discoveries of the age. I don't know if you recollect some experiments of mine in New Haven, many years ago, when I had my painting-room next to Professor Silliman's—experiments to ascertain if it were possible to fix the image of the *camera obscura.* I was able to produce different degrees of shade on paper, dipped into a solution of nitrate of silver, by means of different degrees of light; but, finding that light produced dark, and dark light, I presumed the production of a true image to be impracticable, and gave up the attempt. M. Daguerre has realized in the most exquisite manner this idea.

"A few days ago I addressed a note to Mr. D., requesting as a stranger the favor to see his results, and inviting him in turn to see my Telegraph. I was politely invited to see them under these circumstances, for he had determined not to show them until the Chambers had passed definitely on a proposition for the Government to purchase the secret of the discovery, and make it public. The day before yesterday, the 17th, I called on M. Daguerre at his rooms in the Diorama, to see these admirable results. They are produced on a metallic surface, the principal pieces, about seven inches by five, and they resemble aquatint engravings, for they are in simple *chiaro-oscuro* and not in colors. But the exquisite minuteness of the delineation cannot be conceived. No painting or engraving ever approached it. For example: in a view up the street a distant sign would be perceived, and the eye could just discern that there were lines of letters upon it, but so minute as not to be read with the naked eye. By the assistance of a powerful lens, which magnified fifty times, applied to the delineation, every letter was clearly and distinctly legible, and so also were the minutest breaks and lines in the walls of the buildings and the pavements of the street. The effect of the lens upon the picture was in a great degree like that of the telescope in Nature. Objects moving are not impressed. The boulevard, so constantly filled with a moving throng of pedestrians and carriages, was perfectly solitary, except an individual who was having his boots brushed. His feet were of course compelled to be stationary for some time, one being on the box of the boot-black, and the other on the ground. Consequently his boots and legs are well defined, but he is without body or head, because these were in motion.

"The impressions of interior views are Rembrandt perfected. One of Mr. D.'s plates is an impression of a spider. The spider was not bigger than the head of a large pin, but the image, magnified by the solar microscope to the size of the palm of the hand, having been impressed on the plate, and examined through a lens, was further magnified, and showed a minuteness of organization hitherto not seen to exist. You perceive how this discovery is, therefore, about to open a new field of research in the depths of microscopic Nature. We are soon to see if the minute has discoverable limits. The naturalist is to have a new kingdom to explore, as much beyond the microscope as the microscope is beyond the naked eye. But I am near the end of my paper, and I have unhappily to give a melancholy close to my account of this ingenious discovery. M. Daguerre appointed yesterday at noon to see my Telegraph. He came, and passed more than an hour with me, expressing himself highly gratified at its operation. But, while he was thus employed, the great building of the Diorama, with his own house, all his beautiful works, his valuable notes and papers, the labor of years of experiment, were, unknown to him, at that moment the prey of the flames. His secret indeed is still safe with him, but the steps of his progress in the discovery, and his valuable researches in science, are lost to the

26

scientific world. I learn that his Diorama was insured, but to what extent I know not. I am sure all friends of science and improvement will unite in expressing the deepest sympathy in M. Daguerre's loss, and the sincere hope that such a liberal sum will be awarded him by his Government as shall enable him in some degree at least to recover from his loss."

In the same vessel which brought this letter the writer himself arrived in this country, and the letter was published in the *New York Observer*, April 20, 1839. In the month of June of the same year, within four months of the date of this letter, the French Government, Louis Philippe being the king, completed its negotiations with M. Daguerre for the purchase of his secret, that the beautiful discovery might be given to the world for its use and enjoyment. Arago was a member of the Chamber of Deputies, and chairman of the committee to whom was referred the subject. He made an elaborate report, in which the value of the discovery was set forth, and the indebtedness of the world to the discoverer. The report concluded with a recommendation that the discoverer be rewarded by the Govurement on his making public the process by which the results were reached.

Many years before, a Frenchman named Niepce had discovered the art of obtaining the outline of images, but he could not succeed in permanently fixing them. Daguerre had received from him the information which he had availed himself of in making the next great step, the more important one, of permauently impressing them on the plate. Niepce and Daguerre executed an agreement binding each other to divide between them the advantages that might result from their discoveries. Before any advantages were reached, Niepce died, but Daguerre recognized the continued validity of the contract, and was ready to share with the son of Niepce the fruits of the perfected discovery. It was by mutual consent agreed that a pension of ten thousand francs should be paid to them, six thousand to M. Daguerre and four thousand to M. Niepce, and that the widows of both should receive half of the pension that their husbands had enjoyed.

This arrangement being concluded, the process was made public. M. Daguerre hastened to put Professor Morse in possession of all the knowledge necessary to the immediate manipulation of the delicate process, and the Professor without delay proceeded to put the art into practical use. His brothers, Sidney E. and Richard C. Morse, caused to be erected on the roof of their new building, the northeast corner of Nassau and Beekman Streets, New York, "a palace for the sun," as Mr. S. E. Morse was pleased to name it, a room with a glass roof, in which Professor Morse experimented with the new and beautiful art. While this building was in progress, he had pursued his experiments with great success in his rooms at the New York City University on Washington Square. He says in a letter dated February 10, 1855:

"As soon as the necessary apparatus was made, 1 commenced experimenting with it. The greatest obstacle I had to encounter was in the quality of the plates. I obtained the common plated copper in coils at the hardware-shops, which of course was very thinly coated with silver, and that impure. Still I was enabled to verify the truth of Daguerre's revelations. The first experiment crowned with any success was a view of the Unitarian Church, from the window on the staircase from the third story of the New York City University. This, of course, was before the building of the New York Hotel. It was in September, 1839. The time, if I recollect, in which the plate was exposed to the action of light in the camera was about fifteen minutes. The instruments, chemicals, etc., were strictly in accordance with the directions in Daguerre's first book. An English gentleman, whose name at present escapes me, obtained a copy of Daguerre's book about the same time with myself. He commenced experimenting also. But an American, of the name of Walcott, was very successful with a modification of Daguerre's apparatus, substituting a metallic reflector for the lens. Previous, however, to Walcott's experiments, or rather *results*, my friend and colleague, Professor John W. Draper, of the New York City University, was very successful in his investigations, and with him I was engaged, for a time, in attempting portraits.

"In my intercourse with Daguerre, I specially conversed with him in regard to the practicability of taking portraits of living persons. He expressed himself somewhat skeptical as to its practicability, only in consequence of the time necessary for the person to remain immovable. The time for taking an out-door view was from fifteen to twenty minutes, and this he considered too long a time for any one to remain sufficiently still for a successful result. No sooner, however, had I mastered the process of Daguerre, than I commenced to experiment, with a view to accomplish this desirable result. I have now the results of these experiments taken in September, or beginning of October, 1839. They are full-length portraits of my daughter, single and also in group with some of her young friends. They were taken out-of-doors, on the roof of a building, in the full sunlight, and with the eyes closed. The time was from ten to twenty minutes. About the same time Professor Draper was successful in taking portraits, though whether he or myself took the first portrait successfully I cannot say.[1] Soon after we commenced together to take portraits, causing a glass building to be constructed for that purpose on the roof of the University. As our experiments had caused us considerable expense, we made a charge to those who sat for us to defray this expense. Professor Draper's other duties calling him away from the experiments, except as to their bearing on some philosophical investigations which he pursued with great ingenuity and success, I was left to pursue the artistic results of the process, as more in accordance with my profession. My expenses had been great, and for some time, five or six months, I pursued the taking of portraits by the Daguerreotype, as a means of reimbursing these expenses. After this object had been attained, I abandoned the practice to give my exclusive attention to the Telegraph, which required all my time."

Professor Morse's views of the capabilities of the art were expressed in a letter to his friend Washington Allston:

"I am afraid you will think me remiss in complying with your request by Mr. Hayward, but I have only this moment been able to obtain the album of Mr. Payne, from which I have made a careful tracing of your beautiful design of 'Danger,' and will take the earliest opportunity to transmit it to you, with the volumes of Meng's works also. I had hoped to have seen you long ere this, but my many avocations have kept me constantly employed from morning till night. When I say morning, I mean *half-past four* in the morning! I am afraid you will think me a Goth, but really the hours from that time till twelve at noon are the richest I ever enjoy.

[1] Prof. Draper recollects distinctly that he succeeded in taking the first portrait.

"You have heard of the Daguerreotype. I have the instruments on the point of completion, and if it be possible I will yet bring them with me to Boston and show you the beautiful results of this brilliant discovery. Art is to be wonderfully enriched by this discovery. How narrow and foolish the idea which some express that it will be the ruin of art, or rather artists, for every one will be his own painter. One effect, I think, will undoubtedly be to banish the sketchy, slovenly daubs that pass for spirited and learned; those works which possess mere general effect without detail, because forsooth detail destroys general effect. Nature, in the results of Daguerre's process, has taken the pencil into her own hands, and she shows that the minutest detail disturbs not the general repose. Artists will learn how to paint, and amateurs, or rather connoisseurs, how to criticise, how to look at Nature, and therefore how to estimate the value of true art. Our studies will now be enriched with sketches from Nature which we can store up during the summer, as the bee gathers her sweets for winter, and we shall thus have rich materials for composition, and an exhaustless store for the imagination to feed upon."

DAGUERRE AND ARAGO.

Immediately upon his return to New York in the spring of 1839, Professor Morse, being President of the National Academy of Design, proposed the election, as honorary member of the Academy, of M. Daguerre. On the same day, when he wrote to him announcing the fact of his election, he sent the following letter to Arago. The letters are here inserted in their connection.

To Monsieur Arago.

"My dear Sir: I take advantage of the visit to France of an *attaché* to our legation, to send you for your acceptance a copy of Professor Henry's late contributions to electricity and magnetism; and I also improve the same opportunity to express to you my thanks for the kindness and courtesy which you showed me when I was in Paris with my Electro-Magnetic Telegraph.

"Ever since the misfortune that befell M. Daguerre a few days before I left Paris, and at the very hour, too, when he was with me examining my Telegraph, I have felt a deeper interest in him, and in his most splendid discovery, and a desire, so far as I can be of service to him, to render him substantial aid. His discovery has excited great attention throughout the United States, and I have thought that so soon as his remuneration shall be secured in France and before his secret should be disclosed to the world, that we in the United States might in some way contribute our portion of the reward due to M. Daguerre. An exhibition (which is the mode in this country best adapted for the purpose desired) of a few of his admirable results in several of our cities, I am persuaded, would yield a sum which may not be unimportant in the present state of M. Daguerre's affairs. If, by any gratuitous services of mine in this country in favor of M. Daguerre, I can in any degree return the kindness and liberality I received in France, I hope M. Daguerre and his friends will not hesitate to command me.

" Believe me, etc.

"*May* 20, 1839."

To Monsieur Daguerre.

" MY DEAR SIR : I have the honor to inclose you the note of the secretary of our Academy, informing you of your election, at our last annual meeting, into the body of honorary members of our National Academy of Design. When I proposed your name, it was received with wild enthusiasm, and the vote was *unanimous.* I hope, my dear sir, you will receive this as a testimonial, not merely of my personal esteem and deep sympathy in your late losses, but also as a proof that your genius is in some degree estimated on this side of the water. Notwithstanding the efforts made in England to give to another the credit which is your due, I think I may with confidence assure you that throughout the United States your name alone will be associated with the brilliant discovery which justly bears your name.

" The letter I wrote from Paris, the day after your sad loss, has been published throughout this whole country in hundreds of journals, and has excited great interest. Should any attempts be made here to give to any other than yourself the honor of this discovery, my pen is ever ready in your defense.

" I hope before this reaches you that the French Government, long and deservedly celebrated for its generosity to men of genius, will have amply supplied all your losses by a liberal sum. If, when the proper remuneration shall have been secured to you in France, you should think it may be to your advantage to make an arrange-ment with the Government to hold back the secret for six months or a year, and would consent to an exhibition of your *results* in this country for a short time, the exhibition might be managed, I think, to your pecuniary advantage. If you should think favorably of the plan, I offer you my services gratuitously. In the mean time believe me, etc.

"*May* 20, 1839."

Daguerre to Morse.

"PARIS, *July* 26, 1839.

" MY DEAR SIR : I have received with great pleasure your kind letter, by which you announce to me my election as an honorary member of the National Academy of Design. I beg you will be so good as to express my thanks to· the Academy, and to say that I am very proud of the honor which has been conferred upon me. I shall seize all opportunities of proving my gratitude for it.

" I am particularly indebted to you in this circumstance, and I feel very thankful for this and all the other marks of interest you bestowed upon me. The transaction with the French Government being nearly at an end, my discovery shall soon be made public. This cause, added to the immense distance between us, hinders me from taking the advantage of your good offer to get up at New York an exhibition of my results. Believe me, my dear sir, your very devoted servant,

" DAGUERRE."

Morse to Daguerre.

" MY DEAR SIR : Your letter of July last, acknowledging the receipt of the Academy notification of your election as an honorary member of our body, has been received, and I am truly rejoiced that in any manner we have been able to gratify one who has conferred upon the world so great a boon. Allow me to congratulate you upon the result of the action of your Government, in granting the pension so ably and successfully solicited by that great and truly high-minded man, M. Arago. Your nation, sir, by acts like these, shines more brilliantly than by her achievements in arms. Let me assure you, that in this country the remark is constantly heard in connection with your most popular discovery, ' How nobly the French Government has acted in giving this secret to the world ! ' And not less a subject of remark is the moderation of your own demand for giving to the world that secret, which, but for your disclosure, would, in all probability, have remained a secret. Ever since I saw your admirable results, the day before your disastrous loss, I have felt an absorbing interest in it, and the first *brochure* which was opened in

America at the booksellers', containing your *exposé* of your process, I possess. I have been experimenting, but with indifferent success, mostly, I believe, for the want of a proper lens. I hoped to be able to send you by this opportunity a result, but I have not one which I dare send you. You shall have the first that is in any degree perfect. Will you allow me so far to trespass on your kindness as to request you to choose for me two lenses, such as you can recommend; I have requested my friend M. Lovering, of the firm of Messrs. Edward & Co., No. 9 Rue de Clery, to receive them and pay for them, and transmit them to me. If, after receiving the result which I will send you, you should deem it worthy of an exchange, I need not say how gratified I should be to receive one from your own hand, either for myself personally, or for the National Academy of Design.

"Any communication at any time will reach me through the house of Messrs. Edward & Co., 9 Rue de Clery, or through the ambassador of the United States. Yours, etc.

"*November* 16, 1839."

His artist friends and the National Academy of Design were on his mind and in his heart, while the Telegraph, the Photograph, and his own profession as a painter, were all demanding his attention and anxious care. Thomas Sully and Washington Allston acknowledged his letters, in which he tendered to them the use of the Academy's gallery for the exhibition of their paintings; and Mr. Allston expressed his strong anxieties for the success of his friend in his telegraphic pursuits. As the Daguerreotype was not patented, but was free to all who would master the art, a large number of young men, with the enterprise of American youth, flocked to Professor Morse to be instructed in the mysteries of the process, that they might traverse the country and reap the first fruits of its introduction. Men of science, also, charmed with the wonderful results, pursued the subject with enthusiasm, and entered into correspondence with Professor Morse as the father of the art in the United States. Professor E. N. Horsford writes to him from Albany, November 18, 1840:

"I learn, with equal astonishment and gratification, that you have succeeded in taking likenesses in *ten* seconds with diffused light. Pray reveal to me the wondrous discovery. So capricious has our sunlight been, that we have done very little since I last saw you."

During several years immediately succeeding, Professor Morse was often and intently engaged in the improvement of the photographic art, giving to the practical operators the benefit of his studies and experiments. Many letters addressed to him on this subject indicate the amount of time which was thus consumed. Early in 1848 he received from Baron Gerolt the following translation of an article from the *Prussian Universal Gazette* (*Allgemeine Preussische Zeitung*), December 21, 1847:

"In the last session of the Academy of Sciences at Paris, MM. Biot, Arago, and Thenard, reported a new discovery made by M. Niepce de Saint-Victor, the same chemist who was formerly rewarded by the state, together with Daguerre, for the discovery of the Daguerreotype. M. Niepce has discovered an action of the iodine-vapors upon the black and white color that hitherto had been entirely unknown. When he caused iodine-vapors to pass over a copperplate print or a lithography, or when he plunged a copperplate print or a lithography in a solution of iodine-water, the iodine united quicker and more intensive with the black than with the white. When he then laid the original, prepared in this way, with iodine, upon a paper lined with starch, and pressed it, the iodine parted from the black and united with the starch, so that now the original appeared upon the starch-paper in its most delicate shadowings, and in the violet-blue color of the iodine. When, furthermore, this paper was pressed upon a copperplate, the iodine again parted from the starch, and now the whole drawing (print) was fixed upon the copperplate with complete exactness. The commission, which had been charged by the Academy with the examination of the discovery, declared that, in looking at these exact copies, nobody could keep himself from the highest astonishment."

But nothing diverted Morse from the one great object, the perfection of his Telegraph. Distressed by the long delay of intelligence from Russia, and still more grieved at the indifference of his own country to the invention which was to shed lustre upon it, as well as upon him, he wrote to Mr. Smith, August 12, 1839:

"I received yours of the 2d instant, and the paper accompanying it, containing the notice of Mr. Chamberlain. I had previously been apprised that my forebodings were true in regard to his fate. We shall hear, doubtless, from Mr. Brown, when he returns, what was done by Mr. C. in regard to the Telegraph in the East. Our enterprise abroad is destined to give us anxiety, if not to end in disappointment.

"I have just received a letter from M. Amyot, who was to have been my companion to Russia, and learn from him the unwelcome news that the emperor has decided against the Telegraph. I have been expecting a letter from the Baron Meyendorff every day, for M. Amyot informs me that he intended writing to me. The emperor's objections were, it seems, that 'malevolence can easily interrupt the communication.' M. Amyot scouts the idea, and writes that he refuted the objection to the satisfaction of the baron, who, indeed, did not need the refutation for himself, for that whole matter was fully discussed between us when in Paris. The baron, I should judge from the tone of M. Amyot's letter, was much disappointed; yet, as a faithful and obedient subject of one whose nay is nay, he will be cautious in so expressing himself as to be self-committed. Thus, my dear sir, prospects abroad look dark. I turn with some faint hope to my own country again. Will Congress do any thing? Or, are my time, your generous zeal, and pecuniary sacrifice, to end only in disappointment? If so, I can bear it for myself, but I feel it more keenly for those who have been engaged with me for years— for the Messrs. Vail and Dr. Gale. But I will yet hope. I don't know that our enterprise looks darker than Fulton's once appeared. There is no *intrinsic* difficulty—the depressing causes are extrinsic. I hope to see you soon, and talk over all our affairs. You wish me to bring the telegraph with me. In the hope of doing this, I have delayed my journey for some days, and shall endeavor to bring the new instrument, which has been unavoidably retarded by the mechanician. My present purpose is to leave for the East on this day week (Monday), and probably by Saturday or the Monday following may see you in Portland."

Unavoidable hinderances intervened, and he did not make his promised journey. Mr. Smith says:

"The allusion made in the letter just given, to the fate of Mr. Chamberlain, was another depressing disappointment which occurred to the Professor contemporaneously with those of the Russian contract. Before I left Paris we had closed a contract with Mr.

Chamberlain to carry the telegraph to Austria, Prussia, the principal cities of Greece and of Egypt, and put it upon exhibition with a view to its utilization there. He was an American gentleman (from Vermont, I think), of large wealth, of eminent business capacities, of pleasing personal address, and sustaining a character for strict integrity. He parted with Professor Morse, in Paris, to enter upon his expedition, with high expectations of both pleasure and profit, shortly after my own departure from Paris, in October, 1838. He had subsequently apprised Professor Morse of very interesting exhibitions of the telegraph which he had made, and under date of ' Athens, January 5, 1839,' wrote as follows:

" ' We exhibited your telegraph to the learned of Florence, much to their gratification. Yesterday evening the King and Queen of Greece were highly delighted with its performance. We had shown it also to the principal inhabitants of Athens, by all of whom it was much admired. Fame is all you will get for it in these poor countries. We think of starting in a few days for Alexandria, and hope to get something worth having from Mehemet Ali. It is, however, doubtful. Nations appear as poor as individuals, and as unwilling to risk their money upon such matters. I hope the French will avail themselves of the benefits you offer them. It is truly strange that it is not grasped at with more avidity. If I can do any thing in Egypt, I will try Turkey and St. Petersburg.' "

In the letter communicating the above intelligence, Professor Morse also wrote as follows:

" In another letter from Mr. Chamberlain to Mr. Lovering, dated Syra, January 9th, he says: ' The pretty little Queen of Greece was delighted with Morse's telegraph. The string which carried the cannon-ball used for a weight broke, and came near falling on her Majesty's toes, but happily missed, and we, perhaps, escaped a prison. My best respects to Mr. Morse, and say 1 shall ask Mehemet Ali for a purse, a beauty from his seraglio, and something else.' I will add that, if he will bring me the purse just now, I can dispense with the beauty and the something else."

Early in July of the same year intelligence was received of a fatal calamity that occurred on the Danube, in which six of a select party of nine gentlemen on a boat-excursion of pleasure were drowned, and of which Mr. Chamberlain was one. On July 29, 1839, Professor Morse wrote as follows:

"Our hopes from that quarter are thus darkened by this melancholy event, and in all probability (unless Mr. Brown, when he returns, can give us information) we shall not know what has been done with the Telegraph in Constantinople, or Egypt."

These numerous discouragements to the Professor's ardent hopes for progress with the Telegraph, poverty, the failure of the Russian contract, the annoyance of Dr. Jackson's pretensions to the invention, the progress of Wheatstone in England and Steinheil in Bavaria, with their rival projects, the death of Mr. Chamberlain in the East, and the seeming imperturbable torpor of the American mind on the Telegraph, concurred in depressing his spirits grievously, and there were times when it appeared not unlikely that he would sink beneath the accumulated pressure of anxiety, disappointment, and want.

On the 14th of November, 1839, he wrote to his partner, Mr. Vail, in these despondent words:

"As to the Telegraph, I have been compelled from necessity to apply myself to those duties which yield immediate pecuniary relief. I feel the pressure as well as others, and, having several pupils at the University, I must attend to them. Nevertheless, I shall hold myself ready in case of need to go to Washington during the next session with it. The one I was constructing is completed except the rotary batteries, and the pen-and-ink apparatus, which I shall soon find time to add if required.

"Mr. Smith expects me in Portland, but I have not the means to visit him. The telegraph of Wheatstone is going ahead in England, even with all its complication. So I presume is the one of Steinheil in Bavaria. Whether ours is to be adopted depends on the Government or on a company, and the times are not favorable for the formation of a company. Perhaps it is the part of wisdom to let the matter rest and watch for an opportunity when times look better, and which I hope will be soon."

And to Mr. Smith he wrote in the same spirit, November 20, 1839:

"I feel the want of that sum which Congress ought to have appropriated two years ago, to enable me to compete with my European rivals. Wheatstone and Steinheil have money for their projects, the former by a company, and the latter by the King of Bavaria. Is there any national feeling with us on the subject? I will not say there is not, until after the next session of Congress. But if there is any cause for national exultation in being not merely *first* in the invention as to time, but *best,* too, as decided by a foreign tribunal, ought the inventor to be suffered to work with his hands tied? Is it honorable to the nation to boast of its inventors, to contend for the credit of their inventions, as national property, and not lift a finger to assist them to perfect that of which they boast? But I will not complain for myself—I can bear it, because I made up my mind from the very first for this issue, the common fate of all inventors. But I do not feel so agreeable in seeing those who have interested themselves in it, especially yourself, suffer also. Perhaps I look too much on the unfavorable side. I often thus look, not to discourage others, or myself, but to check those too sanguine expectations which, with me, would rise 'to an inordinate height unless thus reined in and disciplined.

" Shall you not be in New York soon? I wish much to see you and to concoct plans for future operations. I am at present much straitened in means, or I should yet endeavor to see you in Portland; but I must yield to necessity, and hope another season to be in different and more prosperous circumstances.

The following letter, under date of March 23, 1840, inclosed copies of two letters, one from Mr. Wm. F. Cooke, and the other from his partner, Professor C. Wheatstone, the inventors and patentees of the English needle system of Electric Telegraphs in England, proposing a consolidation of the two systems, Professor Morse's and their own, in the United States:

"I send you copies of two letters just received from England. What shall I say in answer? Can we make any arrangements with them? Need we do it? Does not our patent secure us against foreign interference? Or are we to be defeated not only in England, but in our country, by the subsequent inventions of Wheatstone? I feel my hands tied. I know not what to say. Do advise immediately, so that I can send by the British Queen, which sails on the 1st prox. I feel that, if funds and a company, or our Government, would sustain our operations, something yet could be made for all of us. The success of Electric Telegraphs is, you perceive, put beyond doubt. If we could make a reciprocal request for our Telegraph for England, perhaps it would do. I only suggest it.

"I received a letter from M. Amyot, in Paris, a few days ago, advising me that he had constructed one of my Telegraphs, with some improvements, and intrusted it to the Baron Meyendorff, at his earnest request, to carry with him to St. Petersburg to show it to the emperor. I also received a line from the baron, asking my approval of the course taken, urging that, if the emperor could see it in action, he might change his mind. I wrote each by the Great Western, approving the course taken, not having time to advise with any of my associates previous to writing."

The letters of Professor Wheatstone and Mr. Cooke are as follows:

"SUSSEX COTTAGE, NEAR LONDON, *January* 17, 1840.

"*Professor* F. B. MORSE, *of the New York City University, N. Y.*

"SIR: I address you on the subject of the Electro-Magnetic Telegraph, of which, as you are aware, Professor Wheatstone and myself are patentees in this country. We consider that its efficacy and value are now fully established here. It is in constant and successful operation for a distance of twelve or thirteen miles upon the Great Western Railway, and we are about to lay it down, under Mr. Robert Stevenson's sanction, upon the Blackwall Railway, a line on which its certainty of action may be essential to the success of the undertaking.

"It has always been our wish and intention to introduce this invention into the United States, and with that view we made arrangements rather more than two years ago with three American gentlemen for taking out a patent there. In consequence of their not having done so, we are under the necessity of entering into a new arrangement; and I have therefore to propose that you should join us upon similar terms, viz., that you should be entitled to a half share of our American patent, upon exerting yourself to obtain it, and bearing all expenses connected with the invention so far as regards the United States. Your own patent, if you have obtained one, and all improvements which may be made by either party during either patent-right, should be put upon the same footing, so far as regards the whole continuance of any United States patents which may be obtained for them. Should you be disposed to entertain this proposal, it will probably be necessary for you to obtain an act of Congress to sanction the granting of the patent later than six months after the enrollment of the specifications of our English patents of 1837 and 1838; but Mr. Stevenson, the American Minister, thinks that such an act might be obtained, and we presume that the expense of it would be inconsiderable in comparison with the value of the invention.

"My agreement with Mr. Wheatstone has thrown upon me the management of this business; but I also indorse a letter which he has written to you upon the same subject. Requesting the favor of a reply at your early convenience,

"I remain sir, your obedient servant,

"WM. F. COOKE."

"P. S.—We have recently obtained a third English patent (it is to be sealed in a day or two) for very important improvements which have not yet been specified, so important indeed that we think an American patent for them alone might be a valuable one.

"W. F. C."

"KING'S COLLEGE, LONDON, *January* 17, 1840.

"*Professor* F. B. MORSE, *New York.*

"DEAR SIR: For the reasons mentioned in Mr. Cooke's letter, it is necessary we should make fresh arrangements for the introduction of the improvements on the Electro-Magnetic Telegraph, for which we have obtained several English patents, into the United States. I have recommended that the application shall, in the first instance, be made to you, on account of the great attention you have already paid to the same subject, and that you might have the merit of introducing into America the only invention of the kind of which the success has been put beyond all doubt. It is our present intention to take out a patent in the United States for a new Telegraph arrangement totally different to that you have seen, which has occupied me almost entirely during the last twelve months in bringing to completion; and for which, with other improvements, we have just obtained a new English patent. This, of itself, would be extremely valuable; but, if you united with us in asking for the privilege, less difficulty would be experienced in obtaining an act of Congress to include our already published inventions, which, on account of the neglect of the parties with whom we formerly agreed, it would now be necessary to do; the same act might also include whatever you have done. Mr. Stevenson informs me that such an act will be readily granted.

"If any agreement should be entered into between us, as a matter of course, all expenses to which you may be put, in obtaining a patent or an act of Congress, would be deducted from the first proceeds. We will undertake to furnish you with any instruments you

may require, the expenses being defrayed by yourself, and to give
you every information our experience has put us in possession of.

"I remain, dear sir, yours very truly,

(Signed)   "C. WHEATSTONE."

This proposition was declined without hesitation, but its effect was to stimulate the inventor to increased diligence to secure his rights, and to bring his own system into early use.   As
time wore away, and foreign enterprise in European countries
slowly pushed the feeble systems of Wheatstone and Steinheil
upon the public, an occasional scintillation of interest in the Telegraph in this country shot up to the watchful vision of Professor Morse, reinspiring hope, but, like the aurora borealis, again
falling from sight below the horizon.   The following letters to
Mr. Smith will trace some of these tantalizing flickerings through
his mind:

"*August* 16, 1841.—Our Telegraph matters are in a situation
to do none of us any good, unless some understanding can be entered into among the proprietors.   I have recently received a letter
from Mr. Isaac N. Coffin, from Washington, with a commendatory
letter from Hon. R. McClellan, of the House.   Mr. Coffin proposes to
take upon himself the labor of urging through the two Houses the
bill relating to my Telegraph, which you know has long been before
Congress.   He will press it and let his compensation depend on his
success.   He says: 'I will attend to the claim most vigorously at
the usual compensation of a commission on the amount in case it is
obtained, and if not obtained, even after many years of trouble,
time, expense, and fatigue, nothing, or no remuneration, will be
asked if not obtained.'

" I have also other propositions from private individuals to put
down a line for the distance of about 120 miles; they are men of
capital who have opened their eyes to the advantages of the enterprise, and I know not what to say, for I have no authority to act
except for myself.   I wish I could see you.   Would it not be well
to let the first line be established without asking patent fees, in order to encourage others, for, if one line is successfully established,
others will follow, and the enterprise will, after so long delay, produce us something?   Please write and tell me what to do.   Give
me a power of attorney to act for you, if you cannot come on conveniently; I promise to do as well as I can, and yet I should prefer

to have your business tact at hand to see that I did not defraud my-self.

" You may wish to know the condition of the instruments, etc. I have the instruments, two registers and two correspondents, nearly completed at my brother's expense, who owns them, but will of course loan them as long as we wish, or sell them at cost, to us, for he procured them solely to encourage the matter. I have said *nearly completed.* The instruments want the mounting of the mag-nets, pens, paper-rolls, etc., and the glass cases to protect the work from the dust, etc. I have not the means to proceed with them. I am endeavoring to accumulate a little, that I may see at least one line, even if it be but a few miles, in successful operation. 'The destruction of the poor is their poverty;' so says Solomon, and it is true. But I think there is land ahead, and, if the matter could but be pressed in the proper quarter, we should each of us realize all that the most sanguine of us anticipated."

" *December* 3, 1841.—I have just received another letter from Mr. Isaac N. Coffin, from Washington, in relation to the Telegraph. I gave him to understand, last summer, that 1 was favorable to his propositions, but that I could do nothing without consulting the other proprietors. From you I received a definite answer, and power to propose certain terms, but not from Mr. Alfred Vail, who wished to consult his brother. It is, perhaps, my fault that he has not answered definitely, as I perceive, on recently reading his letter, he waited for a reply to my letter, so I have not a power of attorney to act for him. From Dr. Gale I expect one in a few days. In-deed, my dear sir, something ought to be done to carry forward this enterprise, that we all may receive what I think we all deserve. The whole labor and expense of shoving at all devolves on me, and I have nothing in the world. Completely crippled in means, I have scarcely (indeed, I have not at all) the means to pay even the post-age of letters on the subject. I feel it most tantalizing to find that there is a movement in Washington on the subject—to know that Telegraphs will be before Congress this session, and, from the means possessed by Gonon and Wheatstone (yes, Wheatstone who suc-cessfully headed us in England!), one or the other of these two plans will probably be adopted. Wheatstone, I suppose you know, has a patent here, and has expended a thousand dollars to get every thing prepared for a campaign to carry his project into operation, and, more than this, his patent is dated before mine! My dear sir, to speak as I feel, I am sick at heart to perceive how easily others, foreigners,

27

can manage our Congress, and can contrive to cheat our country out of the honor of a discovery of which the country boasts, and our countrymen out of the profits which are our due; to perceive how easily they can find men and means to help them in their plans, and how difficult, nay, impossible for us to find either. Is it really so? Or am I deceived? What can be done? Do write immediately, and propose something. Will you not be in Washington this winter? Will you not call on me as you pass through New York, if you do go?

"Gonon has his telegraph on the Capitol, and a committee of the Senate reported in favor of trying his for a short distance, and will pass a bill this session, if we are not doing something. Some means, somehow, must be raised. I have been compelled to stop my machine just at the moment of competition. I cannot move a step without running in debt, and that I cannot do.

"As to the company that was thought of to carry the Telegraph into operation here, it is another of those *ignes fatui* that have just led me to waste a little more time, money, and patience, and then vanished. The gentleman who proposed the matter was doubtless friendly disposed, but he lacks judgment and perseverance in a matter of this sort.

"If Congress would but pass the bill of thirty thousand dollars before them, there would be no difficulty. There is no difficulty in the scientific or mechanical part of the matter—*that is a problem solved*. The only difficulty that remains is, in obtaining the funds which Congress can furnish, to carry it into execution. I have a great deal to say, but must stop for want of time to write more. Every thing done by me in regard to the Telegraph is at arm's-length. I can do nothing without consultation, and, when I write to consult on the most trivial thing, I have three letters to write, and a week or ten days to wait before I can receive an answer. I feel at times almost ready to cast the whole matter to the winds, and turn my attention forever from the subject. Indeed, I feel almost induced at times to destroy the evidences of priority of invention in my possession, and let Wheatstone and England take the credit of it. For it is tantalizing in the highest degree to find the papers and the lecturers boasting of the invention as one of the greatest of the age, and as an honor to America, and yet to have the nation, by its representatives, leave the inventor without either the means to put the invention fairly before his countrymen, or to defend himself against foreign attacks! If I had the means in any way of support in Washington this winter, I would go on in the middle of January and push the matter; but I cannot run the risk. I would write a detailed history of the invention, which would be an interesting document to have printed in the congressional documents, and establish beyond contradiction both priority and superiority of my invention. Has not the Postmaster-General, or Secretary of War, or Treasury, the power to pay a few hundred dollars from a contingent fund for such a purpose?

"Whatever becomes of the invention through the neglect of those who could but will not lend a helping hand, you, my dear sir, will have the reflection that you did all in your power to aid me, and I am deterred from giving up the matter as desperate, most of all from the consideration that those who kindly lent their aid when the invention was in its infancy, would suffer, and therefore I should not be dealing right by them. If this is a little *blue*, forgive it."

During the absence of Professor Morse in Europe in the winter of 1838–'39, his partner Dr. Gale had lent to Professor Henry, of Princeton, a reel or spool of Professor Morse's Telegraph wire five miles in length, with which Professor Henry made some interesting scientific experiments at Princeton. The results of these were reported by him in a paper read before the American Philosophical Society, November 2, 1838, and published early in 1839, under the title of "Contributions to Electricity and Magnetism." Says Professor Morse: "On my return from Europe, I found awaiting me a copy of Professor Henry's 'Contributions,' directed to 'Professor Morse, with the respects of the author.' I had returned from Europe in the expectation of proceeding within five or six weeks to Russia, under a contract with a Russian Government agent in Paris— the Baron Meyendorff—to establish the Telegraph in that country. Dr. Gale, my confidential scientific friend, had sailed for New Orleans on the very day of my return. I could not therefore have my usual consultations with him, for I was naturally anxious to review and revise all the scientific facts that lay at the foundation of my invention, to make assurance doubly sure, before risking in a foreign country either my own or my country's reputation by possible failure. In this conjuncture I wrote the following letter to Professor Henry:

"'New York, *April* 24, 1839.

"' My dear Sir : On my return, a few days since, from Europe, I found directed to me, through your politeness, a copy of your valuable " Contributions," for which I beg you to accept my warmest thanks. The various cares consequent upon so long an absence from home, and which have demanded my more immediate attention, have prevented me from more than a cursory perusal of its interesting contents ; yet I perceive many things of great interest to me in my telegraphic enterprise. I was glad to learn, by a letter received in Paris, from Dr. Gale, that a spool of five miles of my wire was loaned to you, and I perceive that you have already made some interesting experiments with it. In the absence of Dr. Gale, who has gone South, I feel a great desire to consult some scientific gentleman on points of importance bearing upon my Telegraph which I am about to establish in Russia, being under an engagement with the Russian Government agent in Paris to return to Europe for that purpose in a few weeks. I should be exceedingly happy to see you, and am tempted to break away from my absorbing engagements here to find you at Princeton. In case I should be able to visit Princeton for a few days, a week or two hence, how should I find you engaged ? I should come as a learner, and could bring no " contributions" to your stock of experiments of any value, nor any means of furthering your experiments, except, perhaps, the loan of an additional five miles of wire which it may be desirable for you to have.

"' I have many questions to ask, but should be happy, in your reply to this letter, of an answer to this general one : Have you met with any facts in your experiments, thus far, that would lead you to think that my mode of Telegraphic communication will prove impracticable ? So far as I have consulted the *savants* of Paris, they have suggested no insurmountable difficulties. I have, however, quite as much confidence in your judgment, from your valuable experience, as in that of any one I have met abroad. I think that you have pursued an original course of experiment, and discovered facts of more value to me than any that have been published abroad. I will not trouble you at this time with my questions until I know your engagements. Accompanying this is a copy of a report, made by the Academy of Industry, of Paris, on my Telegraph, which I beg you to accept. Believe me, dear sir, with the highest respect, your most obedient servant,

"'Samuel F. B. Morse.

"'To Professor Joseph Henry, *Princeton.*'"

" To this letter I received the following reply :

" ' PRINCETON, *May* 6, 1839.

" ' DEAR SIR : Your favor of the 24th ult. came to Princeton during my absence, which will account for the long delay of my answer. I am pleased to learn that you fully sanction the loan which I obtained from Dr. Gale, of your wire, and I shall be happy if any of the results are found to have a practical bearing on the Electrical Telegraph. It will give me much pleasure to see you in Princeton after this week ; my engagements will not then interfere with our communications on the subject of electricity. During this week I shall be almost constantly engaged with a friend in some scientific labors which we are prosecuting together. I am acquainted with no fact which would lead me to suppose that the project of the Electro-Magnetic Telegraph is impracticable ; on the contrary, I believe that science is now ripe for the application, and that there are no difficulties in the way, but such as ingenuity and enterprise may obviate. But what form of the apparatus, or what application of the power will prove best, can, I believe, be only determined by careful experiment. I can say, however, that, so far as I am acquainted with the minutiæ of your plan, I see no practical difficulty in the way of its application for comparatively short distances ; but if the length of the wire between the stations be great, I think that some other modification will be found necessary, in order to develop a sufficient power at the farther end of the line. I shall, however, be happy to converse freely with you on these points when we meet. In the mean time I remain, with much respect, yours, etc.,

" ' JOSEPH HENRY.

" ' To Professor MORSE.'

" A few days after the receipt of this letter, I visited him, having prepared beforehand a few questions, the better to economize his time :

" *Questions prepared to ask Professor Henry, and shown him in my visit May,* 1839, *and his answers, on reading them to him.*

" ' 1. Have you any reason to think that magnetism cannot be induced in soft iron, at the distance of a hundred miles or more, by a single impulse, or from a single battery apparatus ? ' ' No.'

" ' 2. Suppose that a horseshoe magnet of soft iron, of a given size, receive its maximum of magnetism by a given number of coils around it, of wire, or of ribbon, and by a given sized battery, or number of batteries, at a given distance from the battery, does a succession of magnets introduced into the circuit diminish the magnetism in each ?' 'No.'

"'3. Have you ascertained the law which regulates the proportion of quantity and intensity from the voltaic battery, necessary to overcome the resistance of the wire in long distances, in inducing magnetism in soft iron ?' 'Ohm has determined it.'

"'4. Is it quantity or intensity which has most effect in inducing magnetism in soft iron ?' 'Quantity with short, intensity with long wires.'"

A few days after receiving Professor Henry's kind invitation, Professor Morse went to Princeton, and, passing the afternoon and evening with the great philosopher, returned the next morning to New York. Previous to this time Professor Morse had successfully operated his telegraph in New York, London, and Paris, before the most learned, scientific, and distinguished men of the age. Statesmen, engineers, philosophers, and mechanics, had minutely examined it, and pronounced it original, practicable, and successful. Its claims had already been compared with all other telegraphic inventions, and its superiority demonstrated and confessed. Two years after Professor Morse first consulted with Professor Henry, he received from him the following letter:

Professor Henry to Professor Morse.

"Princeton College, *February* 24, 1842.

"My dear Sir: I am pleased to learn that you have again petitioned Congress, in reference to your telegraph, and I most sincerely hope you will succeed in convincing our representatives of the importance of the invention. In this you may, perhaps, find some difficulty, since, in the minds of many, the electro-magnetic telegraph is associated with the various chimerical projects constantly presented to the public, and particularly with the schemes so popular a year or two ago, for the application of electricity as a moving power in the arts. I have asserted, from the first, that all attempts of this kind are premature, and made without a proper knowledge of scientific principles. The case is, however, entirely different in regard to the electro-magnetic telegraph. *Science is now fully ripe for this application,* and I have not the least doubt, if proper means be afforded, of the perfect success of the invention.

"The idea of transmitting intelligence to a distance, by means of electrical action, has been suggested by various persons, from the time of Franklin to the present; but until within the last few years, or since the principal discoveries in electro-magnetism, all attempts to reduce it to practice were necessarily unsuccessful. The mere suggestion, however, of a scheme of this kind is a matter for which little credit can be claimed, since it is one which would naturally arise in the mind of almost any person familiar with the phenomena of electricity; but the bringing it forward at the proper moment, when the developments of science are able to furnish the means of certain success, and the devising a plan for carrying it into practical operation, are the grounds of a just claim to scientific reputation as well as to public patronage.

"About the same time with yourself, Professor Wheatstone, of London, and Dr. Steinheil, of Germany, proposed plans of the electro-magnetic telegraph; but these differ as much from yours as the nature of the common principle would well permit; and, unless some essential improvements have lately been made in these European plans, I SHOULD PREFER THE ONE INVENTED BY YOURSELF.

"With my best wishes for your success, I remain, with much esteem, yours truly,

"JOSEPH HENRY.

"Professor MORSE."

This was the most encouraging communication Professor Morse received during the dark ages between 1839 and 1843.

The perfect indifference of his countrymen, and the impossibility of success without aid, overwhelmed him. A young artist speaks of his finding the rooms of Professor Morse while in search of apartments for his own use:

"In the spring of 1841 I was searching for a studio in which to set up my easel. My 'house-hunting' ended at the New York University, where I found what I wanted in one of the turrets of that stately edifice. When I had fixed my choice, the janitor, who accompanied me in my examination of the rooms, threw open a door on the opposite side of the hall and invited me to enter. I found myself in what was evidently an artist's studio, but every object in it bore indubitable signs of unthrift and neglect. The statuettes, busts, and models of various kinds, were covered with dust and cobwebs; dusty canvases were faced to the wall, and stumps of brushes and scraps of paper littered the floor. The only signs of industry consisted of a few masterly crayon drawings and little luscious studies of color pinned to the wall. 'You will have an artist for your neighbor,' said the janitor, 'though he is not here much of late; he seems to be getting rather shiftless, he is wasting his time over some silly invention, a machine by which he expects to send messages from one place to another. He is a very good painter, and might do well if he would only stick to his business; but, Lord!' he added, with a sneer of contempt, 'the idea of telling by a little streak of lightning what a body is saying at the other end of it!' Judge of my astonishment when he informed me that the 'shiftless individual,' whose foolish waste of time so much excited his commiseration, was none other than the President of the National Academy of Design—the most exalted position, in my youthful artistic fancy, it was possible for mortal to attain—S. F. B. Morse, since much better known as the inventor of the Electric Telegraph. But a little while after this his fame was flashing through the world, and the unbelievers who voted him insane were forced to confess that there was at least 'method in his madness.' "

General Strother, of Virginia, "Porte Crayon,' in one of his pen-pictures, shows the state of Professor Morse's private treasury during these years:

"I engaged to become Morse's pupil, and subsequently went to New York and found him in a room in University Place. He had three other pupils, and I soon found that our professor had very little patronage. I paid my fifty dollars; that settled for one quarter's instruction. Morse was a faithful teacher, and took as much interest in our progress as—more, indeed, than—we did ourselves. But he was very poor. I remember that when my second quarter's pay was due my remittance from home did not come as expected, and one day the professor came in, and said, courteously:

" ' Well, Strother, my boy, how are we off for money?'

" ' Why, professor,' I answered, 'I am sorry to say I have been disappointed; but I expect a remittance next week.'

" ' Next week!' he repeated, sadly; 'I shall be dead by that time.'

" ' Dead, sir?'

" ' Yes, dead by starvation!'

"I was distressed and astonished. I said, hurriedly:

" ' Would ten dollars be of any service?'

" 'Ten dollars would save my life; that is all it would do.'

"I paid the money, all that I had, and we dined together. It was a modest meal, but good, and, after he had finished, he said:

" 'This is my first meal for twenty-four hours. Strother, don't be an artist. It means beggary. Your life depends upon people who know nothing of your art, and care nothing for you. A house-dog lives better, and the very sensitiveness that stimulates an artist to work, keeps him alive to suffering.'

"I remained with Professor Morse three years, and then we separated. Some time afterward I met him on Broadway, one day. He was about the same as before, a trifle older, and somewhat ruddier. I asked him how he was getting along with his painting, and he told me that he had abandoned it; that he had something better, he believed; and told me about the proposed telegraph. I accompanied him to his room, and there found several miles of wire twisted about, and the battery, which he explained to me. His pictures, finished and unfinished, were lying about covered with dust. Shortly afterward Congress made an appropriation, and Morse was on the high-road to wealth and immortality."

Professor Morse's letters to Mr. Vail, during this crisis in the life of the Telegraph and its inventor, are full of the same fears and hopes that were revealed in those to Mr. Smith. He says:

"I have been compelled to apply myself to those duties which yield immediate pecuniary relief. I feel the *pressure* as well as others, and having several pupils at the University I must attend to them. Nevertheless, I shall hold myself ready to go to Washington during the next session with the instrument. The one I was constructing is completed, except the rotary batteries and the pen-and-ink apparatus, which I shall soon find time to adapt if required. I hear not a word from Mr. Smith, and have not for several months; he, perhaps, expects me in Portland, but I have not the means to visit him. The telegraph of Wheatstone is going ahead in England, even with all its complications. So I presume is the one of Steinheil in Bavaria. Whether ours is to be adopted depends on the Government, or on a company, and the times are not favorable for the formation of a company. Perhaps it is the part of wisdom to let the matter rest, and watch for an opportunity when times look better, and which I hope will be soon.

"*September* 7, 1840.—I am tied hand and foot through the day endeavoring to realize something from the Daguerreotype portrait. . . . As to the telegraph I know not what to say. I suppose something might be done in Washington next session, if I or some of you would go on, but I have expended so much time in vain there and in Europe, that I feel almost discouraged from pressing it any further—only, however, from want of funds. I have none myself, and I dislike to ask of the rest of you. You are all so scattered, that there is no consultation, and I am under the necessity of attending to duties which will give me the means of living. The reason of its not being in operation is not the *fault of the invention*, nor is it *my neglect*—my faith is not only unshaken in its *eventual adoption throughout the world*, but it is confirmed by every new discovery in the science of electricity."

The year 1840 was made memorable in the history of the American Electro-Magnetic Telegraph by the actual issue of the first patent to Samuel F. B. Morse. In the spring of the year Professor Morse addressed this letter to the Commissioner of Patents, his old friend and classmate:

" NEW YORK, May 2, 1840.

" *Hon.* H. L. ELLSWORTH, *Commissioner*, etc.

"MY DEAR SIR: I have never received my patent-papers from your office. I believe there was something to be done on my part, in relation to a drawing for one of the duplicates, which I was prevented from accomplishing by the necessity of preparing suddenly for my visit to Europe, with the Telegraph. I have nearly completed an improved apparatus, for which I intend to take out a patent, adding it to my patent already executed, as an improvement. I should long since have visited Washington with my apparatus, and asked for some action upon the matter by Congress, but for the low state of financial affairs, private and public. So far as the approbation of the scientific and mechanical world goes, I have had the gratification of having it loudly and substantially expressed, that my Telegraph is the best of all that had been examined. But while in England the very complicated and deficient apparatus of Wheatstone is carried into operation by a wealthy company for thirteen miles, and is in further progress, and while the Telegraph of Steinheil, at Munich, is adopted, and is carried into effect by the Bavarian Government, I am fettered and prevented from bringing the *American Telegraph* (*the first invented*, as dates conclusively show, and the *best*, according to the opinion of the best judges of the case here and in Europe, as I can also show) into operation for want of a little assistance from our Government. I was first encouraged to offer my Telegraph to the Government by letters from the Secretary of the Treasury, drawing my attention to the subject, then by the report of the committees in Congress, to whom the subject was referred, and by the report of a bill for a sum sufficient to test its practicability. I have been hoping that an invention which is to succeed just as surely as steam-traveling has succeeded, an invention which is truly an American invention, would be in a sense adopted by the Government, and an opportunity given me to bring it forth, in full operation, to the honor of the country. I have spent time, strength, and money, to accomplish this; have been exercised with the alternate hopes and disappointments of an inventor; and, unless something is done to help me forward, the more wealthy Englishmen will have it in their power not merely to deprive me of the profit of my discovery in my own country, as they have already in their own, by a gross act of injustice, but, as in the case of Halley's quadrant, the Telegraph will be an English, not an American invention.

" I could tell you a long story on this point, but long stories are not for gentlemen in official stations, who have their time often too thoughtlessly consumed by the intrusion of time-killers. Please tell me what I am to do in order to have my letters-patent for the Telegraph, and I will do it.

" Your old friend and classmate,

" SAMUEL F. B. MORSE."

The Commissioner returned this answer :

" PATENT-OFFICE, *May* 14, 1840.

" SIR : The specifications and drawings of your alleged improvement, in the mode of communicating signals by the application of Electro-Magnetism, are herewith returned to you, the explanatory reference in the same not being sufficient to properly illustrate the invention. Some annotations, pointing out the parts where these are wanting, are marked in pencil in the margin of the description.

" Your favor of the 2d inst. has been received, in reply to which the office has to state that the delay attending the granting of your application has not been caused by any want of attention on its part. Some two years since, when your patent was about being issued, a request was made by you that the case might be postponed, until you should have received letters-patent from the European governments. This request was complied with ; and, as no communication has been received from you since, in relation to the issuing of the patent, the case has been permitted to lie over. The patent will be issued, however, immediately on the return of the papers.   H. L. ELLSWORTH.

" Professor S. F. B. MORSE, New York City, N. Y."

The corrections suggested by the Commissioner having been made, and the duplicate set of drawings prepared, Mr. Morse returned them to the Patent-Office, with this letter to the Commissioner :

" NEW YORK, *May* 18, 1840.

" DEAR SIR : I herewith return you the specifications of my telegraphic invention, which you sent me to correct, and to add a duplicate set of drawings. I hope all will be found correct. My improvements shall be specified and accompanied with drawings, and sent you as soon as I can complete the new apparatus, which is in progress, and which I hoped to have had the pleasure of showing you in Washington this spring. But it is now so late in the session, and you are all so engaged at headquarters in fighting the presidential battle, that I fear my lightning will not have a fair chance till next fall. Hoping to see you at the class meeting in New Haven, in August next, to celebrate our thirty years exit from college, I remain truly as ever, your friend and classmate,

" SAMUEL F. B. MORSE."

" PATENT-OFFICE, *May* 26, 1840.

" SIR : On reviewing the specification of your Magnetic Telegraph, before ordering the case to issue, a slight defect has been found in the oath, which it will be necessary to correct, and which, on the previous examination, escaped the attention of the examiner. The defect in the oath is in its being without a date : the blank left for that purpose never having been filled up. And as it might affect the validity of your patent, were the office to let it pass in its present form, your better plan will be to make a new affidavit, which must be taken before the mayor or recorder of your city, as justices of the peace in your State are not authorized to administer general oaths. It would be well, also, were you to make the alteration in the specifications suggested in the note, which you have made in the margin of it, as it would make the description more clear.   HENRY L. ELLSWORTH."

This is the affidavit annexed to the petition or application for the patent, and description and specification of the invention, which it was supposed was defective :

"UNITED STATES OF AMERICA,   } ss.
"DISTRICT OF COLUMBIA, COUNTY OF WASHINGTON, }

" On this   day of   , 1838, before the subscriber, a justice of the peace in and for said county, personally appeared the within-named Samuel F. B. Morse, and made solemn oath that he believes himself to be the first and original inventor of the several parts, and application thereof, of the American Electro-Magnetic telegraph, above mentioned and described in the specification of claims thereto by him subscribed, and that he does not know or believe that the same was ever before known or used, and that he is a citizen of the United States.

" C. H. WILTBERGER, *Justice of the Peace.*"

On receiving this letter, a new affidavit was made, and the certificate thereof added upon the documents so returned for the purpose, immediately following the original affidavit, in these words :

"COUNTY OF NEW YORK, *ss.*

"On this 29th day of May, 1840, before the subscriber, the Mayor of the city of New York, personally appeared the within-named Samuel F. B. Morse, and made solemn oath that he believes himself to be the first and original inventor of the several parts and applications thereof, of the American Electro-Magnetic Telegraph above mentioned and described in the specification of claim thereto by him subscribed, and that he does not know or believe that the same was ever before known or used, and that he is a citizen of the United States.   ISAAC L. VARIAN, *Mayor.*"

The direction being complied with, the papers were returned by Mr. Morse on the same day the affidavit was made and certified. The patents were then issued, as already stated. These formalities and vexatious delays are thus minutely rehearsed for the special benefit of future inventors.

Professor Morse, in applying to his partners for their consent to an arrangement with an agent, had spoken with great freedom of the desperate state of his affairs. To Mr. Vail he wrote:

"NEW YORK, *December* 13, 1841.

"I am endeavoring to do something with the Telegraph at Washington, but am much embarrassed for want of a power of attorney from you, to act for you in this matter. The prospects of doing any thing with a company here, which seemed to dawn for a few moments last summer, have vanished. I am now in treaty with the person whom I mentioned to you in my letter last summer—Mr. Coffin, at Washington, who offers his services to get the bill through Congress, which was reported by the Committee of Commerce some years ago when we were in Washington. I have written to Mr. Smith, and he assents to any arrangement I may make. Dr. Gale also assents. I wish you would, therefore, empower me on your part to conclude the arrangement with Mr. Coffin. He comes well recommended, as understanding his business, and he asks ten per cent. if he gets the bill through all the stages; *nothing*, if he does not succeed. As matters now stand, can we do better? We all seem somewhat crippled, and I most of all, being obliged to superintend the getting up of a set of machinery complete, and to make the greater part myself, and without a cent of means. I am now at work upon it, and for the purpose of lecturing upon it. If I should get it completed, I may visit you with it in Philadelphia some time before the winter closes. Mr. Smith is without means, and cannot advance any thing. He suggests that if I could raise two or three hundred dollars to enable me to visit Washington with the new machines, it would be well, and he assented to my receiving the first receipts from the Telegraph to repay the sum. If I give my time and attention to the matter, is it not fair that I should receive a compensation? All the burden now rests on my shoulders, after years of time devoted to the enterprise, and I am willing, so far as I am able, to bear my share, if the other proprietors will lend a helping hand, and give me facilities to act, and a reasonable recompense for my services in case of success. Please answer by return of mail, as I cannot write definitely to Mr. Coffin until I hear from you, and he ought to know immediately, that he may act without delay, for there are two plans that interfere with ours that will be entertained by Congress, and their agents are on the ground, and busy. It is necessary that our agent should break ground at once."

The letter which Mr. Morse addressed to Mr. Coffin, after the assent of the partners was obtained, will show the principle by which he was governed. He offers to give the agent one-half all he (Morse) should receive from his invention, until Coffin has received a sum equal to five per cent. of the appropriation for the experimental Telegraph. The Professor was to pay from his own subsequent receipts the expenses of the agent, instead of allowing the agent to receive a portion of the appropriation.

" New York, *December* 23, 1841.

" Dear Sir : I have just received yours of the 21st inst., and I have also received answers and authority from the different proprietors of the Telegraph, to agree to give you, which I hereby agree to do, one-half of all I receive from the Government, either for my personal services, or for purchase-money of the patent-right, until you shall have received five per cent. on the sum which Congress shall appropriate at their present session for the purpose of testing my Electro-Magnetic Telegraph, provided you shall succeed in getting the bill through all its stages till it becomes a law.

" I send you herewith the report of the French Academy of Industry, in which it will be seen that the commission appointed by them to examine my Telegraph not only give it the preference over Wheatstone's, but they recommend that my name be presented to the Committee of Premiums for reward, which was done, and at the annual meeting the great medal of honor was voted me for the invention.

" I have much which is important bearing on the subject, but which it will require a little time to prepare—such, for example, as the opinion of the commission appointed by the French Government to examine and report on all the plans of electric telegraphs which had been submitted to the Government, among which was Wheatstone's, and, after careful examination, they recommend mine ' *as the simplest and the best.*' I will prepare a paper for you with as little delay as possible. How soon will it do? I have, say, over one hundred of these French reports, which, perhaps, might be distributed in Congress to advantage. If you will designate to whom they may be sent, on a printed list of members which may be sent me, I will send a copy to such as you mark."

In giving his consent to the proposed arrangement with Coffin, Mr. Alfred Vail had written to Professor Morse a week before this last letter was sent, and had said :

"I have recently given considerable thought to the subject of the Telegraph, and was intending to get permission of you, if there is any thing to the contrary in 'our articles of agreement, to build for myself and my private use a telegraph upon your plan. Now I should be glad to have your assent to it. It would be some time before I could make it at any rate, and therefore can do the general cause no harm. I will write to my brother that I give my assent for him to give you the power of attorney to act for us. I hope there will be no embarrassment thrown in the way of your and our ultimate success in the Telegraph. I should be very much pleased to have you come to Philadelphia, and make your stay at my house, and I will endeavor to render you every assistance in my power."

In the course of his answer, Professor Morse says to Mr. Vail:

"I have to do all the labor of the whole enterprise at present, and *have not a cent of money in the world.* I am giving my time and skill in getting the instrument in order to act in case it is required at Washington, and I think it but fair that I should have my burdens made as light as possible. You can see in a moment that if I have to write to all the scattered proprietors of the Telegraph every time any movement is made, what a burden falls upon me both of expense of time and money, which I cannot afford. In acting for my own interest in this matter, I, of course, act for the interest of all. If we can get that thirty thousand dollars bill through Congress, the experiment (if it can any longer be called such) can then be tried on such a scale as to insure its success. You ask permission to make a telegraph for your own use. I have no objection. But, before you commence one, I think you had better see me, and the improvements which I have made, and I can suggest a few more, rather of an ornamental character, and some economical arrangements which may be of use to you. I thank you for your kind invitation, and when I come to Philadelphia shall *A Vail* myself of your politeness. I suppose by this time you have a brood of chickens around you. Well, go on and prosper. As for me I am not well, am much depressed at times, and have many cares, anxieties, and disappointments, in which I am aware I am not alone. But all will work for the best if we only look through the cloud and see a kind Parent directing all. This reflection alone cheers me, and gives me renewed strength.'

The business was put into the hands of Mr. Coffin, who spent the winter in prosecuting it. But the energy and tact, of which he had spoken so confidently in his letters to Professor Morse, amounted to nothing. The only means that he proposed to employ, or was allowed to employ, were argument and persuasion, and these were lost upon the minds of members. The session of 1841–'42 wore away and the Telegraph was untouched. In the early part of this dismal year, in a letter to a friend, giving him a commission, Professor Morse discloses the secret sorrow over an old misfortune, from which he never fully recovered. He said:

"Your letter, containing a draft for three hundred dollars, I received yesterday, for which accept my sincere thanks. I have hesitated about receiving it because I had begun to despair of ever being able to touch the pencil again. The blow I received from Congress when the decision was made concerning the pictures for the Rotunda, has almost destroyed my enthusiasm for my art, or rather I should say turned it into a different channel, laboring for the younger artists, that they may not have the same kind of obstacles to overcome, against which I have contended. In this I find indeed great pleasure, so far as my art is concerned. I have not painted a picture since that decision, and I presume that the mechanical skill I once possessed in the art has suffered by the neglect. I may possibly recover my skill, and if any thing will tend to this end it is the consciousness of having the sympathy of those who can understand the circumstances that have operated against me.

"When I applied to paint one of the Rotunda pictures, I was in my full vigor. I had just returned from three years' hard study in Italy, which I considered as completing my studies as an historical painter, and felt a consciousness of ability to execute a work creditable to my country. I hazarded every thing almost for this single object. When so unexpectedly I was repelled, I staggered under the blow. I have endeavored in every way to prevent its effects upon my mind, but it is a thorn which perpetually obtrudes its point, and would goad me to death were it not for its aspect in the light of God's overruling providence. Then all is right."

In the summer of 1842 Professor Morse communicated to the Hon. W. W. Boardman, member of the House of Representatives in Congress, the encouraging letter from Professor

28

Henry, of February 24, 1842, which has been previously copied. Again he wrote :

Professor Morse to Mr. Boardman.

"NEW YORK, *August* 10, 1842.

" MY DEAR SIR : I inclose you a copy of the *Tribune*, in which you will see a notice of my Telegraph. I have showed its operation to a few friends occasionally within a few weeks ; among others to Professor Henry, of Princeton (a copy of whose letter to me on this subject I sent you some time since) ; he had never seen it in operation, but had only heard from description the principle on which it is founded. He is not of an enthusiastic temperament, but exceedingly cautious in giving an opinion on scientific inventions, yet in this case he expressed himself in the warmest terms, and told my friend Dr. Chilton (who informed me of it) that he had just been witnessing the operation of the most beautiful and ingenious instrument he had ever seen. Indeed, since I last wrote you, I have been wholly occupied in perfecting its details, and making myself familiar with the whole system. There is not a shadow of doubt as to its performing all that I have promised in regard to it, and indeed all that has been conceived of it. Few can understand the obstacles arising from want of pecuniary means that I have had to encounter the past winter.

" To avoid debt (which I will never incur) I have been compelled to make with my own hands a great part of my machinery, but at an expense of time of very serious consideration to me. I have executed in six months what a good machinist, if I had the means to employ him, would have performed in as many weeks, and performed much better.

" I had hoped to be able to show my perfected instrument in Washington long before this, and was (until this morning) contemplating its transportation thither next week. The news just received of the proposed adjournment of Congress has stopped my preparations, and interposes, I fear, another year of anxious suspense.

" Now, my dear sir, as your time is precious, I will state in few words what I desire. The Government will eventually, without doubt, become possessed of this invention, for it will be necessary from many considerations, not merely as a direct advantage to the Government and public at large, if regulated by the Government, but as a preventive of the evil effects which must result if it be a monopoly of a company. To this latter mode of remunerating myself I shall be compelled to resort if the Government should not eventually act upon it. You were so good as to call the attention of the House to the subject by a resolution of inquiry, early in the session. I wrote you some time after, requesting a stay of action on the part of the committee, in the hope that long before this I could show them the Telegraph in Washington, but, just as I am ready, I find that Congress will adjourn before I can reach Washington, and put the instrument in order for their inspection. Will it be possible, before Congress rises, to appropriate a small sum, say thirty-five hundred dollars, under the direction of the Secretary of the Treasury, to put my Telegraph in operation for the inspection of Congress the next session? If Congress will grant this sum, I will engage to have a complete Telegraph on my electro-magnetic plan between the President's house, or one of the departments, and the Capitol and the Navy-Yard, so that instantaneous communication can be held between these three points at pleasure, at any time of day or night, at any season, in clear or rainy weather, and ready for their examination during the next session of Congress, so that the whole subject may be fairly understood. I believe that, did the great majority of Congress but consider seriously the results of this invention of the Electric Telegraph on all the interests of society; did they suffer themselves to dwell but for a moment on the vast consequences of the instantaneous communication of intelligence from one part to the other of the land in a commercial point of view, and as facilitating the defenses of the country, which my invention renders certain, they would not hesitate to pass all the acts necessary to secure its control to the Government. I ask not this until they have thoroughly examined its merits, but will they not assist me in placing the matter fairly before them? Surely so small a sum to the Government for so great an object cannot reasonably be denied.

"I hardly know in what form this request of mine should be made. Should it be by petition to Congress? or will this letter handed in to the committee be sufficient? If a petition is required for form's sake to be referred to the committee to report, shall I ask the favor of you to make such petition in proper form? You know, my dear sir, just what I wish, and I know, from the kind and friendly feeling you have shown toward my invention, I may count on your aid. If on your return you stop a day or two in New York, I shall be glad to show you the operation of the Telegraph as it is.

"With sincere respect and esteem, your obedient servant,
"SAMUEL F. B. MORSE.
"Hon. W. W. BOARDMAN, Washington."

To this letter Mr. Boardman replied:

         "HOUSE OF REPRESENTATIVES, *August* 12, 1842.

"DEAR SIR: Yours of the 10th is received. I had already seen the notice of your Telegraph in the *Tribune*, and was prepared for such a report. This is not the time to commence any new project before Congress. We are, I trust, within ten days of adjournment. There is no prospect of a tariff this session, and, as that matter appears settled, the sooner Congress adjourns the better. The subject of your Telegraph was some months ago, as you know, referred to the Committee on Commerce, and by that committee it was referred to Mr. Ferris, one of the members of that committee, from the city of New York, and who, by-the-way, is now at home in the city, and will be glad to see you on the subject. I cannot give you his address, but you can easily find him. The Treasury and the Government are both bankrupt, and that foolish Tyler has vetoed the tariff bill—the House is in bad humor, and nothing of the kind you propose could be done. The only chance would be for the Committee on Commerce to report such a plan, but there would be little or no chance of getting such an appropriation through this session. I have much faith in your plan, and hope you will continue to push it toward Congress.   Truly yours, etc.,

            "W. W. BOARDMAN.
"Professor SAMUEL F. B. MORSE, New York."

In a letter to Mr. Smith, in July of this year (1842), he communicates the most important results of his experiments with a greater length of wire than he had ever used before. And the encouragement he received from Professor Henry is here announced with intense satisfaction. He said:

"You are doubtless desirous of knowing what progress is made in the telegraphic enterprise. I have been compelled, for want of means, to proceed very, very slowly, and to great disadvantage, in maturing the instruments for a fair exhibition of its powers to Congress, and, although I have devoted all my time for nearly a year past in the hope of proceeding to Washington before the close of the session, and by a fresh effort to induce Congress to grant me an appropriation sufficient at least to show them the use of the Telegraph for a short distance, I have been unable to complete the correspondent, solely for want of funds, and have many times been tempted to give up the whole matter, not from any difficulty inherent in the invention itself, but from the accumulation of extraneous obstacles to so heavy an amount that it seemed utterly impossible to move another step. I have oftentimes risen in the morning, not knowing where the means were to come from for the common expenses of the day. Reflect one moment on my situation in regard to the invention. Compelled from the first, from my want of the means to carry out the invention to a practical result, to ask assistance from those who had means, I associated with me the Messrs. Vails and Dr. Gale, by making over to them, on certain conditions, a portion of the patent-right. These means enabled me to carry it successfully forward to a certain point; at this point you were also admitted into a share of the patent, on certain conditions, which carried the enterprise forward successfully still further; since then disappointments have occurred, and disasters to the property of every one concerned in the enterprise, but of a character not touching the intrinsic merits of the invention in the least, yet bearing on its progress so fatally as for several years to paralyze all attempts to proceed. The depressed situation of all my associates in the invention has thrown the whole burden of again attempting a movement entirely on me. With the trifling sum of five hundred dollars I could have had my instrument perfected and before Congress six months ago, but I was unable to run the risk, and I therefore chose to go forward more slowly, but at a great waste of time. In all these remarks, understand me as not throwing the least blame on any individual. I believe that the situation in which you all are thrown is altogether providential—that human foresight could not avert it, and I firmly believe, too, that the delays, tantalizing and trying as they have been, will, in the end, turn out to be beneficial. During the last few months I have availed myself of the means which Mr. Samuel Colt has had at his command in experimenting with wire circuits for testing his submarine batteries; also to test some very important matters in relation to the Telegraph. I loaned him, in the first instance, my two reels of wire, which, by-the-by, is reduced to eight and a quarter miles. In the first place, the wire was taken to a ropewalk, and stretched back and forth, keeping each thread at least six inches apart from its neighbor, in order to ascertain if the coil had any effect in the result we obtained. The experiments were highly satisfactory, the magnetism and the heating effects, which latter Mr. Colt desired, being apparently stronger when the wire was stretched out than when in coil. We also found that when one wire was coated, the other might be naked, and passed to any distance.

"This result induced Mr. Colt to contract, for his purposes, for the purchase of forty miles of wire. This quantity, with two that he had already procured, and my eight miles, make fifty miles! Twenty miles have already been finished, and we have experimented with perfectly satisfactory results on this distance. In a few days (it may be weeks, however) he expects the remainder, when we shall pursue our experiments. I have invented a battery which will delight you: it is the most powerful of its size ever invented, and this part of my telegraphic apparatus the results of experiments have enabled me to simplify, and truly to perfect. Dear sir, I am just now in a dilemma in consequence of an application from an energetic and enterprising engineer, Mr. John P. Monroe, who is so delighted with the operation of the telegraph that he desires to form a company, and at once put it in operation from New York to Washington. He thinks there is no doubt but capital could be raised for this purpose. He is just the person to enter upon the plan, and Mr. Monroe is a substantial man, a successful contractor on the New York & Erie Railroad. He is in earnest, and I promised to write you on the subject. If you could come on (and apprise me when you can be here), I will endeavor to have Mr. Vail here also, and, if Dr. Gale is on the spot, we could put all our matters into a state less embarrassing than they are at present. It seems to me that there is now an opportunity for doing something advantageous to all. You must perceive at what disadvantage I do business when, before I can make any answer to queries from persons who feel disposed to take hold of the enterprise, I must write two or three letters of particulars to different parts of the country, and wait days for an answer. *The necessity of our Telegraph* is made evident in this very case. If you had in your parlor one of my registers, there would be no need of a long journey, or of waiting three or four days for an answer. In brief, I can say that the cost per mile we have ascertained to be as follows, and the wire you will perceive is to be tied in a most substantial manner:

Lead pipe, and the joinings large enough to contain four or even eight wires per mile................................$250 00	
Wire completely prepared, by winding with twine saturated in tar and in India-rubber, per mile.......................	150 00
Passing the wire, thus prepared, into the pipe, per mile.........	5 00
Delivery of pipe and wire......................................	10 00
Excavation and filling in again, about one thousand yards, per mile, three feet deep....................................	150 00
At fifteen cents per yard, laying the pipe.....................	3 00

$568 00

—or say, in round numbers, six hundred dollars per mile. Mr. Monroe proposes that a company be formed to carry the Telegraph into operation from New York to Washington; that about ten thousand dollars be raised at first to lay it down as far as Newark—nine miles; that the certain operation of it at this distance will insure the subscription to the rest of the stock in Philadelphia, New York, and Baltimore; that the expenses of each of the proprietors should be summed up, and they all should be reimbursed by the stock, which he thinks would give confidence. The shares, he thinks, should be low, in order to interest a great number in the enterprise. Please think over the plan, and write me on the subject immediately, but do come on, if possible. ´ Mr. Monroe will be in the city a few days at present, and I wish to give him some kind of reply.

"Yours, etc., S. F. B. MORSE."

"P. S.—I have not heard a word from Mr. Coffin, at Washington, since I saw you. I presume he has abandoned the idea of doing any thing in the time we proposed, and so has given it up. Well, so be it—I am content.

"I have much to tell you of the most gratifying character in relation to the certainty of success, and, as for my telegraphic system, all my experiments go to confirm its entire practicability. Professor Henry visited me a day or two ago. He knew the principles of the Telegraph, but had never before seen its operation. He told a gentleman, who mentioned it again to me, that without exception it was the most beautiful and ingenious instrument he had ever seen. He says mine is the only truly practical plan. He has been experimenting and making discoveries on celestial electricity, and he says that Wheatstone and Steinheil's Telegraph must so be influenced in a highly-electrical state of the atmosphere as at times to be useless, they using the deflection of the needle; while mine, from the use of the magnet, is not subject to this disturbing influence. I believe, if the truth were known, some such cause is operating to prevent our hearing more of their telegraphs.

"Truly your friend, etc.,

"S. F. B. M.

"NEW YORK, *July* 16, 1842."

In the autumn Professor Morse submitted his telegraphic instrument to the American Institute, and the following report and resolution were adopted by that body:

Report of the American Institute on the Electro-Magnetic Telegraph.

NEW YORK, *September* 12, 1842.

The undersigned, the Committee of Arts and Sciences of the American Institute, respectfully report:

That, by virtue of the power of adding to their numbers, they called to their aid the gentlemen whose names are hereunto annexed, with those of the original members of the committee, and proceeded to examine Professor Morse's Electro-Magnetic Telegraph. Having investigated the scientific principles on which it is founded, inspected the mechanism by which these principles are brought into practical operation, and seen the instruments in use in the transmission and return of various messages, they have come to the conclusion that it is admirably adapted to the purposes for which it is intended, being capable of forming words, numbers, and sentences, nearly as fast as they can be written in ordinary characters, and of transmitting them to great distances with a velocity equal to that of light. They, therefore, beg leave to recommend the Telegraph of Professor Morse for such testimonials of the approbation of the American Institute as may in its judgment be due to a most important practical application of high science, brought into successful operation by the exercise of much mechanical skill and ingenuity.

All which is respectfully submitted:

JAMES RENWICK, LL. D.,
Prof. Chem. and Nat. Phil., Columbia Col., N. Y.
JOHN W. DRAPER, M. D.,
Prof. Chem.-and Min., University City of New York.
WILLIAM H. ELLET, M. D.,
Prof. Chem., etc., Col. of Columbia, S. C.
JAMES R. CHILTON, M. D.,
Chemistry, etc., New York.
G. C. SCHAEFFER,
Associate Prof. Chem., Columbia College, N. Y.
EDWARD CLARK.
CHARLES A. LEE, M. D.

Such a report as this should have inspired public confidence in the invention, but it did not; and, in a very few days after it was made, the Professor wrote to his partner, Mr. Smith, a letter in which he appears on the point of abandoning it as a hopeless enterprise. His own confidence in it was undiminished, but it must perish if he could not obtain aid:

" While, so far as the invention itself is concerned, every thing is favorable, I find myself without sympathy or help from any who are associated with me, whose interest one would think would impel them at least to inquire if they could render some assistance. For nearly two years past, I have devoted all my time and scanty means, living on a mere pittance, denying myself all pleasures, and even necessary food, that I might have a sum to put my Telegraph into such a position before Congress as to insure success to the common enterprise. I am crushed for want of means, and means of so trifling a character, too, that they who know how to ask (which I do not) could obtain in a few hours. One year more has gone, for want of these means. I have now ascertained that, however unpromising were the times last session, if I could but have gone to Washington I could have got some aid to enable me to insure success at the next session. As it is, although every thing is favorable, although I have no competition, and no opposition—on the contrary, although every member of Congress, as far as I can learn, is favorable—yet I fear all will fail because I am too poor to risk the trifling expense which my journey and residence in Washington will occasion me. *I will not run in debt*, if I lose the whole matter. So, unless I have the means from some source, I shall be compelled, however reluctantly, to leave it; and, if I get once engaged in my proper profession again, the Telegraph and its proprietors will urge me from it in vain. No one can tell the days and months of anxiety and labor I have had in perfecting my telegraphic apparatus. For want of means, I have been compelled to make with my own hands (and to labor for weeks) a piece of mechanism which could be made much better, and in a tenth part of the time, by a good mechanician, thus wasting *time*—time which I cannot recall, and which seems double-winged to me.

" ' Hope deferred maketh the heart sick.' It is true, and I have known the full meaning of it. Nothing but the consciousness that I have an invention which is to mark an era in human civilization, and which is to contribute to the happiness of millions, would have sustained me through so many and such lengthened trials of patience in perfecting it."

SUBMARINE CABLE.

During the summer of this year (1842), Professor Morse had been making great preparations for an experiment destined to give wonderful development to his invention. This was no less

than a submarine wire, to demonstrate the fact that the current
of electricity could be conducted as well under water as through
the air.   Of this he had entertained no doubt.   " If I can make
it work ten miles, I can make it go around the globe," was a
favorite expression of his in the infancy of his enterprise.   But
he wished to prove it.   He insulated his wire as well as he could
with hempen strands well covered with pitch, tar, and India-rubber.   In the course of the autumn he was prepared to put the
question to the test of actual experiment.   The wire was only
the twelfth of an inch in diameter, as may be seen from the
annexed engraving of the lateral and end sections :

The copper wire is represented by the white space in the end-
section.   About two miles of this, wound on a reel, was placed
in a small row-boat, and, with one man at the oars and Professor
Morse at the stern, the work of paying out the cable was commenced.   It was a beautiful moonlight night, and those who
had prolonged their evening rambles on the Battery wondered,
as they gazed at the proceedings in the boat, what kind of fishing
the two men could be engaged in that required so long a line.
In somewhat less than two hours, on that eventful evening of
the 18th of October, 1842, "the cable" was laid.   Professor
Morse returned to his lodgings and waited with some anxiety
the time when he should be able to test the experiment fully
and fairly.   The next morning the *New York Herald* contained the following editorial announcement :

"MORSE'S ELECTRO-MAGNETIC TELEGRAPH.

"This important invention is to be exhibited in operation at Castle Garden between the hours of twelve and one o'clock to-day.   One
telegraph will be erected on Governor's Island, and one at the Castle, and messages will be interchanged and orders transmitted during the day.   Many have been incredulous as to the powers of this
wonderful triumph of science and art.   All such may now have an
opportunity of fairly testing it.   *It is destined to work a complete
revolution in the mode of transmitting intelligence throughout the
civilized world.*"

At daybreak the Professor was on the Battery, and had just
demonstrated his success by the transmission of three or four

characters between the termini of the line, when the communication was suddenly interrupted, and it was found impossible to send any messages through the conductor. The cause of this was explained by his observing no less than seven vessels lying along the line of the submerged cable, one of which, in getting under way, had raised it on her anchor. The sailors, unable to divine its meaning, hauled in about two hundred feet of it on deck, and, finding no end, cut off that portion, and carried it away with them. Thus ended the first attempt at submarine telegraphing. The crowd that had assembled on the Battery dispersed with jeers, the most of .them believing they had been made the victims of a hoax. A few only, and the patient inventor was one of the very few, hoped on, while the prospect of success was darkened by this public failure. He knew that it was successful; and believed the world would yet acknowledge it. The Professor renewed the experiment in Washington, in December, by carrying his wires through the canal, and then with perfect success. Both of these experiments are mentioned in detail in his letter to the Secretary of the Treasury, December 23, 1844.

The Vails had been among his best friends, and were still warmly attached to him and his work. To them he turned in the hope of obtaining the means to enable him to go to Washington, and make one more effort to secure the assistance of Government. To his application for a small sum of money, he received the following reply, which showed him very clearly that, hereafter, his only reliance must be on God and himself:

Hon. George Vail to Professor Morse.

"SPEEDWELL IRON-WORKS, *December* 3, 1842.

"S. F. B. MORSE, Esq.

"DEAR SIR: Your favor is at hand. I had expected that my father would visit you, but he could not go out in the snow-storm of Wednesday, and, if he had, I do not think any thing could induce him to raise the needful for the prosecution of our object. He says: 'Tell Mr. Morse that there is no one that I would sooner assist than him, if I could, but, in the present posture of my affairs, I am not warranted in undertaking any thing more than to make my payments as they become due, of which they are not a few.' He thinks that Mr. S—— might soon learn how to manage it; and, as he is there, it would save a great expense. I do not myself know that he could learn ; but, as my means are nothing at the present time, I can only wish you success, if you go on.

"I am yours truly,   ` GEORGE VAIL."

This letter cut off the last earthly hope of the disappointed and despairing inventor. There was a double significance in its last words. Mr. Vail referred merely to Professor Morse's wish to go on to Washington to make his last appeal for Government assistance. But, to his sensitive mind, it was a suggestion that all he could expect of aid was the good wishes of his friends, if he were to go on with his fond scheme of an electric telegraph to cover the earth. Mr. Coffin, the agent who had promised so much aid, and had been so unsuccessful in the previous session of Congress, renewed his application to be again employed. But Professor Morse wrote to him that he had determined to go to Washington himself, and that he believed it indispensable to success that he should give his personal attention to the business.

The Hon. C. G. Ferris, of New York, of the Committee on Commerce, having taken a deep interest in the Telegraph, and fully appreciating its prospective value to the world, sought to make himself thoroughly acquainted with all the principles and facts involved, that he might intelligently press the subject upon the attention of Congress. At his request, Professor Morse wrote the following letter and petition :

S. F. B. Morse to the Hon. C. G. Ferris.

"NEW YORK, *December* 6, 1842.

"DEAR SIR : In compliance with your request, I give you a slight history of my electro-magnetic telegraph, since it was presented for the consideration of Congress, in the year 1838.

"During the session of the Twenty-fifth Congress, a report was made by the Committee on Commerce of the House, which concluded by unanimously submitting a bill appropriating thirty thousand dollars for the purpose of testing my system of electro-magnetic telegraphs. The pressure of business at the close of that session prevented any action being taken upon it.

"Before the session closed, I visited England and France, for the double purpose of submitting my invention to the test of

European criticism, and to secure to myself some remuneration for my large expenditures of time and money in elaborating my invention. In France, after a patent had been secured in that country, my telegraph first attracted the attention of the Academy of Sciences, and its operation was shown, and its principles were explained, by the celebrated philosopher, Arago, in the session of that distinguished body of learned men, on September 10, 1838. Its reception was of the most enthusiastic character. Several other societies, among which were the Academy of Industry and the Philotechnic Society, appointed committees to examine and report upon the invention, from all of which I received votes of thanks, and from the former the large medal of honor. The French Government at this time had its attention drawn to the subject of electric telegraphs, several systems having been presented for its consideration, from England, Germany, and France. Through the kind offices of our minister at the French Court, General Cass, my telegraph was also submitted; and the Minister of the Interior (M. Montalivet) appointed a commission, at the head of which was placed M. Alphonse Foy, the administrator-in-chief of the telegraphs of France, with directions to examine and report upon all the various systems which had been presented. The result of this examination (in which the ingenious systems of Professor Wheatstone, of London, of Professor Steinheil, of Munich, and Professor Masson, of Caen, passed in review) was a report to the minister in favor of mine. In a note addressed to me by M. Foy, who had expressed his warmest admiration of my telegraph in my presence, he thus writes:

" 'I take a true pleasure in confirming to you in writing that which I have already had the honor to say to you *viva voce*, that I have prominently presented (*signalé*) to monsieur the Minister of the Interior your electro-magnetic telegraph, as being the system which presents the best chance of a practical application; and I have stated to him that, if some trials are to be made with electric telegraphs, I hesitate not to recommend that they should be made with your apparatus.'

" In England my application for a patent for my invention was opposed before the Attorney-General by Professor Wheatstone and Mr. Davy, each of whom had systems already patented, essentially like each other, but very different from mine. A patent was denied me by the Attorney-General, Sir John Campbell, on a plea which I am confident will not bear a legal examination. But there being no appeal from the Attorney-General's decision, nor remedy, except at enormous expense, I am deprived of all benefit from my invention in England. Other causes than impartial justice evidently operated against me. An interest for my invention, however, sprung up voluntarily, and quite unexpectedly, among the English nobility and gentry in Paris, and, had I possessed the requisite funds to prosecute my rights before the British Parliament, I could scarcely have failed to secure them, so powerfully was I supported by this interest in my favor; and I should be ungrateful did I not take every opportunity to acknowledge the kindness of the several noblemen and gentlemen who volunteered to aid me in obtaining my rights in England, among the foremost of whom were the Earl of Lincoln, the late celebrated Earl of Elgin, and the Hon. Henry Drummond.

"I returned to the United States in the spring of 1839, under an engagement entered into in Paris with the Russian Councilor of State, the Baron Alexandre de Meyendorf, to visit St. Petersburg with a distinguished French *savant*, M. Amyot, for the purpose of establishing my telegraphic system in that country. The contract, formally entered into, was transmitted to St. Petersburg, for the signature of the emperor, which I was led to believe would be given without a doubt; and, that no time should be lost in my preparations, the contract, duly signed, was to be transmitted to me in New York, through the Russian ambassador in the United States, in four or five weeks, at farthest, after my arrival home.

"After waiting, in anxious suspense, for as many months, without any intelligence, I learned *indirectly* that the emperor, from causes not satisfactorily explained, refused to sign the contract.

"These disappointments (not at all affecting the scientific or practical character of my invention), combined with the financial depression of the country, compelled me to rest a while from further prosecuting my enterprise. For the last two years, however, under many discouraging circumstances, from want of the requisite funds for more thoroughly investigating some of the principles involved in the invention, I have, nevertheless, been able to resolve all the doubts that lingered in my own mind, in regard to the perfect practicability of establishing my telegraphic system to any extent on the globe. I say, 'doubts that lingered in my own mind;' the principle, and indeed the only one of a scientific character, which at all troubled me, I will state, and the manner in which it has been resolved:

"At an early stage of my experiments, I found that the magnetic power produced in an electro-magnet, by a single galvanic pair, diminished rapidly as the length of the conductors increased. Ordinary reasoning on this fact would lead to a conclusion fatal to the whole invention, since at a great distance I could not operate at all, or, in order to operate, I should be compelled to make use of a battery of such a size as would render the whole plan in effect impracticable. I was, indeed, aware that, by multiplying the pairs in the battery—that is, increasing the intensity of its propulsive power—certain effects could be produced at great distances, such as the decomposition of water, a visible spark, and the deflection of the magnetic needle. But as magnetic effects, except in the latter case, had not, to my knowledge, been made the subject of careful experiment, and as these various effects of electrical action seemed, in some respects, to ,be obedient to different laws, I did not feel entirely assured that magnetism could be produced by a multiplication of pairs sufficiently powerful at a great distance to effect my purpose. From a series of experiments which I made, in conjunction with Professor Fisher, during the last summer, upon thirty three miles of wire, the interesting fact so favorable to my telegraphic system was fully verified, that, *while the distance increased in an arithmetical ratio, an addition to the series of galvanic pairs of plates increased the magnetic power in a geometric ratio.* Fifty pairs of plates were used as a constant power. Two miles of conductors at a time, from two to thirty-three, were successively added to the distance. The weight upheld by the magnet from the magnetism produced by fifty pairs, gradually diminished up to the distance of ten miles ; after which, *the addition of miles of wire up to thirty-three miles* (the extent to which we were able to try it) *caused no further visible diminution of power.* The weight then sustained was a constant quantity. The practical deduction from these experiments is the fact that, with a very small battery, all the effects I desire, and at any distance, can be produced. In the experiments alluded to, the fifty pairs did not occupy a space of more than eight cubic inches, and they comprised but fifty square inches of active surface.

"The practicability of establishing my telegraphic system is thus relieved from all scientific objections.

"Let me now turn your attention, sir, one moment, to a consideration of the telegraph as a source of revenue. The imperfections of the common systems, particularly their uselessness, on account of the weather, three-quarters of the time, have concealed from view so natural a fruit of a perfected telegraphic system. So uncertain are the common telegraphs as to time, and so meagre in the quantity of intelligence they can transmit under the most favorable circumstances, that the idea of making them a source of revenue would not be likely to occur. So far, indeed, from being a source of revenue, the systems in common use in Europe are sustained at great expense; an expense which, imperfect as they are, is justified, in the view of the Government, by the great political advantages which they produce. Telegraphs with them are a government monopoly, and used only for government purposes. They are in harmony with the genius of those governments. The people have no advantage from them, except indirectly as the government is benefited. Were our mails used solely for the purpose of the Government, and private individuals forbidden to correspond by them, they would furnish a good illustration of the operation of the common European telegraphic systems.

"The Electro-Magnetic Telegraph, I would fain think, is more in consonance with the political institutions under which we live, and is fitted, like the mail system, to diffuse its benefits alike to the Government and to the people at large.

"As a source of *revenue*, then, to the Government, few, I believe, have seriously computed the great profits to be derived from such a system of telegraphs as I propose; and yet there are sure data already obtained by which they can be demonstrated.

"The first fact is, that every minute of the twenty-four hours is available to send intelligence.

"The second fact is, that twelve signs, at least, can be sent in a minute, instantaneously, as any one may have proof by actual demonstration of the fact, on the instrument now operating in the Capitol.[1]

"There can be no doubt that the cases, where such speedy transmission of intelligence from one distant city to another is desirable, are so numerous, that, when once the line is made for such transmission, it will be in constant use, and a demand made for a greater number of lines.

"The paramount convenience, to commercial agents and others, of thus corresponding at a distance, will authorize *a rate of postage proportionate to the distance*, on the principle of rating postage by the mails.

[1] Ninety-eight, per minute, can now be sent (1845).

"To illustrate the operation of the telegraph in increasing the revenue, let us suppose that but eighteen hours of the twenty-four are efficiently used for the actual purposes of revenue; that six hours are allowed for repetitions and other purposes, which is a large allowance. This would give, upon a single circuit, 12,960 signs per day, upon which a rate of postage is to be charged. Intelligence of great extent may be comprised in a few signs. Suppose the following commercial communication is to be transmitted from New York to New Orleans:

" ' Yrs., Dec. 21, rec. Buy 25 bales c., at 9, and 300 pork, at 8.'

"Here are thirty-six signs, which take three minutes in the transmission from New York to New Orleans, and which informs the New York merchant's correspondent at New Orleans of the receipt of a certain document, and gives him orders to purchase twenty-five bales of cotton at nine cents per pound, and three hundred barrels of pork at eight cents per pound. Thus may be completed, in three minutes, a transaction in business which now would take at least four or five weeks to accomplish. .

"Suppose that one cent per sign be charged for the first 100 miles, increasing the charge at the rate of half a cent. each additional 100 miles, the postage of the above communication would be $2.88 for a distance of 1,500 miles. It would be sent 100 miles for 36 cents. Would any merchant grudge so small a sum for sending such an amount of information in so short a time to such a distance? If time is money, and to save time is to save money, surely such an immense saving of time is the saving of an immense sum of money. A telegraphic line of a single circuit only, from New York to New Orleans, would realize, then, to the Government, *daily*, in the correspondence between those two cities alone, over *one thousand dollars*, gross receipts, or over $300,000 per annum.

"But it is a well-established fact that, as facilities of intercourse increase between different parts of the country, the greater is that intercourse. Thousands travel, in this day of railroads and steamboats, who never thought of leaving their homes before. Establish, then, the means of instantaneous communication between the most distant places, and the telegraphic line of a single circuit will very soon be insufficient to supply the demands of the public—they will require more.

"Two circuits will of course *double the facilities, and double the revenue ;* but it is an important fact that the expense of afterward establishing a second, or any number of circuits, does not proceed

29

on the *doubling* principle. If a channel for conveying a single circuit be made, in the first instance, of sufficient capacity to contain
many more circuits, which can easily be done, additional circuits
can be laid as fast as they are called for, at but little more than the
cost of the prepared wire. The recent discovery of Professor Fisher
and myself shows that a single wire may be made the common conductor for at least six circuits. How many more we have not yet
ascertained. So that to add another circuit is but to add another
wire. Fifty dollars per mile, under these circumstances, would,
therefore, add the means of doubling the facilities and the revenue.

"Between New York and Philadelphia, for example, the whole
cost of laying such an additional circuit would be but $5,000, which
would be more than defrayed by *two months'* receipts only from the
telegraphs between these two cities.

"There are two modes of establishing the line of conductors.

"The first and cheapest is doubtless that of erecting spars about
30 feet in height and 350 feet apart, extending the conductors along
the tops of the spars. This method has some obvious disadvantages. The expense would be from $350 to $400 per mile.

"The second method is that of inclosing the conductors in leaden
tubes, and laying them in the earth. I have made the following
estimate of the cost of this method:

Wire, prepared, per mile	$150 00
Lead pipe, with solderings	250 00
Delivery of the pipe and wire	25 00
Passing wire into the pipes	5 00
Excavations and filling in about 1,000 yards per mile, or 3 feet	
deep, at 15 cents per square yard . . . . . -	150 00
Laying down the pipe	3 00
	$583 00

One register, with its machinery, comprising a galvanic battery	
of four pairs of my double-cup battery	$100 00
One battery of 200 pairs	100 00

Expense for thirty-nine miles	$22,837 00
Two registers	200 00
Two batteries	200 00
Services of chief superintendent of construction per annum .	2,000 00
Services of three assistants, at $1,500 each, per annum .	4,500 00
	$29,637 00

"As experience alone can determine the best mode of securing the conductors, I should wish the means and opportunity of trying various modes to such an extent as will demonstrate the best.

"Before closing my letter, sir, I ought to give you the proofs I possess that the American Telegraph has the *priority in the time of its invention.*

"The two European Telegraphs in practical operation are Professor Steinheil's, of Munich, and Professor Wheatstone's, of London. The former is adopted by the Bavarian Government; the latter is established about 200 miles in England, under the direction of a company in London. In a highly-interesting paper on the subject of telegraphs, translated and inserted in the *London Annals of Electricity,* March and April, 1839, Professor Steinheil gives a brief sketch of the various projects of electric telegraphs, from the time of Franklin's electrical experiments to the present day. Until the birth of the science of electro-magnetism, generated by the important discovery of Oersted, in 1820, of the action of electric currents upon the magnetic needle, the Electric Telegraph was but a philosophic toy, complicated and practically useless. Let it be here noticed that, after the discovery of Oersted, the *deflection of the needle* became the principle upon which the *savants* of Europe based all their attempts to construct an electric telegraph. The celebrated Ampère, in the same year of Oersted's discovery, suggested a plan of telegraphs, to consist of a magnetic needle, and a circuit for each letter of the alphabet and the numerals—making it necessary to have some sixty or seventy wires between the two termini of the telegraphic line.

"The suggestion of Ampère is, doubtless, the parent of all the attempts in Europe, both abortive and successful, for constructing an electric telegraph.

"Under this head may be arranged the Baron Schilling's at St. Petersburg, consisting of thirty-six needles, and upward of sixty metallic conductors, and invented, it seems, at the same date with my Electro-Magnetic. Telegraph, in the autumn of 1832. Under the same head comes that of Professors Gauss and Weber, of Göttingen, in 1833, who simplified the plan by using but a single needle and a single circuit. Professor Wheatstone's, of London, invented in 1837, comes under the same category; he employs five needles and six conductors. Professor Steinheil's, also invented in 1837, employs two needles and two conductors.

"But there was another discovery in the infancy of the science of electro-magnetism, by Ampère and Arago, immediately cousequent on that of Oersted, namely, the *electro-magnet*, which none of the *savants* of Europe who have planned electric telegraphs ever thought of applying, until within two years past, for the purpose of signals. My Telegraph is essentially based on this latter discovery.

"Supposing my Telegraph to be based on the same principle with the European electric telegraphs, which it is not, mine, having been invented in 1832, would still have the precedence, by some months at least, of Gauss and Weber's, to whom Steinheil gives the credit of being the first to simplify and make practicable the Electric Telegraph. But when it is considered that all the European telegraphs make use of the deflection of the needle to accomplish their results, and that none use *the attractive power of the electro-magnet to write in legible characters*, I think I can claim, without injustice to others, to be the first inventor of the *Electro-Magnetic Telegraph*.

"In 1839 I visited London, on my return from France, and, through the polite solicitations of the Earl of Lincoln, showed and explained its operation at his house, on the 19th of March, 1839, to a large company which he had expressly invited for the purpose, composed of Lords of the Admiralty, members of the Royal Society, and members of both Houses of Parliament.

"Professor Wheatstone has announced that he has recently (in 1840) also invented and patented an *electro-magnetic telegraph*, differing altogether from his invention of 1837, which he calls his *Magnetic-Needle Telegraph*. His is, therefore, the first European electro-magnetic telegraph, and was invented, as is perceived, eight years subsequent to mine, and one year after my Telegraph *was exhibited in the public manner described at the Earl of Lincoln's residence in London*.

"I am the more minute in adducing this evidence of priority of invention to you, sir, since I have frequently been charged by Europeans, in my own country, with merely imitating long-known European inventions. It is, therefore, due to my own country, as well as to myself, that in this matter the facts should be known.

"Professor Steinheil's telegraph is the only European telegraph that professes to *write* the intelligence. He records, however, by the delicate touch of the needle in its deflections, with what practical effect I am unable to say; but I should think that it was too delicate and uncertain, especially as compared with the strong and efficient power which may be produced in any degree by the electro-magnet.

"I have devoted many years of my life to this invention, sustained in many of the disappointments by the belief that it is destined eventually to confer immense benefits upon my country and the world. "

"I am persuaded that whatever facilitates intercourse between the different portions of the human family will have the effect, under the guidance of sound moral principles, to promote the best interests of man. I ask of Congress the means of demonstrating its efficiency.

"I remain, sir, with great respect, your most obedient servant,

"SAMUEL F. B. MORSE.

"Hon. CHARLES G. FERRIS,

"*Member of the House of Representatives from the city of New York, and one of the Committee on Commerce, to whom was referred the subject of the expediency of adopting a system of electro-magnetic telegraphs for the United States.*"

Immediately after this letter was sent, Professor Morse once more appeared at the seat of government, to press his importunate suit for aid. Christopher Columbus was not more persistent under discouragements. In the Capitol Professor Morse again mounted his wires and implored the members of Congress and officers of the Government to come and see. An incident occurred at this time that greatly cheered him, though it was in itself of very little moment. Mr. Tuckerman, in his "Lives of the Painters," records it as having occurred after the appropriation by Congress was made, but it happened while making preparations for the exhibition of the instrument:

"A striking evidence of the waywardness of destiny is afforded by the experience of this artist, if we pass at once from this early and hopeful moment to a more recent incident. He then aimed at renown, through devotion to the beautiful; but it would seem as if the genius of his country, in spite of himself, led him to this object by the less flowery path of utility. He desired to identify his name with art, but it has become far more widely associated with science. A series of bitter disappointments obliged him to 'coin his mind for bread,' for a long period of exclusive attention to portrait-painting, although at rare intervals he accomplished something more satisfactory. More than thirty years since, on a voyage from Europe, in a conversation with his fellow-passengers, the theme of discourse happened to be the electro-magnet;

and one gentleman present related some experiments he had lately witnessed at Paris, which proved the almost incalculable rapidity of movement with which electricity was disseminated. The idea suggested itself to the active mind of the artist, that this wonderful and but partially explored agent might be rendered subservient to that system of intercommunication which had become so important a principle of modern civilization. He brooded over the subject as he walked the deck, or lay wakeful in his berth, and, by the time he arrived at New York, had so far matured his invention as to have decided upon a telegraph of signs, which is essentially that now in use. After having sufficiently demonstrated his discovery to the scientific, a long period of toil, anxiety, and suspense, intervened before he obtained the requisite facilities for the establishment of the magnetic telegraph. It is now in daily operation in the United States, and its superiority over all similar inventions abroad was confirmed by the testimony of Arago and the appropriation made for its erection by the French Government.

" By one of those coincidences which would be thought appropriate for romance, but which are more common, in fact, than the unobservant are disposed to confess, these two most brilliant events in the painter's life—his first successful work of art and the triumph of his scientific discovery—were brought together, as it were, in a manner singularly fitted to impress the imagination. Six copies of his ' Dying Hercules ' had been made in London, and the mould was then destroyed. Four of these were distributed by the artist to academies, one he retained, and the last was given to Mr. Bulfinch, the architect of the Capitol, who was engaged at the time upon that building. After the lapse of many years, an accident ruined Morse's own copy, and a similar fate had overtaken the others, at least in America. After vain efforts to regain one of these trophies of his youthful career, he at length despaired of seeing again what could not fail to be endeared to his memory by the most interesting associations. One day he was superintending the preparations for the first establishment of his telegraph in the room assigned at the Capitol. His perseverance and self-denying labor had at length met its just reward, and he was taking the first active step to obtain a substantial benefit from his invention. It became necessary, in locating the wires, to descend into a vault beneath the apartment, which had not been opened for a long period. A man preceded the artist with a lamp. As they passed along the subterranean chamber, the latter's attention was attracted by something white glimmering through the darkness. In approaching the object, what was his surprise to find himself gazing upon his long-lost Hercules, which he had not seen 'for twenty years! A little reflection explained the apparent miracle. This was undoubtedly the copy given to his deceased friend the architect, and temporarily deposited in the vault for safety, and undiscovered until after his death."

On the last day but one of this year, 1842, Mr. Ferris submitted to Congress the report and·bill which resulted in favorable action. It is in these words:

Mr. Ferris, from the Committee on Commerce, made the following Report, December 30, 1842:

That they regard the question, as to the general utility of the telegraphic system, settled by its adoption by the most civilized nations; and experience has fully demonstrated the great advantages which may be derived from its use. Its capability of speedily transmitting intelligence to great distances, for national defense, and for other purposes, where celerity is desirable, is decidedly superior to any of the ordinary modes of communication in use. By it, the first warning of approaching danger, and the appearance of hostile fleets and armies on our coasts and borders, may be announced simultaneously and at the most distant points of our widely-extended empire, thus affording time and opportunity for concentrating the military force of the country, for facilitating military and naval movements, and for transmitting orders suitable to the emergency.

In the commercial and social affairs of the community, occasions frequently arise in which the speedy transmission of intelligence may be of the highest importance for the regulation of business transactions, and in relieving the anxious solicitude of friends, as to the health and condition of those in whose fortunes they feel an interest.

The practicability of establishing telegraphs on the electric principle is no longer a question. Wheatstone, of London, and his associates, have been more fortunate than our American inventor, in procuring the means to put his ingenious system into practical use for two or three hundred miles, in Great Britain; and the movements of the cars on the Blackwall Railroad are at this time directed with great economy, and perfect safety to life and property, by means of his magnetic needle telegraph. If a system more complicated and less efficient than the American telegraph is operated for great distances in England, with such eminent success and advantage, there can be no reasonable doubt that, if the means be furnished for putting in operation the system of Professor Samuel F. B. Morse, of New York, the original inventor of the electro-magnetic telegraph, the same, if not·greater success, will be the result. Your committee are of opinion that it is but justice to Professor Morse, who is alike distinguished for his attainments in science and excellence in the arts of design, and who has patiently devoted many years of unremitting study, and freely spent his private fortune, in inventing and bringing to perfection a system of telegraphs which is calculated to advance the scientific reputation of the country, and to be eminently useful, both to the Government and the people, that he should be furnished with the means of competing with his European rivals.

Professor Morse bases his system upon the two following facts in science :

1. That a current of electricity will pass to any distance along a conductor connecting the two poles of a voltaic battery or generator of electricity, and produce visible effects at any desired points on that conductor.

2. That magnetism is produced in a piece of soft iron (around which the conductor, in its progress, is made to pass) when the electric current is permitted to flow, and that the magnetism ceases when the current of electricity is prevented from flowing. This current of electricity is produced and destroyed by breaking and closing the galvanic circuit at the pleasure of the operator of the telegraph, who in this manner directs and controls the operation of a simple and compact piece of mechanism, styled the register, which, at the will of the operator at the point of communication, is made to record, at the point of reception, legible characters, on a roll of paper put in motion at the same time with the writing instrument. These characters the inventor has arranged into a conventional *alphabet*, and which is capable of being learned and used with very little practice.

Professor Morse has submitted his telegraphic plan to the severe scrutiny of European criticism; and the Academy of Sciences, of Paris, the highest scientific tribunal in the world, hailed it with enthusiasm and approbation, when its operation was exhibited, and its principles explained, by their distinguished perpetual secretary, M. Arago.

It appears, from documents produced by Professor Morse, that the thanks of the several learned bodies in France were voted to him for his invention, and the large medal of honor was awarded to him by the Academy of Industry. It further appears that several other systems of telegraphs on the electric plan (among which were Wheatstone's, of London; Steinheil's, of Munich; and Masson's, of Caen) had been submitted at various times for the consideration of the French Government, who appointed a commission to examine and report on them all, at the head of which commission was placed the administrator-in-chief of the telegraphs of France (M. Foy), who, in a note to Professor Morse, thus writes:

"I take a true pleasure in confirming to you in writing that which I have already had the honor to say to you *viva voce*—that I have prominently presented to Monsieur the Minister of the Interior your electro-magnetic telegraph, as being the system which presents the best chance of a practical application; and I have declared to him that, if some trials are to be made with electric telegraphs, I do not hesitate to recommend that they should be made with your apparatus."

Your committee, in producing further evidence of the approbation by the scientific world of the system of Professor Morse, would cite the letter of Professor Henry, of Princeton College, well known for his eminent attainments in electrical science, in the appendix of this report.

More recently, a committee, consisting of some of our most distinguished scientific citizens, was appointed by the American Institute, of New York, to examine and report upon this telegraph, who made the report in the appendix. In compliance with the recommendation of this report, the Institute awarded to Professor Morse the gold medal.

Besides the evidence these testimonials furnish of the excellence of Professor Morse's system, your committee, as well as the greater part of the members of both Houses of Congress, have had a practical demonstration of the operation of the electro-magnetic telegraph, and have witnessed the perfect facility and extraordinary rapidity with which a message can be sent by means of it from one extremity of the Capitol to the other. This rapidity is not confined in its effects to a few hundred feet, but science makes it certain that the same effects can be produced at any distance on the globe, between any two given points connected by the conductors.

Your committee have alluded to other electric telegraphs; for, as is not uncommon in the birth of great inventions, scientific minds have, at nearly the same period of time, in various parts of Europe, conceived and planned electric telegraphs; but it is a matter of national pride, that the invention of the *first electro-magnetic telegraph*, by Professor Morse, as well as the *first conception* of using electricity as the means of transmitting intelligence, by Doctor Franklin, is the offspring of American genius.

Your committee beg leave to refer to the letter of Professor Morse, in the appendix, to C. G. Ferris, one of the committee, giving, at his request, a brief history of the telegraph since it was before Congress in 1838, for some interesting information concerning it, and for Professor Morse's estimate of the probable expense of establishing his system of telegraphs for thirty or forty miles.

They would also refer to the House document, No. 15 (December 6, 1837), and to House report, No. 753 (April 6, 1838), for valuable information on the subject of telegraphs.

Your committee invite special attention to that part of Professor Morse's letter which details the plan of a *revenue* which may be derived from his telegraphic system, when established to an extent sufficient for the purpose of commercial and general intelligence. From these calculations, made upon safe data, it is probable that an income would be derived from its use by merchants and citizens more than sufficient to defray the interest of the capital expended in its establishment. So inviting, indeed, are the prospects of profit to individual enterprise, that it is a matter of serious consideration, whether the Government should not, on this account alone, seize the present opportunity of securing to itself the regulation of a system which, if monopolized by a private company, might be used to the serious injury of the Post-Office Department, and which could not be prevented without such an interference with the rights of the inventor and of the stockholders as could not be sustained by justice or public opinion.

After the ordeal to which the electro-magnetic telegraph system has been subjected, both in Europe and in America, and the voice of the scientific world in its favor, it is scarcely necessary for your committee to say that they have the fullest confidence in Professor Morse's plan, and they earnestly recommend the adoption of it by the Government of the United States. They deem it most fortunate that no definite system of telegraphs should hitherto have been adopted by the Government, since it enables them to establish this improved system, which, in the opinion of your committee, is decidedly superior to any other now in use, possessing an advantage over telegraphs depending on vision, inasmuch as it may be used both by night and day, in all weathers, and in all seasons of the year, with equal convenience; and, also, possessing an advantage over electric telegraphs heretofore in use, inasmuch as it records, in permanent legible characters on paper, any communication which may be made by it, without the aid of any agent at the place of recording, except the apparatus which is put in motion at the point of communication. Thus, the recording apparatus, called the register, may be left in a closed chamber, where it will give notice of its commencing to write, by a bell, and the communication may be found on opening the apartment. Possessing these great advantages, and the means of communication not being liable to interruption by the ordinary contingencies which may impede or prevent the successful action of other telegraphs, the advantages to be derived from it will soon be apparent to the community, and it will become the successful rival of the Post-Office, when celerity of communication is desired, and create a revenue from which this system of telegraphs may be extended and ramified through all parts of the country, without imposing any burden upon the people or draughts on the treasury, beyond the outlay for its first establishment.

As a first step toward the adoption of this system of telegraphs by the Government, your committee recommend the appropriation of thirty thousand dollars, to be expended under the direction of the Postmaster-General, in constructing a line of electro-magnetic telegraphs, under the superintendence of Professor Samuel F. B. Morse, of such length, and between such points, as shall fully test its practicability and utility; and for this purpose they respectfully submit the following bill:

A Bill to test the Practicability of establishing a System of Electro-Magnetic Telegraphs by the United States.

Be it enacted by the Senate and House of Representatives of the United States in Congress assembled, That the sum of thirty thousand dollars be, and is hereby appropriated, out of any moneys in the Treasury not otherwise appropriated, for testing the capacity and usefulness of the system of electro-magnetic telegraphs invented by Samuel F. B. Morse, of New York, for the use of the Government of the United States, by constructing a line of said electro-magnetic telegraphs, under the superintendence of Professor Samuel F. B. Morse, of such length and between such points as shall fully test its practicability and utility; and that the same shall be expended under the direction of the Postmaster-General upon the application of said Morse.

Sec. 2. *And be it further enacted,* That the Postmaster-General be, and he is hereby authorized to pay, out of the aforesaid thirty thousand dollars, to the said Samuel F. B. Morse, and the persons employed under him, such sums of money as he may deem to be a fair compensation for the services of the said Samuel F. B. Morse and the persons employed under him, in constructing and in superintending the construction of the said line of telegraphs authorized by this bill.

To us, with the triumphs of the Telegraph before us, and its incorporation into the business and intercourse of the world, so as to have become as essential as steam, it seems incredible, after the complete success of the initial experiment, that Congress should have so little faith as to hesitate to make the slight appropriation required to test it practically over a space of thirty or forty miles. But it had some believing friends. The Commissioner of Patents, Hon. H. L. Ellsworth, was one of its earliest and firmest supporters. He was ardently interested in the inventor. He received him into his own family, cheered him in his retirement, sustained his flagging energies, and smoothed his path with unceasing kindness and hopes of ultimate success. Several members of Congress—Kennedy, of Maryland; Mason, of Ohio; Wallace, of Indiana; Ferris and Boardman, of New York; Holmes, of South Carolina; Aycrigg, of New Jersey, and others—supported the measure with energy and ability. The favorable report of the bill from the Committee of Commerce was the closing and encouraging point in the history of the Telegraph for the year 1842. Ten years had elapsed since, on board the ship, the scheme of the Telegraph, connecting cities and continents, had dawned upon the mind of the inventor. Apparently he had often been upon the point of seeing his dreams made real by the practical faith of his country. Doomed to disappointment and driven to the verge of despair, he persevered with that energy which faith only inspires. Another year—1843 —the year of success, the year to be hereafter associated with that of 1832 in the history of the Telegraph, at length opened in the life of the inventor. Day after day he stood at his instrument, meekly and sometimes tearfully explaining to successive visitors its operations. One and another member of Congress came, saw, heard, and went away believing. Others mocked. The most were silent, waiting to see what would come of it. Two months of the year were nearly spent, and Congress would expire within a week. Hope was more slowly expiring in the breast of the anxious inventor. In vain were his entreaties. His predictions were as those of a mad prophet. At last, on the 21st day of February, 1843, the Hon. John P. Kennedy submitted a resolution, that "the bill appropriating thirty thousand dollars, to be expended under the direction of the Secretary of the Treasury, in a series of experiments to test the expediency of the Telegraph projected by Professor Morse, should be passed." The debate that followed is fortunately not preserved in the journals of the day nor in the official reports. That it was exceedingly discreditable to the intelligence of an American Congress is abundantly evident in the meagre report that remains. The *Congressional Globe*, professing to give *verbatim* reports of the proceedings, disposes of the discussion in a few lines, and this fact is perhaps the most striking evidence of the utter indifference of the public to the subject. Every word of the debate in the *Globe* is here given:

[*From the Congressional Globe, February* 21, 1843.]

ELECTRO AND ANIMAL MAGNETISM.

On motion of Mr. Kennedy, of Maryland, the committee took up the bill to authorize a series of experiments to be made, in order to test the merits of Morse's electro-magnetic telegraph. The bill appropriates thirty thousand dollars, to be expended under the direction of the Postmaster-General.

On motion of Mr. Kennedy, the words "Postmaster-General" were stricken out and Secretary of the Treasury inserted.

Mr. Cave Johnson wished to have a word to say upon the bill. As the present had done much to encourage science, he did not wish to see the science of mesmerism neglected and overlooked. He therefore proposed that one-half of the appropriation be given to Mr. Fisk, to enable him to carry on experiments, as well as Professor Morse.

Mr. Houston thought that Millerism should also be included in the benefits of the appropriation.

Mr. Stanly said he should have no objection to the appropriation for mesmeric experiments, provided the gentleman from Tennessee (Mr. Cave Johnson) was the subject. [A laugh.]

Mr. Cave Johnson said he should have no objection, provided the gentleman from North Carolina (Mr. Stanly) was the operator. [Great laughter.]

Several gentlemen called for the reading of the amendment, and it was read by the clerk, as follows:

" Provided, that one-half of the said sum shall be appropriated for trying mesmeric experiments, under the direction of the Secretary of the Treasury."

Mr. S. Mason rose to a question of order. He maintained that the amendment was not *bona fide*, and that such amendments were calculated to injure the character of the House. He appealed to the Chair to rule the amendment out of order.

The chairman said it was not for him to judge of the motives of members in offering amendments, and he could not, therefore, undertake to pronounce the amendment not *bona fide*. Objections might be raised to it on the ground that it was not sufficiently analogous in character to the bill under consideration, but, in the opinion of the Chair, it would require a scientific analysis to determine how far the magnetism of mesmerism was analogous to that to be employed in telegraph. [Laughter.] He therefore ruled the amendment in order.

On taking the vote, the amendment was rejected—yeas 22, nays not counted.

The bill was then laid aside, to be reported.

ELECTRO-MAGNETIC TELEGRAPH.

February 23, 1843.

On motion by Mr. J. P. Kennedy, the bill making appropriation to test the value of Morse's magnetic telegraph was taken up, and, under the operation of the previous question, passed—yeas 89, nays 83.

Professor Morse sat in the gallery while the vote was taken, his frame trembling with intense anxiety, and his soul struggling at that moment for the aid of an unseen power in which he believed and trusted in his darkest hours. IT WAS CARRIED. The majority was small—only six—but it was on the right side. The bill had passed the House. So far the victory was his. When the votes were recorded, they were found to stand—yeas

90, nays 82—majority 8. Professor Morse subjected them to analysis and classification, and the table remained among his papers throughout his life.

Vote on the Telegraph, February 23, 1843, in the House of Representatives.

	Neutral.	Yeas.	Nays.		Neutral.	Yeas.	Nays.
Maine	2	4	2	Georgia	5	..	4
New Hampshire.	1	..	4	Kentucky	6	3	4
Massachusetts...	6	4	2	Tennessee	3	1	9
Rhode Island....	1	1	..	Ohio...........	2	10	7
Connecticut.....	1	5	..	Louisiana	..	2	1
Vermont	..	4	1	Indiana	3	3	1
New York......	7	22	11	Mississippi	1	..	1
New Jersey.....	..	6	..	Illinois..........	..	1	2
Pennsylvania....	9	15	4	Alabama	3	..	2
Delaware.......	1	..	..	Missouri	2	..	..
Maryland.......	4	3	1	Arkansas	..	..	1
Virginia........	5	3	13	Michigan	..	1	..
North Carolina..	4	1	8				
South Carolina..	4	1	4		70	90	82

This table is suggestive, and will reward a careful study.

On the same day Professor Morse wrote to Hon. F. O. J. Smith:

" The long agony (truly agony to me) is over; for you will perceive, by the papers of to-morrow, that, so far as the House is concerned, the matter is decided. *My bill has passed by a vote of eighty-nine to eighty-three,* a close vote, you will say; but explained upon several grounds, not affecting the disposition of many individual members, who voted against it, to the invention. In matter, six votes are as good as a thousand, so far as the appropriation is concerned. The *yeas* and *nays* will tell you who were friendly, and who adverse to the bill. I shall now bend all my attention to the Senate. There is a good disposition there, and I am now strongly encouraged to think that my invention will be placed before the country in such a position as to be properly appreciated, and to yield to all its proprietors a proper compensation. I have no desire to vaunt my exertions, but I can truly say that I have never passed so trying a period as the last two months. Professor Fisher (who has been of the greatest service to me) and I have been busy from morning till night every day since we have been here.

" I have brought him on with me at my expense, and he will be one of the first assistants in the first experimental line if the bill passes. I shall want to see the proprietors together very soon after my return to New York. Drop me a line after you receive this, and let me know what you now think of matters. I received your letter in answer to mine some time since. I intended to reply, but was prevented by press of business at that time. All I will now say is, it was just such a letter as I expected from my friend Smith. My feelings at the prospect of success are of a joyous character, as you may well believe, and one of the principal elements of my joy is, that I shall be enabled to contribute to the happiness of all who formerly assisted me, some of whom are at present specially depressed."

On the same day the Professor wrote to Mr. Alfred Vail:

"You will perceive, by the papers to-morrow, that my bill appropriating thirty thousand dollars for a trial of the Telegraph, has just passed the House by a vote of eighty-nine to eighty-three. It is read a second time in the Senate, and I am now strongly in hopes that it will be carried through the.latter body, and become a law before the 4th of March. You can have but a faint idea of the sacrifices and trials I have had in getting the Telegraph thus far before the country and the world. I cannot detail them here; I can only say that, for two years, I have labored all my time, and at my own expense, without assistance from the other proprietors (except in obtaining the iron of the magnets for the last instruments obtained of you), to forward our enterprise; my means to defray my expenses, to meet which, every cent I owned in the world was collected, are nearly all gone; and if, by any means, the bill should fail in the Senate, I shall return to New York, with the *fraction of a dollar* in my pocket."

"I watched," says the Professor, writing to a friend in after-years of this memorable day, "with intense interest the progress and vicissitudes of the measure, through the House and then through the Senate. I had staked all I possessed on the issue. After much tantalizing delay the vote was taken in the House amid many attempts, by ridicule, to defeat the measure. One member moved that a portion of the appropriation should be given to a lecturer on animal magnetism, to experiment on that subject, which motion was tested and negatived by a vote and a count by tellers; another motion was made that a portion should be given to experiment on a railroad to the moon; but, after much skirmishing of this sort, the vote was taken on the bill as reported from the committee, and passed by a small majority. Notwithstanding this vote in the House, there seemed to be a determination on the part of some in the House, as was reported to me, to procure its defeat in the Senate. The amount of business before the Senate rendered it more and more doubtful, as the session drew to a close, whether the House bill on the Telegraph would be reached; and on the last day, the 3d of March, 1843, I was advised, by one of my senatorial friends, to make up my mind for failure, as he deemed it next to impossible that it could be reached before the adjournment. The bill, however, was reached a few moments before midnight, and passed. This was the turning-point in the history of the Telegraph. My personal funds were reduced to the fraction of a dollar, and, had the passage of the bill failed from any cause, there would have been little prospect of another attempt on my part to introduce to the world my new invention."

In the gallery of the Senate Professor Morse had sat all the last day and evening of the session. At midnight the session would close. Assured by his friends that there was no possibility of the bill being reached, he left the Capitol and retired to his room at the hotel, dispirited, and wellnigh broken-hearted. As he came down to breakfast the next morning, a young lady entered, and, coming toward him with a smile, exclaimed:

" I have come to congratulate you ! "

" For what, my dear friend ? " asked the Professor, of the young lady, who was Miss Annie G. Ellsworth, daughter of his friend the Commissioner of Patents.

" On the passage of your bill."

The Professor assured her it was not possible, as he remained in the Senate-Chamber until nearly midnight, and it was not reached. She then informed him that her father was present until the close, and, in the last moments of the session, the bill was passed without debate or division. Professor Morse was overcome by the intelligence, so joyful and unexpected, and gave at the moment to his young friend, the bearer of these good tidings, the promise that she should send the first message over the first line of telegraph that was opened. To his partner, Mr. Smith, he announced the result, dating his letter incorrectly, in the excitement of the hour:

30

"WASHINGTON, *March* 3, 1843.

" Well, my dear sir, the matter is decided. *The Senate have just passed my bill without division, and without opposition,* and it will probably be signed by the President in a few hours. This I think is news enough for you at present, and, as I have other letters that I must write before the mail closes, I must say good-by until I see you, or hear from you. Write to me in New York, where I hope to be by the latter part of next week."

On the same day Professor Morse wrote to Mr. Vail these calm but cheerful words :

" You will be glad to learn, doubtless, that my bill has passed the Senate without a division, and without opposition, so that now the telegraphic enterprise begins to look bright. I shall want to see you in New York after my return, which will probably be the latter part of next week. I have other letters to write, so excuse the shortness of this, which, IF SHORT, IS SWEET, at least. My kind regards to your father, mother, brothers, sisters, and wife. The whole delegation of your State, without exception, deserve the highest gratitude of us all."

That is the most cheerful letter he had written in ten years. It is " short, but sweet," and expressed the joy of his heart at the appropriation by Government of the means by which his long and painful struggle was to be made a permanent success.

DEATH OF WASHINGTON ALLSTON.

In the midst of his elation in the prospect of now seeing his Telegraph fully developed, an event occurred that deeply touched him, and with sorrow more intense than the death of any one but his wife had ever brought with it.

The friendship of Allston and Morse had been intimate and beautiful. On the part of Morse it was in some degree filial. The condescension and kindness of the teacher, while Morse was his pupil, were such as to draw him to the heart of Allston as to an equal and friend.

Mr. Morse received the stunning intelligence of the death of Allston, which occurred July 9, 1843, and hastened to Boston and Cambridge to the house of his departed friend. The brush with which Allston was engaged at the time of his departure was still moist with the paint that he was laying upon the last canvas that he had touched, "The Feast of Belshazzar." Mr. Morse begged this as a memorial of his friend. He afterward presented it to the National Academy of Design, where it is preserved with care.

Saddened by this bereavement, he returned after the funeral to New York and Washington, with the feeling that one less was living to rejoice in the success that was now opening before him. Allston had been among the first to congratulate him, when the appropriation bill passed the House. The last letter Professor Morse ever received from him contained these cheering words:

"*March* 24, 1843.

"All your friends here join me in rejoicing at the passing of the act of Congress, appropriating thirty thousand dollars toward carrying out your Electro-Magnetic Telegraph. I congratulate you with all my heart. Shakespeare says, 'There is a tide in the affairs of men that, taken at the flood, leads on to fortune.' You are now fairly launched on what I hope will prove to you another Pactolus. *I pede fausto!* This has been but a melancholy year to me. I have been ill with one complaint or another nearly the whole time; the last disorder, the erysipelas, but this has now nearly disappeared. I hope this letter will meet you as well in health as I take it you are now in spirits."

Professor Morse replied:

"I thank you, my dear sir, for your congratulations in regard to my telegraphic enterprise. I hope I shall not disappoint the expectations of my friends. I shall exert all my energies to show a complete and satisfactory result. When I last wrote you from Washington, I wrote under the apprehension that my bill would not be acted upon, and that I should have another year's perplexing delay, and consequently I wrote in very low spirits. 'What has become of Painting?' I think I hear you ask. Ah, my dear sir, when I have diligently and perseveringly wooed the coquettish jade for twenty years, and she then jilts me, what can I do? But I do her injustice, she is not to blame, but her guardian for the time being. I shall not give her up yet in despair, but pursue her even with lightning, and so overtake her at last. I am now absorbed in my arrangements for fulfiling my designs with the Telegraph, in accordance with the act of Congress. I know not that I shall be able to complete my experiment before Congress meet again, but I shall endeavor to show it to them at their next session."

Professor Morse requested the brother-in-law of Mr. Allston to write him a letter, giving a minute account of the last moments in the life of the illustrious painter, and Mr. Dana complied with his request within a week after the mournful event occurred. It is in these beautiful words:

"Boston, *July* 14, 1843.

"My dear Sir: Your old friend, and one who spoke of you often with deep affection, was taken from us most suddenly, and I may say most unexpectedly; for, though he seemed to be failing fast, his friends had no suspicion of a disease of the organs that would take him away instantly. The great arteries were not essentially impaired; but one or two that fed the heart itself were ossified. While none of the intestinal organs would be said to be in a healthy state, none, with the exception of those I have mentioned as being ossified, were in so diseased a condition that he might not have lived some years longer. So long ago as when —— took a bust of him, his friends thought he would not live long; but he recruited. The winter before last he was severely ill, and we feared for him then. From that attack he but partially recovered, and from that time was plainly, with short terms of a better state, a broken-down, failing man. His strength was not sufficient for his labor; and, while his intellect was as clear as ever, it was evident that the servant, the body, was too much weakened to do its appointed work. He spoke of himself as an old, broken-down man. It was plain, his wife says, from the dreadful depression he was under for the last ten months, when his friends were not round him, that he was suffering under the apprehension he should not have strength to finish what he was about. God, in his mercy, spared him from living on with this thought to prey upon him, and took him away in a moment, but with a touch as gentle as the breaking morning light. Both my sisters and my daughter were there, preparatory to leaving him for the summer. All but my daughter went to bed. She sat talking with him. He was strongly attached to her; and had spoken of her most affectionately, as he was wont to do, the last time I saw him. 'I like to talk to her, for she always takes my meaning at once,' he said to me. He said many kind things to her this last night. 'You are my niece,' said he. 'You are more to me—you are my child. There are relations nearer than those of blood.' Twice he put his arms gently round her, and the second time kissed her forehead, and then lowered his head for her to kiss his cheek. He then looked upward, and his eyes were as if he was seeing into the world of holiness and all peace, and he said, 'I want you to be perfect, perfect.' . . . 'I do not feel like talking,' he soon added, sat down, drew a chair to him for her to sit by him, took her hand, and occasionally spoke in somewhat the same strain. Between twelve and one o'clock he complained of a pain in the chest; he had felt the same once before, about three weeks previous to this. She advised his taking something for it, not thinking of it, however, as any thing of much importance; so that, when he went up to his wife's chamber to get what she recommended, she herself went off to bed. He moved about as usual, and, when his wife offered to go down and prepare something, he answered: 'Oh, no! I can do it just as well myself.' He went down again. She stopped to get something which she thought he might want, and followed him in five minutes. She found him sitting in his usual place, with his writing apparatus, which he had just taken out, near him, his feet on the hearth, and his head resting on the back of his chair, in just the position in which he often took his nap. She went up to him; his eyes were open, and, from their appearance, she thought he might have fainted. They were all instantly with him. One of my sisters said to him, 'Mr. Allston, we are all here.' 'His eyes soon closed. A physician was called, they, in the mean time, doing all they could to revive him. There is very little doubt that life had stopped when his wife reached him. His physician says that he must have gone without a moment's pain—that it was a mere closing.

"So beautiful an expression as was on his face, as he lay sleeping in Jesus, I never saw on the face of man. Spirits were with his spirit. And a most humble being he was before his God. In Christ and the great atonement was his only trust. Trust, do I say? it was his realized, fervid life. Not a fortnight before his death he opened his whole soul to the clergyman here—a most interesting man—who told me that such childlike, undoubting faith, it was delightful to sit and hear poured forth. Let us all pray that we may be prepared to meet him in that world where anguish of mind which the circumstances of life brought upon him, and which was the prime cause that broke him down, is all passed away, and he now a blessed spirit among the blessed!

" I am aware how much your time is occupied, yet I must beg
of you to look over your letters, and to let me have any that you
may have of Allston. Depend upon it they will not be used in any
way that you would think objectionable. I must further request
of you to begin from your first acquaintance with him, and to write
me all that you can recollect about him—his doings—his sayings.
And I beg of you to give me your views of him as an artist; there
are very few qualified to do this. It will be in safe hands; and I
trust some memoir of him will be prepared. I need not urge this
a second time; for, busy as you are, I know that love can find time
to do what it would, and I know that you loved Allston exceedingly. My heart can hardly bear it when I think what his beautiful spirit suffered, and yet it is continually going back to it. The
God of peace be with you!   RICHARD H. DANA.
    "To SAMUEL F. B. MORSE, Esq."

A few days afterward Mr. Dana wrote again:

" MY DEAR SIR: I wrote you a few days ago. Since that time
I have seen the account of the meeting of your Academy, and find
that a committee is appointed to procure a bust of our departed
friend. I write again thus early to make you acquainted with the
fact that we employed Brackett, the afternoon of poor Allston's
death, to take a cast from the face. We did this because, all the
time that Clevenger was here, Allston was in a wretched state
of health, suffering under almost continual pain in the face, producing an expression of distress and a rigid state of the muscles.
So ill was he, that a friend, who had seen him for two or three
months, upon coming out of the painting-room, where he was sitting to Clevenger, said to me: 'Allston cannot stay with us much
longer; that Clevenger did so well as he has done in the marble, is
surprising.' But so beautiful was the countenance after death, so
softened the muscles, and rounded and smoothed the face, that he
looked as he did years back, before disease and distress of mind had
so preyed upon him. Brackett has this advantage, besides having
seen Mr. A. in better states of health than C. was fortunate enough
to see him in. He has long had a great desire to model Mr. A.'s
head; and of his power his bust of me, but especially that of Bryant, may be said to settle the question. . . . I have written to you
rather than to the committee, as I am but slightly acquainted with
only one of them, Mr. Gray; and what I might say to you, as Mr.
A.'s friend, I could not say without some appearance of improper
interference.

"My sister is calm; it seems almost as if he had left her the influence of his spirit as he departed. But in Christ is her, and, I trust, our support.

"I cannot seal this without telling you how deeply touched we all were with what you said of poor A. It was the heart pouring out its sorrows. You know not, my dear sir, with what affection Allston always spoke of you, and, let me add, how highly he thought of your powers as an artist.

"Very sincerely yours,

"RICHARD H. DANA."

The condition in which Allston's "Belshazzar" was left by his sudden death led to an earnest request from the family that Professor Morse would come and give his opinion as to the best course to be pursued in putting it into a state for exhibition. He went immediately, upon receiving a request to that effect from Mr. Franklin Dexter, and on his return Mr. Dana writes to him:

"Your coming immediately upon a line from Mr. Dexter was no more than what we expected; for we knew well how deep was your love for our departed friend, and that you would not account any thing as labor or trouble which concerned his memory. At the same time it was very gratifying to us *all*, and a true comfort. . . .

"I wish you could have seen more of Allston, particularly within the last year of his life. Frequent use of terms, and especially a cant use of them, is apt to deaden their force and significancy, even with those who have a spirit fitted for them; yet, let me say, that, if ever *heavenly-mindedness* showed itself in its *life* and *beauty*, it made itself visible in the mind of Allston—humble, child-like—himself nothing, Christ all things—love overflowed him, and the harmony of the upper world permeated him, and harmonized for him all Nature and all art. These were not separated from his religious life, because they were taken up into it and sanctified and made beautiful. How few really feel and understand that term, *the beauty of holiness!*' Yet one is almost afraid to speak in this way, so mournfully has a self-presuming spiritualism desecrated spiritual things. May God bless you, my dear sir; and, through the trials which He has laid upon you, may you be fitted for that prosperity which, in his good providence, I trust, is now awaiting you!"

That Allston lived to see the great work of his pupil and

friend accomplished was a source of the highest satisfaction to Mr. Morse. It was his justification for having turned away from his profession as an artist to make an achievement in science which was destined to confer happiness upon his fellow-men. The appropriation of the money by Congress for building the line from Baltimore to Washington was the act that gave not only the pledge of success, but also the means of its final accomplishment. Mr. Morse was now emphatically alone in the world. His wife, his parents, Leslie, Allston, West, and all those to whom his early years of struggle had been known, were dead. He had made new acquaintances and associations, but friendships formed after middle life never take the place of those with which the pursuits and aspirations of youth are identified.

CHAPTER XI.

1843-1844.

PREPARATIONS TO LAY THE FIRST LINE—USE OF TUBES UNDERGROUND—
EZRA CORNELL—TUBES ABANDONED—LINES PUT UPON POLES—EXPERI-
MENTS WITH 160 MILES OF WIRE—PROFESSOR HENRY'S LETTER—PROGRESS
OF THE WORK—NATIONAL WHIG CONVENTION—NOMINATION OF HENRY
CLAY ANNOUNCED AT WASHINGTON BY TELEGRAPH—THE LINE COMPLETE
—THE FIRST MESSAGE — TRIUMPH OF THE INVENTOR—HIS LETTER TO
BISHOP STEVENS—NATIONAL DEMOCRATIO CONVENTION—JAMES K. POLK
NOMINATED—CONFERENCE WITH SILAS WRIGHT—WORKING OF THE TELE-
GRAPH—PROFESSOR MORSE'S REPORT OF THE COMPLETION OF THE LINE
—ENTHUSIASM OF THE PRESS AND THE PUBLIC—TELEGRAPH OFFERED TO
THE GOVERNMENT—DETERMINING THE LONGITUDE.

THE appropriation by Congress having been made, Professor Morse proceeded with energy and delight to construct the first line of his Electric Telegraph. It was obviously important that it should be laid where it would the most powerfully attract the attention of the Government, the country, and the world, and this consideration decided the question in favor of a line between Washington and Baltimore. Professor Morse, without any delay, addressed these communications to the Secretary of the Treasury:

"WASHINGTON, *March* 8, 1843.

" *To the Hon. the Secretary of the Treasury.*

"SIR: I have the honor to inclose to you the report of the House Committee of Commerce, on the subject of my Electro-Magnetic Telegraph. The bill which accompanies the report has become a law, and I am desirous, with the least possible delay, to commence my operations, that I may have the telegraphic line contemplated by the bill completed, ready for your next report, and for the examination of the next Congress. I am aware that just at this moment your valuable time must be occupied in the more pressing duties of your new office, and I am therefore unwilling to intrude upon you. But as there is some preliminary information necessary in order that you may form the better judgment on those subjects submitted to you, particularly as to the eligibility of the route to be determined for the trial, I will proceed immediately to ascertain these points, and will return to Washington and wait upon you again when you are more at leisure. I have thought, if it should meet your approbation, of establishing the telegraphic line between Baltimore and Washington, but whether along the line of the turnpike or railroad, cannot well be determined until I can have an interview with the stockholders of the two companies.

"With sincere respect, your obedient servant,

"SAMUEL F. B. MORSE."

"WASHINGTON, D. C., *March* 10, 1843.

"DEAR SIR: In compliance with your request this morning, I give you the plan I propose for my operations, in fulfillment of the design contemplated by the act of the late Congress 'to test the practicability and efficacy' of my system of Electro-Magnetic Telegraphs. I propose immediately to procure the necessary quantity of wire, which must first be prepared with its insulating covering before the subsequent operation of inclosing in tubes, or laying them in the earth, can be performed. Many interesting experiments bearing upon the general result can then be tried before the wire is inclosed. When inclosed in tubes other experiments of the same character may be tried before laying them in the ground. The telegraphic instruments should also be in progress of making. I propose to lay the experimental line between Baltimore and Washington. I propose to make some experiments on the forms of galvanic batteries, and magnets, and in modes of crossing rivers, with the electric fluid. I desire to have two assistants, to aid me in my labors, Professor Fisher and Professor Gale, of New York, who have been for a long time associated with me in my experiments.

"In regard to the kind of tubes necessary, Colonel Talcott, to whom you had the kindness to give me a letter, is decidedly of opinion that *lead* is preferable to all other substances, both for durability and cheapness. For the proposed experiment at least, I think *lead* is preferable.

"I have copied below the general estimate.

"I would say in conclusion that I shall remain in the city until

Monday morning, and will call at the chief clerk's office in the Department before three o'clock to-morrow (Saturday) for the Honorable Secretary's answer, if ready; if not, I should feel obliged to have his answer forwarded to me in New York, where my address is No. 142 Nassau Street.

"I remain with sincere respect, your obedient servant,

"S. F. B. MORSE.

" *To the Hon. J. C. SPENCER, Secretary of the Treasury.*

" *General Estimate for the Experimental Essay with the Electro-Magnetic Telegraph, provided for by the Act of Twenty-seventh Congress, Third Session, House Bill* 641.

1. Rooms to be rented for preparing the work, per annum, . $600 00
2. Copper wire, No. 16, and its preparation with cotton and insulating varnish, four lengths of forty miles, ·. . 6,000 00
3. Lead pipe for forty miles, ... 10,000 00
4. Delivery of the pipe and wire, and passing the wire into the pipe, ... 1,400 00
5. Machinery, registers, and correspondents, galvanic batteries, magnets, acids, etc., ... 500 00
6. Survey of the route between Baltimore and Washington, both railroad and turnpike, uncertain, say, . . . 300 00
7. Engineering, laying down and protecting wires, . . 6,120 00
8. Experiments on forms of batteries, etc., not more than . 500 00

$25,420 00 "

To this letter he received the following reply:

" TREASURY DEPARTMENT, WASHINGTON, *March* 14, 1843.

" SIR : I have received your communication of the 10th instant, stating the plan of operations you propose, for fulfilling the object of the act of Congress to test the practicability of establishing a system of Electro-Magnetic Telegraphs by the United States.

" In general, I approve the plan proposed by you. The compensation of the two assistants whom you propose to employ ought, however, to be fixed before they are engaged, and you will report to the Department the amount or rate which you deem reasonable. Some arrangement in respect to your own compensation should also be made, either in reference to the whole undertaking, or to the time which may be devoted to it.

" In order to preserve a proper check over the expenditures, and to conform to the established practice of the Department, previous to the conclusion of any contract for materials, or for any work by the job, you will submit the same to this Department for its approval.

Of course this does not apply to the hiring of laborers by the day or the month, although the rates of wages proposed to be paid, in such case, should be submitted to the Department. An advance of a reasonable sum, to enable you to commence your operations, will be made on your requisition, stating the amount and object, and designating the place at which you desire the same to be paid or transmitted to you. And, as the operations proceed, such sums will be paid from time to time, as may be necessary, on similar requisitions. As you will be held accountable for all moneys paid on your application, you will find it necessary to be exceedingly careful to take vouchers in duplicate for all sums expended by you. You will be required to account monthly, at least, for the amounts received, and no advance or payments will be made while there shall remain any considerable sum unaccounted for. It may be well for you to devolve on one of your assistants the duties of a disbursing agent, and of keeping the accounts of the experiment.

" Very respectfully, your obedient servant,

" J. C. SPENCER, *Secretary of the Treasury.*

" To SAMUEL F. B. MORSE, Esq."

Returning to New York, Mr. Morse proceeded without delay to organize the system for the construction of the experimental line. He writes to Mr. Vail:

"NEW YORK, *March* 15, 1843.

" You will not fail, with your brother, and, if possible, your father, to be in New York on Tuesday, the 21st, to meet the proprietors of the Telegraph. I was upon the point of coming out this afternoon to Speedwell to see you, with young Mr. Serrell, the patentee of the lead-pipe machine, which I think promises to be the best for our purposes, of all that have been invented, as to it can be applied ' *a mode of filling lead-pipes with wire,*' for which Professor Fisher and myself have entered a caveat at the Patent-Office.'

Mr. Vail replied:

" As an assistant in the telegraphic experiment contemplated by act of Congress, lately passed, I can superintend and procure the making of the instruments complete according to your direction, namely, the register, the correspondents with their magnets, the batteries, the reels and the paper, and will attend to the procuring of the acids, the ink, and the preparation of the various stations. I will assist in fitting the tubes with wire, and the resinous coating, etc., and I will devote my whole time and attention to the business, so as to secure a favorable result, and, should you wish to devolve upon me any other business connected with the Telegraph, I will cheerfully undertake it. Three dollars per diem, with travelling expenses, I shall deem a satisfactory salary."

Mr. Morse immediately appointed as his assistants Professor L. D. Gale and Professor J. C. Fisher. Mr. Vail was to devote his time and attention to the making of instruments under the direction of Mr. Morse, and to the purchase of materials. Professor Fisher was to superintend the preparation of the wire, from its manufacture to the placing of it in the tubes, as originally proposed. Professor Gale was to give his personal attention to the work of construction at such points as Mr. Morse should consider necessary. Mr. Morse himself, as general superintendent, under the appointment of the Government, gave attention to the minutest details. Every cent that was disbursed passed through his hands. In point of accuracy, attention to the smallest expenditures, the preservation of vouchers, and the presentation of accounts, General Washington himself, whose books are models for all disbursing officers, was not more precise, lucid, and correct. Mr. Morse made monthly reports to the Secretary of the Treasury, presenting the exact state of his accounts, together with vouchers for all his expenditures. Duplicates of these, carefully preserved, present the most beautiful evidence of his particularity in the management of business matters, and his fidelity in public trusts.

Mr. Ezra Cornell[1] had invented a machine to lay pipe, to contain conducting-lines for telegraphic purposes, and he was employed to take charge of the works, under the superintendence of Mr. Morse. The work was commenced at the old Baltimore and Washington Depot, on the hill, on the east side of the railroad-track, and was continued until it was satisfactorily proved, by repeated experiments, that the plan of tubes in the earth would not succeed. Two-thirds of the appropria-

---

[1] Mr. Cornell, who was thus early connected with the Telegraph, being employed at a salary of one thousand dollars a year, became one of the most successful constructors and largest proprietors of telegraphs, and the founder of Cornell University.

tion were expended, and it was estimated that it would require nearly as large a sum as the original appropriation to complete the work, with no prospect of success when it was finished. When the pipe had been laid as far as the Relay House, Pro- . fessor Morse came to Mr. Cornell and expressed a desire to have the work arrested until he could try further experiments, but he was very anxious that nothing should be said or done to give to the public the impression that the enterprise had failed. Mr. Cornell said he could easily manage it, and stepping up to the machine, which was drawn by a team of eight mules, he cried out, " Hurrah, boys! we must lay another length of pipe before we quit." The teamsters cracked their whips over the mules, and they started on a lively pace. Mr. Cornell grasped the handles of the plough, and, watching an opportunity, canted it so as to catch the point of a rock, and broke it to pieces, while Professor Morse stood looking on. Consultations, long and painful, followed. The anxiety of Professor Morse at this period was greater than at any previous hour known in the history of his invention. Some that were around him had serious apprehensions that he would not stand up under the pressure. Professor Morse's account of the abandonment of the tubes and the employment of poles was given in these words :

" Much time and expense were lost in consequence of my following the plan adopted in England of laying the conductors beneath the ground. At the time the Telegraph bill was passed, there had been about thirteen miles of telegraph-conductors, for Professor Wheatstone's telegraph system in England, put into tubes and interred in the earth; and there was no hint publicly given that that mode was not perfectly successful. I did not feel, therefore, at liberty to expend the public moneys in useless experiments on a plan which seemed to be already settled as effective in England. Hence I fixed upon this mode as one supposed to be the best. It was prosecuted till the winter of 1843–'44. It was abandoned, among other reasons, in consequence of ascertaining that, in the process of inserting the wire into the leaden tubes (which was at the moment of forming the tube from the lead at melting heat), the insulating covering of the wires had become charged at various and numerous points of the line to such an extent that greater delay and expense would be necessary to repair the damage than to put the wire on posts. In my letter to the Secretary of the Treasury, of September 27, 1837, one of the modes of laying the conductors for the Telegraph was the present almost universal one of extending them on posts set about two hundred feet apart. This mode was adopted with success."

In his letter to the Secretary of the Treasury, dated September 27, 1837, he said : "If the circuit is laid through the air, the first cost would, doubtless, be much. lessened. Stout spars, of some thirty feet in height, well planted in the ground, and placed about three hundred and fifty feet apart, would, in this case, be required, along the tops of which the circuit might be stretched." Mr. Cornell remembers an interesting discussion which now arose as to the mode of *fastening the wires to the poles.* He says :

"In the latter part of March Professor Morse gave me the order to put the wires on poles, and the question at once arose as to the mode of *fastening the wires to the poles,* and the insulation of them at the point of fastening. I submitted a plan to the Professor which, I was confident, would be successful as an insulating medium, and which was easily available then, and inexpensive. Mr. Vail also submitted a plan for the same purpose, which involved the necessity of going to New York or New Jersey to get it executed. Professor Morse gave preference to Mr. Vail's plan, and started for New York to get the fixtures, directing me to get the wire ready for use, and arrange for setting the poles. At the end of a week Professor Morse returned from New York, and came to the shop where I was at work, and said he wanted to provide the insulators for putting the wires on the poles upon the plan I had suggested, to which I responded: 'How is that, Professor? I thought you had decided to use Mr. Vail's plan.' Professor Morse replied: 'Yes, I did so decide, and on my way to New York, where I went to order the fixtures, I stopped at Princeton, and called on my old friend Professor Henry, who inquired how I was getting along with my Telegraph. I explained to him the failure of the insulation in the pipes, and stated that I had decided to place the wires on poles in the air. He then inquired how I proposed to insulate the wires when they were attached to the poles. I showed him the model I had of Mr. Vail's plan, and he said, "It will not do; you will meet the same difficulty you had in the pipes." I then explained to him your plan, which he said would answer.'"

In August, 1843, he wrote to the Secretary of the Treasury, giving the result of some important experiments:

"NEW YORK, *August* 10, 1843.

"SIR: I have the honor herewith to transmit my fifth monthly report of expenditures, under the act of the last Congress, for 'testing the practicability of establishing a system of Electro-Magnetic Telegraphs for the United States.'

"I also take this opportunity of communicating to the Honorable Secretary the result of the experiments, made on the 8th instant, with the prepared wire in one continuous line of one hundred and sixty miles. Professors Renwick, Draper, Ellet, and Schaeffer, with my assistants, Professors Fisher and Gale, were present by invitation; Professors Silliman, Henry, Torrey, and Dr. Chilton, were also invited, but were prevented by official duties from attending.

"In the letter to the Honorable Secretary, dated March 10, 1843, in which I propose my general plan, I have this remark, speaking of the wire after its insulating preparations should be completed: 'Many interesting *experiments* bearing upon the general result can then be tried before the wire is inclosed.'

"The experiments alluded to were tried on Tuesday, and with perfect success. I had prepared a galvanic battery of three hundred pairs, in order to have ample power at command, but to my great gratification I found that one hundred pairs were sufficient to produce all the effects I desired through the whole distance of one hundred and sixty miles!

"It may be well to observe that the hundred and sixty miles of wire are to be divided into four lengths of forty miles each, forming a fourfold cord from Washington to Baltimore. Two wires form a circuit; the electricity, therefore, in producing its effects at Washington from Baltimore, passes from Baltimore to Washington, and back again to Baltimore, of course traveling eighty miles to produce its result. One hundred and sixty miles, therefore, gives me an actual distance of eighty miles, double the distance from Washington to Baltimore. The result, then, of my experiments on Tuesday is, that a battery of only hundred pairs at Washington will operate a Telegraph on my plan eighty miles distant with certainty, and without requiring any intermediate station!

" Some careful experiments on the decomposing power of various distances were made, from which the law of propulsion has been deduced, verifying the results of Ohm, and those which I made in the summer of 1842, and alluded to in my letter to the Hon. C. G. Ferris, and published in the House Report, No. 17, of the last Congress.

" *The practical inference from this law is, that a telegraphic communication on the Electro-Magnetic plan may with certainty be established* ACROSS THE ATLANTIC OCEAN! Startling as this may now seem, I am confident the time will come when this project will be realized.

" The wire is now in its last process of preparation for inclosing in the lead tube, which will be commenced on Tuesday, the 15th instant. I have the honor to be, sir, with sincere respect, your most obedient servant,

" SAMUEL F. B. MORSE,
" *Superintendent of Electro-Magnetic Telegraph.*
" To the Hon. JOHN C. SPENCER, *Secretary of the Treasury of the United States.*"

" TREASURY DEPARTMENT, *August* 15, 1843.

" *Professor S. F. B. Morse, Superintendent of Electro-Magnetic Telegraph, New York.*

" SIR: The accounts and vouchers inclosed in your letter of the 10th instant, have been referred to the First Auditor for adjustment. I am gratified with the result of the experiments made with the Electro-Magnetic Telegraph, and trust the country will have reason to be satisfied with the result of your labors.
" I am, etc.,
(Signed)   " J. C. SPENCER, *Secretary of the Treasury.*"

The important experiments alluded to in this letter were illustrated in a communication made by him to *Silliman's Journal of Science.*

" NEW YORK, *September* 4, 1843.

" DEAR SIRS : On the 8th of August, having completed my preparations of one hundred and sixty miles of copper wire for the Electro-Magnetic Telegraph, which I am constructing for the Government, I invited several scientific friends to witness some experiments in verification of the law of Lenz, of the action of galvanic electricity

31

through wires of great lengths. I put in action a cup battery of one hundred pairs, which I had constructed, based on the excellent plan of Professor Grove, but with some modifications of my own, economizing the platinum. The wire was reeled upon eighty reels, containing two miles upon each reel, so that any length, from two to one hundred and sixty miles, could be made at pleasure to constitute the circuit. My first trial of the battery was through the entire length of one hundred and sixty miles, making of course a circuit of eighty miles, and the magnetism induced in my electro-magnet,[1] which formed a part of the circuit, was sufficient to move with great strength my telegraphic lever. Even forty-eight cups produced action in the lever, but not so promptly or surely.

"We then commenced a series of experiments upon decomposition, at various distances. The battery alone (one hundred pairs) gave, in the measuring-gauge, in one minute, 5.20 inches of gas. When four miles of wire were interposed, the result was 1.20 inches; ten miles of wire, .57; twenty miles, .30 inches; fifty miles, .094. The results obtained from a battery of one hundred pairs are projected in the following curve:

[1] In Professor Daniel's "Introduction to the Study of Chemical Philosophy," second edition, 1843, there are these facts to be noticed:

In the preface, there are these words: "It only remains for me now, to acknowledge my obligations to my friends and colleagues, *Professor Wheatstone* and Dr. Todd, for their great kindness in undergoing the disagreeable labor of revising and correcting the proof-sheets. They have thereby prevented many errors which would have otherwise deformed the work."

No statement then of Professor Daniel's, particularly in that part of his work which related especially to Wheatstone's Telegraph, would be allowed to pass unnoticed by Mr. Wheatstone, and we are authorized in considering any such statement as having his sanction.

We then find, page 576, the following statement: "Ingenious as Professor Wheatstone's contrivances are, they would have been of no avail for telegraphic purposes, without the investigation which he was the first to make of the laws of electro-magnets, when acted on through great lengths of wire. *Electro-magnets of the greatest power, even when the most energetic batteries are employed, utterly cease to act when they are connected by considerable lengths of wire with the battery.*"

If any thing were needed to show that Professor Wheatstone was not the inventor of the *Electro-Magnetic Telegraph*, it is this assertion (under the supervision of Professor Wheatstone) made by Professor Daniel. In 1843 Professor Wheatstone had not made the discovery upon which Professor Morse bases his invention, viz., that *electro-magnets can be made to act, with an inconsiderable battery too, when the latter is connected with the former by considerable lengths of wire;* eighty miles may certainly be considered as of *considerable length.*

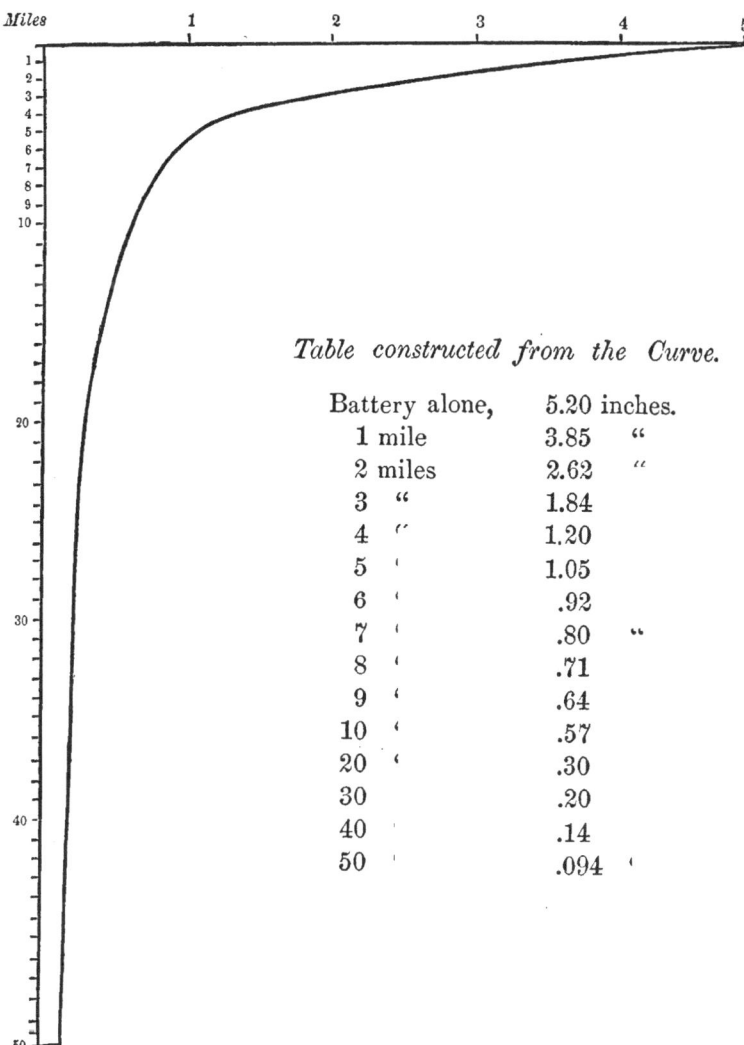

Table constructed from the Curve.

Battery alone,	5.20 inches.	
1 mile	3.85	"
2 miles	2.62	"
3 "	1.84	
4 "	1.20	
5 '	1.05	
6 '	.92	
7 '	.80	"
8 '	.71	
9 '	.64	
10 '	.57	
20 '	.30	
30	.20	
40 '	.14	
50 '	.094	'

"During the previous summer, I made the following experi-ments, upon a line of thirty-three miles, of No. 17 copper wire, with a battery of fifty pairs. In this case, I used a small steel-yard, with weights, with which I was enabled to weigh, with a good degree of accuracy, the greater magnetic forces, but not the lesser, yet sufficiently approximating the recent results to confirm the law in question.

Table of Results.

" 50 pairs through 2 miles attracted and raised 9 ozs.
		4	"	"		"	4	"
		6	"	"	''	3	"
	"	8	"	"			$2\frac{1}{2}$	"
	"	10	"	"			$2\frac{1}{4}$	"
	"	12	"	"			$\frac{1}{8}$	"
"	"	14	"	"	"		$\frac{1}{8}$	"

and each successive addition of two miles, up to 33, still gave an
attractive and lifting power of one-eighth of an ounce.

Curve from these Results.

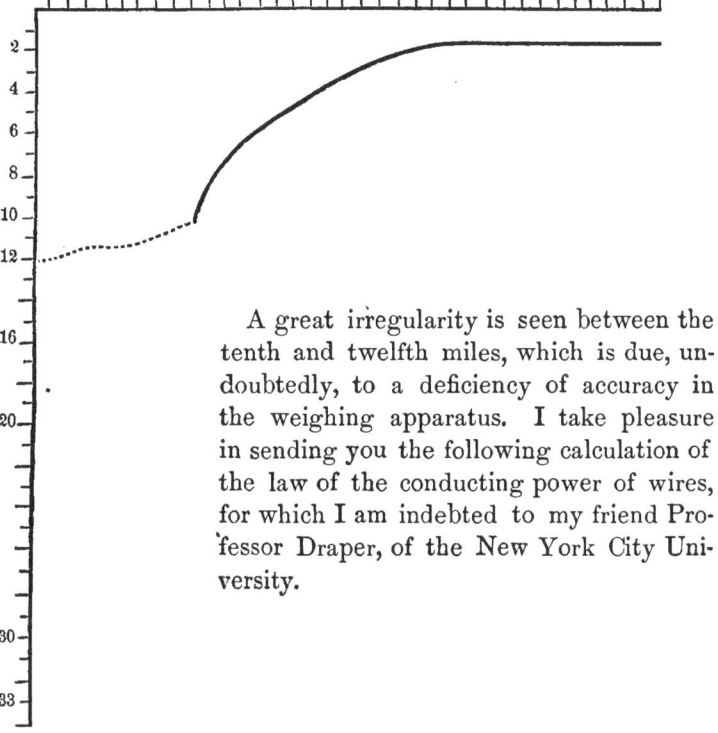

A great irregularity is seen between the tenth and twelfth miles, which is due, undoubtedly, to a deficiency of accuracy in the weighing apparatus. I take pleasure in sending you the following calculation of the law of the conducting power of wires, for which I am indebted to my friend Professor Draper, of the New York City University.

" ' It has been objected that, if the conducting power of wires `for electricity was inversely as their length, and directly as their section, the transmission of telegraphic signals, through long wires, could not be carried into effect, and even the galvanic multiplier, which consists, essentially, of a wire making several convolutions round a needle, could have no existence. This last objection was brought forward by Professor Ritchie, of the University of London, as an absolute proof that the law referred to is incorrect. There is, however, an exceedingly simple method of proving that signals may be dispatched through very long wires, and that the galvanic multiplier, so far from controverting the law in question, depends for its very existence upon it.

" ' Assuming the truth of the law of Lenz, the *quantities* of electricity which can be urged by a constant electro-motoric source through a series of wires, the length of which constitutes an arithmetical ratio, will always be in a geometrical ratio. Now, the curve whose ordinates and abscissas bear this relation to each other, is the logarithmic curve whose equation is $ay=x$.

" ' 1. If we suppose the base of the system, which the curve under discussion represents, be greater than unity, the values of y taken between $x=0$, and $x=1$, must be all negative.

" ' 2. By taking $y=0$, we find that the curve will intersect the axis of the x's at a distance from the origin, equal to unity.

" ' 3. By making $x=0$, we find y to be infinite and negative. Now, these are the properties of the logarithmic curve, which furnish an explanation of the case in hand. Assuming that the x's represent the quantities of electricity, and the y's the length of the wires, we perceive at once that those parts of the curve which we have to consider lie wholly in the fourth quadrant, where the abscissas are positive and the ordinates negative. When, therefore, the battery-current passes without the intervention of any obstructing wire, its value is equal to unity. But, as successive lengths of wire are continually added, the quantities of electricity passing undergo a diminution, at first rapid, and then more and more slow. And it is not until the wire becomes infinitely long that it ceases to conduct at all; for the ordinate y, when $x=0$, is an asymptote to the curve. In point of practice, therefore, when a certain limit is reached, the diminution of the intensity of the forces becomes *very small*, while the increase in the lengths of the wire is vastly great. It is, therefore, possible to conceive a wire to be a million times as long as another, and yet the two shall transmit quantities of electricity not perceptibly different, when measured by a delicate galvanometer. But, under these circumstances, if the long wire be coiled, so as to act as a multiplier, its influence on the needle will be inexpressibly greater than the one so much shorter than it.

Further, from this we gather that for telegraphic dispatches, with a battery of given electro-motoric power, when a certain distance is reached, the diminution of effect for an increased distance becomes inappreciable.' "

To the invitation of Professor Morse to assist at the great experiment mentioned in the foregoing letter, Professor Henry replied:

"PRINCETON, *August* 22, 1843.

"MY DEAR SIR: I hope you will pardon me for not before acknowledging the receipt of your kind letters of invitation to attend your galvanic exhibition. My time has been so much occupied during the last three weeks, with an extra course of lectures, and our senior examination, and so little at my own disposal, that I was unable to say whether I could be in the city on the day you mentioned or not. I did hope, however, to get away, but the examination prevented. Dr. Torrey was also engaged, and could not leave. I do not know, however, that I could have done much in the way of original experiments in the course of a single day. I am not quick in the process of inventing experiments, unless my mind is thoroughly aroused to the subject by several days' exclusive attention to the work, and then I am often obliged to pause between each effort. I have not been able, since I last saw you, to devise a satisfactory process for determining the velocity of *galvanic* electricity, and, on reflection, I did not think it worth the expense which would be incurred to have a machine constructed for the mere repetition of the experiments of Wheatstone.

"I think it probable that I shall visit the city next week, as I shall be unemployed from this time until a week from next Monday. If there is any prospect of your repeating any of your experiments previous to that time, I will be with you on any day you may appoint. With much respect and esteem, yours truly,

"JOSEPH HENRY.

"Professor MORSE.

"P. S.—I have found no mention in my number of the *Comptes Rendus*, of the French Academy, of the proofs you mention relative to the increasing of the power of the electro-magnet, and do not believe that any thing new of any importance has lately been published on that subject.   J. H."

The experimental line was now approaching its completion.

Professor Morse issued the following order to Mr. Cornell, dated in Washington, March 13, 1844:

"SIR: After you have had the wire for the pipe drawn in, sufficient to reach the Capitol from the Patent-Office, or *at farthest by next Monday morning*, you will proceed at once to the preparation of the wire for the posts, passing it through the insulating medium, soldering and covering the joints, and have it reeled up in such a manner as in your judgment shall be most convenient to place on the posts where they are set. You will take the superintendence of this part, and put on as much force as shall be consistent with safety, so as to have the whole of the wire prepared by the end of the week ending March 23, 1844. Report to me what additional force you need before."

The work went on. Among the loose papers of Professor Morse are lying the memoranda of those days when he was watching the progress of the work, and noting, for his own guidance, every minute event that bore upon the science and art of the Telegraph. It was a grand as well as novel experiment on which he was entering, and these transient records of impressions are intensely interesting:

"1844: *April 15th, evening, about 4.30 o'clock.*—It struck 1, then 2, and soon after, about twelve or fifteen times quite rapid, and about half an hour after it commenced again, and, at intervals, struck 1, 3, 5, 1, 1, 1, 1, 3, three times 3; repeated the same after my striking three times 3, again 3; 3 they again answered me several times without my returning it.

"*April 16th.*—At 5 minutes past 9 action of magnet commenced; thought I received word that the connection was this side yesterday's work. Afterward many strikings, but no answer to my question, 'Is all right?' At about 9.25 connection was broken, and the lever up, so that I could not communicate.

" At 25 minutes of 11, lever in action, but could not understand signals. Had previously doubled the pairs for quantity, and, upon connecting the 35 again in a single battery, found action of lever. At 18 minutes to 11, action; again asked 'If all is right?' No answer. At 8½ minutes to 11 action ceased, lever being up. Went, at 11.15, to depot for Mr. Cornell's letter. On return found it in action from Beltsville; at 12.30 put 49 pairs in action, 30 of them being fresh. My magnet moved strongly, but no answers from the other end.

"At 22 minutes to 1 o'clock tried 39 pairs—30 fresh and 9 old. The magnet moved strongly, but still no answers from Beltsville.

"At 16 minutes to 1 tried the 30 fresh pairs alone; moved magnet strongly, but still no answers from Beltsville.

"Tried 20 pairs, moved magnet *once*, feebly; added, successively up to 30, and found that 25 would move magnet well.

"*7 minutes to* 1.—Still no answers.

"*5 minutes to* 1.—Still no answer.

"*4 minutes to* 1.—Received signals, but not intelligible.

"*3 minutes to* 1.—Asked if all was right; no answer.

"*1 minute to* 1.—The same.

"*1 o'clock.*—The same. Gave many signals, but no answer returned.

"*7 minutes after* 1.—The same.

"*10 minutes after* 1.—Announced cars of freight-train leaving for Baltimore.

"*16 minutes after* 1.—Not disconnected.

"*17½ minutes after* 1.—Signals received.

"*25 minutes after* 1.—I stopped for the morning.

"From 2 till 20 minutes past, signals were given better, but difficult to understand.

"*April 18th.*—30-cup battery in action at 20 minutes to 9; quarter to 9, lever struck several times, probably from Bladensburg. Shows good insulation, notwithstanding the rain.

"*April 26, 1844.*—Attempted two circuits, according to Mr. Vail's arrangement. Put the batteries in action. My large magnet did not work well. There were attempts to write from Bladensburg (which I could not detect by the ear), producing a slight click at the great magnet, showing that the lever wanted adjusting. After adjustment, the lever worked well, and I obtained a few markings on the register, but all stopped after this.

"At first, Vail's battery gave a feeble spark, but mine none; and in touching with Vail's no effect was produced on my magnet or register; soon after, both batteries gave a vivid spark, and both equally moved the lever; then, soon after, the batteries were in the same state as at first.

"At 11.10 the batteries were again in a similar state, both operating my magnet; 23 in one battery, and 24 in another—47 cups in all.

"At 12 changed the circuit to the distant terminus—20 miles; found it sound. Received signals, but not intelligible, owing

doubtless to persons there not acquainted with the mode of operation; Mr. Cornell not there; battery perhaps too weak. At 24
minutes to 1 added 6 more plates; the magnet worked much
stronger. Experiment showed the integrity of the circuit 20 miles.

· "*April* 29, 1844; *Monday*. — Day calm and fine. Learned
this morning that a wire had drawn apart at a bad joint near Beltsville, which was doubtless the cause of the difficulty on Saturday.
Saturday was a rainy and windy day. The galvanometer showed
deflection of needle two or three degrees with 60 pairs; a slight
spark was also visible, which may be accounted for by the ends of
the wire being on the ground, and a slight current being returned
through the ground. Mr. Cornell is to repair the wire at 1
o'clock, having the whole circuit closed at the Junction. I have
prepared 80 pairs for trial: 80 operates the magnet powerfully, 65
operates well, 70 better. Kept in action from 12 o'clock; at 5.30
o'clock battery strong, 67 pairs sufficient to operate well; 65 operates small magnet quick, but not the large magnet. Near 6 o'clock
Mr. Vail operated from Junction, and announced the cars as at the
junction at 2 minutes to 6 o'clock, and that he was coming in.
Made various experiments to-day with different arrangement of circuits. Crossed tub of water without wires; water acidulated.

"*May* 3*d*.—Went to Junction to see arrangements there, and ascertain the cause of difficulty of conversing yesterday during the rain.

"Learned that, during the thunder and lightning in the night,
the electricity was heard 'snapping like a chestnut-fire in the tele-
graph-room.' The persons there did not awaken Mr. Vail, and did
not dare to go into the room of the telegraph. Mrs. Sumwalt says
she saw the line of wires surrounded with light. The electricity
of the atmosphere may have had something to do with the effects
yesterday, but it is doubtful. The magnet of Mr. Vail at Junction operated when I touched, but mine did not when he touched.
The reason of this is yet involved in mystery. Returned in 10
o'clock train.

"The ground circuit was put in operation with the east wire,
and the result is that the effect is stronger than when the two wires
are used as the circuit. The telegraph has operated finely to-day."

It was a brief work to build a line forty miles long, when
the system of poles was adopted. In expectation of the meeting
of the National Whig Convention, May 1st, to nominate candidates for the presidency and vice-presidency, redoubled ener-

gies were put forth, and by that time the wires were in working
order twenty-two miles from Washington toward Baltimore.
The day before the convention met, Professor Morse wrote to
Mr. Vail:

"Get every thing ready in the morning for the day, and do not
be out of hearing of your bell. When you learn the name of the
candidate nominated, see if you cannot give it to me, and receive
from me an acknowledgment of its receipt before the cars leave
you. If you can, it will do more to excite the wonder of those
in the cars than the mere announcement that the news is gone to
Washington. When the cars are in sight from Baltimore, which
will be about 10 A. M. and 5 P. M., prepare me for the announcement
by the letter ····· deliberately struck, after the usual beginning
and ending. When they arrive at your station get the name of the
Vice-President of Mr. Evans; write simply · ··—·— —·
··· or Mr. Davis —·· ·— ···—·· ··· and I will acknowledge by ·· ··· which means 'Very well,' as well as 'Yes.' Afterward you can repeat the name and any other information you may
have received, but the name of the Vice-President is of most importance. There will be hours when it is of more importance *to be
attentive* at the register than at other times—at 10 A. M. until
12 M., from 1 to 3, and from 5 to 6, or 6½. At 12 M. disconnect, so
that Mr. Cornell may test the wires to the point where he is at
work, and continue disconnected one hour. Tell Mr. Cornell this.
Do not forget to keep your circuit closed after writing."

And the next day:

"Things went well to-day. Your last writing was good. You
did not correct your error of running your letters together until
some time. Better be deliberate; we have time to spare, since we
do not spend upon our stock. Get ready to-morrow (Thursday) as
to-day. There is great excitement about the Telegraph, and my
room is thronged; therefore it is important to have it in action
during the hours named. I may have some of the Cabinet to-
morrow. I told Mr. Brown to go to post-office for you and bring
me the letter if there. He has not brought it, so I fear there is
none. Add the following to your list of phrases . . . . Get from
passengers in the cars from Baltimore or elsewhere all the news you
can, and transmit. A good way of exciting wonder will be to tell
the passengers to give you some short sentence to send me; let

them note time, and call at the Capitol to verify the time I received it. Before transmitting, notify me with (48). Your message to-day that 'the passengers in the cars gave three cheers for Henry Clay,' excited the highest wonder in the passenger who gave it to you to send, when he found it verified at the Capitol.

" When you correct your register again at 1 o'clock, after Mr. Cornell has tried the wires, notify me at once by the word '*Junction*' —— ——. . . . — — . . — . . . . —. I was bothered some time at noon to-day to know who was writing, whether you from the Junction, or Mr. Cornell from the extremity, and many persons were waiting to have you write."

A few days of private practice and experiment followed, the interest of the public rising daily as the results were reported. On the 11th of May Professor Morse said in a letter to Mr. Vail

"Every thing worked well yesterday, but there is one defect in your writing. Make a *longer* space between each letter, and a still longer space between each word. I shall have a great crowd to-day, and wish all things to go off well. Many *M. C.'s* will be present, perhaps Mr. Clay ; give me news by the cars. When the cars come along, try and get a newspaper from Philadelphia or New York, and give items of intelligence. The arrival of the cars at the Junction begins to excite here the greatest interest, and both morning and evening I have had my room thronged."

The back of one of these letters is covered with pencil-notes that indicate the " trials and tribulations " of those anxious hours: " Wires crossed." " At Junction the electricity of the atmosphere was observed upon the line and snapping like a chestnut-fire during the storm last night." " Wires twisted near Bladensburg." But the experiment was approaching its crisis. The convention assembled, and Henry Clay was nominated by acclamation for the presidency. The news was conveyed on the railroad to the point reached by the Telegraph, and thence instantly transmitted over the wires to Washington. An hour afterward passengers arriving at the capital, and supposing that they had brought the first intelligence, were surprised to find that the announcement had been made already and that they were the bearers of old news ! The convention shortly afterward nominated Theodore Frelinghuysen as Vice-President, and the intelligence was sent to Washington in the same manner. The astonishment of the public was great. The fact was to many minds incredible.

Before the month of May had passed, the junction of the lines that had been started from each city was effected, and the communication between Washington and Baltimore was complete and perfect.

THE FIRST MESSAGE.

On the 24th day of May, 1844, Professor Morse was prepared to put to the test the great experiment on which his mind had been laboring for twelve anxious, weary years. Mr. Vail, his assistant, was at the Baltimore terminus, in the Mount Clare depot. Professor Morse had invited his friends to assemble in the chamber of the U. S. Supreme Court, where he had his instrument, from which the wires extended to Baltimore. He had promised his young friend, Miss Ellsworth, that she should indite the first message over the wires. Her mother suggested the familiar words of Scripture (Numbers xxiii. 23): "What hath God wrought!" The whole verse from which this message was taken is in these words: "Surely there is no enchantment against Jacob, neither is there any divination against Israel: according to this time it shall be said of Jacob and of Israel, What hath God wrought!"

The words were chosen without consultation with the inventor, but were singularly expressive of his own sentiment in regard to the invention, and his own experience in bringing it to a successful accomplishment. From the moment of its conception he had been under the serious and sincere impression that he was guided and controlled by supernatural power in this great work. Profoundly religious in his convictions, and trained from earliest childhood to believe in the special superintendence of Providence in the minutest affairs of men, he had acted throughout the whole of his struggles under the firm persuasion that God was working in him to will and to do His own pleasure in this thing. In conversation with intimate personal friends and in private letters to those dear to him, he was free to acknowledge this dependence, and to declare his confidence that the final result would be a complete triumph.

Mrs. Ellsworth had often heard these expressions from the lips of the great inventor. She knew that he would appreciate the propriety of ascribing the honor of this wonderful invention to Him whose lightning shineth out of the east even unto the west, and whose words have gone out through all the earth. It was with such reverential emotion, that the words " What hath God wrought ! " were selected from the pages of Holy Scripture, and accepted by the inventor as the first message to be recorded on a completed line of telegraph. In the room were assembled many of the most distinguished officers of the Government, and the personal friends of the inventor, with various emotions of doubt, anxiety, hope, and faith. The calmest person in the company was Professor Morse.

Taking his seat by the instrument, he proceeded to manipulate it. Slowly, steadily, and successfully, he wrote the selected words, in the Morse telegraphic alphabet, as follows :

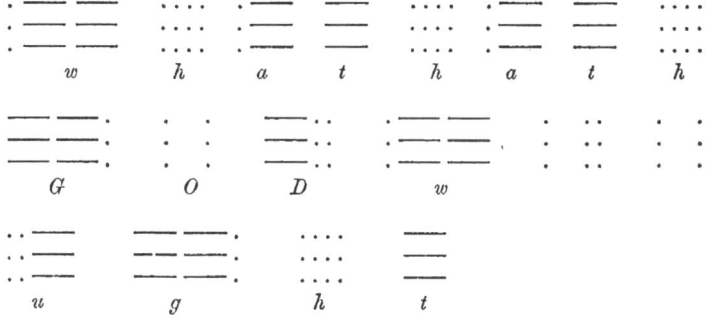

It was instantaneously received by Mr. Vail in Baltimore, who was ignorant of the message to be sent. He returned it immediately to Washington ; so that within a single moment of time, those inspired and inspiring words were carried back and forth through a circuit of eighty miles.

Again the triumph of the inventor was sublime. His confidence had been so unshaken that the surprise of his friends in the result was not shared by him. He knew what the instrument would do, and the fact accomplished was but the confirmation to others of what to him was a certainty on the packet-ship Sully, in 1832. But the result was not the less gratifying and sufficient; had his labors ceased at that moment, he would have cheerfully exclaimed in the words of Simeon, " Lord, now lettest thou thy servant depart in peace, for mine eyes have seen thy salvation."

The congratulations of his friends followed. He received them with modesty, in perfect harmony with the simplicity of his character. Neither then, nor at any subsequent period of his life, did his language or manner indicate exultation. He believed himself an instrument employed by Heaven to achieve a great result, and, having accomplished it, he claimed simply to be the original and only instrument by which that result had been reached. With the same steadiness of purpose, tenacity, and perseverance, with which he had pursued the idea by which he was inspired in 1832, he adhered to his claim to the paternity of that idea, and to the merit of bringing it to a successful issue. Denied, he asserted it; assailed, he defended it. Through long years of controversy, discussion, and litigation, he maintained his right. Equable alike in success and discouragement, calm in the midst of victories, and undismayed by the number, the violence, and the power of those who sought to deprive him of the honor and the reward of his work, he manfully maintained his ground until, by the verdict of the highest courts of his country, and of academies of science, and the practical adoption and indorsement of his system by his own and foreign nations, those wires which were now speaking only forty miles from Washington to Baltimore, were stretched over continents and under oceans, making a net-work to encompass and unite, in instantaneous intercourse for business and enjoyment, all parts of the civilized world.

Professor Morse said of the first dispatch, " It baptized the American Telegraph with the name of its author." The author, as he believed, was God. Twenty-two years afterward, Bishop Stevens, of Pennsylvania, having requested Professor Morse to write his recollections of the birth of the Telegraph, received the following narrative :

"PARIS, *November*, 1866.

"I cheerfully comply with the request you made last evening, to give you in writing the incidents I related to you connected with the *first telegram* transmitted by the Electro-Magnetic Recording Telegraph, the first ever practically in public use, on the first line constructed in the United States, or indeed in the world.

"I had spent at Washington two entire sessions of Congress, one in 1837–'38, the other in 1842–'43, in the endeavor so far to interest the Government in the novel Telegraph as to furnish me with the means to construct a line of sufficient length to test its practicability and utility.

" The last days of the last session of that Congress were about to close. A bill appropriating thirty thousand dollars for my purpose had passed the House, and was before the Senate for concurrence, waiting its turn on the calendar. On the last day of the session (3d of March, 1843), I had spent the whole day and part of the evening in the Senate-chamber, anxiously watching the progress of the passing of the various bills, of which there were, in the morning of that day, over one hundred and forty to be acted upon, before the one in which I was interested would be reached; and a resolution had a few days before been passed, to proceed with the bills on the calendar in their regular order, forbidding any bill to be taken up out of its regular place. As evening approached, there seemed to be but little chance that the Telegraph Bill would be reached before the adjournment, and consequently I had the prospect of the delay of another year, with the loss of time, and all my means already expended. In my anxiety, I consulted with two of my senatorial friends—Senator Huntington, of Connecticut, and Senator Wright, of New York—asking their opinion of the probability of reaching the bill before the close of the session. Their answers were discouraging, and their advice was to prepare myself for disappointment. In this state of mind I retired to my chamber, and made all my arrangements for leaving Washington the next day. Painful as was this prospect of renewed disappointment, you, my dear sir, will understand me when I say that, knowing from experience whence my help must come in any difficulty, I soon disposed of my cares, and slept as quietly as a child.

" In the morning, as I had just gone into the breakfast-room, the servant called me out, announcing that a young lady was in the parlor, wishing to speak with me. I was at once greeted with the smiling face of my young friend, the daughter of my old and valued friend and classmate, the Hon. H. L. Ellsworth, the Commissioner of Patents. On expressing my surprise at so early a call, she said, 'I have come to congratulate you.' 'Indeed, for what?' 'On the passage of your bill.' 'Oh, no, my young friend, you are mistaken; I was in the Senate-chamber till after the lamps were lighted, and my senatorial friends assured me there was no chance for me.'

'But,' she replied, 'it is you that are mistaken. Father was there at the adjournment, at midnight, and saw the President put his name to your bill; and I asked father if I might come and tell you, and he gave me leave. Am I the first to tell you?' The news was so unexpected that for some moments I could not speak. At length I replied: 'Yes, Annie, you are the first to inform me; and now I am going to make you a promise: the first dispatch on the completed line from Washington to Baltimore shall be yours.' 'Well,' said she, 'I shall hold you to your promise.'

"In about a year from that time, the line from Washington to Baltimore was completed. I was in Baltimore when the wires were brought into the office, and attached to the instrument. I proceeded to Washington, leaving word that no dispatch should be sent through the line until I had sent one from Washington. On my arrival there, I sent a note to Miss Ellsworth, announcing to her that every thing was ready, and I was prepared to fulfill my promise of sending the first dispatch over the wires, which she was to indite. The answer was immediately returned. The dispatch was, ' *What hath God wrought!* ' It was sent to Baltimore, and repeated to Washington, and the strip of paper upon which the telegraphic characters are printed, was claimed by Governor Seymour, of Hartford, Connecticut, then a member of the House, on the ground that Miss Ellsworth was a native of Hartford. It was delivered to him by Miss Ellsworth, and is now preserved in the archives of the Hartford Museum, or Athenæum.

"I need only add that no words could have been selected more expressive of the disposition of my own mind at that time, to ascribe all the honor to Him to whom it truly belongs.

"With sincere respect, your most obedient servant,

"To the Rt. Rev. Bishop STEVENS."   "SAMUEL F. B. MORSE.

When Mr. Vail, at Baltimore, had received and returned the first dispatch, "What hath God wrought!" a familiar conversation followed, which proved to the company that the dispatches had not been agreed upon previously by the operators. Professor Morse said, "Stop a few minutes." Mr. Vail replied, "Yes."

"Have you any news?" "No." "Mr. Seaton's respects to you." "My respects to him." "What is your time?" "Nine o'clock, twenty-eight minutes." "What weather have you?" "Cloudy."

"Separate your words more." "Oil your clock-work." "Buchanan stock said to be rising." "I have a great crowd at my window." "Van Buren cannon in front, with a fox-tail on it."

Two days afterward, May 26th, the National Democratic Convention for the nomination of candidates assembled in Baltimore. Mr. Morse was at the terminus of the line in Washington. Mr. Alfred Vail, his assistant, was at the terminus in Baltimore. The most anxious and careful correspondence had passed between them by mail and messenger, as well as by the wires, that every thing might be in perfect order for the success of the first great experiment of the public use of the invention. In private it had been worked to their complete satisfaction. They had not a doubt of its ability to do all they had ever claimed for it; but they well knew that so much depended upon the success of its first appearance in public, it was of the highest importance that no failure should now occur.

The convention had a long and exciting struggle over the nomination of a candidate for the presidency. A rule was adopted, requiring a majority of two-thirds to make a nomination. Mr. Van Buren, failing to receive this number, although he was the first choice of a majority of the convention, was dropped, and James K. Polk, of Tennessee, was finally nominated with great unanimity. The convention, then, having rejected Mr. Van Buren for the presidency, nominated his friend Silas Wright, of New York, for the vice-presidency. Mr. Wright was at that time in the Senate of the United States, and in Washington. The fact of his nomination was immediately communicated by Mr. Vail to Mr. Morse, through the Telegraph, and by Mr. Morse to Mr. Wright. In a few moments the convention was astonished by receiving a message from Mr. Wright, that he respectfully declined the nomination. The president of that body read to them the dispatch, but so incredulous were the members as to the authority of the evidence before them, many utterly disbelieving it to be possible that intelligence could have gone to Washington and an answer returned in the few minutes that had elapsed since the nomination was made, that the convention adjourned over to the following day, to await the report of a committee sent to Washington to get

32

reliable information upon the subject. The committee returned
in the morning, and their report confirmed the correctness and
capacity of the Telegraph, and at once gave it such an advertisement and certificate as its inventor had desired.

Then followed a scene of scientific and moral sublimity.
The convention having reassembled in the morning, and the
refusal of Mr. Wright to accept their nomination having been
communicated, a conference with him was held, by his friends,
through the medium of the wires. In Washington Mr. Wright
and Mr. Morse were closeted with the instrument; at Baltimore
the committee of conference surrounded Mr. Vail and the instrument. Spectators and auditors were excluded. The committee communicated to Mr. Wright their reasons for urging
his acceptance of the nomination. In a moment he received
their communication in writing and as quickly returned to them
his answer. Again and again these confidential messages passed,
and the result was finally announced to the convention that
Mr. Wright was inflexible. Mr. Dallas then received the nomination and accepted it. The ticket thus nominated was successful at the election in November of that year.

The original slips of paper, on which some of the messages
were written at the Baltimore Convention, are still preserved,
and have an interest of their own:

"Governor Morton, of Massachusetts, is now addressing the
convention in favor of taking the question now on the two-thirds
rule. He is in favor of a majority as the rule. Governor Morton
closed at five minutes to ten.

"Mr. Walker is now (fifteen minutes before eleven) speaking in
favor of the two-thirds rule, in answer to Benjamin F. Butler, at
fifteen minutes past ten.

"Senator Walker closed his last speech thirty minutes past ten.

"Robert Rantoul is addressing the convention in favor of the
two-thirds rule.

"Lieutenant-Governor Dickinson, of New Jersey, is speaking in
favor of the majority rule.

"Some firm Democrats here think Henry Dodge, of Wisconsin,
is the man to unite upon.   B. B. FRENCH."

"State Polk's vote at eighth ballot.

"Where will the convention meet on Monday?

"Mr. Morehead's respects, in return, to Mr. Atwill, with his thanks for the box of cigars.

"As a rumor is prevalent here this morning that Mr. Eugene Boyle (son of Mr. John Boyle, of this place) was shot at Baltimore, last evening, Professor Morse will confer a *great favor* upon the family by making inquiry by means of his 'Electro-Magnetic Telegraph' if such is the fact."

Mr. Holmes, member of Congress from South Carolina, had been very active in promoting the passage of the bill for the appropriation; and his brother, a venerable citizen of Charleston, relates the following incident on the opening of the Telegraph:

"My brother, Isaac Edward Holmes, warmly supported Mr. Morse's application to Congress for an appropriation which enabled him to erect the first telegraph-wires between Washington and Baltimore. These first-erected wires were operated on by Morse in person. I stood with him in his room under the Senate-chamber at Washington, saw him operate by dipping into a phial of quicksilver the end of one wire from the battery in the corner of the room, while the same phial held, immersed in the quicksilver, the end of the other wire from the same battery. A reel held, wound up, a paper ribbon which, as it was unwound, passed over a roller having three grooves corresponding to three prongs of a dull-pointed fork which was passed upon the paper, and, according to the time, made dots or lines, which was the alphabet invented by Morse. Morse dismissed us (the spectators) that, as he said, he might assist Lieutenant afterward Commodore Wilkes in determining by the Telegraph the relative longitude in time of Washington and Baltimore. I attempted after the exhibition to explain to one of the Senators of South Carolina, McDuffie, the mode of operation. I failed, for, though he listened, I am sure he did not heed, since, at the conclusion, he exclaimed—

"'I don't understand one word you've said!'

"Which produced an explosive laugh from our other Senator, Huger, who was quietly smoking his cigar, expecting just such a result."

Mr. Vail kept a diary in those early days of the Telegraph, and we have his reminiscences:

"The Telegraph first put in operation, between Washington and Baltimore, in the spring of 1844, was shown, without charge, until

April 1, 1845. Congress, during the session of 1844–'45, made an appropriation of eight thousand dollars to keep it in operation during the year, placing it, at the same time, under the supervision of the Postmaster-General. He, at the close of the session, ordered a tariff of charges of one cent for every four characters made by or through the telegraph, appointing also the operators of the line, Mr. Vail for the Washington station, and Mr. H. J. Rogers for Baltimore. This new order of things commenced on April 1, 1845, and the object was to test the profitableness of the enterprise.

" Mr. Polk had just been inaugurated, and, as is always the case on the advent of a new Administration, the city was filled with persons seeking for office. A gentleman of Virginia, who stated that to be his errand to the city, came to the office on the 1st day of April, and desired to see its operation. The oath of office being fresh in the mind of the operator, and he being determined to fulfill it to the very letter, the gentleman was told of the rates of charges, and that he would see its operation by sending his name to Baltimore, and having it sent back, at the rate of four letters or figures for a cent, or he might ask Baltimore regarding the weather, etc. This he refused to do, and coaxed, argued, and threatened. He said there could be no harm in showing him its operation, as that was all he wanted. He was told of the oath just taken by the incumbent, and of his intention to observe it faithfully; and that, if it was shown to him by the passage of a communication gratuitously, it would be in violation of his oath of office. He stated that he had no change. In reply he was told that, if he would call upon the Postmaster-General, and obtain his consent that the operation should be shown him gratis, the operator would cheerfully comply to almost any extent. He stated, in reply, that he knew the Postmaster-General, and had considerable influence with some of the officers of the Government, and that he, the operator, had better show it to him at once, intimating that he might be subjected to some peril by refusing. He was told that no regard would be paid to the extent of his influence, etc., be it great or little; that he did not think he was at liberty to use the property of the Government for individual benefit when under oath to exact pay, and cited the rules of the post-office in relation to the carriage of letters; but that he was willing to do as directed by the Postmaster-General (Hon. Cave Johnson). The discussion lasted almost an hour, when the gentleman left the office in no pleasant mood.

" This was the patronage received by the Washington office on the 1st, 2d, and 3d of April. On the 4th the same gentleman 'turned up' again, and repeated some of his former arguments. He was asked if he had seen the Postmaster-General, and obtained his consent to his request; to which he replied he had not. After considerable discussion, which was rather amusing than vexatious, he said that he had nothing less than a twenty-dollar bill, and one cent, all of which he pulled out of his breeches-pocket. He was told that he could have a cent's worth of telegraphing, if that would answer, to which he agreed. After his many manœuvres, and his long agony, the gentleman was finally gratified in the following manner: Washington asked Baltimore, ' 4,' which means, in the list of signals, ' *What time is it ?* ' Baltimore replied ' 1,' which meant ' *one o'clock.*' The amount of the operation was one character each way, making two in all, which, at the rate of four for a cent, would amount to half a cent exactly. He laid down his cent, but was told that half a cent would suffice, if he could produce the change. This he declined to do, and gave the whole cent, after which, being satisfied, he left the office.

"Such was the income of the Washington office for the first four days of April, 1845. On the 5th, twelve and a half cents were received. The 6th was the Sabbath. On the 7th, the receipts ran up to sixty cents; on the 8th, to one dollar and thirty-two cents; on the 9th, to one dollar and four cents. It is worthy of remark," concludes Mr. Vail, "that more business was done by the merchants after the tariff was laid than when the service was gratuitous."

The most amusing incidents are related in the early history of this new and unintelligible mode of communication. Many of the published incidents are undoubtedly fictitious, inventions of those who are fond of extracting amusement from the gravest events. Among those preserved by Professor Morse himself, and therefore worthy of being credited, is the following:

A pretty little girl tripped into the Washington City termination, and, after a great deal of hesitation and blushing, asked how long it would "take to send to Baltimore?" The interesting appearance of the little questioner attracted Mr. Morse's attention, and he very blandly replied, "*One second.*"

"Oh, how delightful, how delightful!" ejaculated the little beauty, her eyes glistening with delight. "One second, only—here, send this even *quicker*, if you can." And Mr. Morse found in his hand a neatly-folded, gilt-edged note, the very perfume and shape of which told a volume of love.

" I cannot send this note," said Mr. Morse, with some feeling; "it is impossible."

"Oh, do, *do!*" implored the distracted girl; "William and I have had a quarrel, and I shall die if he don't know that I forgive him in a second—I know I shall."

Mr. Morse still objected to sending the note, when the fair one, brightening up, asked, "You will then send *me* on, won't you?"

"Perhaps," said one of the clerks, "it would take your breath away to travel forty miles in a second!"

"Oh, no, it won't—no, it won't, if it carries me to William! The cars in the morning go *so slow* I can't wait for them."

Mr. Morse now comprehended the mistake which the petitioner was laboring under, and attempted to explain the process of conveying important information along the wires. The letter-writer listened a few moments impatiently, and then rolled her burning epistle into a ball, in the excitement under which she labored, and thrust it into her bosom.

"It's too slow," she finally exclaimed, "it's too slow, and my heart will break before William knows I forgive him; and you are a cruel man, Mr. Morse," said the fair creature, the tears coming into her eyes, "that you won't let me travel by the telegraph to see William." And full of emotion she left the office, illustrating the truth of the poet's wish—

> " Annihilate but space and time,
> And make two lovers happy."

Many of the letters of Professor Morse to Mr. Vail during these few weeks before and after opening the first line, are the reflection of the inner life and history of the invention as it was approaching its introduction to the world :

" *May* 15, 1844.

" Every thing operated finely last evening, and this too without additional cups. We will try this morning, after the train has passed you for Washington, the number of cups necessary. Yesterday there were 80, and a less number I think will answer. When I am ready, I will tell you as I did a few days ago. I will first say, ' Try 70,' — · · · · ·· — — · · —— then I will go into the battery-room and change to 70—return and write ' 70 ' —— — · · —— then of 65; ' try 65 ' — · · · · · · · · · · · – – – and so on, waiting between each time to get your answer. If I do not get it, I will go and change to a higher number, and give you that number. *East* and *Ground* is the present circuit. I want to try the others, but we must understand, if a change does not operate in five minutes after we have made it, put back the wires to *East* and *Ground* again. I will give you to-day the doings in the Capitol occasionally, and I wish you to be particular in writing down in your note-book the time . you receive each piece of news, with the news, as this will verify the fact to many minds. We will set watches by Capitol time to-day."

"*May* 25, 1844.

"Inclosed are some abbreviations. You had better put upon your door a notice to this effect: ' In order to report the principal events of the conventions, it will be absolutely necessary to keep the doors closed except to assistants and messengers.' Mr. Houghton, of Detroit, will call on you, and you can arrange with him and Mr. Cornell the best mode of getting from the conventions such facts as will be interesting here. If necessary, employ two or three persons as messengers and door-keeper. Do not experiment for persons, or explain, until after the conventions have adjourned, but request those who desire to see the operation, to wait till afterward. Condense your information, but not so as to be obscure. Select the most important facts, if you are crowded with matter, and leave the rest to be transmitted at leisure. Prepare to be pretty busy, and, if possible, take the time of adjournment for dinner-time. Write your communication first on paper, in the abbreviated form, thus : 'T. com. sess. 2 K. P. Conv. Gov.—250 mem. Walker, Sen. Mo. ⅔d. maj.—A. N.' If any confusion arises from using abbreviations, use the more lengthened form. I will apprise you of this, by writing '*NO abbrev.*,' and if I wish you to try again, I will write ' Abbrev.' "

" *May* 28th.—Things went off well, on the whole, yesterday. You confound your *ms*, *ts*, and *ls*, and do not separate your words. Sometimes your dots were not made. It is not the fault of local battery here, for at other times it worked perfectly well, but for want, I think, of perfect contact in touching at your end. No time to add. Be particular to-day."

" *May* 29th.—Every thing worked finely yesterday. You have little conception of the sensation produced by telegraphic dispatches. The wonders of the Telegraph, since it is discovered it is no humbug, are in everybody's mouth. Your *ms*, *ts*, and *ls*, were

better yesterday, but still might be improved by attention to proportionate length. Separate your words a little more. Strike your
dots firmer, and do not separate the two dots of the *O* so far apart.
Condense your language more, leave out '*the*,' whenever you can,
and when *h* follows *t*, separate them so that they shall not be 8.
The beginning of a long common word, will generally be sufficient
—if not, I can easily ask you to repeat the whole, *o*, for example.
Butler made communication in favor of majority rule.—' Butler
made com– in fav– of maj.–' '*rule*,' or similar words, are unnecessary to repeat, when the subject has just been considered."

The Telegraph was now a reality. Its completion was hailed
with enthusiasm. The newspapers of the day announced the
annihilation of time and space in the intercourse of men. The
name of the inventor was lauded to the skies. Resolutions of
thanks and applause were adopted by popular assemblies. Language was found too feeble to express the wonder and joy of
the people.

It was a favorite idea with Professor Morse, from the inception of his enterprise, that the Telegraph should belong to the
General Government. In pursuance of this intention, on the
same day when he communicated to the Secretary of the Treasury the completion of the work between Baltimore and Washington, he sent a communication to Congress, making a formal
overture of the Telegraph to the Government.

Professor Morse to Hon. McClintock Young.

"WASHINGTON, *June* 3, 1844.

"SIR: I have the honor to report that the experimental essay
authorized by the act of Congress on March 3, 1843, appropriating
thirty thousand dollars for 'testing' my 'system of Electro-Magnetic Telegraphs, and of such length, and between such points, as
shall test its *practicability* and *utility*,' has been made between
Washington and Baltimore—a distance of forty miles—connecting
the Capitol, in the former city, with the railroad depot in Pratt
Street, in the latter city.

" On the first point proposed to be settled by the experiment, to
wit, its *practicability*, it is scarcely necessary to say (since the public demonstration which has been given of its efficacy, for some
days past, during the session of the different conventions in the city
of Baltimore), that it is fully proved.

"Items of intelligence of all kinds have been transmitted back and forth, from the simple sending of names, to the more lengthened details of the proceedings of Congress and the conventions. One fact will, perhaps, be sufficient to illustrate the efficiency and speed with which intelligence can be communicated by the telegraph.

"In the proceedings of the Democratic Convention at Baltimore for the nomination of a candidate for President of the United States at the next election, the result of the votes, in the nomination of the Hon. J. K. Polk, was conveyed from the convention to the telegraphic terminus in Baltimore, transmitted to Washington, announced to the hundreds assembled in front of the terminus at the Capitol, and to both Houses of Congress; the reception of the news at Washington was then transmitted to Baltimore, sent to the convention and circulated among its members—all before the nomination of the successful candidate was *officially announced* by the presiding officer of the convention.

"In regard to the *utility* of the Telegraph, time alone can determine and develop the whole capacity for good of so perfect a system. In the few days of its infancy, it has already casually shown its usefulness in the relief, in various ways, of the anxieties of thousands; and, when such a sure means of relief is available to the public at large, the amount of its usefulness becomes incalculable. An instance or two will best illustrate this quality of the telegraph:

"A family in Washington was thrown into great distress by a rumor that one of its members had met with a violent death in Baltimore the evening before. Several hours must have elapsed ere their state of suspense could be relieved by the ordinary means of conveyance. A note was dispatched to the telegraph-rooms at the Capitol, requesting to have inquiry made at Baltimore. The messenger had occasion to wait but *ten minutes*, when the proper inquiry was made at Baltimore, and the answer returned that the rumor was without foundation. Thus was a worthy family relieved immediately from a state of distressing suspense.

"An inquiry from a person in Baltimore holding the check of a gentleman in Washington, upon the Bank of Washington, was sent by telegraph, to ascertain if the gentleman in question had funds in that bank. A messenger was instantly dispatched from the Capitol, who returned in a few minutes with an affirmative answer which was returned to Baltimore instantly; thus establishing a confidence in a money arrangement which might have affected unfavorably (for many hours at least) the business transactions of a man in good credit.

" Other cases might be given; but these are deemed sufficient to illustrate the point of utility, and to suggest to those who will reflect upon them, thousands of cases in the public business, in commercial operations, and in private and social transactions, which establish beyond a doubt the immense advantages of such a speedy mode of conveying intelligence.

" In the construction of this *first line of conductors,* it was necessary that experiments should be made to ascertain the best mode of establishing them.   The plan I first suggested in my letter to the Secretary of the Treasury in 1837 (*see* House Report, No. 6, April 6, 1838), of placing my conductors upon posts thirty feet high, and some three hundred feet apart, is, after experiment, proved to be the most eligible.   The objection, so strongly urged in the outset, that, by being exposed aboveground, the conductors were in danger from evil-disposed persons, had such weight with me, in the absence of experience on the subject, as early to turn my whole attention to the practicability of placing my conductors in tubes beneath the earth, as the best means of safety.   The adoption of the latter mode, for some thirteen miles in England, by the projectors of the English Telegraph, confirmed me in the belief that this would be best.   I was thus led to contract for lead pipe sufficient to contain my conductors through the whole route.   Experience, however, has shown that this mode is attended with disadvantages far outweighing any advantages from its fancied security beneath the ground. If apparently more secure, an injury once sustained is much more difficult of access, and of repair; while upon posts, if injury is sustained, it is at once seen, and can be repaired, ordinarily almost without cost.   But the great advantage of the mode on posts over that beneath the ground is the cheapness of its construction. This will be manifest from the following comparative estimate of the two modes in England and in America :

" *Cost of English Telegraph.*—In pipe, £287 6s., or $1,275 per mile.   On posts, £149 5s., or $662 per mile.

" *Cost of American Telegraph, as estimated in House Report, No. 17, Twenty-seventh Congress, Third Session.*—In pipe, $583 per mile.   On posts, from $350 to $400 per mile.

"These comparisons also show how much less is the cost of the American Telegraph, even at the highest estimate.

"But these estimates of the cost of construction largely exceed the actual cost, under the improved modes recently suggested by experiment, and now adopted; and the cost of the line between Baltimore and Washington, already constructed, involves numerous expenditures of an experimental character, which will not be incident to an extension of the line onward to New York, if that shall be deemed desirable.

"Of the appropriation made, there will remain in the Treasury, after the settlement of outstanding accounts, about $3,500, which may be needed for contingent liabilities, and for sustaining the line already constructed, until provision by law shall be made for such an organization of a telegraphic department or bureau as shall enable the Telegraph at least to support itself, if not to become a profitable source of revenue to the Government.

"I will conclude by saying that I feel grateful for the generous confidence which Congress has thus far extended toward me and my enterprise; and I will cheerfully afford any further and more detailed information on the subject of the Telegraph, when desired, and will be prepared to make and execute any desirable arrangements for the extension of it that Congress shall require.

"With great respect, your obedient servant,

"SAMUEL. F. B. MORSE,
"*Superintendent of Electro-Magnetic Telegraph.*
"To the Hon. McCLINTOCK YOUNG, *Secretary of the Treasury, ad interim.*"

Accompanying the report, Professor Morse addressed the following memorial:

"WASHINGTON, *June* 3, 1844.
"*To the Congress of the United States.*

"The undersigned, for himself and coproprietors of Morse's Electro-Magnetic Telegraph, represents that the report of the Superintendent of the Telegraph from Washington City to Baltimore has been made of its completion to the Secretary of the Treasury; and the proprietors now ask the further action of Congress upon the subject. That report will furnish full information of the proceedings that have been had, under and by virtue of the former appropriation made for the purpose of testing the feasibility of the Telegraph, and of the present satisfactory and successful operation of it.

"The proprietors respectfully suggest that it is an engine of power, for good or for evil, which all opinions seem to concur in desiring to have subject to the control of the Government, rather than have it in the hands of private individuals and associations;

and, to this end, the proprietors respectfully submit their willingness to transfer the exclusive use and control of it from Washing-
ington City to the city of New York to the United States, together
with such improvements as shall be made by the proprietors, or
either of them, if Congress shall proceed to cause its construction,
and upon either of the following terms:

"1. By Congress paying the proprietors such remuneration for
it as may be justly due to its value and importance, and the years
of anxious toil and expense it has cost to bring it to its present
state of perfection.

"And in case of this arrangement, the Government will proceed
to construct it at their own expense, and under their own direction,
without imposing any care or responsibility of it on the proprietors; or—

"2. The proprietors will contract with the Government to construct it, complete for use as soon as may be done, from Baltimore
to some point in, or opposite to (as may be found most practicable),
the city of New York, including a sufficient number of wires, to
establish distinct communications to and from Washington and
each of the following places, viz.: Baltimore in Maryland, Wilmington in Delaware, Philadelphia in Pennsylvania, Trenton in New
Jersey, and New York City, or a point most practicable opposite
thereto, including a supply of all necessary instruments to put the
same in complete operation, delivering it into the charge of the
Government as fast as each successive section of ten miles shall be
completed, and relinquish to the Government the exclusive right
and property in the use of the same, with the improvements aforesaid, for the sum of   dollars, and the unexpended
balance of the former appropriation, subject to the payment of all
unliquidated claims outstanding against such balance; said sums
shall be in full compensation for all materials, labor, and every
expense of construction, up to the delivery of every section to the
Government ready for use as aforesaid.

"The work and the materials to be upon the plan, and in all
respects equal to the line, constructed between Washington and
Baltimore City, and the points of communications to be in said
several cities and towns mentioned at such places as the Government, by its proper officer, shall provide and determine, the terms
of payment to be ten per cent. at the commencement of the work,
or signing of the contract, and a *pro-rata* sum for every successive
ten miles when completed.

" The undersigned will add that he will take pleasure in affording any further information than is contained in the two former reports made on the subject.

"SAMUEL F. B. MORSE,
" *Superintendent of Electro-Magnetic Telegraph.*"

The overture was not accepted, as it will soon appear.

Professor Morse suggested to Arago, in 1839, that the Electro-Magnetic Telegraph would be the means of determining the *difference of longitude* between places with an accuracy hitherto unattained. By the following letter from Captain Charles Wilkes to Professor Morse, it will be perceived that the first experiment of the kind resulted in the fulfillment of the Professor's prediction :

"WASHINGTON, *June* 13, 1844.

"MY DEAR SIR: The interesting experiments for obtaining the difference of longitude through your Magnetic Telegraph were finished yesterday, and have proved very satisfactory. They resulted in placing the Battle Monument Square, Baltimore, 1' 34".868 east of the Capitol.

" The time of the two places was carefully obtained by transit observations. Lieutenants Carr and Eld assisted me in these observations. The latter was engaged in those at Baltimore. The comparisons were made through chronometers, and without any difficulty. They were had in three days, and their accuracy proved in the intervals marked and recorded at both places. I have adopted the results of the last day's observations and comparisons, from the elapsed time having been less.

" The difference from former results found in the *American Almanac* is .732 of a second. After these experiments I am well satisfied that your Telegraph offers the means for determining *meridian distances* more accurately than was before within the power of instruments and observers.

" Accept my thanks and those of Lieutenant Eld for yourself and Mr. Vail, for your kindness and attention in affording us the facilities to obtain these results.

" With great respect and esteem, your friend,

"CHARLES WILKES.
"Professor S. F. B. MORSE, Capitol, Washington."

CHAPTER XII.

1845.

CONGRESS REFUSES FURTHER APPROPRIATIONS—LETTER OF PROFESSOR MORSE
TO HIS DAUGHTER—HON. AMOS KENDALL ENGAGED AS AGENT—FORMATION
OF THE MAGNETIC TELEGRAPH COMPANY—LETTERS TO MR. VAIL—MR.
VAIL'S REPLIES—PROFESSOR MORSE GOES ABROAD—IN LONDON—GENERAL
COMMERCIAL TELEGRAPH COMPANY — HON. LOUIS MCLANE — PROFESSOR
MORSE IN HAMBURG—RETURNS TO LONDON—EXHIBITIONS OF THE TELE-
GRAPH IN HAMBURG, ST. PETERSBURG, BERLIN, AND VIENNA—MR. FLEISCH-
MANN'S ACCOUNT OF ITS RECEPTION—PROFESSOR MORSE IN PARIS—ARAGO
—EXHIBITION BEFORE CHAMBER OF DEPUTIES—RETURN TO AMERICA.

THE Telegraph, no longer an experiment, was an accomplished fact. Speaking for itself, it required no champions on the floor of Congress, or in the public press. The extension of the line from Baltimore to Philadelphia and New York, and to all the cities of the land, was only a work of time. But the aid of Congress was sought in vain. An appropriation of $8,000 was made to support the line between the capital and Baltimore, while in its infancy, but further than that the Government declined to go. The sum named as the price for which the Morse Company would sell the Telegraph to the Government, was $100,000. The subject was discussed in the report of Hon. Cave Johnson, the Postmaster-General, under President Polk. He was a member of Congress when the bill was before the House appropriating $30,000 for the experimental line, and was one of those who ridiculed the whole subject as unworthy the notice of sensible men! As Postmaster-General he said in his report, after the experiment had succeeded to the admiration of mankind: "That the operation of the Telegraph between

Washington and Baltimore had not satisfied him that, under any rate of postage that could be adopted, its revenues could be made equal to its expenditures."

Such an opinion, with the evidence then in the possession of the Department, would appear to be the limit of official blindness. But it was undoubtedly fortunate for the inventor, and for the country, that the development of the Telegraph was left to private enterprise. A quarter of a century after the Government had declined to take the Telegraph at the price of $100,000, a project was started to establish lines of. Telegraph to be used by the Government as part of the mail postal system, or to take possession of the lines already established. And in 1873 the Postmaster-General, Mr. Cresswell, stated in his report that the entire cost of all the lines in the country, including patents, was less than $10,000,000, and that the cost of a new system, equal in extent to the present, would be $11,800,000. At the time this estimate was made, the property of the existing Telegraph companies was worth in the market, $50,000,000.

In a letter to his daughter, who had removed with her husband to Porto Rico, in the West Indies, Professor Morse wrote, February 8, 1845:

" The Telegraph operates to the perfect satisfaction of the public, as you perhaps see by the laudatory notices of the papers in all parts of the country. I am now in a state of unpleasant suspense, waiting the passage of the 'bill for the extension of the Telegraph to New York.' I am in hopes they will take it up and pass it next week; if they should not, I shall at once enter into arrangements with private companies to take it and extend it. I do long for the time, if it shall be permitted, to have you with your husband, and little Charles, around me; I feel my loneliness more and more keenly every day. Fame and money are, in themselves, a poor substitute for domestic happiness; as means to that end, I value them. Yesterday was the sad anniversary (the twentieth) of your dear mother's death, and I spent the most of it in thinking of her. How I should like to look in upon you! You must describe your situation, so that I can form an idea of what you are doing daily. I wish you were not so far off; I get discouraged almost in writing to you, it seems so like an age before I can get an answer, and so uncertain as to the fate of my letters.

"I dine on Tuesday with the Russian Minister, Mr. Bodisco; both the Russian and French Governments are taking an interest in Electric Telegraphs, and I may have to visit both these countries. It is one of the possible things that we may meet in Europe.

"*Thursday, February* 12.—I dined at the Russian ambassador's Tuesday. It was the most gorgeous dinner-party I ever attended in any country. Thirty-six sat down to table; there were eleven Senators (nearly half the Senate). I will give you their names, Evans, Woodbury, Webster, Huntington, Buchanan, Bayard, Archer, Huger, Berrien, Crittenden, Benton, and Barrow; Mr. Webster is Senator-elect; then there were General Scott, Captain Shubrick, Captain Morris, Seaton, Mayor of Washington, Judge McLane, of the Supreme Court, Dickens, Secretary of the Senate, and many members of the House. The table, some twenty or twenty-five feet long, was decorated with immense gilt vases of flowers, on a splendid plateau of richly-chased gilt ornaments, and candelabra with about a hundred and fifty lights. We were ushered into the house through eight liveried servants, who afterward waited on us at table.

"I go to-morrow evening to Mr. Wickliffe's, Postmaster-General, and probably, on Wednesday evening next, to the President's. The new President, Polk, arrived this evening amid the roar of cannon; he will be·inaugurated on the 4th of March, and I presume I shall be here. I am most anxiously waiting the action of Congress on the Telegraph; it is exceedingly tantalizing to suffer so much loss of precious time that cannot be recalled.

"Your affectionate father,   SAMUEL F. B. MORSE."

Professor Morse had long known that his pecuniary interests required him to commit them to the hands of skillful, able, and honest men of business. While the invention was in progress, his mind was far more engrossed with it than with its future possible advantage to himself, though he was never insensible to the charms of fame and fortune. But no one could *invent* for him. That labor he bore in solitude and unaided, save by the divine spirit, which he believed to be continually at work with him to produce the result he sought. But now that the Telegraph was in operation, and his own agency in its production acknowledged by the Government, he perceived at once the necessity of confiding his business to the hands of a competent agent, who should administer the trust to their mutual advantage. Such a man he found. The Hon. Amos Kendall was a native of Massachusetts, a graduate of Dartmouth College, New Hampshire. He had spent his active life in Kentucky, and had been called to Washington by General Jackson, when that distinguished man became President of the United States. Mr. Kendall had acquired a national reputation by his able, wise, and energetic administration as Postmaster-General of the United States under President Jackson. In that office he had become thoroughly familiar with the postal affairs of the country, and had demonstrated executive ability that commanded the admiration of the friends and opponents of the Administration. Professor Morse was peculiarly happy in securing the services of such a man, and in March, 1845, he constituted Mr. Kendall his attorney, and committed his telegraphic interests to his control. A contract was concluded with the original proprietors, S. F. B. Morse, Alfred Vail, and L. D. Gale, and Amos Kendall, by which Mr. Kendall became their agent, and was clothed with full powers to manage the business according to his own judgment.

The proprietors of the Morse patent, despairing of action by Congress for the adoption of the Telegraph which it had called into existence, on the 15th day of May, 1845, organized a joint-stock company under the name of "The Magnetic Telegraph Company, for the purpose of constructing and carrying on a line of said Telegraph from New York to Washington." The following persons constituted this first telegraphic organization in the United States, viz., Samuel F. B. Morse, Leonard D. Gale, Alfred Vail, by their attorneys in fact, Amos Kendall, Francis O. J. Smith, B. B. French, Keller, and Greenough, by J. J. Greenough, Charles Monroe, David Gold, E. Cornell, A. Warren Paine, James A. McLaughlin, Charles G. Page, T. L. & A. Thos. Smith, Jno. M. Broadhead, J. C. Broadhead, by J. M. Broadhead, Amos Kendall, P. G. Washington, John E. Kendall, Corcoran & Riggs, John J. Waley, Eliphalet Case, by F. O. J. Smith. An act of incorporation was obtained from the Maryland Legislature, and the first list of subscribers to the stock of the company antedating the act of incorporation, and under the articles of association, was as follows:

Corcoran & Riggs	$1,000	John M. Broadhead	$1,000
B. B. French	1,000	Chas. G. Page	500
Eliphalet Case	1,000	Geo. Templeman	200
Charles Monroe	1,000	Henry J. Rogers, Baltimore	100
Peter G. Washington	200	J. W. Murphy, Baltimore	100
John J. Waley, New York	500	A. W. Paine	500
John E. Kendall	300	F. O. J. Smith	2,750
James A. McLaughlin	350	J. Black	200
Amos Kendall	500	Keller & Greenough	500
E. Cornell, New York	500	J. G. Broadhead, Boston	500
Daniel Gold	1,000	T. L. & A. T. Smith	200
Simon Brown	500	A. Thos. Smith	100
J. J. Glossbrenner	500		
			$15,000

From this time the extension of the Telegraph proceeded step by step, and sometimes with rapid strides, over the United States of America. Professor Morse had the proud satisfaction of seeing his invention acknowledged before the world as an American invention. He felt ambitious to secure that honor to his country, which he loved with the devotion of a child to its parent. " When you arrive in sight of dear America," he said, in a letter from Paris under date of October 13, 1839, to Mr. Smith embarking in Liverpool homeward bound, " bless it for me ; and when you land, kiss the very ground for me. Land of lands! Oh, that all our countrymen would but know their blessings! God hath not dealt so with any nation. We ought to be the *best*, as well as the happiest and most prosperous, of all nations. Nor should we forget to whom we are indebted, either as a nation, or as individuals, for these more distinguished favors. ' Righteousness exalteth a nation, but sin is a reproach to any people.' "

" The Secret Corresponding Vocabulary, adapted for Use to Morse's Electro-Magnetic Telegraph, and also in conducting Written Correspondence transmitted by the Mails, or otherwise," was now printed in a volume, prepared by Francis O. J. Smith, Esq., and published at Portland, Maine. The dedication of the work is in these words :

To Professor Samuel F. B. Morse, Inventor of the American Electro-Magnetic Telegraph.

" SIR : The homage of the world during the last half-century has been, and will ever continue to be, accorded to the name and genius of the illustrious American philosopher, Benjamin Franklin, for having first taught mankind that the wild and terrific ways and forces of the electric fluid, as it flies and flashes through the rent atmosphere, or descends to the surface of the earth, are guided by positive and fixed laws, as much as the movements of more sluggish matter in the physical creation ; and that its terrible death-strokes may be rendered harmless by proper scientific precautions.

" To another name of another generation, yet of the same proud national nativity, the glory has been reserved of having first taught mankind to reach even beyond the results of Franklin, and to subdue in a modified state, into the familiar and practical uses of a household servant, who runs at his master's bidding, this same once frightful and tremendous element. Indeed, the great work of science which Franklin commenced for the protection of man, you have most triumphantly subdued to his convenience. And it needs not the gift of prophecy to foresee, nor the spirit of personal flattery to declare, that the names of Franklin and Morse are destined to glide down the declivity of time together, the equals in the renown of inventive achievements, until the hand of History shall become palsied, and whatever pertains to humanity shall be lost in the general dissolution of matter.

" Of one thus rich in the present applause of his countrymen, and in the prospect of their future gratitude, it affords the author of the following compilation, which is designed to contribute in a degree to the practical usefulness of your invention, a high gratification to speak in the presence of an enlightened public feeling.

" That you may live to witness the full consummation of the vast revolution in the social and business relations of your countrymen, which your genius has proved to be feasible, under the liberal encouragement of our national councils, and that you may, with this great gratification, also realize from it the substantial reward which inventive merit too seldom acquires, in the shape of pecuniary independence, is the sincere wish of,

"Your most respectful and obedient servant,

"Forest Home, Westbrook, Me., }
November 23, 1844."   THE AUTHOR.

The Telegraph must have suddenly asserted itself before the world to justify such language as this in the first year of its actual operation. Judge Wayne, of the Supreme Court of the United States, on receiving a copy of this work, wrote to Mr.

Morse : "No one has watched your career in the arts and in philosophy with more interest than I have done, or with stronger wishes for your success, and the eminence which you have attained in both, I trust, will be followed by substantial advantages, as I know it will be by durable fame."

The spring and summer of 1845 were passed by Professor Morse in the discharge of his duties as superintendent of the Telegraph between Washington and Baltimore, and it was more important than ever to keep a watchful eye upon attempts to invade the rights of the patentees, by pretended improvements or actual manufacture of the Morse instruments. The Professor wrote to Mr. Vail, in July:

"You need have no printing-telegraph. I have studied the principles of our *writing* as well as our *printing* telegraph very thoroughly, and the single key must beat all others, about in the ratio that a man can write faster than he can set up *type*—perhaps a little slower, yet at least half as fast again. I wrote to-day 122 (S's.) in succession in one minute. It is all humbug that House, even if he were a *meeting-house* as big as Trinity Church, can print 120 in a minute. I doubt if he can print 30. Depend upon it, all these printing-telegraphs will explode. Mark my predictions. . . . I have just received a letter from Mr. Fleischman. Wheatstone was going to bring out *one like mine, in about a week* from the time he wrote, that is, if he can make it. I am exceedingly anxious to be beforehand with him : I believe I shall be, for he cannot 'conceive how I produce my marks, or how I produce so powerful a magnet.' Fleischman has gone to Paris, and hopes to do something in Germany for us. I have not the least doubt but I can produce, on my principle of alphabetic writing or printing, a rapidity of communication as far beyond any thing the printing-telegraph men have dreamt of, as lightning is beyond railroad speed ; and it is by methods known to you and me. But keep dark upon the subject. Give me specimens of *timed writers* to take with me. Try your best. I sail on the 6th of August in the Ashburton, for Liverpool."

"NEW YORK, *July* 30, 1845.

"I have a capital letter from the Russian Minister Bodisco, who has given me a letter to Count Nesselrode, the Prime-Minister of Russia, and next in power to the emperor. I would not be sanguine, but still I hope to effect something. I have received Dr.

Page's letter, for which thank him for me, and say : ' Doctor, I stick to it and can prove it mathematically, that the mode of suspending the rotating keeper which I suggested, is the STEADIEST ! ! ! and on the other side of this sheet I think I can show that the *bevel* is also as effective, if not more so, than the other plan.' The doctor has erred in supposing that the keeper and the magnet were of the same size."

Professor Morse left New York for Europe August 6, 1845, and arrived in Liverpool on the 25th. He wrote to Mr. Vail from London as soon as he arrived :

" London, *September* 1, 1845.

" I have just taken lodgings with my brother and his family, preparatory to looking about for a week, when I shall continue my journey to Stockholm and St. Petersburg, by the way of Hamburg direct from London. On my way from Liverpool, I saw at Rugby the telegraph-wires of Wheatstone, which extend, I understood, as far as Northampton. I went into the office as the train stopped a moment, and had a glimpse of the instrument, as we have seen it in the *Illustrated Times*. The place was the ticket-office, and the man very uncommunicative ; but he told me it was not in operation, and that they did not use it much. This is easily accounted for, from the fact that the two termini are inconsiderable places, and Wheatstone's system clumsy and complicated. The advantage of record-ing is incalculable, and in this I have the undisputed superiority. As soon I can visit the telegraph-office here, I will give you the result of my observation. I shall probably do nothing until I re-turn from the North."

Professor Morse immediately placed himself in communica-tion with the " General Commercial Telegraph Company " in London, and submitted to them a proposition to demonstrate the superiority of his instrument over those in use in England, and to receive for the use of his instrument a small sum in hand, and only one-quarter of what the company would save by sub-stituting his apparatus for their own ! He was invited to meet a committee of that company September 11th, and, accepting the invitation, he made to them the following proposition in writing :

" In prefacing my proposition to you, I would beg leave to ask, if Mr. Wheatstone or Davy in their systems can give a certain amount of intelligence with *two wires* in one minute, is not a system which gives double the amount with *one wire* in the same time worth *four times* as much?

" I will guarantee that my apparatus shall accomplish what I promise it shall do, and ocular demonstration shall be given.

" I have with me the apparatus complete for establishing my system of Electro-Magnetic Telegraphs, now in such successful operation in the United States. I have a part of the apparatus never revealed to the public, and which is essential to the efficacy of my plan. I can put it in operation (if arrangements are concluded with a company) in a few days. If we can agree on terms, I will delay my visit to Russia; put in order the apparatus; fully explain it to those authorized by you to take out the patent for you, and leave my whole apparatus with you. I will also instruct two persons whom you may designate in the use of it.

" On the delivery of the apparatus into your possession, you shall pay me *one thousand pounds sterling*, and further guarantee to pay me one-fourth part of the savings derived from the use of my system. That is to say, ascertain the utmost amount of intelligence under the most favorable circumstances that Messrs. Wheatstone & Cooke, or Mr. Davy, can give in a minute, and the number of wires necessary to produce their result. If I cannot give more under the same circumstances in the same time, I will ask no more than the one thousand pounds to be paid down on delivery to you of the apparatus, although the advantage alone of recording in so simple and easy a manner is very greatly in favor of mine. If I can give more, then I must be paid, in addition, a certain proportion of the savings by my system. For example, say that Messrs. W. & C. or Mr. D., by giving the signals complete for twenty-five letters of the alphabet in one minute, enable you to realize fifteen per cent. on your capital; if I can by my system give you fifty letters per minute, I enable you to realize a much larger per cent., and I will then ask *one-fourth part* of your savings derived from the use of my system. To illustrate my proposition, say that the expense of one wire from London to Birmingham will cost £500. Four will cost £2,000. Suppose that I can communicate with *two* wires as much information as W. or D. can give with *four*. Here would be a saving of £1,000 to you. Of this I propose you should pay me £250. Say that W. & C. or D's apparatus at each station cost £80, and mine but £40, here would be a saving of £40. I propose you should pay, on account of this saving, £10.

"Say that *two attendants* are necessary at each station with W. & C.'s or D.'s apparatus with salary of £100 per annum each, and mine should require but *one*, here would be a saving of £100 per annum at each station. Of this sum I propose you should pay me £25 per annum, and so for the saving in any other item of expense."

The Hon. Louis McLane was at that time the American Minister in England, and with him Professor Morse had repeated interviews in regard to the introduction of his system into European countries. To meet some difficulties in the mind of Mr. McLane in regard to the chronology of telegraphs, Professor Morse addressed him this important letter :

"13 BROMPTON SQUARE, *September* 15, 1845.

" MY DEAR SIR : Accompanying this are the documents I promised in conversation with you this morning, and I have procured and reëxamined with some attention the article in the *Electrical Magazine*, to which you had the kindness to direct my notice. There is so much obscurity in the description of his arrangements, arising probably from the translation, that I am really in doubt whether M. Matteucci's experiments are a repetition of mine or not. His experiments, in repetition of M. Mangrini's, and made with so many precautions, appear to me to have no novelty in them. Franklin made the ground for a distance of three or four miles a part of an electrical circuit, for the passage of common electricity, and Professor Steinheil, of Munich, as far back as 1837, showed that galvanic electricity was subject to the same law. My telegraphic circuit, as you well know, is constructed on this well-known fact in science, the ground for forty miles making one-half of my circuit since the earliest moment of its construction; and I am a little surprised that at this late date so much wonder at a result so long known should be manifested by so distinguished a man of science as Matteucci.

" In regard to *crossing rivers without wires*, whether M. Matteucci's experiments are a repetition of mine or not, the dates of his experiments and mine are now in your possession, and will resolve any doubt whether his or mine were earliest. Matteucci's seem to have been performed in the early part of the present year, while mine were made in 1842, and were announced at the time in the *Journal of Commerce*, long before they were presented to Congress in the form you have (in document 24), which bears date 1844.

There was ample time intervening between this late date and the date of M. M.'s experiment to have reached Europe and to circulate through the scientific world.

"From the magazine on your table, page 78, paragraph ' *Chess by Telegraph*,' you will observe an instance of the mode in which the public here are made to believe in the priority of experiments on their Telegraph. When I have mentioned in conversation the games of chess played by means of my Telegraph between B. and W., the answer has uniformly been, ' Oh, ah, yes, we have had that experiment on ours long ago.' This English game of chess and its precise date I saw announced in a paper published a few days after it occurred, with a great flourish, as marking an era in the game of chess. The date, as you perceive, is Wednesday and Thursday, April 9 and 10, 1845. The date of one of our games of chess (*see* page 3, document 24) is December 5, 1844.

" On the last page of the magazine, page 80, and the last paragraph but one, you will see a notice of my discovery of a mode of causing electricity to cross rivers."

Professor Morse, having accomplished nothing in London, continued his journey to the north of Europe, and his letters to his daughter, gave a lively account of his journey to Hamburg and his return.

"HAMBURG, *September* 27, 1845.

"MY DEAR SUSAN: Every thing being ready on the morning of the 17th instant (September), we left Brompton Square in very rainy and stormy weather, and drove down to the Custom-house Wharf, and went on board our destined steamer, the William Joliffe, a dirty, black-looking, tub-like thing, about as large but not half so neat as a North-River wood-sloop. The wind was fresh from the southwest, blowing a gale, with rain, and I confess I did not much fancy leaving land in so unpromising a craft, and in such weather; yet our vessel proved an excellent sea-boat, and, although all were sea-sick on board but Mr. Ellsworth and myself, we had a safe but rough passage across the boisterous North Sea. The weather cleared up, however, before we arrived in mid-channel, and the moon, breaking through the clouds, made the latter part of our voyage more agreeable. We made the light on the island of Schouwen, on the Dutch shore, a little after midnight, and at daylight found ourselves in smooth water opposite Helvoetsluis. We were compelled, on account of the tide, to make a circuitous route to this place, close to Dort, and, passing Delft Haven, arrived at the Hôtel des Pays Bas in Rotterdam, about half-past two o'clock, on the 18th instant. On the morning of the 19th we took a carriage, and drove about the city. There is nothing like a Dutch city on our side of the water. The wide and deep canals, in which the largest class of vessels, as well as the smaller craft, lie opposite your windows; the singular rig of their vessels, the sides, and masts, and blocks of which are all brightly polished and varnished (even the anchors being rubbed bright), give to their streets a very novel appearance. We went in the afternoon to Delft Haven, a place I was very desirous of seeing on account of its associations with the embarkation of the Pilgrims. I presume we were on the spot whence they embarked, and where the distinguished Robinson knelt and prayed with them before they went on board the Speedwell. In the evening we left Rotterdam for the Hague in a carriage, and at the latter place arrived in the nick of time to take the cars for Haarlem and Amsterdam. At Haarlem I saw a single wire on small posts, not so high as the railroad-cars, which I learned was an electric telegraph. It is on Mr. Wheatstone's plan, and I have since had ocular demonstration that it is far less efficient than mine.[1] We arrived late in the evening, and, finding the principal

[1] Professor Morse made the following memorandum at the time:

"AMSTERDAM, *Monday, September* 22, 1845.

"Went to see the Telegraph which is established here between Amsterdam and Haarlem. The Amsterdam terminus is at the railway-depot, and used for the purposes of the road only. It has been established six weeks. It communicates a distance of only ten miles English. The system is Wheatstone's ratchet-wheel instrument, slightly modified from the instrument shown me at the Southampton terminus in London. A dial-plate, with the letters marked upon the outer edge, is turned to the desired point for each letter, and then stopped a moment to be recognized. After each word a period is shown, and after each message a cross +. I inquired how many letters could be shown in a minute; the answer was *fifteen* ordinarily, but they could give *twenty-four* in a minute. A single wire is used in this case; it is said to be iron. A battery of six cups was shown me, which required replenishing every few days. The cost, the conductor told me, was about twenty pounds sterling per mile. The posts are about three inches diameter, and not more than eight or nine feet high; they are planted along the railroad, not so high as the tops of the cars. The telegraph is not used at present for general purposes, but the Government has been petitioned to grant them the privilege, and it is expected to be granted. It is used exclusively for the service of the railroad. The wire is covered with *silk*, and of iron; so said the superintendent. It is larger than mine—about No. 12.

"Remarks: In this instrument Wheatstone has left his needles, and taken up the electro-magnet, the basis of my system. The conductor told me that Mr. Wheatstone was engaged upon an instrument which would print the letter, and that it would be ready in about two weeks. From what I could learn it might possibly

hotels full, at length got lodged at the Hôtel Rondeel. The next day (Saturday), having ascertained that we must remain till Wednesday of the next week, we determined to see a little of the vicinity of Amsterdam. We had heard much of the singular Dutch village of Broek; so, taking a boat, we crossed the harbor, and hired a carriage to take us six miles to the village. On the way we turned aside for a few moments to look into the interior of a Dutch farm-house, and to learn a little of its economy. You cannot conceive of its extreme neatness and order. I thought of Aunt Salisbury all the while I was there, wishing she could be with me, for she would have enjoyed it of all things. The stalls of the cows are kept with as much care as any parlor. The dairy, or rather the cheese-room, is in the *same room* with the cows, and is set round with the crockery-ware. All the iron and brass utensils, every chair and nail-head, are polished perfectly. The floors in the stalls are of clean shells and gravel. It is difficult to imagine what is done with all the litter of a cow-house, unless the Dutch cows have learned the rare secret of living without eating and drinking. Every part of the process of cheese-making is conducted with such superlative neatness and cleanliness, that I think I shall eat Dutch cheeses in preference to all other kinds. We purchased two, at a guilder (forty cents) each. We were shown also the apartments of the family. The tables, chairs, bureaus, floors, all were of the same character of neatness. Not a spot or particle of dirt, not a fly or spider, or any insect, could be found in any nook or corner of the whole house. One would suppose it had been expressly fitted up for exhibition, and yet we were told this was but a fair specimen of all Dutch farm-houses.

print as fast as it now shows a letter; that is, ordinarily, about fifteen letters per minute, while mine ordinarily prints forty-five, and can print eighty, and, with some new arrangements of my first mechanism, at least one hundred and fifty letters per minute. I have, therefore, still the advantage. I have adhered strictly to the plan of mine first conceived in 1832. I still retain my *single circuit* of *one wire ;* my *alphabet* invented to suit my system, my power the *electro-magnet*, and with this arrangement I now print in legible characters at least sixty letters per minute ; while Mr. Wheatstone, whose first invention of an electric telegraph was in 1837, first used five magnetic needles and six conducting wires. He has been varying his system until he has first reduced his needles to three, and then to two, with as many conductors, and at length has, in 1840, adopted the electro-magnet, the basis of *mine*, as the basis of *his* new arrangement ; by which he only shows fifteen, or, at the most, twenty-four letters per minute, and is expecting to print as many by another modification of his invention. With these facts, the scientific world may form their judgment who was the inventor of the Electro-Magnetic Telegraph."

"The inn at Broek was another example of the same neatness. Here we took a little refreshment before going into the village. We walked, of course, for no carriage, not even a wheelbarrow, appeared to be allowed, any more than in a gentleman's parlor. Every thing about the exterior of the houses and gardens was as carefully cared for as the furniture and embellishments of the interior. The streets (or rather alleys, like those of a garden) were narrow, and paved with small, variously-colored bricks, forming every variety of ornamental figures. The houses, from the highest to the lowest class, exhibited not merely comfort, but luxury; yet, it was a selfish sort of luxury. The perpetually-closed door, and shut-up room of ceremony, the largest and most conspicuous of all in the house, gave an air of inhospitableness which, I should hope, was not indicative of the real character of the inhabitants; yet it seemed to be a deserted village, a place of the dead, rather than of the living, an ornamented graveyard. The liveliness of social beings was absent and was even inconsistent with the superlative neatness of all around us. It was a best parlor out-of-doors, where the gayety of frolicking children would derange the set order of the furniture, or an accidental touch of a sacrilegious foot might scratch the polish of a fresh-varnished fence, or flatten down the nap of the green carpet of grass, every blade of which is trained to grow *exactly so*. The grounds and gardens of a Mr. Vander Beck were, indeed, a curiosity from the strange mixture of the useful with the *ridiculously ornamental*. Here were the beautiful banks of a lake, and Nature's embellishment of reeds and water-plants, which, for a wonder, were left to grow in their native luxuriance, and in the midst a huge pasteboard or wooden swan, and a wooden mermaid of tasteless proportions, blowing from a conch-shell. In another part were a cottage with puppets, the size of life, moving by clock-work, a peasant smoking and turning a reel to wind off the thread which his " goed vrow " is spinning upon a wheel, while a most sheep-like dog is made to open his mouth and to bark—a dog which is, doubtless, the progenitor of all the barking, toy-shop dogs of the world; and directly in the vicinity is a beautiful grapery, with the richest clusters of grapes literally covering the top, sides, and walls of the greenhouse, which stands in the midst of a garden, gay with dahlias and amaranths, and every variety of flowers, with delicious fruits thickly studding the well-trained trees. Every thing, however, was cut up into miniature landscapes; little bridges and little temples adorned little canals, and little mounds, miniature representations of streams and hills.

" We visited the residence of the burgomaster. He was away, and his servants permitted us to see the house. It was *cleaning-day*. Every thing in the house was in keeping with the character of the village. But, the kitchen! how shall I describe it? The polished marble floor, the dressers, with glass doors like a book-case, to keep the least particle of dust from the bright-polished utensils of brass and copper. The varnished mahogany handle of the brass spigot, lest the moisture of the hand in turning it should soil its polish: and, will you believe it, the very pot-hooks as well as the cranes (for there were two) in the fireplace were as bright as your scissors! Broek is, certainly, a curiosity. It is unique, but the impression left upon me is not, on the whole, agreeable. I should not be contented to live there. It is too ridiculously and uncomfortably nice. Fancy a lady always dressed throughout the day in her best evening-party dress, and say if she could move about with that ease which she would like. Such, however, must be the feeling of the inhabitants of Broek; they must be in perpetual fear, not only of soiling or deranging their clothes merely, but their very streets, every step they take. But, good-by to Broek. I would not have missed seeing it, but do not care to see it again.

" In Amsterdam we were compelled to stay four or five days to take the steamer to Hamburg, which goes but twice a week. I found here an American artist of great merit, Mr. Schwartze, of Philadelphia. I went with him to see some of the galleries of pictures. I also went one evening to a place of amusement called *Frascati's*, after a celebrated *café* of that name in Paris. A large room fitted up with evergreens and statuary, and a fine band of music, is the evening resort of the citizens to take coffee and other refreshments, and to hear the music.

> "WEDNESDAY, *September* 24, SIX O'CLOCK, P. M.
> On board Steamer Willem de Ernest for Hamburg.

" We have just embarked on board the steamer for Hamburg. The weather, so essential in the life of a traveler, is beautifully calm, and as we lie at anchor off the booms in the harbor, awaiting the hour of midnight to get under way, the chimes of the clocks, so famous in the Dutch cities, give us a serenade every half-hour.

> " HAMBURG, *September* 26*th.*

" At midnight we set sail from Amsterdam yesterday, and had not proceeded five miles before we ran aground, and were unable to proceed for five or six hours. We at length got under way

again, and pushed out into the North Sea through the outlet between Wieland and Ter Schilling, sailing over the Zuyder-Zee,
which is a large expanse of water, the effect of an inundation many
centuries ago, which deluged many cities and fields like those now
existing in Holland, destroying some eighty thousand lives. One
feels in Holland like being in a ship, constantly liable to spring a
leak. We had some pleasant passengers on board, principally
Danes. Count Blücher, aide-de-camp to the King of Denmark, and
cousin to the celebrated general of that name who led the Prus-
sians at the battle of Waterloo. Hamburg, you may remember,
was nearly destroyed by fire in 1842. It is now almost rebuilt, and
in a most splendid style of architecture. I am much prepossessed in
its favor. We have taken up our quarters at the Victoria Hotel,
one of the splendid new hotels of the city. I find the season so
far advanced in these northern regions that I am thinking of giving
up my journey farther north. My matters in London will demand
all my spare time.

"*September 30th.*

"The windows of my hotel look out upon the Alster Basin, a
beautiful sheet of water; three sides of which are surrounded with
splendid houses. Boats and swans are gliding over the glassy surface, giving, with the well-dressed promenaders along the shores, an
air of gayety and liveliness to the scene.

" LONDON, *October 9, 1845.*

"I am once more seated at the table at No. 13 Brompton Square,
after my journey and voyage to Hamburg, and continue my letter,
which has been written at such intervals of time as I could catch
from out-door duties. Mrs. Overmann and family left on the 30th
ultimo, in the August, to go down the Elbe. I went on board
the steamer Caledonia, for London, on the evening of the 3d instant, having parted most reluctantly from my friends, the Ellsworths, on the 30th ultimo, they having left that day for Lubeck
and Stockholm. On going on board, Mr. Miller brought a little
girl, and introduced her to me as Miss Axelina Murdoch, a niece
of Mr. Lind, and said she was to be a fellow-passenger with me
to London, where she is going to school. She is quite a pretty and
intelligent little girl, of fourteen years, and we had a great deal to
say about St. Thomas, and ' Uncle Edward,' and her school in London. I took charge of her. We set sail in the night, and in the
morning, after passing a great number of vessels, we saw several
ships ahead. I told Axelina we must look out for the August; for

I was sure she could not yet have got out of the river, as the wind had been contrary ever since they sailed from Hamburg, and, sure enough, just as we were about to sit down to breakfast, we were coming up fast with a ship under full sail, and, just off Cuxhaven, as soon as we came near enough to read her name, I found it, indeed, to be the August. We passed so near as to distinguish the persons on board. I saw only Mr. Lunt on deck, the rest being below on account of the weather, which was a little rainy. We shook our handkerchief, and Mr. Lunt, after surveying us with the spy-glass, disappeared, and in a moment after the whole family were at the side of the ship shaking handkerchiefs, and nodding farewell to Axelina and myself, whom they recognized. We were soon past them, but we had the gratification thus of once more greeting them before they sailed for the West Indies.

"We had a boisterous and disagreeable day, but a still more boisterous night; the sea was so high and the vessel so uneasy, that I could not lie in my berth, and at midnight I opened the door of the companion-way and looked out on the tempest, for it was then blowing a perfect gale. I had no sooner opened the door than I saw a brilliant rocket go up from a vessel close to us, and a blue light from the same vessel showed us a large steamer coming toward us. Our captain at once gave orders to our helmsman to put up the helm, which was done, and a rocket and blue light were burned on board ours. I supposed at first it was a signal of distress, but in a few moments I learned that it was the steamer for Hamburg from London which we were meeting, and these rockets and blue lights were to prevent us from running foul of each other. Edward was on board that steamer, and thus we met, without seeing each other, at midnight in a storm in the midst of the North Sea. The wind was fair for him, and he probably arrived in the morning or during the day at Cuxhaven, and passed as near to his friends in the August without knowing it. We arrived in London on Monday, and I carried little Axelina to her aunt Napier's. Mrs. Napier is sister of Axelina's father, and Mr. Napier is the celebrated machinist and inventor of the Napier press, and a very wealthy and distinguished man. I mean to call and see them all before I leave London. Edward had been there, and they supposed he was still in London; but I found, as soon as I got to Brompton Square, that he had sailed in the Neptune steamer for Hamburg, which was the one we met, as I have described.

"I have thought of you a great deal, my dear daughter, and

how disappointed you must have felt, on finding us all gone (when you arrived in New York). I really could have cried, myself, to think of your disappointment; but cheer up, dear Susan, I hope we shall have a meeting all the pleasanter for these disappointments. We live, indeed, in a changing world; there is nothing stable or settled here, and yet we look to being settled as a great desideratum. I do hope yet to have a home, where I can have my children visit me, and have the comforts of home around them. I often feel sad to think of my privation in this respect; but I have so much to be thankful.for, that I would repress all sad feelings of this sort, lest they savor of repining and unthankfulness.

"I know not what to say of my telegraphic matters here yet. There is nothing decided upon, and I have many obstacles to contend against, particularly the opposition of the proprietors of existing telegraphs. But that mine is the best system, I have now no doubt; all that I have seen, while they are ingenious, are more complicated, more expensive, less efficient, and easier deranged. It may take some time to establish the superiority of mine over the others, for there is the usual array of prejudice and interest against a system which throws others out of use."

The Morse Telegraph was becoming well known on the Continent of Europe, through the agency of two young Americans, Charles Robinson and Charles L. Chapin, who went abroad with the hope of securing its introduction. They visited Hamburg, St. Petersburg, and Berlin. After two years they returned to America, with abundant evidence that they had been successful in demonstrating to scientific men and to the commercial public the decided superiority of the American system.

In 1845 Charles T. Fleischmann, Esq., agent of the United States Patent-Office, was in Europe, and collecting valuable information on agriculture, arts, and education. He took with him the Telegraph of Professor Morse, the fame of which had preceded him, and in letters to his family he gave sketches of the effects of its operation, and of the distinguished persons to whom he exhibited the instrument. From Vienna he wrote:

"*October* 9, 1845.—I was told I must see Baron Huegel, counselor of the court, and friend of Prince Metternich. I found the baron already acquainted with my arrival in Vienna, and my object; he received me very politely and requested me to partake of his

breakfast, but I declined; and he then invited me to see the curiosities of his rooms, the walls of which are literally covered with old
paintings, and of collections of antiquities of great interest and variety.   After he was dressed he ordered his carriage, and we went
to see Prince Metternich, at his villa near the city.   We arrived,
and I waited in a beautiful room adjoining the prince's office; but,
after waiting an hour, Baron Huegel returned and stated that the
prince could not now see me, as he was engaged to go to the archduke, but to-morrow he would be pleased to see me.   The princess
also went to town, and then the Baron Huegel took me over the
whole house, showing me all the different departments.   Beautiful
and rare statuary was everywhere displayed.   We went into the
princess's sitting-room, a large apartment tastily arranged.   Her
writing-desk, especially, struck me; it was surrounded by a screen
of ivy, which made a kind of bower, and gave the whole an air of
enchantment.   The prince's office is likewise tastily arranged, and
no one would suppose that in that room the deepest and most important diplomatic schemes are projected and carried out—schemes
upon which the destinies of nations depend.   The villa is one-story
high, and the wings contain the saloons for receptions on great occasions.   The family live in a house adjoining.   The grounds which
surround this charming villa are extensive and delightful.   We
returned to the city, and the baron very kindly placed me at my
own door, inviting me to see him to-morrow to make another attempt to see the prince.   Baron Huegel is the brother of the gentleman who paid his addresses to the princess before she married
the Prince Metternich, and he has great influence with the prince.
He advised me to postpone my tour into Hungary, and attend to
the matter of the Telegraph, as it is just now before the Government, to which I consented.   Thus you see I am brought in contact
with the most influential and distinguished men in Austria.

"*Friday.*—At two o'clock I went to the palace of the prince in
the city.   I sent in my card to the Baron Huegel, who sent me
word that after a few minutes he would see me and introduce me
to the prince.   I was with several gentlemen who were also waiting in the antechamber; every thing here looked well kept, *distin-
gué* without being showy or extravagant.   After waiting an hour,
the Baron Huegel came to me and announced that the prince was
ready to receive me.   I passed through one room, and entering another I found the prince at his desk, and the princess, also, who was
engaged in arranging her own desk.   The prince rose, and, saying

he was pleased to make my acquaintance, alluded to the letter
which I brought him from Count Uoyna, ambassador at Brussels.
I told him I had the honor of showing to Count Uoyna the Telegraph, and that he was so much pleased with it that he recommended me to show it to the prince. We conversed on the merits
of the different systems of Telegraphs. I explained to him the superiority of Morse's, and said I should be happy to show him the
instrument, and make an experiment with it before him. He said,
'Have you an instrument with you?' I told him that I had
brought a full apparatus with me, and was ready at any time to exhibit it at his command, and asked if he would allow me to put it
up somewhere; and when I told him I could put it up in his palace,
he was exceedingly pleased, and immediately ordered that every
facility should be given me. He said it was highly interesting just
at this moment to see the American Telegraph, since his Majesty
has given orders that Electro-Magnetic Telegraphs should be put
up along the railroads, and, if the American Telegraph should prove
to be what it was reported to be, it should be applied. After several other questions in regard to its construction, its practicability,
etc., I took my leave. He followed me to the antechamber, where
he asked me if this was my only object of coming here. I told him
that I was sent by our Government to examine into agriculture,
etc., and we had some conversation about locomotives, and then I
left the prince and his lady. The prince is a noble-looking, highly-
intelligent, elderly gentleman; his conversation is precise, like that
of a great diplomatist; every word has its bearing, not more and
not less. His lady is young, about thirty-eight, and handsome.
She was very busily engaged with papers, and I had only once or
twice a chance to see her face. The prince told me that he had
spoken to the High Kammer, President Baron Kucbeck, about me,
and I shall go and see him, and I was informed that next Thursday
at three o'clock he would see me. *Voilà!* my first interview with
great statesmen. Next week I put the Telegraph in operation,
which will excite great curiosity, as I have begun at the head of
society, and shall have everybody of distinction to see it. To-
morrow I have an interview with Baron Huegel about the place in
the palace, and the necessary battery. The baron is very friendly
toward me.

. " *Thursday.*—At three o'clock I went to see Baron Kucbeck,
the Minister of Finance, the next highest officer to the Prince Metternich. I found the antechamber full of gentlemen, waiting for

34

audience, many with great parade, and all sorts of uniforms, among which the Hungarian magnate was the most conspicuous. I gave my name to the usher, and made up my mind to wait until five o'clock, till my turn should come. After a few minutes the bell rang, the usher went in with his long list, and soon the door opened and my name was called loud enough to be heard by the whole city. I was quite flattered, and every one looked at me, especially the uniformed gentlemen, already fixing their swords to be in readiness when their names should be called. I went in, found the Baron Kucbeck standing in the centre of the room. He received me very politely, and, after exchanging the usual 'How do you do's?' he said he was glad to see me, and especially at the moment when the subject of the construction of the Telegraphs was before him. He offered me a chair, and we went from A to Z about telegraphs, America, etc. He requested me to show him the experiments, and if the American Telegraph showed advantages over others he would be happy to see it go into operation. He requested me to come and see him again.

"*Saturday.*—Prince Metternich is moving into the city, and next week I shall make the experiments with the Telegraph before his highness. I saw Baron Huegel this morning, who told me that Baron Kucbeck wished to see me about the experiments, and that he would like to show me the greenhouses of his brother at Heilzing, and he invited me to ride out with him to that place to-morrow, to which I consented. I accordingly went. His brother has in his greenhouses forty thousand specimens of plants, and in his whole garden over three hundred thousand plants. It is said it is the greatest collection of plants on the Continent. His apartments are beautifully furnished, and stored with Indian and Chinese curiosities which he collected when in those countries. The greenhouses extend from the dwelling, and are beautifully arranged, and enlivened with birds and fountains.

"*October* 27, 1845.—At length, yesterday, I exhibited the Telegraph before the Minister of Finance, a most admirable and accomplished statesman. He seemed to be pleased with it, and requested me to show it as soon as possible to Prince Metternich. To-day I was called upon and informed that the prince was ready to see the experiments. The carriage was announced which was to take me to the palace of the prince. I had to wait two hours before the council was over. At last the prince appeared with his counselors. I explained the Telegraph to them, pointing out the difference of Morse's system from that of others, and its advantages over every other. The prince listened with great interest. He sent for the princess and his family to look at this wonderful instrument. My experiments went off well. The prince exhibited great satisfaction. He expressed several times his astonishment at the simplicity of the instrument, and thanked me very politely for the opportunity I had given him to see the 'beautiful Telegraph,' and wished that I would be so kind as to show it to the brother of the emperor, and to the emperor himself, saying that he should tell them of it, and he would send me word at what time I could exhibit it to them.

"*Monday, November 3d.*—I hoped by this time to give you some account of my interview with the emperor; but such great personages are not easy to approach. Count Colobrant, the Minister of the Interior, sent to inquire if I would be so kind as to show him the Telegraph. I assented, but I know not when he expects me.

"*November 5th.*—I received an invitation this morning to be at one o'clock at the emperor's palace, to show the Telegraph to the uncle of the emperor, the Archduke Louis, and Count Colobrant, the Minister of the Interior. I had scarcely put the apparatus in motion when his imperial highness was announced, an elderly gentleman, dressed as plainly as a bourgeois could be, having the real features of the imperial family. He requested me to explain the Telegraph to him, so I explained it, having some difficulty in bringing out of my mouth his long titles. He was very much interested, and he was a long time with me. I told him there was nothing like it in the world. He observed that he had been very curious to see it, and that he was exceedingly pleased with its simplicity and practicability. I gave him a regular lecture on electricity and magnetism, etc. The Count Colobrant was exceedingly polite, and thanked me for my interesting explanations.

"I had almost given up the idea that I should see the emperor, but it seems that the whole court is anxious to see this wonder from America, and to-day I am requested to appear to-morrow at one o'clock at the palace, as his Majesty and his family have expressed a desire to see the Telegraph. I had an interview with the gentleman who has the business in his hands to report on the subject, and he told me that he proposed two telegraphs, Morse's, of America, and Bain's, of England—Morse's for the principal stations, and Bain's for the intermediate places. There is, in fact, a great deal of interest shown just now in the Telegraph, and in what the court takes an interest the whole country does.

"*November* 8*th.*—According to my promise, I give you a description of my interview with the imperial family. Prince Metternich found the Telegraph so exceedingly interesting that he mentioned it to the whole court, which opened all doors to me. I consequently had interviews with Baron Kucbeck, Minister of Finance, Count Colobrant, Minister of the Interior, and his imperial highness Archduke Louis, who all agreed in Prince Metternich's account, and the imperial family invited me to bring the instrument to the court. I went there at one o'clock to set it up. I passed through the guards. The page in waiting opened the door leading into the great reception-room of Maria Theresa. The chamberlain in waiting ordered the servants to bring me tables, and in a few minutes the apparatus was ready. Prince Metternich passed through with the Archduke Louis and his aide-de-camp. Soon after the emperor and empress were announced, followed by Prince Metternich, the Archduke Louis, and many others. Prince Metternich explained the Telegraph to the empress in Italian, as she does not speak the German language, and I explained it to the emperor. After the empress had examined and admired it, she withdrew, followed by the whole party; but in a moment the emperor returned with his suite, and I showed him again the method of writing, etc. He was very much pleased, and he understood it very well. He is good-natured and polite, and thanked me repeatedly for the opportunity I had afforded him to see an instrument of which he had heard so much. Prince Metternich repeated to him the advantages it had over all others, and, after I had written for each one some words, they took the strips of paper with them and retired. The emperor, in retiring, bowed many times, repeating his thanks, and wishing me good success.

"I have thus had an opportunity of seeing the great Emperor of Austria. He is a small man, delicate, but apparently enjoying good health. His head is the most remarkable part about him; it is very large, and the forehead of uncommon shape and circumference. His eyes are hid under heavy eyebrows, and when he looks at a person he turns up his eyes without lifting up his head, which gives him a peculiar expression. His lips are large, a family feature of the imperial family. His voice is sharp and feeble; he moves very quick, and seems somewhat nervous. He was dressed in a blue dress-coat, and had the order of the Golden Fleece in his button-hole. I forgot to mention that the Duchess de Berri came in while the empress was present. The empress is tall and thin, of about forty years of age. She seems very amiable, and is very kind to the poor.

"The chamberlain requested me to wait a few moments longer for his highness the Archduke Charles, the hero of Austria, who faced Napoleon's armies, and who is distinguished both as a warrior and a diplomatist. He soon appeared with his son's daughter on his arm, and with two sons of his. Then came the Archduke Francis Charles, brother of the present emperor, and the heir to the crown; his son, a young man of twenty-five years, with his wife, a Bavarian princess, a charming woman; and then a whole set of *dames d'honneur*. They all seemed to be interested, and I gave them a full lecture on subjects connected with the Telegraph. They then retired. I am told that very few persons have had such an opportunity of seeing the whole imperial family as I have had, and that I should consider it a great honor.

"The Imperial Palace is an old building, but exceedingly comfortable. The room in which I exhibited the Telegraph was the room of Maria Theresa, and her morning reception-room was next to it, in which every thing is as it was in the time of that great woman. The walls are of red velvet, embroidered with gold. In the centre stands a large bed of red velvet, and heavily embroidered with gold and pearl. This is only a show-bed. Several busts of her children are placed round the room. Near the bed stands a kind of altar for devotion, which consists of bass-reliefs in marble, representing Christ leaning on Mary, from the chisel of an Italian artist. Instead of bureaus, there are large trunks of wood, or boxes, highly ornamented. The room was not used as a bedchamber, but as a reception-room for favored persons and friends of Maria Theresa. It was at that time considered a great honor and distinction to have an audience in the bedchamber, where the empress received in her *négligé*. One thing reminded me of America amid this gorgeous display of royalty. It was a large fireplace, in which a real Western country fire was made up. A large pile of wood was placed on each side, which had more the appearance of a genuine Kentucky fireplace than an imperial mode of heating their apartments.

"I passed through muskets, drawn swords, and servants, to my carriage, and in a few moments I was in my room to give you an account of what had happened.

"I must wait now to know what the commission will determine about the Telegraph. If they should adopt Morse's, much must not be expected, since they could adopt another plan, which is not so good, but which would answer their purpose. I shall, therefore, leave it to their generosity. I shall be glad to see Morse have the honor to have his system employed in a country which abounds with scientific men."

"VIENNA, *November* 20, 1845.

"In my last letter I stated that the emperor and family, etc., had seen the Telegraph, and there is no doubt that Morse's system will be adopted, since it has excited universal admiration among all who have witnessed its operation. Ten days ago I exhibited it before all the foreign diplomatists present at Vienna, among whom was the ambassador of the pope. I was requested to write all the names of the crowned heads with telegraphic signs, which these gentlemen sent to their sovereigns as a curiosity. Many of their ladies and friends were also present, and I gave a regular lecture on telegraphs, and made Morse's name sound from one corner of Europe to the other.

"This morning I received a note, requesting me to bring the Telegraph once more to the palace of the Archduke Stephen, Governor of Bohemia, the young prince who is to marry the daughter of the Emperor of Russia. He is very anxious to see it during his stay in Vienna, since it is proposed to establish the Telegraph between Prague, which is his residence, and Vienna. At the appointed hour I went to the palace, and arranged the instrument in one of the apartments for the prince's inspection. He was not in, but his chamberlain was expecting him every moment to return from Prince Metternich, with whom he had probably some interview relative to his marriage—for Metternich is not only the great diplomat, but also the great match-maker for the European monarchs. The Princess Olga has twice refused Archduke Stephen on account of a condition of the house of Austria that every princess must be a Roman Catholic; as she is a member of the Greek Church (which is the religion of the Russian court), the proposed marriage could not take place unless one of the parties yielded to the other in religious views. But, of late, the Emperor of Russia seems desirous that his daughter should marry the prince, and she has consented to join the Catholic Church. Having waited his return for some time in vain, I left, promising to call again at half-past five, at which time I was told he would be at leisure. I did so, and was soon ushered through several apartments to the audience-room, where the prince received me with much courtesy, expressing his regret that he had troubled me to come a second time, and then requested me to ex-, plain to him the Telegraph and its operation. This was all done with so much politeness and frankness, such freedom from all *hauteur*, that I felt quite at ease. He is about six feet in height, rather a slender figure; his features are not handsome, but pleasing; his eyes are dark, very expressive, and full of vivacity; his voice is agreeable, and he expresses himself with facility, and, what is best of all, he is very intelligent, and, unlike many of the Austrian princes, he is active. He took great interest in Morse's invention, expressed many times his gratification at having seen it and his admiration of its simplicity and beautiful contrivance. He asked me if Mr. Morse was a professor of a university; and when I told him he had no public employment until lately, and that this was only a temporary office, he expressed his astonishment that such ingenious men were not provided for by our Government. He was really delighted with the Telegraph: he said that such an invention was more interesting to him than all other machinery, where matter alone is made to produce matter; but here was an element subdued to the will of man, and made the medium of transmitting his thoughts over land and sea.

"The prince informed me that Baron Kucbeck, the Minister of Finance, who has this matter to decide, is quite in favor of Morse's system, and he has promised that all his own influence shall be exerted in my behalf to have it adopted.

"Prince Metternich's power and influence are undiminished; his decisions require only the signed envelope of the emperor. His antechamber is a proof of his power: there you find the ambassadors and *chargés* of all nations; the clerical *savants* of the pope, in all their different-colored robes; the veteran generals of the army; the mantled and mustached Hungarian magnates; the highest functionaries of the state; the speculative banker, whose fortune depends on a single mark of his pen; the enterprising manufacturer; the artist, exhibiting his productions of brush or chisel to his inspection; Asiatics, Africans, and Americans, all are assembled, to wait patiently until their names are called out, to be admitted before him. But this continual care and responsibility have worn down his constitution, and in a few more years his course will be run, and Austria will lose its preserver."

These letters give us a vivid idea of the interest already excited in the heart of Europe by the Morse Telegraph, so early as the year 1845. Professor Morse continues the history of his own operations, writing to Mr. Vail:

"London, *October* 8, 1845.

"I have just reached here on my return from the North of Europe. I went no farther than Hamburg, finding that if I visited St. Petersburg I should probably be belated in my return to the United States. I was also influenced in my determination to go no farther by the improbability, under all circumstances, of accomplishing any thing with Russia; and the probability that in England I should be able to do something. I know not what the issue of the present negotiations here may be, but I will say, in brief, that there is a 'General Telegraph Commercial Company' forming here, with a capital of six hundred thousand pounds sterling. They are auxious to make arrangements with me. I have offered them liberal terms. One thousand pounds down in cash, and a percentage on the profits, or, rather, one-fourth part of *the savings* to the company from the use of mine over Wheatstone's : that is, if Wheatstone uses four wires and I use but one, one-fourth of the savings thus made shall be mine. If Wheatstone gives but twenty-four letters per minute with four wires, and I can give sixty per minute with one, one-fourth of the savings thus made is mine, and so on. Should they accept these terms, the result will be favorable to us in many ways. I have stipulated that they take out the patent in their own name; so that I am at no risk. If one Telegraph can once be successfully established on a line in England, we command the Continent also, where electric telegraphs have been established on Wheatstone's principle, for the best must succeed. Whether we shall derive any benefit direct from their establishment on the Continent is, perhaps, a question, since publicity must be so far given to our method that it will be seized without acknowledgment or reward. There is no mistake about the superiority of my system. I saw a line of Wheatstone's electric telegraph between Haarlem and Amsterdam, ten miles. It is a single wire, and he uses his ratchet-wheel plan. The ratchet-wheel is urged forward by the *power of the magnet*, thus adopting the basis of my system as the basis of his improvement. He could not use his improvement in the United States, as it would conflict with our prior right. I believe I told you in my former letter that the *number* of signals which Wheatstone can give, and which Mr. Fleischmann says in his letter was fifty or sixty, are *not letters*, but parts of a letter. I timed his improved method at Amsterdam, the other day. The utmost number he could possibly give was twenty four letters in a minute, but ordinarily only fifteen. Cooke and Wheatstone are aware that I am here, and the *latter*, I learn, is quite busy denouncing my system as inferior to theirs—as, indeed, IMPRACTICABLE and ABSURD! Is not this truly laughable? I shall see what I can do here; then take a hasty run to Paris, and be back in season to take one of the steamers of November home."

Before he went to Paris, Professor Morse addressed the following letter to M. Arago, then the Astronomer Royal:

"LONDON, *October* 20, 1845.

"DEAR SIR: In *Galignani's Messenger*, of the 18th instant, I perceive that the subject of electric telegraphs is before the commission of the French Government, who are to decide on the best system of electric telegraphs for France. You will, doubtless, remember my visit to you in Paris, in the autumn of 1838, with my telegraphic system; and I shall not myself forget the kindness with which you explained its action at the *séance* of the Academy on September 10th of that year. You are, doubtless, aware that my system is since in successful operation in the United States; but you may not be aware of the extent to which it has been projected, and which is in process of construction. My time has necessarily been directed to the operations for its extension in the United States, where a line of over thirteen hundred English miles are under contract, the greater part of which is expected to be completed before the 1st of January of the coming year. I should be glad of an opportunity of showing to the commission my improved instruments, and hope to be in Paris within a fortnight from date. I am fully persuaded, from a personal examination of the English system in use here, that my system is much more simple in its apparatus, and far more efficient, as well as less expensive. Of this, however, I am willing that those naturally less biased should be the judge. In a note to my friend Mr. Walsh, United States consul in Paris, I have requested him to send you a copy of my letter to the Secretary of the Treasury, transmitted by him to Congress, at the last session, containing some facts in relation to the operation of the telegraphic line belonging to the Government, and under my superintendence."

In Paris Professor Morse was kindly received by Arago, to whom he was so largely indebted in the year 1838, when he was, in the same city, a stranger and foreigner, seeking to introduce a new invention. Now he came with all the prestige of victory. His Telegraph had been tried on a line of forty miles in length, and had demonstrated its almost miraculous powers. It was not now begging the favor of governments, but was commanding the admiration of the world. Arago introduced the inventor and the invention to the French Chamber of Deputies, and in its presence Professor Morse exhibited his Telegraph, November 10, 1845. It received the loudest encomiums of the Chamber and of the press, as its superiority over all other systems was easily demonstrated. But there was no other inducement than a sense of justice to grant a patent to an American citizen, whose invention the European nations were at liberty to employ at their own pleasure, and the disappointed Professor was obliged to return to his own country, loaded with honor, and nothing else.

CHAPTER XIII.

1846-1847.

EXTENSION OF PATENT—THE INVENTOR'S CLAIM—NEW LINES ESTABLISHED—
SIDNEY E. MORSE'S PREDICTIONS—REPORT TO THE POSTMASTER-GENERAL—
ARTISTS' PETITION—LINE BETWEEN BALTIMORE, PHILADELPHIA, AND NEW
YORK—FRENCH CHAMBERS DEBATE—LETTER TO ARAGO—FIRST FRUITS—
SMITHSONIAN INSTITUTION—PROFESSOR HENRY APPOINTED SECRETARY—
PRINTING-TELEGRAPH—LETTER TO DANIEL LORD—PIRATICAL INVASIONS—
OCEAN-TELEGRAPH.

THE year 1846 was signalized by the reissue of Morse's patent, in which he defined with great exactness the nature of his claim. He said in his statement :

" Having fully described my invention, I wish it to be understood that I do not claim the use of the galvanic current or currents of electricity for the purpose of telegraphic communication ; but what I specially claim as my invention and improvement is, making use of the motive power of magnetism when developed by the action of such current or currents, as a means of operating or giving motion to machinery, which may be used to imprint signals upon paper or other suitable material, or to produce sounds in any desired manner for the purpose of telegraphic communication.

" The only way in which the galvanic current has heretofore been proposed to be used is by decomposition, and the action or exercise of the deflective force of a current upon a magnetized bar or needle ; and the decompositions and deflections thus produced were the subject of inspection, and had no power of recording the communication. I therefore characterize my invention as the first recording or printing Telegraph, by means of electro-magnetism.

" There are various known modes of producing motions by electro-magnetism, but none of these have hitherto been applied to actuate or give motion to printing or recording machinery, which is the chief point of my invention and improvement.

" I also claim the system of signs, consisting of dots and lines, substantially as herein set forth, and illustrated in combination with telegraph for recording signals.

" I also claim the types and rule in combination with the signal levers, as herein described, for the purpose of connecting and breaking the current of galvanism and electricity.

" I also claim, in combination with an electro-magnet used for telegraphic purposes, the train of clock-work actuated by a weight or spring, for the purpose of carrying the material on which the record is to be made, under the registering pen, substantially in the manner specified.

" I also claim the combination of two or more circuits of galvanism or electricity, generated by independent batteries by means of electro-magnets, as above described.

" In testimony whereof," etc.

Professor Morse was now watching the progress of new lines of telegraph, gradually extending from city to city. Mr. Cornell was putting up the wires between New York and Philadelphia. The great problem, as it was then regarded, of crossing the Hudson River, was not satisfactorily solved. On the 10th of January Professor Morse wrote to Mr. Cornell :

" I have just received a letter from Mr. Vail, who is desirous of having us communicate with him from Newark ; but I shall write him by to-day's mail that we will try through to Fort Lee, and if possible to New York. I have written him the following regulations : At twelve o'clock on Monday, and the same on Tuesday at ten o'clock, strike the letter P . . . . successively for five minutes, then rest five minutes, and thus alternately till four o'clock, unless the desired result is realized. I will strike the letter Y . . . . from New York in the same way, if all is clear for that purpose at Fort Lee—if not, you will strike the letter .—. F in the same way from Fort Lee to Philadelphia, and also to me at New York. It will thus be known at each station whence the communication comes. If at either station the signals are recognized, then add . . . s after each, for example : if at Fort Lee you get from Philadelphia, p. p., etc, then return f. s—f. s., until it is recognized.

"Batteries { Platinum plate, and ground at Philadelphia.
{ Zinc plate, and ground at New York."

Thus he was feeling his way along, step by step, with firm confidence that no insuperable difficulties remained. His friends the Ellsworths, whose sympathy and aid in Washington during his struggles with Congress had been so precious, were now residing in Indiana. Mrs. Ellsworth wrote to the Professor : " Oh, might we think you would ever come out into this Western world, how delighted we should be ! We talk daily of you and the Telegraph, and rejoice with something of a *personal pride* in its success. You, my dear friend, stand on a high and enviable round of the ladder—you are just now the nation's idol ; but I have no fear of the blighting influence of such fame on you ; therefore, I pray you be happy in this good that God permits to you."

" The nation's idol ! " This was the language of warm personal friendship, but it expresses the sentiment of admiration with which the inventor was at this moment regarded. New lines of his Telegraph were established from month to month. Each city, on its first enjoyment of instantaneous communication with the metropolis, was thrilled with joy, and raised its voice in honor of the genius that had conferred the boon.

The details of business being now in the hands of Mr. Kendall, the Professor continued his labors as superintendent of the United States Telegraph. His brother, Sidney E. Morse, being in Europe, wrote to him respecting its progress, and, true to the genius of the family, foreshadowed other inventions, venturing a prediction to be fulfilled within fifty years. More than half the time has passed away, and the vision is yet unrealized :

" LONDON, *March* 3, 1846.

" Your letter of January 30th, with the information of the rapid progress of the Telegraph in the United States, and the prospect that it would be profitable property, gave us all much pleasure. It is of the first importance to you to perfect the plan of writing with the *utmost rapidity*, which occupied so much of our thought and conversation last summer in New York. You then told me, you recollect, that, while still using only *one wire*, variety might be given to the written character by using two or more pens to be acted upon by batteries and magnets of different strength, the character of course being in *two or more lines* instead of in *one line*, as at present. I have thought much of this since, and, in connection with your saw-teeth type moving in grooves, I am satisfied that you can at least double, and perhaps *treble* or *quadruple*, the number of letters you now write in any given time. Perfect and patent this mode by all means. I can see clearly how the rapidity can be *doubled* by this method, but, when it comes to trebling and quadrupling by means of three or four varieties in the strength of the magnets and batteries, I see some difficulties. Therefore, to make sure of the utmost possible rapidity, I should patent the use of four wires with four pens (one to each wire), marking upon the same paper in four different parallel lines. With these you can unquestionably make three hundred and twenty letters in a minute, or more, if you can make your lever-pen vibrate and distinctly dot upon the paper more than three hundred and twenty times in a minute. Perhaps, in practice, two wires and two varieties of strength in the magnet or battery will be found best. I write in haste, and cannot explain.

"When we get through with telegraphy and cerography, I think, among other matters, we may turn our thoughts to the perfection of submarine navigation. I have some thoughts on this subject, and will venture to prophesy, that in less than fifty years submarine voyages will be made across the Atlantic, and that improvements in submarine navigation will revolutionize the military and commercial policy of all maritime powers. This is an American invention—Bushnell, of Connecticut, being, I believe, the first who experimented to any effect in this way."

In a communication to the Postmaster-General, the Professor now gave some facts to show the claims which the Telegraph had upon the Government, and the satisfactory results thus far secured:

"In paying over to the Department the receipts of the Telegraph-offices at Washington and Baltimore for the last quarter (which were only $203.43), ending 31st of March, 1846, I have the honor of presenting to the Department a few considerations in relation to the Telegraph generally.

"The line now belonging to the Government is but the experimental line authorized by the act of Congress of March 3, 1843, the principal design of which was to test the 'practicability and utility' of my system of Electro-Magnetic Telegraphs. The first quality, its 'practicability,' was proved when the first communication was made by means of its conductors, from Washington to Baltimore. Its 'utility' required a longer probationary period, and circumstances have arisen which I think will require yet further time satisfactorily to test this point in the experiment. Already, indeed, numerous cases have almost daily occurred, which have demonstrated this quality within the limited extent of forty miles, perhaps enough, in the minds of the thinking, to foreshadow its vast increase as the lines become more and more extended. The revenue to be derived from the use of the Telegraph is by no means the only criterion to judge of its utility. From the character of many of the thousands of messages already transmitted, when the rapidity of transmitting intelligence has been essential often to the security of property of great amounts, directly and indirectly, and to the convenience of business of all kinds, can be derived a powerful argument for its public utility, when more extensively established. It will be gratifying, however, to know that, merely in point of revenue, the receipts of the last quarter have been one fourth greater than those of the previous quarter, and I am sanguine in the belief that when the great lines (now nearly completed by private companies), extending from the lakes to Boston, and from Boston to this city, shall be connected at Baltimore with the Government line, the increase of telegraph business thus brought to Baltimore will increase the revenue far beyond the expenses necessary to sustain it.

"By a reference to the statement of the total receipts for the year ending 31st of March, 1846, it will be seen that there has been a regular increase of the business of the office from the first to the last quarter, and the last month has produced the largest amount of any month in the year. If there is this regular increase without any influence from lines beyond Baltimore, is it not reasonable to expect a vastly greater increase when the business of Philadelphia, New York, and Boston, shall be brought to Baltimore? At any rate, would it be policy, in this stage of the progress of the Telegraph, to stop the Government Telegraph at the moment when these other lines are about to be connected with it?

"The experience we have had upon the Utica and Albany line, and the Philadelphia and New York line, with all the temporary disadvantages of comparatively inexperienced operators (who are, however, daily becoming more expert), and some physical obstacles temporarily encountered, shows that, in point of revenue, the Telegraph will undoubtedly realize the expectations of those who have engaged in the enterprise. The receipts of a single day have amounted to $38.85 on the latter line, and this while laboring under the disadvantages of crossing the Hudson River with the messages in boats.

"In regard to the state of the telegraph-line, an inspection of the daily receipts for the last three quarters (nine months) shows that not a minute during that time has the line been so out of repair as to prevent its use for correspondence. It has been in working order at any moment, showing, among other things, that the danger which many have apprehended of wanton or other injury to the conducting wires, is unfounded; and, in this connection, I would beg leave to correct, once for all, most of the erroneous statements of some of the newspapers, in attributing the breaking of the conductors on the new lines to design. In nine cases out of ten the breaks are attributable to defective wire, and to unforeseen, or rather unprovided-for, effects of frost and sleet upon the conductors. As far as my observation goes, the telegraphic conductors are protected by the favorable feelings of the people; for one instance, where any local cause of unfriendly feeling has resulted in injury to the line, there are five where accident has been kindly remedied by casual passers-by, and information given in the proper quarter of the place and nature of the injury.

"During the last year, I made a rapid tour in England, Holland, and France, mainly for the purpose of personally ascertaining whether any system of Electric Telegraphs, recently adopted there, possessed any advantages over mine. I think I may say, without a boast, that mine is palpably superior to any as yet devised. The recent adoption of my system by the Austrian Government, and, after a careful examination of all the European systems, may be cited as corroborative of my opinion. For a detailed description of the differences between mine and the English and French systems, I beg to refer to my letter to the Commissioner of Patents, in his forthcoming report, printing by order of Congress.

"Should Congress deem it expedient to sustain for another year the telegraph-line between Baltimore and Washington, I would suggest the expediency of increasing the number of messengers at the Washington terminus, and imposing a small additional charge for the delivery of messages within certain limits. I would also suggest that the Telegraph be made available at all times, day and night, and that a relief of two or more operators should be employed to give a constant attendance in the offices. I have reason to believe that the increase of revenue consequent on such an arrangement will more than defray the additional expense."

His old friends the artists, determined to win him back from his wires to his studio and pencil, rallied in force and laid before Congress a petition that Professor Morse be employed to execute the painting to fill the panel in the Rotunda of the Capitol assigned to Mr. Inman, who had been removed by death. The memorial was signed by A. B. Durand, President National Academy of Design, Thomas S. Cummings, Jno. G. Chapman, Jno. L. Morton, F. W. Edmonds, G. C. Verplanck, J. F. E. Prudhomme, Jona. Goodhue, P. Perit, Philip Hone, Frederick R. Spencer, Alfred Jones, James Harper, Chas. C. Ingham, V. P. N. A., S. DeWitt Bloodgood, R. Watts, Jr., M. D., Professor of Anatomy, Regis Giejewus, Jasper F. Cropsey, Chas. L. Elliott, Jas. J. Mapes, Jas. Renwick, Clinton Roosevelt, Geo. P. Morris, and Henry C. Shumway. But it came to nothing. "There's a divinity that shapes our ends," and Morse was never to take his brush in hand again.

The first money that he received, in any way, as the avails of his invention of the Telegraph, was the sum of forty-five dollars, being his share of the amount paid for the right to use his patent on a short line from the Post-Office in Washington City to the National Observatory. The use he made of this money was characteristic of the man. To the Rev. Dr. Sprole, then a pastor in Washington, and afterward chaplain of the Military Academy at West Point, he sent fifty dollars, requesting him to apply it to the benefit of the church. Dr. Sprole says that he added fifty dollars as a personal gift to himself.

June 8, 1846, Professor Morse received from the Controller of the Treasury of the United States, J. W. M. Cullough, a letter stating that his accounts were adjusted. This letter is indorsed "final adjustment closing the books of the Treasury, and settling all my accounts with the Treasury of the United States, in relation to the thirty thousand dollars appropriation for testing the Telegraph."

Early in June, the line from Baltimore to Philadelphia was in operation, Philadelphia and New York being already united by the same tie. Mr. Henry O'Rielly, to whose indefatigable

35

energy and enterprise the public was largely indebted for the success of the undertaking, sent the following dispatch to Professor Morse in Washington:

"*Philadelphia, June* 5, 1846, 10 A. M.—Mr. H. O'Rielly congratulates Professor Morse on the completion of the Telegraph, and on the connection of the Hudson and Potomac by links of lightning."

In five minutes after, the following was received in Philadelphia:

" *Washington, June* 5, 1846, A. M.—Professor Morse congratulates Mr. O'Rielly on the success of his labors."

Communications were sent backward and forward. After a full test had been made between Baltimore and Philadelphia, the wires were connected with the Washington line, and a number of uninterrupted communications made directly with the same impulse between those two cities.

While these extensions were going on with great rapidity, Professor Morse's time was largely occupied by correspondence with those who made inquiries respecting his invention, or sought his aid in perfecting their own. The number of men was great who desired his personal examination of their inventions, and his commendation, that they might, under the auspices of so successful an inventor, secure public attention. To the end of his life, this was one of the most irksome offices which were thrust upon him. His natural kindness and intense dislike of giving pain to others, inclined him to permit these applications to be made, and to yield to them as much consideration as he could with any propriety afford. Some of these schemes were, on their face, absurd, and some of them ridiculous, but perhaps no one of them would appear more preposterous than his own when first proposed. As he remembered, with a chill, the coldness and unbelief with which his own scheme was received, he was the more disposed to listen favorably to the conceptions of others. One man requests him to examine a writing-machine, another a flying-machine ; another begs his attention to a caloric-engine, a steam-boiler improvement, or a cable-stopper. Some propose Telegraphs to supersede his own, and kindly offer him an interest in their inventions. To them all he had a kind word, but few of them are known to have been successful. One of these letters reads:

"BOSTON, *March* 18, 1846.

"I too have invented a Telegraph, so far as to have an *idea* of it; and, though I have made no experiments, I am very confident of its practicability. To put it in operation I want none of your lightning, and can do very well without your apparatus for writing, but not so well as with it. Its operation, I think, cannot be quite so rapid as yours; but the difference will be too small to be very important. In some situations yours will be decidedly the best; in most, it will be at least as good; and in some, I think mine will have the advantage. I *can* go through the air, but shall usually prefer to go underground; and, except some additional expense of construction, I care nothing for swamps and rivers. In the expense of first construction, there will probably be no very great difference, though I have made no estimates. The expense of working mine will probably be less than yours. If mine should ever go into operation, it ought to be in connection with yours, as parts of one system, using for each line and part of a line the plan best adapted to that particular locality."

Nothing ever came of the proposition, but almost at the same time a learned professor of one of the colleges of New England wrote to Professor Morse of an invention for carrying the lines of telegraph-wire across rivers. His plan was in all respects worthy of a man of science, and received the attention it merited. He wrote to Professor Morse:

"The principle of it is as simple as A, B, C. This is ordinarily deemed a recommendation. However, it is very possible that in the multitude of your thoughts and experiments you may find something closely resembling my idea—I do not know that you will—for nothing is more common than for one man to run *close to* an idea which, after all, does not *come out* till years afterward in the original conceptions of some other man."

To this letter Professor Morse replied, and in answer received a very extended communication, with drawings, which he carefully examined and reported upon, as if he had nothing else to do.

Abroad the system was working its way steadily into general favor. Prejudice yielded gradually to the resistless power of self-interest. The cheapest and best mode was sure to secure the palm. In the month of June, 1846, in the French Chamber of Deputies, upon a proposed appropriation for an Electrical Telegraph, the eminent statesman, M. Berryer, opposed it, on the ground *that the experiment of the new system was not complete.* The French Government were then trying experiments with Electrical Telegraphs (not Morse's), but were not successful. Two years after Morse's Telegraph was successfully established and in daily use in this country, there was no reliable Electric Telegraph in France. This opposition of M. Berryer was met by M. Arago, who rose and said:

"The experiment is consummated. In the United States the matter is settled. I received three days ago the *Sun* of Baltimore, accompanying a letter from Mr. Morse, one of the most honorable men of his country; and here is the President's message printed from the Telegraph in two or three hours. The message would fill four columns of the *Moniteur*. It could not have been copied by the most rapid penman in a shorter time than it was transmitted."

The appropriation of nearly half a million francs was passed with but few dissentient voices. While the French Government was introducing and employing the Morse system, an ingenious Frenchman, M. Brequet, was very innocently proposing to make use of Morse's mechanism to operate a telegraph which he hoped to call his own. M. Brequet had taken a deep interest in the Morse Telegraph, and had been using it on the line between Paris and Rouen. He was in correspondence with Professor Morse, and to him the Professor was in the habit of communicating freely the progress of his system. April 20, 1846, Professor Morse wrote to him: '

"I know not if you get information through the American papers of the progress of my Telegraph. I have every reason to be gratified with its success. A few weeks more, and Boston, New York, Philadelphia, Baltimore, and Washington, will be connected, 428 miles, and also New York, Albany, and Buffalo, 433 miles; these main lines extend 861 miles. There are beside these main lines many branch lines of 30 or 40 miles each. I have not much of importance to communicate in relation to the action of the Telegraph;

I have always preferred to underrate rather than overrate its efficiency; I have already shown before the Academy of Sciences a telegraphic communication in which 50 characters or signs were given *in one minute*. I inclose you one written in the same time, of 85 characters, and I have several operators who perform at that rate. I have one in which 94 characters are distinctly written in one minute. The power of battery which I require is very small. I tried in one instance a battery of *two elements* (two cups of my arrangement such as are described in the book I sent you), and operated the Telegraph a distance of 130 miles with perfect success. One pair has operated well 40 miles, and with a plate of zinc in the ground at one extremity, and a plate of copper in the ground at the other, I have operated the Telegraph well. I shall be much obliged to you for any drawings and specifications illustrative of the system you have in operation between Paris and Rouen, and for any information on the general subject of Telegraphs which you may think of interest to me."

Upon the receipt of M. Brequet's answer, Professor Morse wrote to Arago:

"My dear Sir: By the English steamer Caledonia, which takes this, I also send a small packet containing cuttings from newspapers, to illustrate the practical effect as well as efficiency of my system of Magnetic Telegraphs. You will perceive the same date and the same news in all these extracts, from newspapers published in cities at the distance of hundreds of miles from each other. By reference to a map, the place at which each journal is published will be easily recognized. The Cambria steamer arrives in Boston on September 18th. Her news, in the minutest details, is at once transmitted along the telegraphic lines, ready for publication the next morning (the 19th) in the next papers that are issued in the various cities. I thought I could not give you a better tangible proof of the success of my system. I received from the ingenious M. Brequet a letter by the last steamer, in which he relates to me his manner of overcoming the difficulty in obtaining *magnetic force at a distance sufficient to impress paper.*

"The method he proposes is precisely the method I have always had in operation, and which was devised and ready for use from the earliest stages of my invention, and by which I have accomplished all my results. I allude to the use of my first battery and magnet, to break and close the circuit of a second magnet, where

the first magnet, in consequence of the length of the circuit connecting it with the distant battery, has but a feeble magnetism, yet is
sufficient to produce a feeble motion. Power can be obtained to
any extent by means of the size of the magnet and battery.

"This mode, as I have said, was early devised to obviate a supposed and anticipated difficulty, long before experiments demonstrated its necessity.

"In my '*Brevet d'Invention*,' dated Paris, August 18, 1838,
which is of course recorded in Paris, this mode of interposing a second battery and magnet for the purpose of obviating the difficulty
which might arise from the enfeebling of the magnetism at a distance, is fully set forth with a diagram. It has been practically
applied by me from the commencement of my telegraphic operations, and I have always considered it essential to the effective result of my system. I give to the magnet, which is operated from a
distance, the name of *receiving magnet*, because it receives its impulse from the main battery, and it is used to break and close what
I call the *local battery*, which battery operates the magnet of the
register. In the hope that a decision in favor of my system would
soon be given by the commissioners of the Academy of Science and
'Chambers,' and a more complete detail of my arrangements called
for, I took with me to Paris, when I had the pleasure of seeing you,
one of these receiving magnets. I deposited it in the consulate of
the United States, in Paris, that it might be ready when called for.
It is still there, and I have requested my friend, R. Walsh, Esq.,
the consul, to unseal it and show it whenever desired. The magnet in his possession is a modification, by Professor Page, of my
original one, which, though efficient, was too cumbersome to suit
my taste. I have it now reduced to a very small size, and I may
here remark that, although the wire of the helices of these receiving magnets is so much smaller than the wire of the main conductors (No. 15), and although a magnet with two helices of this kind
is interposed at each of the following eleven places along the line,
to wit, New York, Poughkeepsie, Troy, Albany, Schenectady, Utica, Rome, Syracuse, Auburn, Rochester, Buffalo, yet the magnetic
power of the electrical current seems not to be diminished; each
and all act simultaneously, and act efficiently. I still look with
anxiety for the decision of the question, 'Whose system will be
adopted by the French Government?' The practical results of the
Telegraph in this country have realized my most sanguine expectations, and I have every reason to believe that the next session of

our Congress will not pass by without some decision on the subject.

" With the highest respect, your most obedient servant,

"SAMUEL F. B. MORSE."

PROFESSOR HENRY.

The Smithsonian Institution at Washington was founded on the acceptance by the Government of the United States of a donation by a gentleman in England, whose name, Smithson, was perpetuated in the name of the institution. The trustees, appointed by Congress, well knowing that its success and usefulness would depend mainly upon the man whom they should select as the secretary, who was also to be their presiding officer, adopted the following resolution:

" *Resolved*, That it is essential for the advancement of the proper interests of the trust that the Secretary of the Smithsonian Institution be a man possessing weight of character and a high grade of talent; and that it is further desirable that he possess eminent scientific and general acquirements; that he be a man capable of advancing science and promoting letters by original research and effort, well qualified to act as a respectable channel of communication between the Institution and scientific and literary individuals and societies in this and foreign countries; and, in a word, a man worthy to represent, before the world of science and of letters, the Institution over which this Board presides."

Professor Morse, being in Washington at the time of the election, communicated the result to the *New York Observer*, in the following letter:

" WASHINGTON, *December* 3, 1846.

" As there is a well-founded anxiety in regard to the character which the new national institution—the Smithsonian—is to assume, I am sure it will gratify you, as well as the friends of science throughout the country, to learn that this day the trustees have unanimously elected Professor Joseph Henry, of Nassau Hall, as the Secretary of the Institution. By this choice to the most responsible, and, I may say, the highest, scientific post in the country, the trustees have but given utterance to the universal voice of the scientific world. The trustees deserve the thanks of the community for their impartiality, and the judiciousness of their selection. I fear not the arousing of any jealousy in his contemporaries, when I assert that no man in the country has all the qualifications for this high trust in a greater degree than Professor Henry. The fear has been expressed that he may not accept the office, for there have been no seekings on his part; it has been an election where merit has shown forth preëminently above all the common and much-abused forms of recommendation, and asserted its own inherent right to preferment; it is a case where native no-bility of mind has commanded the willing homage of kindred minds. I trust that Professor Henry will accept the office.   M."

More than a quarter of a century has elapsed since the ap-pointment thus announced by Professor Morse was made. The result has justified the wisdom of the trustees and Professor Morse's opinion expressed in this letter. For his own personal contributions to useful knowledge; for patient, persevering, and successful pursuit of science by experiment, research, and original thought; for the power of analysis, and of reducing to order and available use the contributions which he has called forth from others, in wielding the resources and instrumental-ities of the Institution of which he has been the chief, Professor Henry has won the appreciating homage of the world of science. Professor Morse well said twenty-eight years ago that the choice of Professor Henry was "the voice of the scientific world," and it is still the same.

THE PRINTING-TELEGRAPH.

Professor Morse was now quietly pursuing his work of super-intending and improving his invention. He mentions in a letter (December 15, 1846) his views upon printing-telegraphs:

"I noticed an announcement in the papers, that I had recently made 'some improvements in my Telegraph for which I had entered a caveat at the Patent-Office.' It is true that I am taking measures to secure by patent some recent modifications of my telegraphic apparatus, simplifying the printing of my telegraphic alphabet; my experiments on that point have been satisfactory. It is true, also, that I have applied a fact in electro-magnetism (never to my knowledge before applied) in the construction of an apparatus for *printing the common letter of the alphabet*, and I have devised an apparatus of the greatest simplicity.

"But, simple as it is, incomparably more so than any contrivance for that purpose as yet published, I really do not attach any great importance to it, for the reason that it is mathematically demonstrable that, from the very nature of such a contrivance, it cannot successfully compete in the rapidity of recording intelligence with the simple mode I have in use, and which is a consequence mainly of the intention of my telegraphic alphabet. For example, the President's message, entire, on the subject of the war with Mexico, was transmitted with perfect accuracy [exclusively for and at the expense of the *Baltimore Sun*] at the rate of 99 letters per minute. My skillful operators in Washington and Baltimore have printed these characters at the rate of 98, 101, 111, and one of them actually printed 117 letters per minute, and I have little doubt that the accomplished operators in the Philadelphia office could easily show similar results. He must be an expert penman who can write legibly more than 100 letters per minute; consequently, my mode of communication equals, or nearly equals, the *most expeditious mode known of recording thought.*

"A Rochester paper recently contained a paragraph, which has been extensively copied, to the effect that there was a new invention about to appear, which was to 'impress every letter perfectly distinct on paper,' and, '*of course*,' do away with the characters to represent the alphabet. This effect of any such invention is by no means such a *matter of course* as the writer supposes. Allow me a word on that point.

"My very earliest conception of the Telegraph embodied this idea, to wit: '*The marking, in a permanent manner, of a character*, to denote the intelligence transmitted.' It was certainly very natural, then, that *the marking of the common letter of the alphabet* should be suggested to my mind, and I of course expended suficient thought upon the subject to perceive that it was practicable in several ways, but also that any way (at that time) was necessarily complicated. I was intent on *simplicity*, and adopted my present system because of its simplicity and greater efficiency.

"My friend and co-proprietor in the Telegraph, Mr. Vail, some time in the spring of 1837, was intent on producing an instrument of this kind, and gave the project much thought. I uniformly discouraged him, however, on the ground, not that such a plan was impracticable, but, in comparison with the method I had devised, *worthless*, since, were such a mode perfectly accomplished and in actual use, my more simple mode would inevitably supersede the more complicated mode. Mr. Vail, in his work entitled 'The

American Electro-Magnetic Telegraph,' discusses the whole matter from pages 157 to 171. Experience has proved that when my system has been put to the test in competition with the common letter-printing telegraphs in Europe, mine has been proved superior. In Vienna, for example, Mr. Bain's letter-printing telegraph (the most ingenious as yet published) was examined with mine publicly before one of the largest and most learned assemblies ever convened in that capital, comprising the court and notables of Austria, and the American Telegraph carried the day *by acclamation*, and is now adopted by that Government.

"I wish it distinctly understood, therefore, that my recent invention of an apparatus for printing the common Roman letter was not induced by any expectation that it will supersede my present plan, but solely to give the choice to any (if there are any) who, after all the evidence which has long been published of the *intrinsic unimportance* of such a result, may be desirous of seeing the common Roman letter printed, instead of my simple character signifying the same thing. I accomplish this result by means of an apparatus very far less complicated than any yet published here or in Europe."

This was only the beginning of the trials that disturbed his peace, and made many subsequent years of his life almost incessant war. Attempts to use his invention in whole or in part, by rival and opposing parties, to deprive him of the honor and the profit which were justly his, and to destroy his property and his good name, were powerful, persistent, and often malignant. Whatever could be done was done by the use of wealth, in the employment of legal talent and learning of the highest order, and of scientific experts, to invalidate his claims to originality in the invention and construction of the Electro-Magnetic Telegraph. The annals of litigation furnish no example of greater energy, perseverance, and failure of effort to wrest from the hands of a deserving, modest, and successful inventor the fruits of a work that had cost him long years of toil, and had at last conferred unspeakable blessings upon the world.

His brother, Sidney E. Morse, being in London, wrote to the Professor, February 3, 1847: "In a little time your Telegraph will be introduced here, but the people will be made to believe that it is an English invention, and that the Americans copied it." The prediction was fulfilled. England is the last of the countries to admit the claims of Morse and America to the honor of the invention. And to this day, although the Morse system has gradually been adopted from the manifested evidences of its superiority, the power of prejudice is so great that on many lines the Wheatstone Telegraph is employed. But the verdict of the world has long since been pronounced, and the Morse system is without a formidable rival.

Not a month passed without an attempt being made in some way to turn the new invention to account for the advantage of others, and the injury of the inventor. To one who had actually gone into the business of manufacturing the instrument, Professor Morse wrote this very gentle but decided remonstrance and warning:

" I have just seen an instrument of my patent made by you and numbered 15, with your name upon it, in the hands of one who informed me that he purchased it of you. Are you not aware that you are infringing on my patent? I have learned also that you are making some other instruments for other persons. I regret exceedingly this state of things, but you must see that, if continued, you are incurring a very heavy responsibility, for the patentees (if the others become acquainted with these facts) will most assuredly proceed against you. I am personally disposed to be lenient to unintentional errors in this respect, and now write to learn from you the true state of matters, that if possible any evil consequences to yourself may be averted. A moment's reflection will convince you of the irregularity of your proceeding, if you are making them without authority of the patentees. If you desire to make the telegraphic instruments, you must have some understanding with the patentees."

Such violations of his rights were only the beginning of troubles. More formidable enemies rose to meet him. To Daniel Lord, Esq., his legal counsel, Professor Morse gave expression to his private griefs over the persecutions to which he and his invention were subjected:

" The plot thickens all around me; I think a *dénoûment* not far off. I remember your consoling me under these attacks with bidding me think that I had invented something worth contending for. Alas! my dear sir, what encouragement is there to an inventor, if, after years of toil and anxiety, he has only purchased for himself the pleasure of being a target for every vile fellow to shoot at, and in proportion as his invention is of public utility so much the greater effort is to be made to defame, that the robbery may excite the less sympathy? I know, however, that beyond all this there is a clear sky, but the clouds may not break away till I am no longer personally interested whether it be foul or fair. I wish not to complain, but I have feelings, and cannot play the stoic if I would."

THE OCEAN-TELEGRAPH.

In the early part of this year Professor Morse revived in conversation his early idea of an ocean-Telegraph to connect the Old World with the New. B. F. Hall, Esq., of Auburn, N. Y., wrote to him to say that " Captain George B. Chase, of Auburn, who has navigated the ocean for many years, has hit upon a plan that appears to be, and which he and others who know what it is are confident is, FEASIBLE; that it will protect the wire from vessels, icebergs, and other obstructions, and at the same time be permanent and cheap. If you will confer with him, it is believed that his nautical information and experience will enable him to be of service to you in the stupendous plan of tying together the continents." Professor Morse replied that he was not at present engaging in the project, but had it before him for future action, and would be glad to see Captain Chase on the subject. As the conception of the ocean-line was Professor Morse's, and was suggested by him in his early letters on the subject of the Telegraph, he never lost sight of it, and lived to see it successfully accomplished.

CHAPTER XIV.

RIVAL CLAIMS AND LAWSUITS.

INVASION OF PATENT-RIGHT—O'RIELLY CONTRACT—INJUNCTION—LAWSUIT
IN DISTRICT COURT OF KENTUCKY—DECISION—MORSE PATENT SUSTAINED
—INCIDENTS OF THE TRIAL—DISTINGUISHED MEN ENGAGED—JUDGE PIR-
TLE'S EPIGRAM—THE CASE APPEALED—SUPREME COURT OF THE UNITED
STATES SUSTAINS THE MORSE PATENT—OPINION—FRENCH AND ROGERS
CASE—JUDGE KANE'S OPINION—SUSTAINS MORSE PATENT—HOUSE'S AND
BAIN'S INSTRUMENTS—DR. JACKSON'S PRETENSIONS—INPROVEMENTS IN
THE TELEGRAPHIC INSTRUMENT—EXTENT AND VALUE OF THE TELEGRAPH
BUSINESS—MORSE INSTRUMENTS COMPARED WITH OTHERS—WESTERN
UNION TELEGRAPH COMPANY—WILLIAM ORTON—GEORGE B. PRESCOTT—
THE WORLD'S VERDICT—ONLY ONE SYSTEM, THAT OF MORSE.

THE most painful chapter in the life of Mr. Morse is the
history of the lawsuits in which he was involved in defense
of his rights. Having intrusted his business interests to the
hands of Mr. Kendall, he would gladly have left the details,
with the burdens of anxiety and responsibility, to his agent and
attorney. But this was not in human nature. No one could
relieve him of the care caused by assaults upon his reputation
as well as his property. Exceedingly sensitive to these attacks
upon his good name and his rights, the lawsuits that followed
the success of his Telegraph cost him inexpressible distress. It
was some compensation for his sufferings that he was triumphant. His rights were established by the most learned and
impartial legal tribunals to which they could be submitted, and
by the higher test of practical adoption and use throughout the
world!

The first lawsuit had this origin. Professor Morse and his
partners made a contract, June 13, 1845, with Henry O'Rielly,

under which the latter was to construct a line of Telegraph, to
be operated with the Morse instrument, from Philadelphia to
St. Louis, and to the chief towns on the great Western lakes.
Nothing in the contract permitted the use of the Morse patent
on any other line than those mentioned. The line was completed to St. Louis in December, 1847. The Morse owners then
contracted with Colonel T. P. Shaffner and William Tanner to
construct a line of Telegraph from Louisville, Kentucky, to
Nashville, Tennessee, to be a section of a line to New Orleans.
O'Rielly commenced and pushed on a line in the same direction,
without authority in his contract. Immediately a struggle began between the Shaffner Company and O'Rielly in a race for
New Orleans. The O'Rielly, called the People's Line, was completed to Nashville in February, 1848. A telegraphic instrument, named the Columbian Telegraph, and claimed to be another
instrument than Morse's, was adopted by the O'Rielly Company.
The equivalent for the relay-magnet of Morse was a series of
electro-magnetic multipliers, each being composed of a magnetic
needle delicately suspended, and placed within a longitudinal
coil of copper wire, covered with silk thread. In this arrangement, the needle is extremely sensitive to the least current transmitted through the coil. The wire, passing many times above
and below the needle, tends to move its poles with the united
influence of the whole, and in the same direction; so that the
effect of a single wire becomes multiplied in nearly the proportion of the number of times the coil passes above and below the
needle. A needle thus circumstanced, with a divided circle to
measure the angle of deviation, constitutes an instrument termed
a galvanometer, or, as it was first termed, *electro-magnetic multiplier*. Faraday, by means of a delicate instrument of this
kind, succeeded in identifying common and voltaic electricity
as a source of electro-magnetic action. The application of this
instrument as a part of the Columbian proved defective. The
mutator was then introduced in its place, to perform the functions of a relay-magnet.

The public mind was excited with apprehension that the
Morse Company was to be a gigantic monopoly, oppressive and
dangerous, and the cry was raised that the People's Line was to
be the protection of the people's rights. Then it was alleged

that the Telegraph itself was not Morse's, but the invention of
STEINHEIL, of Bavaria, and PAGE, of the Patent-Office, at Washington. The former had employed the electro-magnet; and it
was asserted that Dr. Page invented the *receiving-magnet*, essential to the success of Morse's instrument. Hon. Amos Kendall addressed a letter of inquiry to Dr. Page on this point, and
received the following answer, which refutes the assertion respecting the claims of Dr. Page.[1]

"WASHINGTON, D. C., *February* 22, 1848.

" *Hon. Amos Kendall—*

"SIR: In reply to your inquiry if I laid any claim to the invention of the receiving-magnet used in Morse's Telegraph, I will state
briefly that I have never claimed that invention publicly or privately, directly or indirectly. Yours respectfully,

"CHARLES G. PAGE."

As the attempt had been persistently made to attribute to
another the merit of this vital part of the Morse Telegraph, the
letter of Dr. Page, the original of which is preserved, put the
question at rest during his lifetime. His important contributions to the art and science of magneto-electricity are set forth
in his work, "The American Claim to the Induction-coil and its
Electro-static Developments." In 1843 he applied to Congress
for leave to take out a patent for his improvements, but he was
debarred by law, being an officer in the Patent-Office. After
his death a law securing his claims by patent to his heirs was
passed. But this attack upon Morse's rights, which was made
in the Western newspapers, though speedily answered by publication of the facts, was now followed by the actual construction
of a line of Telegraph in defiance of the patent secured. Argument, evidence, appeals to the public sense of justice, had no
effect. Morse's patent was denounced as a "remorseless monopoly" which must be put down by the popular will. Nothing
was left to the owners but an appeal to the courts of law. With
great reluctance, they applied for an injunction against the
O'Rielly line. This brought to judicial inquiry the claim of
Professor Morse to be the original inventor of the Electro-Magnetic Telegraph, and also the question whether the Columbian

[1] For a similar disclaimer by Steinheil, *see* page 687.

Telegraph was an infringement of the Morse patent. The trial commenced in Louisville, Kentucky, August 24, 1848, and continued sixteen days. The preparation for this trial involved the most expensive and protracted labor. Men, eminent in science, in distant parts of the country, were examined at great length, and their testimony, filling large volumes, is on record and easily accessible to those who desire to make themselves acquainted with it.[1] All systems of telegraphy employed in Europe previous to Morse's were investigated by those competent to form an intelligent opinion. The ingenuity of the most learned counsel was exhausted in the effort to show that the Morse instrument was not original with its inventor.

The parties present were, Hon. Thomas B. Monroe, presiding judge; Professor Morse, Amos Kendall; for counsel, Preston S. Loughborough, of Louisville, ex-Judge Benjamin Monroe, of Frankfort (brother of the judge on the bench), ex-Judge Woolley, of Lexington, and Colonel Shaffner, on the Morse side. On the other were H. O'Rielly, ex-Judge Henry Pirtle, of Louisville, Madison C. Johnson, of Lexington, and D. Y. Gholson, of Cincinnati. O'Rielly had, as experts, E. F. Barnes and Anson Stager. Colonel Shaffner afterward became distinguished for his gigantic enterprises in the extension of the telegraphic system in this country and in Europe, and is the author of the most valuable works which are used in the study of the art and science of telegraphy. He has related to the writer the incidents of this great Kentucky trial:

"All the parties not residing in Frankfort stopped at the Weisiger House. They mingled at all times as at a social meeting. After adjournment of the court, the counsel and others generally met in front of the hotel, and, sitting beneath the shade-trees, gave reciprocal intellectual entertainments. Jefferson Davis was visiting his friends in Kentucky, and, fresh from the Mexican War, he entertained the company much of the time, in his turn, with the most exciting descriptions of the incidents of the war. Woolley was a

[1] Mr. Henry O'Rielly has deposited in the Library of the New York Historical Society more than one hundred volumes, containing a complete history of telegraphic litigation in the United States. These records are at all times accessible to any persons who wish to investigate the claims and rights of individuals or companies. The *testimony* alone in the various suits fills several volumes, each as large as this.

scholar of rare merits, and his fluency in conversation seemed enchanting. Loughborough, one of the oldest lawyers in Kentucky, was mathematical, and often proposed problems for solution. Kendall gave incidents of the Kitchen Cabinet of Jackson, and the part he occasionally performed. One of them had reference to Duane, of the cabinet. Jackson wanted Taney to be Secretary of the Treasury, but was not sure of his opinions. Kendall was authorized to ascertain, and he reported that they were in accord with the President's. Kendall was then sent to request Taney to accept of the secretaryship of the Treasury, and in answer he said to Mr. Kendall : 'You can say to the President that I will accept of the positiou, but, in doing so, I sacrifice and abandon the ambition of my life, and that is to be on the Supreme Court bench.' The new position placed him in political line, and off from the legal, as then considered. Marshall subsequently died, and Taney was appointed by Jackson in his place, which exceeded his expectations and ambitiou. Taney told me of the circumstance in 1853. Pirtle generally indulged in references to the early settlement of Kentucky. He was the senior of all, and knew in his early days its founders. Johnson was familiar with the judicial history of the State, and well acquainted with many of the early statesmen. Gholson was a young man and very quiet—a Virginian of Cincinnati association, and not so open as Kentuckians. He measured his words. Morse engaged their attention in the early invention of the Telegraph, his meeting with Arago, Humboldt, and his acquaintance with West (the artist), and his invention of the use of colors to represent temperature.

"As for myself, I was a silent listener, capable only of studying the pending suit, and listening to the conversations of those great men. Besides the above, Governor Charles S. Morehead, John J. Crittenden, Rev. Robert J. Breckenridge, 'Tom' Marshall, Hon. W. J. Graves (of the Cilley duel), ex-Governor Metcalf, ex-Governor Letcher, and many others, from time to time joined the sidewalk sociables.

"The Morse line alone connected Louisville and Frankfort, and I gave directions to the officers to transmit free all dispatches handed in by O'Rielly and his friends, and I requested him to use the lines to any extent ·that he desired, which he did. From 10 A. M., until 3 P. M., the judge occupied his seat in the court-room, hearing the case in chambers. The case was conducted with the most respectful consideration to all parties, and on all issues.

None of the lawyers had ever had a patent case before, and, having had considerable experience in patent suits since then, I am surprised to see at this date how correctly the case was then conducted. After the court adjourned each day, the counsel and the parties on each side, respectively, met in their accustomed rooms and discussed the proceedings to be observed the next day. Supper was at 6 P. M., and after that all met as before described, and held intellectual entertainments.

"Mrs. Morse (then a bride) was the centre of attraction, and received the polite attentions of all; counsel and friends on both sides endeavored to make the time agreeable to her.

"Of these men, Woolley died in 1849, of cholera; Loughborough became demented and committed suicide by hanging himself, in a stable, in the interior of Missouri; Ben Monroe died about 1860; Kendall died some few years since; Morse in 1872. I am the only one alive that took an active part in the suit on the side of Morse."

It was during one of these pleasant and social hours that Judge Pirtle, of the counsel for O'Rielly, wrote upon a sheet of paper this sentence in Latin, and passed it across the table to Mrs. Morse, in compliment to her husband:

"Et non 'eripuit cælo fulmen'
Fulguri mentem fudit, et orbem lumine cinxit."

"Though he did not 'snatch the thunder from heaven,' he gave the electric current thought, and bound the earth in light."

After the case had been argued with consummate ability on both sides, Judge Monroe gave his opinion sustaining the Morse patent, and granting an injunction against the O'Rielly line. The parties thus enjoined sought to evade its force by receiving intelligence by *sound*. This was one of the original modes of telegraphy secured to Morse as its inventor, and the use of it by the O'Rielly line was pronounced by the court to be a mere evasion of the injunction. It is now the plan almost universally in use in this country. The parties were then arrested and placed under bonds for contempt. A second attempt at evasion was made by removing the instruments outside the district of Kentucky to Jeffersonville, Indiana, while the posts and wires continued on the other side of the river Ohio as before. The line operators were arrested, a fine imposed, and they were placed under bonds again. The marshal of the district was directed to take possession of the posts and wires, to break the circuit of electricity, and prevent the defendants from further operations upon their Telegraph. An appeal was taken from the decision of the District Court of Kentucky to the Supreme Court of the United States.

We now approach the great trial by which the right and title of Samuel F. B. Morse to the invention of the Electro-Magnetic Recording Telegraph were settled, so for as human knowledge can determine any question. The opinion of the Supreme Court of the United States in full is here recited, because the case in all its relations and bearings is set forth with such clearness that the general reader, as well as scientific, will readily receive and appreciate the justice and intelligence of the decision. With great force and propriety did Mr. Kendall say in his argument submitted to the Supreme Court:

"Seldom, if ever, has a more important case been brought before the Supreme Court of the United States for its decision. It is important on account of the pecuniary interests involved in it; it is important as involving the fame of a distinguished citizen, and through him, to some extent, the fame of our common country. It is transcendently important in the principles of patent-law which it presents for final decision by this tribunal. It is now to be tested whether Professor Morse is to share the fate of so many distinguished inventors who have gone before him; whether individuals or the public, eager to possess the fruits of his mental labor before they rightfully become public property, shall be permitted to gratify their cupidity; whether Professor Morse, like the inventor of the cotton-gin, is to lose the profits of his invention, while thousands of his instruments, the originality of which no man doubts, resound throughout the land, almost in the presence of the tribunal which must decide upon his patents. It is now to be tested whether American courts are hereafter to consider patent privileges as the price paid by the Government for the fruits of mental labor, to be held as sacred from piracy, theft, or trespass, as any other species of private property; or whether, like the English courts for a long period, now happily at an end, they are still to confound them with odious monopolies of what, before the issue of the special grants, had become the property of the public."

The case was argued by General R. H. Gillett and Hon. Salmon P. Chase in favor of O'Rielly, and George Harding, St. George T. Campbell, and George Gifford, Esqrs., for the Morse partners. Mr. Chase afterward became Chief-Justice of the United States, and the decision which he rendered, not on the bench, but at the dinner-table, will be found in the subsequent pages of this volume, where he is to be seen presiding at a banquet given to Professor Morse, in the city of New York. It is quite as decisive as the following, rendered by his immediate predecessor. The decision of the Supreme Court was unanimous on all the points involving the right of Professor Morse to the claim of being the original inventor of the Electro-Magnetic Recording Telegraph. A minority of the court went still further, and gave him the right to the motive power of magnetism as a means of operating machinery to imprint signals or to produce sounds for telegraphic purposes.

The testimony of experts in science and art is not introduced, because it was thoroughly weighed and sifted by intelligent and impartial men, whose judgment must be accepted as final and sufficient. The justice of the decision has never been impugned. Each succeeding year has confirmed it with accumulating evidence. One point was decided against the Morse patent, and it is worthy of being noticed that this decision which denied to Morse the right to the *exclusive* use of electro-magnetism for recording telegraphs has never been of injury to his instrument, because no other inventor has devised an instrument to supersede his. The court decided that the Electro-Magnetic Telegraph was the sole and exclusive invention of Samuel F. B. Morse. If others could make better instruments for the same purpose, they were at liberty to use electro-magnetism. Twenty years have elapsed since this decision was rendered, the Morse patent has expired by limitation of time, but it is still without a rival in any part of the world.

DECISION OF SUPREME COURT OF THE UNITED STATES.

SAMUEL F. B. MORSE *vs.* HENRY O'RIELLY.

Appeal from the District Court of Kentucky, wherein Morse was granted an Injunction against O'Rielly, for an Infringement of the Morse Patents, by the Use of the Columbian Telegraph. The Supreme Court perpetuates that Injunction.

Counsel for Morse.—George Gifford, St. George T. Campbell, George Harding.

Counsel for O'Rielly.—Salmon P. Chase, R. H. Gillett.

DECISION RENDERED JANUARY 80, 1854.

December Term, 1853. — Henry O'Rielly, Eugene L. Whitman, and W. F. B. Hastings, Appellants, *vs.* Samuel F. B. Morse, Alfred Vail, and Francis O. J. Smith, Appellees.

Appeal from the Circuit Court of the United States for the District of Kentucky.

Chief-Justice Taney delivered the opinion, which was concurred in by Justices Daniel, Catron, and McLean.

"In proceeding to pronounce judgment in this case, the court is sensible, not only of its importance, but of the difficulties in some of the questions which it presents for decision. The case was argued at the last term, and continued over by the court for the purpose of giving it a more deliberate examination. And since the continuance, we have received from the counsel on both sides printed arguments, in which all of the questions raised on the trial have been fully and elaborately discussed.

"The appellants take three grounds of defense: In the first place, they deny that Professor Morse was the first and original inventor of the Electro-Magnetic Telegraph, described in his two reissued patents of 1848. Secondly, they insist that, if he was the original inventor, the patents under which he claims have not been issued conformably to the acts of Congress, and do not confer on him the right to the exclusive use. And, thirdly, if these two propositions are decided against them, they insist that the Telegraph of O'Rielly is substantially different from that of Professor Morse, and the use of it, therefore, no infringement of his rights.

"In determining these questions, we shall, in the first instance, confine our attention to the patent which Professor Morse obtained in 1840, and which was reissued in 1848. The main dispute between the parties is upon the validity of this patent; and the decision upon it will dispose of the chief points in controversy in the other.

"In relation to the first point (the originality of the invention), many witnesses have been examined on both sides.

"It is obvious that, for some years before Professor Morse made his invention, scientific men in different parts of Europe were earnestly engaged in the same pursuit. Electro-Magnetism itself was a recent discovery, and opened to them a new and unexplored field for their labors, and minds of a high order were engaged in developing its power, and the purposes to which it might be applied.

"Professor Henry, of the Smithsonian Institution, states in his testimony that, prior to the winter of 1819–'20, an Electro-Magnetic Telegraph—that is to say, a Telegraph operating by the combined influence of electricity and magnetism—was not possible; that the scientific principles on which it is founded were until then unknown; and that the first fact af Electro-Magnetism was discovered by Oersted, of Copenhagen, in that winter, and was widely published, and the account everywhere received with interest.

"He also gives an account of the various discoveries subsequently made from time to time, by different persons in different places, developing its properties and powers; and among them his own. He commenced his researches in 1828, and pursued them with ardor and success from that time until the Telegraph of Professor Morse was established and in actual operation. And it is due to him to say that no one has contributed more to enlarge the knowledge of Electro-Magnetism, and to lay the foundations of the great invention of which we are speaking, than the professor himself.

"It is unnecessary, however, to give in detail the discoveries enumerated by him—either his own or those of others. But it appears from his testimony that, very soon after the discovery made by Oersted, it was believed by men of science that this newly-discovered power might be used to communicate intelligence to distant places. And, before the year 1823, Ampère, of Paris, one of the most successful cultivators of physical science, proposed to the French Academy a plan for that purpose. But his project was never reduced to practice. And the discovery made by Barlow, of the Royal Military Academy at Woolwich, England, in 1825, that the galvanic current greatly diminished in power as the distance increased, put at rest for a time all attempts to construct an Electro-Magnetic Telegraph. Subsequent discoveries, however, revived the hope; and in the year 1832, when Professor Morse appears to have devoted himself to the subject, the conviction was general, among men of science everywhere, that the object could and, sooner or later, would be accomplished.

"The great difficulty in their way was the fact that the galvanic current, however strong in the beginning, became gradually weaker as it advanced on the wire; and was not strong enough to produce a mechanical effect after a certain distance had been traversed. But encouraged by the discoveries which were made from time to time, and strong in the belief that an Electro-Magnetic Telegraph was practicable, many eminent and scientific men in Europe, as well as in this country, became deeply engaged in endeavoring to surmount what appeared to be the chief obstacle to its success. And, in this state of things, it ought not to be a matter of surprise that four different Magnetic Telegraphs, purporting to have overcome the difficulty, should be invented, and made public so nearly at the same time that each has claimed a priority, and that a close and careful scrutiny of the facts in each case is necessary to decide between them. The inventions were so nearly simultaneous, that neither inventor can be justly accused of having derived any aid from the discoveries of the other.

"One of these inventors, Doctor Steinheil, of Munich, in Germany, communicated his discovery to the Academy of Sciences in Paris, on the

19th of July, 1838, and states in his communication that it had been in operation more than a year.

"Another of the European inventors, Professor Wheatstone, of London, in the month of April, 1837, explained to Professors Henry and Bache, who were then in London, his plan of an Electro-Magnetic Telegraph, and exhibited to them his method of bringing into action a second galvanic circuit in order to provide a remedy for the diminution of force in a long circuit; but it appears by the testimony of Professor Gale that the patent to Wheatstone & Cooke was not sealed until January 21, 1840, and their specification was not filed until the 21st of July, in the same year; and there is no evidence that any description of it was published before 1839.

"The remaining European patent is that of Edward Davy. His patent, it appears, was sealed on the 4th of July, 1838, but his specification was not filed until January 4, 1839; and when these two English patents are brought into competition with that of Morse, they must take date from the time of filing their respective specifications. For it must be borne in mind that, as the law then stood in England, the inventor was allowed six months to file the description of his invention after his patent was sealed, while, in this country, the filing of the specification is simultaneous with the application for patents.

"The defendants contend that all, or at least some one of these European Telegraphs, were invented and made public before the discovery claimed by Morse; and that the process and method by which he conveys intelligence to a distance is substantially the same, with the exception only of its capacity for impressing upon paper the marks or signs described in the alphabet he invented.

"Waiving, for the present, any remarks upon the identity or similitude of these inventions, the court is of opinion that the first branch of the objection cannot be maintained, and that Morse was the first and original inventor of the Telegraph described in his specification, and preceded the three European inventions relied on by the defendants.

"The evidence is full and clear that, when he was returning from a visit to Europe in 1832, he was deeply engaged upon this subject during the voyage; and that the process and means were so far developed and arranged in his own mind that he was confident of ultimate success. It is in proof that he pursued these investigations with unremitting ardor and industry, interrupted occasionally by pecuniary embarrassments; and we think that it is established, by the testimony of Professor Gale and others, that early in the spring of 1837 Morse had invented his plan for combining two or more electric or galvanic circuits, with independent batteries, for the purpose of overcoming the diminished force of electro-magnetism in long circuits, although it was not disclosed to the witness until afterward; and that there is reasonable ground for believing that he had so far completed his invention, that the whole process, combination, powers, and machinery, were arranged in his mind, and that the delay in bringing it out arose from his want of means; for it required the highest order of mechanical skill to execute and adjust the nice and delicate work necessary to put the Telegraph into operation, and the slightest error or defect would have been fatal to its success. He had not the means at that time to procure the services of workmen of that character; and without their aid no model could be prepared which would do justice to his invention; and it, moreover, required a large sum of money to procure proper materials for the work. He, however, filed his caveat on the 6th of October, 1837, and on the 7th of April, 1838, applied for his patent, accompanying his application with a specification of his invention, and describing the process and means used to produce the effect. It is true that O'Rielly in his

answer alleges that the plan by which he now combines two or more galvanic or electric currents, with independent batteries, was not contained in
that specification, but discovered and interpolated afterward; but there is
no evidence whatever to support this charge. And we are satisfied from
the testimony that the plan, as it now appears in his specification, had
then been invented, and was actually intended to be described.

"With this evidence before us, we think it is evident that the invention of Morse was prior to that of Steinheil, Wheatstone, or Davy. The
discovery of Steinheil, taking the time which he himself gave to the
French Academy of Sciences, cannot be understood as carrying it back
beyond the months of May or June, 1837; and that of Wheatstone, as
exhibited to Professors Henry and Bache, goes back only to April in that
year. And there is nothing in the evidence to carry back the invention
of Davy beyond the 4th of January, 1839, when his specification was filed,
except a publication said to have been made in the *London Mechanics'
Magazine*, January 20, 1838; and the invention of Morse is justly entitled
to take date from early in the spring of 1837. And in the description of
Davy's invention, as given in the publication of January 20, 1838, there is
nothing specified which Morse could have borrowed; and we have no
evidence to show that his invention ever was or could be carried into
successful operation.

"In relation to Wheatstone, there would seem to be some discrepancy
in the testimony. According to Professor Gale's testimony, as before
mentioned, the specification of Wheatstone and Cooke was not filed until
July 21, 1840, and his information is derived from the *London Journal of
Arts and Sciences*. But it appears by the testimony of Edward F. Barnes
that this Telegraph was in actual operation in 1839. And in the case of
the Electric Telegraph Company *vs.* Brett & Little, 10 Common Pleas
Reports, by Scott, his specification is said to have been filed December 12,
1837. But if the last-mentioned date is taken as the true one, it would
not make his invention prior to that of Morse. And even if it would, yet
this case must be decided by the testimony in the record, and we cannot
go out of it, and take into consideration a fact stated in a book of reports.
Moreover, we have noticed this case merely because it has been pressed
into the argument. The appellants do not mention it in their answer, nor
put their defense on it. And if the evidence of its priority was conclusive,
it would not avail them in this suit. For they cannot be allowed to surprise the patentee by evidence of a prior invention of which they gave
him no notice.

"But if the priority of Morse's invention was more doubtful, and it
was conceded that in fact some one of the European inventors had preceded him a few months or a few weeks, it would not invalidate his
patent. The act of Congress provides that when the patentee believes
himself to be the first inventor, a previous discovery in a foreign country
shall not render his patent void, unless such discovery or some substantial
part of it had been before patented or described in a printed publication.

"Now we suppose no one will doubt that Morse believed himself to
be the original inventor when he applied for his patent in April, 1838.
Steinheil's discovery does not appear to have been ever patented, nor to
have been described in any printed publication until July of that year.
And neither of the English inventions is shown by the testimony to have
been patented until after Morse's application for a patent, nor to have
been so described in any previous publication as to embrace any substantial part of his invention. And if his application for a patent was made
under such circumstances, the patent is good, even if, in point of fact, he
was not the first inventor.

"In this view of the subject, it is unnecessary to compare the Telegraph of Morse with these European inventions, to ascertain whether they are substantially the same or not. If they were the same in every particular, it would not impair his rights. But it is impossible to examine them, and look at the process and the machinery and results of each, so far as the facts are before us, without perceiving at once the substantial and essential difference between them, and the decided superiority of the one invented by Professor Morse.

"Neither can the inquiries he made, nor the information or advice he received from men of science, in the course of his researches, impair his right to the character of an inventor. No invention can possibly be made, consisting of a combination of different elements of power, without a thorough knowledge of the properties of each of them, and the mode in which they operate on each other. And it can make no difference in this respect whether he derives his information from books, or from conversation with men skilled in the science. If it were otherwise, no patent in which a combination of different elements is used could ever be obtained. For no man ever made such an invention without having first obtained this information, unless it was discovered by some fortunate accident. And it is evident that such an invention as the Electro-Magnetic Telegraph could never have been brought into action without it. For a very high degree of scientific knowledge, and the nicest skill in the mechanic arts, are combined in it, and were both necessary to bring it into successful operation. And the fact that Morse sought and obtained the necessary information and counsel from the best sources, and acted upon it, neither impairs his rights as an inventor, nor detracts from his merits.

"Regarding Professor Morse as the first and original inventor of the Telegraph, we come to the objections which have been made to the validity of his patent.

"We do not think it necessary to dwell upon the objections taken to the proceedings upon which the first patent was issued, or to the additional specifications in the reissued patent of 1848. In relation to the first, if there was any alteration, at the suggestion of the commissioner, it appears to have been in a matter of form rather than of substance; and, as regards the second, there is nothing in the proof, or on the face of the reissued patent, to show that the invention therein described is not the same with the one intended to be secured by the original patent. It was reissued by the proper authority, and it was the duty of the Commissioner of Patents to see that it did not cover more than the original invention. It must be presumed, therefore, that it does not, until the contrary appears. Variations from the description given in the former specification do not necessarily imply that it is for a different discovery. The right to surrender the old patent, and receive another in its place, was given for the purpose of enabling the patentee to give a more perfect description of his invention, when any mistake or oversight was committed in his first. It necessarily, therefore, varies from it. And we see nothing in the reissued patent that may not, without proof to the contrary, be regarded as a more careful description than the former one, explaining more fully the nice and delicate manner in which the different elements of power are arranged and combined together and act upon one another, in order to produce the effect described in the specification. Nor is it void because it does not bear the same date with his French patent. It is not necessary to inquire whether the application of Professor Morse to the Patent-Office, in 1838, before he went to France, does or does not exempt his patent from the operation of the act of Congress upon this subject. For, if it should be decided that it does not exempt it, the only effect of that decision would be to limit the monopoly to fourteen years from the date of the foreign patent. And in either case the patent was in full force at the time the injunction was granted by the Circuit Court, and when the present appeal stood regularly for hearing in this court.

"And this brings us to the exceptions taken to the specification and claims of the patentee in the reissued patent of 1848.

"We perceive no well-founded objection to the description which is given of the whole invention and its separate parts, nor to his right to a patent for the first seven inventions set forth in the specification of his claims. The difficulty arises on the eighth.

"It is in the following words:

"'Eighth. I do not propose to limit myself to the specific machinery or parts of machinery described in the foregoing specification and claims; the essence of my invention being the use of the motive power of the electric or galvanic current, which I call Electro-Magnetism, however developed, for marking or printing intelligible characters, signs, or letters, at any distances, being a new application of that power of which I claim to be the first inventor or discoverer.'

"It is impossible to misunderstand the extent of this claim. He claims the exclusive right to every improvement where the motive power is the electric or galvanic current, and the result is the marking or printing intelligible characters, signs, or letters, at a distance.

"If this claim can be maintained, it matters not by what process or machinery the result is accomplished. For aught that we now know, some future inventor in the onward march of science may discover a mode of writing or printing at a distance, by means of the electric or galvanic current, without using any part of the process or combination set forth in the plaintiff's specification. His invention may be less complicated—less liable to get out of order—less expensive in construction and in its operation. But yet, if it is covered by this patent, the inventor could not use it, nor the public have the benefit of it, without the permission of this patentee.

"Nor is this all. While he shuts the door against inventions of other persons, the patentee would be able to avail himself of new discoveries in the properties and powers of electro-magnetism which scientific men might bring to light. For he says he does not confine his claims to the machinery or parts of machinery which he specifies: but claims for himself a monopoly in its use, however developed, for the purpose of printing at a distance. New discoveries in physical science may enable him to combine it with new agents and new elements, and by that means attain the object in a manner superior to the present process, and altogether different from it. And if he can secure the exclusive use, by his present patent, he may vary it with every new discovery and development of the science, and need place no description of the new manner, processs, or machinery, upon the records of the Patent-Office. And when his patent expires, the public must apply to him to learn what it is. In fine, he claims an exclusive right to use a manner and process which he has not described, and indeed had not invented, and therefore could not describe when he obtained his patent. The court is of opinion that the claim is too broad, and not warranted by law.

"No one, we suppose, will maintain that Fulton could have taken out a patent for his invention of propelling vessels by steam, describing the process and machinery he used, and claimed under it the exclusive right to use the motive power of steam, however developed, for the purpose of propelling vessels. It can hardly be supposed that under such a patent he could have prevented the use of the improved machinery which science has since introduced, although the motive power is steam, and the result is the propulsion of vessels. Neither could the man who first discovered that steam might, by a proper arrangement of machinery, be used as a motive power to grind corn or spin cotton, claim the right to the exclusive use of steam, as a motive power, for the purpose of producing such effects.

"Again, the use of steam, as a motive power in printing-presses, is comparatively a modern discovery. Was the first inventor of a machine or process of this kind entitled to a patent, giving him the exclusive right to use steam as a motive power, however developed, for the purpose of marking or printing intelligible characters? Could he have prevented the use of any other press subsequently invented, where steam was used? Yet, so far as patentable rights are concerned, both improvements must stand on the same principles. Both use a known motive power to print intelligible marks or letters; and it can make no difference, in their legal rights under the patent laws, whether the printing is done near at hand or at a distance. Both depend for success not merely upon the motive power, but upon the machinery with which it is combined. And it has never, we believe, been supposed by any one that the first inventor of a steam printing-press was entitled to the exclusive use of steam, as a motive power, however developed, for marking or printing intelligible characters.

"Indeed, the acts of the patentee himself are inconsistent with the claim made in his behalf. For in 1846 he took out a patent for his new improvement of local circuits, by means of which intelligence could be printed at intermediate places along the main line of the Telegraph; and he obtained a reissued patent for this invention in 1848. Yet in this new invention the electric or galvanic current was the motive power, and writing at a distance the effect. The power was undoubtedly developed by new machinery and new combinations. But if his eighth claim could be sustained, this improvement would be embraced by his first patent. And if it was so embraced, his patent for the local circuits would be illegal and void. For he could not take out a subsequent patent for a portion of his first invention, and thereby extend his monopoly beyond the period limited by law.

"Many cases have been referred to in the argument, which have been decided upon this subject, in the English and American courts. We shall speak of those only which seem to be considered as leading ones. And those most relied on, and pressed upon the court, in behalf of the patentee, are the cases which arose in England upon Neilson's patent for the introduction of heated air between the blowing apparatus and the furnace in the manufacture of iron.

"The leading case upon this patent is that of Neilson and others vs. Harford and others, in the English Court of Exchequer. It was elaborately argued, and appears to have been carefully considered by the court. The case was this:

"Neilson in his specification described his invention as one for the improved application of air to produce heat in fires, forges, and furnaces, where a blowing-apparatus is required. And it was to be applied as follows: The blast or current of air produced by the blowing-apparatus was to be passed from it into an air-vessel or receptacle made sufficiently strong to endure the blast; and through or from that vessel or receptacle, by means of a tube, pipe, or aperture, into the fire: the receptacle to be kept artificially heated to a considerable temperature by heat externally applied. He then described in rather general terms the manner in which the receptacle might be constructed and heated, and the air conducted through it to the fire : stating that the form of the receptacle was not material, nor the manner of applying heat to it.   In the action above mentioned for the infringement of this patent, the defendant, among other defenses, insisted that the machinery for heating the air and throwing it hot into the furnace was not sufficiently described in the specification, and the patent void on that account ; and also, that a patent for throwing hot air into the furnace, instead of cold, and thereby increasing the intensity of the heat, is a patent for a principle, and that a principle was not patentable.

" Upon the first of these defenses the jury found that a man of ordinary skill and knowledge of the subject, looking at the specification alone, could construct such an apparatus as would be productive of a beneficial result sufficient to make it worth while to adapt it to the machinery in all cases of forges, cupolas, and furnaces, where the blast is used.

" And upon the second ground of defense, Baron Parke, who delivered the opinion of the court, said :

" ' It is very difficult to distinguish it from the specification of a patent for a principle, and this at first created in the minds of the court much difficulty ; but, after full consideration, we think that the plaintiff does not merely claim a principle, but a machine embodying a principle, and a very valuable one.   We think the case must be considered as if, the principle being well known, the plaintiff had first invented a mode of applying it by a mechanical apparatus to furnaces ; and his invention then consists in this : by interposing a receptacle for heated air between the blowing-apparatus and the furnace.   In this receptacle he directs the air to be heated by the application of heat externally to the receptacle, and thus he accomplishes the object of applying the blast, which was before cold air, in a heated state to the furnace.'

" We see nothing in this opinion differing in any degree from the familiar principles of law applicable to patent cases.   Neilson claimed no particular mode of constructing the receptacle, or of heating it.   He pointed out the manner in which it might be done ; but admitted that it might also be done in a variety of ways ; and at a higher or lower temperature ; and that all of them would produce the effect in a greater or less degree, provided the air was heated by passing through a heated receptacle.   And hence it seems that the court first doubted whether it was a patent for any thing more than the discovery that hot air would promote the ignition of fuel better than cold.   And if this had been the construction, the court, it appears, would have held his patent to be void ; because the discovery of a principle in natural philosophy or physical science is not patentable.

" But after much consideration, it was finally decided that this principle must be regarded as well known, and that the plaintiff had invented a mechanical mode of applying it to furnaces ; and that his invention consisted in interposing a heated receptacle between the blower and the furnace, and by this means heating the air after it left the blower, and before it was thrown into the fire.   Whoever, therefore, used this method of throwing hot air into the furnace, used the process he had invented, and thereby infringed his patent, although the form of the receptacle or the mechanical arrangements for heating it might be different from those described by the patentee.   For whatever form was adopted for the receptacle, or whatever mechanical arrangements were made for heating it, the effect would be produced in a greater or less degree, if the heated receptacle was placed between the blower and the furnace, and the current of air passed through it.

" Undoubtedly the principle that hot air will promote the ignition of fuel better than cold, was embodied in this machine.   But the patent was not supported because this principle was embodied in it. He would have been equally entitled to a patent if he had invented an improvement in the mechanical arrangements of the blowing-apparatus, or in the furnace, while a cold current of air was still used. But his patent was supported, because he had invented a mechanical apparatus by which a current of hot air instead of cold could be thrown in. And this new method was protected by his patent. The interposition of a heated receptacle in any form was the novelty he invented.

" We do not perceive how the claim, in the case before us, can derive any countenance from this decision. If the Court of Exchequer had said that Neilson's patent was for the discovery that hot air would promote ignition better than cold, and that he had an exclusive right to use it for that purpose, there might, perhaps, have been some reason to rely upon it. But the court emphatically denied his right to such a patent; and his claim, as the patent was construed and supported by the court, is altogether unlike that of the patentee before us.

" For Neilson discovered that by interposing a heated receptacle between the blower and the furnace, and conducting the current of air through it, the heat in the furnace was increased. And this effect was always produced, whatever might be the form of the receptacle, or the mechanical contrivances for heating it, or for passing the current of air through it, and into the furnace.

" But Professor Morse has not discovered that the electric or galvanic current will always print at a distance, no matter what may be the form of the machinery or mechanical contrivances through which it passes. You may use electro-magnetism as a motive power, and yet not produce the described effect—that is, print at a distance intelligible marks or signs. To produce that effect it must be combined with and passed through and operate upon certain complicated and delicate machinery adjusted and arranged upon philosophical principles, and prepared by the highest mechanical skill. And it is the high praise of Professor Morse, that he has been able by a new combination of known powers, of which electro-magnetism is one, to discover a method by which intelligible marks or signs may be printed at a distance. And for the method or process thus discovered he is entitled to a patent. But he has not discovered that the electro-magnetic current, used as a motive power, in any other method, and with any other combination, will do as well.

" We have commented on the case in the Court of Exchequer more fully, because it has attracted much attention in the courts of this country as well as in the English courts, and has been differently understood. And perhaps a mistaken construction of that decision has led to the broad claim in the patent now under consideration.

" We do not deem it necessary to remark upon the other English decisions in relation to Neilson's patent, nor upon the other cases referred to, which stand upon similar principles. The observations we have made on the case in the Court of Exchequer will equally apply to all of them.

" We proceed to the American decisions; and the principles herein stated were fully recognized by this court in the case of Leroy *et al. vs.* Tatham and others, decided at the last term, 14 How., 156.

" It appeared in that case that the patentee had discovered that lead, recently set, would, under heat and pressure in a close vessel, reunite perfectly after a separation of its parts, so as to make wrought instead of cast pipe. And the court held that he was not entitled to a patent for this newly-discovered principle or quality in lead; and that such a discovery was not patentable; but that he was entitled to a patent for the new process or method in the art of making lead pipe, which this discovery enabled him to invent and employ; and was bound to describe such process or method fully in his specification.

"Many cases have also been referred to which were decided in the Circuit Courts. It will be found, we think, upon careful examination, that all of them, previous to the decision on Neilson's patent, maintain the principles on which this decision is made. Since that case was reported, it is admitted that decisions have been made which would seem to extend patentable rights beyond the limits here marked out. As we have already said, we see nothing in that opinion which would sanction the introduction of any new principle in the law of patents; but if it were otherwise, it would not justify this court in departing from what we consider as established principles in the American courts. And to show what was heretofore the doctrine upon this subject, we refer to the annexed cases. We do not stop to comment on them, because such an examination would extend this opinion beyond all reasonable bounds. 1 Stor. Rep. 270, 285; Wyeth *vs.* Stone, 3 Sumu. 540; Blanchard *vs.* Sprague. The first-mentioned case is directly in point.

"Indeed, independently of judicial authority, we do not think that the language used in the act of Congress can justly be expounded otherwise.

"The fifth section of the act of 1836 declares that a patent shall convey to the inventor, for a term not exceeding fourteen years, the exclusive right of making, using, and vending to others to be used, his invention or discovery, referring to the specification for the particulars thereof.

"The sixth section directs who shall be entitled to a patent, and the terms and conditions on which it may be obtained. It provides that any person shall be entitled to a patent who has discovered or invented a new and useful art, machine, manufacture, or composition of matter, or a new and useful improvement on any previous discovery in either of them. But before he receives a patent he shall deliver a written description of his invention or discovery, '*and of the manner and process of making, constructing, using, and compounding the same,*' in such exact terms as to enable any person skilled in the art or science to which it appertains, or with which it is most nearly connected, to make, construct, compound, and use the same.

"'This court has decided that the specification required by this law is a part of the patent, and that the patent issues for the invention described in the specification.

"Now, whether the Telegraph is regarded as an art or machine, the manner and process of making or using it must be set forth in exact terms. The act of Congress makes no difference in this respect between an art and a machine. An improvement in the art of making bar-iron or spinning cotton must be so described, and so must the art of printing by the motive power of steam. And in all of these cases it has always been held that the patent embraces nothing more than the improvement described and claimed as new, and that any one who afterward discovered a method of accomplishing the same object, substantially and essentially differing from the one described, had a right to use it. Can there be any good reason why the art of printing at a distance, by means of the motive power of the electric or galvanic current, should stand on different principles? Is there any reason why the inventor's patent should cover broader ground? It would be difficult to discover any thing in the act of Congress which would justify this distinction. The specification of this patentee describes his invention or discovery, and the manner and process of constructing and using it, and his patent, like inventions in the other arts above mentioned, covers nothing more.

"The provisions of the acts of Congress in relation to patents may be summed up in a few words.

"Whoever discovers that a certain useful result will be produced in any art, machine, manufacture or composition of matter, by the use of certain means, is entitled to a patent for it; provided he specifies the means he uses in a manner so full and exact, that any one skilled in the science to which it appertains can, by using the means he specifies, without any addition to or subtraction from them, produce precisely the result he describes. And if this cannot be done by the means he describes, the patent is void. And if it can be done, then the patent confers on him the exclusive right to use the means he specifies to produce the result or effect he describes, and nothing more. And it makes no difference in this respect whether the effect is produced by chemical agency or combination; or by the application of discoveries or principles in natural philosophy, known or unknown before his invention; or by machinery acting altogether upon mechanical principles. In either case, he must describe the manner and process as above mentioned, and the end it accomplishes. And any one may lawfully accomplish the same end without infringing the patent, if he uses means substantially different from those described.

"Indeed, if the eighth claim of the patentee can be maintained, there was no necessity for any specification, further than to say that he had discovered that by using the motive power of electro-magnetism he could print intelligible characters at any distance. We presume it will be admitted on all hands that no patent could have issued on such a specification. Yet this claim can derive no aid from the specification filed. It is outside of it, and the patentee claims beyond it. And if it stands, it must stand simply on the ground that the broad terms above mentioned were a sufficient description, and entitled him to a patent in terms equally broad. In our judgment, the act of Congress cannot be so construed.

"The patent then being illegal and void, so far as respects the eighth claim, the question arises whether the whole patent is void, unless this portion of it is disclaimed in a reasonable time after the patent issued.

"It has been urged on the part of the complainants that there is no necessity for a disclaimer in a case of this kind. That it is required in those cases only in which the party commits an error in fact, in claiming something which was known before, and of which he was not the first discoverer; that in this case he was the first to discover that the motive power of electro-magnetism might be used to write at a distance; and that his error, if any, was a mistake in law in supposing his invention, as described in his specification, authorized this broad claim of exclusive privilege; and that the claim, therefore, may be regarded as a nullity, and allowed to stand in the patent without a disclaimer, and without affecting the validity of the patent.

"This distinction can hardly be maintained. The act of Congress above recited requires that the invention shall be so described, that a person skilled in the science to which it appertains, or with which it is most nearly connected, shall be able to construct the improvement from the description given by the inventor.

"Now, in this case, there is no description but one of a process by which signs or letters may be printed at a distance. And yet he claims the exclusive right to any other mode, and any other process, although not described by him, by which the end can be accomplished, if electro-magnetism is used as the motive power. That is to say, he claims a patent for an effect produced by the use of electro-magnetism, distinct from the process or machinery necessary to produce it. The words of the act of Congress, above quoted, show that no patent can lawfully issue upon such a claim. For he claims what he has not described in the manner required by law. And a patent for such a claim is as strongly forbidden by the act of Congress as if some other person had invented it before him.

"Why, therefore, should he be required and permitted to disclaim in the one case and not in the other? The evil is the same if he claims more than he has invented, although no other person has invented it before him. He prevents others from attempting to improve upon the manner and process which he has described in his specification, and may deter the public from using it, even if discovered. He can lawfully claim only what he has invented and described, and if he claims more his patent is void. And the judgment in this case must be against the patentee, unless he is within the act of Congress which gives the right to disclaim.

"The law which requires and permits him to disclaim is not penal, but remedial. It is intended for the protection of the patentee as well as the public, and ought not, therefore, to receive a construction that would restrict its operation within narrower limits than its words fairly import. It provides 'that when any patentee shall have in his specification claimed to be the first and original inventor or discoverer of any material or substantial part of the thing patented, of which he was not the first and original inventor, and shall have no legal or just claim to the same,' he must disclaim in order to protect so much of the claim as is legally patented.

"Whether, therefore, the patent is illegal in part, because he claims more than he has sufficiently described, or more than he invented, he must in either case disclaim, in order to save the portion to which he is entitled; and he is allowed to do so when the error was committed by mistake.

"A different construction would be unjust to the public, as well as to the patentee, and defeat the manifest object of the law, and produce the very evil against which it is intended to guard.

"It appears that no disclaimer has yet been entered at the Patent-Office. But the delay in entering it is not unreasonable. For the objectionable claim was sanctioned by the head of the office; it has been held to be valid by a Circuit Court, and differences of opinion in relation to it are found to exist among the justices of this court. Under such circumstances, the patentee had a right to insist upon it, and not disclaim it until the highest court to which it could be carried had pronounced its judgment. The omission to disclaim, therefore, does not render the patent altogether void, and he is entitled to proceed in this suit for an infringement of that part of his invention which is legally claimed and described. But as no disclaimer was entered in the Patent-Office before this suit was instituted, he cannot, under the act of Congress, be allowed costs against the wrong-doer, although the infringement should be proved. And we think it is proved by the testimony. But as the question of infringement embraces both of the reissued patents, it is proper, before we proceed to that part of the case, to notice the objections made to the second patent for the local circuits, which was originally obtained in 1846, and reissued in 1848.

"It is certainly no objection to this patent, that the improvement is embraced by the eighth claim in the former one. We have already said that this claim is void, and that the former patent covers nothing but the first seven inventions specifically mentioned.

"Nor can its validity be impeached upon the ground that it is an improvement upon a former invention, for which the patentee had himself already obtained a patent. It is true that, under the act of 1836, sec. 3, it was in the power of Professor Morse, if he desired it, to annex this improvement to his former specification, so as to make it from that time a part of the original patent. But there is nothing in the act that forbids him to take out a new patent for the improvement, if he prefers it. Any other inventor might do so; and there can be no reason, in justice or in policy, for refusing the like privilege to the original inventor. And when there is no positive law to the contrary, he must stand on the same footing with any other inventor of an improvement upon a previous discovery. Nor is he bound in his new patent to refer specially to his former one. All that the law requires of him is, that he shall not claim as new what is covered by a former invention, whether made by himself or any other person.

"It is said, however, that this alleged improvement is not new, and is embraced in his former specification; and that, if some portion of it is new, it is not so described as to distinguish the new from the old.

"It is difficult, perhaps impossible, to discuss this part of the case so as to be understood by any one who has not a model before him, or perfectly familiar with the machinery and operations of the Telegraph. We shall not, therefore, attempt to describe minutely the machinery or its mode of operation. So far as this can be done intelligibly, without the aid of a model to point to, it has been fully and well done, in the opinion delivered by the learned judge who decided this case in the Circuit Court. All that we think it useful or necessary to say is, that, after a careful examination of the patents, we think the objection on this ground is not tenable. The force of the objection is mainly directed upon the receiving-magnet, which, it is said, is a part of the machinery of the first patent, and performs the same office. But the receiving-magnet is not of itself claimed as a new invention. It is claimed as a part of a new combination or arrangement to produce a new result. And this combination does produce a new and useful result. For by this new combination, and the arrangement and position of the receiving-magnet, the local independent circuit is opened by the electric or galvanic current as it passes on the main line, without interrupting it in its course, and the intelligence it conveys is recorded almost at the same moment at the end of the line of the Telegraph and at the different local offices on its way. And it hardly needs a model or a minute examination of the machinery to be satisfied that a Telegraph which prints the intelligence it conveys, at different places, by means of the current as it passes along on the main line, must necessarily require a different combination and arrangement of powers from the one that prints only at the end. The elements which compose it may all have been used in the former invention, but it is evident that their arrangement and combination must be different to produce this new effect. The new patent for the local circuits was, therefore, properly granted, and we perceive no well-founded objection to the specification or claim contained in the reissued patent of 1848.

"The two reissued patents of 1848, being both valid, with the exception of the eighth claim in the first, the only remaining question is, whether they, or either of them, have been infringed by the defendants.

"The same difficulty arises in this part of the case which we have already stated in speaking of the specification and claims in the patent for the local circuits. It is difficult to convey a clear idea of the similitude or differences in the two Telegraphs to any one not familiarly acquainted with the machinery of both. The court must content itself, therefore, with general terms, referring to the patents themselves for a more special description of the matters in controversy.

"It is a well-settled principle of law, that the mere change in the form of the machinery (unless a particular form is specified as the means by which the effect described is produced), or an alteration in some of its unessential parts, or in the use of known equivalent powers, not varying essentially the machine, or its mode of operation or organization, will not make the new machine a new invention. It may be an improvement upon the former, but that will not justify its use without the consent of the first patentee.

37

" The Columbian (O'Rielly's) Telegraph does not profess to accomplish a new purpose or produce a new result. Its object and effect is to communicate intelligence at a distance, at the end of the main line and at the local circuits on its way. And this is done by means of signs or letters impressed on paper or other material. The object and purpose of the Telegraph is the same with that of Professor Morse.

" Does he use the same means ? Substantially, we think he does, both upon the main line and in the local circuits. He uses upon the main line the combination of two or more galvanic or electric circuits, with independent batteries, for the purpose of obviating the diminished force of the galvanic current, and in a manner varying very little in form from the invention of Professor Morse. And indeed the same may be said of the entire combination set forth in the patentee's third claim. For O'Rielly's can hardly be said to differ substantially and essentially from it. He uses the combination which composes the register, with no material change in the arrangement, or in the elements of which it consists ; and with the aid of these means he conveys intelligence, by impressing marks or signs upon paper ; these marks or signs being capable of being read and understood by means of an alphabet, or signs adapted to the purpose. And as regards the second patent of Professor Morse, for the local circuits, the mutator of the defendant does not vary from it in any essential particular. All of the efficient elements of the combination are retained, or their places supplied by well-known equivalents. Its organization is essentially the same.

" Neither is the substitution of marks and signs differing from those invented by Professor Morse any defense to this action. His patent is not for the invention of a new alphabet, but for a combination of powers composed of tangible and intangible elements, described in his specification, by means of which marks or signs may be impressed upon paper at a distance, which can there be read and understood. And if any marks, or signs, or letters, are impressed in that manner, by means of a process substantially the same with his invention, or with any particular part of it covered by his patent, and those marks or signs can be read, and thus communicate intelligence, it is an infringement of his patent. The variation in the character of the marks would not protect it, if the marks could be read and understood.

" We deem it unnecessary to pursue further the comparison between the machinery of the patents. The invasion of the plaintiff's rights, already stated, authorized the injunction granted by the Circuit Court, and so much of its decree must be affirmed. But for the reasons hereinbefore assigned, the complainants are not entitled to costs, and that portion of the decree must be reversed, and a decree passed by this Court, directing each party to pay his own costs in this and in the Circuit Court."

The opinion of Justice Grier, concurred in by Justices Nelson and Wayne, contained these additional points :

" I entirely concur with the majority of the court that the appellee and complainant below, Samuel F. B. Morse, is the true and first inventor of the recording telegraph, and the first who has successfully applied the agent or element of Nature, called electro-magnetism, to printing and recording intelligible characters at a distance ; and that his patent of 1840, finally reissued in 1848, and his patent for his improvements, as reissued in the same year, are good and valid ; and that the appellants have infringed the rights secured to the patentee by both his patents. But, as I do not concur in the views of the majority of the court, in regard to two great points of the case, I shall proceed to express my own."

Having given his reasons at length, Judge Grier says:

"It is not a composition of matter, or a manufacture, or a machine. It is the application of a known element or power of Nature to a new and useful purpose by means of various processes, instruments, and devices, and, if patentable at all, it must come within the category of '*a new and useful art.*' It is as much entitled to this denomination as the original art of printing itself. The name given to it in the patent is generally the act of the commissioner, and in this, as in many other cases, a wrong one. The true nature of the invention must be sought in the specification. The word *telegraph* is derived from the Greek, and signifies to 'write afar off, or at a distance.' It has heretofore been applied to various contrivances or devices to communicate intelligence by means of signals or semaphores which speak to the eye for a moment; but in its primary and literal signification of *writing, printing, or recording at a distance*, it never was invented, perfected, or put into practical operation, till it was done by Morse. He preceded Steinheil, Cooke, Wheatstone, and Davy, in the successful application of the mysterious power or element of electro-magnetism to this purpose; and his invention has entirely superseded their inefficient contrivances. It is not only 'a new and useful art,' if that term means any thing, but a most wonderful and astonishing invention, requiring tenfold more ingenuity and patient experiment to perfect it, than the art of printing with types and press, as originally invented."

This opinion of the Supreme Court established the rights of Professor Morse. Subsequent attempts to disturb the decision were in vain, and the inventor lived to know that this judgment of the highest legal tribunal to which his claims could be submitted, was also the enlightened verdict of the nations of the earth.

ROGERS'S MODIFICATION.

In the year 1848, Henry J. Rogers, Josiah Lee, and Zenas Barnum, contracted with Alexander Bain, for the right and privilege of using his inventions and improvements, then made and patented, in operating a line of Telegraphs between the cities of Washington, Baltimore, Wilmington, Philadelphia, and New York, and did construct a line of Telegraph between those cities; the line was finished from Washington to Baltimore in March, 1849; from Baltimore to Wilmington in May, 1849; thence to Philadelphia in July, 1849; and from Philadelphia to New York in December, 1849. Mr. Rogers being a skillful telegraphic engineer, and not finding the telegraph of Mr. Bain to work satisfactorily, he so modified this form of telegraph as to make it operate with great satisfaction. The recording was effected by means of the conjoined influence of electro-chemical and chemical composition and decomposition—the electro-chemical decomposition arising from an electrical current being transmitted through bibulous paper, saturated with a solution of yellow prussiate of potash, a small quantity of dilute nitric acid, and a small quantity of a solution of cream-of-tartar. This paper was placed upon the recording instrument, consisting essentially of a metallic disk, connected with clock-work, capable of rotation on its axis, and a mechanical connection with one of the wires of the branch (or local) circuit above the plate, and the other wire of the branch circuit beneath. The upper wire of the branch circuit, consisting principally of a covered copper wire, was terminated by a very fine short iron wire, acting as the stylus, at the end of which, in contact with the prepared paper, and on its upper surface, dark-blue marks were made as the battery contacts were made or broken during the rotation of the disk.

The foregoing statement, by Professor Rogers, presents the material points in a trial which occurred in Philadelphia, September, 1851, involving the originality of the invention claimed by Professor Morse. The plaintiffs, who represented the Magnetic Telegraph Company using Morse's patents, alleged that the defendants, who represented the " Bain Line " from Washington to New York, had violated the patents granted to Morse. The counsel on both sides were:

For Plaintiffs.—Hon. Amos Kendall, of Washington; St. George T. Campbell, Esq., of Philadelphia; George Gifford, Esq., of New York; and George Harding, Esq., of Philadelphia.

For Defendants.—Hon. William M. Meredith, of Philadelphia; Peter McCall, Esq., of Philadelphia; and Hon. R. H. Gillett, of Washington.

The Judges were Hon. R. C. Grier and Hon. J. K. Kane. The plaintiffs, B. B. French and others, represented the " Magnetic Company," and claimed damages from the defendants, Henry J. Rogers and others, who represented the Bain Line Telegraph between Washington and New York, for alleged violations by them of the several patents granted to Professor Morse, whose assignees the plaintiffs claimed to be. After a protracted trial, in which voluminous testimony was taken, and the ablest counsel heard, on the 3d of November Judge Kane delivered the opinion of the court, Judge Grier expressing his concurrence therein. A few paragraphs only from these opinions will be cited here:

" That he, Mr. Morse, was the first to devise and practise the art of recording language, at telegraphic distances, by the dynamic force of the electro-magnet; or, indeed, by any agency whatever, is, to our minds, plain upon all the evidence. It is unnecessary to review the testimony for the purpose of showing this. His application for a patent, in April, 1838, was preceded by a series of experiments, results, illustrations, and proofs of final success, which leave no doubt whatever but that his great invention was consummated before the early spring of 1837. There is no one person, whose invention has been spoken of by any witness or referred to in any book, as involving the principle of Mr. Morse's discovery, but must yield precedence of date to this. Neither Steinheil, nor Cooke and Wheatstone, nor Davy, nor Dyar, nor Henry, had at this time made a recording telegraph of any sort. The devices then known were merely *semaphores*, that spoke to the eye for the moment—bearing about the same relation to the great discovery now before us, as the Abbé Sicard's invention of a visual alphabet for the purposes of conversation bore to the art of printing with movable types. Mr. Dyar's had no recording apparatus, as he expressly tells us; and Professor Henry had contented himself with the abundant honors of his laboratory and lecture-rooms.

"When, therefore, Mr. Morse claimed, in his first specification, 'the application of electro-magnets' 'for transmitting, by signs and sounds, intelligence between distant points,' and 'the mode and process of recording or making permanently signs of intelligence transmitted between distant points;' and when in his second specification he claimed 'the making use of the motive power of magnetism, when developed by the action of currents of electricity, as a means of operating and giving motion to machinery, which may be used to imprint signals upon paper or other suitable material,' 'for the purpose of telegraphic communication;' characterizing his 'invention as the first recording or printing telegraph by means of electro-magnetism;' and when, in his third, after again describing his machinery and process, he once more characterized it in the same terms, and claimed 'as the essence of his invention the use of the motive power of the electric or galvanic current' (electro-magnetism as he now terms it), 'however developed, for marking or printing intelligible characters, signs of letters at any distance;' through these several forms of specification, claiming and renewing his claim of property in the same invention, as it seems to us—and claiming in each and all of them no more, as it also seems to us, than he was justly entitled to claim—he declared the existence of a new art, asserted his right as its inventor and owner, and, announcing fully its nature and elements, invoked in return the contracted protection of the laws.

"From this time his title was vested as patentee of the art, and other men became competitors with him only in the work of diversifying and perfecting his details. He himself used the *stylus*, to impress paper or parchment, or wax-coated tablets, it may be; though he sometimes made a colored record by the friction of a pencil: another substitutes a liquid pigment, or stains his paper with a chemical ink: the next perhaps stains his paper beforehand, and writes on it by decomposing the coloring matter: and another yet, more studious of originality than the rest, writes in a cyclovolute, instead of a straight line, and manufactures his ink as he goes along, by decomposing the tip of his stylus on a chemically-moistened paper. They are no doubt all of them inventors; as was the man who first cast types in a mould, or first bent metal into the practical semblance of the gray goose-quill, or first devised sympathetic ink, that the curious in letter-writing might veil their secrets from the profane. All these toiled ingeniously and well, to advance and embellish a preëxisting art. But they had no share in the discovery of the art itself, and can no more claim to share the property, which its discovery may have conferred on another, than he who has devised some appropriate setting for a gem, can assert an interest in the gem itself.

" That the local or independent circuit, as we have described it, and as it is more accurately and perhaps more intelligibly set out by Mr. Morse in his specification, was original with him, cannot be seriously questioned. The devices referred to in the patents of Cooke and Wheatstone, and Davy, are at least imperfect modifications of the combined series of Mr. Morse's first patent ; one of them not improbably borrowed from it. The adjustable receiving magnet, the indispensable and characteristic element of the local circuit patent, no one has claimed but himself.

" It is only to make the first approach to a controversy on this point, to prove to us that Professor Henry had as early as 1828 made the *intensity magnet*, with which the scientific world is now familiar—or that he afterward, and before Mr. Morse's first application for a patent, had illustrated before his classes at Princeton, the manner in which one circuit could operate to hold another closed or to break it at pleasure—or that he had foreseen the applicability of his discoveries to the purposes of a telegraph. The question is not one of scientific precedence ; and, if it were, this is not the forum that could add to or detract from the eminent fame of Mr. Henry. It is purely a question of invention applied in a practical form to a specific use ; and, so regarded, it admits but of a single answer."

After we have given these judicial decisions, so intelligent, discriminating, impartial, and exhaustive, demonstrating the sole and indisputable right of Samuel F. B. Morse to the invention of the recording Telegraph, it is certainly not necessary for us to argue the question. Envy or ignorance may still deny to the inventor the honor which the courts and the world have awarded him, but the verdict is irreversible.

BAIN AND HOUSE.

Two suits for infringement were conducted by the proprietors of Professor Morse's patents, in which their applications for injunction were denied. They are known as the House and Bain cases. House devised an instrument of wonderful ingenuity for printing messages in Roman letters, employing axial magnetism, a device developed by Dr. Charles G. Page. It was claimed that Professor Morse, having been the first to invent a method of recording the message, by means of electro-magnetism, was entitled to the exclusive use of the electrical force as a telegraphic agent, by whatever device a current might record the message. The phraseology of the patent, in the judgment of the court, did not sustain the claim. While the invention dated back to 1832, the patent was not applied for until 1837, and was not issued till 1840. Steinheil had used a recording magneto-electric telegraph in 1837, and Gauss and Weber had pointed out in print, the device by which to accomplish it, in 1833. Bain had succeeded in employing the electric current to effect the solution of an iron wire, resting upon paper in motion, saturated with yellow prussiate of potash and weak nitric acid. When the current flowed, the iron dissolved, and at the instant, by the action of the acid and prussiate of potash, a blue stain was produced. If the contact was but for a moment, a dot was produced; if for an appreciable interval of time, a line was produced. Bain used Morse's alphabet, but he effected a visible record by a method wholly his own. The decisions do not apply to any thing Professor Morse did. While acquiescing in his claims, they simply assert that House's and Bain's modes were each new as regards that of Professor Morse, and that the language of his patent could not be construed to exclude all possible forms of using electrical force to produce a recorded telegraphic message. The question was in the phraseology of the patent; the working invention going back to 1835, two years before Steinheil's successful exhibition of his invention, was unquestionably the first electro-magnetic recording telegraph.

The House invention is now employed only in a modified form in combination with other inventions in stock-reporting instruments. The Bain principle is employed to a limited extent only in various systems of automatic telegraphs, but for the general business of telegraphing, it has been, like the House, superseded by the Morse system.

DR. JACKSON'S PRETENSIONS.

More annoying than any of these lawsuits, was a claim set up by Dr. Charles T. Jackson, as the original inventor of the Telegraph. He was one of the passengers on the Sully, and took a leading part in the conversation which led Mr. Morse to conceive the idea of the instrument which he afterward constructed. The pertinacity with which Dr. Jackson insisted upon his right to the honor of the invention, in spite of the clearest evidence to the contrary, led Mr. Morse to state publicly that he believed the claim to be the result of a disordered intellect. Subsequent events make it evident that this charitable view was also just. The same claimant asserted his right to the discovery of gun-cotton, anæsthetic agents and the circulation of the blood. As his pretensions to the invention of the Telegraph were exploded by the courts, and exposed in a document by Hon. Amos Kendall, widely published, it is not necessary to burden these pages with the correspondence between the claimant and the inventor.

Nor is it important to report the various lawsuits which arose in the extension of the Telegraph by rival lines, with conflicting claims. It was the practice of the Morse Company to grant the use of their instruments to parties constructing lines of telegraph, and to take stock in such lines as the consideration for the use of their patent. Conflicts naturally arose. The Morse partners themselves became divided in interest. Complicated and protracted litigations ensued. Large sums of money were expended. The life of the great inventor was embittered. At times he apprehended that he would be reduced again to abject poverty. But in the end justice was triumphant. Whatever reward of merit the world can bestow, was secured to Professor Morse in his lifetime—a lot that falls to few great inventors. The decision of the courts, and testimony that is now incontrovertible, justify the following

SUMMARY OF PROFESSOR MORSE'S ACHIEVEMENTS.

1. The Electro-Magnetic Recording Telegraph. This involved the fillet of paper moving by clock-work with uniform velocity under the lever-pen, rising and falling at measured intervals, controlled by the transmitting key operating the electro-magnet through the opening and closing of the galvanic circuit. It included the mathematical and mechanical conception of the combination of dots, lines, and spaces, to stand for letters, whether recorded chemically or by pressure.

2. The combined series, or *relay*, which made it practical to transmit from any station intelligence to any point, however far, and to receive and record messages at the end, and at all intermediate points, however numerous.

3. The first practical determination that the galvanic force could be made actually operative through sufficiently great distances without repetition, to render the recording telegraph a practical success, suited to public use.

4. The electro-magnetic sounder, or acoustic semaphore, with an alphabet corresponding to dots, lines, and spaces.

5. The stopping apparatus, for controlling the movement of the fillet of paper at a distant station through the key of the transmitting office.

6. The *combination* of the battery of Volta, improved by Daniell; the electro-magnet of Sturgeon; the multiplied insulated coil, and the battery of many pairs and long-conducting wire of Henry; and the single wire and earth circuit of Steinheil, with his own writing and registering apparatus, including the key, lever-pen, moving fillet of paper, stopping apparatus, and register-magnet; his own alphabet of dots, lines, and spaces, and his own relay working with an intensity battery—all proportioned and adjusted in a harmonious whole of extreme simplicity, and adapted to practical working for every-day public use.

7. He suggested to Arago, in 1839, the use of the electro-magnetic recording telegraph for determinations of longitude.

8. He was the first to lay a working submarine cable.

9. He is entitled to the further honor of having fought and conquered the difficulties, scientific, pecuniary, material, and in the way of legislation and litigation, which the effort to make the invention *useful* and *successful* encountered.

MORSE'S PATENTS AND INSTRUMENTS.

1. Professor Morse's first caveat was dated October 3, 1837; first application for a patent April 7, 1838; patent granted June, 20, 1840; patent of June 20, 1840, was reissued January 15, 1846; patent granted April 11, 1846; patent of June 20, 1840, reissued June 13, 1848; patent granted May 1, 1849; patent of 1840 extended in 1854 for seven years; patent of April 11, 1846, extended in 1860 for seven years.

2. The Morse Telegraph is employed (1874) in America upon about 110,000 miles of line, and 250,000 miles of wire, and in foreign countries upon about 200,000 miles of line, and upon 600,000 miles of wire. It is not much used upon long submarine lines; Sir William Thomson's Mirror Galvanometer being used as a receiving instrument upon all long submarine circuits.

3. The total Telegraph receipts throughout the world (in 1874) are about $40,000,000 per annum. The total number of messages is about 75,000,000.

4. The Morse Telegraph apparatus and alphabet now used in the United States are the same, and in Europe are substantially the same, as invented by him. Receiving by sound is the general

practice in America, and receiving on paper in Europe. As a rule, the Morse's ink-writer has superseded the embossing instrument in England and on the Continent of Europe.

5. The principal improvements applied to the Morse system are, the Repeater, through the use of which messages may be sent over distances ranging from 500 to 10,000 miles without rewriting, and the Duplex apparatus, invented by Joseph B. Stearns, of Boston, for the transmission of two messages in opposite directions, over one wire, at the same time. This latter invention, which is the greatest addition made to telegraphy since the great invention of Professor Morse, is now successfully operated throughout the United States, the Canadas, Great Britain, and Ireland, and is being introduced upon the Continent of Europe.

6. In England the Post-Office Telegraph continues to use a variety of systems of telegraphs, although the bulk of the traffic is performed by the Morse apparatus. Of the 8,284 instruments in use there, 3,582 are Wheatstone needle instruments, 2,367 Wheatstone's A B C, 394 Bright's bell, 98 Wheatstone's automatic, 23 Hughes's letter-printing, and 1,720 Morse ink-writers and sounder. On the Continent of Europe 12,938 Morse apparatus are employed, against 508 Hughes's letter-printing, and 2,529 telegraph instruments of all other kinds !

TELEGRAPH COMPANIES IN THE UNITED STATES.

Within the first seven years of the operations of Morse's Telegraph, there were more than fifty separate organizations in the United States in actual existence at the same time. In the year 1851 a few of them were consolidated under one management. Still, the great number of separate lines in operation prevented that unity and dispatch in conducting the business so essential to its success, and the public failed to secure everywhere the benefits of direct and reliable communication. Telegraphic correspondence between the Eastern, Western, and Southern sections, was not only burdened with several tariffs, but with unnecessary delays. Messages under this system required copying and retransmission at the termini of each local line, and this process not only occupied time, but was frequently the cause of errors, which rendered the service of little value. The Western Union Telegraph Company was originally organized as the New York and Mississippi Valley Printing Telegraph Company, on the 1st of April, 1851, for the purpose of building a line from Buffalo, New York, to St. Louis, Missouri. On the. 30th of March, 1854, they purchased the lines of the Lake Erie Telegraph Company, extending from Buffalo to Detroit, and from Cleveland to Pittsburg; and, on the 29th of April, 1854, secured control of the lines of the Cleveland and Cincinnati, the Cincinnati and St. Louis, and the Ohio Telegraph Companies. The Western Union gradually swallowed up more and more of the various lines, until, in twenty years, it effected a complete unification of the great majority of the telegraph-lines in the United States, and rendered the system the most extensive and efficient in the world. The territory now occupied by the lines of this company embraces almost the entire civilized portion of the Continent of North America. On the eastern coast its lines extend from Plaister Cove, on the Gulf of the St. Lawrence, to Brownsville, on the Rio Grande ; and, on the western coast, from San Diego, California, to the fisheries on the Kishyox River, eight hundred miles north of New Westminster, British Columbia. They reach across the continent, from the Atlantic to the Pacific Ocean, and embrace every State and Territory in the Union. The consolidations which have resulted in the Western Union connect with the British provinces, and by the Cuba and the Atlantic cables with the whole world. The management of this immense organization is in the hands of William Orton, Esq., president of the company, a gentleman of great executive ability, whose administration has given to this company a success without a parallel in the history of telegraphic enterprise. The accomplished electrician of the company, George B. Prescott, Esq., has charge of all matters of a scientific or technical character pertaining to the service, including the investigation of new inventions in telegraphy, and from time to time authorizes such changes and modifications of the instruments, insulators, and other parts of the apparatus, as to enable the company to fully keep pace with the progress of discovery.

In the report of the Western Union Telegraph Company to its stockholders, 1869, the following testimony is borne to the superiority of the invention of Professor Morse, and its practical indorsement by other companies :

"Nearly all the machinery employed by the company belongs to the Morse system. This telegraph, indeed, *is now used almost exclusively everywhere*, and the time will probably never come when it will cease to be *the leading system of the world.* Of more than a hundred devices that have been made to supersede it, not one has succeeded in accomplishing its purpose, and it is used at the present time upon more than ninety-five per cent. of all the telegraph lines in existence. The almost universal use of this apparatus is due to its simplicity and peculiar adaptability to the telegraphic traffic of every country. It employs electro-magnetism in the simplest form ; and its alphabet, when produced at a distance through the aid of the electric current, is read with equal facility by sight and sound, and can be readily interpreted by two of the other senses."

Thus have we seen, in the rapid review of this chapter, that the invention of Professor Morse, by the decision of the most competent scientists, and the highest judicial tribunals, is *distinct* and *different* from all others that claim priority to his, and by the more practical and absolutely impartial and irreversible verdict of *use*, its superiority is attested by ninety-five out of every hundred telegraph-lines on the face of the earth ! More than one hundred devices have been made to supersede it ; not one has succeeded in accomplishing its purpose. This fact is stronger proof than the arguments of counsel, the opinions of judges, or the claims of science, and renders it certain that in all future ages the present Recording Telegraph will be recognized as exclusively the invention of MORSE.

CHAPTER XV.

1847–1854.—REST AND REWARDS.

A HOME AT LAST—PURCHASE OF A COUNTRY-SEAT AND FARM AT POUGH-KEEPSIE—MARRIAGE—SOCIAL AND DOMESTIC LIFE—LOVE OF NATURE—BIRDS—HIS NEIGHBORS' ESTEEM—LETTER TO HIS DAUGHTER—REMBRANDT PEALE VISITS MORSE—LETTER OF BENSON J. LOSSING—HOUSE IN THE CITY OF NEW YORK—LETTER TO ARAGO—ADOPTION OF THE MORSE SYSTEM BY THE GERMAN CONVENTION—EXTENSION INTO DENMARK, SWEDEN, RUSSIA, AND AUSTRALIA—HONORARY DISTINCTIONS AND TESTIMONIALS—SCIENTIFIC BODIES—YALE COLLEGE—FOREIGN GOVERNMENTS.

UP to this time, 1847, Mr. Morse had never enjoyed a home since in youth he left his father's house. For brief periods, at intervals, he had found rest under the paternal roof, and after his first marriage he established his family in New Haven; but his own occupations were elsewhere, and he was only an occasional visitor, where he desired to be at home. His letters to his wife were full of ardent longings for the time when he should be no longer an exile. His domestic attachments were intense, and the separation from his family in the highest degree painful. After the death of his wife, when his children were scattered, the sense of desolation was greater still. He was a stranger everywhere. Poverty forbade him to have a home. When the Telegraph began to yield him a moderate income with the prospect of indefinite increase, he sought without delay for a spot where he might gather his children around him, and at last enjoy the luxury of his own house. He was now fifty-six years old. It was high time that he found a home if he would have one on earth. He consulted with his brothers and other friends as to the location. His brother Richard wrote to him: "Wherever we settle ourselves, obligations of a social and religious character will be imposed upon us. Our children must have as good institutions as we have enjoyed. Our standard of religious habits and conduct must be as high as in the best parts of New England." His attention was directed to a place near Poughkeepsie, on the eastern bank of the Hudson River, in Dutchess County and State of New York, about seventy-five miles north of the city. Here he purchased about two hundred acres of land. A farm-house on it was his abode while he completed a mansion adapted to his wants, his tastes, and his means. He gave to the place the name of " Locust Grove," not knowing that it had borne the same name in former years. There he gathered his children and their children, and for the first time knew what it was to have a house and home of his own. In the year following this purchase he was married to Miss Sarah E. Griswold, the daughter of his cousin. She was born December 25, 1822, at Fort Brady, Sault St. Mary's, at the foot of Lake Superior. Her father was an officer in the U. S. Army. Her grandfather was Arthur Breese, Esq., of Utica, New York, and her grandmother was Catharine Livingston, of Poughkeepsie. After his marriage Professor Morse discovered that the place he had purchased had once been the property of his wife's great-grandfather, who had called his place " Locust Grove." Her grandmother, Catharine Livingston, when a child, had fallen into the well, near the old cottage, and was rescued by the nurse, who descended into the well by the bucket, and saved the life of the girl. When the child grew up and was engaged to be married to Arthur Breese, she was wont to stand beneath an immense oak-tree and with her handkerchief wave a welcome to her lover as he came up the river on a sloop, which was then the mode of travel up and down the Hudson. This tree was called the " Breese tree," and stood there until within a few years, when it was unhappily destroyed by a stroke of lightning. A spacious and beautiful house, in the style of an Italian villa, being finished, Mr. Morse removed from the cottage, and in the midst of his family and friends sat down to the enjoyment of that rest and peace which had hitherto been denied him. His business affairs were in the hands of a trusted, faithful, and able agent, and he fondly hoped that they would be conducted without his care. But so wide-spread had become the relations of the Telegraph in the affairs of the country and the world, it was necessary for him to be constantly on the alert for the protection of his own interests, and to defeat the arts of those who sought to deprive him of the fame as well as the fortune which he had fairly won. The battle of life was only begun when he thought it was ended and the victory secure. His correspondence with Mr. Kendall was incessant and voluminous. The lawsuits in which he was compelled to engage required of him a vast amount of personal labor, preparing argument and illustration, searching and arranging testimony, and meeting the objections which the selfishness, the envy, or the ignorance of his opponents interposed to rob him of his due.

. The retirement of his place on the Hudson was favorable to study, and his habits of industry were such that he made the most of his time. Into a large and beautiful library he brought all the fruits of science and art that would aid him in his inquiries, and with plodding. perseverance he worked as steadily in his age and leisure, as when struggling under the burden of poverty to bring out his great invention. The wires of the Telegraph that connected Poughkeepsie with New York, passed near his house, and by-and-by one of them was led into his library! Here, with the instrument of his own invention on the table at his right hand, he sat and conversed at his ease with friends and correspondents in distant parts of the land! As years rolled on, and these wires were stretched still farther, and by-and-by beneath the ocean to foreign shores, making a reality of every prophecy he had uttered when wise men thought him deluded or mad, he still sat in his chair, in his own house in the country, far from the city and the sea, and, when he would, he could speak to men in Europe as if they were in an adjoining room! He believed he would, when he was in the ship Sully in 1832. He said he would, when he was in his garret in 1837. It was done in the year 1866. Nothing in the history of human progress is more sublime and beautiful than this! Never were the visions of imagination, the calculations of reason, and the deductions of science, more completely and practically accomplished within the lifetime of the seer, the philosopher, and the sage.

Identifying himself as a neighbor, a citizen, and Christian, with the community of which he had now became a member, he bore the responsibilities, discharged the duties, and enjoyed the pleasures of his new position with earnestness, ability, and zest. His hand and heart were always open to every good work, and his fellow-citizens delighted to know him as a model of every manly and generous virtue. William H. Crosby, Esq., of Poughkeepsie, in a note to the author, speaks of Professor Morse in these just and graceful words:

"His quiet, unostentatious life, among us, displayed no prominent incidents that would find employment for the pen of a biographer, while at the same time it was sufficiently marked to reveal to all, who were thown into his company, the liberal, kind-hearted, courteous, unpresuming, Christian gentleman. Though his name was blazed abroad in every land as that of one whose invention had been the source of so many blessings to his fellow-creatures, though crowned heads had vied with each other in loading him with honors, no pride nor arrogance displayed itself in his social intercourse; on the contrary, his whole conduct and conversation proved him to be actuated by the spirit of his first electric and electrifying message, and to be ever ready to give to God all the glory. His house was a place of delightful resort, and his uniform kindness and courtesy to his visitors, of whatever rank or station, coupled with an easy dignity of manners, always left upon their minds the impression that they had been in the presence, if not of a brilliant, yet of a truly great man. As wealth and honors poured in upon him, his neighbors and friends found little or no change in his social conduct, although his mode of life and style of equipage had kept pace with the increase of his means. His liberality was not confined to the outlay of his purse. He was ever ready to do a kindness to a neighbor, even at the cost of great personal inconvenience and toil. I will mention but one instance out of many of his self-denying kindness. While riding into town one day his attention was arrested by observing that the woods of Mrs. L—— were on fire, and that, if not speedily extinguished, the mansion would be endangered. Regardless of his years, of the business that was taking him to town, of the quality of his apparel, he sprang from his carriage, and went to work with such a will that, with the assistance of a few others, in a little while the danger was over. As my informant remarked, he worked harder and more efficiently than any common laborer on the ground. One striking characteristic of Professor Morse—and one which, no doubt, has already claimed your attention—was his love of Nature, in all her varied aspects, and it is probable that regret for the loss of those noble forest-trees mingled with his kind feelings to a neighbor, and had its share in prompting him to active exertion on the occasion above mentioned."

One of the many letters to his beloved daughter, Mrs. Lind, residing in the West Indies, was written when, having completed the payments on his estate, he was able to call it his own:

"LOCUST GROVE, *May* 14, 1848.

"I snatch a few moments, my dear Susan, to commence a letter to you, and to thank you for your frequent and most acceptable letters. Locust Grove is now *mine*, that is to say, it is loaned to me by our heavenly Father, just so long as he shall see fit to permit us to enjoy it. I have paid off the bond and mortgage on the 1st instant, and it is now free of incumbrance, but it has drained my money-cistern quite dry. Economy, at all times and under all circumstances right and proper, is now more than ever necessary. I have fresh attacks on my rights, and I am kept in a continual attitude of defense, and from so many quarters, that were it not for the trust I have in him who has thus far carried me through difficulties that seemed at the time perfectly insurmountable, I should almost give up in despair so persevering and so reckless and vindictive is the opposition that is made to me. Within a few weeks a new and more threatening attack has come from the other side of the water. Mr. Bain, a Scotchman, who has succeeded in England in an ingenious piece of mechanism, has applied for a patent for a mode of marking. It seems that it is the very mode which I first devised on board the ship, applied in 1836, and in January, 1847, entered a caveat and applied for a patent at our Patent-Office in July last. Mr. Bain has just applied for a patent for the same thing; he is allowed to go back in his proofs to the date of his English patent, which is in December, 1846, about *one* month before my caveat. I must prove my invention before that date (December, 1846), or he gets his patent and I lose mine (the one last applied for). But, I can prove priority, so that I think I shall defeat him. The case comes on at Washington in July. Thus you see, my dear children, my invention gives me little ease, and much vexation and anxiety, or would, were it not that I can view all as ordered by a kind and wise Father. If it is his will, he can continue to me the

38

credit and the profits of the Telegraph, or I see that by unforeseen incidents, easily brought about by infinite power, he can so throw a cloud over both as to deprive me entirely of the latter, and temporarily deprive me also of the former.   If I use the influence and the property he has bestowed, merely for selfish purposes, merely for self-aggrandizement, and selfish pleasure, he will take them away if I am a child of his, for he will not let these things interfere with my eternal interest.   I have been thinking much of the duties which devolve on me in this juncture.   I have wealth in stock, and now what portion ought to be devoted sacredly to the cause of God?   I have decided deliberately, and believe that I shall have the hearty concurrence of my dear children, when I tell them that *one-tenth* is the portion that must be set apart and consecrated to the cause of Christian benevolence.   All, indeed, should be consecrated to him, but this must be a fund. from which all applications for religious benevolent objects are to be answered.   Days of trial may come, nay, will come, but, as our day is our strength will be, if we look with steady faith for help in every time of need.

"You may judge, from what I have told you of my affairs, that I have not much time to write. I leave in the morning for New York and Washington, to look after matters and prepare for defense.   With all the piracies and frauds upon me, I hope to save enough to give my children a welcome reception in their father's house at all times.   Years are passing; age is on its way; how long I may be spared I know not, but I am beginning to feel a stronger desire than ever to have the society of my dear children."

His life in the country was very simple and quiet.   His hour of rising was half-past six o'clock in the morning, and he was in his library alone until breakfast at eight.   He loved to hear the birds in their native songs, and he could distinguish the notes of each species of birds, and would speak of the quality of their respective music.   He spent most of the day in reading and writing, rarely taking exercise, except walking in his garden to visit his graperies, in which he took special pride; or to the stables to see if his horses were well cared for.   He did not ride out regularly with his family, preferring the repose of his own grounds and the labors of his study.   But when he walked or rode in the country, he was constantly disposed to speak of the beauty and glory around him, as revealing to his mind the beneficence, wisdom, and power of the infinite Creator, who had made all these things for the use and enjoyment of man. One of his daughters writes of him in these simple and tender words: "He loved flowers. He would take one in his hand, and talk for hours about its beauty, its wonderful construction, and the wisdom and love of God in making so many varied forms of life and color to please our eyes. In his later years he became deeply interested in the microscope, and purchased one of great excellence and power. For whole hours, all the afternoon or evening, he would sit over it, examining flowers, or the animalcula in different fluids. Then, he would gather his children about him and give us a sort of *extempore* lecture on the wonders of creation, invisible to the naked eye, but so clearly brought to view by the magnifying power of the microscope. He was very fond of animals, cats and birds in particular. He tamed a little flying-squirrel, and it became so fond of him that it would sit on his shoulder while he was at his studies, and would eat out of his hand and sleep in his pocket. To this little animal he became so much attached that we took it with us to Europe, where it came to an untimely end in Paris, by running into an open fire."

Years passed by in this delightful retreat, out of the world but in it, so in it and of it that every day, and if needs be every hour or moment, brought to him intelligence of what was transpiring in his own country and in distant lands. He had but to touch the keys of the instrument at his side, and he had the attention of far-away friends with whom he was in instant communion. He had filled the earth with a new nervous system that responded to his touch in every part, as if it were a living, sensitive being. He dispensed a generous hospitality, which was enjoyed by his friends, and not seldom by strangers who came from distant countries and desired to make the acquaintance of a man whose fame was now as extensive as civilization itself. The companions of his early years, who were with him in his contests with the world, delighted to see him in the evening of his days, prosperous, honored, and happy. Benson J. Lossing, Esq., the historian of the American Revolution, and a resident of Poughkeepsie, has furnished a sketch of an interview which he enjoyed with Professor Morse and the distinguished artist,

REMBRANDT PEALE.   Mr. Lossing shall speak with his pen and pencil:

MORSE AND PEALE.

"THE RIDGE, DOVER PLAINS, N. Y., April, 1873.

" You ask me to unfold into a record the hint I gave you the other day about a notable picture. Memory always recalls that picture with delight. It was a marvelous grouping of landscape and figures by the pencil of God, in forms and colors of exquisite beauty and interest. It was a midsummer evening scene. Oberon and Titania, Puck and Peas-Blossom, Cobweb, Moth, and Mustard-seed, were all there among the shrubs and flowers, for it was the home of a great magician—a conjurer more potent than the King of the Fairies. He had conquered Saturn and Neptune, and his chief minister had already gone out to ' put a girdle round the earth in forty minutes.'

" The time was toward sunset. The place was a beautiful country-seat on the banks of the Hudson. The grounds and the outlook from them formed the landscape. Green lawns, neat hedges, beds of gay flowers, and graveled paths, with aged men, accomplished women, and young children on them, composed the foreground. These were on the verge of a plateau a hundred feet above the river. There stood magnificent trees which had been young denizens of the primal forest, perhaps, when the Mohican hunted among them. From their huge stems shadows stretched many a perch eastward in the slanting sunbeams. Beyond these giants, westward, abrupt and gentle slopes bowed to the lowly meadows, wedded to the broken crags which skirted the margin of the river. Beyond the shining waters, wooded precipices arose among golden wheat-fields; and, far away on the northwestern horizon, slumbered in misty azure the lofty Catskill Mountains. The singing-birds were nearly all silent, for it was July; but the throat of the swamp-robin sent its clear notes far away through the vistas.

" The chief figures in the group were two old men. They had been friends in their younger days, but had not seen each other's faces in forty years. They had been pupils of Benjamin West at the Royal Academy in England, one of them half a century before this meeting; and their countrymen were proud of the achievements of both in art and science. One was in the eighty-second year of his age; the other was on the verge of seventy. The elder was quite erect in figure, handsome in features, with eyes of mildest blue, the complexion of a young woman, a sweet voice, and was

wearing a crown of•flowing white locks. The younger was tall and slender, lithe in limb, with dark, magnetic eyes, benevolence beaming from his face, and a long white beard covering his bosom. The elder was REMBRANDT PEALE, who had painted a portrait of Washington from the living man. The younger was Professor MORSE, then (1859) at the zenith of his fame.

" Mr. Peale and his wife (an accomplished artist, full thirty years his junior) were spending a few days with us at Poughkeepsie. ' Locust Grove,' the country-seat of Professor Morse, the scene of the picture, is about two miles below that city. We rode down there with our guests toward the close of a summer day ; and at the ' artist's hour,' when the shadows are long and thick, we strolled about the grounds and saw the beautiful vision so dear to memory.

" It was delightful to hear those venerable men, as they walked among the flowers, call up recollections of the past. Peale was with West ten years before Morse became that master's favorite pupil ; and Peale's father had been West's pupil thirty years before his son entered his studio.

" They talked of the venerable Copley, with whom the elder Peale had studied, in Boston ; of his sweet though wrinkled face, and tender eyes, and kindly manner. ' He was like a father to me while I was in London,' said Peale. ' A Tory in America, he was a republican in England. He said to me one day, " I was the first to display the American standard in England, after the independence of the United States was acknowledged by this. government." " How and where ? " I asked. " On my easel," he replied, " as part of the back-ground to a portrait of your countryman, Elkanah Watson. It was painted on the day when the king sanctioned the acknowledgment.' "

" ' To me,' Morse said, ' Copley was a mentor in art. His dying hand and feeble voice helped me in professional difficulties on several occasions while in London. He was then painting his last picture—the portrait of his son, who was created Lord Lyndhurst in 1827.'

" They talked of Northcote, whose bold aquiline nose, lustrous eyes, and bald head, were notable at a chop-house in Cheapside, where he dined at five o'clock in the afternoon, and whose pictures were annually a conspicuous part of the exhibition at Somerset House.

" Of pale little Flaxman, the classic sculptor, they spoke tenderly. His genius claimed their admiration, but his goodness was their favorite theme, for his abounding piety was like a fragrant blossom, ever exhaling pure delight. They talked graciously of handsome Sir Thomas Lawrence, the 'painter to the king,' and the favorite of the ladies as a limner of feminine portraits, for he made the plainest appear attractive. They had mutual reminiscences of the irritable and excitable Fuseli (the intimate friend of Lavater, and the originator of Alderman Boydell's 'Shakespeare Gallery'), who was appointed Keeper of the Royal Academy at about the time when Peale left London for Paris in 1804.

"'He often looked over my shoulder,' said Peale, 'while I was at work, and criticised my drawing; and whenever he saw a glaring error, he would fly into a passion, declare I was an unworthy son of a worthy father, and end by inviting me to sup with him at his lodgings in a back room in Ivy Lane.'

"'I well remember the waspish Switzer,' Morse said. 'He was a bundle of paradoxes. Learned, yet ignorant; a good artist, with glaring faults; quarrelsome, but placable; always scolding, yet always kind-hearted. He would reproach President West for some fancied remissness in duty, and with the next breath declare that he was the most faithful man he knew. We all laughed at his storms and enjoyed his sunshine. West said to me gravely one day, after Fuseli's tongue had run its course: "I verily believe the good man (then seventy-four years of age) does not desire to go to heaven, because he may find no occasion there for storming; he would not endure the eternal serenity that prevails in the Land of the Blest."'

"Concerning our own artists who were their contemporaries, these venerable men exchanged opinions freely. They spoke most kindly of the blunt, erratic Stuart, under whose rugged exterior beat a heart of sweetest nature. The memory of the ethereal Allston they cherished with the devotion of worshipers, and confirmed the verdict of contemporary critics, that in coloring he was justly styled the 'American Titian.' Trumbull, as an artist and a man, was not spoken of in terms of admiration; but of the genial, erring Jarvis, the generous Inman, and the noble Sully, they talked lovingly. Concerning the irascible and soured bachelor, Vanderlyn, they uttered words of mingled praise as an artist and pity as a man.

"I was particularly interested in listening to their estimate of the painters who have filled the eight panels in the rotunda of the national Capitol with historical pictures. They were agreed in the opinion that Weir's picture of the 'Embarkation of the Pilgrims' is the best among them as a work of art, history, and sentiment. They regarded Trumbull's four pictures as works of great intrinsic value, because of the portraits. Chapman's 'Marriage of Pocahontas' they considered more pleasing to the less-cultivated popular taste than to the judgment of the skilled art-critic. Vanderlyn's 'Landing of Columbus' seemed to them to be weak, and Powell's 'De Soto on the Mississippi' as a good painting, but an historical improbability in its composition.

"But I will not weary you with further details of my recollections of their conversation upon art themes and social memories. For forty years these eminent Americans had been pursuing their respective courses in life, within a few leagues of each other, but without meeting face to face in all that time. The elder, gentle, quiet, timid, unassuming, lacking in self-assertion, and eminently good in all the relations of life, had moved almost noiselessly along the flowery pathways of art, and was then near the end of his long journey, for he died in the early autumn of the next year. The younger was more actively ambitious and restless, tenacious of his rights, and quick to assert and defend them; but he was patient, plodding, persevering, modest, and eminently good. He had, by his achievements, made the whole earth, as it were, resonant with his praises, for he had answered affirmatively the great question put by God to the Chaldean emir, 'Canst thou send lightnings, that they may go, and say unto thee, Here we are?' He had trained for the intellectual uses of man that subtile 'soul of the universe' to which the prophet of Twickenham alluded when he wrote:

'It warms in the sun, refreshes in the breeze,
Glows in the stars, and blossoms in the trees;
Lives through all life, extends through all extent,
Spreads undivided, operates unspent.'

"The men, the landscape, the hour, made a picture which will never fade from memory. We returned home in the evening twilight, with hearts full of thanksgiving for the opportunity we had enjoyed. Yours faithfully,

"BENSON J. LOSSING."

In the home to which his heart had so fondly turned in all the years of his struggles with poverty, and the severer contests with those who sought to deprive him of his rewards, the life of Professor Morse was now tranquilly flowing. Several years after his purchase in Poughkeepsie, he bought a large and beau-

tiful house, No. 5 West Twenty-second Street, in the city of
New York. On a vacant lot adjoining, he erected an elegant
building for his library and study. Here he established his
winter residence. Among his papers, found after his death, is a
prayer which he wrote and used on the occasion of entering
upon possession of his house in town. It was in the central
part of the city, adjacent to Madison Square, and it soon became the frequent resort of the learned and the good, who
sought the society of the now famous inventor, recognized as a
great public benefactor. But for the vexatious lawsuits that
for several years disturbed his peace, the life of the retired philosopher would have been as pleasant as the former years had
been dark and stormy. But he was reminded constantly that
this world was not his rest ; and he took things as they came,
in the firm persuasion that all would be well in the end. His
correspondence with men of science at home and abroad increased rapidly and greatly. His letters during these years of
rest indicate the progress of the Telegraph, and his own pursuits. Writing to Arago in 1851, he said:

"At this moment my system of telegraphing comprises about
fifteen thousand English miles of conductors on this continent.
How far the essential parts of my system have been adopted in
Europe and Asia, I am unable to say. In Russia, it has been intimated to me that it is in operation; and at Constantinople the
Sublime Porte has it in operation between two of his military
schools. Making all due allowance for the partiality naturally felt
for one's own offspring, may I not say that the Recording Telegraph
is the most efficient as well as simplest form of the Telegraph yet invented? It ought to be noticed, as a striking peculiarity of my system, that the *sound* given out by the lever in recording is as readily
understood by a practised ear as the recorded characters are by the
eye. Many, and indeed most, of the operators read from the sound
only, and many will thus read long dispatches, while every one understands, when his station is called, as readily as if spoken to by
the human voice. There is a practical advantage in this talking
hourly experienced in every telegraph-office on the lines. This
characteristic of voice connected with *recording*, has led me to
designate the principle of my invention as Telegraphic Speech by
Electricity—*speech* comprehending *intelligible sounds* and *written*

marks. The *Recording Telegraph,* as a distinct genus, I have ever claimed as my invention. There was no Recording Telegraph previous to the invention of mine; and it is this function, *par excellence,* to wit, '*recording,*' that gives to it both its peculiarity and great efficiency. . . . As a commercial enterprise, telegraph stock in the Morse lines has paid valuable dividends. Their business has lately been embarrassed by temporary and local causes not affecting the merits of the invention, but mainly in consequence of the attempts to compete with and to supplant by rival modes.

"A *brochure,* entitled 'Full Exposure of Dr. Charles T. Jackson's Pretensions to the Invention of the American Electro-Magnetic Telegraph,' was sent to you and to the Academy some time since at my request. The *brochure* was prepared from the evidence before the courts, by the Hon. Amos Kendall, formerly Postmaster-General of the United States. Much more, indeed, is admitted as fact, in this *exposé* in favor of Jackson's pretensions, than truth will warrant. I never met with a case of such reckless disregard of truth as this of Dr. Jackson's. He is not sustained by any witness in a single important assertion. The only explanation which can be given that shall not implicate his moral character is *monomania,* and to this misfortune I have been willing, with many of his friends, to attribute his conduct, provided I may have the benefit which is usually accorded to the sane, of protection against the insane.

"I have not learned that the Academy of Sciences has ever passed a decision upon the subject of Electric Telegraphs. While anxious, of course, that justice should be done to me and to my country, by a tribunal to whose decisions the civilized world does willing homage, I yet desire that equal justice should be accorded to those distinguished discoverers of principles in science, of whatever country, without which the inventor would lack the materials for his invention."

In the month of October, 1851, a convention of deputies from the German states of Austria, Prussia, Bavaria, Wurtemberg, and Saxony, met at Vienna to establish a German-Austrian Telegraphic Union. The various systems of telegraphy then in use were subjected to the most thorough examination and discussion, by men well qualified to illustrate the principles of the several plans. They reached the conclusion with great unanimity that the American (or Morse system) was the only one to meet their wants. Professor Steinheil, the administrator-in-chief of the Austrian telegraphs, although himself the inventor of an electric telegraph, which has procured for him well-deserved fame, with a magnanimity which does him high honor, gave his opinion in favor of adopting the American system in Germany. This was to Professor Morse a most gratifying fact. In the lawsuits involving his rights, great stress had been laid upon the Steinheil invention as something anterior to Morse's; but Steinheil himself never made such pretensions, and freely supported Morse's system as having advantages superior to his own. And by the same steamer that brought this gratifying intelligence, the inventor received the news that it had been decided in the Denmark House of Representatives that the Electric Telegraph, in continuation of the German lines, should be immediately extended from Elsinore, *via* Copenhagen, to Rendsberg.

Extract from the Protocol of the Convention of Deputies from the German Governments which met at Vienna in the month of October, 1851, for the establishment of a German-Austrian Telegraphic Union, etc., etc.:

"*Articles* 2 *and* 3.—The Governments of this Union give their mutual assurance to bring into operation, at the latest, on the 1st of July, 1852, the direct transmission of telegraphic communications between the central stations of the respective governments, so that transfers upon intermediate stations will be no longer required, whenever the lines are not previously occupied, so that each of the central stations can enter into direct communication with every other. To accomplish this, *all the Governments of the Telegraph Union* adopt for the International Correspondence *upon each line, for the present,* MORSE'S TELEGRAPH, *with receiving magnets, registers, and uniform alphabet.*"

In August, 1854, Mr. Fleischmann, who had introduced the Telegraph into Austria, wrote from Paris to Professor Morse:

"I saw this day the agent of the submarine Telegraph between England and France, and he told me that they came to the conclusion to adopt *Morse's Telegraph* in preference to any known and tried system. They have experimented with your system and find it the most perfect. They have already some of your machines working, and the *French Government* is about to adopt it also. So much for you and your glory. My prediction comes to pass—'Morse's Telegraph must be universally adopted.'"

And Professor Morse, inclosing Mr. F.'s letter to his friend T. R. Walker, Esq., of Utica, said:

"My Telegraph system, as you may be aware, had been previously adopted throughout all Germany, and extended into Denmark, Sweden, and lately into Russia. It has been introduced also by choice of the government throughout Australia, and in Europe the only countries not using my system were England and France. The facts, therefore, revealed by the inclosed letter, show that without any aid of an extrinsic character on my part, my system, from its own inherent qualities, is pervading the globe, and this in my own lifetime. I believed from the beginning that this would eventually be the case, but I did not dream of its so rapid accomplishment; I did not expect to live to see its diffusion over the whole world. So far as it regards England, I confess to having had some skepticism on the fact of her doing away with her own systems and acknowledging an American one better than her own. 'Can any good thing come out of Nazareth?' has been her uniform question regarding any thing American; but in confirmation of the fact that she is actually about to adopt my system, not only on her submarine lines, but also on her other lines, I have the authority of a gentleman, a member of the Royal Society and secretary of the Great English Company, whom I met in New York last week, that this is the fact; and he assured me that in England the opinion was rife that my system would supersede all the others as the simplest and best. This is gratifying, after all the injustice at home and abroad which I have been called to endure."

HONORARY DISTINCTIONS.

As the Morse system of telegraphing made its way into foreign lands, readily demonstrating its superiority, and superseding other systems, the merit of the inventor was acknowledged by one and another government, until it may be safely asserted that Professor Morse received a greater number of honorary distinctions from foreign powers than were ever bestowed upon any other private citizen. Before he became generally known as the inventor of the Telegraph he was (December 25, 1835) elected a corresponding member of the Historical Institute of France.

January 12, 1837, he was elected a member of the Royal Academy of Fine Arts of Belgium. The certificate of this election he preserved with a care that reveals his secret love for distinction in the line of his first pursuit, in which he would gladly have passed his life.

July 15, 1839, the Great Silver Medal of the " Academy of Industry" of Paris was voted to him, for his invention of the Telegraph. This medal he never received.

October 12, 1841, he was made a corresponding member of the National Institution for the Promotion of Science, established at Washington.

October 18, 1842, a record was made by the American Institute, showing the use of the submarine Telegraph by Professor Morse in 1842, and on the 20th day of the same month the thanks of the Institute were voted to him for placing at the disposal of the Institute his Telegraph to communicate between the Battery and Governor's Island, and the Gold Medal of the Institute was awarded to him for his successful experiments.

June 12, 1845, he was elected a corresponding member of the Archæological Society of Belgium; April 21, 1848, a member of the American Philosophical Society, Philadelphia; November 14, 1849, a Fellow of the American Academy of Arts and Sciences, Boston.

Foreign distinctions were afterward conferred on Professor Morse in great numbers and in the most flattering terms, but none gave him more pleasure than the reception of the following letter from the wise and good man who also gave him his first lessons in the science of electricity:

"YALE COLLEGE, *August* 27, 1846.

" DEAR SIR : Permit me to inform you that the corporation of this college, at our late public commencement, conferred on you the degree of Doctor of Laws. College distinctions, I am aware, are becoming very common in this country. But Yale College aims to proceed on the principle of selecting those who will *confer* honor, rather than receive it, by being enrolled in the list of its favorites. We present you this testimony of our regard, as a tribute of respect and gratitude for what you have done to obviate the reproach which we sometimes hear, that discoveries and inventions of great public utility do not proceed from men who have imbibed the principles of their education within the walls of a college. I have the honor to be, with affectionate regard, your friend and servant,   J. DAY.

"Professor S. F. B. MORSE, LL. D."

Professor Morse acknowledged the receipt of this honor in these words:

"Permit me to return, through you, my sincere thanks to the honorable corporation for the high honor they have conferred upon me at the late commencement, in bestowing upon me the degree of Doctor of Laws. I esteem it doubly valuable as emanating from my much-loved and venerated *alma mater.* In the success with which it has pleased God to crown my telegraphic invention, it is not the least gratifying circumstance that you consider the invention as reflecting credit on my collegiate instruction, and I may therefore say that, in reviewing the mental processes by which I arrived at the final result, I can distinctly trace them back to their incipiency, in the lessons of my esteemed instructors in natural philosophy and in chemistry. Later developments in electro-magnetism in the lectures of Professor J. F. Dana were, indeed, the more immediate sources whence I drew much of my material, but this was dependent for its efficacy on my earlier college instruction. Be pleased to accept my sincere thanks for the flattering and friendly manner in which you have communicated to me the act of the corporation. In common with all the friends of learning, I sincerely deplore the necessity, which you conceive to exist, of your resignation of the presidency of the college over whose interests you have so long watched. May the blessing of God accompany you in your retirement!"

TURKEY.—March 1, 1848, the Hon. John P. Brown, dragoman of the United States, addressed a letter to the American Oriental Society, relating the incidents of an exhibition of Professor Morse's Telegraph before the Sultan of Turkey, and the remarkable results that followed:

"I do myself the pleasure," he said, "to subjoin herewith a copy of a diploma, called in Turkish a *berait*, bestowing upon Professor Morse, of New York, a decoration (or *nichan*) of honor, together with a translation of it into English. As this is the first and only decoration which the Sultan of the Ottoman Empire has conferred upon a citizen of the United States, it struck me, when translating it for the legation, that some account of it would not prove uninteresting to our Society. There is a young American in the service of the Sultan, as a geologist, etc., Dr. James Lawrence Smith, who was sent out here, by the present Hon. Secretary of

State, at the request of the Sultan, made through me during the absence of the Minister Resident. This gentleman, who stands high here in his profession, and has already been able to render the Sultan some important services, being desirous of procuring something from the United States which would be entirely new to his Majesty, and of scientific interest to him, sent for a specimen of the electric telegraph, as perfected by our celebrated countryman Mr. Morse. On its arrival here, the Minister Resident confided its presentation to the Sultan to my care and management; and, having soon afterward an occasion to see his Majesty, I embraced it to inform him of the desire of Dr. Smith to have the honor of exhibiting the telegraph before him. The Sultan immediately named the following day for receiving it; and Dr. Smith, kindly aided by Rev. C. Hamlin, of the Armenian Seminary at Bebek, who, to use his own words, lent his assistance on the occasion *con amore*, accompanied me to the palace of the Sultan at Beglerbey, on the Asiatic shore of the Bosporus. The wires were stretched from the principal entrance of the palace to its union with the harem, a distance of some thirty or forty paces, and the performers were completely concealed from each other by the angle of a door-way, so that, had the Sultan been disposed to doubt the reality of the powers of the instrument, it would nevertheless have been evident to him, that the operators communicated with each other only by means of its wires. The Sultan was attended by his own personal employés and domestic officers. He was in excellent spirits, and treated us all with the amiableness and graciousness of disposition for which he is much beloved by all who have the honor of approaching him. I may here add for your information that the Sultan, now about twenty-six years of age, is of middle stature, rather lightly built, and thin, simple in his manners, with dark eyes and beard, and a face slightly marked with the small-pox; and, though he has but little of the dignified air supposed to belong to all sovereigns, his countenance indicates that his feelings all partake of the most pure benevolence and generosity. Indeed, it is quite impossible to converse with his Majesty, and not be forcibly struck with the evidence, in his own demeanor and personal conduct, of the immense change which has taken place in this country, and particularly in the character of its sovereigns, in the course of the past century, or even half century. The exhibition of Mr. Morse's telegraph, on this occasion, was perfectly successful and much to the satisfaction of the young Sultan, who remarked that he had often heard of the wonderful invention, but had never been able until then to comprehend its nature. I am happy to say that his Majesty understood very well the properties of the electric fluid, and, perceiving that the alphabet used (which I had explained in Turkish) was a purely conventional one, composed a few letters himself, which he desired to have used. So much was he gratified with the exhibition, that he requested me, in a very kind manner, to leave the telegraph as it was, and come again on the following day, saying he would send invitations to all his ministers and other officers to assemble, on the following morning, to witness its operations. I remarked, during this interview with the Sultan, that those about him were quite at their ease, and conversed freely with him. He addressed several questions to me about the United States, and its war with Mexico, expressing great regret that there should ever be a necessity for war. On the following morning, all the officers of the Government, from the Grand-Vizier and the Sheik-ul-Islam down, assembled at the palace; and Dr. Smith and Rev. Mr. Hamlin again worked the telegraph with entire success. Some of those present, such as the Grand-Vizier, Reshid Pasha, formerly ambassador at London and Paris, Ali Effendi, now Pasha, also formerly ambassador at London, and Sarim Pasha, Minister of Finance, formerly ambassador at London, had already seen electric telegraphs in those places. All, however, seemed much pleased with that of Mr. Morse. I was then consulted by the secretary of the Sultan about offering a recompense to Dr. Smith, for his trouble in procuring the telegraph from the United States. The doctor, to whom, of course, the matter was left, generously disclaimed all desire of receiving any thing for himself, as he had simply sent for the telegraph, and the honor of exbibiting it before the Sultan was all he wished. He requested that whatever honor the Sultan was disposed to confer upon him might be given to the talented inventor of the telegraph; and I took occasion to recommend this to the secretary, as a course which would do honor both to the Sultan as a patron of science, and to Mr. Morse as a person of distinguished talents. The object to be conferred, I thought at the moment, would be a snuff-box in diamonds, but I was agreeably surprised to learn from the secretary, on his return from reporting the result of our conversation to the Sultan, that he had been pleased to confer upon Mr. Morse a *nichan*, or decoration of a superior grade, in diamonds."

The ingenuous and high-minded gentleman who thus refused the decoration which he believed to be due to the inventor of the Telegraph, rather than to himself who had illustrated it to the Sultan, Professor J. Lawrence Smith, has since been the President of the American Scientific Association, and is a resident of Louisville, Ky. He states that, after the decoration had been promised to Professor Morse, some delay in its presentation occurred, and Professor Smith, inquiring for the cause, was informed by the Minister of Foreign Affairs that the *English* legation had stated to the Turkish Government that Professor Morse was not the inventor! Professor Smith then argued the question in a communication to the Turkish minister, Ali Pasha, and fully satisfied that intelligent statesman of the rights of the American. In ten days after this paper was submitted, the decoration was placed in the hands of Professor Smith to be forwarded officially to Professor Morse. The original diploma which Professor Morse received with the diamond decoration of the order is given in *fac-simile*, of which the following is a translation:

[TRANSLATION.]

" IN THE NAME OF HIM:

" SULTAN ABDUL MAJID KHAN, Son of Mahmoud Khan, Son of Abdul Hamid Khan—may he ever be victorious!

" The object of the present sovereign decoration of Noble Exalted Glory, of Elevated Place and of this Illustrious, World Conquering Monogram, is as follows:

" The Bearer of this Imperial Monogram of exalted character, Mr. Morse, an American, a man of science and of talents, and who is a Model of the Chiefs of the nation of the Messiah—may his grade be increased—having invented an Electrical Telegraph, a specimen of which has been exhibited in my Imperial presence; and it being proper to patronize knowledge, and to express my sense of the value of the attainments of the Inventor, as well as to distinguish those persons who are the Inventors of such objects as serve to extend and facilitate the relations of mankind, I have conferred upon him, on my exalted part, an honorable decoration in diamonds, and issued also this present diploma, as a token of my benevolence for him.

" Written in the middle of the moon Sefer, the fortunate, the year of the Flight one thousand two hundred and sixty-four (22 January, 1848). In Constantinople the well-guarded.

" Signed on the face of the Diploma by the SULTAN.

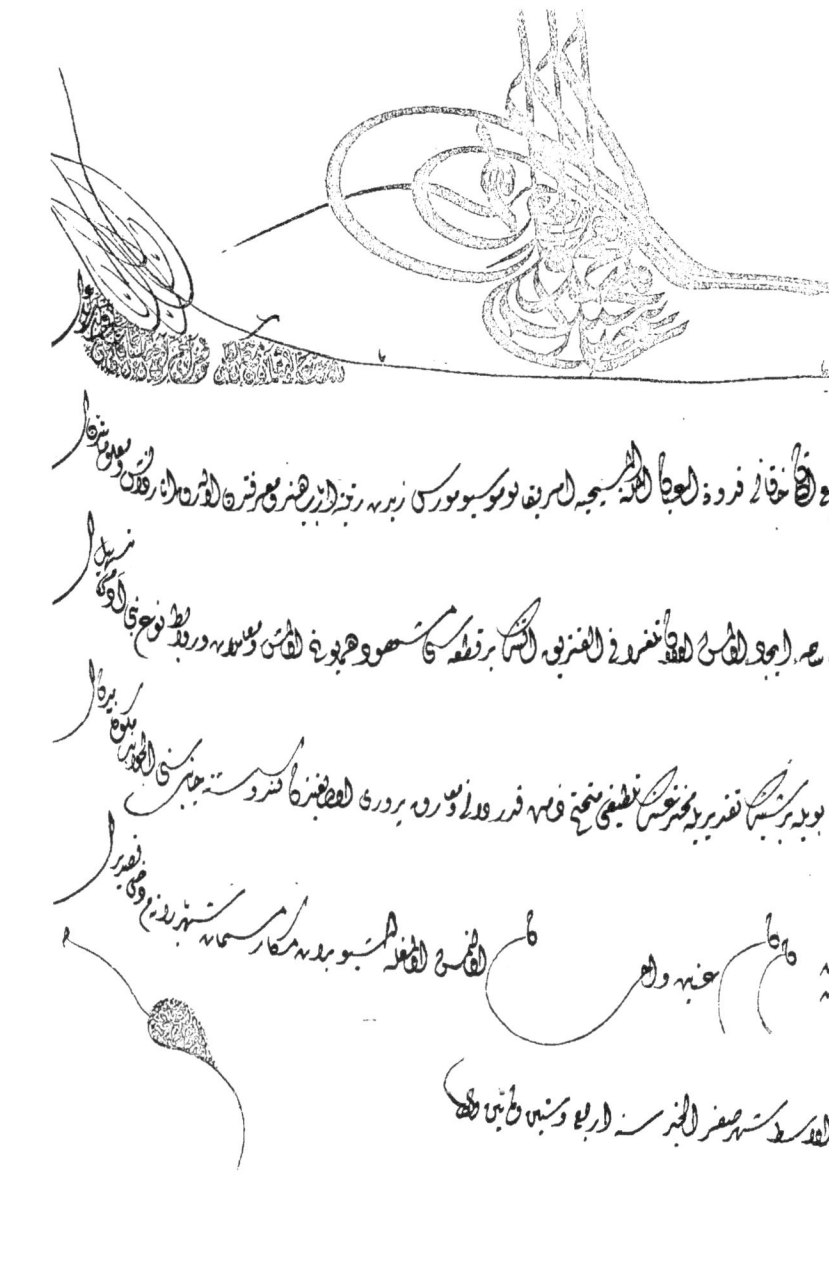

" On the back by

" MOHAMMED ALI PASHA, *Minister of Foreign Affairs;* CHEO-KEL BEY, *Vice-Chancellor of the Sublime Porte.*

" THE REGISTRAR *of the Sublime Porte.*"

Thus the first recognition of the Telegraph by a monarch of the Old World, was made by the Sultan of Turkey! Professor Morse acknowledged the honor in a letter closing with these words : " That God may grant a long and prosperous reign to your Majesty, is the sincere prayer of your Majesty's most humble and obedient servant."

In the year 1851 Professor Morse, having learned that the American Electro-Magnetic Telegraph had been adopted in Prussia as the most efficient yet devised, directed a letter of inquiry into the truth of the report to the Baron Gerolt, the Prussian Minister at Washington ; at the same time transmitting, as a specimen of the efficiency of Morse's Telegraph, a pamphlet containing a full report of the trial of Professor Webster for the murder of Dr. Parkman, which had just been transmitted from Boston and printed in the New-York *Globe,* being the longest consecutive document then ever sent over a line of telegraph. The following reply to his inquiry was received by Professor Morse a few days afterward:

" PRUSSIAN LEGATION AT WASHINGTON, *April* 15, 1851.

" DEAR SIR : On the 26th of April, 1850, I informed you that I had communicated to his Majesty's Government the pamphlet which you had sent to me as an example of the efficiency of your Electric Telegraph system. In answer to your inquiries about the adoption of your Telegraph in Prussia, I beg to inclose a copy of the report made on the subject by Mr. Nottebohm, who was charged with the establishing of telegraphic lines in Prussia. You will see by that report *that your Telegraph has been found the most efficient for great distances.*

" It gives me great satisfaction to inform you at the same time that his Majesty the king, as an acknowledgment of your great merits for the improvement of the Electro-Magnetic Telegraphs, has ordered me to present to you *a golden snuff-box containing the Prussian golden medal for scientific merit.*

" The said box is now in possession of his Majesty's consul-

39

general, F. W. Schmidt, Esq., at New York, No. 56 New Street, who will deliver it to you, and receive your receipt for it.

"I avail myself of this opportunity to renew to you the assurances of my high consideration and personal esteem.

"Your most obedient servant,   GEROLT.

"Professor S. F. B. MORSE, Poughkeepsie, Dutchess County, New York."

To this Professor Morse returned the following reply:

"POUGHKEEPSIE, DUTCHESS COUNTY, N. Y., *April* 21, 1851.

"MY DEAR BARON: On my return home on Saturday evening, I received your most gratifying letter of the 15th instant, announcing to me the doubly flattering intelligence that the American Electro-Magnetic Telegraph had been adopted throughout the Prussian dominions, by his Majesty the king, 'as the most efficient for great distances,' and that his Majesty had been pleased, through you, to present to me as the inventor such a valuable mark of his consideration. The box, with its inclosed medal, is not yet received. I shall take the earliest opportunity to call and receive it from the Prussian consul, when I next visit the city of New York.

"Be pleased, my dear baron, to present to his Majesty the king my sincere thanks, with my unfeigned wishes that the Electric Telegraph may be a means, under God, in the hands of his Majesty, and of the other governments of the world, of adding greatly to the convenience, the security, and the substantial happiness of mankind.

"Accept also for yourself, my dear baron, my thanks for this additional token of your personal friendliness, and kind interest in the success of my invention.

"Believe me, with the highest consideration and personal esteem, your most obedient servant,

"SAMUEL F. B. MORSE.

"To his Excellency the Baron GEROLT."

WURTEMBERG.—The third European Government recognizing the inventor of the Telegraph was Wurtemberg. The following is a translation of the letter informing Professor Morse of the honor:

"STUTTGART, *February* 24, 1852.

"*To his Excellency Professor* MORSE, *at Washington.*

"YOUR EXCELLENCY: His Majesty the King of Wurtemberg, upon the report of the Minister of Finance relative to your Excellency *as the inventor of the best Recording Telegraph known to him,* and which, on account *of its simplicity and efficiency, is adopted and used throughout all Germany,* and particularly in Wurtemberg, has graciously bestowed upon you the Great Gold Medal of Arts and Sciences, for your meritorious services in the art of Telegraphing. While it affords me special satisfaction most respectfully to inform your Excellency of this, in inclosing to you the medal, and to present my sincere congratulations on this deserved distinction, I seize gladly the opportunity to assure you of my perfect esteem.

"The Chief of the Royal Wurtemberg Finance Department and Chancellor of State, KNAPP."

AUSTRIA.—In 1855 the Emperor of Austria sent to Professor Morse the Great Gold Medal of Science and Art. It is a massive and beautiful piece of work. On one side is a medallion head of the young emperor, crowned with laurel, with the inscription, "Franciscus Josephus I., D. G., Austriæ Imperator;" and, on the obverse, a wreath of laurel surrounding the imperial crown, with the inscription, "Literis et Artibus." This was the fourth token of acknowledgment from European sovereigns accorded to Professor Morse. It was accompanied by this letter:

"BOSTON, *August* 4, 1855.

"SIR: I have much pleasure in transmitting to you, by order of the Imperial Government, the Great Golden Medal for Science and Arts, which his Majesty the Emperor of Austria has been pleased to confer upon you, in acknowledgment of your eminent merits concerning the telegraphic system in general, as well as its development in Austria in particular. It is very satisfactory to myself to be the organ of the Imperial Government on this agreeable occasion; and I beg you will at the same time permit me to express to you my great personal regard. Remaining, sir, very respectfully, your obedient servant, HULSEMANN,

" *Chargé d'Affaires of his Majesty the Emperor of Austria.*

"To Professor MORSE, Poughkeepsie, New York."

FRANCE.—In the year 1856 the Emperor of France conferred upon Professor Morse the brevet and decoration as Chevalier of the Imperial Order of the Legion of Honor. The Hon. J. Y. Mason was at that time the Minister of the United States in France, and through him the Order was conferred. Mr. Mason, in acknowledging it, wrote to the Minister of the Interior a letter, in which were these words:

"My distinguished compatriot, Professor Morse, having returned to his home in the United States, I will hasten to send to him the letter addressed to him by his Excellency Count Walewski, Minister of Foreign Affairs, and with it the brevet and decoration which his Majesty has deigned to confer on him as a Chevalier de l'Ordre Impérial de la Légion d'Honneur. The success of Professor Morse's invention, in promoting the interests of mankind, in facilitating the art of telegraphic communication, has given him fame, and made him friends in all countries. This gracious act of consideration on the part of his Majesty will, I am assured, be acknowledged by him and them as peculiarly gratifying. Professor Morse deserves to be regarded as the benefactor of his race, and the rewards bestowed on one so highly gifted, and yet so modest, can never be unworthily conferred."

DENMARK.—The King of Denmark honored the inventor in the same year, 1856. Professor Morse received the Cross of the Order of Dannebrog, with the following letter

"LEGATION OF DENMARK, PHILADELPHIA, *December* 29, 1856.

"SIR: I have the honor to inform you that his Majesty the King of Denmark, having been pleased to confer on you the Cross of a Knight of the Order of the Dannebrog, in acknowledgment of the services you have rendered the world by the invention and successful establishment of the Electrical Telegraph, I have received for you from his Majesty's Ministry of Foreign Affairs the Cross of the Dannebrog, together with an official communication from the Chapter of the Order, which his Majesty's consul at New York, Mr. Ed. Beck, will have the honor of handing to you.

"Begging you to accept my compliments, and the assurance of my distinguished consideration, I have the honor to be, sir, your most obedient servant, TUBENS BILL,

"*H. D. Minister Chargé d'Affaires.*

"Professor SAMUEL MORSE, Poughkeepsie, New York."

SWEDEN.—October 3, 1858, Professor Morse was elected a member of the Royal Academy of Sciences in Sweden, and the fact communicated to him in the most flattering terms by the secretary.

Convention of European Powers.—The pecuniary testimonial awarded to Professor Morse in 1858, by a convention of the

European Governments, is made the subject of a subsequent chapter.

SPAIN.—May 11, 1859, Isabella II., Queen of Spain, on the occasion of the adoption of the Morse system of Telegraphs in her dominions, issued a decree conferring on Samuel F. B. Morse, the inventor, the order of Knighthood and Commander of the First Class of the Royal Order of Isabella the Catholic.

PORTUGAL.—September 20, 1860, the King of Portugal with his own hand addressed a letter to Professor Morse, thanking him for the great benefit he had conferred upon the human race by his invention, and making him Knight of the Tower and Sword, as a mark of his "appreciation of the Professor's scientific merit and the service he had rendered the world at large."

ITALY.—March 31, 1864, his Majesty Victor Emmanuel II., King of Italy, conferred on Professor Morse the brevet and the insignia of Chevalier of the Royal Order of *S. S. Maurizio et Lazare.*

SWITZERLAND.—December 20, 1866, Professor Morse was elected honorary member of the "Société de Physique et d'Histoire Naturelle" of Geneva, Switzerland.

These honorable distinctions are grouped in the order of their dates, and presented in connection, that it may be seen at a glance how generally and thoroughly the merits of Morse as the inventor were comprehended, and the value of his labors appreciated among the nations of the earth. And all this in his own life-time!

CHAPTER XVI.

1854–1855.

SUBMARINE TELEGRAPH—THE FIRST EXPERIMENT—NEWFOUNDLAND ELECTRIC TELEGRAPH—CYRUS W. FIELD—LIEUTENANT MAURY'S OPINION—FORMATION OF A NEW COMPANY—MORSE TO FARADAY—EXTENSION OF PATENT— LETTERS TO MR. FIELD AND MR. WHITE—DR. STEINHEIL'S LETTER—HON. D. D. BARNARD—PROFESSOR MORSE'S PREDICTIONS—EXPEDITION TO NEW-FOUNDLAND—ATTEMPT TO LAY THE CABLE—FAILURE—RENEWED ATTEMPT, AND SUCCESS.

IN a letter to the Hon. Levi Woodbury, dated September 27, 1837, Professor Morse remarked, in speaking of the construction of the lines of Telegraph: "Where the stream is wide, and no bridge, *the circuit* inclosed in lead *may be sunk to the bottom;*" and again, speaking of the mode of stretching the lines upon posts, to connect different parts of the country together, he says, "This mode would be as cheap, probably, as any other, unless the *laying of the circuit in the water* should be found to be most eligible." Professor Morse then contemplated a submarine line between New York and Charleston, along the coast. He proceeds: "A series of experiments to ascertain the practicability of this mode, I am about to commence with Professor Gale—we are preparing a circuit of twenty miles. The result of our experiments I will have the honor of reporting to you."

This letter, with other documents, was published and circulated in the year 1837. There was ample time in two years for such a suggestion, published in a congressional document, to reach Europe, and to be perused by those interested in the subject. That the result of the proposed experiments was satisfactory is subsequently proved, although it does not appear to have been reported to the department.

Early in the spring of 1838 Professor Morse went to Europe with his Telegraph for the purpose of procuring patents, and to explain its operation to the scientific world. Our consul in Paris at that date was Robert Walsh, Esq., well known as a distinguished scholar and writer. He was the correspondent for many years of the New-York *Journal of Commerce*. In the summer of 1858 the *Journal of Commerce* quoted Professor Morse's letter of August 10, 1843, to the Secretary of the Treasury, in which this passage occurs: "The practical inference from this law is that a telegraphic communication on the electro-magnetic plan may with certainty be established across the Atlantic Ocean! Startling as this may now seem, I am confident the time will come when this project will be realized." When this number of the *Journal* reached Paris, Mr. Walsh, in his correspondence to the *Journal* (1858), alluding to the letter of Professor Morse, says: "His letter to Mr. Spencer (Secretary of the Treasury), dated in August, 1843, which I read in your *Journal*, is most remarkable and opportunely produced. Many years ago, in 1838, when the Professor endeavored to cause his invention and practice to be understood by the French dignitaries, I held frequent converse with him, and I can distinctly recollect that he expressed to me that firm persuasion of the practicability and ultimate execution of an Atlantic Telegraph which is so confidently stated in the penultimate paragraph of his letter." The conversations thus alluded to and *distinctly recollected* by Mr. Walsh, and the predictions of a future Atlantic Telegraph, were undoubtedly based upon the success of the experiments proposed and tried by Professor Morse in 1837, just before he left for Europe. In an article in the *Telegrapher* of August 12, 1871, the attempt is made on the authority of Mr. N. J. Holmes to show that the first suggestion of "conveying messages under the sea" was due to Sir C. Wheatstone, in 1840, who, it is for the first time alleged, made an experiment at that date in Swansea Bay, and the article thus concludes: "From the results of that trial has proceeded the great submarine telegraph system, now extending over so large a portion of the globe." Even if this experiment was made at that time and in that manner by

Sir C. Wheatstone, it was at least two or three years subsequent to the successful experiments for that same purpose by Professor Morse. But in 1840, the year in which this experiment of Professor Wheatstone is said to have been made, a select committee of the House of Commons was raised on railways, of which Lord Seymour was chairman, and Sir John Guest a member. Professor Wheatstone was called before this committee to answer some questions respecting telegraphs. Question 340 was proposed by Sir John Guest:

"Have you tried to pass the line through water?" To which Professor Wheatstone made this reply:

"*There would be no difficulty in doing so*, but THE EXPERIMENT HAS NOT YET BEEN TRIED."

Question 341, by Lord Seymour: "Could you communicate from Dover to Calais, in that way?"

The answer of Professor Wheatstone was, "I think it perfectly practicable."

These two questions and the answers were all that were proposed before that committee, relative to submarine telegraphy. Alluding to this examination before the committee, an article in an English scientific journal of 1865 commences with this remark:

"Twenty-four years have elapsed since Professor Wheatstone suggested, to the select committee of the House of Commons on railways, the construction of a submarine telegraph between Dover and Calais." Now, if the question of Sir John Guest was the suggestion, because he alluded to "*the line through water*," it was Sir John Guest, and not Professor Wheatstone, who suggested it. If it was the question whether communication could be made between Dover and Calais, it was the suggestion of Lord Seymour, and not of Professor Wheatstone. There is no published account of any submarine telegraph experiments until the year 1842. Professor Morse said in a public address: "In October, 1842, the first submarine telegraph cable was laid by me on one moonlight night in the harbor of this city, which proved experimentally the practicability of submarine telegraphy."

For this experiment Professor Morse received the Gold Medal of the American Institute, and the result was published in the journals of the day. A submarine telegraph, with an instrument and battery at Castle Garden, and an instrument in the fort at Governor's Island, was successfully operated. This was the commencement of Submarine Telegraphy. The first practical demonstration of a submarine telegraph belongs to Professor Morse.

In the year 1852 the Legislature of Newfoundland incorporated a company under the title of the "Newfoundland Electric Telegraph Company," its object being to connect the island with the American Continent. The company failed to accomplish its purpose, and never proposed to cross the ocean with its lines. In the month of January, 1854, Mr. F. N. Gisborne, one of the officers of that company, came to the city of New York, and meeting Mr. Matthew D. Field, a civil-engineer, sought to interest him in an effort to revive the fortunes of the Newfoundland company. Mr. Field spoke of the subject to his brother, CYRUS W. FIELD, who invited Mr. Gisborne to his house to consider the subject. An evening was spent in its discussion. After Mr. Gisborne had left the house, Mr. Field took a terrestrial globe, and, while studying it with reference to the connection of Newfoundland with New York, he said to himself, "Why not cross the ocean, and connect the New World with the Old?" Professor Morse had long ago declared it practicable, and predicted its accomplishment. The idea took possession of the mind of Mr. Field, as the original conception of the Telegraph had absorbed the mind of Professor Morse in 1832. Mr. Field immediately applied to Professor Morse for his opinion as to the feasibility of the scheme. The Professor, being in Washington at the time, replied that he had "perfect faith in the feasibility of the enterprise;" and that he had consulted with Lieutenant Maury, of the United States Navy, on the subject, and obtained from him a letter which he would show to Mr. Field when he returned to New York. The letter, which was addressed to the Secretary of the Navy, described the beautiful plateau which deep sea-soundings had disclosed, extending from Newfoundland to Ireland, on which could be laid a cable, to rest as quietly as at the bottom of a mill-pond. This was conclusive. Hon. David Dudley Field embarked with his brother, Cyrus W. Field, with great enthusiasm in the project, and became the legal ad-

viser of the company formed to prosecute the work. He and
his brother, Cyrus W., Peter Cooper, Moses Taylor, M. O. Roberts, and Chandler White, met, and around a table covered with
maps, plans, and estimates, the subject was discussed for four
successive evenings—the practicability of the undertaking examined, its advantages, its cost, and the means of its accomplishment. The result of the conference was the agreement of all
the six gentlemen to enter upon the undertaking. Mr. Cyrus W.,
and David D. Field, and Mr. White, went to Newfoundland to
procure a charter and such aid in money and privileges as the
government of that island could be induced to give.

At St. John's they met Mr. Edward M. Archibald, then
Attorney-General of the colony. He entered warmly into the
subject, introduced them to the Governor, Kerr Bailey Hamilton,
who convoked the Council to hear an explanation of their views
and wishes. As the result of these negotiations a liberal charter
was secured from the Assembly. To the six gentlemen already
named as corporators were now added Professor Morse, Mr. Robert W. Lowber, Mr. Wilson G. Hunt, and Mr. John W. Brett.
Immediately, Mr. Cyrus W. Field went to England, and pro-
.cured specimens of cable, and engaged men of capital and influence in the enterprise. Mr. Brett, Mr. Whitehouse, and Mr.
Bright, gentlemen of high scientific attainments, were enlisted.
The Atlantic Telegraph Company was formed to coöperate with
the company already organized in America. Mr. Field obtained
from the British Government the promise of ships to aid in laying the cable, and a fixed yearly sum for the service of the Ocean
Telegraph. On his return to the United States, he succeeded in
obtaining from Congress similar pledges of assistance, though
by a majority of *one* only in the Senate. The two companies
were now acting in harmony. Morse was appointed ELECTRICIAN
of the company on this side. Faraday held the same responsible
office on the other. They compared views by frequent correspondence. Morse, in writing to Faraday, Sept. 30, 1854, says :

"Taking for granted a successful result of the experiment on
the propulsion of a current to the required distance, that is to say,
from Newfoundland to Ireland, I have proposed that the cable conductor be constructed in the following manner, to wit :

"The conducting wires of the circuit I propose to be of the

purest copper, each not less than one-eighth ($\frac{1}{8}$) of an inch in sectional diameter. Each wire to be insulated to the thickness also of one-eighth of an inch with gutta-percha. If it should be decided by the company that in the first instance a *single conductor* shall be laid down, then a thin tube of lead, about one-sixteenth ($\frac{1}{16}$) of an inch in thickness, is drawn over the wire conductor and its gutta-percha covering, and then a series of strands of common iron wire and of hempen cord, or rope yarn of the same size, say four or five of the former and the rest of the latter, are to be laid parallel with the interior conducting wire, on the exterior of the tube (Fig. 6), and these are to be confined in place by two spiral cords wound in contrary directions and crossing each other around the cable at intervals, say of nine or twelve inches.

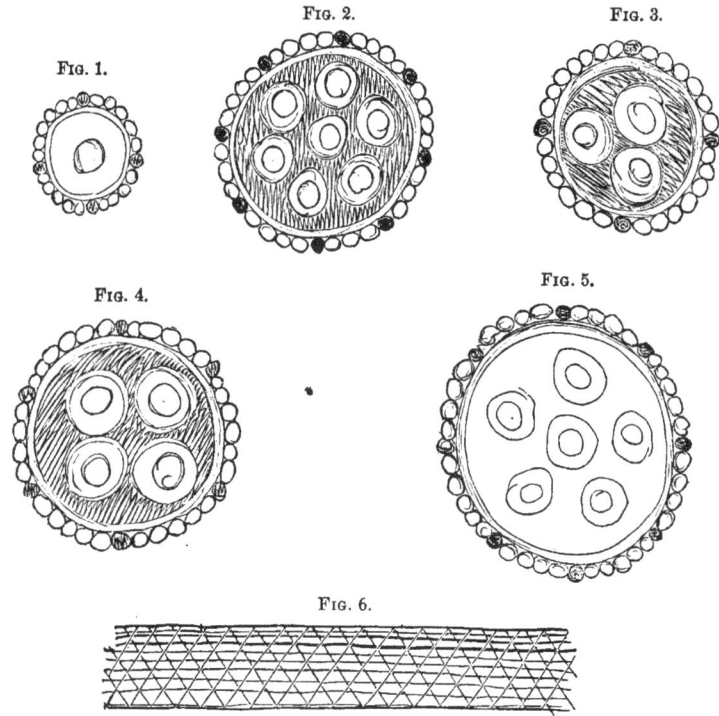

Fig. 1. Fig. 2. Fig. 3. Fig. 4. Fig. 5. Fig. 6.

"If it is thought best to lay down, in the first instance, more than one conductor in the same package, or fascis, then the number chosen may be three, as in Fig. 3, or seven, as in Fig. 2; these being the numbers most economically packed in a tube to form the fascis of conductors. Six wires, as in Fig. 5, and four wires, as in Fig. 4, do not pa. k ·   t   micall · "

Professor Steinheil, of Munich, whose Telegraph approached that of Professor Morse more nearly than any other, and who had so magnanimously insisted upon the superiority of the Morse instrument in the German Telegraph Convention of 1852, communicated to Colonel Shaffner in this summer of 1854 a letter giving a minute account of the progress of the Telegraph on the Continent of Europe, through his instrumentality, and closing with the following declaration: "*In this way I have been able effectually to labor for the adoption of the Morse system throughout all Europe ; and that I have thereby extended his well-earned fame has been to me the source of peculiar pleasure, which I beg you to testify to Professor Morse in proper time, together with my most friendly respects.*"

This declaration is certainly sufficient to silence forever the oft-repeated assertion that Morse's system is the same as Steinheil's. But a letter from Dr. Steinheil, subsequently received by Morse himself, is still more explicit.[1]

Hon. D. D. Barnard, who had been the Minister of the United States at the court of Prussia, wrote to Professor Morse communicating information which greatly cheered him :

" I have been an indignant observer, from the beginning of the outrageous piracies to which you have been subjected at the hands of your countrymen, and of the infamous course of the public press of this country toward you, in reference to your wonderful invention of the Telegraph. It was, therefore, with peculiar satisfaction that, during my residence abroad, I was accustomed to hear your name pronounced with emphasis and honor everywhere on the Continent where I chanced to be, and in whatever circle, whenever the subject of the Electric Telegraph was named. I became entirely satisfied that the general sentiment of the European world did not fail or hesitate to award to you the chief merit of this grand invention, and that your name was as sure of unrivaled immortality in connection with it, as that of Galileo or Newton with astronomy, or that of Bacon with philosophy. I spoke to you briefly of this when I had the pleasure of meeting you, but I have wished to express to you the same thing in a more substantial form.

" In Germany, after the most mature and elaborate investigation by the aid of the profoundest learning and wisdom of the age, your

[1] *See* page 687.

Telegraph was adopted in a general convention of all the states assembled expressly to consider that subject. And I can give you the assurance, without attempting to detail particular conversations, that had you visited Berlin while I was there, and when I had hoped to have seen you, you would have met from such a man as the illustrious Humboldt, and from the King of Prussia himself, such a distinguished and honored reception as would only be accorded from such quarters to the few who have made themselves eminent and immortal by such rare benefactions of their genius to the world as have satisfactorily passed the ordeal of trial and time.

"Regretting the necessity I am under of writing thus briefly, and wishing you all honor and prosperity, I am, my dear sir, most truly yours, D. D. BARNARD."

Professor Morse to Mr. Barnard.

"POUGHKEEPSIE, *July* 26, 1854.

"MY DEAR SIR: I return you my hearty thanks for your most acceptable letter. I had supposed that mine, to which it was in reply, had by some means miscarried. Any evil merely of delay, however, has now been more than overbalanced. I regret only the cause of the delay, and this most sincerely, and I trust your valuable life and health may long be preserved to the country and to your family. ·Your letter is to me, indeed, most gratifying as a most valuable addition to the substantial and munificent proof of regard already in my possession from his Majesty the King of Prussia. To have such an attestation of priority of invention of the Telegraph from so distinguished a quarter, and supported by the opinion of that excellent and world-renowned *savant*, the Baron Humboldt, is indeed cheering, yet in some respects a mortifying contrast with the denial of this claim by some of my own countrymen who stand high in attainments in science. But the courts of my country, especially our noble Supreme Court, have at length fully sustained the foreign verdict, but alas! I fear their decision will be of little personal benefit, except as it may favorably affect my family after I am gone.

"I feel the loss of time, and the habits of mind generated by long-continued litigation more than all else, as unfitting me for consummating other projects of usefulness, and when I consider that my age must ere long, in the natural course of things, disqualify me from undertaking them with any prospect of success, I feel a sadness I cannot express."

Professor Morse to Mr. Kendall.

" A most important arrangement has been entered into between the American and English, or rather *Continental* Submarine Telegraph Companies. Our New York, Newfoundland, and London Telegraph Company has been united with the Continental or Great Telegraph Union of Europe. A deputation or rather agent was sent over to concert a plan of union. Mr. C. D. Archibald, F. R. S., and secretary of the British company, met us at Mr. Field's. I was present at the meetings, and after much consultation a plan of union was adopted. They have the control of all the lines of Great Britain, France, and the Continent generally, and are the company carrying out the Mediterranean and Asiatic lines.

" Mr. Archibald gave me the first information that the British lines were about to discard all other systems but mine, and that the scientific mind of Britain was disposed at length to do us the justice to acknowledge that we were far ahead of all the world in telegraphy. A letter also just received from him commences thus: ' I feel bound to express my acknowledgments of your kindness in initiating me into the mysteries of electric telegraphy, of which I regard you as the great high-priest.' I had shown him the operation of the Telegraph in our various offices, and he was enthusiastic in his admiration of the simplicity of my system, and was strong in his expressions of its superiority over their systems, which he as strongly condemned. Mr. A. is an intimate and personal friend of Faraday, who proposed him as a member of the Royal Society, and who by-the-by is the electrician of the British company."

Professor Morse to Mr. Fleischmann.

" *September* 21, 1854.

" Many thanks for your letter of the 25th August, which came safely to hand, and for the most gratifying intelligence which it gives me of the near prospect of the universality of my Telegraph system. I am now engaged in the great enterprise of the *Oceanic Telegraph*, and in investigating and, overcoming the difficulties of such a work. The two companies, European and American, have united on satisfactory terms, and, as great capital is embarked to carry it through, I do not despair of witnessing myself, as *un fait accompli*, my prediction to the Secretary of the Treasury, in my letter to him of August 10, 1843, fulfilled, that, ' startling as it may *now* seem (a telegraph *across the Atlantic*), the project will eventually be realized.' "

In the autumn of this year Professor Morse was nominated for Congress by a portion of the Democratic party, and the result he expresses, very concisely but correctly, in a letter written to a friend abroad : "I came near being in Congress at the late election, but had not quite votes enough, which is the usual cause of failure on such occasions."

His mind was constantly absorbed in experiments and correspondence, meeting new difficulties, encouraging doubtful capitalists, and combating adverse suggestions by men of science. The winter of 1854–'55 was passed in New York, in the midst of intense labors, such as few' young students would endure. In the spring he wrote to his friend T. R. Walker, Esq., of Utica :

"Our *Atlantic line* is in a fair way. We have the governments and capitalists of Europe zealously and warmly engaged to carry it through. *Three years* will not pass before a *submarine telegraph communication will be had with Europe;* and I do not despair of sitting in my office, and, by a touch of the telegraph-key, asking a question simultaneously to persons in London, Paris, Cairo, Calcutta, and Canton, and getting the answer from all of them in *five minutes* after the question is asked. Does this seem strange ? I presume, if I had even suggested the thought some twenty years ago, I might have had a quiet residence in a big building in your vicinity."

The "big building" is the Lunatic Asylum. To Mr. Field he wrote:

"I am happy to learn the progress of the Telegraph, and hope, in 1858, to accomplish what I have so often predicted I should do in three years from this, to wit: ask a question from my office, in my house in Poughkeepsie, to London, Paris, Vienna, Constantinople, and Calcutta, if not to Canton, and get my answer back in five minutes."

And in July Professor Morse wrote to N. Green, Esq., in New Orleans:

"I am about to leave home for some weeks to sail for Newfoundland, to assist in laying down the submarine-cable, to connect Newfoundland and Nova Scotia across the Gulf of St. Lawrence, a

distance of about sixty miles.   When this is laid, we shall bring
Europe within six days of America; and this is preparatory to the
great enterprise across the Atlantic, which I confidently anticipate
seeing in operation within two years from the present time. Should
this enterprise succeed, as I have no doubt it will, a great impulse
will be given to telegraph business throughout all the country; indeed, I may say, throughout the world. The effects of the Telegraph
on the interests of the world, political, social, and commercial, have
as yet scarcely begun to be apprehended, even by the most speculative minds.   I trust that one of its effects will be to bind man to
his fellow-man in such bonds of amity as to put an end to war; I
think I can predict this effect as in a not distant future."

On the 7th day of August, 1855, Professor Morse, with his
wife and one of his sons, embarked on the steamer James
Adger, with a large number of friends, for Newfoundland.
The party was one of business and pleasure combined.   The
company was represented by Messrs. Peter Cooper, Cyrus W.
Field, David Dudley Field, Robert W. Lowber, and Professor
Morse; and the invited guests included Rev. Drs. Spring and
H. M. Field, Rev. J. M. Sherwood, and others.   Professor Morse
was in high spirits.   He had a telegraphic instrument on board,
which he illustrated to the company.   The voyage was delightful.   The steamer touched at Halifax, and then went on to
Port au Basque, near Cape Ray, where the Sarah L. Bryant
was expected from England with the cable, to be laid across
the Gulf of St. Lawrence.   She had not arrived; and the party
proceeded to St. John's, where they were entertained with great
hospitality.   In return, a banquet was given on board the
James Adger to the principal inhabitants of the town.   The
Morning Post of August 18th, gave an animated sketch of the
occasion, and records the toast that called out the inventor of
the Electric Telegraph—

> " The steed, called Lightning (say the Fates),
> Was tamed in the United States;
> 'Twas Franklin's hand that caught the horse,   ·
> 'Twas harnessed by Professor Morse."

Returning from St. John's to Port au Basque, the expected
ship was found, with the cable on board.   The work of laying

it was begun August 23, 1855, and prosecuted four days, when, in the midst of a terrific storm, it was necessary to sever the cable and abandon the attempt. The James Adger arrived at New York, September 5th, on her return from this first and unsuccessful expedition. The next summer a second and quiet attempt was crowned with success.

40

CHAPTER XVII.

1856.

PROFESSOR MORSE VISITS HIS NATIVE PLACE—GOES TO EUROPE—CONSULTA-
TIONS IN LONDON ON THE ATLANTIC TELEGRAPH—MR. PEABODY'S DINNER
—LANDSEER AND LESLIE—WHITEBAIT DINNER—LETTER TO THE CHILDREN
—GOES TO PARIS AND HAMBURG—ATTENTIONS SHOWN TO HIM THERE—
COPENHAGEN—VISIT TO THE KING OF DENMARK—GOES TO RUSSIA—RE-
CEPTION—PRESENTATION TO THE EMPEROR—VISIT TO BERLIN—RECEP-
TION BY HUMBOLDT—RETURN TO LONDON—SCIENTIFIC EXPERIMENTS—
LETTERS TO MR. FIELD—BANQUET TO MORSE—LEGION OF HONOR—TUP-
PER'S SONNET—LONDON TIMES—ROBERT OWEN.

BEING in Boston on business in the spring of 1856, Professor
Morse employed a leisure afternoon in visiting the house in
which he was born. In a letter written at the Revere House
the same evening, he describes the interesting incidents of the
visit:

"BOSTON, *Wednesday, May* 13, 1856.

"After dinner, to-day, I walked over to Charlestown, not having visited the place for some eighteen years, and then but for a
few hours, after an absence of many years. The changes in the
north part of Boston, and in Charlestown, were so great, that I
found my way across the old Charles River bridge with some difficulty, and, standing on the bridge and looking on each side, could
scarcely recognize any of the former landmarks. I paid my penny-
toll to the toll-taker, and said to him: 'I find some alterations here
since I used to pay my tolls to old Deacon Miller, at the toll-house
on the opposite side of this bridge.' 'Ah!' said he; 'that was a
great while ago; the old deacon has been dead many years; my
grandfather was deacon with him in the same church.' 'In what
church?' said I. 'In Dr. Morse's church,' said he, 'where I used

to go when I was a boy.' 'Indeed,' said I; 'and who was your grandfather?' 'Deacon Frothingham,' said he. 'Are you a grandson of old Deacon Frothingham? I knew the good old man well; he was one of my father's firmest friends' 'And who was your father, then, sir?' said he. 'Dr. Morse,' I replied. 'Are you a son of Dr. Morse?' said he; 'which one? He had a son a painter; and my brother also is a painter.' 'I am the painter,' I said; 'and your brother, then, is James Frothingham?' 'Yes.' 'Where is he? Is he living?' 'Yes; he lives in Brooklyn, New York.' 'Indeed! and can you tell me where the portrait is which he took of my father?—for I think it was one of the best ever taken of him; and I am very anxious to know where I can find it.' 'No,' said he; 'I cannot tell you where it is.' After shaking hands with him, I passed on into the square of Charlestown. I stopped and looked round. A pump used to stand in the centre. It was no longer there. The eastern part of the square was entirely changed. The north showed the Salem turnpike, passing between a new building, the Bunker Hill Bank, and an old building, which seemed unchanged amid the changes that surrounded it, the old store of Skinner & Hurd, the same in all respects as of old, except a new firm upon the sign over the door. Directly opposite, on the south of the square, more changes struck me; a new bridge-way occupied the space where the house of Richard Carey, and old Aunt Dowse, as she was familiarly called, formerly stood, leaving a venerable reminiscence of the ancient aristocracy of Charlestown on the right, in the old mansion of the Russell family; it is now a tavern, the words 'Innholder,' in small letters, are over the door. What a change was here! In that house I had seen the venerable Judge Russell, and his two maiden daughters, Sally and Mary Russell. I recalled the days when, with my parents, I used to visit at that house, and the pleasure, when a child, with which I heard my mother say, 'If you are good, you shall go and see Aunt Russell this afternoon;' for Aunt Sally and Aunt Mary were sure to fill our pockets with cakes and apples. So vividly did the sight of this old mansion bring up the faces of the good old people, that I think now I could paint each of their portraits from recollection: the large features of the old judge, with his bushy eyebrows, his prominent under lip, and his bending form; Aunt Mary, with her wide face, pale, and somewhat sad; and Aunt Sally, with a sharper physiognomy, and expression of more vivacity, and quicker and more bustling in her movement; their dress models of neatness and pro-

priety, and their demeanor kind and courteous, yet sufficiently reserved to restrain any disposition on our part to childish excess.

"Separated from the old mansion by a passage to a wharf, still
stands in all its gloomy, unattractive shabbiness, an old house,
which I well remember possessed, from my earliest recollection of
it, the same repulsive characteristics which it now has. For fifty
years it seems never to have had a coat of paint, nor any attempt
at change.

"I passed up the hill where, formerly on the right, was the garden of my father's house. All trace of this garden and the house
is gone; the site of both is covered by a row of brick houses; all on
that side was new. On the left, however, still stands, apparently
unchanged, the garden and house of Matthew Bridge, our opposite
neighbor—unchanged I mean in their general characteristics, but
bearing marks of decay and neglect. The house toward the west
has also the same general features as it had forty years ago, but
now decayed and dilapidated, the fence down, and every thing
about it slovenly.

"The church where my father preached has long since been removed, and on its site the present neat, substantial, and commodious house of worship erected. I had not time to give it more
than a passing glance. I went on, desirous of finding the house in
which I was born, for my parents occupied a different house from
the parsonage, when they first came to Charlestown, and during the
time the parsonage was being built. I proceeded down the hill
toward the main street, leaving on the right the house in which our
family physician, Dr. Josiah Bartlett, once lived, and, on the left,
the site where once stood the little shanty of a school-house, kept by
old Ma'am Rand, which was standing not many years ago, and when
my first attempts at drawing, from the injudicious choice I had
made of my pencil and canvas, which were a pin and a bureau,
were rewarded by a smart rap on the shoulders by her long rattan.

"Passing into the main street, I soon found, after proceeding beyond the church on the right, the substantial, though wooden, house
of two stories, which I had been told in earlier days was the house
in which I was born. It is now painted brown, but formerly was
white. I stood for a short time on the opposite side of the street,
reconnoitring it, to be assured that it was the house. I then
crossed over, and, finding on the door-plate 'R. B. Edes,' I was confirmed in my assurance, and rang the bell. It was opened by a
lady, to whom I apologized for the liberty I had taken, stating that

I knew she would excuse me when she learned my errand, which was to visit a room in which I first saw the light, and in which I had not been for more than sixty years. She at once exclaimed, 'Surely this is not Mr. Morse!' 'Yes, madam, you have spoken my name.' 'Walk in, walk in,' she exclaimed, 'I am rejoiced to see you. I well remember your good father and mother, and have often heard that you were born in this house.' So I walked into a neatly-furnished parlor, and found that the lady was Mrs. Edes, the wife of Captain Robert Edes, whom we all well knew in our younger days. He was not at home, but two of their daughters, with each a sweet child, were soon called and introduced to me. I soon found that I was among friends, and, while talking with them, one suddenly ran to the window, exclaiming, 'There is Mr. Hooper; I wonder if he is coming here?' She had scarcely spoken, before he turned to the door and came in. The moment he recognized me he manifested the greatest pleasure, and was full of inquiries after all the family. I told him my errand in coming to this house. 'Oh!' said he, 'I can tell you all about it, for I was here when you were born, and used to take you out-of-doors to take the air, before your mother was well of her confinement.' 'In which room, then, was I born?' said I, 'for I had the impression it was the east front chamber.' 'No,' said he, 'it was the east rear chamber, and it is unchanged, except new papering and painting. I have good reason to remember the time of your birth: your father wished a boy to go to the post-office in Boston daily for him, and also to carry the proofs and copy to the printers. I was then about nine years old,' said he, 'and your father employed me for those purposes, and I lived in the family. Nancy Shepherd was the nurse, and was always active in the kitchen. One day she was roasting peas to free them from the weevil, preparatory to burning them for coffee, for,' said he, 'real coffee at that time was very scarce. I was sitting by the fire, when one of these little bugs flew into my ear, and it caused me so great pain that I feared for my life. I ran across the street to a doctor who poured some spirits of wine into my ear, which soon drove the weevil out.' After a few anecdotes of this kind I went up-stairs to see the room. I was first shown into the east front room, overlooking the street, which I had supposed was the room. Then into the east rear room, which communicated with the other by a small entry. There was nothing peculiar in the room; the ceiling is low, the walls substantial, as is the whole house, in striking contrast with modern buildings.

"I then visited Mr. Hooper's residence, where I found that Mr. Henry C. Pratt (my former pupil in painting) and his family were boarding. While there, Mrs. Benjamin Brown came in, one of father's old friends; she was greatly rejoiced to see me, and insisted that I must call with her upon Mrs. Hovey, the widow of Abijah Hovey, and one of the strongest friends of father and mother in their last days in Charlestown. I observed that I could not think of coming to Charlestown without calling upon her; so Mrs. Brown piloted me to Mrs. Hovey's, saying, as we knocked at the door, ' Do not mention your name ; see if she will know you.' When I went into the parlor, and while waiting for the appearance of Mrs. Hovey, I cast my eyes upon the picture of my father, by Frothingham, the identical portrait about which I had inquired of the toll-keeper of the bridge, the brother of the painter ; and, on the opposite side of the room, is my earliest picture of a group, being our own family, my father, mother, my brother Sidney, Richard, and myself, in water-colors; this picture had been the subject of inquiry by myself and brothers just previous to my coming to Boston ; we were speculating where it could be. I remembered giving it to Nancy Shepherd, and it seems that Nancy just previously to her death gave it to Mrs. Hovey. My father's likeness, but especially my mother's, were good likenesses still; Richard's was tolerable, but Sidney's and my own did not strike me agreeably. My father's figure is without legs, the picture having been abruptly left before completing it. On the whole, I had a most agreeable, and to me exceedingly exciting, visit, which I shall remember to the end of my life."

On the 5th of June, 1856, Professor Morse sailed for Liverpool in the steamship Baltic, Captain Comstock. Among the passengers were William H. Appleton, Esq., of New York, Dr. Hull, and Colonel Cobb. The Professor was accompanied by his wife and his niece, Miss Louisa Morse, daughter of his brother Richard. On board the ship, at the request of the passengers, Professor Morse gave a discourse in the cabin on the history of the Telegraph, the circumstances of its invention at sea, and its progress thus far in the several countries. His time in London was largely occupied with the gentlemen who were then engaged in the construction of the cable for the Atlantic, Messrs. Glass, Bright, Whitehouse, Statham, and others. On the 4th of July he was one of the guests of George Peabody, Esq., at dinner, at the Star and Garter Tavern, Richmond Hill. When the toast, " The Telegraph," was suddenly proposed, he was unexpectedly called upon to respond, and, being unable to make a speech, he rose, and with modesty and dignity recited these words from the 19th Psalm : " Their line is gone out through all the earth, and their words to the end of the world."

Landseer was a boy when Morse was a student with West in London, and Morse knew him at that time. The great artist now sought him and paid him deserved honors as the President of the National Academy of Design in the United States. He gathered the artists of London and men of science and letters at his own house, and presented to them his distinguished friend Professor Morse. C. R. Leslie, his fellow-student and roommate in early youth, when they were both taking lessons of West, was now in the country at the seat of the Earl of Egremont. It was a few miles by stage-coach, and an invitation from his old companion was readily accepted. The reunion was like that of boys meeting after a few years only of separation. They wandered arm-in-arm over the grounds, and through the halls, recalling the thousand pleasant memories of youth, and repeating to one another the incidents that had marked the intervening years. A white-bait dinner at Greenwich, given to Morse by the Telegraph managers, brought together several gentlemen who had been actively engaged in the extension of the system abroad, and, in a private letter to his children at home, Professor Morse gives natural expression to his gratification in the testimonies of these practical men to the great success of his invention.

From London he journeyed toward the north of Europe, spending a few days only in Paris, and at Hamburg. In neither of these cities did he find at this season of the year the men whom he would have been most pleased to meet; but, with a definite purpose before him, he pursued his journey to Copenhagen. His niece, Miss Morse, in one of her letters, says:

" We reached Copenhagen after two night's tossing in the most wretched dog-kennel of a boat, and when we arrived at the gloomy hotel on a damp, drizzling day, and looked out of our parlor-window upon the long canal-wharf, and the prison-like palace on the other side, we were a most homesick, as we had been a seasick, party.

But after this forbidding introduction, Copenhagen proved to be one of the pleasantest, if not the pleasantest place, of our journey thus far. We were immediately surrounded by warm friends, who made us feel at once as if we were at home. Every day and hour was filled up with entertainments, which these hospitable friends were delighted to give to uncle and his party. Commodore Michelsen and Mr. Froliche were devoted in their attentions. All spoke the English language so naturally that we could not believe ourselves in a strange country."

Professor Morse's own letters, in the familiar and confidential words of a father to his children, give a pleasant account of his presentation to the king:

" Captain Raastoff and I arrived at Fredericksborg at 11.30, near midnight. The aide and chamberlain of the king had already retired for the night, but, leaving our letters to be delivered to the aide in the morning, we retired to rest.

" In the morning, while at breakfast, we received a message from the king to see him in his audience-chamber in half an hour; so, dressing for the occasion, the captain wearing his orders as Knight of the Dannebrog, and I my Turkish Nishan (by advice), we proceeded to the palace in the Castle of Fredericksborg, where we were received in the anteroom by the king's aide. The aide told us that the king had been apprised of my visit to Copenhagen, and was expecting to see me the day before, which would have been the case had we not been misdirected to Jæger's Priis instead of Fredericksborg. After a few minutes the captain was called into the presence of the king, and in a few minutes more I was requested to go into the audience-chamber, and was introduced by the captain to Ferdinand VII., King of Denmark. The king received me standing, and very courteously. He is a man of middle stature, thick-set, and resembles more in the features of his face the busts and pictures of Christian IV. than those of any of his predecessors, judging as I did from the numerous busts and portraits of the Kings of Denmark which adorn the city palace and the Castle of Fredericksborg.

" The king expressed his pleasure at seeing the inventor of the Telegraph, and regretted he could not speak English, as he wished to ask me many questions. He thanked me, he said, for the beautiful instrument I had sent him; told me that a telegraph-line was now in progress from the castle to his royal residence in Copenhagen;

that when it was completed, he had decided on using my instrument, which I had given him, in his own private apartments. He then spoke of the invention as a most wonderful achievement, and wished me to inform him how I came to invent it. I accordingly in a few words gave him the early history of it, to which he listened most attentively, and thanked me, expressing himself highly gratified. He asked me what I thought of the practicability of the Transatlantic Telegraph. I told him it was an enterprise sure to be accomplished. After a few minutes more of conversation of the same character, the king shook me warmly by the hand, and we took our leave. After the king and his *cortége* had left the castle, the governor of the castle, who speaks English, as if it were his native language, politely accompanied us through the rooms of the palace, and the gorgeous old church attached to it. It is impossible to give in description any idea of its richness. The altar has all the splendor of many of the most ornate old Roman Catholic churches, and it was difficult to believe it to be a Lutheran church.

" We returned to Fredericksborg, which we left after passing through the royal apartments, and arrived in the afternoon at Copenhagen. Mrs. F—— called in her carriage. We drove to the Thorwaldsen Museum or Depository, where are all the works of this great man. This collection of the greatest sculptor since the best period of Greek art is attraction enough in itself to call travelers of taste to Copenhagen. After spending some hours in Thorwaldsen's Museum, I went to see the study of Oersted, where his most important discovery of the *deflection of the needle* by a galvanic current was made, which laid the foundation of the science of electro-magnetism, and without which my invention could not have been made. It is now a drawing-school. I sat at the table where he made his discovery. We went to the Porcelain Manufactory, and singularly enough met there the daughter of Oersted, to whom I had the pleasure of an introduction. Oersted was a most amiable man, and universally beloved. The daughter is said to resemble her father in her features, and I traced a resemblance to him in the small porcelain bust, which I came to the manufactory to purchase. Mr. B—— kindly gave me a medallion struck in honor of Oersted's discovery.

"I feel under great obligations to all these good people. We left Copenhagen and its hospitable people with reluctance. But our time was limited, and so on the 24th of July (dear Arthur's birthday) we embarked on a neat little steamer that had arrived at Copenhagen on its way to St. Petersburg from Hull in England.

Her name is *Falcon*, and her commander has an appropriate name as her captain, Captain *Fowler;* we find him a worthy and obliging man. Such a passage I never before made up to this date (July 27th, noon); for three days and three nights the weather has been perfectly clear and calm, the sea smooth; not once has the vessel been off an even keel; we have had a whole .cabin to ourselves, good food, and but three other passengers in the other cabin, a gentleman and two ladies, Scotch, quiet and agreeable. Last night Louisa and I sat up till after midnight to witness a night without darkness. Though somewhat late in the season to see the night of these northern latitudes in the longest days to the greatest advantage, yet we witnessed such a one as we never before saw. The sun dipped below the horizon in the northwest at half-past eight o'clock, but the twilight continued so bright, gradually passing to the north and northeast, that at midnight we could read large printed letters without difficulty. To vary the scene, the moon, in its last quarter, arose in the northeast on the eastern edge of the twilight, a very unusual place (as you will perceive on reflection) to see an *evening moon*. A few clouds of the stratus character, low down, lent an additional lustre to the red and apple-colored twilight by their contrasted darkness. All else was clear and calm. We staid on deck till the *evening* twilight became the *morning* twilight; and, when it had so far brightened that we could see to read print of a less size, we retired to rest, and found ourselves, on waking this beautiful calm Sunday morning, rapidly closing our pleasant passage, three o'clock P. M. finding us within sight of the formidable and extensive fortress of Cronstadt.

"St. PETERSBURG, *August* 8, 1856.

" My letter was abruptly interrupted by the bustle and confusion of our arrival in a strange and unimagined country, and studying its novel forms and customs. Americans are particularly struck with the strictness of the custom-house and police regulations, although as it regards the former we had less trouble and were treated with more politeness and less inconvenience than we have been in most other countries. We were detained at Cronstadt about two hours, passing the ordeal of the police, and, leaving our steamer, with our luggage, embarked on board another steamer for St. Petersburg, seventeen miles distant. We passed up the Neva about eight o'clock and landed amid hundreds of people at the custom-house landing, when our luggage went through a very slight examination, the fact that we were Americans finding us favor with all, with officers and people. We took two or three droskies and drove to a house kept by an Englishwoman of the name of Benson, but which we found full, so that we were compelled to take to our droskies again and drive to the Hôtel de Russie, where we are well lodged, and shall remain during our stay here; we were tired enough when we entered our rooms, and glad to go to our beds.

"Up to this date we have been in one constant round of visits to the truly wonderful objects of curiosity in this magnificent city. I have seen, as you know, most of the great and marvelous cities of Europe, but, I can truly say, none of them can at all compare in splendor and beauty to St. Petersburg. It is a city of palaces, and palaces of the most gorgeous character. The display of wealth in the palaces and churches is so great that the simple truth told about them would incur to the narrator the suspicion of romancing. England boasts of her regalia in the Tower, her crown jewels, her Kohinoor diamond, etc. I can assure you they fade into insignificance, as a rushlight before the sun, when brought before the wealth in jewels and gold seen here in such profusion. What think you of nosegays, as large as those our young ladies take to parties, composed entirely of diamonds, rubies, emeralds, sapphires, and other precious stones, chosen to represent accurately the colors of various flowers — the imperial crown, globular in shape, composed of diamonds, and containing in the centre of the Greek cross which surmounts it an unwrought ruby at least two inches in diameter? The sceptre has a diamond very nearly as large as the Kohinoor. At the Arsenal at Tsarskoe-selo we saw the trappings of a horse, bridle, saddle, and all the harness, with an immense saddle-cloth, set with tens of thousands of diamonds; on those parts of the harness where we have rosettes, or knobs, or buckles, were rosettes of diamonds an inch and a half to two inches in diameter, with a diamond in the centre as large as the first joint of your thumb, or say three-quarters of an inch in diameter. Other trappings were as rich. Indeed, there seemed to be no end to the diamonds. All the churches are decorated in the most costly manner with diamonds, and pearls, and precious stones."

Hon. Thomas H. Seymour was the United States Minister at St. Petersburg at this time, and Mr. J. Pierce, Jr., the secretary of legation. They received Mr. Morse and his party with the greatest cordiality, and extended to them every courtesy that would be accorded to the most distinguished Americans. Dinners, parties, and receptions, followed each other in rapid succession. In a letter to his children at home, Professor Morse gives a brilliant description of his presentation at court, and his account is the more entertaining because of those minute and delicate touches which a father writing to his children, and to them only, would give:

PROFESSOR MORSE TO HIS CHILDREN.

"PETERHOFF, SEVENTEEN MILES FROM ST. PETERSBURG (RUSSIA),
"*August* 14, 1856.

"MY DEAR DAUGHTER SUSAN, AND THE GROVITES GENERALLY: Yesterday I received notice from Prince Gortchakoff, Minister of Foreign Affairs, through our minister, Mr. Seymour, that his imperial Majesty the Emperor had appointed the hour of half-past one this day to see me at his palace at Peterhoff.

"On our arrival at the quay at Peterhoff, we found, somewhat to my surprise, the imperial carriages in waiting for us, each carriage with a coachman and two footmen in imperial livery, which is scarlet and gold lace, with towering *chapeaux bras*, edged with broad gold-lace. Our party occupied two of the carriages, which drove rapidly by all other carriages, and through people with their heads uncovered as we passed, which, to us republicans, was something new; and were set down at our quarters in one of the palace buildings in the extensive gardens specially appropriated to our party. Here we were attended by four or five servants in scarlet livery loaded with gold lace, and shown to our apartments, upon the doors of which were our names respectively. After throwing off our overcoats, the servants inquired if we would have breakfast—to which, of course, we had no objection; and an excellent one, of coffee and sandwiches, was soon upon the table, served up on silver, with the imperial arms upon the waiter, spoons, etc. Every thing about our rooms—which consisted of a parlor and bedrooms attached—was plain, but exceedingly clean and neat. After seeing us well housed, our attendant chamberlain left us to prepare ourselves for the presentation, saying he would call for us at the proper time. As there were two or three hours to spare, I took occasion to improve the time, to commence this brief notice of the events of the day.

"About two o'clock, our attendant, who gave his name as Thorner, an officer under the principal chamberlain, called to say our carriages were ready. On descending our staircase, through rows of liveried servants, we found three carriages in waiting, with the imperial livery, and splendid black horses, three servants to each carriage, as before, but in blue and gold-lace two inches at least broad, and the double-headed eagle emblazoned upon it at intervals of about four inches. We seated ourselves in the carriages, which were then driven at a rapid rate to the great and principal palace, the entrance to which is most picturesquely placed to overlook the numerous and magnificent fountains so celebrated at Peterhoff. Hundreds of well-dressed people thronged each side of the carriage-way, as we drove up to the door, where we were set down in turn. After alighting, we were ushered through a long hall by an officer richly dressed, and having upon his head a cap with black feathers, much like the Highlander's cap; we passed through two lines of liveried servants, that manned the sides of the hall and staircase, to the entrance of the anteroom—the last two of these officials being Africans of the darkest complexion, and dressed with Turkish turban, etc. We passed through the anteroom to a large and magnificent room, where were assembled those who were to be presented. The master of ceremonies led the way to the southern veranda, which overlooked the gardens, ranging us in a line, and reading our names from a list, to see if we were truly mustered, after which a door suddenly opened, and the Emperor Alexander II. entered. He was dressed in military costume, a blue sash was across his breast, passing over the right shoulder; on his left breast were stars and orders. He commenced at the head of the column, which consisted of some fourteen or fifteen persons, and on the pronouncing of the name by the master of ceremonies, he addressed a few words to each. When he came to me, the master of ceremonies mistook my name, calling me Mr. Moore; I instantly corrected him, and said, 'No, Morse.' The emperor at once said, kindly, 'Ah, that name is well known here; your system of telegraph is in use in Russia. How long have you been in St. Petersburg, and how have you enjoyed yourself?' To which I appropriately replied. After a few more unimportant questions and answers, the emperor addressed himself to the other gentlemen, and retired. After remaining a few moments, the master of ceremonies—who, by-the-by, apologized to me for miscalling my name—opened a door from the veranda into the large drawing-room of the empress, where we were again put in line to await the appearance of her imperial Majesty. The doors of an adjoining room were suddenly thrown open, and the empress, gorgeously but appropriately attired, advanced toward us. She addressed a few words gracefully.

to each of us in succession, approaching us as our names were called. The impression left upon my mind in regard to both the emperor and empress is that they are amiable and kind-hearted, with sufficient firmness in the emperor's temperament to prevent these gentle virtues from degenerating into weakness. After speaking to each of us in perfect English, she gracefully bowed (we, of course, returning the salutation) and retired, followed by her maids-of-honor, her long train sweeping the floor for a distance of several yards behind her. . . .

"On our return to our rooms, we dressed for dinner, and proceeded in the same manner to the palace in the gardens, called the English Palace. Here we found assembled, in the great reception-room, the distinguished company, in number forty-seven, of many nations, who were to sit down to table together. When dinner was announced, we entered the grand dining-hall, and found a table most gorgeously prepared with gold and silver service and flowers. At table, I found myself opposite three princes, an Austrian, a Hungarian, and one from some other German state; and second from me, on my left, was Lord Ward, of England, with whom I had a good deal of conversation. Opposite to me, and farther to my right, was Prince Esterhazy, seated between Lady Granville and the beautiful Lady Emily Peel; on the other side of Lady Peel was Lord Granville, the principal and special delegate from England to the coronation ceremonies at Moscow, and near him sat Sir Robert Peel. Among the guests, a list of which I regret I could not obtain, was the young Earl of Lincoln, and several other noblemen, in the suite of Lord Granville. Here, then, was a rare assemblage; English, French, Austrians, Sardinians, Italians, and Americans, gathered at table in a palace of the Emperor of Russia. Some twenty servants in the imperial scarlet livery waited upon the table, which was served in a truly royal profusion and costliness. The rarest dishes and the costliest wines, in every variety, were put before us. I need not say that, in such an assemblage, every thing was conducted with the highest decorum. No noise, no boisterous mirth, no loud laughing or talking, but a quiet cheerfulness and perfect ease characterized the whole entertainment. After the dinner, all arose, both ladies and gentlemen, and left the room together.

"We remained in the large hall for coffee, but, being fearful that we should be too late for the last steamer from Peterhoff to St. Petersburg, we were hurrying to get through and to leave, but the moment our fears came to the knowledge of Lord Granville, he most kindly came to us and told us to feel at ease, as his steam-yacht was lying off the quay to take them up to the city, and he was but too proud to have the opportunity of offering us a place on board—an offer which we of course accepted with thanks. Having thus been entertained with truly imperial hospitality for the entire day, ending with this sumptuous entertainment, we descended once more to the carriages, and drove to the quay, where a large and commodious barge, belonging to the English man-of-war Jean d'Acre (the ship put in commission for the service of Lord Granville), manned by stalwart man-of-war's men, was waiting to take the English party of nobles on board the steam-yacht. When all were collected on the quay, we left Peterhoff in the barge, and were soon on board the yacht. The weather was fine, and the moon soon rose over the palace of Peterhoff, looking for a moment like one of the splended gilded domes of the palace. On board the yacht, I had much conversation with Lord Granville, who brought the various members of his suite and introduced me to them—to Sir Robert Peel; to the young Earl of Lincoln, the son of the Duke of Newcastle, who, when himself the Earl of Lincoln, in 1839, showed me so much courtesy and kindness in London; to Mr. Acton, a nephew of Lord Granville, with whom I had some interesting conversation. We landed at the quay in St. Petersburg about eleven o'clock P. M., and I reached my lodgings at the Hôtel de Russie about midnight, thus ending a day of incidents which I shall remember with great gratification.

"Having completed, as far as such a flying visit would allow, our sight-seeing in this beautiful and interesting city, we the next day, August 15th, prepared for our departure for Stettin, on our return toward home, having remained longer than we originally intended in this part of the world. In the evening, we paid our parting visit to our amiable and kind Minister, Mr. Seymour, taking tea with many Americans at his house.

"In the morning we took our leave of St. Petersburg, embarking with Major Barnes and lady, of Springfield, Massachusetts, and Mr. Edward Bell and lady, of New York, on board the steamer for Cronstadt, to be received at Cronstadt on board the Prussian mail-steamer Prussian Eagle, for Stettin. The morning of Saturday, the 16th of August, was somewhat unpromising, threatening rain, but, accompanied by Mr. and Mrs. Shaffner, and young Nicolai Bodisco, a son of the late Baron Bodisco, Russian Minister in the

United States, we set out for Cronstadt, leaving the quay and the Neva at twelve o'clock. Mr. Seymour intended to accompany us as far as Cronstadt, but, supposing our boat did not leave till one o'clock, he was left behind. Before we reached Cronstadt, a settled rain set in, much to our discomfort, and we got on board the steamer Prussian Eagle not under the most favorable circumstances, but the boat was large, neat, and generally commodious, one with an obliging captain; there was one exception, and a very important one, too, to the commodiousness of the boat; the sleeping-apartments were the smallest I ever saw on any boat, even a Long Island Sound wood-boat contains larger and better accommodations in this respect; they have no conveniences of shelves or hooks to stow away our clothing. The berths were so narrow that I lay in mine as I would in a coffin, with no room to raise my head any more than if lying between two shelves.

"In the evening, to our gratification, the weather cleared, and the voyage, from Saturday noon till Monday night, was like the voyage from Copenhagen to St. Petersburg, beautifully clear and calm, with a smooth sea, and I began to have quite a favorable idea of the character of the Baltic Sea, as a most amiable and gentle piece of water; but, as if conscience-stricken that such a false impression of its real character should go forth to the world, the sky on Monday evening put on a frown of clouds; the wind rose, and our little steamer began to dance to the piping winds so ungracefully that most of our passengers (some fifty in number) were glad to retire early to their berths. The morning of Tuesday, the 19th, broke in tears, but not until we had made good our landfall, and the Swinemunde lighthouse loomed up in the fog, and showed us our entrance into the Oder, into which we soon entered upon smooth water, and moored for a few moments at the custom-house wharf. We then proceeded up the winding river for two or three hours, and arrived at *Stettin just in time to be too late* for the noon train to Berlin. So we quietly wended our way to the Hôtel de Prussie, had a good dinner, rested ourselves comfortably, and at six took our seats in the cars for Berlin, where we arrived in the rain, which more or less pursued us all the day, at ten o'clock, and at this present writing, the morning of August 20th, find ourselves comfortably housed at the excellent Hôtel St.-Pétersbourg, on the Unter den Linden.

"*Saturday Evening, August 23d.*—Yesterday we had a pleasant dinner-party at our excellent Minister's, Governor Vroom, and met there several Americans. To-day I went to Potsdam to see

Eng^d by W G Jackman from a Photograph from Life

BARON VON HUMBOLDT.

Baron Humboldt, and had a delightful interview with this wonderful man. Although I had met with him at the house of Baron Gerard, the distinguished painter, in Paris, in 1839, and afterward at the Academy of Sciences, when my Telegraph was exhibited to the assembled academicians in 1838, I took letters of introduction to him from Baron Gerolt, the Prussian Minister, but they were unnecessary, for the moment I entered his room, which is in the Royal Palace, he called me by name and greeted me most kindly, saying, as I presented my letters, 'Oh, sir, you need no letters, your name is a sufficient introduction;' and, so seating myself, he rapidly touched upon various topics relating to America. He was enthusiastic in his praise of Professor Dana's work on the geology of the countries he visited with Captain Wilkes, saying it was the most splendid contribution to science of the present day; a compliment of some significance, when we consider the source whence it comes.

"And now good-by; kiss those dear little ones for me. Arthur, I hope, is a good boy, and gives you no trouble, and sweet Leila, tell her she must not forget her papa . . . . darling

in his way to bed, and hear him . . . . . . Well, in good time, it is well, we shall all meet again . . . . . . our love to . . . . the assurance of every . . . . and . . . . May we . . . . they seem to

. . . .

. . . . Mrs. . . . . makes, in one of her . . . . . the study of Humboldt, which has been . . . . She writes:

'He came forward and received us very cordially, with no stiffness or formality. He is quite short, stoops a little, and holds his head slightly toward one side. He talked very fast, so that I could scarcely understand him. His library was very simply furnished, the walls on all sides were lined with bookcases; two or three tables, in the middle of the room, were strewed with papers, pamphlets, etc. Before we left, the baron presented uncle with an imperial photograph of himself, on the margin of which he wrote an inscription in French.

Baron Humboldt, and had a delightful interview with this wonderful man. Although I had met with him at the *soirées* of Baron Gerard, the distinguished painter, in Paris, in 1832, and afterward at the Academy of Sciences, when my Telegraph was exhibited to the assembled academicians in 1838, I took letters of introduction to him from Baron Gerolt, the Prussian Minister, but they were unnecessary, for the moment I entered his room, which is in the Royal Palace, he called me by name and greeted me most kindly, saying, as I presented my letters, ' Oh, sir, you need no letters, your name is a sufficient introduction;' and, so seating myself, he rapidly touched upon various topics relating to America. He was enthusiastic in his praise of Professor Dana's work on the geology of the countries he visited with Captain Wilkes, saying it was the most splendid contribution to science of the present day; a compliment of some significance, when we consider the source whence it comes.

"And now good-by; kiss those dear little ones for me. Arthur, I hope, is a good boy, and gives you no trouble; and sweet Leila, tell her she must not forget dear papa and mamma; and my darling little Willie, tell him papa loves him dearly, and longs to carry him in his arms to bed, and hear him say his prayers. Well, in good time, if God wills, we shall all meet again. I cannot send my love to *little* Charley any more, but to *tall* Charley, and to him give grandpapa's hearty love, and indeed to all the dear ones of every degree and connection, both at the Grove and at Newark. May we not look for another *deluge ?* In our family, at least, they seem to be ' *marrying and giving in marriage.*'

"Your affectionate father,

"SAMUEL F. B. MORSE."

Professor Morse's niece (now Mrs. Parmalee), in one of her letters mentions the visit to the study of Humboldt, which has been alluded to above. She writes:

"He came forward and received us very cordially, with no stiffness or formality. He is quite short, stoops a little, and holds his head slightly toward one side. He talked very fast, so that I could scarcely understand him. His library was very simply furnished, the walls on all sides were lined with bookcases; two or three tables, in the middle of the room, were strewed with papers, pamphlets, etc. Before we left, the baron presented uncle with an imperial photograph of himself, on the margin of which he wrote an inscription in French:

41

"'To Mr. S. F. B. Morse, whose philosophic and useful labors have rendered his name illustrious in two worlds. The homage of the high and affectionate esteem of

"'ALEXANDER HUMBOLDT.

"'POTSDAM, *August,* 1856.'

"His secretary accompanied us through the gardens of Sans-Souci, and from him we learned something of the habits of this remarkable man. He told us how he portioned off each day exactly, saying that Humboldt only allowed four hours for sleep—from two o'clock A. M. till six o'clock. Then he arose, breakfasted at nine o'clock; then walked till ten o'clock; read his letters and papers till one o'clock; received visitors till four o'clock; then dressed, and, when he had no other engagement, dined with the king at six o'clock, and spent the evening there till ten o'clock. From that time till two o'clock in the morning, he passed in his library at his studies. This had been his rule for years."

This journey of pleasure was extended to Cologne, Aix-la-Chapelle, Brussels, Paris, and then to London, where Professor Morse arrived in the latter part of the month of September, 1856. The Atlantic cable enterprise was the engrossing topic among men of science at that moment. A letter of Professor Morse to Baron Humboldt indicates the minute attention he was giving to this work:

"LONDON, *October* 7, 1856.

"MY DEAR BARON: You will doubtless have read of the achievement of *sounding the Atlantic Ocean* between Newfoundland and Ireland, by order of the American Secretary of the Navy, expressly for the New York, Newfoundland, and London Telegraph Cable, under the immediate direction of that expert navigator, Lieutenant O. H. Berryman, of the American Navy, in the U. S. steamer Arctic, with a view to explore '*the telegraphic plateau*' of our distinguished *savant,* Lieutenant Maury, whose ingenious speculations respecting its character, from a partial previous survey, have been so beautifully verified by a more complete survey. It is with great pleasure that I am enabled to send you a copy of the draft made of this survey by Lieutenant Berryman, which I had made expressly to send you, knowing the great interest you feel in every advance in science. I could have wished to send you at the same time a specimen of the bottom obtained from each sounding, and, if possible, will yet do so before I embark for the United States.

There will shortly be published engravings of some of the infusoria, as viewed in the microscope, copies of which I have requested shall be forwarded to you.

"You will be gratified also to learn that experiments made under the direction of Dr. Whitehouse, an acute investigator of electrical phenomena, and Mr. Bright, the experienced and ingenious Superintendent of the Electric Telegraphs, assisted by myself, on Thursday last, most satisfactorily solved the problem of the practicability of telegraphing from Newfoundland to Ireland. A subterranean line of one continuous conductor of more than two thousand English miles, was at our disposal, and we succeeded in passing signals through its entire length at the rate of 210, 241, and at one moment of 270, per minute. The scientific and commercial problem of an ocean-telegraph, I conceive, is thus satisfactorily solved. The pecuniary aid for its practical accomplishment is at hand, and there only remains that service which the proper manufacture of the cable and the nautical skill in laying it in its ocean-bed demand, to insure the accomplishment of the grand enterprise of uniting the two worlds in telegraphic bonds.

"You will excuse my enthusiasm, my dear baron, if I say that I confidently anticipate the successful accomplishment of this enterprise in *less than one year* from this time, and the possibility of sending you a dispatch from my home on the Hudson River to Potsdam in less than five minutes of time. I look with sanguine hopes to this consummation."

These scientific experiments, conducted by Professor Morse and the gentlemen with whom he was associated while in London, were reported to Mr. Field:

"LONDON, FIVE O'CLOCK A. M., *October* 2, 1856.

"As the electrician of the New York, Newfoundland, and London Telegraph Company, it is with the highest gratification that I have to apprise you of the result of our experiments of this morning upon a single continuous conductor of more than two thousand miles in extent, a distance you will perceive sufficient to cross the Atlantic Ocean from Newfoundland to Ireland.

"The admirable arrangements made at the Magnetic Telegraph-Office in Old Broad Street, for connecting ten subterranean gutta-percha insulated conductors, of over two hundred miles each, so as to give one continuous length of more than two thousand miles during the hours of the night, when the Telegraph is not commercially employed, furnished us the means of conclusively settling, by actual experiment, the question of the practicability as well as the practicality of telegraphing through our proposed Atlantic cable.

"'This result had been thrown into some doubt by the discovery, more than two years since, of certain phenomena upon subterranean and submarine conductors, and had attracted the attention of electricians, particularly of that most eminent philosopher, Professor Faraday, and that clear-sighted investigator of electrical phenomena, Dr. Whitehouse; and one of these phenomena, to wit, the perceptible retardation of the electric current, threatened to perplex our operations, and required careful investigation before we could pronounce with certainty the commercial practicability of the Ocean-Telegraph.

"I am most happy to inform you that, as a crowning result of a long series of experimental investigation and inductive reasoning upon this subject, the experiments under the direction of Dr. Whitehouse and Mr. Bright, which I witnessed this morning—in which the induction-coils and receiving-magnets, as modified by these gentlemen, were made to actuate one of my recording instruments—have most satisfactorily resolved all doubts of the practicability as well as practicality of operating the Telegraph from Newfoundland to Ireland.

"Although we telegraphed signals at the rate of 210, 241, and, according to the count at one time, even of 270 per minute upon my telegraphic register (which speed, you will perceive, is at a rate commercially advantageous), these results were accomplished notwithstanding many disadvantages in our arrangements of a temporary and local character—disadvantages which will not occur in the use of our submarine cable.

"Having passed the whole night with my active and agreeable collaborators, Dr. Whitehouse and Mr. Bright, without sleep, you will excuse the hurried and brief character of this note, which I could not refrain from sending you, since our experiments this morning settle the scientific and commercial points of our enterprise satisfactorily.

"With respect and esteem, your obedient servant,

"SAMUEL F. B. MORSE."

A week later he writes again:

"LONDON, *October* 10, 1856.

"MY DEAR SIR: After having given the deepest consideration to the subject of our successful experiment the other night, when we signaled clearly and rapidly through an unbroken circuit of subterranean wire over two thousand miles in length, I sit down to give you the result of my reflections and calculations.

"There can be no question but that, with a cable containing a single conducting wire, of a size not exceeding that through which we worked, and with equal insulation, it would be easy to telegraph from Ireland to Newfoundland at a speed of at least from eight to ten words per minute; nay, more: the varying rates of speed at which we worked, depending as they did upon differences in the arrangement of the apparatus employed, do of themselves prove that even a higher rate than this is attainable. Take it, however, at ten words in the minute, and allowing ten words for name and address, we can safely calculate upon the transmission of a twenty-word message in three minutes;

"Twenty such messages in the hour;

"Four hundred and eighty in the twenty-four hours, or fourteen thousand four hundred words per day.

"Such are the capabilities of a single-wire cable fairly and moderately computed.

"It is, however, evident to me, that, by improvements in the arrangement of the signals themselves, aided by the adoption of a code or system constructed upon the principles of the best nautical code, as suggested by Dr. Whitehouse, we may at least double the speed in the transmission of our messages.

"As to the structure of the cable itself, the last specimen which I examined with you seemed to combine so admirably the necessary qualities of strength, flexibility, and lightness, with perfect insulation, that I can no longer have any misgivings about the ease and safety with which it will be submerged.

"In one word, the doubts are resolved, the difficulties overcome, success is within our reach, and the great feat of the century must shortly be accomplished.

"I would urge you, if the manufacture can be completed within the time (and all things are possible now), to press forward the good work, and not to lose the chance of laying it during the ensuing summer.

"Before the close of the present month, I hope to be again landed safely on the other side of the water, and I full well know that on all hands the inquiries of most interest with which I shall be met will be about the Ocean Telegraph.

"Much as I have enjoyed my European trip this year, it would enhance the gratification which I have derived from it more than I can describe to you, if, on my return to America, I could be the first bearer to my friends of the welcome intelligence that the great work had been begun, by the commencement of the manufacture of the cable to connect Ireland with the line of the New York, Newfoundland, and London Telegraph Company, now so successfully completed to St. John's. Respectfully, your obedient servant,

"SAMUEL F. B. MORSE.

"To CYRUS W. FIELD, Esq, Vice-President, etc."

These experiments scattered the last doubts of the practicability of the enterprise. Individuals and governments yielded to the force of truth, and the work was begun.

BANQUET IN LONDON TO PROFESSOR MORSE.

The last place where Professor Morse could reasonably have expected the honor of a public dinner was the city of London. His most ungracious and unjust treatment there when a patent was refused him in 1838, was a life-long grievance. But now, eighteen years afterward, he comes back in triumph. The world has pronounced upon his merits and his rights, and accorded to him the honor which England had persistently denied. He was now invited to a banquet by the Telegraph companies, in distinct acknowledgment of his services! And at the head of the table, as the chairman, sat Mr. W. F. Cooke, who had been the partner of Wheatstone, whose claims had been preferred in England to those of Professor Morse. The dinner was given October 9, 1856, at the Albion Tavern. The chairman, in presenting Professor Morse to the company, bore this extraordinary testimony:

"I was consulted only a few months ago on the subject of a telegraph, for a country in which no telegraph at present exists. I recommended the system of Professor Morse. I believe that system to be one of the simplest in the world, and in that lies its permanency and certainty. [Cheers.] There are others which may be as good in other circumstances, but for a wide country I hesitate not to say Professor Morse's is the best adapted. It is a great thing to say, and I do so after twenty years' experience, that Professor Morse's system is one of the simplest that ever has been, and I think ever will be, conceived. [Cheers.] It was a great thing for me, after having been so long connected with the electric telegraph, to be invited to preside at this interesting meeting; and I have traveled upward of one hundred miles, in order to be present to-day, having, when asked to preside, replied by electric telegraph, 'I will.' [Cheers.] But I may lower your idea of the sacrifice I made in so doing when I tell you that I knew the talents of Professor Morse, and was only too glad to accept an invitation to do honor to a man I really honored in my heart. [Cheers.] I have been thinking, during the last few days, on what Professor Morse has done. He stands alone in America as the originator and carrier out of a grand conception. We know that America is an enormous country, and we know the value of the telegraph, but I think we have a right to quarrel with Professor Morse for not being content with giving the benefit of it to his own country, but that he extended it to Canada and Newfoundland; and, even beyond that, his system has been adopted all over Europe—[cheers]—and the nuisance is, that we in England are obliged to communicate by means of his system. [Cheers and laughter.] I, as a director of an electric telegraph company, however, should be ashamed of myself if I did not acknowledge what we owe him. But he threatens to go further still, and promises that, if we do not, he will carry out a communication between England and Newfoundland across the Atlantic. I am nearly pledged to pay him a visit on the other side of the Atlantic to see what he is about; and, if he perseveres in his obstinate attempt to reach England, I believe I must join him in his endeavors. [Cheers.] To think that he has united all the stripes and stars of America, which are increasing day by day—and I hope they will increase until they are too numerous to mention—that he has extended his system to Canada, and is about to unite those portions of the world to Europe, is a glorious thing for any man; and, although I have done something in the same cause myself, I confess I almost envy Professor Morse for having forced from an unwilling rival a willing acknowledgment of his services. [Cheers.] I am proud to see Professor Morse this side of the water. I beg to give you 'The health of Professor Morse,' and may he long live to enjoy the high reputation he has attained throughout the world!'"

Speeches by distinguished gentlemen followed, all of them bearing the highest testimony to the merits of the great American inventor, whose claims were now beyond question, and whose system commanded the unqualified favor of the best-informed and most practical electricians in the world. On the day of this banquet, Professor Morse received from Paris, through Mr. Mason, the American Minister, the information that the Emperor Napoleon III. had made him a *Chevalier of the Legion of Honor;* and the next day Mr. Tupper sent him the following lines: ·

TO PROFESSOR MORSE,

IN PLEASANT MEMORY OF OCTOBER 9, 1856, AT THE ALBION.

A good and generous spirit ruled the hour;
    Old jealousies were drowned in brotherhood;
Philanthropy rejoiced that Skill and Power,
    Servants to Science, compass all men's good;
    And over all Religion's banner stood,
Upheld by *thee*, true patriarch of the plan
Which in two hemispheres was schemed to shower
Mercies from God on universal man.
    Yes; this electric chain from East to West
More than mere metal, more than mammon can,
    Binds us together—kinsmen, in the best,
As most affectionate and frankest bond;
Brethren as one; and looking far beyond
    The world in an Electric Union blest!

MARTIN F. TUPPER.

ALBURY, GUILFORD.

The London *Times* of October 13th gave noble testimony to the fact that the labors of Professor Morse were understood and appreciated by men of intelligence in England. The banquet itself was proof of this, and the verdict of the press confirmed it. The distinguished philanthropist, Robert Owen, from his retirement, wrote to the Professor, giving his congratulations. And Mr. Morse considered his success as complete, now that England's men of science and men of letters, her greatest and wisest men, had honored him publicly as the inventor of the Recording Telegraph.

CHAPTER XVIII.

1857.

SUBMARINE CABLES—EARLY ATTEMPTS—CONSTRUCTION OF THE CABLES—CON-
GRESSIONAL ACTION—PROFESSOR MORSE, THE ELECTRICIAN—EMBARKS ON
THE NIAGARA—LETTERS TO MRS. MORSE—EXPERIMENTS WITH DR. WHITE-
HOUSE IN LONDON—LORD MAYOR'S BANQUET—IN PARIS—MR. MASON—
PROFESSOR MORSE'S CLAIM—RETURN TO LONDON—EMBARKING—NARROW
ESCAPES—CABLE FESTIVAL—COVE OF CORK—AN ACCIDENT—VALENTIA—
SAILING OF THE EXPEDITION—PARTING OF THE CABLE—ATTEMPT ABAN-
DONED FOR THE SEASON—RETURN TO NEW YORK—MR. FIELD'S EFFORTS—
THE SECOND EXPEDITION—FAILURE—THIRD EXPEDITION—THE CABLE LAID
— THE CONTINENTS CONNECTED—FIRST MESSAGE—GREAT REJOICING—
CELEBRATION—THE CABLE SILENT EIGHT YEARS—FOURTH EXPEDITION
—GREAT EASTERN—FAILURE—RETURN—FIFTH EXPEDITION—SUCCESS AT
LAST.

FROM the laying of the first submarine cable, the work of
Professor Morse in the harbor of New York in 1842, we
hear of no successful attempts until 1849, when it was proposed
to unite Dover and Calais by a line across the British Channel.
"The wire, it was proved by frequent attempts, could not be
wholly insulated, and the electric fluid, as it passed along the exposed portions, was so diffused by contact with the water as to
lose its efficacy. Hemp, saturated with tar, was employed; but
in course of time it was found that the water penetrated through
that covering, and the project was about being abandoned as
hopeless, when a new material was discovered, which was found
to answer the purpose when every thing else had failed. Fortunately, at this very time, when it was most needed, the valuable properties of gutta-percha, and its entire adaptability to this
purpose, were made known. It was tested with the most signal

success—found not only to resist the action of the water, but
that it was a perfect non-conductor. This important fact once
established, the attempt to construct a submarine telegraph between France and England was made, and with the most gratifying result. A factory for the manufacture of ' the submarine
telegraph cable,' as it was called, was erected in England in
1850, and by September of that year twenty-four miles of it were
made and ready to be laid down from Calais to Dover. This
cable consisted simply of the copper wire, which was about the
thickness of an ordinary knitting-needle, and was encased with
gutta-percha. At either end, where it lay in shallow water near
the shore, it was protected by a covering of thick iron wire.
The engraving presents the lateral and end sections of this cable
without the wire protector.

" In the following engravings, the inner core, or conductor,
with its gutta-percha coating, is preserved from the action of the
water, and from attrition, by the wire protector.

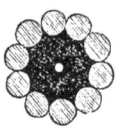 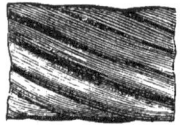

" This cable was laid in the latter part of August, 1850, between Dover and Calais. Two small steamers were employed
in laying it, and the work was accomplished in from six to seven
hours. For the purpose of sinking the cable, chunks or weights,
of from fourteen to twenty-four pounds each, were fastened to
it at distances of the sixteenth of a mile apart. This was an
easy matter, the greatest depth not exceeding two hundred feet
along the course of the line. In the whole length not more
than twenty-four miles of cable were paid out, which was only
three more than the actual distance between the two points. It
was found, however, a short time after it was laid, that a por-

tion of it had given way, and the communication was interrupted. Under these circumstances, it was deemed advisable to manufacture a cable which would be able to resist all the straining it might be subjected to, and in a comparatively brief period the required article was produced and successfully laid down between the points already named. This cable was composed of four copper wires, or conductors, each insulated with gutta-percha, and afterward bound together with hemp steeped in a solution of tar and tallow. In this condition it had the appearance of a rope about an inch in diameter. Outside of the hemp was the iron wire protector, which increased the diameter to nearly an inch and a half. Nine miles of this cable were manufactured every day. In the latter part of May, 1852, Great Britain and Ireland were brought into instant communication through the same wonderful agent, the submarine telegraph. The distance between the points of connection—Holyhead and Howth—is sixty-five miles, and the greatest depth five hundred and four feet. There was only one wire in this cable, with the indispensable coating of gutta-percha, which was protected and strengthened by the iron wire covering the outside. It was laid at the rate of four miles an hour, and fell so evenly that only three miles more than the actual distance traversed was required. Scotland and Ireland were connected by a cable of six wires, in May, 1853. The distance is about thirty miles, and was traversed by the steamer in not more than ten hours. The following June a cable was laid from Oxfordness, in England, to the Hague, in Holland, a distance of one hundred and fifteen miles. This task was accomplished in thirty-four hours, and only four and a half miles of cable were required in the paying out over the actual length from point to point, making hardly one hundred and twenty miles altogether. It has been already stated that the New York, Newfoundland and London Telegraph Company made an attempt in August, 1855, to unite the islands of Newfoundland and Cape Breton, but the vessels employed in the work were caught in a gale, the cable was obliged to be cut, and the undertaking abandoned for that time. The cable, as may be seen by the accompanying engravings, which show the exact size, had three conductors, and was protected in the same manner, by iron wire, as those already described.

THE FIRST GULF-CABLE.

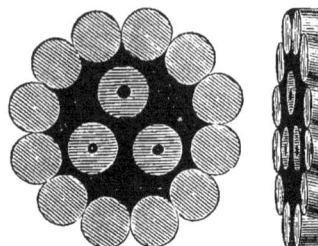

" In 1856 the company succeeded in making the desired telegraphic connection between the opposite shores of Newfoundland and Cape Breton.   This time they rejected the three-wire
cable and procured a much lighter one, with a single wire, consisting of seven strands.   This strand was covered with three
layers of the purest gutta-percha, separately applied.   In the sub-
joined engraving is a correct representation of this cable and of
its exact size.

THE SECOND GULF-CABLE.

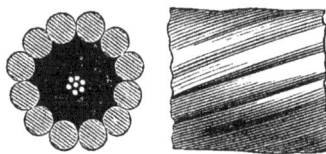

" A few weeks after the allied army entered the Crimea, a
single-wire cable was laid across the Black Sea, a distance of
three hundred and seventy-four miles, between Varna and Ba-
laklava, and it was through this that the English and French
Governments were apprised every day of the movements of the
belligerent forces on either side."

This brief outline of the progress of submarine cables was
prepared under the eye of Professor Morse when the great expedition of 1857 was about to sail, to lay the cable across the
Atlantic Ocean.   It was accompanied also with a minute description of the great Atlantic cable.   The core, or conductor,
was composed, like that of the gulf-cable, of seven copper wires,
wound together in the same manner.   The cable was twenty-

five hundred miles in length, the surplus over the actual distance to be traversed being considered necessary in case of emergency to make up for the inequalities in the bed of the ocean and the variations that might be caused by the winds and currents. The protecting wires were made into strands, each

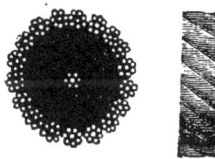

composed of seven of the best charcoal-iron wires. The aggregate length of the smaller wires required in the manufacture of one mile of the cable was one hundred and twenty-six miles, and the *whole cable required three hundred and fifteen thousand miles of this wire.*

"The flexibility of this cable was so great that it could be made as manageable as a small rope, and was capable of being tied round the arm without injury. Its weight was but 1,800 pounds to the mile, and its strength such that it would bear in water over six miles of its own length if suspended vertically."

As the electrician of the company, Mr. Morse's responsibility was great, but, the cable having been made in England, the officers there had it in charge. He embarked at New York on the steam-frigate Niagara, April 21, 1857, to go abroad and give personal attention to the great work. The daily letters that he wrote on board the ship, to his family at home, disclose the intense anxiety he felt at every stage of the enterprise. On arriving in London he was hospitably received by Dr. Whitehouse, and entertained at his house in Greenwich. He was invited to dine at the Lord Mayor's, and honored with every attention by men who appreciated the work he had done and was doing. While the vessels were delayed in taking the cable on board, he visited Paris by invitation of Mr. Mason, the American Minister, and had interviews with the Prime-Minister of France. In one of his playful letters to his family, he writes:

"While I was at Mr. Mason's, one of the young ladies came running to me and said that Lady Elgin was at the door, to make a call; so I went with Mr. Mason to the hall-door, and was introduced to Lady Elgin, the widow of Lord Elgin, who was so kind to me in Paris in 1838-'39. She had an attack of paralysis, which rendered her lower limbs useless, about the same time that Mr. Mason suffered from a like attack a few years ago. She was drawn to the door in a little hand-carriage, and did not alight; so we all sat on the steps, and had a pleasant conversation with her. When my name was mentioned, she said she had often heard her husband speak of me and of the Telegraph. She put me very much in mind of my mother, in her last days. I learned an anecdote of her and Lord Elgin, after she had left. It seems she was the second wife of Lord Elgin, who had first married a very beautiful woman. This first wife was about to visit Italy with her husband. Their preparations had all been made, but, owing to some unforeseen circumstance, Lord Elgin was obliged to remain some weeks longer, and, not wishing to disappoint his wife, gave her in charge of a friend of his (a Mr. Patterson), to accompany her to Italy, where he proposed to join them in the course of two or three weeks. Mr. Patterson was a good-looking man, while Lord Elgin was far from being so. Mr. Patterson proved himself a villain; he took advantage of his position, and betrayed the confidence of Lord Elgin, and prevailed on the lady to elope with him. Of course the result was divorce; and Lord Elgin then married the lady whom I saw. The first Lady Elgin, after the divorce, married Patterson. It so happened that Lord and Lady Elgin were in a part of the country where his former wife and Patterson lived, and had proposed to visit a family, which the Pattersons also visited. Something prevented Lord and Lady Elgin from fulfilling their engagement with punctuality, and they did not arrive at their friend's house until some hours after the time. The first salutation of the lady of the house to Lady Elgin was, 'I am so glad that you did not come at the time you had appointed, for if you had you would have met here Mrs. Patterson, and I have been nervous all the time lest you should encounter her; it would have been so disagreeable to you.' 'Not at all,' said Lady Elgin, 'I should have been glad of the opportunity to thank her, for surrendering to me so excellent a husband.'"

Returning to London, and still delayed, he writes again to his wife and children :

"GREENWICH, *July* 24, 1857.

"Yesterday was a most exciting day. Sir Culling Eardley, whose name is well known in the religious world, and who lives at Erith, in Kent, not many miles from here, invited the officers and crew of the Agamemnon, the principals and men of the manufacturers of the cable, Messrs. Glass & Co., to a grand *fête champêtre* at his splendid place. Besides these, invitations were sent to a large circle of the nobility, ladies and gentlemen, to the Atlantic Telegraph Company, to the officers of the American frigates, etc. The account of the whole matter will be in the papers this morning."

At this festival, when Professor Morse was called out to speak for the scientific men of the expedition, he was received with great applause, and is reported in the papers as saying in the course of his remarks : " We may not then concentrate our plaudits upon any one individual. Many divide the honors. Time would fail me were I to mention their names, and time must not be taken from the enjoyments of the occasion so generously and magnificently provided by our noble host. [Cheers.] It is an unusual spectacle to see England and America, with blended flags, thus united with ships-of-war, not for conquest, nor in hostile array, but in the great interest of universal peace. Is it not an omen of good to mankind ? May God bless the enterprise ! If he bless it, it succeeds ; if not, it surely fails."

The departure of the expedition was also attended with solemn religious services in which the Divine favor was humbly invoked. From the Cove of Cork he wrote to his wife :

" When I wrote the finishing sentence of my last letter I was suffering a little from a slight accident to my leg. We were laying out the cable from the two ships, the Agamemnon and Niagara, to connect the two halves of the cable together, to experiment through the whole length of twenty-five hundred miles for the first time. In going down the sides of the Agamemnon, I had to cross over several small boats to reach the outer one, which was to take me on board the tug which had the connecting cable on board ; in stepping from one to the other of the small boats, the water being very rough, and the boats having a good deal of motion, I made a misstep, my right leg being on board the outer boat, and my left leg went down between the two boats, scraping the skin from the upper part of the leg near the knee for some two or three inches. It pained me a little, but not much. Still, I knew from experience that, however slight, and comparatively painless at the time, I should be laid up the next day, and possibly for several days. My warm-hearted, generous friend, Sir William O'Shaughnessy, was on board, and, being a surgeon, he at once took it in hand, and dressed it, tell Susan, in good *hydropathic* style, with cold water. I felt so little inconvenience from it at the time, that I assisted throughout the day in laying the cable, and operating through it after it was joined, and had the satisfaction of witnessing the successful result of passing the electricity through twenty-five hundred miles, at the rate of one signal in one and a quarter second. Since then, Dr. Whitehouse has succeeded in telegraphing a message through it at the rate of a single signal in three-quarters of a second. If the cable, therefore, is successfully laid, so as to preserve continuity throughout, there is no doubt of our being able to telegraph through, and at a good commercial speed. I have been on my back for two days, and am still confined to the ship. To-morrow I hope to be well enough to hobble on board the Agamemnon, and assist in some experiments.

"*August 3d, Monday morning, eleven o'clock* A. M.—I am still confined, most of the time on my back in my berth, quite to my annoyance in one respect, to wit, that I am unable to be on board the Agamemnon with Dr. Whitehouse to assist at the experiments. Yet, I have so much to be thankful for that gratitude is the prevailing feeling.

"Our success in the electrical experiments is most gratifying. Mrs. Whitehouse showed me a strip of paper marked on my register with my alphabetic characters, beautifully made, through the whole cable of twenty-five hundred miles, and with a feeble sand-battery of only twelve plates, like one of those in gutta-percha boxes in my instrument-room. If the nautical and engineering departments perform their part successfully, we are now sure of success.

"*Seven o'clock.*—All the ships are under way from the Cove of Cork; the Leopard left first, then the Agamemnon, then the Susquehanna, and the Niagara last; and at this moment we are all off the Head of Kinsale, in the following order: Niagara, Leopard, Agamemnon, Susquehanna. The Cyclops and another vessel, the Advice, left for Valentia on Saturday evening, and with a beautiful night before us we hope to be there also by noon to-morrow. This day, three hundred and sixty-five years ago, Columbus sailed on his first voyage of discovery, and discovered America. Goodnight, my beloved.

"*Tuesday morning, August 4th, ten* A. M.—Off the Skilligs light, of which I send you a sketch. A beautiful morning, with head wind and heavy sea, making many sea-sick. We are about fifteen miles from our point of destination. Our companion-ships are out of sight astern, except the Susquehanna, which is behind us only about a mile. In a few hours we hope to reach our expectant friends in Valentia, and to commence the great work in earnest. Our ship is crowded with engineers and operators, and delegates from the Governments of Russia and France; and the deck is a bewildering mass of machinery, steam-engines, cog-wheels, breaks, boilers, ropes of hemp and ropes of wire, buoys and boys, pulleys and sheaves of wood and iron, cylinders of wood and cylinders of iron, meters of all kinds, anemometers, thermometers, barometers, electrometers, steam-gauges, speed-measurers, strain-gauges, ships' logs, from the common log to Massey's log, and Friend's log, to our friend Whitehouse's electro-magnetic log, which I think will prove to be the best of all, with a modification I have suggested; and, thus freighted, we expect to disgorge most of our solid cargo before reaching mid-ocean. I am keeping ready to close this at a moment's warning; so give all manner of love to all friends, kisses to whom kisses are due. I am getting almost impatient at the delays we necessarily encounter. But our great work must not be neglected. I have seen enough to know now that the Atlantic Telegraph is sure to be established, *for it is practicable. We may not succeed in our first attempt,* some little neglect or accident may foil our present efforts, but the present enterprise will result in gathering stores of experience which will make the next effort certain. Not that I do not expect success now, but accidental failure now will not be the evidence of its impracticability. Our principal electrical difficulty is the slowness with which we must manipulate in order to be intelligible. *Twenty words in sixteen minutes* is now the rate; I am confident we can get more after a while, but the Atlantic Telegraph has its own rate of talking, and cannot be urged to speak faster any more than any other orator, without danger of becoming unintelligible.

" *Three o'clock* P. M.—We are in Valentia harbor. We shall soon come to anchor. A pilot who has just come to show us our anchorage-ground says, ' There are a power of people ashore.' "

In other letters he gives the minutest details of the delays, accidents, and fears, by which they were beset, and at length he writes:

" *August 8th.*—Yesterday, at half-past six P. M., all being right,

42

we commenced again paying out the heavy shore-end, of which we
had about eight miles to be left on the rocky bottom of the coast,
to bear the attrition of the waves, and to prevent injury to the delicate nerve which it incloses in its iron mail, and which is the living
principle of the whole work. A critical time was approaching; it
was when the end of the massive cable should pass overboard at
the point where it joins the main and smaller cable. I was in my
berth by order of the surgeon, lest my injured limb, which was
somewhat inflamed by the excitement of the day and too much
walking about, should become worse. Above my head, the heavy
rumbling of the great wheels over which the cable was passing, and
was being regulated, every now and then giving a tremendous
thump, like the discharge of artillery, kept me from sleep, and I
knew they were approaching the critical point. Presently it came;
the machinery stopped; and soon amid the voices I heard the unwelcome intelligence, 'The cable is broke.' Sure enough, the smaller cable at this point had parted; but, owing to the prudent precautions of those superintending, the end of the great cable had
been buoyed, and the hawsers which had been attached secured it.
The sea was moderate, the moonlight gave a clear sight of all, and
in half an hour the joyous sound of ' All right ! ' was heard, the machinery commenced a low and regular rumbling, like the purring of
a great cat, which has continued from that moment (midnight) till
the present moment uninterrupted. The coil on deck is most beautifully uncoiling, at the rate of three nautical miles an hour. The
day is magnificent, the land has almost disappeared, and our companion-ships are leisurely sailing with us at equal pace, and we are
all of course in fine spirits. I sent you a telegraph dispatch this
morning, thirty miles out, which you will duly receive, with others
that I shall send if all continues to go on without interruption. If
you do receive any, *preserve them with the greatest care*, for they
will be great curiosities."

" *August* 10*th*, *Monday*.—Thus far, we have had most delightful weather, and every thing goes on regularly and satisfactorily.
You are aware we cannot stop night nor day in paying out. On
Saturday we made our calculations that the first great coil, which is
upon the main deck, would be completely paid out, and one of our
critical moments, to wit, the change from this coil to the next,
which is far forward, would be made by seven or eight o'clock yesterday morning (Sunday). So we were up and watching the last
flake of the first coil gradually diminishing. Every thing had been

well prepared: the men were at their posts; it was an anxious moment, lest a kink might occur, but, as the last round came up, the motion of the ship was slightly slackened, the men handled the slack cable handsomely, and in two minutes the change was made with perfect order, and the paying out from the second coil was as regularly commenced, and at this moment continues, and at an increased rate to-day of five miles per hour.

"Last night, however, was another critical moment. On examining our chart of soundings, we found the depth of the ocean gradually increasing up to about four hundred fathoms, and then the chart showed a sudden and great increase to seventeen hundred fathoms, and then a further increase to two thousand and fifty, nearly the greatest depth with which we should meet in the whole distance. We had, therefore, to watch the effect of this additional depth upon the straining of the cable. At two in the morning, the effect showed itself in a greater strain, and a more rapid tendency to run fast. We could check its speed, but it is a dangerous process. Too sudden a check would inevitably snap the cable. Too slack a rein would allow of its egress at such a wasting rate, and at such a violent speed, that we should lose too great a portion of the cable, and its future stopping within controllable limits be almost impossible. Hence our anxiety. All were on the alert; our expert engineers applied the brakes most judiciously, and at the moment I write— latitude 52° 28'—the cable is being laid at the depth of two miles in its ocean-bed as regularly, and with as much facility, as it was in the depth of a few fathoms. After the critical point of change yesterday from coil one to coil two (there are five coils altogether), we had our Sunday services on deck. Read the portion of the Psalms, morning prayer for 9th of the month; you will see there is much appositeness in its tone and character to our situation. The more I contemplate this great undertaking, the more I feel my own littleness, and the more I perceive the hand of God in it, and how he has assigned to various persons their duties, he being the great controller, all others his honored instruments. No single human being can appropriate to himself the exclusive honors of this enterprise, for in no human being do the various and almost opposite qualities exist necessary to be combined before it can be consummated. Hence our dependence first of all on God, then on each other.

"*Six* P. M.—We have just had a fearful alarm. 'Stop her! stop her!' was reiterated from many voices on deck. On going up I perceived the cable had got out of its sheaves, and was running out at great speed. All was confusion for a few moments. Mr. Canning, our friend, who was the engineer of the Newfoundland cable, showed great presence of mind, and to his coolness and skill I think is due the remedying of the evil. By rope-stoppers, the cable was at length brought to a stand-still, and it strained most ominously, perspiring at every part large tar-drops. But it held together long enough to put the cable on its sheaves again.

" *Tuesday, August* 11*th.*—Abruptly, indeed, am I stopped in my letter. This morning, at 3.45, the cable parted, and we shall soon be on our way back to England."

Mr. Charles T. Bright, who was in charge of the paying-out machine, gave a minute account of the fatal accident. "Its origin," he says, " was no doubt the amount of retarding strain upon the cable, but had the machine been properly manipulated at the time it could not possibly have taken place. I had attended personally to the regulation of the breaks; but, finding that all was going on well, and it being necessary that I should be temporarily away from the machine to ascertain the rate of the ship, and to see how the cable was coming out of the hold, and also to visit the electrician, the machine was for the moment left in charge of a mechanic who had been engaged from the first in its construction and fitting, and was acquainted with its operation. I was proceeding to the fore-part of the ship, when I heard the machine stop; I immediately called out to ease the break and reverse the engine of the ship, but when I reached the spot the cable was broken." Professor Morse, the next day, wrote again to his wife:

" You will perhaps be surprised to learn that I have not left my berth for three days. The accident to my leg, in the Cove of Cork, when engaged in connecting the two halves of the cable, is the cause. Athough apparently slight, I took too much exercise with it, and consequently have now been compelled to lie quiet. I do not suffer except from the irksomeness of the confinement, while so much of interest has been enacted on deck, which I have not visited since the parting of the cable. And, moreover, my hurt on the leg is healing kindly and rapidly."

" *August* 13, *three o'clock* P. M.—A beautiful day, and we are now under full steam and sail for Plymouth. The Agamemnon and

Susquehanna are in sight for the same destination. The Cyclops took Mr. Field to Valentia, and the Leopard at the same time sailed for Plymouth, leaving us to make several important experiments bearing upon the Atlantic Telegraph, which consumed nearly the whole day. I was unable to be on deck, but I learned the results, which are for the most part very satisfactory. Our accident will delay the enterprise, but will not defeat it. I consider it a settled fact, from all I have seen, that it is perfectly practicable. It will surely be accomplished. There is no insurmountable difficulty that has for a moment appeared, none that has shaken my faith in it in the slightest degree. My report to the company, as co-electrician, will show every thing right in that department. We got an electric current through till the moment of parting, so that electric connection was perfect, and yet the farther we paid out the feebler were the currents, indicating a difficulty which, however, I do not consider serious, while it is of a nature to require attentive investigation."

PROFESSOR MORSE TO MR. SAWARD.

In the midst of this disappointment, and while still confined to his berth, Professor Morse addressed a letter to the company:

"UNITED STATES STEAM-FRIGATE NIAGARA, }
PLYMOUTH HARBOR, *August* 18, 1857. }

"DEAR SIR: Your letter of the 17th instant is just received, and to it I send a brief answer by telegraph, as you requested. I take advantage of Captain Hudson's departure for London to write to you, since the hurt I received in the Cove of Cork, while connecting the two parts of the cable, has shown itself to be more serious than I anticipated, and so confining me to my berth now for a week, with an uncertain prospect of release; I am thus unable, most unfortunately for myself, to be with you in your consultation; nevertheless, although deprived of being present in person, I will venture a few remarks by letter, giving the conclusions to which I have come in reflecting upon the condition of our enterprise.

" We have met with a misfortune, viewed in some of its aspects, but in others a providential interference to insure final success. It is not in accordance with the law of success in any great enterprise that every part of our plans should go smoothly forward. Partial failures ought to be expected, and it is neither wise nor just to leave such probable failures out of our calculations. What, then, is the state of the enterprise? We had a cable of some 2,300 miles. We still have some 2,000 miles left, so that the loss is but about 300 miles. What had been gained by this loss? An amount of experieuce and knowledge for which the loss of 300 miles of cable is a cheap purchase. Better to lose 300 miles than the whole cable. It has been shown by our experience that the rate of safe paying out will require more surplusage than had been provided. In the deepest soundings it has been demonstrated that to check the speed of the cable to accommodate it to the speed of the ship is fatal, and it has taught us that the proper remedy in such an exigency is to increase the speed of the ship, even at the sacrifice of the deposit of more cable.

" I would say it with all deference, too, that the instructions devolving so much of duty and responsibility upon the engineers, and at the same time depriving the nautical department of duties and responsibilities which appropriately belonged to it, have been shown by the event to have been injudicious. The safe deposit of the cable from on shipboard involves duties, it is true, of a mixed character; but the duties are more nautical than engineering, and ought not to have been devolved upon any one individual unless possessed of the rare qualifications of a knowledge of both departments. Had our ingenious engineer possessed the nautical knowledge which experienced seamen have at command, as it were by instinct, the engineering remedy, the fatal brake, would not have been applied without making account of the nautical risk of such an act, engendered by the rate of the ship's progress and the surging of the sea. We learn by mistakes. My object is by no means to censure the past, but to hint a remedy for the future.

" Have we not gained as well as lost by this check? We have demonstrated that the cable, so far as strength and capability of being paid out is concerned, is well devised and well made. No change for the present is desirable, although future cables may doubtless be better constructed to accomplish better telegraphic results by taking advantage of the discoveries and additions of science.

" We have demonstrated that either of the two plans of splicing in mid-ocean is practicable.

" We have demonstrated that the cable, once paid out from the ship, is not recoverable with any certainty by the means at present devised on board.

" We have demonstrated that the cable can be laid out.

" Now with regard to the future :

" The advanced state of the season opposes an obstacle to any further attempt at laying the cable this year.

" Before a supply of the quantity lost can be had and coiled on board ship the season of rough weather sets in, adding untried difficulties to the undertaking. Hence a postponement till the mild season of June or July of another year would seem desirable. There may be inconveniences, but there are also advantages in the delay. Not the least of the latter is the furnishing our worthy electrician, Dr. Whitehouse, with his other scientific associates, an opportunity to experiment during the winter with the entire cable, and to devise means for more rapid transmission and in greater quantity in a given time. Compelled as I am to return to my home, I can derive no benefit immediately in my own studies from this arrangement, but it would be most gratifying to me if this accident, so called, should prove in this way a means of benefiting the company to an amount far exceeding the cost of the entire enterprise. That this, with such opportunities, is likely to be the result of scientific investigation, I have the strongest faith, and, should this happen as one of the effects of what otherwise is a disappiontment and seems a frown, we shall all derive a most salutary lesson to trust in him who disposes of all events for the greatest good, and with whom—if we were indeed sincere in our trust and in our submission to his will— we professed to leave the disposal of our whole enterprise. With sincere respect, your most obedient servant,

" SAMUEL F. B. MORSE.

" To GEORGE SAWARD, Esq., *Secretary of the Atlantic Telegraph Company, etc.*"

Professor Morse's letters to his family continue the history of the enterprise, the discouragements, the heroic endeavors, the perseverance, and hopes of its friends. In September he returned to New York in the steamer Arabia. The London directors ordered seven hundred miles of cable to be manufactured to supply the place of what had been lost. Mr. Field returned to the United States and secured the continued assistance of our Government in the use of the ships to repeat the experiment. He then went to London, and was made general manager of the company. This office he accepted, but declined to receive any salary or any extra compensation for his services. He engaged the efficient services of Mr. William E. Everett, the American engineer of the steamship Niagara. Mr. Everett constructed a machine for paying out the cable, which promised to obviate all the difficulties and the dangers attending the one in use the year before. The American ship, the Susquehanna, being detained in the West Indies with the yellow fever on board, the British Government supplied her place with the Valorous, and the new squadron sailed from Plymouth May 29, 1858, on the second Atlantic-Telegraph expedition. After putting out to sea and making a few experiments by way of testing the new machinery, the squadron set off on its mission June 10, 1858, the Niagara and the Agamemnon being followed by the Valorous and the Gorgon. Three days of fair weather were succeeded by a fearful storm. A series of gales scattered the little fleet. Some of the vessels narrowly escaped destruction. On the 25th of June they found each other again. The Agamemnon had suffered severely, and so had the cable on board of her. After repairing damages the vessels proceeded to mid-ocean. The Niagara and the Agamemnon, having joined the cable, parted company, each steaming away with its portion of the mighty coil, to its own country. Fifty, one hundred, two hundred miles were paid out, and, at the moment when all doubt of success had disappeared, the cable gave way at the stern of the Agamemnon!

The fleet returned to Queenstown. But Mr. Field and his associates would not abandon the attempt. Every failure was met with fresh resolution. The world never saw sublimer heroism. July 17, 1858, the third expedition left the Cove of Cork, with the agreement among the commanders of the several vessels to rendezvous in mid-ocean, which was reached by the last of the vessels in eleven days. The splice was soon effected, and again the two old friends, the Niagara and Agamemnon, bade each other a brief "good-by" and started with their burdens for their own lands. Signals were constantly passed between the two ships. On the 4th day of August the Niagara safely entered Trinity Bay, Newfoundland, with her precious freight, and on the next day the cable was made fast to the American shore. *On the same day* the Agamemnon landed her end of the cable at Valentia, and the continents of Europe and America were united!

The enthusiastic joy of the American people on this result found expression in thanksgiving to him who rules the winds

and waves. Several days of great anxiety were passed while
preparations were made for the practical working of the cable,
and on the 16th day of August, 1858, a message from the Qeeen
of England was received, addressed to the President of the
United States. Celebrations followed. In the city of New
York the demonstration was on a scale of magnificence rarely
surpassed by festivities that have signalized the most important
events in its history. The successful efforts of Mr. Cyrus W.
Field were acknowledged with every token of grateful recognition.

In the midst of these rejoicings the Atlantic cable suddenly
ceased to do its duty. It died and made no sign. Consterna-
tion, then distrust, filled the public mind. Several private and
a few public messages had been received by it from Europe.
On the 27th day of August intelligence was received of a British
treaty with China, allowing the Christian religion. But on the
1st day of September the cable ceased to speak. The cause of
this sad failure has been a mystery to the public. It was even
asserted that the cable was never operated at all, and many still
believe that no messages were received by it from the other side.
But the cable did work, although very imperfectly and irregularly,
twenty days. In that time 129 messages were received at Newfoundland from Valentia, containing 1,474 words and 7,253 letters, and a still larger number were sent from this to the other
side and there received. The intended return of two regiments
of the British army from Canada was countermanded by a cable
message, saving to the Government the sum of £250,000. Mr.
George B. Prescott, the eminent American electrician, attributes
the failure to the imperfect mode in which the cable was manufactured, and the improper manner in which it was cared for
afterward, the conducting wire being left so much exposed by
the melting and breaking of the gutta-percha that its insulation
was destroyed.

In January, 1864, Mr. Field was once more on his way to
England. In the mean time he had toiled with indefatigable
perseverance, to serve an enterprise which to all appearance was
as dead as the host of Pharaoh in the Red Sea. When public
confidence began to revive, and it was believed that the British
Government would guarantee the interest on the stock of the

Telegraph Company, if their cable should be laid successfully, the Red-Sea-Telegraph cable, which had been laid by a company having a government guarantee, died suddenly in its bed, as the Atlantic cable had perished. But the British Government was always disposed to promote the Atlantic Telegraph, and did engage to pay eight per cent. on £600,000 of new capital, for twenty-five years, if the cable were successfully laid, and made to operate during that time. Mr. Field enlisted Mr. Thomas Brassey in the great work, with Mr. John Pender, Mr. John Chatterton, and others, and, by a union of the Gutta-Percha Company with Glass, Elliot & Co., a new cable was made. The Great Eastern, the largest steamship in the world, was purchased; the cable was put on board, and the command was given to Captain Anderson. On the 15th day of July, 1865, the Great Eastern set off for Valentia Bay; there the cable was secured to the shore, and on the 23d day of July she left for the New World. The expedition had reached a point within six hundred miles of Newfoundland, when the cable parted, and twelve hundred miles of it were left in the bottom of the sea. To recover it seemed the most hopeless of all human undertakings. The attempt was made; three times it was caught and raised toward the surface, but as often the ropes by which it was drawn up failed to bear the strain, and the cable sank again into its ocean-bed. The Great Eastern returned to England. A new company was formed, called the Anglo-American Telegraph Company. A new cable was made. The Great Eastern received it, and on Friday, July 13, 1866, after solemn religous services in which the favor of God was heartily invoked, once more it left Valentia Bay for the Bay of Newfoundland. The work proceeded daily without interruption by accident. Messages from all parts of Europe and the East were daily received on the Great Eastern. On Friday, July 27, 1866, the cable was safely landed on the American shore. Again the Eastern and Western Hemispheres were united. The great work was successfully accomplished. From that day to this the Atlantic cable has done its duty.

CHAPTER XIX.

1858–1859.

RETURN TO AMERICA—WINTER IN NEW YORK—BRIDAL PARTY AND FESTIVITIES —INVITED TO PARIS—PREPARATIONS FOR THE JOURNEY—INSTRUCTION TO FARMER AND COACHMAN—VOYAGE—REMARKABLE PREDICTION AND FUL- FILLMENT—PARIS—BANQUET—MEMORIAL TO FOREIGN POWERS—HON. LEWIS CASS—HON. JOHN Y. MASON—THE FRENCH GOVERNMENT—CON- VENTION CALLED—GOVERNMENTS REPRESENTED—COUNT WALEWSKI'S LET- TER TO PROFESSOR MORSE—PROCEEDINGS OF THE CONVENTION—AMOUNT OF AWARD—PROPORTION OF THE SEVERAL GOVERNMENTS—SUMMARY OF FOREIGN DISTINCTIONS—VISIT TO THE WEST INDIES—ERECTION OF A TELE- GRAPH—SOUTHERN ATLANTIC TELEGRAPH—CORRESPONDENCE—LETTER FROM PROFESSOR STEINHEIL—MORSE'S REPLY—PROPOSAL TO RAISE A TES- TIMONIAL TO STEINHEIL—PROFESSOR MORSE'S RETURN—RECEPTION AT POUGHKEEPSIE.

THE official connection of Professor Morse with the Atlantic cable enterprise was terminated when the new company was organized in London, in 1857. He was not elected an honorary director. The reason assigned for his omission was that he had taken no stock in the new company. As the company was not formed until after he had left England, and he had no opportunity to subscribe, the reason was not satisfactory to him. In the midst of rivalries and jealousies among companies, capitalists, scientists, and others interested, it is possible that his services in the board, and as electrician, were dispensed with for some other reason than the one assigned. Whatever was the real cause, the fact was personally mortifying to the great inventor of the enterprise, if it were not also injurious to the interests of the new company.

Arriving in New York early in October from England, he

passed a few weeks at his country-seat, and then removed to the city, where he spent the winter. His correspondence occupied all the time that he could save from public and social duties. Among the many and curious applications made to him at this moment was one from a French countess, who claimed that in 1832, a quarter of a century before, she had consigned a number of prints to his care, with a request that he would place them in the hands of some dealer in New York, to be sold for her benefit. He had forgotten to whom he confided them, and had no means of knowing whether they had ever been sold or not. As he was informed that the countess was in distress, he sent her the full amount of her claim for the value of the prints, placing the matter upon grounds of personal obligation, so that there should be no hesitation on her part in receiving the money. He says to the consul who had brought the subject to his notice: "The letter of the countess which you have obligingly forwarded to me, informs me that she is in distress, having lost her sister and her fortune. There are other obligations than those of an equitable pecuniary character, which prompt me to view her claim upon me as more than equitable. I have grateful recollections of kindness shown to me by these amiable ladies during the prevalence of the cholera scourge in Paris in 1832, and I feel happy in having an opportunity of showing my sense of that kindness."

The spring and early summer of 1858 at Locust Grove were enlivened by a wedding-party from New Orleans; Mrs. Morse's brother-in-law, Mr. Goodrich, coming North with his bride. Professor Wier, of West Point, who had won the honor, which Professor Morse had so ardently desired, of painting the picture for the Rotunda of the Capitol, was invited to his house, with Gouverneur Kemble, Esq., of Cold Spring, and others. The mansion was a scene of prolonged festivity, and the most refined and elegant hospitalities.

At this time, a congress of European Governments was discussing at Paris the question of giving to this private citizen, on the banks of the Hudson River, a pecuniary testimonial of the distinguished benefits which those foreign peoples had received from his invention of the Telegraph.

The Hon. J. Y. Mason, Minister of the United States to

France, wrote to Professor Morse, advising him to come immediately to Paris. He says: " The prospects of success are brighter than ever; come over as soon as you can." Yielding to this suggestion, he made preparations for the journey, and for a protracted absence, should he find it desirable to remain abroad. If it has been supposed that his mind was absorbed in the Telegraph to the exclusion of the petty details of ordinary life, the idea will be dispelled by observing the minute instructions which he left in writing for the management of his farm while he was absent. He rented the mansion and immediate grounds to B. Hinckley, Esq., and in a note to him says: " May I ask your attention to the condition of my carriages, wagons, sleighs, etc., occasionally asking Thomas Bennett about them, simply to show that he has one supervising him? And so of the others." To his hired men he gave written directions, going into the most minute details of the farm and stock. A few extracts will illustrate his prudent care:

" *Instructions to Mr. Luckey.*

" In the conduct of the farm while I am gone, I wish the *old bay horse* and *old cream horse* to be under your care and use for farming purposes, and for Thomas the gardener's service for the garden and grapery. I do not wish your son Frank to use or drive any of my horses. The hay and grain I wish to have estimated, and an accurate account kept of their use, to be shown me when I return. The hogs, after being slaughtered at the proper time, may be sold for me. So also those cattle it may be advisable to fatten for sale. Offer them to Messrs. Pine & Spencer, and, if they will give a fair price, let them take them on account. I leave funds and directions with Mr. Hinckley to pay you every month. In case of any emergency, ask advice of Mr. Hinckley, who is authorized by me to direct respecting all matters about the place. The milk, cream, and butter, dispose of for me to Mr. Hinckley's family, or others, if he does not take all. Keep account also of these articles, and all the produce of the farm. Store away potatoes enough to last me from May until potatoes come in again. In winter see to having the ice-house filled with good ice, with the assistance of Thomas Bennett and Thomas Devoy. Cut down dead trees and remove stumps. Put the embankment against the fence in good order. Select out the larger stone from the wall that was taken away, such as will do for building-stone, and draw them into the yard, piling them up for future use. The smaller stone may remain and be broken up for a foundation for a pathway on the road. Leave a culvert through it and a drain (open), for the water to flow off on the south side of the road down the north dell. You may get from Collinwood the usual quantity of coal (four tons), and have it charged to me. I have given orders to that effect, and for Thomas Devoy also (two tons). When the time comes for paying tax, direct the collector to call on Mr. Hinckley for mine, as he is authorized to pay it for me. Thomas Bennett and Thomas Devoy will both be paid by Mr. Hinckley, who has funds of mine for the purpose."

" *Thomas Devoy.*

" I wish you to take care of the garden and grapery, and lawns, as usual; and you may dispose of the produce of the garden to the best advantage to Messrs. Carpenters & Brothers, Main Street, or to Mr. Pine, or to others, if better terms can be had. Send to my son Charles, through Mr. Luckey, by the barge, corn, squashes, beets, and early potatoes, and also a few grapes. I have requested Mr. Luckey to allow you, as you can agree with each other, as to time, the use of the *old cream horse*, and the *old bay horse*, to draw muck and bones, and manure for the garden and grapery. I wish that there may be mutual helping of each other in this and other respects, and, in case of needing advice, advise with Mr. Hinckley, who, while he rents my house, is chief supervisor of the place. When melons, and corn, squashes, beets, and grapes, are ripe, make up a liberal parcel in a large basket, and send same to the directress of the ' Home of the Friendless.' And send also a basket of vegetables and fruits occasionally to Rev. Mr. Ludlow, while he is in Poughkeepsie. You may get from Mr. Haggerty three hundred asparagus-plants of the best kind, say about a dollar per hundred, and twelve hyacinth-flower bulbs, at not over twenty-five cents apiece, and one hundred tulip-bulbs, at not over seventy-five cents per hundred. Take good care of the tools, and every thing in your department."

" *Thomas Bennett.*

" I wish you to take charge of the *span of horses* while I am absent, letting them rest, except such exercise as may be good for them, taking off their shoes and letting them run when proper in the field. Also take under your charge the pony in the same way;

and old bay (Tommy) keep for the use of Mr. Hinckley, who, if he uses him, will be at the expense of his feed. Look after the carriages, wagons, and sleighs; see that they are housed in good order. Assist Mr. Luckey on the farm, and Thomas Devoy in the garden, as you and they can arrange to the best advantage. In case of any difficulty, apply to Mr. Hinckley for advice, who has the chief supervision of my place while he rents my house. I know that you are an industrious man, and I have full confidence that you will lend your aid cheerfully in any labors on the farm and in the garden, as well as about the horses and barns. Mr. Hinckley has funds to pay you your monthly wages on the 1st of each month, according to a schedule I have left with him."

July 24, 1858, Professor Morse, with his family and other relatives, making a party of fifteen, sailed from New York, in the steamer Fulton, for Havre. On the steamer with him was one of his neighbors from Poughkeepsie, who has furnished a remarkable incident illustrating the penetration and judgment of the Professor. It will be remembered that the Atlantic cable was landed on both shores of the ocean on the same day, August 5, 1858, and that after messages had passed through the cable about twenty days, each way, it suddenly ceased to speak, and has remained dumb to this day. On the day that messages began to pass, the steamer Fulton, with Mr. Morse on board, was approaching the coast of England. Jacob S. Jewett, Esq., in a letter to the author of this memoir, dated March 18, 1874, writes:

"I thought it might interest you to know when and how Professor Morse received the first tidings of the success of the Atlantic cable. I accompanied him to Europe on the steamer Fulton, which sailed from New York July 24, 1858. We were nearing Southampton, when a sail-boat was noticed approaching, and soon our vessel was boarded by a young man who sought an interview with Professor Morse, and announced to him that a message from America had just been received, the first that had passed along the wire lying upon the bed of the ocean. Professor Morse was, of course, greatly delighted, but, turning to me, said, '*This is very gratifying, but it is doubtful whether many more messages will be received,*' and gave as his reason that '*the cable had been* so long stored in an improper place, that much of the coating had been destroyed,

and the cable was in other respects injured.' His prediction proved
to be true."

Probably Professor Morse was the only man living who entertained that opinion at that time. But with the evidence before
him that the cable had been successfully laid; that a message,
fulfilling his early predictions, had been received; with every
motive for wishing it to be permanently successful; and at
a crisis when he was hoping for a testimonial from the European powers, which might be defeated by the failure of the
cable, he expressed his belief that *the cable would not continue
to do its work*, and that the first few messages would be the last.
Had he been in the Board of Direction, had his judgment and
experience as electrician been employed, that great calamity
which cost millions of money and eight years of delay in the
use of the Ocean Telegraph would, in all human probability,
have been averted.

Landing at Southampton, he went to the Continent. On his
arrival in Paris he was received with enthusiasm by his countrymen residing there. They tendered him the honor of a banquet,
saying in their note that they desired to give him " some special
mark of their exalted appreciation of his personal character, and
the achievements of his genius." At this banquet Colonel John
S. Preston presided. The vice-president was the Hon. Hamilton
Fish, and the guests especially invited were Hon. J. Y. Mason,
Hon. J. R. Chandler, and Rev. R. H. Seeley, of the American
chapel. Senator Charles Sumner was in Paris, but, his physician
not allowing him to attend any public occasions of excitement,
he sent a letter to Professor Morse, in which he said : " Through
you, civilization has made one of her surest and grandest triumphs, beyond any ever won on any field of blood ; nor do I go
beyond the line of most cautious truth, when I add that, if mankind had yet arrived at a just appreciation of its benefactors, it
would welcome such a conqueror with more than a marshal's *bâ-
ton.*" The speeches that were made on this occasion by Mr. Fish,
Mr. Seeley, and others, have been referred to already in the testimony which they furnished as to the time when Professor Morse
first brought his Telegraph into actual operation. In his own
remarks Professor Morse took occasion to speak in warm terms

of commendation of other inventors, and especially of the magnanimous and amiable Bavarian philosopher, Steinheil. "He alone," said Professor Morse, "of all the projectors, entertained the thought in 1837 of a recording Telegraph. It is to the magnanimity of Steinheil that I owe much of my European fame."

THE EUROPEAN TESTIMONIAL.

In the year 1857, by the advice of friends holding high official stations, Professor Morse had issued a memorial, setting forth the grounds on which he based a claim to some indemnity from the different governments of the European states within whose territories his Telegraph was in use. General Cass, Secretary of State, with great kindness, sent copies of the memorial to the several diplomatic representatives of the United States at the courts in Europe, with a personal letter intimating to each of the ministers that no objection is entertained to their forwarding Mr. Morse's views by means of unofficial oral communications, and other personal good offices with the authorities of the several governments. Hon. John Y. Mason, American Minister in France, entered very heartily into the service, and in a letter to Mr. Cass, dated August 22, 1857, recites the steps that were taken to bring about a convention of the several powers to take the subject into consideration, and secure substantial justice to Professor Morse. Mr. Mason wrote:

"Mr. Morse submitted his claim to the French Government through the Minister of the Interior. He presented a statement of facts prepared by himself, which was so equitable that it was hardly possible for the emperor's Government to deny relief. He showed that he complied with the French law, paid the usual charges and obtained a patent; that this patent gave to him the exclusive use of the invention in France; that the Government had forbidden his putting it in operation for reasons of state policy, which destroyed his privilege; that the Government had subsequently adopted the invention, to the exclusion of all other modes of telegraphic communication, openly acknowledging it as the Morse system, without arrangement with him or making compensation for thus taking his acknowledged private property for public use. The use of his system had promoted facility and accuracy in transmission of telegraphic communications, and produced great economy. The

Minister of the Interior, who has charge of the whole system of telegraphing, of which the Government is a monopolist, after considering his petition for many months, announced to Mr. Morse that the French Government would confer with the different governments of Europe, and unite in a compensation to him bearing some proportion to the benefits conferred by the result of his genius.

"The minister suggested that this should be done at Paris. This decision necessarily implied that Mr. Morse was to be rewarded ; that the French Government would make compensation, and that other governments ought to do the same. But it presented a serious difficulty in this, that the ministers representing other governments in Paris would not engage in the execution of the proposed plan without instructions of their respective governments ; he could not approach them, and I could not aid him in promoting such cooperation, and thus a modest and meritorious citizen, whose genius had produced an invention, by general consent his property, which reflected honor on him and on his country, was likely to lose an acknowledged demand simply because the suggested plan for his relief was impracticable to him. I am persuaded that the instructions which you have given will relieve him of these difficulties, thrown in his way by a suggestion generously and in good faith made by the French minister. Believing that the reward is well deserved, I shall be gratified to contribute to its accomplishment. But I will take care to observe strictly the caution and keep within the limits prescribed by your instruction."

More than a year elapsed, and Mr. Mason again wrote to Mr. Cass, announcing the result.

Mr. Mason to Mr. Cass.

"Legation of the United States, Paris, *September* 9, 1858.

"*Hon. Lewis Cass, Secretary of State:*

"Sir: After receiving your dispatch No. 122, which you addressed to me under date of July 31, 1857, I availed myself of the first opportunity, in conversation with the Minister of Foreign Affairs, to inform him of my precise position in reference to the affair of Professor S. F. B. Morse, in which I was assured that the Imperial Government had generously manifested an interest. His excellency appreciated the reasons which had influenced my Government in its instructions to the ministers of the United States in Europe.

"I have, in the progress of the affair, more than once conversed with Count Walewski, in regard to it, but always at his own instance, and have been happy to find that ten of the European governments have, without solicitation, united in an act not more honorable to Professor Morse than to themselves. Professor Morse is at present in Switzerland. A few days since the *chef du cabinet* of Count Walewski called at my house, and informed me that the final sitting of the ministers had taken place, and his excellency desired to know if it would be agreeable to me to receive and communicate to Mr. Morse a letter and a *procès-verbal* of the proceedings of the conference. I replied that it always gave me pleasure to comply with his excellency's wishes, and never more so than when made the organ of a communication showing that the Imperial Government has generously and earnestly interested itself in doing honor to a distinguished and esteemed fellow-citizen. I have since received from Count Walewski a letter, of which I send you a copy. I have placed the letter addressed to him and the *procès-verbal* intended for him in the hands of Professor Morse's agent here, and the professor will, I presume, acknowledge their receipt directly to the Minister of Foreign Affairs. If he desires me to do so, I will transmit his reply. I am gratified at the result of an affair which seemed, and would have been, hopeless, but for the action and generous support voluntarily given to Mr. Morse by the Imperial Government.

" I have the honor to be your obedient servant,

"J. Y. MASON."

The letter of Count Walewski to Professor Morse, and the proceedings of the convention, form the most brilliant chapter in the life of a private individual.

Letter of Count Walewski to Professor Morse.

"MINISTRY OF FOREIGN AFFAIRS, PARIS, *September* 1, 1858.

" SIR : It is with a lively satisfaction that I have the honor to announce to you that a sum of four hundred thousand francs will be remitted to you, in four annuities, in the name of France, of Austria, of Belgium, of the Netherlands, of Piedmont, of Russia, of the Holy See, of Sweden, of Tuscany, and of Turkey, as an honorary gratuity, and as a reward, altogether personal, of your useful labors. Nothing can better mark, than this collective act of reward, the sentiment of public gratitude which your invention has so justly excited.

"The emperor has already given you a testimonial of his high esteem, when he conferred upon you, more than a year ago, the decoration of a Chevalier of his order of the Legion of Honor. You will find a new mark of it in the initiative which his Majesty wished that his Government should take in this conjuncture; and the decision that I charge myself to bring to your knowledge is a brilliant proof of the eager and sympathetic adhesion that his proposition has met with from the states I have just enumerated.

"I pray you to accept on this occasion, sir, my personal congratulations, as well as the assurance of my sentiments of the most distinguished consideration.   A. WALEWSKI.

"Monsieur MORSE."

[TRANSLATION.]

"Report of proceedings at the meeting of the representatives of Austria, Belgium, France, the Netherlands, Piedmont, Russia, the Holy See, Sweden, Tuscany, and Turkey, held for the purpose of considering the proposition made in behalf of Dr. Morse.

"Sitting of April 27, 1858.

"*Present*—For Austria, Baron HUBNER; for Belgium, Mr. FIRMIN ROGIER; for France, Count WALEWSKI; for the Netherlands, Mr. LIGHTENVELT; for Piedmont, Count VILLAMARINA; for Russia, Count KISSELEFF; for the Holy See, his Grace Mr. SACCONI; for Sweden, Count DE PIPER; for Tuscany, Marquis TANAY DE NERLI; for Turkey, HAÏDAR EFFENDI.

"Count Walewski stated, in the first place, the reasons which had induced the emperor's Government to support, along with other governments, the claim advanced by Mr. Morse, with the view of procuring a pecuniary remuneration to be made to him for the services which the process of his electro-magnetic telegraph has already rendered in the greater part of the European states. The discovery of the principles upon which the process that has received the name of Mr. Morse rests, unquestionably, said Count Walewski, does not belong to him; but he was the first to contrive to carry this discovery out of the speculative dominion of reason into that of material application. It is owing to labors and studies, the honor of which belongs indisputably to him, that electric communication, which, previous to him, was only, so to speak, a simple affirmation of science, has become a reality, and one of the most useful acquisitions that our epoch has made, and that must bind it to the future.

Results have already spoken sufficiently loud, and the admiration which they have excited has been too universal for it to be necessary to insist on the importance of the service that Mr. Morse has rendered to everybody, private persons and governments. But the more manifest this service is, the more equitable does it seem that it should not be left without a recompense proportionate to its magnitude. Now, if Mr. Morse has seen the Supreme Court of the United States establish, by a patent, his right to the invention of the process which has taken his name, and if he has been able, consequently, to derive some profit from its application in that country, it has not been the same with that which has been made of it in Europe. Nearly all the governments here having reserved to themselves the exclusive use of the Telegraph, or the faculty of alone conceding its employment to private persons or to companies, the knowledge which they have had of Mr. Morse's process could not obtain for him the material advantages which would not have failed to follow, had an invention of a different character been in question. The honorary distinctions which several of the sovereigns have deigned to confer on him have, beyond any doubt, been to him valuable marks of a lofty esteem; but they have been insufficient to supply the place of the pecuniary compensations which his sacrifices and his labors seemed destined to assure to him, and which are so much the more justly called for, since electro-magnetic telegraphing, independently of the immense services which it renders by the rapidity of transmitting news and correspondence, also obtains, by its operation under the governments having the monopoly of it, profits in money, already considerable, and which must continue to increase. It is, therefore, under a conviction that there is justice as well as generosity in acceding to the claim of Mr. Morse, whom the infirmities of age have now reached, after he has entirely devoted his small fortune to experiments and voyages necessary to arrive at the discovery and application of his process, that the emperor's Government has solicited various states, to whose gratitude Mr. Morse has acquired rights, to join in the remuneration which is due to him. The answer to this appeal must permit a hope that an agreement will easily be established, in regard to the collection itself which it will be expedient to adopt.

"After unfolding these considerations, Count Walewski indicated the two questions which, when the principle of indemnity is once admitted, must invite the attention of the meeting:

" 1. What ought to be the amount of the indemnity, and in

what manner should the payment be made? Shall it be in the shape of a pension for life, or in that of a sum paid at once?

" 2. What is the most equitable mode of apportionment to be established among the various governments which will contribute to the payment of the indemnity?

" The meeting, having heard this statement, entered into discussion, under a reservation that the determinations should only be accepted *ad referendum* by each of its members.

" Count Walewski proposed that, for indemnity, there be allowed to Mr. Morse either a pension for life of sixty to seventy thousand francs, or a single sum of four hundred thousand francs, payable in four annuities.

" Baron Hubner declared himself in favor of the latter mode of allowance, in preference to the establishment of a pension for life. This opinion met with general assent.

" In regard to the amount of the indemnity, his Grace Mr. Sacconi observed that, from the moment in which various governments united for the purpose of recompensing a discovery, it was necessary that a suitable sum should evince this union of several states in a measure of remuneration.

" The meeting having consulted in regard to the sum of four hundred thousand francs proposed, in case the system of a sum to be given at once should be chosen, no objection was offered to this assessment.

" In regard to the question of apportionment, two systems were proposed: to fix the apportionment by the number of apparatuses employed in each country, or to determine it according to the population and extent of each state.

" Count de Kisseleff, after remarking that, in the view of his government, the Morse process is an improvement of electric telegraphing, and not the invention itself, declared that it was, however, disposed, in consideration of the practical utility of this process, and of the personal use which was made of it, to concur in a reasonable and collective remuneration of it, apportioning the remuneration in each country by the number of apparatuses which are in use therein. There was, in fact, in each state employing the Morse process, a question of revenue; but the greater the number of apparatuses in use, the more considerable the revenue must be.

" Baron Hubner earnestly concurred in the opinion expressed by Count Kisseleff. The number of apparatuses was, in his judgment, the most practical basis to adopt for an apportionment, for it corresponded exactly with the expenses and profits of which the electro-magnetic Telegraph was the source for every government. There was, in the establishment of the Morse process, an amount of capital invested, of which the number of machines in use must represent the interest. It was on that number, therefore, that it was just to rely in the apportionment.

"The Marquis of Villamarina thought that his government would also prefer, in the assessment of its share in a collective remuneration, a proportion based on the number of apparatuses, as being more in accordance with the advantages obtained by employing the process in question.

" Count Walewski was of the same opinion, and again adduced, in its favor, the consideration that the Morse process has, besides the increase of celerity in the transmission of dispatches which is due to it, produced, by being substituted for previous systems of telegraphing, remarkable savings to all the governments, and that the number of apparatuses gives the measure of the savings realized by each government; and this furnishes the surest means of proving what proportionate part it ought to bear in a collective remuneration.

" His Grace Mr. Sacconi did not think that this mode of valuation would answer the purpose intended. He rather inclined to the other system. He feared that the number of apparatuses would not furnish a basis of apportionment as equitable as had been said, inasmuch as a state of less importance, relatively, might find that it was its lot to pay more than a more considerable state, because it had more apparatuses than the latter.

" Mr. Firmin Rogier likewise thought that the number of apparatuses was not the most just basis to adopt. He preferred that account should be taken of the distance to be run by the telegraphic lines, or of the amount of the population, and of the extent of the territory. There would then be no liability of a state with a smaller number of inhabitants paying more than a state which was manifestly more populous.

" The Marquis de Nerli was also of opinion that the share of each, in the indemnity to be allowed, should be proportionate to the extent of territory, and to the number of the population. What seemed to him most satisfactory would be an apportionment which should take into account the number only of those who availed themselves of telegraphing—the very considerable agricultural population of Tuscany making no use of it.

" Mr. Lightenvelt limited himself to stating that the concurrence of his government was obtained in the measure of remuneration solicited by Mr. Morse, provided that the various governments which profited by the discovery of his process contributed simultaneously to recompense it.

"Haïdar Effendi and Count de Piper were in like manner satisfied by declaring that their governments would accede to any equitable proposition of remuneration. Their personal opinion as to the mode of apportionment was, however, in favor of the number of apparatuses.

"His Grace Mr. Sacconi and Mr. Firmin Rogier, in the course of the discussion, again advanced the idea of adopting a middle term between the sum resulting from the number of apparatuses and that afforded by the population and extent of territory.

"Baron Hubner proposed to take into consideration the opinion of the majority, by rallying in favor of the mode of apportionment by the number of apparatuses, except that each one should consult his government on this subject, and bring forward subsequently the observations thereon, when he shall have gathered the information which this mode of assessment requires.

"This opinion was unanimously adopted, and it was decided, consequently, that the members of the meeting should transmit *ad referendum* to their respective governments the proposition for an indemnity of four hundred thousand francs, payable in four annuities, the apportionment of which to each state should be made in the ratio of the number of apparatuses. It was, moreover, understood that, if on account of new applications of his process Mr. Morse should hereafter think proper to make other claims, he would have to make them himself of the governments or companies from which he should claim compensation.

"After these resolutions, the meeting adjourned until the time when the members should have received an answer from their governments.

"The present report of proceedings having been read at the second sitting of the meeting, on the 23d of August, 1858, it was signed — OITTENFELS, Austria; Baron DE BEYENS, Belgium; Count WALEWSKI, France; LIGHTENVELT, Netherlands; Marquis DE VILLAMARINA, Sardinia; BALABINE, Russia; Archbishop of Nice, Holy See; E. DE PIPER, Sweden; Marquis TANAY DE NERLI, Tuscany; HAÏDAR EFFENDI, Turkey.

"Count Walewski, after the proceedings of the first sitting had been read, consulted the various members of the meeting in regard to the answers which they had received from their governments on the matters contained in the resolutions previously adopted *ad referendum*. The members of the meeting, with the exception of the Minister of the Netherlands, stated that their governments concurred in the mode of the proposed apportionment, and in the sum of four hundred thousand francs.

" Mr. de Balabine observed that, only having positive instructions to concur in the mode of apportionment, he awaited, so far as concerned the amount of the indemnity, the opinion of his government.

" The Minister of the Netherlands regretted that he was unable, in his answer, to unite entirely· in the statements of the other members of the meeting. His government, while accepting the proposed basis of apportionment, considered the amount of the remuneration as too high.[1] It feared that it might call forth, on the part of its people, similar claims for inventions of a different character.

" Count Walewski, on declaring that, with the exception of the Minister of the Netherlands, all the members of the meeting agreed on the same mode of apportionment, and, no objection being made to the sum brought forward, proposed to order an apportionment based on the figures which, after an exchange of their respective reports of investigation, should indicate the exact number of apparatuses in use in each country. The comparative estimate which results therefrom is contained in the table herewith annexed. It was understood that, if the Government of the Netherlands should still think of reducing the amount of the sum placed to its account in the common apportionment, the apportionment should not be affected thereby, but that it would only result in a reduction of the allowance made to Mr. Morse.

" Count Walewski called to mind that Mr. Morse could, moreover, make direct application to the governments which have not joined in the generous measure adopted by the present meeting.

" On motion of his Grace the Nuncio of the Holy See, it was agreed that the time for the payments should be fixed, and it was arranged that they should be made in four annuities commencing on the 1st of January, merely in order to leave to the various governments the care of regulating this expenditure according to the constitutional requirements to which they have to pay attention.

[1] Subsequently the Minister of the Netherlands acceded to the arrangement, and the vote was unanimous.

" It was, moreover, agreed that the payment of each state should be made at said periods, to the Department of Foreign Affairs, at Paris, which would be charged with the duty of delivering to Mr. Morse, in the name of all the governments, the actual amount of the annuity falling due.

" Done at Paris, on the 23d of August, 1858."

The signatures follow.

Table of the Proportionate Distribution.

The total number of apparatuses being twelve hundred and eighty-four, if the indemnity of four hundred thousand francs to be allowed be divided by this number, the sum which each government has to contribute is three hundred and eleven francs fifty-five centimes for each apparatus, which gives the following proportions:

COUNTRIES.	Number of Appara- tuses.	Amount to be paid in Four Annuities.
Austria........................	224	$69,787 20
Belgium	52	16,200 60
France	462	143,936 10
Netherlands....................	72	22,431 60
Piedmont	73	22,743 15
Russia	110	34,270 50
Holy See	17	5,296 35
Sweden........................	191	59,506 05
Tuscany.......................	14	4,361 70
Turkey........................	69	21,496 95
	1,284	$400,030 20

This result was communicated to Mr. Morse by Mr. Mason, and the gratified recipient immediately addressed the following letter to the French Minister:

Professor Morse to Count Walewski.

" Paris, Grand Hôtel du Louvre, September 15, 1858.

" Monsieur le Ministre : On my return to Paris from Switzerland, I have this day received from the Minister of the United States the most gratifying information which your Excellency did me the honor to send to me through him, respecting the decision of the congress of the distinguished diplomatic representatives of ten of the august Governments of Europe, held in special reference to myself.

" You have had the considerate kindness to communicate to me a proceeding which reflects the highest honor upon the Imperial Government and its noble associates, and I am at a loss for language adequately to express to them my feelings of profound gratitude.

"But especially, your Excellency, do I want words to express toward the august head of the Imperial Government and to your Excellency the thankful sentiments of my heart for the part so prominently taken by his Imperial Majesty, and by your Excellency, in so generously initiating this measure for my honor in inviting the governments of Europe to a conference on the subject, and for so zealously and warmly advocating and perseveringly conducting to a successful termination the measure in which the Imperial Government so magnanimously took the initiative.

"I accept the gratuity thus tendered on the basis of an honorary testimonial, and a personal reward, with tenfold more gratification than could have been produced by a sum of money, however large, offered on the basis of a commercial negotiation.

"I beg your Excellency to receive my thanks, however inadequately expressed, and to believe that I appreciate your Excellency's kind and generous services, performed in the midst of your high official duties, consummating a proceeding so unique, and in a manner so graceful, that personal kindness has been beautifully blended with official dignity.

"I will address respectively to the honorable ministers who were your Excellency's colleagues a letter of thanks for their participation in this act of high honor to me.

"I beg your Excellency to accept the assurances of my lasting gratitude, and highest consideration, in subscribing myself

"Your Excellency's most obedient, humble servant,

"SAMUEL F. B. MORSE.'

We may fittingly close this portion of the history with a list of the *nations* which acknowledged the Telegraph as the invention of Professor Morse, and the *mode* of acknowledgment:

France.— The Emperor Napoleon III. convened in Paris in 1858 a special congress, inviting the different nations to concur in a united testimonial to the inventor, at the same time conferring upon him the decoration of the Legion of Honor. The result of the congressional deliberations was an *honorary gratuity*, from ten of the principal powers, of four hundred thousand francs.

Prussia.—The King of Prussia sent him the "Scientific Gold Medal" of Prussia, set in the lid of a gold snuff-box.

Austria.—A contributor to the "honorary gratuity," and, from the Emperor, the "Scientific Gold Medal" of Austria.

Russia.—A contributor to the "honorary gratuity."

Spain.—The Queen of Spain conferred upon him the Cross of "Knight Commander de Numero," of the Order of Isabella the Catholic.

Portugal.—The King of Portugal conferred upon him the Cross of a "Knight of the Tower and Sword."

Italy.—A contributor to the "honorary gratuity," and the King of Italy conferred upon him the Cross of a "Knight of Saints Lazaro and Mauritio."

Holy See.—A contributor to the "honorary gratuity."

Belgium.—A contributor to the "honorary gratuity."

Holland.—A contributor to the "honorary gratuity."

Denmark.—The King Frederick VII. conferred upon him the Cross of "Knight of the Dannebrog."

Sweden.—A contributor to the "honorary gratuity."

Turkey.—A contributor to the "honorary gratuity," and the late Sultan conferred upon him the decoration in diamonds of the "Nishan Iftichar," or Order of Glory.

Great Britain.—Nationally, *nothing.* The telegraph companies in 1856 gave him a grand banquet in London, presided over by the inventor of the English semaphore, the distinguished William Fothergill Cooke.

Switzerland.—Nationally, *nothing.*

Saxony.—Nothing.

The *Great Convention* in Paris in March and April, 1865, convened to arrange *telegraphic* correspondence between the European nations, was formed from representative delegates from Austria, Baden, Bavaria, Belgium, Denmark, Spain, France, Greece, Hamburg, Hanover, Italy, Holland, Portugal, Prussia, Russia, Saxony, Sweden and Norway, Switzerland, Turkey, and Würtemberg. Article third of this convention is in these words: *The Morse apparatus is provisionally adopted for the use of all the international lines !*

Having received the first installment of the indemnity awarded him by the congress of European powers, and surfeited with honors and attentions, Professor Morse left Europe. By steamer from Southampton, November 17, 1858, he went with his family to Arroyo, Porto Rico, in the West Indies, where his daughter, Mrs. Lind, had been residing for several years. In a letter to Mrs. Morse's mother, he gives a picture of the new scenes to which he was now introduced for the first time:

"In St. Thomas we received every possible attention. The Governor called on us and passed an evening, and invited Edward and myself to breakfast (at 10½ o'clock) the day we left. He lives in a fine mansion on one of the lesser hills that inclose the harbor, having directly beneath him on the slope, and only separated by a wall, the residence of Santa Anna. He was invited to be present, but he was ill (so he said), and excused himself. I presume his illness was occasioned by the thought of meeting an American from the States, for he holds the citizens of the States in perfect hatred, so much so as to refuse to receive United States money in change from his servants on their return from market.

" A few days in change of latitude make wonderful changes in feelings and clothing. When we left England the air was wintry, and thick woolen clothing and fires were necessary. The first night at sea blankets were in great demand. With two extra, and my great-coat over all, I was comfortably warm. In twenty-four hours, the great-coat was dispensed with, then one blanket, then another, until a sheet alone began to be enough; and, the two or three last nights on board, this slight covering was too much. When we got into the harbor of St. Thomas, the temperature was oppressive. Our slightest summer clothing was in demand. Surrounded by pomegranate-trees, magnificent oleanders, cocoa-nut trees, with their large fruit some thirty feet from the ground, the aloe, and innumerable, and to me strange, tropical plants, I could scarcely believe it was December. I felt at first somewhat debilitated from the heat, for St.-Thomas harbor is surounded by conical hills, facing the south, and the sun has full play upon the city, which is built on the slopes of three hills, the houses rising from the shore and occupying about one-quarter of the height.

" We arrived on Thursday morning and remained until Monday evening. Edward " (his son-in-law) " having engaged a Long-Island schooner, which happened to be in port to take us to Arroyo, at four o'clock the Governor sent his official barge, under the charge of the captain of the port, a most excellent, intelligent, scientific gentleman, who had breakfasted with us at the Governor's in the morning, and in a few minutes we were rowed alongside of the schooner Estelle, and before dark were under way and out of the harbor. Our quarters were very small and close, but not so uncomfortable. At daylight in the morning of Tuesday, we were sailing along the shores of Porto Rico, and at sunrise we found we were in sight of Guayama and Arroyo, and with our glasses we saw at a distance the buildings on Edward's estate. Susan "(his daughter) "had been advised of our coming, and a flag was flying on the house in answer to the signal we made from the vessel. In two or three hours we got to the shore, as near as was safe for the vessel, and then, in the doctor's boat, which had paid us an official visit to see that we did not bring yellow fever or other infectious disease, the kind doctor, an Irishman, educated in America, took us ashore at a little temporary landing-place, to avoid the surf. On the shore there were some handkerchiefs shaking, and in a crowd we saw Susan, and Leila, and Charlie, who were waiting for us in carriages, and in a few moments we embraced them all. The sun was hot upon us, but, after a ride of two or three miles, we came to the ' Henrietta,' my dear Edward and Susan's residence, and were soon under the roof of a spacious, elegant, and most commodious mansion. And here we are with midsummer temperature and vegetation, but a tropical vegetation, all around us. Well, we always knew that Edward was a prince of a man, but we did not know, or rather appreciate, that he has a princely estate, and in as fine order as any in the island. When I say ' fine order,' I do not mean that it is laid out like the Bois de Boulogne, nor is there quite so much picturesqueness in a level plain of sugar-canes as in the trees and shrubbery of the gardens of Versailles, but it is a rich and well-cultivated estate of some fourteen hundred acres, gradually rising for two or three miles from the sea-shore to the mountains, including some of them, and stretching into the valleys between them."

While here in the West Indies, Professor Morse received a letter of great value and interest to himself from the distinguished Professor Steinheil. It has the same significance with the letter of Dr. Page,[1] as a disclaimer of any part of the invention peculiar to the Morse instrument. Writing to Mr. Kendall, December 22, 1858, Professor Morse said :

" I have received from Professor Steinheil the letter of which

[1] *See* page 559, *ante.*

the following is a translation, and I send it to you, that, if possible, in this day of rewards, the delicate and righteous hint contained in the latter part may lead to some grateful acknowledgment on the part of those who are profiting by his discovery. Every line in the United States is saved by it one-half the expense of the conductors upon their poles. He has no patent that enables him to demand compensation, but his claims are no less just on that account; they appeal rather with more force to men whose sense of right is not confined to the letter of a statute, and who have any feeling of magnanimity. I know of no public attention which could be shown to me either by the telegraph companies of the United States, or by the American public generally, so personally gratifying to me as the setting on foot an appropriate testimonial for Professor Steinheil's labors in the cause of telegraphy. But to the letter:

" 'MUNICH, *October* 30, 1858.

" 'DEAR SIR: Accept, first of all, my sincere and cordial congratulations on the beautiful results which have followed the acknowledgment of your invention, and which bears your name, and which has at last extended the only important system of telegraphing (as I believe) over the whole world.

" ' When you, at the moment of receiving the well-merited reward of much pains, called to the minds of your countrymen in so friendly a manner my services for the Telegraph, as your speech announces (which was yesterday sent to me by M. Violliet, American consul in Geneva), I regard it as the finest testimony your heart could give, and it is new proof that united powers can effect more than when from selfish considerations they act separately. What we both have done for telegraphy stands side by side. The contributions of the one do not encroach on the contributions of the other —do not make the other superfluous. You have contributed the quickest, simplest, and most beautiful mode of communication. I have reduced to one-half the conducting wire, and also made it surer and cheaper. Now it will be a satisfaction to me if this my contribution toward solving the great problem should be rewarded by my friends in Europe. But I cannot suppress the wish that as I contributed to procure the acknowledgment of your invention in Europe, so you may be inclined to procure my portion of reward in America. It would certainly be a noble example, seldom seen in the world's history, the example of two men who had spent a great part of their lifetime in solving the same problem, appearing, not as rivals, but as friends, each striving that the services of the one should be rewarded in the land of the other.

" ' With the expression of the sincerest respect and esteem,

" ' Dr. C. A. STEINHEIL,

" ' *Ministerial Councilor and Academician.*

" ' To Professor S. F. B. MORSE.'

"The above noble letter from one of Nature's noblemen has excited the strongest desires that some testimonial from our country, appropriate and delicate, should be sent to Professor Steinheil. Many modes have occurred to me, but I wish your judgment, well knowing that in my desires in this respect your feelings are in unison with my own. I now merely throw out hints. Steinheil's discovery of the *earth's circuit,* which, as I have said, and he has also said, has reduced the expense of the conductor one-half, is in use by every telegraph-line in the country as well as in Europe. No patent secures to him his just and natural right to compensation. In this he stands in the same position that I do before the European Governments. See what Europe has done for me! I personally cannot adequately return the honor upon Steinheil, but would it not be a beautiful reciprocation if an American testimonial, proposed by me, if you please, to take from it any appearance of antagonism, should be made by the American public, but especially by the telegraph companies of the United States, for all the lines, legitimate or illegitimate, are using his discovery, and are therefore under obligations in equity to Steinheil? Whatever plan shall be proposed, I wish to contribute to it, and will most cheerfully do so. Another plan would be the adoption by the telegraph companies of a mode of compensation which I have often thought would be a feasible one for remunerating an inventor, such as Fulton, for example. Suppose, in the case of Fulton's heirs, it is desired to give them the benefit of the compensation of which he has been deprived; let *one cent* be added to the fare of every passenger in every steamboat, for a limited number of years, to constitute the inventor's fund, and to be paid over annually or semi-annually for the benefit of his heirs. This is a simple plan, easily adopted, and look at the results! First, it is a tax so light, that no individual, *however poor,* would feel it burdensome; it is levied exactly upon those who are receiving the benefit of the inventor's labors; it does not burden the companies, for it is *additional* to their tariff rates, and by every man who has the least gratitude in his composition would be given, not grudgingly, but with a hearty good-will; and what would be the *aggregate?* Sufficient amply for all purposes of compensation to those who have an equitable claim to public gratitude, and produced in the most equitable way, burdensome to none. Now, to apply the plan for the creation of a Steinheil fund Let it be ordained by every telegraph company that, for a certain number of years, *one cent* additional upon *every message* shall be levied, and the thing is done. Please think of this."

On the same day when he addressed this letter to Mr. Kendall, Professor Morse wrote to Dr. Steinheil these words:

"Arroyo, Porto Rico, West Indies, *December* 22, 1858.

"My dear Professor Steinhéil : Your letter of the 30th of October I have this moment received at this place, it having been forwarded to me from New York by my brother.

"I am passing the winter in these tropical regions, at the residence of my son-in-law, Edward Lind, Esq., a planter of this island, and my address until March 1, 1859, will be to his care.

"Your courteous acknowledgment of my poor attempt to do you justice at the honorary dinner given me in Paris, is exceedingly grateful. I had long wished for the opportunity thus publicly to acknowledge your great kindness. I intended to do it in London, in 1856, when the telegraph companies gave me a public reception, but I was there fettered by the apprehension that I might be treading upon delicate ground, in the country of Wheatstone. In Paris, before my own countrymen, I had no such fear, and therefore carried out my long-cherished wish toward you.

"The suggestion you make in regard to some acknowledgment from America, for your important discovery in telegraphy, is not new to me, but the means of bringing any feasible plan to a result are environed with some peculiar difficulties, which I will briefly state.

"Such a testimonial as has been conceded to me by the congress of powers convened in Paris, could not be enacted in the United States, principally on this ground: Telegraphs on the Continent of Europe are a government monopoly, and are therefore wholly under the control of the governments of the several states; hence the propriety of government action in awarding me the recent testimonials. On the contrary, telegraphs in the United States, as well as in Great Britain, are managed and are under the control of joint-stock companies, who regulate their doings at

44

pleasure, independent of the government, except in some very general particulars.

" The government itself is subject to the tariff rates and regulations of the companies. Hence, you will see, the British and United States Governments are not the parties against whom any equitable claims can be set up by the inventor of a telegraph.

" The *patent* granted by these governments assumes to protect the right of the inventor to compensation, and leaves him to make such terms for his own compensation with joint-stock companies as he and they can agree upon.

" The absence of a patent on your part for your valuable discovery, which you so generously threw open to the world, deprives you, therefore, of all *legal* right to claim compensation for it, but it by no means lessens your *equitable* right to it, from those who are benefited by its use; on the contrary, in my view, it enhances it, while at the same time the difficulties in realizing a just compensation are increased tenfold.

" For it must be through appeals to a sense of justice lying back of legal enactment, and which, to the shame of human nature, is dormant, if not dead, in the hearts of those who look at an enterprise only in the light of a lucrative investment. Yet I am proud to believe that there is a great majority of those capitalists in the United States who have invested their funds in the Telegraph enterprise, whose hearts will respond promptly to an appeal to their magnanimity, if a judicious plan be presented to them, especially with such a noble example as Europe has set, in respect to me.

" At any rate, my dear Dr. Steinheil, your hint shall be fruitful, if any efforts of mine can make it so. I have already indited a letter to my friends in the United States, on the subject. I have suggested several modes of attaining a favorable result, and I cannot but hope something may be done. I would not wish to raise expectations which may be disappointed, but I will say to you that what I have thus initiated I will not allow to rest.

" Some months must elapse before I return to my home at Poughkeepsie, New York. In the mean time I have set my friends in the United States to thinking upon the subject, and on my return I may find them prepared for some decisive action, which I may aid in consummating, and of which you shall be duly advised. In the mean time, my dear sir, accept the assurance of my cordial esteem and friendship, SAMUEL F. B. MORSE.

" Dr. C. A. STEINHEIL, Councilor and Academician, Munich, Bavaria."

Professor Morse was intensely gratified also, while in the West Indies, by receiving notice of his election as a member of the Royal Academy of Sciences of Stockholm, Sweden. The secretary, in sending the diploma, said, " The Academy is happy, sir, to offer you this testimony of the lively interest with which your scientific merits have inspired it, and it hopes you will unite your efforts to those which it has itself made for the advance of the sciences." This was the more acceptable to the Professor, at this moment, because it was at the time when persistent efforts were made in his own country to depreciate his merits as a man of science, and the value of his contributions. A few days afterward came to him the intelligence that the Queen of Spain had conferred upon him the honor of Knight Commander of the Royal Order of Isabella the Catholic.

In a letter to the Hon. J. Y. Mason, United States Minister in France, Professor Morse describes his progress in telegraphic enterprise, while on his visit of pleasure in the West-India islands:

" I have just had the pleasure of completing the first line of Telegraph in this beautiful island, from my son-in-law's house to his place of business, on the bay, about two miles. It excites much interest, and I have been requested to partake of an honorary breakfast by the *intendente* and the military commandant and officials of Guayama and Arroyo to-morrow. This too initiates the grand enterprise of uniting our American Telegraph lines with Europe by a southern route, from Cape St. Vincent, through Madeira, the Canaries, Cape de Verde, and Cape St. Roque in Brazil, thence along the coast, and connecting Barbadoes, Martinique, St. Thomas, Porto Rico, Jamaica, Cuba, and Florida. My friends Sir James Carmichael, Mr. Brett, and Mr. Perry, of Madrid, are the energetic, efficient, and active projectors and promoters of this grand enterprise, in connection with myself, and in a few years I hope, if my life is spared, to see this perfectly feasible plan of telegraphic union accomplished."

The 1st of March, 1859, was a great day in the little island, and in one of his familiar letters Professor Morse describes his own feelings of pleasure in the events which were celebrated.

" ARROYO, PORTO RICO, *March* 2, 1859.

" I have just completed with success the construction and

organization of the short telegraphic line, the first in this island;
initiating the great enterprise of the Southern Telegraph route to
Europe from our shores, so far as to interest the Porto Ricans in
the value of the invention. Yesterday was a day of great excitement here, for this small place. The principal inhabitants of this
place and Guayama determined to celebrate the completion of this
little line, in which they take a great pride, as being the first in the
island, and so they complimented me with a public breakfast, which
was presided over by the lieutenant-colonel commandant of
Guayama, the commandant and alcalde, the collector and captain
of the Port, with all the officials of the place, and the clergy of
Guayama and Arroyo, and gentlemen planters and merchants of the
two towns, numbering in all about forty. We sat down at one
o'clock to a very handsome *breakfast*, and the greatest enthusiasm
and kind and generous feeling were manifested. My portrait was
behind me upon the wall, draped with the Spanish and American
flags. I gave them a short address of thanks, and took the opportunity to interest them in the great Telegraph line which will give
them communication with the whole world. I presume accounts
will be published in the United States, from the Porto-Rico papers.
Thus step by step (shall I not rather say, *stride* by *stride?*) the Telegraph is compassing the world.

" My accounts from Madrid assure me that the Government will
soon have all the papers prepared for granting the concession to
Mr. Perry, our former secretary of legation at Madrid, in connection
with Sir James Carmichael, Mr. John W. Brett, the New York, Newfoundland, and London Telegraph Company, and others. The recent consolidation plan in the United States has removed the only
hesitation I had in sustaining this new enterprise, for I feared that
I might unwittingly injure, by a counter-plan, those it was my duty
to support. Being now in harmony with the American company,
and the Newfoundland company, I presume all my other companies
will derive benefit rather than injury from the success of this new
and grand enterprise. At any rate, I feel impelled to support all
plans that manifestly tend to the complete circumvention of the
globe, and the bringing into telegraphic connection all the nations
of the earth, and this when I am not fully assured that present
personal interests may not temporarily suffer. I am glad to know
that harmonious arrangements are made between the various companies in the United States, although I have been so ill-used. But
let it go. I will have no litigation if I can avoid it. Even —— may

have the field in quiet, unless he has presented a case too flagrantly unjust to leave unanswered."

He endeavored to possess his soul in patience, and, in a letter to one of his near relatives, he said, in regard to one of his severest opponents: "Of the nature of this attack, I am as yet in profound ignorance; but it is rather a damper upon the joy with which I usually return to my loved native land, that I have to encounter the attacks of the envious, and the annoyance of the sordid, and to know that, instead of rest in my old age, I must yet buckle on my armor for self-defense. Well, this is all ordered in wisdom. 'Shall we receive good at the hands of the Lord, and shall we not receive evil?' I would rather ask for proper submission, than be anxious to defeat those opposed to me." And to another he wrote, at the same time: "When I return to Poughkeepsie, it will be sad without your cheerful faces. But all in God's good time. He has purposes to accomplish, of more wisdom, and vaster benefit to his rational universe, than any we, with our selfish hearts, can devise. I return from honors abundant in Europe, to encounter attacks in various shapes at home; but I am not cast down by the prospect. I am most anxious that nothing I may be obliged to do, in self-defense, shall dishonor my Master; and all my hope, all my strength, is in Him. If He undertakes for me—and He certainly will—victory of the highest kind is sure, even if it does not come exactly in the shape I might wish now."

After this delightful visit, the only one that he was ever able to make to the home of his beloved daughter, Professor Morse embarked, in the middle of April, in a sailing-vessel, with his family, and returned to New York. A few days afterward, he went to his country seat in Poughkeepsie. His old neighbors and friends gave him a welcome, as if he were a conquering general returning from war. The *Daily Press* of the city records:.

"For some time previous to the hour at which the train was to arrive, hundreds of people were seen flocking from all directions to the railroad-depot, both in carriages and on foot; and, when the train did arrive, and the familiar and loved form of Professor Morse was recognized on the platform of the car, the air was rent with the cheers of the assembled multitude. As soon as the cheers subsided, Professor Morse was approached by the committee of reception, and welcomed to the country of his birth, and to the home of his adoption. A great procession was then formed, composed of the carriages of citizens. The sidewalks were crowded with people on foot, the children of the public schools, which had been dismissed for the occasion, being quite conspicuous among them. Amid the ringing of bells, the waving of flags, and the gratulations of the people, the procession proceeded through a few of the principal streets, and then drove to the beautiful residence of Professor Morse, the band playing, as they entered the grounds, 'Sweet Home,' and then 'Auld Lang Syne.' The gate-ways at the entrance had been arched with evergreens and wreathed with flowers. As the carriage containing their loved proprietor drove along the graveled roads, we noticed that several of the domestics, unable to restrain their welcomes, ran to his carriage, and gave and received salutations. After a free interchange of salutations, and a general 'shake hands,' the people withdrew, and left their honored guest to the retirement of his own beautiful home. So the world reverences its great men, and so it ought. In Professor Morse we find those simple elements of greatness which elevate him infinitely above the hero of any of the world's sanguinary conflicts, or any of the most successful aspirants after political power. He has benefited not only America and the world, but has dignified and benefited the whole race."

CHAPTER XX.

1860–1870.

AT HOME—VIEWS ON SECESSION AND THE WAR—EDUCATION OF HIS CHIL-
DREN—LETTERS TO THEM—APPLICATIONS FOR AID—LAST VISIT TO EU-
ROPE—DÜSSELDORF AND ARTISTS—PARIS—ATTENTIONS PAID TO HIM—RE-
CEPTION AT COURT—THE GREAT EXHIBITION—HABIT OF LIFE IN PARIS
—LABORS IN THE COMMITTEE ON TELEGRAPHS—ISLE OF WIGHT—DRES-
DEN—PRESENTATION AT COURT—BERLIN AND THE TELEGRAPH CORPS—
RETURN TO AMERICA—PURCHASE OF ALLSTON'S "JEREMIAH" AND PRES-
ENT TO YALE COLLEGE—ALLSTON'S PORTRAIT BY LESLIE HE PRESENTS
TO ACADEMY OF DESIGN—DONATION TO THEOLOGICAL DEPARTMENT OF
YALE COLLEGE—TO NEW YORK UNION THEOLOGICAL SEMINARY—BANQUET
IN NEW YORK—CHIEF-JUSTICE CHASE'S REMARKS—PROFESSOR MORSE'S—
MR. HUNTINGTON'S—SUMMER AT POUGHKEEPSIE—HIS LEG IS BROKEN—
PROSTRATE FOR THREE MONTHS — STATUE OF HUMBOLDT — STATUE OF
MORSE—ERECTED BY TELEGRAPH-OPERATORS—CEREMONIES IN THE CEN-
TRAL PARK—ACADEMY OF MUSIC—ADDRESS BY PROFESSOR MORSE.

ON his return from Europe in 1859, Professor Morse saw distinctly the signs of approaching war between the Northern and Southern portions of the American Union. To prevent the impending conflict, and preserve the peace of the country, was the intense desire of his heart. He was an ardent patriot. In England, during the War of 1812–'14, he had on all occasions been the outspoken defender of his country. In his subsequent career, the recipient of distinguished honors from foreign powers, and the guest of princes, he was still the unchanged, simple republican citizen, and a thorough American. To him the prospect of a civil war was terrible, and he was willing to make any sacrifice to avert it. As the months and years of fierce controversy passed along, and the cloud burst in a fearful

storm, he sought to arrest its course. He was decidedly opposed to secession. Of the abstract right of it under the Constitution, he had doubts, but none as to its justice or expediency.
Associated with men of high standing in social and political life,
he sought, by the diffusion of tracts and books on the relations
of the States to the Federal Government, to reconcile contending parties, and preserve the peace of the country. These efforts, made in the spirit of the purest patriotism, subjected him
to severe reproach. But he bore it with his characteristic patience and equanimity, believing the time would come when
his motives would be understood. And, if they never should
be, he had the testimony of a good conscience that all the ends
he aimed at were *his country's and God's.*

The education of his children occupied a large share of his
attention. When they were at home he was their teacher;
when they were away at school he wrote to them constantly,
entering into their feelings, studying their tastes, and aiming at
the inculcation of those principles which were the basis of his
own character. Writing from Poughkeepsie to one of them,
August 17, 1862, he gave a description of another visit to his
native place:

" My dear Arthur : Here we are again safely at home, after
our journeyings of two weeks. After we left you at Newport, we
arrived in Boston the same evening, and went to the Tremont
House. It was very warm on Saturday and Sunday, but on Saturday your dear mamma and sister went with me over to Charlestown,
to see the town where your good grandfather was so long pastor of
the first church of Charlestown, and where your father was born. I
showed them the house, and, knocking at the door, a neat and
pleasant young woman opened it, and on telling her my errand she
very kindly conducted us up-stairs, and then we were in the room
where your father first saw the light. The house is a large double
house of wood, on the main street, one door opening on the street,
and the other, at which we knocked and entered, on the east side,
to which we had to pass through a gate and small grass-plot. The
other part of the house is occupied by the family of Captain Edes ;
they were all out of town. From thence we went upon Bunker's
Hill, and to the monument, which is within gunshot of the house in
which I was born. Notwithstanding the day was so warm, your

sister and I mounted the two hundred and ninety steps to the top. I was not fatigued, but your mother was fearful that the ascent would be too fatiguing for her, so she did not go up with us. The next day, Sunday, Cornelia and I went over again to Charlestown, as I wished to attend church, on the spot and among the congregation where my excellent father preached. We attended church there, heard an excellent sermon from a stranger, the regular clergyman being out of town. I looked round to see if there was a single face I knew, and not one could I find; every face was strange, but there were two or three old ladies who looked constantly very curiously at me and whispered together. So, when church was over, I put myself in their way, and they said they were sure they knew me. When I told them who I was, the son of their old pastor, they all crowded around me and said, ' Oh, we must shake hands with you, then;' and they seemed overjoyed to see me, invited me to dinner, and would scarcely take no for an answer. I thanked them, but declined, leaving my kind regards for any of my father's friends who were still living.

"On Monday we all left Boston for Nantasket Beach, about nineteen miles from Boston, and found a most beautiful sand-beach, superior in many respects to the beach at Newport; it is some five miles in extent, reaching to a point opposite Boston Light-house. The views here are more extensive and more varied than at Newport, islands and peninsulas varying the view, Boston, Charlestown, and other suburban villages, in the distance, and the light-house, with a beacon, looking like the posts of the great gates forming the entrance to Boston harbor, between which all the great ships pass in and out of the port. The surf is like that at Newport, on quite as shallow and gradual a beach, but the water was purer, without the slimy weeds of the Newport beach; yet the water was much colder; most of the bathers preferred it thus, I did not. I bathed but once, and think I took cold then, but I have recovered from its effects. We returned to Boston after two days; the last day, however, we went on a fishing-excursion. Mother, Cornelia, and I, got up at five o'clock, and, with two gentlemen besides, went off in a large yacht, furnished with lines and bait, about two miles, where we caught in about two hours some dozen of fish ; cod, perch, flounders, and sculpions. I caught the largest, a cod, weighing about eight pounds. We left Boston on Thursday morning, to return home by way of Springfield and Hudson. We passed Thursday night at Springfield, and the next day left for Hudson, by the way of Chatham Four Corners, where we went to take a branch train to Hudson, but, not being notified when we arrived at Chatham Four Corners, we were taken some miles on the way to Albany before we discovered our mistake, so we told the conductor to keep on and we would go to Albany; so we went to Albany while our trunks and other baggage went to Hudson; but, on our arrival at Albany, the Telegraph came to my help, and a few words to Hudson secured the safety of the stray luggage. We dined in Albany, and took the cars at four o'clock, and reached home just as soon as if no mistake had occurred. We were all rejoiced to meet again, thankful to Him who kept us in health and safety in our separation, and brought us together again in so much comfort, while others, no less deserving, have been subjected to all the horrors of this lamentable war. Many inquiries were made after Arthur, and we are all looking forward to October with the hope of having you with us for a while. Good-by, my dear boy; God bless you; and keep you from all harm to body and soul, and early make you one of his chosen ones! You little know how much we love you, and how anxious we are to have you in the way of true happiness. I leave a space for your dear mother to fill. Again good-by.

"Your affectionate father,   SAMUEL F. B. MORSE.
"Master S. ARTHUR B. MORSE."

Another letter to two of his sons shows the father, indulgent and judicious:

"POUGHKEEPSIE, *July* 17, 1864.

"MY DEAR BOYS: William goes to-morrow morning, and he takes 'Ponce,' the pony, for Willie; and little 'Nix,' the terrier, for Arthur, from papa, and I believe there are some other things for Mrs. Choules.

"Arthur, I bought the terrier for you; he is young, about seven months old. He is playful, but has very sharp teeth; you will have to coax him, for I find he does not come readily when called. If you are gentle with him, and feed him yourself, I think he will soon get attached to you, and, as he grows older, will come at your call. Don't tease him, nor let the boys tease him, for it spoils his temper, and he may be savage and bite you.—And, Willie, I hope you will use your dear little pony very kindly and gently; animals love kindness as well as men. Don't whip him or drive him at a racing pace this hot weather, or you may lose him. I hope you will have him where he will be well taken care of.

" You see, my dear boys, what pains and expense we cheerfully incur to make you happy, when we see you have good reports from your teachers. It is on this account we grant these favors to you. If you use them properly and do not let them take you away from your studies, we can indulge you in your reasonable wishes ; but, if we find you abuse these favors, we shall request Mr. Fay to deprive you of them, because it will be necessary for your good. But I won't believe my dear boys will abuse these favors, for they love their father and mother, and I think they won't intentionally pain them, by misusing their kindness.   SAMUEL F. B. MORSE.

" To ARTHUR and WILLIE."

How patiently he bore the burden of applications for counsel and aid which were often made to him by men laboring as he once labored with an unborn invention ! To such a man he wrote :

" Were I a younger man, with less of the cares of a large family, I should feel strongly disposed to examine and understand your project, and, if satisfactory, to aid you with all the means I could spare ; but I am now beyond the allotted age of man, and already burdened with as many cares as I can well sustain.

" Should you visit New York, however, in the course of the winter, I expect to be at my house, 5 West Twenty-second Street, and should be happy to understand your discovery and to put you in the way of aid, by introducing you to those who may be able to assist you, and whose avocations would lead them to be interested in it, more than it can interest me, as I am more interested in it indirectly, and as a general benefit, than directly.

" Inventors are apt to be sanguine, and often yield too much to their imagination. Many projects appear well on paper, which fail in practice from some unlooked-for mechanical difficulty. But these matters you have doubtless considered. If you have indeed discovered a more economical motive-power than is now in use, and have so far tested it as to be certain of success, you can scarcely exaggerate its importance, and no one would feel more gratified than myself to know that its discoverer is amply rewarded by fame and fortune."

His children being now of an age when he thought it would be for their advantage to study in Europe, he went abroad once more. He crossed the ocean with his family in June, 1866, and spent part of the summer at Aix-la-Chapelle. Visiting Düsseldorf, he was received with great enthusiasm by the artists whose favorite seat was in that city. He was now in circumstances to be a patron of art, and he must have taken peculiar pleasure as he remembered his own struggles as an artist, in purchasing of various artists five pictures, which he sent home to the care of Mr. Huntington, President of the National Academy of Design, with permission to exhibit them. A very pleasant incident at Düsseldorf he mentions in a letter to a relative:

"When at Düsseldorf it so happened that, while at the hotel, there was a society having its annual dinner in the *salle à manger*. It was composed of some of the principal citizens of Düsseldorf. The door being open to the reading-room, where I was reading the papers, I could hear (although said in German) the words *America* and *telegraph*, which were never mentioned but with loud applause. It seems Mr. Liech had informed the landlord, on my arrival, of my connection with the Telegraph; so, when the speeches were receiving great applause, the landlord whispered to the president that the American inventor of the Telegraph was at that moment a guest in the hotel. Immediately there was a stir, the president left his seat, and came out to me, and, apologizing for his liberty, he asked if I had any objection to present myself at the table; on replying that, if it would give them any gratification, I would cheerfully comply, he led me into the room, where I was greeted in the most uproarious manner; every one at table rose, three cheers were given, all insisting on touching glasses with mine, which they had filled with champagne. On the first subsidence of this greeting, I was led to the chair by the side of the president, who rose, and in a brief speech paid me and the United States some handsome compliments, to which I briefly replied by thanks in English, which he rendered into German; I then begged leave to retire, but could not until the ceremony of once more touching glasses had been performed, by every one at table, about forty persons."

The remainder of the summer was spent in Switzerland. In the autumn he went to Paris, and took apartments at No. 10 Avenue du Roi de Rome. His arrival was recognized by such attentions as are only extended to the most distinguished personages. The Emperor of the French, then in the zenith of his glory, omitted no opportunity to do him honor. Professor Morse was invited on all state occasions, and the best places were reserved for him and his family. At the court parties, they were placed with the imperial family and the diplomatic corps.

This (1867), the year of the great Exposition in Paris, he spent with his family, in the enjoyment of all which a good, prosperous, and great man could desire. Identifying himself with American society—contributing freely to the support of the American chapel, with which he and his family were connected—he sought to be useful in the various departments of society, as he would be if he were in his own country, and at home. He was now at the summit of human fame. It has oftentimes been said, and with truth, that no private individual was ever more highly honored among men than he. His name was familiar as that of the great benefactor of his race in all countries of the civilized world. Strangers of distinction, visiting Paris, sought him, to pay their respects. Members of royal families sent to know when it would be convenient for him to receive them; and, at the hour appointed, they called in state, to express to him the honor in which he was held. It was his custom to devote the morning of every day to his study. At this time, he prepared a pamphlet of nearly a hundred pages, containing a defense of himself, as the inventor of the Telegraph, in reply to attacks which were made upon him by English claimants. He consulted his friends, in relation to his duty in this matter. He had now reached that period in life, and that position in the esteem of the world, when he was far more disposed to rest quietly upon the good sense and intelligent judgment of mankind, and to consider the question as to his claims as fairly settled by the verdict of the world, than to prolong the controversy, and to reiterate the evidence which had been so frequently produced and published. But the advice which he received from all those with whom he conferred upon the subject encouraged him to take up his pen, and to give a history of the steps by which he accomplished the great work of his life. This pamphlet was printed and published in Paris, circulated among the scientific societies of Europe, and placed in the hands of thoughtful men, who were competent to weigh the evidence, and to judge candidly as to the claims of the inventor. No attempt was ever afterward made to interfere with the just claims of Mr. Morse to the honor which he had firmly claimed, as his own right, and that of the country which he loved. Extracts from this pamphlet, giving the process of the invention, with numerous drawings, form an Appendix to this volume, and should be studiously examined by every intelligent reader.

His morning studies being completed, he was in the habit, daily, of visiting the great Exposition, and spending several hours in the examination of an almost infinite variety of mechanical inventions. He was one of the committee upon telegraphic instruments. He earnestly desired to be excused from serving, from the fact that his prejudices were, naturally, greatly influenced by his relations to the various inventions which were before the public, and were now upon exhibition. But it was pressed upon him, as he was, of all men, the most thoroughly qualified to sit in judgment upon the comparative merits of the several contrivances. He consented to serve; and, with industry and patience, he devoted himself to an investigation of the several instruments, and prepared a report at great length—exhaustive in its research and comparisons—which was published with the official reports of the Exhibition.

At the close of the Exposition, Mr. Morse made another tour on the Continent. Now, as before, wherever he went, he was received with marks of attention from governments and people, as if he himself were the representative of a nation, or a royal personage upon his travels. His modesty was equal to his merit. Honored with marks of distinction from the various governments of Europe, which would have made him more conspicuous, in the midst of public assemblies, than any other individual, of whatever official rank, he steadily avoided, in his dress and equipage, any thing which might attract to himself the notice of the public, or which, in any manner, would distinguish him from his countrymen. On one occasion, he was called to a consultation with the official representatives of several European countries, in relation to telegraphic matters; and he asked me whether it would be proper for him, on this occasion, to wear the insignia which had been conferred upon him, by the several governments, on account of his invention. He said that there were two reasons why it seemed to him that it might be desirable for him, on such an occasion, to'display them. In the first place, it would mark, in the presence of the representatives of these governments, his sense of the honor which he had received from their several sovereigns; and, in the second place, such was the estimate of these marks of distinction in Europe, that he would be, perhaps, more respected, and therefore more influential, in the conference in which he was to engage. I concurred in this opinion, and advised him that it would be, not only proper, but useful, to put them on. But his native modesty controlled his action, and, when I asked him, afterward, whether he wore his decorations, he laughingly replied that, when it came to the point, he was unable to be reconciled to what he thought was a humiliation rather than an enviable distinction, and he went in ordinary citizen's dress—perhaps with nothing more than the ribbon of the Legion of Honor in his button-hole.

After passing a few months on the Isle of Wight, the Professor and family went to Dresden for the winter of 1867. Three months were spent in that delightful city. His presentation at the court of the King of Saxony was a compliment paid to his distinguished services.

From Dresden, Professor Morse repaired to Berlin, where he was specially honored by those who were the best qualified to appreciate the magnitude and importance of his work. From Mr. Bancroft, the United States Minister, and members of the Prussian Government, he received constant attentions. He remained but a few days in Berlin, and was obliged to decline a presentation at court which was tendered him.

But anxious to learn the latest views in the science of telegraphy, he called upon General (then Colonel) von Chauvin, the distinguished chief of the German telegraphic system, which, as in most European countries, is a government monopoly and administered by government officials. Before the interview was concluded, a messenger came in and spoke in German to the chief, who, as Mr. Morse was about to depart, said that the "operators" had heard of his presence in the building, and exceedingly desired to see him. Having kindly assented to the presentation,

Mr. Morse was led by the chief into a neighboring apartment, and there found himself facing several hundred gentlemen seated in a vast hall, the largest operating-room in the world. At a signal, the instruments ceased clicking, and each person stood erect and à la militaire.

"Gentlemen," began Colonel von Chauvin, "you have the honor to see before you the Father of the Telegraph."

All bowed profoundly again and again with such reverence that, as says a letter writer, who relates the incident, "the fond parent was quite embarrassed in the presence of so much of his children."

Not to recount the many tributes of esteem and respect paid him by Dr. Siemens and other gentlemen eminent in the specialty of telegraphy, one other unexpected compliment may be mentioned. The Professor was presented to the accomplished General Director of the Posts of the North-German Bund, Privy-Councilor von Phillipsborn, in whose department the telegraph had been comprised before Prussia became so great, and the centre of a powerful confederation. At the time of their visit, the director was so engaged, and that, too, in another part of the Post-Amt, that the porter said it was useless to trouble him with the cards. The names had not been long sent up, however, before the director himself came hurriedly down the corridor into the antechamber, and, scarcely waiting for the hastiest of introductions, enthusiastically grasped both the Professor's hands in his own, asking whether he had "the honor of speaking to Doctor Morse," or, as he pronounced it, "Morzey."

When, after a brief conversation, Mr. Morse rose to go, the director said that he had just left a conference over a new post and telegraph treaty in negotiation between Belgium and the Bund, and that it would afford him great pleasure to be permitted to present his guest to the assembled gentlemen, including the Belgian envoy and the Belgian postmaster-general.

There followed, accordingly, a formal presentation, with an introductory address by the director, who, in excellent English, thanked Mr. Morse, in the name of Prussia and of all Germany, for his great services; and speeches by the principal persons present, the Belgian envoy, Baron de Nothomb, very felicitously complimenting the Professor in French.

Succeeding the hand-shaking, the director spoke again, and, in reply, Mr. Morse gratefully acknowledged the courtesy shown to him, adding: "It is very gratifying to me to hear you say that the Telegraph has been and is a means of promoting peace among men. Believe me, gentlemen, my remaining days shall be devoted to this great object."

Before Mr. Morse withdrew, the director said he had a further request to make : In the adjoining room was the Councilor ——, the principal adviser of the department in legal questions connected with the Telegraph, especially in reference to international relations ; and the councilor would consider it an event in his life to be presented to Mr. Morse. The gentleman was therefore summoned, and soon entered ; supposing, doubtless, that his professional assistance was required. When told that the venerable gentleman before him was Professor Morse, he gave expression to his surprise and pleasure. The director then led his visitors into a small, cozily furnished room, saying as they entered, "Here I have so often thought of you, Mr. Morse, but I never thought I should have the honor of receiving you in my own private room."

After they were seated, the host, tapping upon a small table, continued, "Over this passed the important telegrams of the War of 1866." Then, approaching a large telegraph-map on the wall, he added : "Upon this you can see how invaluable was the telegraph in the war. Here," pointing with the forefinger of his right hand, "here the crown prince came down through Silesia. This," indicating, with the other forefinger, a passage through Bohemia, "was the line of march of Prince Friedrich Carl. From this station, the crown prince telegraphed Prince Friedrich Carl, always over Berlin, 'Where are you?' The answer from this station reached him also over Berlin.

"The Austrians were here," placing the thumb on the map below, and between the two fingers. "The next day Prince Friedrich Charles comes here," the left forefinger joined the thumb, "and telegraphs the fact, always over Berlin, to the crown prince, who hurries forward here," the forefinger of the right hand slipped quickly under the thumb as if to pinch something, and the narrator looked up significantly. Perhaps the patriotic director thought of the July afternoon, when,

45

eagerly listening at the little mahogany-topped table, over which passed so many momentous messages, he learned that the royal cousins had effected a junction at Königsgrätz, a junction that decided the fate of Germany and secured Prussia its present proud position,—a junction which, but for his modest visitor's invention, the telegraph "always over Berlin," would have been impossible.

Leaving Berlin, Professor Morse came to Paris, and passed a few weeks before embarking for New York. While here he had the great pleasure of receiving his portrait of Thorwaldsen, and of forwarding it to General Raastoff, the Danish Minister of War. In his letter to the minister he begged him to present the portrait to the king as "an acknowledgment on my part of Danish hospitality in 1856, and a mark of my own personal veneration for the names and labors of those noble Danes, Thorwaldsen and Oersted." He was now turning his face toward the west, to the setting sun ; the close of his career on earth he felt to be necessarily not far off. The honors that came from men had been enjoyed throughout this journey. In every city his presence had been marked with the attentions of men of learning and position. If justice had not been done in bestowing pecuniary rewards that he deserved, the full measure of honor had been awarded, and he was prepared to go home, with the assurance that the world had at last given Morse and America the credit of inventing the Recording Telegraph.

He left Havre in the St.-Laurent, in the latter part of May, 1868, and in early June was once more welcomed by his neighbors and friends in Poughkeepsie. Never was his rural home more lovely and inviting than when he entered again into its delights, and, far from palaces, courts, and kings, he sat down to its quiet enjoyment. He was not to be idle, though free from the cares of office and business. He was one to whom men came for advice and aid, in every variety of useful work. One letter to an applicant for pecuniary assistance and counsel might serve as a circular to be addressed to many others seeking the same favors. To a gentleman in Virginia he wrote a few days after he arrived at home :

"I received this morning your letter of yesterday, with its inclosures, and, while I was deeply interested in the details of your beautiful invention, I could not but regret that it is entirely out of my power to give you the aid you desire. You would understand my position in regard to applications from all quarters for aid toward projects of every kind, if you could see the pile of letters soliciting aid, which daily accumulates upon my table. It has become utterly impossible to answer favorably the tenth part of these applications made to me. You could scarcely have taken a more unfortunate time to solicit me at this moment of my return when, from the condition of my property, after an absence of two years, I am compelled to disburse some thousands to put it in repair, and this after having, as late as the 16th instant, subscribed to the utmost of my ability, a large sum, which will require the utmost care and economy on my part to pay during the remainder of my life.

"Let me say, nevertheless, that I consider your discovery, and the invention based upon it, as one of great value, as one which, in an eminent degree, has demands *upon the attention of the Government*, in the departments having care of the public lands and the protection of our navigation. Have you made it known to the Secretary of the Navy, the Secretary of War, and the Secretary of the Interior? Each one of these departments is directly interested in the results of your invention, and, if they have a contingent fund at their disposal, so small a sum comparatively as you desire could not be better bestowed than in enabling you to bring it before the world in its perfected shape. You have, at least, my hearty wishes for your success."

He was a willing and loving patron of art. Especially dear to him were the memories of Allston and Leslie, his teacher and his fellow-student in the days of his early struggles. Before he went abroad on his last visit, he had learned that a project was on foot to purchase Allston's portrait by Leslie, to be presented to the National Academy of Design. Instantly he determined to purchase the picture of his teacher, painted by his friend, and to give it to the Academy which he founded and cherished with parental affection and pride. In his letter to the committee having it in charge, he said: "There are associations in my mind with those two eminent and beloved names which appeal too strongly to me to be resisted. Now I have a favor to ask which I hope will not be denied. It is that I may be allowed to present to the Academy that portrait in my own name. You can appreciate the arguments which have influenced my wishes in this respect. Allston was more than any other person my master in art. Leslie was my life-long cherished friend and fellow-pupil, whom I loved as a brother. We all lived together for years in the closest intimacy and in the same house. Is there not, then, a fitness that the portrait of the master by one distinguished pupil should be presented by the surviving pupil to the Academy over which he presided in its infancy, as well as assisted in its birth? and, although divorced from art, cannot so easily be divorced from the memories of an intercourse with these distinguished friends, an intercourse which never for one moment suffered interruption, even from a shadow of estrangement. I inclose you my check for five hundred dollars, leaving you and the gentlemen in charge of the purchase to act your pleasure in the matter."

While Professor Morse was in Europe in 1866, the celebrated painting of " Jeremiah," by Allston, came before the public under circumstances of peculiar interest. In consequence of the death of a lady of Newport, Rhode Island, for whom it was painted fifty years before, it was placed in the Redwood Library at Newport, with a view to its being sold; when a lady and gentleman of New Haven happened to see it, who brought back word that this prize might be secured for the Yale School of Art at the price of seven thousand dollars. This matter was accordingly taken up, and, after some subscriptions for the purchase had been obtained, the council of the school, through the great liberality of ex-Governor Gibbs, of Newport, administrator of the estate to which the picture belonged, were allowed to have possession of it for a limited time, in the hope that the proceeds of exhibition, together with such subscriptions as might be added by visitors, would make up the amount required for the purchase. The painting represents the prophet, seated in " the court of the prison," where he was shut up for the testimony which he bore against the lying prophets and recreant priests of his generation, and is supposed to be transported with a vision of the capture and spoiling of Jerusalem by the King of Babylon. After the picture had been exhibited for some time at New Haven, subscriptions were solicited for the purpose of purchasing it for the college. When Professor

Morse returned from Europe (in 1868) the subject was brought
to his attention, and he requested permission to present the picture to the college. With the consent of those who had subscribed already, he assumed the entire expense, and, purchasing
the picture by his beloved teacher, for seven thousand dollars,
gave it to his *Alma Mater.*

Thus, by these two gifts in honor of his teacher, he endowed
his child, the Academy, and the College, his mother, with memo-
rials of Allston. This gift of the picture was soon followed by a
donation of ten thousand dollars to the building fund of the Theological Department of Yale College. President Woolsey wrote
to the Professor July 27, 1868, and said : " I write as instructed
by the corporation of Yale College, to express their gratitude to
you for your very generous subscription to the fund for the
Theological building. Permit me also to add my own personal
sense of your munificence. I had the honor last commencement
to convey the thanks of the Fellows to you for your gift of Allston's picture, and I did not think that this would be followed
by a still greater gift."

To the Union Theological Seminary, in the city of New
York, he also presented the sum of ten thousand dollars, endow-
ing a lectureship on the " Relation of the Bible to the Sciences,"
and to be named in honor of his father, the Rev. Dr. Morse,
whose labors in the cause of theological education and geographical science rendered the testimonial peculiarly appropriate.

BANQUET IN NEW YORK.

Toward the close of this year (1868) his fellow-citizens invited Professor Morse to meet them at a public dinner. The
letter of invitation was addressed to him by a large number
of distinguished gentlemen, who united in saying: " Many of
your countrymen, and numerous personal friends, desire to give
a definite expression of the fact that this country is in full accord with European nations in acknowledging your title to the
position of the Father of the Modern Telegraphs, and at the
same time, in a fitting manner, to welcome you to your home."
The invitation was accepted, and the day designated for the
banquet was December 30, 1868. It was designed as the crowning honor of the great inventor's life, by his own countrymen.

The Chief-Justice of the United States, who had been the leading counsel *against* Professor Morse in the first lawsuit brought
to defend his rights, was now called to preside at a banquet
which was to testify that, in the judgment of his country and the
world, the Telegraph was the child of Morse and America. The
dinner was given at Delmonico's, on the corner of Fifth Avenue and Fourteenth Street, New York. Some of the most eminent persons in the country were present; the speeches and general proceedings were marked with good sense and good feeling.
The Hon. Salmon P. Chase, Chief-Justice, presided, having on
his right Professor Morse, and on his left Sir Edward Thornton,
H. B. M. Minister to the United States. About two hundred
gentlemen sat down at the dinner. After the blessing had been
invoked by the Rev. William Adams, D. D., the banquet enjoyed, and thanks returned by the Rev. A. H. Vinton, D. D.,
Mr. Field presented letters from the President of the United
States; from General Grant; from Speaker Colfax; from Admiral Farragut, and others, and then read a telegram from the Governor of Massachusetts, the State in which Professor Morse was
born :

"Massachusetts honors her two sons—Franklin and Morse. The
one conducted the lightning safely from the sky; the other con-
ducts it beneath the ocean, from continent to continent. The one
tamed the lightning; the other makes it minister to human wants
and human progress.   Alexander H. Bullock, *Governor.*"

"This morning," said Mr. Field, "I sent a telegram to London, giving information that we were to meet this evening to
honor our fellow-citizen, Professor Morse." The following reply was received :

"'London, 4 o'clock p. m., *December* 29, 1868.

"'Cyrus W. Field, New York: The members of the Joint Committee of the Anglo-American and Atlantic Telegraph Companies
hear with pleasure of the banquet to be given this evening to Professor Morse, and desire to greet that distinguished telegraphist,
and wish him all the compliments of the season.'

"This telegram was sent from London at four o'clock this afternoon, and was delivered into the hands of your committee at
12.50." (Applause and laughter.)

The speeches that followed were made by men representing various countries and interests. Sir Edward Thornton, the British Minister, said that he "had great satisfaction in being able to contribute his mite of that admiration and esteem for Professor Morse which must be felt by all for so great a benefactor of his fellow-creatures and of posterity." When Chief-Justice Chase was about to introduce the guest of the evening, he made a few remarks, in which he said:

"Many shining names will at once occur to any one at all familiar with the history of the Telegraph. Among them 1 can pause to mention only those of Volta, the Italian, to whose discoveries the battery is due; Oersted, the Dane, who first discovered the magnetic properties of the electric current; Ampère and Arago, the Frenchmen, who prosecuted still further and most successfully similar researches; then Sturgeon, the Englishman, who may be said to have made the first electro-magnet; next, and not least illustrious among these illustrious men, our countryman, Henry, who first showed the practicability of producing electro-magnetic effects by means of the galvanic current, at distances indefinitely great; and finally, Steinheil, the German, who, after the invention of the Telegraph in all its material parts was complete, taught, in 1837, the use of the ground as a part of the circuit. These are some of those searchers for truth whose names will be long held in grateful memory, and not among the least of their titles to gratitude and remembrance will be the discoveries which contributed to the possibility of the modern Telegraph.

" But these discoveries only made the Telegraph possible. They offered the brilliant opportunity; there was needed a man to bring into being the new art and the new interest to which they pointed. And it is the providential distinction and splendid honor of the eminent American who is our guest to-night that, happily prepared by previous acquirements and pursuits, he was quick to seize the opportunity and give to the world the first recording Telegraph. Fortunate man! thus to link his name forever with the greatest wonder and the greatest benefit of the age!" (Great applause.) " I give you, ' Our guest, Professor S. B. Morse—the man of science, who explored the laws of Nature, wrested electricity from her embrace, and made it a missionary in the cause of human progress.'"

The venerable Professor, the father of the Telegraph, arose, under emotion too strong to be concealed, and his rising was hailed with deafening applause. The whole company, on their feet, gave cheer after cheer, and when the applause had in a measure subsided it broke out again and again, as the opportunity was taken by the entire assembly to express their grateful admiration of the illustrious man before them. And in that body of eminent men, had he been unknown, he would have been distinguished by his majestic, patriarchal appearance and bearing. At last silence was obtained and the Professor began. As much that he said in his sketch of the invention and progress of the Telegraph has been already rehearsed, a few passages only from his speech will be given :

" Various and conflicting memories crowd upon me at this moment—memories which this demonstration has quickened into life. What train of thought, what incidents of the past, in the brief moments allotted to me, can I select from this mass of recollections which may contribute either to your profit or your pleasure?"

He then recounted the evidences he had received from foreign countries of their sense of indebtedness to him ; he told the story of the invention of the Telegraph on board the Sully in 1832; of its exhibition in 1835 and 1837, and its final triumph in 1844. He spoke of the great scientific men whose discoveries made the Telegraph possible, and acknowledged his own indebtedness to them ; of his early struggles, of the reluctance of the Government to aid the experiment ; of the debate in Congress ; of his offer to the Government of the Telegraph for postal service ; of the services of Alfred Vail and Amos Kendall and others who had sustained him in his labors, and he concluded his address by saying:

" I have claimed for America the origination of the modern telegraph system of the world. Impartial history, I think, will support that claim. Do not misunderstand me as disparaging or disregarding the labors and ingenious modifications of others in various countries, employed in the same field of invention. Gladly, did time permit, would I descant upon their great and varied merits. Yet, in tracing the birth and pedigree of the modern Telegraph, ' American ' is not the highest term of the series that connects the past with the present; there is at least one higher term, the highest of all, which cannot and must not be ignored. If not a sparrow falls to the ground without a definite purpose in the plans of Infinite Wisdom, can the creation of an instrumentality, so vitally affecting the interests of the whole human race, have an origin less humble than the Father of every good and perfect gift? I am sure I have the sympathy of such an assembly as is here gathered, if, in all humility and in the sincerity of a grateful heart, I use the words of inspiration in ascribing honor and praise to Him to whom first of all and most of all it is preëminently due. ' Not unto us, not unto us, but to God be all the glory.' Not what hath man, but ' *What hath God wrought?* ' "

The Professor resumed his seat in the midst of long-continued and hearty applause. Speeches were then made by Professor Goldwin Smith, Hon. William M. Evarts, A. A. Low, Esq., William Cullen Bryant, Esq., William Orton, Esq., David Dudley Field, Esq., Hon. William E. Dodge, Hugh Allan, Esq., Daniel Huntington, Esq., and Governor Curtin, of Pennsylvania. Mr. Huntington, the artist, a former pupil of Morse, alluded in beautiful terms to his early associations with the Professor:

"Every studio," he said, "is more or less a laboratory. The painter is a chemist, delving into the secrets of pigments, varnishes, mixtures of tints, and mysterious preparations of grounds and over-laying of colors; occult arts, by which the inward light is made to gleam from the canvas and the warm flesh to glow and palpitate. The studio of my beloved master, in whose honor we have met to-night, was indeed a laboratory. Vigorous, life-like portraits, poetic and historic groups, occasionally grew upon his easel; but there were many hours—yes, days—when, absorbed in study among galvanic batteries and mysterious lines of wire, he seemed to us like an alchemist of the middle ages in search of the philosopher's stone. I can never forget the occasion when he called his pupils together to witness one of the first, if not the first, successful experiment with the electric Telegraph. It was in the winter of 1835–'36. I can now see that rude instrument, constructed with an old stretching-frame, a wooden clock, a home-made battery, and the wire stretched many times round the walls of the studio. With eager interest we gathered about it, as our master explained its operation, while with a click, click, the pencil, by a succession of dots and lines, recorded the message in cipher. The idea was born. The words circled that upper chamber as they do now the globe. But we had little faith. To us it seemed a dream of enthusiasm. We grieved to see the sketch upon the canvas untouched. We longed to see him again calling into life events in our country's history, but it was not to be. God's purposes were being accomplished, and now the world is witness to his triumph. Yet the love of art still lives in some inner corner of his heart, and I know he can never enter the studio of a painter and see the artist silently bringing from the canvas forms of life and beauty, but he feels a tender twinge as one who catches a glimpse of the beautiful girl he loved in his youth whom another has snatched away.

"Finally, my dear master and father in art, allow me, in this moment of your triumph in the field of discovery, to greet you in the name of your brother artists with 'All hail!' As an artist you might have spent life worthily in turning God's blessed daylight into sweet hues of rainbow colors and into breathing forms for the delight and consolation of men, but it has been his will that you should train the lightnings, the sharp arrows of his anger, into the swift yet gentle messengers of peace and love."

When Mr. Huntington had concluded, the ladies, who had graced the banquet by their presence, began to retire. The president, however, announced the last toast, "The Ladies," and said: "This is the most inspiring theme of all; but the theme itself seems to be vanishing from us—indeed" (after a pause), "has already vanished" (after another pause and a glance around the room), "and the gentleman who was to have responded seems also to have vanished with his theme. I may assume, therefrom, that the duties of the evening are performed, and its enjoyments are at an end."

This testimonial by his own countrymen, calling forth, as it did, expressions from the press and from men of science and practical knowledge of the Telegraph in all parts of his own country and in distant lands, was justly regarded by Professor Morse as the final verdict in his case. He accepted it with grateful appreciation, esteeming it one of the most valuable as well as pleasing testimonies to the greatness and usefulness of his labors. He had, however, no relaxation from the work of his life. The report of his examination of the telegraphic instruments at the Paris Exposition was still unfinished. He had begun it in Paris and continued it on the Isle of Wight, where he fled for rest. He wrought upon it in Dresden. He brought it home with him and spent his summer days upon it in his rural home at Poughkeepsie. It was now his daily task. He completed it in the course of the year 1869 and it was published by the Government of the United States, making a document of nearly two hundred pages, illustrated with numerous drawings, and stored with valuable information. Nor was this the chief labor with which the man of nearly fourscore years was burdened. "Such is the weight of my correspondence," he writes in a letter to a friend, in February, 1869, "I have the pen in my hand from the earliest daylight until twelve at midnight." But his patience and perseverance were sufficient for the day and the burden. He was conscious of the progress of time, and he worked on steadily, that when the end came he might be found doing.

In the latter part of May he went up to his country-seat with his family, and enjoyed again the delights of the country he so much loved. The summer was sadly broken in upon by an accident that would have been easily fatal to most men of his great age. His foot tripped upon the stair and he fell, breaking both bones of his leg below the knee. It was supposed, almost as a matter of course, that he could not survive the shock. He was laid upon his bed for three months, with his leg in the stocks. But the months were cheerful and peaceful. He received his friends with cordiality. He made no complaints, but quietly waited the recuperating powers of Nature. In due time he was about again on crutches; then these were laid aside and he walked erect, firm and freely as ever. This accident prevented him from assisting at the inauguration of the statue of Alexander Humboldt in the Central Park, to which he had contributed, but his letter was deposited in the pediment. He expressed his regret at being unable to be present, and said :

"I owed my personal acquaintance with Humboldt to his knowledge of my father by correspondence many, many years ago, and when I was a student in the arts in Paris, in the years 1831, 1832, he took pains to find me out, and I have since often called to mind the friendly interest he manifested in the progress of my studies of the works of the old masters in the Louvre. It was his custom, for some time in the winter of the years 1831–1832, to recreate during a portion of the day in that splendid gallery, and more than once did he linger by my easel, and, requesting me to relieve myself awhile from my studies, he desired me to accompany him in the examination of some of the masterpieces of art. At this time I frequently met him at the *soirées* of the Baron Gerard, where not merely the distinguished artist, but men illustrious in all the departments of science, and of various nations, weekly assembled. At these *soirées* I was first struck with the wonderful readiness of the learned Humboldt, in conversing in so many different languages; Spaniards, Turks, Swedes, Danes, Russians, as well as Germans, French, and English, would address him in almost the same breath, and the promptitude of his passing from one language to another, and the fluency and vivacity with which he alike conversed with all of them, were the source of frequent remark and admiration. When, after an interval of six years, I revisited Paris in 1838, in a different capacity, with my Telegraph invention, I again met at the Academy of Sciences with Baron Humboldt. Invited by the Perpetual Secretary, the renowned Arago, to a seat within the pale of assembled members, I sat at a short distance from Baron Humboldt, and I can never forget the feelings of encouragement, in those anxious moments, when, after the lucid explanation of my Telegraph to the Academy by M. Arago, the Baron Humboldt arose, and, taking my hand, congratulated me and thanked me before them all. It was not until the summer of 1856 that, traveling in the north of Europe, I visited Berlin, and again saw, and for the last time, this illustrious man, in one of his homes in the Royal Palace of Potsdam. I was received with his usual kindness of manner. He spoke with enthusiasm of the probable future of American science, and warmed with more than usual enthusiasm in expatiating with praise upon the scientific labors of Maury and Dana. Of the latter, he said that his then recent work was one of the most valuable contributions to science of the age. In parting with him, he alluded to his advancing years, spoke with feeling of the probability that we should never meet again, and, presenting me with his photographic portrait, and his autograph upon it, bade me farewell."

STATUE OF MORSE.

Few men are permitted to see their own statues, erected by their grateful contemporaries. And of many inventors it is said that, wanting bread, they receive only a stone, and not even that until long after they have been starved to death. It was the good fortune of Professor Morse to live until thousands of his fellow-creatures were enjoying the substantial benefits resulting from his labors. The affection with which he regarded all those who were employed in developing and using his invention was reciprocated by the tens of thousands of operators and officers in every land, and especially in all parts of his native land. To a vast number of men and women, his Telegraph furnished, as means of support, a simple, useful, agreeable, and remunerative employment. It was an invention of their own to make some testimonial of their gratitude and appreciation of his service to them as well as to the whole world. In the year 1869 an organization was formed in Alleghany City, Pennsylvania, " to testify to Professor Morse the veneration and respect entertained for him by the operators, and others." This association was soon made national, with Mr. James D. Reid, of New York, as chairman; Mr. John Horner, New York, treasurer; and Mr. Robert B. Hoover, who originated the movement, as secretary. An executive committee, covering the whole country, was appointed. The Hon. William Orton, President of the Western Union Telegraph Company, issued a letter, saying: " The movement is one which merits, and will receive, my warmest sympathy, and most hearty encouragement. The venerable ' Father of all the Telegraphs' has long since passed the meridian of life; and, although his step is firm and his eye undimmed, he is nearing rapidly the verge of that dark river from whose farther shore no message ever comes. It becomes, therefore, all who know and love him, as all who know him do, not to delay their tributes of respect and affection. And I am confident that all connected with us will take pleasure in rendering whatever assistance they are able." The shape the testimonial would finally take was not then determined. A circular was telegraphed over the land proposing that each person connected with the lines should contribute ONE DOLLAR, although more or less would be received, with the hope that every one, from the president to the messenger-boy, might have a share in the work. The subscriptions began to come in with the usual speed of the Telegraph. Its fitting motto would be, " What is to be done

must be done quickly." The cheerful and general response justified the contemplation of a memorial worthy of the man and
the country that would do him honor. It was decided to erect
a bronze statue of Professor Morse. The Central Park in the
city of New York was selected as the most appropriate place for
its erection. Permission was cheerfully granted by the Park
Commission. The proposal was hailed by the public press as eminently becoming and deserved. Within two years of the conception of the idea to make the testimonial, the money was raised by
these small contributions, the statue was completed, and the day
appointed for its inauguration. The most extensive and judicious
arrangements were made for the celebration of the day. Delegates, deputed by telegraphic associations, arrived from Pennsylvania, Mississippi, District of Columbia, Maryland, Connecticut, Canada, Louisiana, Massachusetts, Georgia, Ohio, Tennessee, Illinois, New Jersey, Iowa, North Carolina, Michigan, Kentucky, California, Nebraska, Indiana, Vermont, Maine, Rhode
Island, West Virginia, Virginia, Minnesota, and Nova Scotia.
The day (June 10, 1871) was brilliant, cool, and auspicious. A
thousand telegraphic visitors, gentlemen and ladies from abroad,
were received as guests, and spent the forenoon in making an
excursion, on board a steamer, around the city; giving three
cheers for Professor Morse as they landed. The afternoon saw
the park alive with the people of the city and surrounding country, gathered in multitudes; the wealth and fashion of the town,
and masses of people who knew and prized the value of labor,
thought, and patient perseverance, now to be honored. The
statue stood in the angle between two platforms for the invited
guests, and was wrapped in the folds of the Stars and Stripes.
The band from Governor's Island was in attendance and played
a selection of national airs.

Shortly after four o'clock, amid cheers from the multitude
assembled, Governor John T. Hoffman arose and delivered an
eloquent address. He said: "If the inventor of the alphabet be
deserving of the highest honors, so is he whose great achievement marks this epoch in the history of language—the inventor of the Electric Telegraph. We intend, so far as in us lies,
that the men who come after us shall be at no loss to discover
his name for want of recorded testimony."

After Governor Hoffman had closed his address, Governor Claflin and the Hon. Wm. Orton threw aside the drapery, and displayed the statue. A tumultuous outburst of applause followed, the band playing the "Star-Spangled Banner."

The statue is of heroic size, and was modeled by Byron M. Pickett, and cast at the National Fine-Art Foundery of New York, by Maurice I. Power. Professor Morse is represented holding the first message sent over the wires, and devoutly recognizing the truth of its language: "What hath God wrought!" Addresses were then delivered by William Cullen Bryant, Esq., and by the mayor of the city, A. Oakey Hall, Esq. Prayer was offered by Rev. Stephen H. Tyng, D. D. The Christian Doxology was sung by the multitude.

In the evening of the same day the Academy of Music was thronged. The most eminent men of the country participated in the reception given to the venerable Professor, who was greeted with applause as he entered and took his seat upon the platform. Hon. William Orton presided. Rev. Dr. Howard Crosby, Chancellor of the University, offered prayer. Addresses were made by Mr. Orton, Dr. George B. Loring, of Salem, Massachusetts, and Rev. Dr. George W. Samson. At the hour of 9 P. M., the chairman announced that the telegraphic instrument now before him, the *original* register employed in actual service, was connected with all the wires of America, and the touch of the finger on the key would soon vibrate throughout the continent. Miss Sadie E. Cornwell, who had been selected to transmit a message, was then conducted to her place by Mr. Applebaugh, and sent the following dispatch, in the midst of profound silence:

"GREETING AND THANKS TO THE TELEGRAPH FRATERNITY THROUGHOUT THE LAND. GLORY TO GOD IN THE HIGHEST, ON EARTH PEACE, GOOD-WILL TO MEN."

At the last click of the instrument, Professor Morse, escorted by Mr. Orton, approached the table and took his seat. As his fingers touched the key, tremendous cheers rung through the house, but were stopped by a gesture from Mr. Orton. Again impressive silence fell on the house. Slowly the sounder struck "S. F. B. Morse;" the Professor's hand fell from the key, the entire audience rose, and a wild storm of enthusiasm swept through the house, which was continued for some time, ladies waving their handkerchiefs, and venerable men cheering as joyously as the youngest. Professor Morse, visibly affected, resumed his chair beside the president, and for several moments pressed his brow with his hands. When the excitement had subsided, Mr. Orton said: "Thus the Father of the Telegraph bids farewell to his children."

The current was then switched off to an instrument behind the scenes. Quickly along the wires came responses from Milwaukee, Jacksonville, Montreal, Toronto, Quebec, Chicago, Washington, New Orleans, Portsmouth, Louisville, Philadelphia, Charleston, Ottawa, Ontario, San Francisco, Pittsburg, Memphis, Cincinnati, Mobile, Halifax, Havana.

Dispatches were received later in the night from the Hong-Kong Chamber of Commerce, from Bombay, and Singapore.

General N. P. Banks then made an address, and a poem by J. H. Watson was recited. Mr. W. H. Pope, the Rev. H. M. Gallagher, J. K. Walcott, Esq., Mr. J. D. Reid, the chief promoter of the whole movement, and the Hon. Charles P. Daly, made addresses, the latter introducing Professor Morse.

As the venerable Professor arose to respond, the whole audience broke into a warm cheer of salutation. His long white beard falling on his breast, his erect and graceful form, and his evident emotion, commanded the admiring sympathy of the audience. After a few words of introduction, while struggling to control his emotions, he said:

"When I consider that he who rules supreme over the ways and destinies of man often makes use of the feeblest instruments to accomplish his benevolent purposes to man, as if, by grandest contrast, to point the mind with more marked effect to him as their author, I cheerfully take my place on the lowest seat at his footstool. It is his pleasure, however, to work by human instrumentality. You have chosen to impersonate, in the statue this day erected, the invention rather than the inventor, and it is of no small significance that in the attitude so well chosen, and so admirably executed by the talented young sculptor whose work presents him so prominently and so favorably before you, he has given permanence to that pregnant and just sentence which was the first public utterance of the telegraph : .' What hath God wrought!'

"In the carrying out of any plan of improvement, however grand or feasible, no single individual could possibly accomplish it without the aid of others. We are, none of us, so powerful that we can dispense with the assistance, in various departments of the work, of those whose experience and knowledge must supply the needed aid of their expertness. It is not sufficient that a brilliant project be proposed, that its modes of accomplishment are foreseen and properly devised; there are, in every part of the enterprise, other minds, and other agencies to be consulted for information and counsel to protect the whole plan. The Chief-Justice, in delivering the decision of the Supreme Court, says: 'It can make no difference whether he' (the inventor) 'derives his information from books or from conversation with men skilled in the science'—and 'the fact that Morse sought and obtained the necessary information and counsel from the best sources, and acted upon it, neither impairs his rights as an inventor nor detracts from his merits.' The inventor must seek and employ the skilled mechanician in his workshop, to put the invention into practical form, and for this purpose some pecuniary means are required, as well as mechanical skill. Both these were at hand. Alfred Vail, of Morristown, New Jersey, with his father and brother, came to the help of the unclothed infant, and with their funds and mechanical skill put it into a condition creditably to appear before the Congress of the nation. To these New Jersey friends is due the first important aid in the progress of the invention. Aided, also, by the talent and scientific skill of Professor Gale, my esteemed colleague in the University, the Telegraph appeared in Washington in 1838, a suppliant for the means to demonstrate its power. To the Hon. F. O. J. Smith, then chairman of the House Committee of Commerce, belongs the credit of a just appreciation of the new invention, and of a zealous advocacy of an experimental essay and the inditing of an admirably written report in its favor, signed by every member of the committee. It was, nevertheless, thrown aside among the unfinished business of the session; and now commenced days of trial. Years of delay were yet before it. It was not till 1842 that it was again submitted to Congress. Ferris and Kennedy, and Winthrop and Aycrigg, McClay and Wood, and many others in the House, far-seeing statesmen, rallied to its support, and at length, by a bare majority, the bill that was necessary was carried through the ordinary forms, and sent to the Senate, where it met with no opposition, and was passed the last night of the session.

46

" Now commenced a new series of trials, to which it is unnecessary here more than to allude.

" To Ezra Cornell, whose noble benefactions to his State and the country have placed his name by the side of Cooper and Peabody, high on the roll of public .benefactors, is due the credit of early and effective aid in the superintendence and erection of the first public line of telegraph ever established.

" Notwithstanding the success of the experimental essay, another important step was necessary ere the invention could demonstrate its vast utility. It was not until the skill and experience of the best Postmaster-General that had ever held that office, the Hon. Amos Kendall, were brought into requisition, that, amid many discouragements, the various companies were organized, and in the hands of such enterprising men as Sibley, who united the Atlantic and Pacific, and Swain, and Wade, and a host of determined men, whose names would read like the pages of a dictionary, this vast country, from the northern boundaries of Canada to the Gulf of Mexico, and from the shores of the Atlantic to the Pacific, were webbed with telegraphic wires." (Applause.)

" Another grand stride was yet to be taken, ere international communication could be established.

" In October, 1842, the first submarine telegraph cable was laid by me, one moonlight night, in the harbor of this city, which proved experimentally the practicability of submarine telegraphy, and from the result of this success I ventured, the year after, in a letter to the Secretary of the Treasury, to predict the certainty of an Atlantic Telegraph. It was then believed to be a visionary dream; and, had the individual carrying out of so bold an enterprise depended upon me alone, it might still have been a dream. But at this crisis another mind was touched with the necessary enthusiasm, admirably fitted in every particular, by indomitable energy and perseverance, and foresight, as well as financial skill and influence, to undertake the novel attempt. . To Cyrus W. Field, more than to any other individual, belongs the honor of carrying to completion this great undertaking. Associating with himself Cooper, and Taylor, and Roberts, and White, and Hunt, and Dudley Field, and others, on this side of the Atlantic, and, two years later, Peabody, and Brett, and Brooking, and Lamson, and Gurney, and Morgan, and others, in Great Britain, making the ocean but an insignificant ferry by his repeated crossings, undaunted by temporary failures and unforeseen accidents, he rested not till Britain and

America were united in telegraphic bonds—the Old and the New world in instantaneous communication." (Cheers.)

" If modern progress in the arts and sciences have given unprecedented facilities for the diffusion of the Telegraph throughout the world, back of all are the former discoveries and inventions of the scientific minds of Europe and America—Volta, Oersted, Arago, Schweigger, Gauss and Weber, Steinheil, Faraday, Daniell, and Grove, and a host of brilliant minds in Europe, with Professors Dana and Henry, in our own country, in the past, and the more modern discoveries and inventions of Thomson, of Whitehouse, of Cooke, of Varley, of Glass and Canning, and numerous others. These all, in a greater or less degree, contributed to the grand result. There is not a name I have mentioned, and many whom I have not mentioned, whose career in science or experience in mechanical and engineering and nautical tactics, or in financial practice, might not be the theme of volumes, rather than of brief mention in an ephemeral address. To-night you have before you a sublime proof of the grand progress of the Telegraph in its march around the globe.

" It is but a few days since our veritable antipodes became telegraphically united to us. We can speak to and receive an answer in a few seconds of time from Hong-Kong, in China, where ten o'clock to-night here is ten o'clock in the day, and it is perhaps a debatable question whether their ten o'clock is ten to-day or ten to-morrow. China and New York are in interlocutory communication. We know the fact, but can imagination realize the fact? But I must not further trespass on your patience at this late hour.

" I cannot close without the expression of my cordial thanks to my long-known, long-tried, and honored friend Reid, whose unwearied labors early contributed so effectively to the establishment of telegraph-lines, and who in a special manner, as chairman of your Memorial Fund, has so faithfully and successfully and admirably carried to completion your flattering design.

" To the eminent Governors of this State and the State of Massachusetts, who have given to this demonstration their honored presence ; to my excellent friend the distinguished orator of the day; to the Mayor and city authorities of New York; to the Park Commissioners ; to the officers and managers of the various and even rival telegraph companies, who have so cordially united on this occasion ; to the numerous citizens, ladies and gentlemen ; and, though last, not least, to every one of my large and increasing family of telegraph children, who have honored me with the proud title of *Father*, I tender my cordial thanks." (Applause.)

At the close of Professor Morse's address, Rev. Dr. Ormiston offered prayer, and the assembly retired, many seeking the opportunity to take the Professor by the hand, and to bid him an affectionate farewell.

CHAPTER XXI.

LITERARY AND RELIGIOUS LIFE.

A READY WRITER — STUDIES IN HIS DEPARTMENT — AUTHORSHIP — LUCRETIA
MARIA DAVIDSON — THE SERENADE — ROMAN CATHOLIC CONTROVERSY —
FOREIGN CONSPIRACY—CONFESSIONS OF A PRIEST—GENERAL LAFAYETTE'S
REMARK—OUR LIBERTIES DEFENDED—IMMINENT DANGERS—DEFENSE OF
HIS INVENTION—RELIGIOUS LIFE—ANALYSIS OF HIS CHRISTIAN CHARAC-
TER—SKETCH BY REV. DR. WHEELER—ANTICIPATIONS OF DEATH—DEATH
OF HIS BROTHER RICHARD—THE THREE BROTHERS—THE TORTOISE AND
HARE—IN HIS LIBRARY — ASIATIC SOCIETY — EVANGELICAL ALLIANCE —
LITERARY AND BENEVOLENT LABORS—DOMESTIC PEACE—THE EVENING
OF LIFE.

PROFESSOR MORSE held the pen of a ready writer. His
genius, learning, and taste, were illustrated by many and
large contributions to the press. At the foundation of the National Academy of Design he was compelled to enter the lists
in a controversy that required careful inquiry, extensive reading,
and mature reflection. He acquitted himself well in a discussion with the *North American Review*, and from that
time onward, notwithstanding his native modesty and timidity,
he did not hesitate to enter the field of debate at the call of
duty. His addresses before the Academy, and his lectures as
Professor of the Arts of Design in the University, are models
of graceful rhetoric and elaborate argument. For these discourses he made preparation by patient and exhaustive research
among the best authors of ancient and modern times, making
copious quotations from them into his note-books, and reprodu-
cing them with great skill and effect.

The first volume that appeared in his name was a Memoir
with the "Remains of Lucretia Maria Davidson." She was a
remarkable young lady, who died at Plattsburg, N. Y., in 1825,

in the seventeenth year of her age, having displayed an extraordinary poetic faculty, and produced many poems of unusual merit. The Hon. Moss Kent, of Plattsburg, becoming acquainted with her wonderful gifts, undertook the office of patron, and at his expense she was placed in the Troy Female Seminary to pursue a thorough course of study. Her health declined, and she was laid in an early grave. Mr. Kent placed all her papers in the hands of Professor Morse, with the request that he would edit them and prepare a biographical sketch of the young author. This work he accomplished with fidelity and delicate sensibility. The volume was published by G. & C. Carvill, New York, 1827.

One of his relatives, a lady, relates an incident in a visit he made to her at Utica, N. Y., in the year 1827. He had been playfully asserting his ability to write poetry as well as to paint portraits, and she denied his possession of any genius in that direction. "Give me a subject," he said, "and I will show you what I can do." It had happened a few nights previously that the young lady had been serenaded, but unfortunately she slept soundly through the whole performance. This had naturally been the subject of much amusing conversation, and she replied to his demand for a subject, "Take the serenade." The next day he produced and read a poem on that theme. A few weeks afterward, being in New York, he was requested by Gulian C. Verplanck, Esq., to make a contribution to "The Talisman," an annual which Mr. Verplanck was editing. Mr. Morse submitted "The Serenade;" Mr. Verplanck was delighted with it, and said, "You must make a picture to accompany it." Mr. Morse then made a picture, which was engraved on steel, and published in "The Talisman" of 1828, with the poem. For a copy of it we are indebted to William C. Bryant, Esq., who kindly copied it with his own hand from "The Talisman," for this volume:

"THE SERENADE.

"Haste! 'tis the stillest hour of night,
The moon sheds down her palest light,
And sleep has chained the lake and hill,
The wood, the plain, the babbling rill;
And where yon ivied lattice shows
My fair one slumbers in repose.

PROFESSOR MORSE IN HIS STUDY.

Come, ye that know the lovely maid,
And help prepare the serenade.
Hither, before the night is flown,
Bring instruments of every tone;
But lest with noise ye wake, not lull
Her dreaming fancy, ye must cull
Such only as shall soothe the mind
And leave the harshest all behind;
Bring not the thundering drum, nor yet
The harshly-shrieking clarionet,
Nor screaming hautboy, trumpet shrill,
Nor clanging cymbals; but with skill
Exclude each one that would disturb
The fairy architects, or curb
The wild creations of their mirth;
All that would wake the soul to earth.
Choose ye the softly-breathing flute,
The mellow horn, the loving lute;
The viol ye must not forget,
And take the sprightly flageolet,
And grave bassoon; choose, too, the fife,
Whose warblings in the tuneful strife,
Mingling in mystery with the words,
May seem like notes of blithest birds.

" Are ye prepared? now lightly tread,
As if by elfin minstrels led,
And fling no sound upon the air
Shall rudely wake my slumbering fair.
Softly! now breathe the symphony—
So gently breathe, the tones may vie
In softness with the magic notes
In visions heard; music that floats
So buoyant that it well may seem,
With strains ethereal in her dream,
One song of such mysterious birth
She doubts it comes from heaven or earth.
Play on! my loved one slumbers still.
Play on! she wakes not with the thrill
Of joy produced by strains so mild;
But fancy moulds them gay and wild;
Now, as the music low declines,
'Tis sighing of the forest-pines;
Or 'tis the fitful, varied roar
Of distant falls, or troubled shore.

Now, as the tone grows full or sharp,
'Tis whispering of the Æolian harp;
The viol swells, now low, now loud,
'Tis spirits chanting on a cloud
That passes by. It dies away;
So gently dies she scarce can say
'Tis gone; listens; 'tis lost, she fears;
Listens, and thinks again she hears.
As dew-drops mingling in a stream
To her 'tis all one blissful dream—
A song of angels throned in light.
Softly! away! fair one, good-night."

While Mr. Morse was in Italy in the years 1830 and 1831, he
became acquainted with several ecclesiastics of the Church of
Rome, one of whom, a cardinal, made a vigorous attack upon
the faith of the young artist. A correspondence between them
ensued, and frequent interviews. Mr. Morse was led to believe,
from what he learned in Rome, that a political conspiracy, under
the cloak of a religious mission, was formed against the United
States of America. When he came to Paris in 1832 and enjoyed the confidence and friendship of Lafayette, he stated
his convictions to the General, who fully concurred with him
in the reality of such a conspiracy. Returning to this country
in the autumn of 1832, inventing the Telegraph on his homeward voyage, he never became so absorbed in his invention as
to forget the impressions made in Italy respecting the danger to
which his country was exposed. The conviction was so strong
that he gave much time in subsequent years to the publication in
periodicals, in pamphlets, and in volumes, of the facts and arguments which, in his judgment, were important to a fair understanding of the subject. In the year 1834 Mr. Morse published
a series of papers, which the year following were issued in a
volume entitled " Foreign Conspiracy against the Liberties of
the United States: revised and corrected, with Notes by the
Author." The motto on the title-page was from Spenser :

    " . . . . oft fire is without smoke,
          And peril without show."

The papers, as they first appeared, were copied widely, and,
pervading the whole country, made a deep and permanent impression. The volume passed through numerous editions, and

has proved one of the most efficient works that has appeared in that prolific discussion.

In the year 1837 Professor Morse edited and published, with an introduction by himself : " Confessions of a French Catholic Priest, to which are added Warnings to the People of the United States, by the same Author." This volume bore upon the title-page the line, " American liberty can be destroyed only by the popish clergy."—*Lafayette*. This declaration was not placed upon the title-page by the editor but by the author of the book. It was subsequently challenged, and Professor Morse, though not responsible for the statement, produced the written testimony of living witnesses, to whom Lafayette made the remark.

In the year 1841 a series of papers from the pen of Professor Morse, first published in the *Journal of Commerce*, was issued in a small volume, with the title : " Our Liberties defended ; the Question discussed ; is the Protestant or Papal System most favorable to Civil and Religious Liberty ? "

In the year 1854 a pamphlet was issued containing a series of papers which Professor Morse contributed to the *Journal of Commerce* in 1835. It was published without his name, under the title of " Imminent Dangers to the Free Institutions of the United States through Foreign Immigration, and the Present State of the Naturalization Laws. By an American."

But these were a very small part of the work that employed the pen of Professor Morse. From the moment that his Telegraph became a fact, his time and strength were required to defend its birthright. The controversies in which rival claims involved him demanded as severe study and patient labor as the original invention. In the newspaper press, in pamphlets, and in private correspondence, he maintained his position with such equanimity, ability, and conclusiveness, as commanded the respect of his opponents. No one could state the case with more clearness, arrange the facts in better order, and make the argument more powerful, than the man in whose mind the whole process had orginally been formed. Had he been endowed with the gift of oratory, no one could have argued his case before a court with more effect than Professor Morse himself. Sincere, transparent, unaffected, modest, he had the confidence of every

one with whom he conferred, and his presentation of a subject
in his letters and publications carried conviction of his integrity
to every candid reader.

RELIGIOUS LIFE.

Professor Morse was a Christian in his faith and practice.
In his long life, there was probably not an hour when his inquiring and inventive mind was perplexed with doubts or fears
in regard to religious truth. The system which he embraced
with all his heart, and held with tenacity and affection, was that
which he derived from his father, and which was scarcely modified by his subsequent reading and reflection. He first made a
public profession of religion in Charlestown, Massachusetts, in the
church of which his father was pastor. He was the superintendent of its Sabbath-school, one of the first established in this
country. When the family removed to New Haven, he became
a member of the First Congregational Church of that city. The
death of his wife and of his parents led to his removal, and, having no fixed residence for many years afterward, he remained in
nominal connection with that church until the year 1847, when
he settled in Poughkeepsie and united with the First Presbyterian Church. But, wherever his residence was, even temporary,
he identified himself with the religious community, and in all
the relations of society was known and recognized as a Christian. Those who knew him most intimately, and held communion with him in hours of retirement from the conflicts of
the world, knew that he was governed in all his actions by the
fear of God and love of his fellow-men. He had a sense of
being surrounded at all times by the Infinite and Eternal, in
whom he lived and moved and had his being. He received the
Word of God, the sacred Scriptures, as the guide and rule of
his life; believing in their inspiration, and never questioning
their authority. He endeavored to regulate his conduct by the
principles of that Word, and especially by that golden rule,
which required him to do unto others as he would have others
do unto him. The firmness with which he maintained his rights
was in harmony with these principles. But he often suffered
wrong in silence, and the strength of character natural to him
and the family to which he belonged availed him when exposed

to the annoyances, perplexities, and injuries of those who sought to deprive him of his property and his good name also. No man was more unjustly assailed by the pen and the tongue of detraction. Yet, under those circumstances, which oftentimes bring out the most unhappy traits of human character, he maintained a composure and calmness, with a forgiving and gentle spirit, beautiful to contemplate. In crowded thoroughfares, in the midst of business, when he was immersed in cares, and distracted with anxieties, it was his pleasure and comfort to converse upon the subject of personal religion, and with the simplicity of a child to confer with a friend on those subjects which immediately concern the relation of the soul to God. He preferred, above the applause and honors which come from man, the possession of a meek and quiet spirit.

Nor was the religious life of Professor Morse one merely of meditation and study. He was active and conscientious in the use of his property, giving largely, as it increased, to the various objects of Christian benevolence. Few men have given more in proportion to their wealth than he did. The first earnings of the Telegraph he gave to the church, as we have seen. From this beginning, the commencement of a flow into his hands of wealth, that afterward placed him above the fears of want, he continued to give of his abundance as before he had given from his penury. Colleges and theological seminaries received liberal donations. Missionary and other religious charities were constant recipients of his benefactions. Nor did he confine his gifts to religious objects only. Art and science were always regarded by him as proper objects for the use of his money; and he sought to encourage in others the development of those tastes which he had himself pursued with so much benefit to himself and mankind.

In the later years of Mr. Morse's life, when he was permitted, in the retirement of his family, to cultivate without interruption those graces which so adorned his character, his religious life rapidly matured. Those who came within the circle of his household, and especially those who were received in his study, found him, when the honors of the world were heaped upon him and his name had gone into all the earth, a humble Christian, anticipating the glories of the heavenly state. Rev. Dr.

Wheeler, his pastor in Poughkeepsie, gives a charming picture of his religious life:

"It was at Locust Grove I knew him best and most. Here among the grand old trees, the fresh, green lawns, and rare plants, which adorned his grounds, the fashion and substance of the man were seen. This home he greatly loved. Writing from one of the capitals in Europe at one time immediately after one of the grandest receptions that scholar or philosopher had received, he says: ' My heart yearns for my dear old home on the Hudson; its calm repose, its sweet walks, where so often I have been with God.' I recall with great satisfaction the many times on his veranda, looking westward upon flood and hills beyond, in large discourse he would dwell upon the 'things unseen,' and his utterances would have such depth and scope, that I marveled at the beauty and strength of that love for God and his realm which rose and fell like mighty tides in his heart.

"Sometimes allusion would be made to his career and the honors that had thickened upon him; a significant smile would steal over his face, and he would gently say: ' It is all of God. He has used me as his hand in all this. I am not indifferent to the rewards of earth and the praise of my fellow-men, but I am more pleased with the fact that my Father in heaven has allowed me to do something for him and his world.' Once he said to me with brimming eyes, and grasping me with both hands: ' Oh, you cannot tell how thankful I have been this morning, in, thinking this matter of the Telegraph all over, that God has permitted me to do something for the help and comfort of my fellows. I have just heard of a family made happy by a telegraphic dispatch from one of its absent members, announcing his safety, when the whole household was in grief over his supposed death; only think of the many homes that may be thus gladdened, relieved from solicitude and pain!' Thus it was that he was accustomed to put away all thought of what might accrue to himself of personal honor and glory from his invention, in the larger consideration of the good and profit grown therefrom to others. Calling upon him one pleasant summer day, the last summer of his earthly life, I found him intent upon microsopical observations; leading me to the instrument, he directed my attention to an insect's wing. 'There,' said he, ' that is enough of itself to satisfy any reasonable mind of God's being, wisdom, and power. It is in these things we call small, I am finding every day fresh proofs that God is in direct and positive agency. I see in all these things God's finger, and I am so glad through them to get hold of God's hand; and then,' he added with tears, 'if God makes all these small things around us here so exquisitely beautiful, what grandeur must attach to the things beyond, unseen and eternal!'

"How refreshing and strengthening the testimony of such a man, so thoughtful, so well read, and thoroughly practical in scientific reasearch as to the being, the presence, and the working of God, whom many, professing to be wise, have politely bowed out of his own universe!

"Professor Morse had no sympathy with such men. His whole being went into protest against them; their views seemed to him blasphemous. Through and through from centre to surface, in his whole make-up, in all the workings of his richly-endowed and versatile intellect, he was a religious man. So, from his own thinking, his own conviction, his own experience, there was nothing superficial about him; no superstition, no binding, controlling force of mere tradition, suffering others to think for him religiously. He thought here for himself, and his belief was the outgrowth of clear and well-defined conviction.

"Soon after his coming to Poughkeepsie for the summer, he fractured one of his limbs, and was confined for most of the season to his room. This was a great trial to him, but he bore it with such resignation, and there ripened upon him during it all such heavenly excellence, that it was a rare privilege to see him in his chamber. His window opened upon the broad and majestic Hudson. As I sat with him one afternoon, looking upon river and hill, in the changing light of the setting sun, he said:

"'I have been looking upon the river of my life. I thank God that it had such beginning; that upon it has fallen such sunshine, and I know whom I have believed, and rejoice that so soon this river will flow out into the broad sea of an everlasting love.'

"His face was pale; he was strapped upon his bed, but, patient and gentle in suffering, there came upon him such a transfiguration of divine love that I almost thought to see him then, with trailing garments of glory, sweep through the gates of pearl into the city of the great King. But he did not then go; he was spared a little longer to gladden all our hearts, and to leave upon us, if possible, a still greater impression of the superior sanctity and loveliness of his life. When at last he did fall asleep, I was not with him, to my great regret, but others caught the inspiration that fell from his lips and shone upon his face, as his Lord led him up from darkness into light, and breathed upon him the everlasting benediction of his acceptance.

"I have spoken of him chiefly as a Christian man; as such, I knew him best. But in his whole character, and in all his relations, he was one of the most remarkable men of his age. He was one who drew all who came in contact with him to his heart, disarming all prejudices, silencing all cavil. In his family he was light, life, and love; with those in his employ, he was ever considerate and kind, never exacting and harsh, but honorable and just, seeking the good of every dependant; in the community, he was a pillar of strength and beauty, commanding the homage of universal respect; in the church he walked with God and men. He is not, for God hath taken him. Blessed for evermore his memory, and blessed those who saw and knew him, not merely as the man of science and the Christian philosopher, but as a *man of God.*

"In bringing this letter to a close, may I mention an incident of his leaving Locust Grove for the last time?

"The family had gone on before; he left last, and with one of his favorite and trusty servants, in a single and open wagon. As they passed through the gate-way into the wood, he stopped, and, rising from his seat, looked fondly back, through the trees, over the lawn, on the old home, and then, resuming his seat, said, 'Drive on.' On passing the cemetery he stopped again, and, looking over 'God's acre,' where the dead were so quietly slumbering, he exclaimed: 'Beautiful! beautiful! but I shall not lie there. I have prepared a place elsewhere.'

"So he passed on and was hurried over iron ways to the great metropolis, where, in the next spring-time, his change was to come."

The absorbing cares of his active and restless life, the honors of the world, and the enjoyments of those rewards which were so largely his, had not served to hide from his sight the evidences of advancing age, and the approach of the end of his earthly career. But this prospect served only to strengthen his faith and brighten his hopes. Writing in 1868 from Dresden, to his grandson, he says: "The nearer I approach to the end of my pilgrimage, the clearer is the evidence of the divine origin of the Bible, the grandeur and sublimity of God's remedy for fallen man are more appreciated, and the future is illumined with hope and joy." And in a letter to his brother, dated

Paris, March 4, 1868, he says: "It cannot be long before all this will be gone. I feel daily the necessity of sitting looser to the world, and taking stronger hold on heaven. The Saviour daily seems more precious; his love, his atonement, his divine power, are themes which occupy my mind in the wakeful hours of the night, and change the time of 'watching for the morning' from irksomeness to joyful communion with him."

In the autumn of that year, his youngest brother, Richard C. Morse, died in a foreign land. There had been three brothers of them, the only children who survived the period of infancy— three brothers bound by the closest fraternal ties, with an affection as rare as beautiful. It is worthy of being written here that they inherited no property from their venerable father, but they did assume a load of debts in which he had been involved by indorsements for friends, and by his own publications. To the payment of these debts these sons with filial piety, though under no legal or moral obligation so to do, devoted all their earnings, until principal and interest were discharged. When Professor Morse became able to bear his part of this burden, he cheerfully returned to his brothers what they had many years before advanced on his account, so that the three brothers shared equally in the payment of their father's debts. They all lived to be old men, rejoicing in each other's success, and in sympathy when trials and misfortunes overtook them.

A playfulness marked their correspondence and intercourse, quite unsuspected in the gravity and dignity of their public life. Between Sidney and the Professor there was always a rivalry in the race for the goal of success. Sidney was slow, meditative, and cautious. The Professor was quick, perceptive, and energetic. Early in life the fable of the tortoise and hare became a familiar illustration between them, of their respective traits and habits. Sidney was fond of laughing with his brother, comparing himself to the tortoise creeping along, and while the hare, wearied with rapid running, has paused to rest and fallen asleep, the tortoise passes him and wins the race. When the Telegraph was triumphant, and the Professor's success was assured, he made a drawing, his delight always, of a hare at the end of a race-course, holding in his forepaws two telegraph wires extending to a tortoise toiling slowly along; the wires touching him up to quicken his steps and to tell him also that the hare has won the race!

In one of the letters of Sidney to the Professor, who had asked his brother if he was expected to pay interest on his portion of the debts, Sidney says to him: "If you still think the *hare* has won the race, you will pay the interest; if you think the *tortoise* is ahead, you need not pay it." The Professor paid the interest.

When the sad tidings came across the ocean by telegraph that the youngest of the brothers had died in Kissingen, the Professor wrote to his brother Sidney:

"And so *the triple cord is broken*, and our dear brother Richard, the youngest, is the first of us to pass the dark valley. A happy spirit now, we have not a doubt, with his Saviour and his friends who have preceded him. It is another call to be also ready. We shall not be long in following him. I feel stirred to more diligent improvement of the remnant of life still graciously granted by infinite love. We must work while it is day, it is far spent, and the night cometh when no man can work. I feel the blow more than I supposed it possible.

"And so he is gone. We shall see his kind face no more this side heaven. Well, it is but a short, a temporary separation. The world, with all its attractions, I find is losing its hold upon me. I wish to think more of that world where sin will no more defile, and sorrow, and the machinations of the wicked, no more annoy."

His time was chiefly spent with his family, or in his library, surrounded with those books and scientific instruments which were the delight of his life. The weight of years was now upon him, but every faculty of his mind and every sense were as acute and apparently as vigorous as ever. His handwriting was as beautiful and legible as copperplate engraving. Under the frontispiece of this volume is a *fac-simile* of his signature. Into his study came men of science and letters who sought his counsel and aid. Philanthropists found in him a friend whose name and purse were always ready to further any good work. As president of the Asiatic Society, he corresponded with officers of Government and men of learning, in the promotion of its important objects. He was ardently devoted to the cause of religious liberty, and was one of the delegation to Russia, appointed by the Evangelical Alliance to obtain concessions to the Protestants in the Baltic provinces. His advanced age rendered it inexpedient for him to make the journey, but, as chairman of the delegation, he wrote the first draft of the memorial to be presented to the Czar. In such works of Christian benevolence, in literary and scientific pursuits, in social and domestic enjoyments, the evening of life came on. His children and theirs were around him—in the summer at Poughkeepsie, in the winter in New York—and his home was the abode of contentment and peace.

47

CHAPTER XXII.

1870-1872.

AN OLD PAINTING—LETTER TO THE CONVENTION IN ROME—LAST PUBLIC SER-
VICE—UNVEILING THE STATUE OF FRANKLIN—SICKNESS—DEATH—FU-
NERAL—MEMORIAL SERVICES IN WASHINGTON—BOSTON—ACTION OF CON-
GRESS—LEGISLATURE OF MASSACHUSETTS—TELEGRAPHIC SYMPATHY—
TRIBUTES OF RESPECT—SKETCH OF CHARACTER.

PROFESSOR MORSE was eighty years old when the statue in his honor was erected in the Central Park. He had been many years contemplating, without apprehension or regret, the end of life. His interest in the present and the past was not diminished by his contemplations of the future. A pleasant incident awakened recollections of his earliest art studies. In Charlestown, his native place, a large painting was found among the rubbish in the lofts of the City Hall, almost incapable of being distinguished by reason of neglect and decay. The name of Morse was found on the back of it; and Hon. G. Washington Warren wrote to the Professor asking information respecting it. A letter was received in reply, which is now preserved in the records of the Charlestown Board of Aldermen.

"NEW YORK, *May* 11, 1870.

"MY DEAR SIR: I take pleasure in replying to your queries, in your favor of yesterday, respecting the painting in the Charlestown City Hall. The subject is, 'The Landing of the Pilgrims at Plymouth.' From the date, February, 1811, you will perceive that it was painted before I commenced my studies in the art. It was my earliest effort at painting an historical picture, and can have no particular merit, being the effort of a boy of nineteen. It may have an historical interest in the fact that it was this painting, and a landscape painted about the same time, that decided my father, by the advice of Stuart and Allston, to permit me to visit Europe with the latter artist, to study art as a profession. I left with him in July of the same year, 1811, arriving in England in August; have not seen this picture since that date; it was painted in the parsonage, which was built near the present church, but which has been for many years removed to another locality. A few years ago I made a very brief visit to Charlestown with my wife and a daughter, who were desirous of seeing the house and room in which I was born ; I then heard that this picture was in the City Hall, and I intended to visit it, but they felt more interest in the house, so the time I had at command was devoted to showing them the house in which I was born, temporarily occupied by my parents, while the parsonage, now removed, was in process of building. This house is on the main street, on the north side, a little west of the Unitarian brick church, and when we visited it it had been occupied by Captain Edes.

I have just entered upon my eightieth year, and can scarcely expect that there are many, if any, of my personal friends and fellow-townsmen still living ; but I cannot forget the place of my birth, nor the kind expressions of remembrance by their descendants.

"Respectfully, your ob't servant,   SAMUEL F. B. MORSE.

"G. WASHINGTON WARREN, Esq., Charlestown, Mass."

The picture is now hung in the mayor's office at Charlestown, and has peculiar interest from the facts presented in this letter. In the year 1871, the Grand-duke Alexis, son of the Emperor of Russia, came to the United States, and, during his visit in the city of New York, Professor Morse assisted largely in showing attentions to the distinguished guest. It was the winter following that an important telegraphic convention was held in the city of Rome, which Professor Morse could not attend. Anxious always to make the Telegraph an instrument of good, and with a heart burning with desires for peace on earth, and good-will among men, he wrote to Cyrus W. Field, Esq., at Rome, a letter which was read to the convention. At its conclusion the convention broke out in prolonged cheers for the illustrious author, and the letter was ordered to be printed among the records of the convention. It is in these words, and is worthy of being preserved as one of the last public communications from the hand of the inventor of the Telegraph.

"NEW YORK, *December* 4, 1871.

"MY DEAR MR. FIELD: Excuse my delay in writing you. The excitement occasioned by the visit of the Grand-duke Alexis has just closed, and I have been wholly engaged by the various duties connected with his presence.

"I have wished for a few calm moments to put on paper some thoughts respecting the doings of the great Telegraphic Convention to which you are a delegate.

"The Telegraph has now assumed such a marvelous position in human affairs throughout the world; its influences are so great and important in all the varied concerns of nations, that its efficient protection from injury has become a necessity. It is a powerful advocate for universal peace. Not that of itself it can command a 'Peace, be still!' to the angry waves of human passions, but that by its rapid interchange of thought and opinion it gives the opportunity of explanations to acts and laws which in their ordinary wording often create doubt and suspicion.

"Were there no means of quick explanation, it is readily seen that doubt and suspicion, working on the susceptibilities of the public mind, would engender misconception, hatred, and strife. How important, then, that in the intercourse of nations there should be the ready means at hand for prompt correction and explanation!

"Could there not be passed, in the great International Convention, some resolution to the effect that, in whatever condition, whether of peace or war between nations, the telegraph should be deemed a sacred thing, to be by common consent effectually protected both on land and beneath the waters?

"In the interest of human happiness, of that 'peace on earth' which, in announcing the advent of the Saviour, the angels proclaimed, with 'good-will to men,' I hope that the convention will not adjourn without adopting a resolution asking of the nations their united effective protection to this great agent of civilization.

"The mode and the terms of such resolution may be safely left to the intelligent members of the honorable and distinguished convention. Believe me, as ever, your friend and servant,

"SAMUEL F. B. MORSE.

"Hon. CYRUS W. FIELD, Rome, Italy."

A few days after this letter was written, his brother Sidney, his only surviving brother, his counselor, comforter, and more than friend, was smitten with apoplexy, and, after lying unconscious for several days, expired. This was a sad blow to the aged survivor, the eldest of the three, and outlasting them all. The writer of this sat on one side of the bed, on the other the venerable Professor, and between us lay the dying man. The Professor spoke in the ear of his brother, but there was no evidence that he was heard. He felt that he was indeed alone when his last brother was gone. His friends thought and said he would not long remain behind. He had been subject to neuralgia, and now the attacks became more frequent and more severe.

The last time that he appeared in public was on the occasion of the inauguration of the statue of Benjamin Franklin in Printing-House Square, in front of the City Hall, January 17, 1872. It was happily conceived by the committee of arrangements that there would be a singular fitness in asking MORSE to unveil to the world a statue of FRANKLIN. Those names, identified with electricity, are to be always associated. The Professor was now in feeble health, and the excitement and exposure of the occasion would be dangerous. But his desire to be present and to perform the service assigned was so great that he said he felt it to be his duty to go, if it were the last public act that he should perform. It proved to be a very cold day. Accompanied by his family, he rode in his carriage to the square, was received by the committee, and escorted to the platform in the open air, by the side of the veiled statue. An immense multitude cheered him as he ascended the steps, and stood uncovered in the midst of them. When the introductory exercises had been performed he drew the cord that removed the covering, and the statue of Franklin and the form of Morse himself stood side by side. Tens of thousands of voices shouted applause. When silence was restored, the vast assembly listened to catch his words, as with tremulous voice he said:

"MR. DE GROOT AND FELLOW-CITIZENS: I esteem it one of my highest honors that I should have been designated to perform the office of unveiling this day the fine statue of our illustrious and immortal Franklin. When requested to accept this duty I was confined to my bed, but I could not refuse, and I said, 'Yes, if I have to be lifted to the spot!' Franklin needs no eulogy from me. No one has more reason to venerate his name than myself. May his illustrious example of devotion to the interest of universal humanity be the seed of further fruit for the good of the world ! "

DEATH.

The last public act of his life was this participation in the ceremony of inaugurating the statue of Benjamin Franklin. His failing health compelled him to decline the invitation to the banquet in the evening, where his name was repeatedly mentioned with that of the old philosopher, and received with the warmest applause. He went home to die. Neuralgia concentrated its attacks in his head, and he walked the floor in agony, holding both hands to his temples, and groaning with excessive pain. Day after day, and weeks, succeeded, while he gradually succumbed to the disease. To the Rev. Dr. Adams, on whose ministry he attended in the city, he expressed unwavering faith, and, in response to a remark concerning the goodness of God to him in the past, he said, with cheerful hope, " The best is yet to come."

The pain in his head, that had nearly distracted him, now ceased, and stupor ensued. His had been a teeming, busy, unclouded brain, for more than eighty years. Sickness had rarely laid its hand upon him. Trouble, trials, anxieties, disappointments, bereavements, carking cares, bitter persecutions, extreme poverty, the birth-pangs of a great invention, toil, discouragement, success, triumph, lawsuits, losses, gains, wealth, luxury, honors, fame, the homage of republics, kingdoms, and empires, laid at his feet—through all these vicissitudes of fortune he had passed, beyond the experience, perhaps, of any private citizen. Through fourscore years he had borne and worn them all, with the grace of a Christian, the calmness of a philosopher, and the simplicity of a child. Conscious of the rectitude of his own purposes and action, charitable toward all, and especially to his enemies, he had been calm when others were excited, and so the vexations that wear out the life of most men failed to shorten his days. But now the end was near. To him, the father of the Telegraph, the last message had come. It was not a sudden summons. He had been always ready, and had often wished that it might not be delayed. And when it came it found him waiting. Peacefully he was sinking into the arms of death.

For some days he was scarcely conscious of surrounding persons, save of his fond wife, on whom he turned his mild blue eyes, with looks of love he could not speak. The birthday of his youngest child arrived; and, to the surprise of all, he recalled it, placed his hands upon his son's head, and caressed him tenderly. A picture made by his niece, as a present to the boy, was produced, and, rousing himself, he asked for his spectacles, put them on, examined the drawing, and pronounced it admirable. So the first passion of his life was almost his last emotion. In childhood he began to draw. He never loved any thing so much as his chosen art. And now, forgetting the honors and rewards of the great invention that had made his name immortal, the expiring man revives at the sight of a little drawing, and, remembering his own work when a boy, gives his dying words to its praise!

Yet once more is the thought of the Telegraph revived! The attending physicians were inspecting his lungs, and one of them, tapping upon his chest to learn their condition, said to him, pleasantly, "This is the way we doctors telegraph."

"VERY GOOD," said the dying man, and never spoke again.

The intelligence that Professor Morse was dying touched the heart of the nation. It was announced wherever his electric wires were stretched—over the country, under the ocean, and to the ends of the world. Bulletins were issued from hour to hour, to meet the anxious inquiries of the people. Every hour of the night, as well as of the day, reporters of the press sought to know his condition. His door was besieged by friends testifying their sympathy. Those he loved were around him with ministries of love. When far past the power of speech, he put up his lips to his loving wife for one more kiss. Holy men commended his departing spirit to Him whom unseen he adored. Tears of affection fell like rain upon his bed. Beauty, serene and majestic, clothed his countenance and lighted his eyes. The image of the heavenly was revealed. His peace was like a river. Not a cloud, not a fear, no care, no want, disturbed the calmness of his passing soul.

He had reached and enjoyed his loftiest and last ambition. Around him were gathered all that art and taste and wealth and love contribute to the delight of men. Office and power he had never wished, but he had sought fame and wealth and honor; and, when gained, he had gladly used them for truth and virtue and philanthropy, counting all he had and was but means of usefulness for the sake of Him in whom he lived.

A long, eventful, brilliant career was closing. The light was going out of those eyes that had so long been bright with the fire of genius and the softer rays of love. The fingers that guided the lightning through the seas had lost their cunning. The brain in which was born the grandest of all conceptions ever made real by the art of man—to annihilate time and space in human intercourse, and bring the ends of the earth into instant union—and that throbbed with conscious triumph when the work was done, was resting now. The heart that never harbored an unkind feeling toward a human being, that always warmed with tender affection for the suffering—that kind, gentle, loving heart, in which wife and children nestled and were blest; where every virtue that gilds human life had its source, and out of which flowed streams of kindness, to gladden home, the social circle, and the world—that great, good heart now ceased to beat.

He died April 2, 1872.

POSTHUMOUS HONORS.

The Legislature of the State of New York being in session at the time, the Governor, Hon. John T. Hoffman, sent to that body the following communication, April 3d:

"The Telegraph to-day announces the death of its inventor, Samuel F. B. Morse. Born in Massachusetts, his home has for many years of his eventful life been in New York. His fame belongs to neither, but to the country and the world; yet it seems fitting that this great State, in which he lived and died, should be the first to pay appropriate honors to his memory. Living, he received from governments everywhere more public honors than were ever paid to any American private citizen; dead, let all the people pay homage to his name. I respectfully recommend to the Legislature the adoption of such resolutions as may be suitable, and the appointment of a joint committee to attend the funeral of the illustrious deceased. JOHN T. HOFFMAN."

In both Houses appropriate resolutions were adopted and a joint committee was appointed to attend the funeral. The funeral services were held Friday, April 5th, at Madison-Square Presbyterian Church, New York. At eleven o'clock the procession entered the church in the following order:

Rev. WM. ADAMS, D. D.; Rev. FRANCIS B. WHEELER, D. D.

Corpse.

Pall-bearers:

WILLIAM ORTON,	CYRUS W. FIELD,
DANIEL HUNTINGTON,	CHARLES BUTLER,
PETER COOPER,	JOHN A. DIX,
CAMBRIDGE LIVINGSTON,	EZRA CORNELL.

The Family.

Governor HOFFMAN and Staff.

Members of the Legislature.

Directors of the New York, Newfoundland, and London Telegraph Company.

Directors of the Western Union Telegraph Company, and officers and operators.

Members of the Academy of Design.

Members of the Evangelical Alliance.

Members of the Chamber of Commerce.

Members of the Association for the Advancement of Science and Art.

Members of the New York Stock Exchange.

Delegations from the Common Councils of New York, Brooklyn, and Poughkeepsie, and many of the Yale Alumni.

The Legislative Committee: Messrs. James W. Husted, L. Bradford Prince, James C. Osgood, Samuel J. Tilden, Severn D. Moulton, and John Simpson.

After preliminary devotional services the funeral address was delivered by Dr. Adams. This oration was one of great eloquence and beauty, reciting the history of the illustrious dead, and giving the appropriate lessons drawn from his remarkable career. In its conclusion Dr. Adams said:

" To-day we part forever with all that is mortal of that man who has done so much in the cause of Christian civilization. Less than one year ago his fellow-citizens, chiefly telegraphic operators, who loved him as children love a father, raised his statue of bronze in Central Park. To-day all we can give him is a grave. That venerable form, that face so saintly in its purity and refinement, we shall see no more. How much we shall miss him in our homes, our churches, in public gatherings, in the streets, and in society which he adorned and blessed! But his life has been so useful, so happy, and so complete, that for him nothing remains to be wished. Congratulate the man who, leaving to his family, friends, and country, a name spotless, untarnished, beloved of nations, to be repeated in foreign tongues, and by sparkling seas, has died in the bright and blessed hope of everlasting life.

"Farewell, beloved friend, honored citizen, public benefactor, good and faithful servant! While thy eulogy shall be pronounced in many languages by thy fellow-men, this, I believe, was your own highest aspiration—to have your name, as an humble disciple, written in the Lamb's Book of Life. There it will shine, and ours also, even the humblest of us all, if united to Christ, above the brightness of the firmament and as the stars forever and ever. A small thing is it to be judged of man's judgment; and all the greatness and glory of this world pass away like a dream. 'God accepteth not the persons of princes, nor regardeth the rich more than the poor; for they all are the work of his hands.' Truly great and immortal is that man, however obscure his earthly lot, who so believes in Jesus Christ that he may appropriate to himself the words of the Lord of Life, 'Because I live, ye shall live also.'

"The three grandest objects which ever can occupy the mind of man are the Divine Redeemer, the human soul, the day of death and judgment. Blessed is that man, and so will he be when all the thrones, monuments, and eulogies of the world are forgotten, who so lives that he shall be able to combine the three and say, as did this true Christian in his last articulation, 'I know whom I have believed, and I am persuaded that he is able to keep that which I have committed to him against that day.'"

Prayer was then offered by the Rev. Dr. Wheeler, and the hymn "Just as I am" was chanted by the choir. The remains were taken to Greenwood Cemetery and deposited in the receiving-vault. The burial service was read and prayer offered by the Rev. J. Aspinwall Hodge, pastor of the Presbyterian Church of Hartford, and son-in-law of Richard C. Morse.

The President of the Western Union Telegraph Company issued the following message:

"NEW YORK, *April* 4, 1872.

" *To all Telegraph Superintendents and Managers in the United States and Canada:* All that is mortal of the venerable and venerated father of the American Telegraph system, Professor Samuel F. B. Morse, will be consigned to the grave on Friday, April 5th. No expression of outward exhibition can give fitting evidence of the sorrow which his death has occasioned among those connected with the Telegraph, or within the reach of its influence, not only in America, but throughout the world; but, in token of respect to his memory, some symbol of mourning should be exhibited at all telegraph-stations on the day of burial; a simple rosette, or a bit of crape, will suffice.　　　　　　　　　　WILLIAM ORTON, *President.*"

The Common Council of the city of New York, the National Academy of Design, the New York Stock Exchange, the New York Chamber of Commerce, and the various scientific, philanthropic, and religious institutions with which he had been associated, adopted resolutions of respect for his memory. In other cities and countries similar tributes were paid. The telegraph-poles in many places were hung with mourning, and the bells were tolled.

CONGRESS OF THE UNITED STATES.

In the House of Representatives, Hon. S. S. Cox offered a concurrent resolution, declaring that Congress has heard "with profound regret of the death of Professor Morse, whose distinguished and varied abilities have contributed more than those of any other person to the development and progress of the practical arts, and that his purity of private life, his loftiness of scientific aims, and his resolute faith in truth, render it highly proper that the Representatives and Senators should solemnly testify to his worth and greatness." This resolution was unanimously agreed to.

Mr. Fernando Wood, of New York City, gave a brief history of the legislation under which Professor Morse's invention was practically tested in this country. The speaker was a member of the Twenty-seventh Congress, to which Professor Morse applied for aid to test his invention. And he expressed the great pride with which he (Mr. Wood) found his name recorded in the affirmative, and he was to-day the only living member of either House who voted in favor of the bill.

In the Senate, on motion of Hon. J. W. Patterson, of New Hampshire, a similar resolution was adopted. A committee, appointed by both Houses, was charged with making arrangements for a suitable service in memory of Morse. The Morse Memorial Association of the city of Washington combined with this committee, and preparations were made for a solemn service in the hall of the House. This was held April 16th.

A crowded audience attended. The Speaker of the House, Mr. Blaine, presided, assisted by Vice-President Colfax. The President and Cabinet, Judges of the Supreme Court, together with the Governors of the States, in person or by proxy, occupied seats on the inner semicircle. Senators and Representatives occupied the other seats on the floor. In front of the main gallery was an oil-painting of Professor Morse, and around the outer frame of the portrait was the legend "What hath God wrought!" The ceremonies were opened with prayer by the Rev. Dr. Adams, of New York, when Speaker Blaine said:

"Less than thirty years ago, a man of genius and learning was an earnest petitioner before Congress for a small pecuniary aid, that enabled him to test certain occult theories of science which he had laboriously evolved. To-night the representatives of forty million people assemble in their legislative hall to do homage and honor to the name of 'Morse.' Great discoverers and inventors rarely live to witness the full development and perfection of their mighty conceptions, but to him whose death we now mourn, and whose fame we celebrate, it was in God's good providence vouchsafed otherwise. The little thread of wire placed as a timid experiment between the national capital and a neighboring city, grew and lengthened, and multiplied with almost the rapidity of the electric current that darted along its iron nerves, until, within his own lifetime, continent was bound unto continent, hemisphere answered through ocean's depths unto hemisphere, and an encircled globe flashed forth his eulogy in the unmatched elements of a grand achievement. Charged by the House of Representatives with the agreeable and honorable duty of presiding here, and of announcing the various participants in the exercises of the evening, I welcome to this hall those who join with us in this expressive tribute to the memory and to the merit of a great man."

The exercises were then conducted in the following order :

Resolutions by Hon. C. C. Cox, M. D., of Washington, D. C.
Address by Hon. J. W. PATTERSON, of New Hampshire.
Address by Hon. FERNANDO WOOD, of New York.
Vocal Music by the Choral Society of Washington.
Address by Hon. J. A. GARFIELD, of Ohio.
Address by Hon. S. S. Cox, of New York.
Address by Hon. D. W. VOORHES, of Indiana.
Address by Hon. N. P. BANKS, of Massachusetts.
Vocal Music by the Choral Society of Washington.
Benediction by the Rev. Dr. WHEELER, of Poughkeepsie, N. Y.

Telegraphic messages came in and were read by Cyrus W. Field, Esq., sent the same day from Europe, Asia, and Africa, to America, paying funeral tributes to the memory of the man whose genius and skill had brought these four quarters of the globe into daily intercourse! From the British Provinces on the North, from California, and the farthest South and East, similar messages came, so that the whole civilized world was actually represented, and in spirit was present, at these memorial services in the Capitol at Washington.

On the same evening with the meeting in the Capitol, memorial meetings were held in various parts of the United States. The lines of telegraph were used freely for direct communication between them, and, the progress of the several meetings being reported to all, they were in perfect sympathy. The idea was novel, and happily carried out.

Massachusetts, the native State of Professor Morse, paid him distinguished honors. Its Legislature adopted the following resolutions :

" *Resolved*, That the Legislature of Massachusetts has learned, with profound regret, of the decease of Samuel Finley Breese Morse, the distinguished inventor of that wonderful system of electric telegraphy which is conferring unspeakable blessings upon the whole human family.

" *Resolved*, That, born upon our soil, and under the very shadow of this capitol, his name will ever be associated by the people of this State with that of another of her illustrious sons, who demonstrated to the world the existence of that mighty but subtile agency which the genius and skill of his peer and successor has brought under subjection and made subservient to the will of man.

"*Resolved*, That with the regrets his death has occasioned are mingled emotions of joy and gratitude that he was permitted, by Him in whose hands are the issues of life and death, to attain to the full age allotted to man upon earth, and that he was thereby enabled to witness the complete triumph of the work to which his life was consecrated—a privilege which has seldom been enjoyed by the world's greatest benefactors.

"*Resolved*, That his Excellency the Governor be requested to transmit a copy of these resolutions to the family of the deceased, with the assurance of the spmpathy of the people of this Common-wealth in the loss they have sustained."

A memorial meeting was held in Faneuil Hall, Boston, at which the mayor of the city presided, supported by Josiah Quincy, G. S. Hillard, and others. Addresses were deliverd by Professor E. N. Horsford, Hon. R. H. Dana, Hon. G. S. Hillard, and S. P. Whipple, Esq. ; and appropriate resolutions were adopted.

In every part of his own country, and in many foreign lands, testimonials of respect and gratitude were offered to his memory—such and so many as were never before laid upon the grave of a man who never held a public office among his fellow-men.

REVIEW OF HIS CHARACTER.

It is not given to mortals to leave a perfect example for the admiration and imitation of posterity. But it is safe to say that the life and character of few men whose history is left on record afford less opportunity for criticisim than is found in the conspicuous career of the inventor of the Telegraph.

Having followed him step by step from his birth to the grave, in public, social, and private relations, in struggles with poverty, enemies, and wrongs; in courts of law, the press, and halls of science ; having seen him tempted, assailed, defeated, and again in victory, honor, and renown ; having read thousands of his private letters, his essays, and pamphlets, and volumes in which his claims are canvassed, his merits discussed, and his character reviewed ; having had access to his most private papers and confidential correspondence, in which all that is most secret and sacred in the life of man is hid—it is right to say that in this mass of testimony by friends and foes there is not a line that requires to be erased or changed to preserve the lustre of his name.

Such is the natural result of those influences which formed and developed his character. Intellectual strength and inflexible integrity were traits that distinguished his ancestry. Virtue and usefulness made the atmosphere of his father's house. There he became familiar with the names and works of illustrious men, in his own and other lands; and to be like them was the aspiration of his young ambition. He studied Plutarch's lives of great men when he was a boy, and drew their protraits with his pen almost as soon as he could write. And in his young mind was a sentiment that Plutarch did not teach—the sense of personal responsibility to the Infinite Creator. Him he acknowledged as the source and end of his being. This became a passion, absorbing his thoughts, infusing into his life a secret power to will and to do. In reverential moments, contemplating the extent and results of the great invention conceived in the recesses of his own mind, he felt, deeply and sincerely, that it was not of himself, but of God. Hence he was always under a sense of personal obligation to use this power for the good of his fellow-men.

Subject to the infirmities of a delicate constitution, often sunk in the depths of despondency, afflicted with nervous disorders that were attended with great physical suffering, and harassed through all his life by vexations disappointments, reverses, and wrongs, his heroic faith in God alone held him up and made him victorious.

It was the device and purpose of those who sought to rob him of his honors and his rights to depreciate his intellectual ability and his scientific attainments. But among all the men of science, and of the men of learning in the law, there was not one who was a match for him when he gave his mind to a subject which required his perfect mastery. His favorite study, in college and afterward, was electricity. And when, in 1827, the powers of electro-magnetism were revealed to him, he comprehended its relations and capabilities, and at the proper time applied them with the skill and precision of an expert. He drew up the brief, with his own hand, for one of the distinguished counsel, in a great lawsuit involving his patent rights, and his lawyer said it was the argument that carried conviction to every unprejudiced mind. Such was the versatility and variety of his mental endowments that he would have been great in any department of human pursuits. His wonderful rapidity of thought was associated with patient, plodding perseverance, a combination rare, but mightily effective. He leaped to a possible conclusion, and then slowly developed the successive steps by which the end was gained and the result made secure. He covered thousands of pages with his pencil-notes, annotated large and numerous volumes, filled huge folios with valuable excerpts from newspapers, illustrated processes of thought with diagrams, and was thus fortified and enriched with stores of knowledge and masses of facts, so digested, combined, and arranged, that he had them at his easy command to defend the past, or to help him onward to fresh conquests in the fields of truth. Yet such was his modesty and reticence in regard to himself that none outside of his household were aware of his resources, and his attainments were only known when displayed in self-defense. Then they never failed to be ample for the occasion, as every opponent had reason to remember.

Yet he was as gentle as he was great. Many thought him weak, because he was simple, childlike, and unworldly. Often he suffered wrong rather than resist, and this disposition to yield was frequently his loss. The firmness, tenacity, and perseverance, with which he fought his foes, were the fruits of his integrity, principle, and profound convictions of right and duty. His nature was tender, loving, and kind. Home, and wife, and children, were his joys. In the midst of foreign triumphs and fiercest conflicts, his heart turned fondly to the banks of the river where his loved ones waited his return.

"More than a quarter of a century," said Mr. Mason, the American Ambassador at the court of France in 1858, "I have had the honor to call Professor Morse my friend, and I venture to say that no man ever lived who more eminently deserved to be pronounced—

'Integer vitæ, scelerisque purus'"
(A man of blameless life and pure).

Indeed, he deserves it, more surely than he on whom Horace pronounced the high eulogium, for Professor Morse is a Christian gentleman."

Leonardo da Vinci was an artist, a painter; and his achievements with the brush are the monuments that preserve his name. But he was also an engineer, a mechanician, a philanthropist, and a statesman. He was great in all that he attempted. A man of marvelous industry, patience, and perseverance, he devised and directed schemes for the good of his country and the benefit of his fellow-men. Morse was endowed with similar powers, and inspired with the same purposes. He was a painter, an artist; and he was also an artisan, an inventor; a mechanician, working in brass with his own hands; an author, writing with masterly ability, measuring his strength and learning with the ablest lawyers, the profoundest theologians, and eminent statesmen, maintaining himself with complete success on all occasions. Leonardo is remembered by his works of art. Morse, as a painter, is lost in his renown as an inventor and benefactor of his race.

In person, Professor Morse was tall, slender, graceful, and attractive. Six feet in stature, he stood erect and firm, even in old age. His blue eyes were expressive of genius and affection. His nature was a rare combination of solid intellect and delicate sensibility. Thoughtful, sober, and quiet, he readily entered into the enjoyments of domestic and social life, indulging in sallies of humor, and readily appreciating and greatly enjoying the wit of others. Dignified in his intercourse with men, courteous and affable with the gentler sex, he was a good husband, a judicious father, a generous and faithful friend. He had the misfortune to incur the hostility of men who would deprive him of the merit and the reward of his labors. But this is the common fate of great inventors. He lived until his rights were vindicated by every tribunal to which they could be referred, and acknowledged by all civilized nations. And he died leaving to his children a spotless and illustrious name, and to his country the honor of having given birth to the only Electro-Magnetic Recording Telegraph whose line is gone out through all the earth, and its words to the end of the world.

48

APPENDIX.

[EXTRACTS FROM A PAMPHLET PREPARED AND PUBLISHED IN PARIS, 1867.]

BY SAMUEL F. B. MORSE.

IN the month of October, 1832, I left France for the United States in the packet-ship Sully. Early in the voyage, in the course of conversations in the cabin, some of the facts in relation to electricity, familiar to me from my college-days, were casually brought to my recollection in describing the then recent discovery of the means of obtaining the electric spark from the magnet, a discovery which demonstrated the intimate relations of magnetism and electricity. The fact that electricity passed with such rapidity through a space of many miles was alluded to, in which Franklin's opinion of the *instantaneity* of the passage of electricity was brought to notice. This led me to remark that, "if that were so, and the presence of electricity could be made visible in any desired part of the circuit, I see no reason why intelligence might not be transmitted instantaneously by electricity." This was the crude seed which at once took root, and with the favoring leisure of a long voyage, and a mind unoccupied with other studies, grew into form, absorbing my thoughts in the sleepless hours of the night, and turning the tedium of the voyage into an agreeable pastime. Before the end of the voyage the invention had the following attributes.

I may observe, in passing, that my aim at the outset was simplicity of means as well as result. Hence I devised a *single circuit of conductors* from some generator of electricity. I planned *a system of signs* consisting of dots or points, and spaces to represent numerals; and *two modes* of causing the electricity *to mark or imprint* these signs upon *a strip or ribbon of paper*. One was by *chemical decomposition of a salt* which should discolor the paper; the other was by *the mechanical action of the electro-magnet*, operating upon the paper by a *lever* charged at one extremity with a *pen or pencil*. I conceived the plan of moving the paper ribbon at a *regular rate* by means of *clock-work machinery* to receive the signs. These processes, as well as the mathematically - calculated *signs*, devised for and adapted to *recording*, were sketched in my sketch-book. I also drew in my sketch-book modes of *interring the conductors in tubes in the earth*, and, soon after landing, planned and drew out the *method upon posts*. This was the general condition of the invention (with the exception of the plan upon posts) when I arrived in New York, on the 15th of November, 1832.

Among the original characteristics of the invention as devised on board the ship, one of the
most important was the mathe-
matically-calculated *signs* adapted to *recording.* As these signs
have ever since played a most
important part in the modern
telegraphs, they would seem to
demand here a more distinct notice of their origin.

In reflecting on the operations
of electricity as a proposed agent
in telegraphy, I·was aware that
its presence in a conductor of *moderate length* could be indicated in
several ways. The physical effects
in a shock; the visible spark; visible bubbles during decomposition,
and marks left from decomposition; its magnetic effects upon
soft iron and steel; and its calo-
rific effects—these were all well-
known phenomena. Could any
of these be made available for
recording, and at a *great* distance?
This was the important problem
to be solved. Electricity had
been flashed many miles through
a conductor, apparently instantaneously, and produced some of
these effects at a distance. May
not all of them, likewise, be produced at a distance? If so, which
of them seemed to promise the
surest result of a *permanent record?* Static electricity, as an
agent, was first proposed, but
was quickly dismissed as too un-
controllable, and I directed my
attention exclusively to the phenomena of dynamic electricity.
The decomposition of a salt hav-

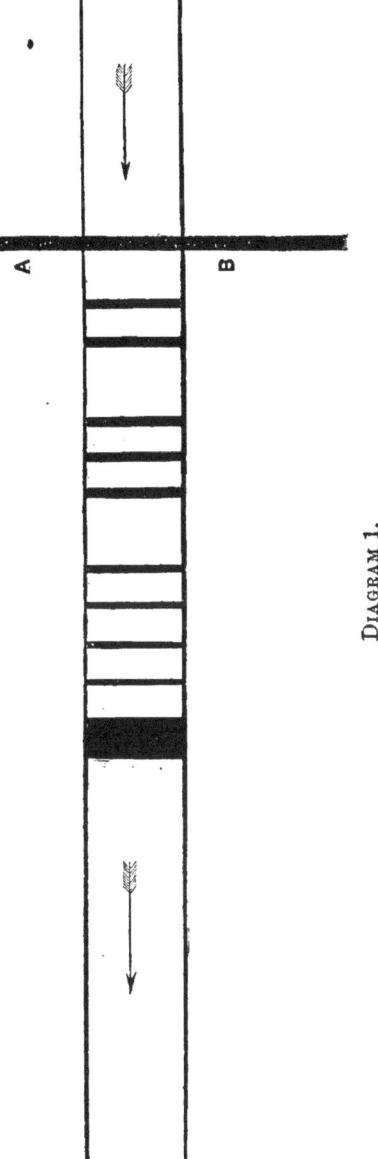

DIAGRAM 1.

ing a metallic basis would leave a mark upon paper or cloth—but what salt? Some would probably answer the purpose. Assuming, therefore, that such a salt could be found, how was it to be used? If a strip of paper or cloth were moistened with the salt, and were then simply *put in contact* with a conductor charged with electricity, would there be any effect upon the paper? A magnetic effect is produced exterior to the charged conductor; is there any salt or substance so sensitive as to be affected either by decomposition, or in any other way, by this magnetic influence, by *simple contact* with an electrically-charged wire? It was doubtful, but worth an experiment.

But, if such effect were verified by experiment, it was conceived that marks like those in the diagram (1) might be made across the moistened paper, as it passed beneath and in contact with the conjunctive wire A B, when the wire was electrically charged and discharged.

It is needless to add that on trial no such effect was produced by the *magnetic* properties of an electrically-charged wire upon any salt that I afterward submitted to the experiment. Nevertheless, it is perceived that, had this device (which was noted down for testing) been verified, the simplest of all modes of *recording* would have been the result.

The nearest approach to this simplicity seemed to be the passing of the chemically-prepared paper between the two broken parts of a circuit so that the electricity should pass through the moistened paper or cloth; this would mark a point or dot when the circuit was closed, and by rapid closing and opening of the circuit, while the paper was moved regularly forward, points or dots, in any required groups, could be made at will. But what salt would best produce this result was to be determined after reaching the end of the voyage. In the mean time, as I originally proposed to record numerals only, intending to indicate *words* and *sentences* by numbers, it was a desideratum to arrange the ten digits to be represented by dots or points within as small a space as possible. The first and most obvious mode seemed to be the following:

```
1  2   3    4     5      7       8        9         10
.  ..  ...  ....  .....  ......  .......  ........  .........  ..........
```

But a few minutes' reflection showed that after *five* dots or points the number of dots became inconveniently numerous in indicating the larger digits; hence it occurred to me that, by extending the spaces appropriated to the five larger digits, giving them a greater space value than was possessed by the five smaller digits, I might reduce the number of dots, necessary to indicate any of the ten digits, within five dots. On this principle, therefore, I constructed the following *signs* for the ten numerals, and devised the TYPES for regulating the opening and closing of an electric circuit. (*See* Diagram 2.)

On inspecting the diagram (2) it will be perceived that the types were to be divided into definite *parts.*

Type 1 contains 4 parts, and appropriates	1 part	to its cog, and 3	to its space.
" 2 " 6 "	3 parts	to its cog, and 3	"
" 3 " 8 "	5 parts	to its cog, and 3	"
" 4 " 10 "	7 parts	to its cog, and 3	"
" 5 " 12	9 parts	to its cog, and 3	"
" 6 " 6	1 part	to its cog, and 5	"
" 7 " 8	3 parts	to its cog, and 5	"
" 8 " 10	5 parts	to its cog, and 5	"
" 9 " 12	7 parts	to its cog, and 5	"
" 0 " 14	9 parts	to its cog, and 5	"

Each of the *first* five digits, therefore, is indicated by a space of three parts, and

Each of the *last* five digits is indicated by a space of five parts.

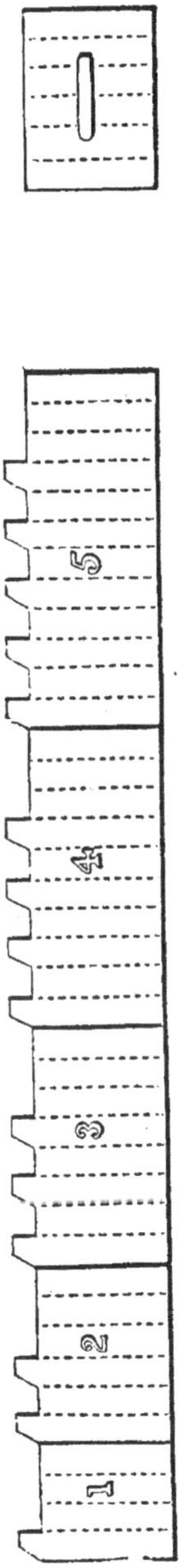

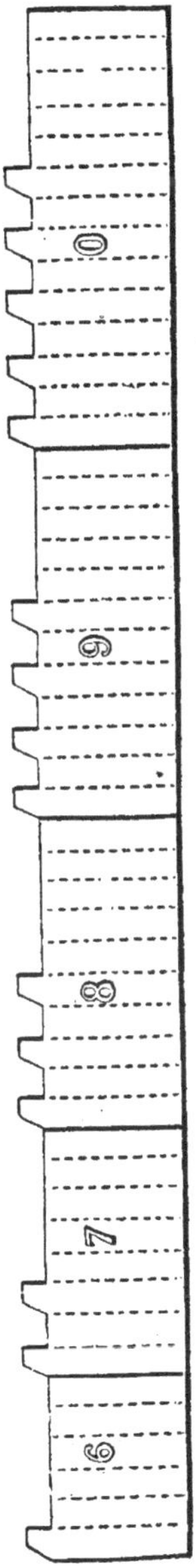

DIAGRAM 2.

DIAGRAM 3.

The *space type* for separating completed numbers, whether single or compounded, contains six parts.

The *length* of the *spaces*, therefore, was an element to be used in determining the difference between the class of the first five digits and the class of the last five digits, and not simply the number of dots or points. Whether one dot was to be read as numeral 1 or as numeral 6 was to be determined by the length of the space after it, and, for the purpose of measuring this space in the last numeral of a dispatch, the single dot or point was to be used as a supernumerary *finale* to every dispatch.

A space of the length of nine or more parts, after a dot or group of dots, indicates the dot or group of dots to be a complete number, whether single or compounded.

A space *less* than the length of the nine parts, after a dot or group of dots, indicates that they are a portion of a compounded number.

An example will illustrate this first mode of recording that was proposed. Suppose the numbers to be telegraphed are

$$77—8—92$$

The type would be arranged as in the above diagram (3). The record would show two dots, then a space of five parts, which, being less than nine parts, determines the two dots to belong to numeral 7, the five parts being its proper or natural space, and that it is one of a compounded number; then follow two similar dots, but followed by a space of eleven parts, which, consisting of more than nine parts, shows that a space type of six parts has been inserted, separating this last group from the next; six parts subtracted from the eleven parts leave five parts for the proper or natural space of the last numeral, showing it to be like the first, the numeral 7. Next come three dots, and also followed by a space of eleven parts, which, consisting of more than nine parts, isolates the numeral, and shows that a space type of six parts must be subtracted from the eleven, leaving five parts for the natural or proper space of the last numeral, indicating, therefore, the numeral 8. Then come four dots, followed by a space of five parts, which, being less than nine parts, shows the four dots to be a numeral belonging to a compounded number, and that it belongs to the class of the five larger digits, and indicates the numeral 9. Next come two dots, followed by a space of three parts, which, being less than nine parts, shows it to belong to the class of the first five digits, and therefore indicates the numeral 2, because it is succeeded by the final 1, which is not to be regarded except as serving to measure the space to determine the character of the previous numeral.

This method (in the light of my improvements of the code, which very soon followed after the first practical test) seems crude and even impractical, especially in view of my perfected alphabetic code devised as early as 1835, and now with some comparatively slight improvements in use throughout the world. But, cumbrous and inconvenient as it was, in its earliest stages, if compared in its results with the results of the semaphoric modes in use at that day, it will be perceived that it was even then a great step in advance.

A day had scarcely passed after my landing, before I commenced the construction of the invention from the plans and drawings made on board the ship. The signs to be recorded or imprinted it was necessary to embody in a species of *type*, the name I gave to the cogged pieces which were to make the required closings and openings of the circuit of conductors, necessary to mark or imprint the points or signs for numerals upon the strip of paper at the regulated intervals of time; the paper or ribbon having a *regular* movement, while the type performed the closing and opening of the circuit at *irregular* intervals (and thus broke the continuous line of the regular movement of the paper into *irregular parts* at pleasure), and furnished the means of breaking the line into dots and spaces, in such variety as at once to enable me not only to construct the numerals, but eventually, as will be seen by the different combinations of long lines, short lines, or points, and spaces, all the different letters of the alphabet. The *type* proposed at this time consisted of thin strips of type-metal with cogs varied at intervals, as seen in Diagram 2. These by means of a mechanical movement (hereinafter described) were made and intended for closing and opening the circuit at the desired times. These types, therefore, for imprinting at a distance, were, at that time, an essential part of the machinery in process of construction; and having more facilities, immediately on my arrival, for elaborating these types than for other parts of the machinery, they were the first constructed. A mould of brass was made and a quantity of the type was cast before the close of the year 1832. The rest of the machinery, except a single-cup battery, and a few yards of wire, and the train of wheels of a wooden clock, which I adapted to the service of unrolling the strip of paper, I was compelled, from the necessities of my profession, to leave in the condition of drawings until I found some more permanent resting-place. From November, 1832, until the summer of 1835 (two and a half years), I had changed my residence three times, and was wholly without the pecuniary means for putting together and embodying the various parts of my invention in one whole. But in July, 1835, I took possession of my new home, in the new building of the New York City University, and I then lost not a day in collecting the parts and putting into practical form the first rude instrument which was to demonstrate the operation of the invention. I was favored with a little leisure from the unfinished condition of the University building, which impeded the access of visitors to my apartments for my usual professional duties.

I ought here to say that, with the aid of a single-cup battery, as early as 1834, previous to my removal to the University, I ascertained that no visible effect was produced upon numerous salts, which I submitted to trial by putting them in *simple contact* with the wire charged with electricity, as shown in the plan of Diagram 1, proposed for experiment on board the ship. I succeeded, however, in marking by chemical decomposition, when the electricity was passed *through* the moistened paper or cloth, in 1836, in the University, but the process was attended with so many inconveniences that it was laid aside for the moment, not *abandoned*, that I might give my attention more directly to the *electro-magnetic mode* of recording.

If my nomadic mode of life for two years previous, and the condition of my pecuniary means, be kept in mind; if, also, it be considered that many of the mechanical facilities in New York, so abundant at the present day, for embodying the invention, did not exist, and therefore were denied to me, it will account both for the slowness in completing the instrumentalities of my invention, and the rudeness of the first-constructed instrument. The *electro-magnet* was not an instrument found for sale in the shops, as at this day ; insulated wire was nowhere to be obtained, except in the smallest quantities, as bonnet-wire of *iron* wound with cotton thread. Copper wire was not in use for that purpose, and was sold in the shops by the pound or yard at high prices and also in very limited quantities.

To form my electro-magnet, I was under the necessity of procuring from the blacksmith a small rod of iron bent in horseshoe form ; of purchasing a few yards of copper wire, and of winding upon it, by hand, its cotton-thread insulation, before I could construct the rude helices of the magnet. I had already purchased a cheap wooden clock and adapted the train of wheels to the rate of movement required for the ribbon of paper.

I needed a proper support for the machinery on which to arrange the various disconnected parts. A stretching-frame for canvas, XX, Diagram 4, (having a bar across the middle), which stood unemployed against the wall of my atelier, suggested to me a rough but convenient method of putting into operation the printing or marking of the signs. I nailed it at the bottom against the edge of a common table. Across the lower part of the frame I constructed a narrow trough to hold three narrow cylinders of wood, A B C ; A and C small, one on each side of the large cylinder B. The wooden clock D was placed at one end of this trough. The small cylinder C next to the clock had a small pulley-wheel fixed upon its prolonged axis, outside the trough ; a similar pulley-wheel was fixed upon the prolonged axis of the slower wheels of the train of wheels outside the clock ; these two pulley-wheels were connected by an endless cord or band.

Upon the other small cylinder A, on the other side of cylinder B, was wound the ribbon of paper, composed of long strips of paper pasted together, end to end. When the clock-train was put in movement, the ribbon of paper was gradually unrolled from its cylinder, and, passing over the cylinder B, was rolled up upon the cylinder C by means of the cord and pulleys. To give the weight which moved the clock-train a sufficiently long space in which to fall, a long rod or strip of wood projecting upward was nailed to the side of the frame, at the top of which rod was a pulley-wheel over which the cord attached to the weight E was passed.

Upon the middle of the cross-bar of the frame there was a small shelf or bracket *h* to hold the electro-magnet, which was the moving power of the marking or printing lever.

The *lever* was an A-shaped pendulum, F, suspended by its apex at *f* from the centre of the top of the frame, directly above the centre of the cylinder B in the trough below. This lever was made of two thin rules of wood meeting at the top *f*, but opening downward about one inch apart, and joined at the bottom by a transverse bar (which was close to the paper as it moved over the large cylinder), and another about one inch above it. Through the centre of these two bars a small tube or pencil-case

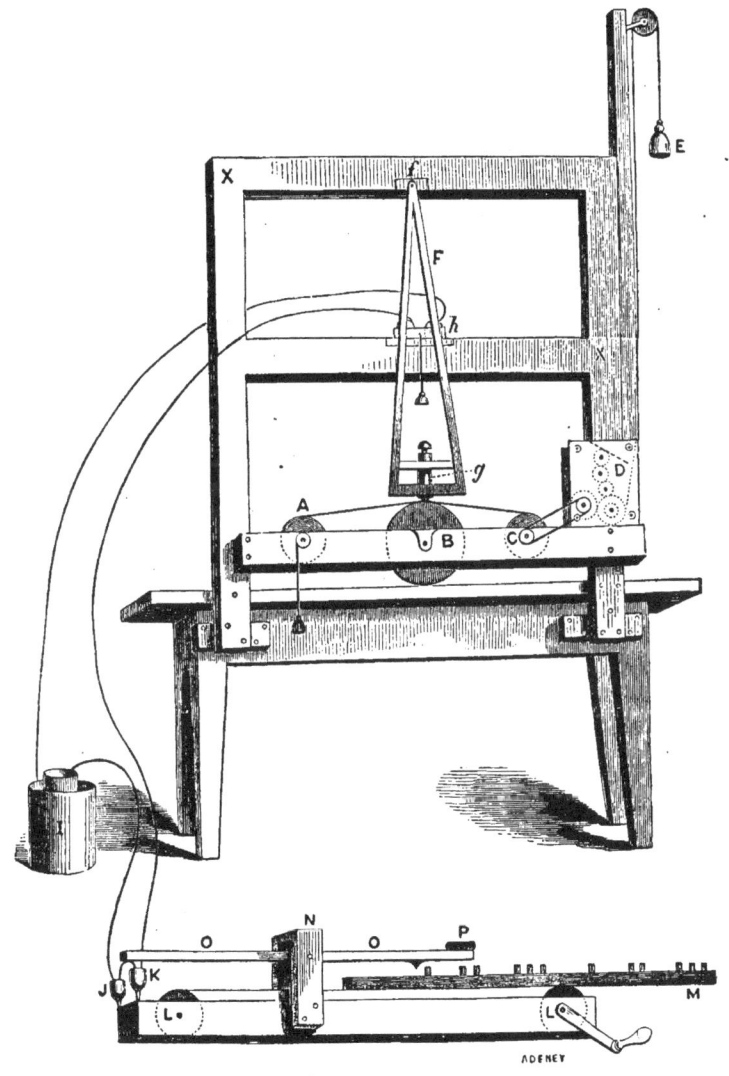

DIAGRAM 4.

TYPE.

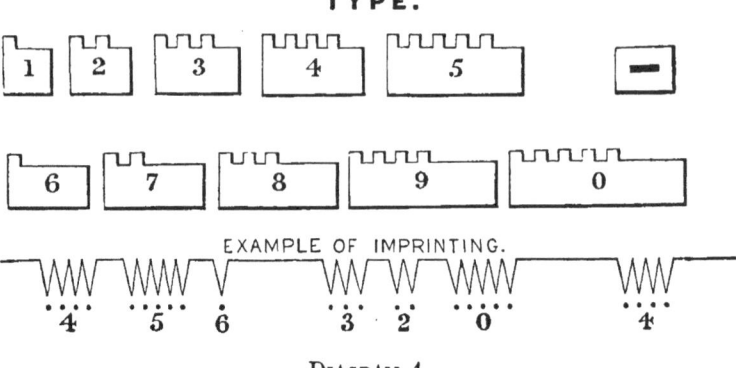

EXAMPLE OF IMPRINTING.

4   5   6   3   2   0   4

DIAGRAM 4.

g was fixed, through which a pencil loosely ·played. The pencil had a small weight upon its top to keep the point in constant contact with the paper ribbon. Upon the lever directly opposite to the poles of the electro-magnet was fastened the *armature* of the magnet, or a small bar of soft iron *h.* The movement of the lever was guided by stops on the frame at the sides of the lever, permitting to it only a movement forward to, and back from, the magnet; the pencil at the bottom of the lever was thus allowed to advance when the magnet was charged, and to retreat when discharged, about one-eighth of an inch. The lever advanced by the attraction of the magnet, and retreated by a weight in the first attempts, but immediately afterward by the action of a spring.

The first voltaic battery or pile[1] was of a single pair, I, having one of its poles connected by a conjunctive wire with one of the helices of the electro-magnet, and the other pole with *one* of *two cups of mercury* K; a conjunctive wire connected with the other helix of the magnet. The only part of the voltaic circuit not completed was between the two cups of mercury J and K. When a forked wire upon the lever 'O O united the two cups J K, the circuit was complete, the magnet was discharged, the armature *h* was attracted, and the lever F drawn toward the magnet. When the forked wire was removed the magnet was discharged, and the spring brought back the lever to its normal position. When the clock-work was put in motion, the ribbon of paper was drawn over the large cylinder B; from the cylinder A, the pencil *g* on the lever, being in constant contact with the ribbon of paper, traced a continuous line lengthwise with the ribbon. When the lever was in a normal position, the line was upon one side of the ribbon, as at *r;* when attracted by the magnet to the other limit of its motion, the line was on the other side, as at *s* in Diagram 5.

---

[1] I had at this time a Cruikshank's battery of twelve pairs, but so out of order as not to be available for experiment.

The *pathway* of the pencil-point (when the lever was attracted toward and held by the magnet for a longer or shorter time, tracing the line *s*) contains the *three* elements of *points*, *spaces*, and *lines*, forming by their various combinations the various conventional characters for *numerals* and *letters*. The other line *r*, traced by the pencil when the lever is in its normal position, may, therefore, be disregarded. Only the variations in the line *s* traced by the pencil when the magnet is charged is of importance. A specimen of these combinations is exhibited in the following diagram (6).

A is the line *r* in Diagram 5 which the pencil traces when the lever is in its normal position.

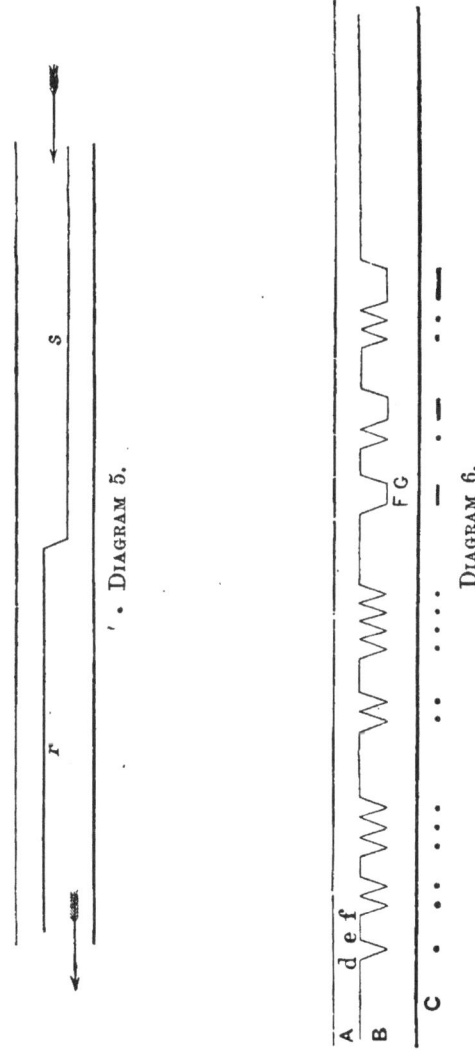

B is the line *s* in the same diagram which is to contain the conventional characters to be read as if marked in points, spaces, and lines, as on the line C below the ribbon of paper. The arrows show the direction of the movement of the ribbon of paper when the clock-work is in motion.

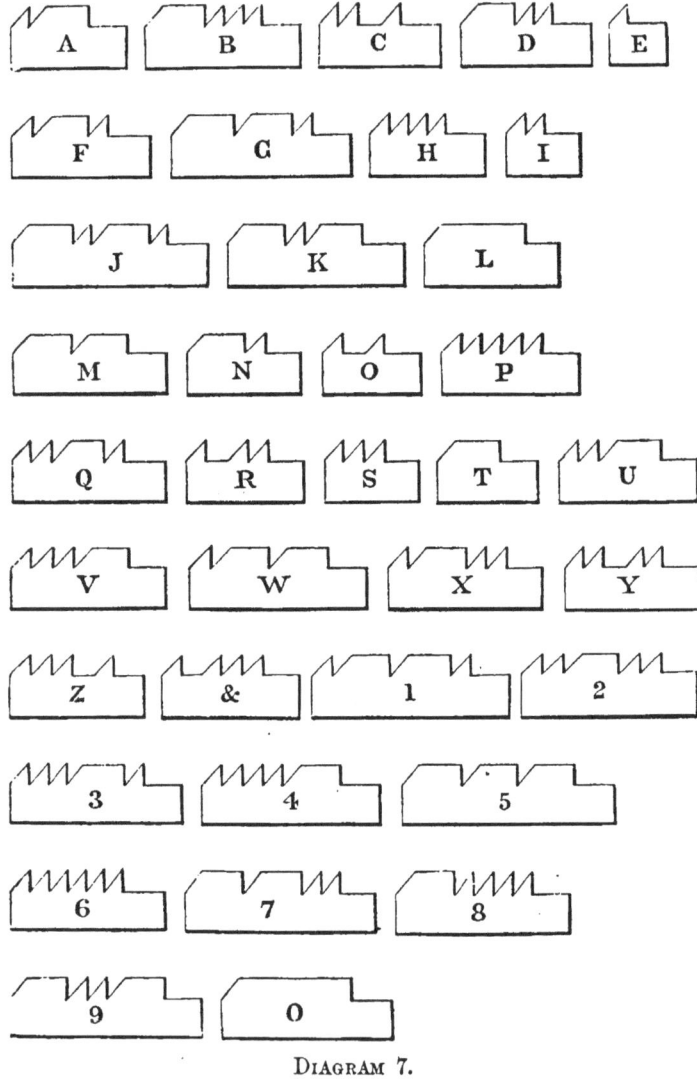

DIAGRAM 7.

Supposing the ribbon of paper in motion while the magnet is not charged, and the pencil to have commenced marking the upper line at A, when arriving at *d*, the circuit is quickly closed and opened again; the pencil is thus drawn a moment to the lower line B, marking a transverse across and back again, leaving a *point* in the lower line B. But, as the ribbon of paper is in motion, the transverse line back again does not return the way it came, but goes back to *e*. From *e* to *f* is a *space*. If the circuit be closed twice, and at each closing be opened quickly again, there will be two *points* left in the line B, followed by another space; if *three* times, there will be *three points*, and then a longer *space*, and so on, making one or more *points* and *spaces* at pleasure. But if, instead of opening the circuit quickly, it be kept closed a moment, and then opened, the pencil leaves a *line* on the line B, as at F G. Thus *points*, *spaces*, and *lines*, are made at will. Combinations of these (strictly speaking, *broken parts of a continuous line*) I made in sufficient variety to form my conventional alphabet. (*See* Diagram 7.)

At the time of the construction of this first telegraphic instrument, I had not conceived the idea of the present *key manipulator* dependent on the skill of the operator, but I presumed that the *accuracy* of the imprinting of signs could only be secured by mechanical mathematical arrangements and by *automatic process*. Hence the first conception, on board the ship, of embodying the signs in type mathematically divided into *points* and *spaces*. (*See* Diagram 2.) Hence also the construction of the type-mould, and castings of the first type, in 1832.

Having ascertained that the machinery I had constructed, rude as it was, would move the ribbon of paper at a regular speed, and that the pencil-lever was obedient to the closing and opening of the circuit, the next thing to construct was the manipulator or regulator of the closing and opening of the circuit.

I had already in abundance the type cast in 1832. These were now to be put in use.

I prepared rules or composing-sticks M (Diagram 4) of about *three* feet in length each, formed by two strips of wood, so placed side by side as to leave a narrow channel large enough to contain the type in desired order and to allow the cogs of the type to project above the upper edge of the rules. Through and along the bottom of the rules, projecting downward, were several needle-points, about one-fourth of an inch in length; their use will be perceived presently.

A long trough L L, sufficiently wide to allow of easy passage of the rules through its length, was constructed with the following parts. Near each end of this trough were two small cylinders, of wood, L L. On the prolonged axle of one of them was a hand-crank, and over the two cylinders an endless band of worsted tape about one and a half inch in width, which, when the crank was turned, passed from end to end of the trough. Midway and across the trough was erected a small frame or bridge N, within which a wooden lever O O was suspended parallel with the endless band, having its fulcrum at N at a point about two-thirds its length, but the longer part reaching from the fulcrum to the end of the trough, on each side of which under the end of the longer part of the lever were placed the *two cups of mercury* J K. Upon the end of the lever and above the cups of mercury was fixed a forked wire so bent as to connect both cups when the end of the lever was depressed, and to disconnect them when it was raised. At the other or shorter end of the lever a weight P overbalanced the longer part, and on the under side beneath the weight was a beveled tooth projecting downward. The rule or composing-stick, having the type set up, was then placed upon the endless band: the needle-points beneath the rule striking through the band and retaining the rule in its place. By turning the crank the rule was made to pass beneath the lever. The first cog of the type, coming in contact with the tooth beneath the weight of the lever, raised that end and depressed the other, causing the forked wire to descend into the two cups of mercury, and *closing* the circuit. When the cog had passed the tooth, the weight caused the tooth to fall into the space between the first and second cogs, and the fork at the other end of the lever to rise out of the cups of mercury, *opening* the circuit. At each dip of the fork into the cups, the circuit was closed, the magnet was charged, the armature on the pendulum lever was attracted, and the pencil passed from the upper line A (Diagram 6) to the lower line B. When the fork was raised out of the cups the circuit was opened, the magnet was discharged, and the pendulum lever with its pencil resumed its normal position by the action of the spring. A repetition of this process, as the rules with the type passed beneath the tooth on the lever, completed the action of the instrument.

This was the construction and mode of operation of the first recording instrument for *imprinting characters at a distance*. In this shape it "*produced a new practical result, seen and felt and appreciated by the senses*," witnessed, and testified to, by many witnesses as seen in operation in 1835, 1836, 1837. It was undoubtedly an imperfect instrument, but it produced, *then*, the same result that is produced more effectively, by more perfectly made instruments, *at this day*. It was a result never conceived nor accomplished before; it was an important practical result for the first time attained.

The recording instruments throughout the world at this hour have the same characteristics as this first rude instrument.

They *record* or *imprint conventional signs, points, spaces, and lines*, upon a *ribbon of paper*, moved by clock *machinery*, and by the action of an *electro-magnet*, charged and discharged through the agency of *electricity*, by means of a *single circuit* of conductors. The mechanism of to-day is indeed more beautiful, more finished, more exact, and as varied in form as the varied forms of the timepiece. The result is consequently more rapidly produced, but the result is the same as in this original instrument. The *semaphore* was then transmuted into a *telegraph*. The *evanescent sign* had become fixed, permanently *written* or *imprinted at a distance*.

I have said that the modern instruments have the same characteristics as the first instrument.

To make clear the *identity* of the modern recording instruments with this recording instrument of 1835, which at first blush may not be so obvious, I have made the diagrams (8, 9).

As in the *timepiece* there is seen every variety of form and arrangement of parts to produce the same result (*the passage of time*), so in the recording instruments of the present day there is the same variety of form and arrangement of parts to produce the *writing* or *imprinting*, the final result in all.

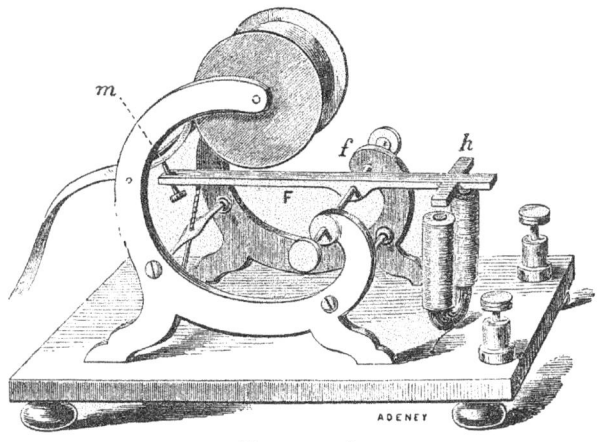

DIAGRAM 8.

Compare Diagrams 8, 9, with Diagram 4. The letters in each diagram refer to similar parts in each, so that, in describing one, all are described. In Diagram 8, the machinery that moves the ribbon of paper is removed in order the better to show the writing or recording apparatus. F is the lever; *f* its fulcrum; *h* the armature of the electro-magnet affixed to the lever; *m* shows the stylus or marking instrument in Diagrams 8, 9, affixed to the extremity of the lever, having the fulcrum *f* between the stylus *m* and the armature *h*. This is the modification in the modern instruments, while in Diagrams 4 and 9 *g* shows the stylus affixed to the other extremity of the lever F, having the armature *h* between the stylus *g* and the fulcrum *f*. If, therefore, as in Diagram 9, two ribbons of paper are put in movement, one before each stylus *g* and *m*, it will be seen that *g* in Diagram 9 makes the zigzag marks represented in Diagram 6 like those of *g* in the original instrument (Diagram 4), while at the same time, by the same movement of the lever, the stylus *m*, at the other exremity of the same lever, marks the alphabet in *points and lines*, or *dots and dashes*, upon its own ribbon of paper, the characters in universal use at the present day.

It is thus perceived that by prolonging the lever of the modern modification of the recording instruments beyond the armature *h* toward the cylinder B, and affixing a stylus, pen or pencil *g*, on its extremity, and allowing it to be in contact with the moving ribbon of paper, as in the original instrument of 1835, the action of the lever F may be made to mark the original zigzag characters at *g*, while the modern points and lines are at the same time marked by *m* on its own ribbon of paper. The dotted lines shadow the original A-shaped lever of Diagram 4, showing the same assemblage and arrangement of parts as in the original instrument.

It may seem singular to some that the plan of direct up-and-down movement of the lever, as in Diagrams 8 and 9 at *m*, to mark upon the paper (the plan devised on board the ship, and which is now the most universal), should not have been the first that was put in operation, since too

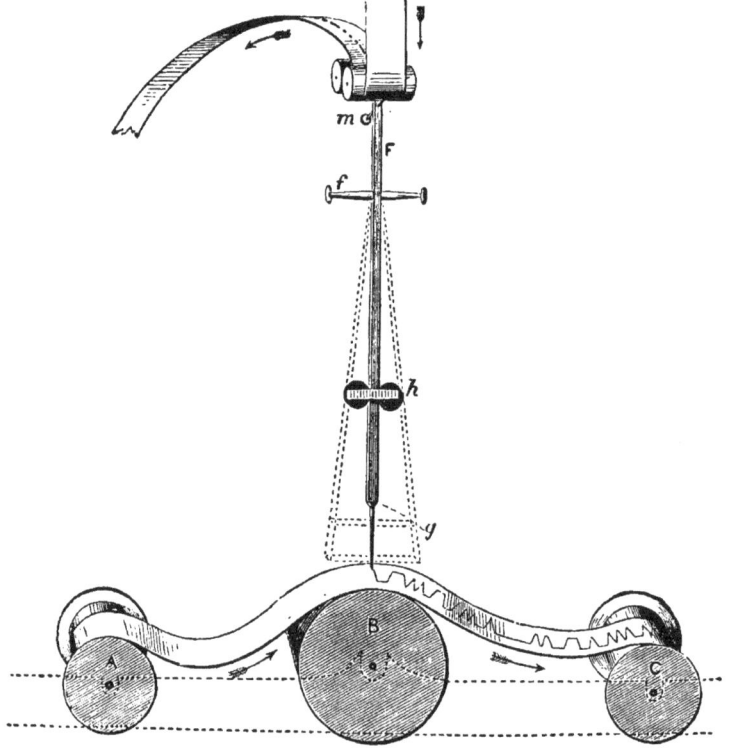

DIAGRAM 9.

it was the first and the most obvious mode devised. Having chosen, however, for economical reasons, the stretching-frame as the most convenient support at hand for the machinery, it was necessary to adapt the parts to this choice, even if my results must be attained in a more indirect manner.

It is easy to see that the direct action of the lever, as at present universally used in the register, would accomplish the result better, and it was put into use almost immediately after the first trial. Lightness in the lever was a desideratum, and this seemed to be easiest attained by suspending it at its fulcrum *f*, but, especially as a *pencil* was chosen as the first marking instrument (Diagram 10), it was supposed to be necessary in some way to avoid the direct blow of the pencil upon the paper, which was produced by this mode, but which endangered the point, and therefore the zigzag

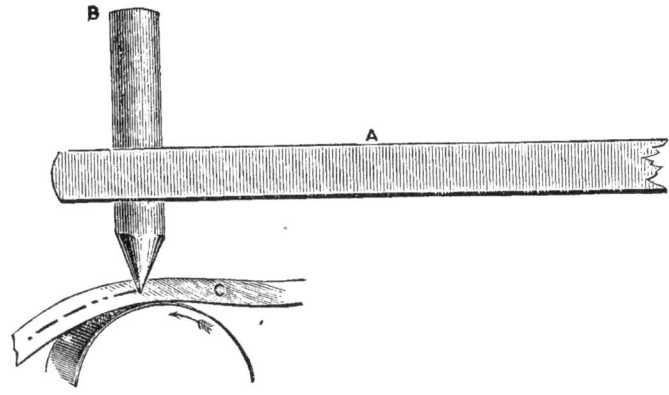

DIAGRAM 10.

sliding movement was adopted. The *pencil as employed* in Diagram 9, at *g*, was not the only marking instrument devised and put in operation in the earlier instruments. Besides the direct action of the pencil as in Diagram 10, *fountain-pens* of various kinds, one of which is shown in Diagram 11,

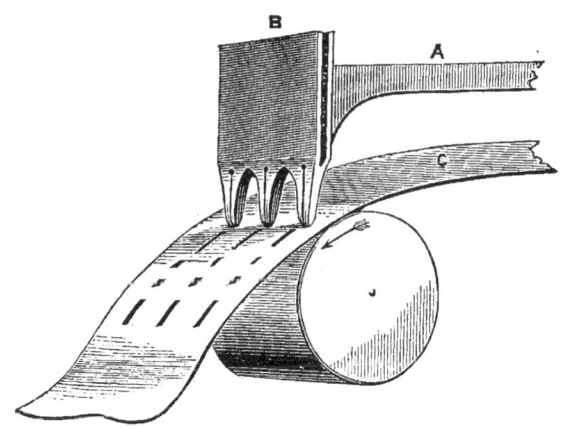

DIAGRAM 11.

and a small *printing-wheel*, as shown in Diagram 12, were used, the latter being supplied with ink from a sponge with which it was in contact. All these were used with more or less of success.

49

The same *result*, however, to wit, *recorded characters* representing
numerals and letters, and words and sentences, was given by each of these
modes in this first-constructed instrument as is given in instruments of the
present day. The instrumentalities are the same, and the result the same;
the only difference is in the mode of using the *marking* lever.

It will be now perceived that my invention of 1832 had certain very important novel characteristics which distinguished it from all inventions of
a previous date. It was not like any of them.

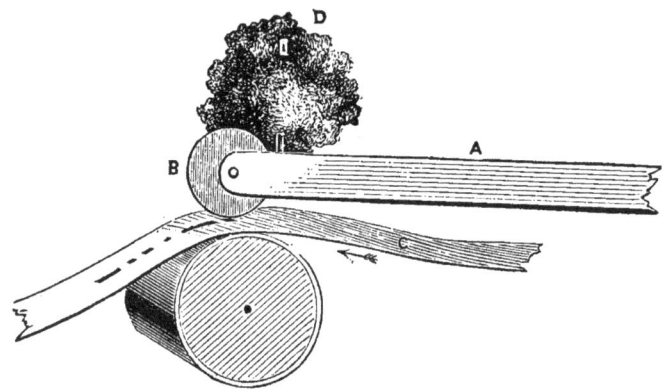

DIAGRAM 12.

Although the contemplation of static electricity as a means of producing
a permanent record at a distance gave rise in my mind to the conception
of the invention on board the ship, it was not the *static* form of electricity,
but its *dynamic* form, which I immediately adopted for carrying into
operation what I had devised. Electricity was proposed to be used by me
neither in the form, nor for the purpose, nor by the same instrumentalities,
as were proposed in the earliest contrivances, say previous to the year 1800.
None of them proposed to *record* their intelligence. None of them proposed or made use of the *electro-magnet*, for it was not then invented, nor
the scientific basis of it discovered. None of them had invented a *system of
signs* adapted to recording, for the necessity for them had not arisen. For
the same reason, none had proposed a *moving ribbon of paper* for receiving
the record. None proposed to use *a single circuit of conductors*.

In the earliest attempts to use electricity for communicating at a distance, *static* electricity was the form proposed and attempted. Failure
was the uniform result, not for the lack of ingenuity in the savants of that
day, but from the intractable nature of the form of electricity to which
they were limited. When the *dynamic* form of electricity became known,
it was at once seized upon as an agent in accomplishing communication at
a distance.

Still, between the years 1800 and 1832, the means by which that end was to be accomplished were all *semaphoric*. *Decomposition* by dynamic electricity in the form of *gas-bubbles*, and the *deflection* of the *magnetic needle*, were the sole novelties in the signals of their proposed plans. No period, therefore, is more strongly isolated from all previous dates than the date 1832 as the epoch of a *new method* of applying electricity by the *electro-magnet* to the *creation of a* NEW ART, of a *new method* of communicating to a distance, to wit, *recording*, a method wholly unlike any previously imagined or invented.

But the instrument I had devised in 1832, and constructed in 1835 (so far at least as to demonstrate its practicability to communicate *from* one station *to* a distant station), did not completely embody my *whole plan*. This *whole plan* was not complete until I could, by a *duplicate* of the instrument, have the means of a return from that distant station. This was necessary in order to *receive from*, as well as to *send to*, a particular station. The *whole plan* comprised intercommunication, or reciprocal communication.

It is true that any ordinary mind could easily comprehend from the operation of the single original apparatus that, if precisely the same apparatus were used from the *receiving* station to the *sending* station, *intercommunication* would be complete. No new appliances were necessary. A duplicate of the instrumentalities already in use from the *sending* station to the *receiving* station was all that was needed to complete my whole plan, and to establish intercommunication. But this was an affair of finance, and not of invention. To supply the duplicate required pecuniary means, and these I had not at command. But the rigidly captious may ask, "Why did you not borrow the pecuniary means?" My reply must be that I preferred the delay, and the hazards of a delay, to the hazard of being unable to repay a loan. I must be pardoned if I state that, even from my earliest youth, I ever had the deepest repugnance to incur debt by borrowing, even from my own relatives. Is it my idiosyncrasy? If so, the reader will excuse it, and my allusion to it.

By dint of the most rigid economy, I was able slowly to complete and to add this duplicate, necessary to complete my *whole plan*. Although the original single instrument was freely shown to my pupils and to many friends, I was reluctant to make any more public exhibitions of the invention until this duplicate should be added, and this was done in the early part of August, 1837. Early in September, I was more free in exhibiting the invention, and on the 2d and on the 4th of September I showed the instruments in operation to some hundreds of persons assembled in the large hall of the University. Most writers on the Telegraph choose to take this date as the date of my *invention*. But why, with the facts before them, is this just? To the existence and previous operation of the essential part of my whole plan, long before this more public operation of 1837, there were many witnesses whose evidence is before the courts on oath. But there are other writers, having ascertained the date of my *caveat* at the Patent-

Office on the 6th of October, 1837, and others again who find the date of the 7th of April, 1838, the date of my application in Washington for letters-patent, who choose to consider this latter date as the date of my invention. To all these I propose a question. Suppose I had never applied for letters-patent for the invention, but had chosen to give it to the public, or suppose I had never brought it to France, would there, therefore, be no invention, and no inventor of it? Their answer will settle that point.

Between the date, 1835, of the completion of the first instrument and 1837, the date of its more public exhibition, there was a very important addition to it, which I had already devised and provided against a fore-shadowed exigency, to meet it if it should occur when the conductors were extended, not to a few hundred feet in length in a room, but to stations many miles distant. I was not ignorant of the possibility that the electro-magnet might be so enfeebled, when charged from a great distance, as to be inoperative for *direct* printing. This possibility was a subject of much thought and anxiety long previous to the year 1836, long previous to my acquaintance or consultations with my friend Professor Gale on the subject, but I had then already conceived and drawn a plan for obviating it. The plan, however, was so simple that it scarcely needed a drawing to illustrate it; a few words sufficed to make it comprehended. If the magnet, say at twenty miles distant, became so enfeebled as to be unable to print *directly*, it yet might have power sufficient to close and open another circuit of twenty miles farther, and so on until it reached the required station. This plan was often spoken of to friends previous to the year 1836, but early in January, 1836, after showing the original instrument in operation to my friend and colleague, Professor Gale, I imparted to him this plan of a relay battery and magnet to resolve his doubts regarding the practicability of producing magnetic power sufficient to write at a distance.

This apprehended difficulty of an enfeebled magnet, as distance increased, was among the very first subjects of discussion with Professor Gale; so soon as my plan for obviating it was revealed to him, it was deemed per-fectly satisfactory. It was not then permanently embodied for use. A moment's reflection will show why. The relay was not then necessary to show the final result of the telegraph in the short circuit of less than a mile arranged around a hall. The operation and result of printing at a dis-tance was complete without it. But the frequent objection made by vis-itors that the instrument shown them might answer well enough for an in-teresting philosophical experiment in a class-room, but would not operate at a distance, at length induced me not merely to explain the *relay* by words and diagrams, but, so soon as I could command another magnet, to embody it in proper form.

This plan of the relay thus made in the spring of 1837 was productive of an important incident of great consequence to me in the prosecution of my invention. A few days after the more public exhibition of the telegraph, the late Alfred Vail, Esq. (then a student in the University, who was pres-ent at the exhibition on the 4th of September), became so fascinated with the invention that he called to have it more perfectly explained to him. The usual objection that it would not operate at a distance was a bar to his belief in its success. No sooner, however, had I explained the operation of the relay, than he desired an interest in the invention, and, to procure this interest, he offered to negotiate with his father and brother to supply the funds necessary to have constructed such a telegraphic instrument as would demonstrate to the United States Congress, and to the country, its practicability and utility. Thus the invention of the relay was the immediate cause of the construction of the apparatus which was shown to Congress in Washington in the winter of 1837–1838.

The simple and effective instruments as modified by Messrs. Digney Frères, of Paris, embody the distinctive features of my invention more to my satisfaction than any of the French instruments. There is a modification which they have made, however, which requires a few remarks to prevent misapprehension in regard to its exact nature. In reading the excellent work of M. Brequet, p. 163, in his chapter "*Morse Register marking the signs in ink*," "*Recepteur Morse faisant les signaux à l'encre*," I find some things to correct. A wrong impression is made in describing the mode of *embossing* the characters by a *a steel point*, "à gaufrage," as if that were my *only* original mode of marking. This is not the fact; *a pencil, a fountain-pen*, and the *small printing-wheel* by which ink was used, were among the first modes of marking. There were many modes of marking which I devised and tried, but experience alone could settle which was best; the pencil and pen and small printing-wheel with ink were the original modes in use; the steel point (Diagram 13), for embossing the character, was invented some time after, and patented as an im-

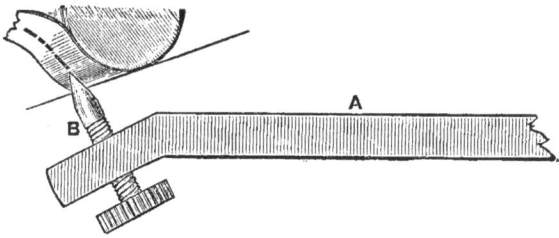

DIAGRAM 13.

provement, since it dispensed with ink; M. Brequet gives to Thomas John, of Prague, the invention of the *small printing-wheel*, "une molette ou roulette," to mark the characters, and states that he received for his invention a platina medal from the Society of Encouragement.

That Mr. Thomas John made his improvement independently, without a knowledge of the fact that I had it in use nearly twenty years before, I have no doubt, but it is nevertheless true that the introduction of this inking wheel is not a novelty: whatever of novelty there is in its present use

consists in the *mode* of its application, and in the beautiful apparatus constructed by Messrs. Digney Frères the mode, so far as I know, is new.
The mode of application of Mr. John is different from mine and from
Messrs. Digneys'. My original mode (its first use) was by *bringing down* the
printing-wheel, inked from a sponge, upon the paper. Mr. John *brings the
printing-wheel* against the paper *from the side.*

My *caveat*, filed in the Patent-Office in Washington on the 6th of October, 1837, in describing the register, specifies: "3. A *pencil*, or *fountain-
pen*, or a *small printing-wheel*, or any other marking material;" and the

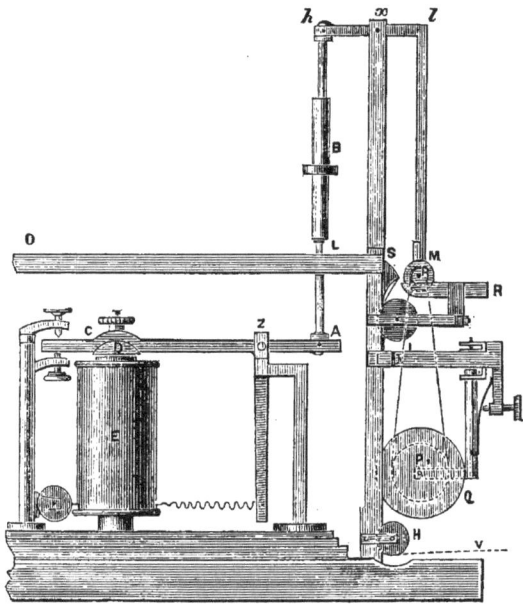

DIAGRAM 14.

mode of using the wheel is also described, thus: "When the *printing-wheel*
is used, the *wheel* is *brought in contact with the paper* by the magnet when
required to mark." The wheel in my first experiments, inked by a sponge,
was *brought down* upon the paper; Mr. John's mode of applying the wheel,
inked in a reservoir, was by bringing it *against* the paper from the side,
while Messrs. Digneys' mode was *bringing the paper* against the wheel
inked by a felt roller. This latter mode I conceive to be a substantial improvement, since it combines delicacy with efficiency, and requires so much
less power for the operation that even the relays can be dispensed with on
lines of considerable extent. My original mode of using the *printing-wheel*
by ink from a sponge I found so inconvenient, from its constant tendency
to soil the paper, and the fountain-pens of every variety of form so unreli-

able, that the *steel point* "à gaufrage" (Diagram 13) I considered at the time a great improvement, since it gave the characters with certainty, without the inconvenience of constant attention and the dirt and accidents of the ink.

If, then, judged by the first rule laid down by Dr. Russell, I claim to be the *inventor of the first recording telegraph* (not to say, strictly speaking, the *first real telegraph*), am I not " the first who produced the practical result which, however imperfect, gave a result which was seen, and felt, and appreciated, by the senses?" Am I not, according to this rule, " the true maker and inventor whom the world should recognize, no matter how much may have been done by others to improve my work?"

Let me not be misunderstood as appropriating to myself the credit of the many modifications of the telegraph that have since been made in every part of the world, because I claim the invention of the *generic telegraph*. I do not pretend that the mechanism of the first forms of the telegraph was not rude, and even uncouth when compared with the beautiful workmanship of the European ateliers, of the hundreds of accomplished mechaniciaus who have brought to the work their incomparable ingenuity and skill, but I think I may justly claim that the essential characteristics of a *new art* were demonstrated even in the rudest instruments, constructed in the earliest times of the invention. So suggestive were the novelties introduced by the promulgation of the *new art*, so wide the field which it opened for investigation in science and mechanics, that it would be strange indeed if modifications of the separate elements that made up the whole invention should not at once be conceived and produced. And yet I may appeal to the fact generally acknowledged that the essential features of the original invention have not been obliterated; they can be easily and distinctly traced through all the improvements made in the various parts by which the different processes of the art have been more easily performed.

MORSE'S TELEGRAPHIC ALPHABET.

The Telegraphic Alphabet represents each letter of the English alphabet, with the numerals, by which any amount of writing or correspondence may be conducted, in all the details of letters and words of the common mode of correspondence, or writing.

ALPHABET.   NUMERALS.

A	· —	1	· — — · ·
B	— · · ·	2	· · — · ·
C	· · ·	3	· · · — ·
D	— · ·	4	· · · · —
E	·	5	— — —
F	· — ·	6	· · · · · ·
G J	— — ·	7	— — · ·
H	· · · ·	8	— · · · · ·
I Y	· ·	9	— · · —
K	— · —	0	——
L	——		
M	— —		
N	— ·		
O	· ·		
P	· · · ·		
Q	· · — ·		
R	· · ·		
S Z	· · ·		
T	—		
U	· · —		
V	· · · —		
W	· — —		
X	· — · ·		
&	· · · ·		

THE END.

SD - #0008 - 051222 - C0 - 229/152/44 - PB - 9781332754267 - Gloss Lamination